The Playbill® Broadway Yearbook

Fifth Annual Edition
2008–2009

ROBERT VIAGAS
EDITOR

AMY ASCH
Assistant Editor

KESLER THIBERT
Art Director

AUBREY REUBEN   BRIAN MAPP   SAMANTHA SOUZA   BEN STROTHMANN
Photographers

DAVID GEWIRTZMAN
Production Coordinator

SAMANTHA SOUZA
Photo Coordinator

The Playbill Broadway Yearbook: Fifth Annual Edition, June 1, 2008–May 31, 2009
Robert Viagas, Editor

ISBN 978-1-4234-8293-2
ISSN 1932-1945

Published by PLAYBILL® BOOKS
525 Seventh Avenue, Suite 1801
New York, NY 10018
Email: yearbook@playbill.com
Internet: www.playbill.com

Published in 2009 by Applause Theatre & Cinema Books
An Imprint of Hal Leonard Corporation
7777 West Bluemound Road
Milwaukee, WI 53213

Trade Book Division Editorial Offices
19 West 21st Street, New York, NY 10010

www.applausepub.com

Printed in the United States of America

Preface to the Fifth Edition

The 2008-2009 season saw the greatest economic stumble since the Great Depression of the 1930s, but Broadway proved to be amazingly resilient. Twenty-first century descendants of the show folk of old got their chance to uphold the tradition that the show must go on—no matter what.

Collapsing financial institutions in the first half of the season made producers wonder whether there would be any audience at all. Fears of a looming Swine Flu epidemic didn't help. Nearly a third of the Broadway shows running at Christmas 2008 were shuttered by the end of January 2009, including Tony-winners *Hairspray*, *Spamalot* and *Spring Awakening*, a fact widely noted with alarm in the mass media. However, so many productions had been launched into the production pipeline in flush times just a few months earlier that nearly all the vacant theatres were quickly rebooked. And audiences somehow found ways to buy tickets. When Broadway finally closed its spreadsheet programs in May 2009 producers found it had been one of the most moneymaking seasons in history, with the most new productions—43—since in the 1982-83 season and with only a slight decline in audience overall. In all, 78 shows (including holdovers) played on the Great White Way during the course of the season, the most so far this century. Broadway had weathered the "Great Recession" with a burst of creativity.

The imploding economy almost spelled the end of the *The Playbill Broadway Yearbook*, too. But, mirroring Broadway, sales continued to be unexpectedly strong, even after the 2008 holidays until the fourth edition was nearly sold out. To our fans we say "Thank you!" for the new lease on publishing life.

During the *Yearbook*'s three-month hiatus we lost editorial assistant Kristen Luciani, who embarked on a career that will someday doubtless make her a truly great Broadway producer. She was succeeded by the charismatic actress (and co-founder of her own Off-Off-Broadway troupe, Company 1B) Samantha Souza, who punctuated her days in the Playbill office with the traditional rounds of auditions.

In the News

Three years after its triumphant debut in London, *Billy Elliot*, Elton John's musical adaptation of the film of the same title, arrived on Broadway in the fall, beginning a juggernaut parade to the Tony Awards. The heart-tugging story of a working class boy from a bleak British coal-mining town who dreams of becoming a ballet dancer left other new musicals struggling to get some traction on the sidelines.

Billy Elliot's main competition proved to be a very dissimilar musical, *Next to Normal*, about a suburban woman's descent into mental illness and its effect on her and her family. Alice Ripley earned a Tony Award for her starring performance. *Rock of Ages* didn't win any Tony Awards, but offered fans of 1980s rock a chance to wave mini flashlights designed to look like lighters as their favorite period songs strutted past.

Photo by Brian Mapp

Photo by Kari Otero

Photo by Aubrey Reuben

THE 2008-2009 YEARBOOK COMMITTEE
Top (L-R): Brian Mapp, Robert Viagas, Samantha Souza, David Gewirtzman
Bottom (L): Amy Asch (R): Aubrey Reuben
Not pictured: Kesler Thibert

Among dramas, Yasmina Reza's *God of Carnage* and Neil LaBute's *reasons to be pretty* examined loyalty and betrayal among people in very different social strata. Moisés Kaufman's *33 Variations* showed a woman trying to unravel the mystery of mother-daughter relations while simultaneously unraveling a mystery of musical history involving classical composer Ludwig van Beethoven.

33 Variations starred Jane Fonda in her first return to Broadway in more than four decades. But she was just one of a constellation of stars brightening Broadway this year. Fans were able to see Liza Minnelli, Angela Lansbury, James Gandolfini, Will Ferrell, Sutton Foster, Jeff Daniels, John Lithgow, Marcia Gay Harden, Patti LuPone, and lots more.

Stars worked their magic offstage as well, with country singer/composer Dolly Parton writing the score for an adaptation of her film *9 to 5*, and Elton John composing *Billy Elliot*.

Also among visiting "stars" was recently-inaugurated President Barack Obama, who fulfilled a campaign promise to take First Lady Michelle Obama to a Broadway show. They picked the revival of August Wilson's *Joe Turner's Come and Gone*.

A resolute absence of stars characterized a little musical called *[title of show]*. The characters who dreamed of writing a musical that would open on Broadway virtually willed themselves onto Broadway with one of the most innovative (and entertaining) web campaigns ever. "The [title of show] Show" added new episodes each month as the four-member cast (plus pianist) breathlessly chronicled their tongue-in-cheek (but eventually successful) campaign to move to Times Square.

Patti LuPone again confirmed her diva status in the final days of the *Gypsy* run, when she interrupted her volcanic "Rose's Turn" to rage at a member of the audience who was taking flash photos of her. Captured by a third party, her withering hoots of "Who do you think you are?!" became a nine-day internet wonder, as raw audio, as a rhythmic remix and, eventually, as a Broadway catch-phrase. Delighted LuPone impersonators quickly incorporated the rant into their acts.

David Mamet's Hollywood sendup *Speed-the-Plow* found itself in the tabloids when co-star Jeremy Piven abruptly quit the show claiming he had suffered mercury poisoning from eating too much sushi. The innovative excuse inspired jokes throughout the year, including a comment from Mamet: "My understanding is that he is leaving show business to pursue a career as a thermometer." Snarks continued right up to Tony night when host Neal Patrick Harris dug into a plate of sushi on camera and crowed about how much energy it was giving him.

Two of the greatest classics in the Broadway canon, *West Side Story* and *Guys and Dolls*, got revivals this season, but both of them wound up taking a back seat at Tony time to the scruffy hippies of *Hair*. Anti-establishment hope was once again in tune with the zeistgeist.

When the books finally closed at the end of May 2009, Broadway was still singing "I'm still here."

Robert Viagas
July 2009

Special Thanks

Special thanks to Amy Asch, David Gewirtzman, Samantha Souza, Brian Mapp, Kristen Luciani, Kesler Thibert, Aubrey Reuben, Ben Strothmann, Pam Karr, Greg Kalafatas, Martha Graebner, Maria Somma, Matt Blank, Andrew Gans, Kenneth Jones, Ernio Hernandez, Adam Hetrick, Jake Hirzel, Catherine Ryan and Jean Kroeper Murphy, whose help made this year's edition possible.

We also thank the Fifth Edition *Yearbook* Correspondents who shared their stories with such wit and insight: John Ahlin, Don Amendolia, Susan Blackwell, Heidi Blickenstaff, Arnie Burton, Al Calderon, Jim Caruso, Adam Chanler-Berat, Alison Cimmet, Natalie Cortez, Lauren Elder, Evan Ensign, Aymee Garcia, Asmeret Ghebremichael, Malik Hammond, Roy Harris (for the third and fourth time), Steven Hauck, Gregory Jbara, Sean Allan Krill, James T. Lane, Baayork Lee, Melissa Rae Mahon, Tyler Maynard, Ken McGee, Charles Means, Elizabeth Moloney, Ira Mont, Javier Muñoz, Kerry O'Malley, Kris Koop Ouellette (for the fifth time), Patrick Page (for the second time), Michael J. Passaro, Brandon Perler, Steve Rosen, Tory Ross (for the second time), Thomas Ryan, Jonathan Sandler, Aaron Serotsky, Judine Somerville, Allison Sommers, Daniel Stewart Sherman, Matthew Silver, Gwen Stewart, Barclay Stiff (for the third time), Emily Walton, Steven Weber, Kirsten Wyatt, Denise Yaney, Michael P. Zaleski and Alissa Zulvergold.

And we thank the folks on each show who shared their photographs and other artwork that lent extra sparkle to the Scrapbook pages: Matt Blank, Susan Blackwell, Jay Brady, Heidi Burns, Suzie Cho-Stanisci, Lauren Elder, Harvey Fierstein, John Funk, Steven Hauck, Owen Iverson, Sean Allan Krill, David LeShay, Claudia Lynch, Melissa Rae Mahon, Wilson Morales, Kerry O'Malley, Elizabeth Pearce, Larry Pressgrove, Steve Rosen, Jonny Rueda, Jeremy Shaffer, Anita Shevett, Steve Shevett, Matthew Silver, Allison Sommers, Barclay Stiff, Tomas Vrzala and Alissa Zulvergold.

Also the Broadway press agents who helped set up interviews and photo sessions: especially Chris Boneau, Adrian Bryan-Brown, John Barlow, Michael Hartman, Richard Kornberg, Jeffrey Richards, Marc Thibodeau, Philip Rinaldi, Sam Rudy, Tony Origlio, Rick Miramontez, Peter Cromarty and their respective staffs.

Plus Joan Marcus, Paul Kolnik, Carol Rosegg and all the fine professional photographers whose work appears on these pages.

And, most of all, thanks to the great show people of Broadway who got into the spirit of the *Yearbook* and took time out of their busy days to pose for our cameras. There's no people like them.

Yearbook User's Manual

Which Shows Are Included? *The Playbill Broadway Yearbook 2008-2009* covers the Broadway season, which ran, as per tradition, from June 1, 2008 to May 31, 2009. Each of the seventy-eight shows that played at a Broadway theatre under a Broadway contract during that time are are profiled in this edition. That includes new shows that opened during that time, like *Billy Elliot*; shows from seasons past that closed during this season, like *Rent;* and shows from seasons past that ran throughout this season and continue into the future (and into the next *Yearbook*), like *The Phantom of the Opera*.

How Is It Decided Which Credits Page Will Be Featured? Each show's credits page (which PLAYBILL calls a "billboard page") changes over the year as cast members come and go. We use the opening-night billboard page for most new shows. For most shows that carry over from the previous season we use the billboard page from the first week in October. Occasionally, at the request of the producer, we use a bill-board page from another part of the season, especially when a major new star joins the cast.

What Are "Alumni" and "Transfer Students"? Over the course of a season some actors leave a production; others take their place. To follow our "Yearbook" concept, the ones who left a show after June 1, 2008 but before the date of the billboard page are listed as "Alumni"; the ones who joined the cast are called "Transfer Students." If you see a photo appearing in both "Alumni" and "Transfer Students" sections, it's not a mistake; it just means that they went in and out of the show during the season and were not present on the billboard date.

What Is a "Correspondent" and How Is One Chosen? We ask each show to appoint a Correspondent to record anecdotes of backstage life at their production. Sometimes the show's press agent picks the Correspondent; sometimes the company manager, the stage manager or the producer does the choosing. Each show gets to decide for itself. A few shows decline to provide a correspondent, fail to respond to our request, or miss the deadline. Correspondents bring a richness of experience to the job and help tell the story of backstage life on Broadway from many different points of view.

Who Gets Their Picture in the Yearbook? Everyone who works on Broadway can get a picture in the *Yearbook*. That includes actors, producers, writers, designers, assistants, stagehands, ushers, box office personnel, stage doormen and anyone else employed at a Broadway show or a support organization. PLAYBILL maintains a database of headshots of all Broadway actors and most creators. We send our staff photographers to all opening nights and all major Broadway-related events. We also offer to schedule in-theatre photo shoots at every production. No one is required to appear in the *Yearbook*, but all are invited. A few shows declined to host a photo shoot this year or were unable to provide material by our deadline. We hope they'll join us in 2010.

TABLE OF CONTENTS

Timeline 2008-2009

Opening Nights, News Headlines and Other Significant Milestones of the Season

June 15, 2008 The 62nd Annual Tony Awards are held at Radio City Music Hall. *In the Heights* is named Best Musical; Tracy Letts' *August: Osage County* is named Best Play; *South Pacific* and *Boeing-Boeing* are named Best Revivals.

June 26, 2008 *Cirque Dreams Jungle Fantasy*, the family-friendly theatrical and musical adventure that evokes exotic, untamed places with acrobats, jugglers, aerialists and contortionists, is the first production of the season.

June 27, 2008 Opening of the animated film *Wall·E*, with songs from the musical *Hello, Dolly!* featured in the story of a lonely robot on abandoned Earth, trying to get a sense of what humanity was like.

July 2, 2008 Actors' Equity Association and The Broadway League reach a tentative, 39-month agreement for the production contract, avoiding a second Broadway strike within a year. The contract covers actors and stage managers in commercial Broadway and touring productions.

July 3, 2008 *The Phantom of the Opera* becomes the first Broadway show to reach 8,500 performances. It's the longest-running show in Broadway history, and sets a new record every night. Since its debut on Jan. 26, 1988, *Phantom* has grossed $690 million in New York and more than $5 billion worldwide, surpassing every Broadway show in history as well as the world's highest-grossing films, such as *Titanic, Jurassic Park* and *Star Wars*. More than 12.5 million people have seen the show at Broadway's Majestic Theatre alone.

July 11, 2008 New York City shuts down two lanes of Broadway between Times Square and Herald Square—the stretch once known as the Rialto, which was the center of Manhattan theatrical activity in the late 19th century—to make a bicycle lane and pedestrian esplanade.

July 17, 2008 *[title of show]*—the musical that "would rather be nine people's favorite thing than a hundred people's ninth favorite thing"—officially opens at the Lyceum Theatre. Originally seen Off-Broadway in 2006, the entire original cast—including co-creators Jeff Bowen and Hunter Bell as well as co-stars Susan Blackwell and Heidi Blickenstaff—make the leap to the Broadway stage. The musical, which tells the story of its own creation, started a campaign to move to Broadway as an internet joke, but real-life producers became interested and on this date the gag became reality.

July 18, 2008 The film adaptation of long-running London and Broadway musical *Mamma Mia!* opens in the U.S. Starring Meryl Streep, the film will eventually earn $150 million in the U.S., $500 million worldwide and will become the top-grossing film in U.K. history.

July 19, 2008 The Tony-nominated Broadway musical *Passing Strange*, which is closing July 20, is captured for posterity. The Saturday matinee and evening performances at the Belasco Theatre are filmed by director Spike Lee, for later release at film festivals.

July 21, 2008 Omigod you guys, Bailey Hanks is totally named the winner of the MTV reality

Times Square Alliance President Tim Tompkins speaks at the opening of the new Father Duffy Square and TKTS booth at Broadway and 47th Street. See October 16, 2008. Among the seated (third from left) is Bernadette Peters.

casting competition, "Legally Blonde The Musical: The Search for Elle Woods." Hanks beats out nine other contestants to succeed Laura Bell Bundy as Elle Woods in the New York production of *Legally Blonde*. She makes her Broadway debut in the musical July 23.

August 13, 2008 Recession begins to bite Broadway as a revival of *Godspell* that had already begun advertising and selling tickets is forced to postpone indefinitely when, ironically, they lose one of their "angels" (investors).

August 17, 2008 The Tony-nominated Broadway revival of *A Chorus Line* closes after 759 performances.

September 4, 2008 The 1925-vintage Biltmore Theatre, Broadway home of the Manhattan Theatre Club, is rechristened the Samuel J. Friedman Theatre after the pioneering Broadway publicist.

September 7, 2008 Closing night for *Rent* after twelve years and 5,123 performances. The event is filmed for later "cinecast" in movie theatres.

Starting September 2008 The slide of world stock exchanges and the loss of thousands of Wall Street jobs leave Broadway producers worrying how box offices will be affected. Within weeks the long-running *Monty Python's Spamalot, Xanadu, Legally Blonde, Hairspray* and *Spring Awakening* announce closings.

September 18, 2008 Something new on Broadway: Inside the Times Square Information Center near the Palace Theatre, theatregoers can now find the Broadway Concierge & Ticket Center which offers free help in picking both shows and restaurants in the theatre district. Information is available in six languages. The center also begins hosting weekly free Broadway concerts in association with Sirius Satellite Radio.

September 18, 2008 Nearly two decades of writing, workshops and rewriting come to a cli-

max with the opening of Jill Santoriello's musical adaptation of the Charles Dickens classic *A Tale of Two Cities*. James Barbour plays drunken lawyer Sydney Carton who is redeemed by his love for a good woman in the musical set in London and Paris during the French Revolution. Also featured in the cast are Gregg Edelman, Brandi Burkhardt and Aaron Lazar.

September 25, 2008 *Harry Potter* film star Daniel Radcliffe and Tony- and Olivier Award-winner Richard Griffiths are featured in a revival of the Tony-winning drama *Equus*. Peter Shaffer's play tells the story of a psychiatrist (Griffiths) who becomes absorbed in the strange case of a young man (Radcliffe) who blinds a stableful of horses.

October 2, 2008 Kristin Scott Thomas and Peter Sarsgaard star in a revival of Anton Chekhov's *The Seagull*. Thomas recreates her performance as Arkadina that won her an Olivier Award when the show originated at the Royal Court Theatre in London. Sarsgaard plays Trigorin. Ian Rickson directs Christopher Hampton's new translation of the drama about a master actress and the writers and artists who gather at her summer home.

October 5, 2008 Jason Robert Brown's musical *13* opens with a 13-member cast of actual teenagers (as was the band). The musical tells the story of a boy facing his 13th birthday and Bar Mitzvah in a new town.

October 7, 2008 In the first Broadway revival of Robert Bolt's *A Man for All Seasons*, three-time Tony Award winner Frank Langella plays the 16th century statesman Sir Thomas More, who stood up to King Henry VIII in his conflicts with the church.

October 8, 2008 The Tony Awards inaugurate a new non-competitive award, The Isabelle Stevenson Award, named for the longtime director of the American Theatre Wing. It will

Timeline 2008-2009

recognize an individual from the theatre community who has made a substantial contribution of volunteered time and effort on behalf of one or more humanitarian, social service or charitable organizations. The award will be presented to one individual per season starting in 2009 and will not necessarily be awarded every season.

October 14, 2008 The first show to open at the newly rechristened Friedman Theatre is *To Be or Not To Be*, Nick Whitby's adaptation of the Ernst Lubitsch film comedy about a Polish acting troupe that tries to escape the Nazis during World War II with nothing but their acting ability to help them. Casey Nicholaw directs a cast including Jan Maxwell, Peter Benson and Rocco Sisto for the Manhattan Theatre Club.

October 16, 2008 The long-awaited new TKTS booth, featuring a luminescent red staircase, opens in the heart of the newly renovated

whose movie pitch is interrupted by a pretty temp worker. When Piven withdraws just a few weeks into the run, claiming mercury poisoning, his role is assumed, in turn, by Jordan Lage, Norbert Leo Butz and William H. Macy.

November 2008 The Broadway League begins charging $1 "League fee" on Broadway tickets sold at the TKTS discount booths.

November 13, 2008 *Billy Elliot*, the hit London musical based on the 2000 film about a working class boy who dreams of becoming a ballet dancer, makes its Broadway debut. *Billy Elliot* has music by Elton John and book and lyrics by Lee Hall, who wrote the film. The demanding part of Billy is rotated among three young actors on a nightly basis. The cast also features London star Haydn Gwynne as the dance teacher, with American stars Gregory Jbara and Carole Shelley as members of Billy's family.

November 17, 2008 John Leguizamo, Cedric

Fuller and Gerald McRaney.

November 23, 2008 Broadway opening night for the stage adaptation of Irving Berlin's holiday film *White Christmas*, about a pair of army buddies who try to help their former commanding officer who has fallen on hard times. Stephen Bogardus and Jeffry Denman star in the production, staged by Walter Bobbie. The score includes songs from the Bing Crosby film, augmented with other tunes, familiar and unfamiliar, from the Irving Berlin songbook.

November 25, 2008 Gerald Schoenfeld, longtime chairman of the theatre-owning Shubert Organization and routinely referred to as the most powerful man on Broadway, dies of a heart attack at age 84. He is succeeded by Philip J. Smith.

December 3, 2008 Liza Minnelli returns to Broadway for the first time in nearly a decade in her concert show *Liza's at the Palace…!*, paying tribute to her godmother, vocal arranger and performer Kay Thompson.

December 7, 2008 It snows on Broadway tonight with the opening of a limited-run transfer of the long-running Off-Broadway clowning theatrical special, *Slava's Snowshow*, starring Slava Polunin.

December 14, 2008 DreamWorks Pictures makes its first foray into Broadway producing with a stage adaptation of its popular animated film *Shrek*, starring Brian d'Arcy James as the green ogre of the title, Sutton Foster as the princess he saves, and Daniel Breaker as his donkey sidekick. *Shrek The Musical* has a score by Jeanine Tesori and Pulitzer Prize winner David Lindsay-Abaire.

December 18, 2008 Roundabout Theatre Company revives Rodgers and Hart's 1940 musical *Pal Joey*, with Stockard Channing, Martha Plimpton and, in the title role, Matthew Risch (who replaced Christian Hoff in previews). The story of a scheming charmer in the world of 1940s Chicago nightclubs, the show has a new book by Richard Greenberg and direction by Joe Mantello.

January 4, 2009 Black Sunday on Broadway as nine shows close, including Tony-winning Best Musical *Hairspray* (after 2,642 performances). A sign of tough economic times, more than a quarter of all shows on Broadway will close during January—though nearly all the theatres are quickly rebooked.

January 15, 2009 *Soul of Shaolin*, an extravaganza of music and martial arts, is imported from Shanghai by the Chinese government.

January 22, 2009 Mercedes Ruehl and Lily Rabe play mother and daughter whose summer vacation is thrown into turmoil by the arrival of a handsome young man in *The American Plan*. David Grindley directs the drama by Richard Greenberg. With *Pal Joey*, it's Greenberg's second Broadway opening in a little over a month.

January 25, 2009 Mary-Louise Parker and Michael Cerveris star in a new production of Henrik Ibsen's classic *Hedda Gabler* at Roundabout Theatre Company.

February 5, 2009 Comedian Will Ferrell marks

Photos by David Gewirtzman

Before and After: (Left): The statue of George M. Cohan watches cabs drive down Broadway at 46th Street for the last time. (Right): Relaxing on the new pedestrian mall on Broadway. See May 24, 2009.

Duffy Square, just under two years after originally promised. The redesigned discount ticket booth features twelve ticket windows under an illuminated red glass staircase where pedestrians can sit. The multimillion dollar redevelopment of the island located in the northern part of Times Square features an expanded and enhanced plaza that continues to honor World War I hero Father Francis P. Duffy and Broadway's George M. Cohan with statues.

October 16, 2008 Also on this date: Opening night for a revival of Arthur Miller's 1947 drama *All My Sons*, the story of an aircraft parts manufacturer who carries a terrible wartime secret. John Lithgow, Dianne Wiest, Patrick Wilson and Katie Holmes star in the production, directed by Simon McBurney.

October 23, 2008 Two decades after its Tony Award-nominated debut, *Speed-the-Plow* returns to Broadway starring Jeremy Piven, Elisabeth Moss and Raúl Esparza. David Mamet's comedy shows two Hollywood sharks

the Entertainer and Haley Joel Osment are featured in a Broadway revival of *American Buffalo*, which, along with *Speed-the-Plow*, means that Broadway hosts two David Mamet classics simultaneously. Robert Falls directs the story of a group of small-time crooks who plot to steal a valuable coin collection.

November 17, 2008 Elijah Wood, Rosie Perez, Terrence McNally and Pablo Schreiber are among the talents taking part in the eighth annual "24 Hour Plays" event at the American Airlines Theatre. As in previous years a group of playwrights, actors and directors write, rehearse and perform a program of one act plays in a single 24-hour period as a fundraiser for Urban Arts Partnership, which brings arts education to New York City classrooms.

November 20, 2008 The battling Gordon clan of Harrison, Texas tries to decide whether to sell the family mansion to developers in Horton Foote's comedy-drama *Dividing the Estate*, starring Elizabeth Ashley, Hallie Foote, Penny

Timeline 2008-2009

the end of the Bush Administration with a sold-out show in which he impersonates and satirizes the forty-third president, *You're Welcome America. A Final Night with George W Bush.*

February 19, 2009 Will Chase and Malcolm Gets star as pals who grow up together, from ages 6 to 35 in the original new musical *The Story of My Life.* Directed by Richard Maltby Jr., the show marks the Broadway debut of the writing team of Neil Bartram (music and lyrics) and Brian Hill (book).

March 1, 2009 Des McAnuff stages an innovative revival of *Guys and Dolls* that uses animated projections and introduces author Damon Runyon as a character. The classic "musical fable of Broadway" stars Craig Bierko as Sky Masterson, Oliver Platt as Nathan Detroit, Kate Jennings Grant as Sarah Brown and Lauren Graham as Miss Adelaide.

March 9, 2009 After an absence of more than forty years, actress Jane Fonda returns to Broadway in *33 Variations,* Moisés Kaufman's drama about a music historian who investigates Beethoven's obsession with a seemingly trivial waltz.

March 11, 2009 Broadway dodges a bullet when New York Governor David Paterson strikes a proposed tax on Broadway theatre tickets from his 2009-10 state budget proposal after an intense lobbying effort by producers, theatre owners and their allies.

March 15, 2009 Four-time Tony winner Angela Lansbury and two-time Tony winner Christine Ebersole return to Broadway in a revival of Noël Coward's "improbable comedy" *Blithe Spirit,* about a novelist (Rupert Everett) doing research with an eccentric medium (Lansbury) who conjures up the ghost of his late first wife (Ebersole), with dire consequences for his second wife (Jayne Atkinson).

March 19, 2009 Revival of the classic musical *West Side Story,* directed by its 90-year-old librettist, Arthur Laurents. Matt Cavenaugh and Josefina Scaglione play Tony and Maria in the Leonard Bernstein/Stephen Sondheim retelling of *Romeo and Juliet.* Laurents stages the scenes of Puerto Rican street gang member in Spanish, with translation supplied by Lin-Manuel Miranda of *In the Heights.* Actress Karen Olivo left the cast of *In the Heights* to play Anita, for which she will win a Tony Award.

March 22, 2009 Transfer of Yasmina Reza's London hit, *God of Carnage,* in which James Gandolfini, Marcia Gay Harden, Jeff Daniels and Hope Davis, play the increasingly belligerent parents of two boys involved in a playground fight.

March 24, 2009 Jeremy Irons and Joan Allen star in Michael Jacobs' play, *Impressionism,* about a photojournalist and a gallery owner who discover each other. Also featured: Marsha Mason and André De Shields.

March 26, 2009 Geoffrey Rush and Susan Sarandon are king and queen on unsteady thrones in a rare revival of Eugene Ionesco's black comedy *Exit the King,* directed by Neil Armfield. Among their court are Lauren

Workers put finishing touches on renovations to Henry Miller's Theatre on 43rd Street.

Ambrose and Andrea Martin.

March 29, 2009 Tovah Feldshuh plays a Polish woman who hides a group of Jews from the Nazis during World War II in a transfer of the Off-Broadway hit, *Irena's Vow.*

March 31, 2009 The "American tribal love-rock musical" *Hair* returns to Broadway in Diane Paulus' production, which originated at the Delacorte Theatre in Central Park in summer 2008. Gavin Creel and Will Swenson are featured in the James Rado/Gerome Ragni/Galt MacDermot musical.

April 2, 2009 Playwright Neil LaBute makes his Broadway debut with a transfer of his Off-Broadway hit, *reasons to be pretty,* part of a trio of plays examining people's obsession with physical beauty. Terry Kinney directs a cast that includes Thomas Sadoski, Marin Ireland, Piper Perabo and Steven Pasquale.

April 7, 2009 Constantine Maroulis, Amy Spanger and James Carpinello are featured in the musical *Rock of Ages* with a score of 1980s hits by rock groups Journey, Bon Jovi, Styx, Pat Benatar and others. The original story follows two fans who come to Los Angeles to pursue their dreams of pop stardom.

April 15, 2009 Alice Ripley plays a suburban woman battling mental illness in Tom Kitt and Brian Yorkey's musical, *Next to Normal,* which enjoyed runs Off-Broadway and in Washington, DC. J. Robert Spencer, Aaron Tveit and Jennifer Damiano are among the supporting cast.

April 16, 2009 A wanderer arrives at a Pittsburgh boarding house in 1911 on a quest to find his lost wife in the first Broadway revival of August Wilson's *Joe Turner's Come and Gone.* Bartlett Sher directs a cast that includes Ernie Hudson, Chad L. Coleman and Aunjanue Ellis.

April 19, 2009 Janet McTeer and Harriet Walter play battling queens of Scotland and England in the U.S. premiere of the hit London revival of Friedrich Schiller's *Mary Stuart.*

April 20, 2009—Lynn Nottage's Off-Broadway drama *Ruined* is named winner of the

2009 Pulitzer Prize for Drama.

April 23, 2009 It takes three visits to see all of Alan Ayckbourn's triptych *The Norman Conquests,* which comes to Broadway's Circle in the Square from a hit revival at London's Old Vic. Directed by Matthew Warchus, the cast includes Amelia Bullmore, Jessica Hynes, Stephen Mangan and Amanda Root.

April 26, 2009 Matthew Broderick leads the cast of *The Philanthropist,* Roundabout Theatre Company's revival of Christopher Hampton's comedy centering on a clueless professor.

April 27, 2009 Two-time Tony winner Brian Dennehy recreates his Goodman Theatre performance in a revival of Eugene O'Neill's New England family drama, *Desire Under the Elms.* Robert Falls directs the production, which also features Carla Gugino and Pablo Schreiber.

April 29, 2009 Tony winner David Hyde Pierce portrays a playwright who finds fresh inspiration in a pretty young secretary in Manhattan Theatre Club's revival of Samson Raphaelson's 1934 comedy *Accent on Youth.* The cast also features Mary Catherine Garrison and Charles Kimbrough, directed by Daniel Sullivan.

April 30, 2009 Country star and actress Dolly Parton makes her Broadway debut as composer-lyricist of the score to *9 to 5: The Musical,* an adaptation of the film in which she once co-starred. Screenwriter Patricia Resnick wrote the libretto to the show about female office workers' conflicts with their male chauvinist boss. Allison Janney, Stephanie J. Block, Megan Hilty star with Marc Kudisch.

April 30, 2009 Theatre fans had to wait—appropriately—for the final production of the season, Roundabout Theatre Company's revival of Samuel Beckett's existential classic *Waiting for Godot,* starring Bill Irwin, Nathan Lane, John Goodman and John Glover.

May 24, 2009 Broadway is closed to automotive traffic from 47th to 42nd Streets as part of a yearlong pilot program to see if the traffic artery works better as a pedestrian mall.

May 26, 2009 The Broadway League announces that, recession notwithstanding, Broadway has enjoyed a record-breaking $943.3 million season at the box office, slightly higher than 2007-2008's $937.5 million, and entailing only a slight decline in the number of ticket buyers, from 12.27 million to 12.15 million. Forty-three productions opened on Broadway during the season, the most since the 1982-1983 season, which saw 50 productions open. The 2008-2009 season comprised ten new musicals, eight new plays, four musical revivals, sixteen play revivals and five special performances.

May 30, 2009 President Barack Obama fulfills a campaign promise to First Lady Michelle Obama and takes her to a Broadway show, *Joe Turner's Come and Gone.*

June 7, 2009 The 63rd Annual Tony Awards are held at Radio City Music Hall. *Billy Elliot* is named Best Musical, *God of Carnage* is named Best Play, and *Hair* and *The Norman Conquests* are named Best Revivals.

Head of the Class

Trends, Extraordinary Achievements and Peculiar Coincidences of the Season

Most Tony Awards to a Musical: *Billy Elliot* (10).

Most Tony Awards to a Play: *God of Carnage* (3).

Shortest Run: *The Story of My Life* (4 regular performances).

By the Numbers: Numerical titles were very popular this season: *13, 9 to 5, 33 Variations, The 39 Steps.*

Awards They Should Give: #1 Best New Showtune: Our nominees: "Nine People's Favorite Thing" from *[title of show].* "What It Means To Be a Friend" from *13.* "Electricity" from *Billy Elliot.* "Who I'd Be" from *Shrek.* "I Miss the Mountains" from *Next to Normal.* "Get Out and Stay Out" from *9 to 5.*

Let It Snow: Shows in Which, at Some Point, It Snows: *Slava's Snowshow, Billy Elliot, White Christmas, Pal Joey, The Soul of Shaolin, To Be or Not To Be, Hair.* Honorable mention: Rain in *Mary Stuart.*

Yes, Your Majesty: Monarchs Attended by Their Faithful Servants: *Exit the King, The Lion King, The Little Mermaid, Mary Stuart, A Man for All Seasons, Spamalot.*

Omigod You Guys! Year III: Shows With Pre-Teen, Teenage or Barely Post-Teen Girls As Lead or Important Characters (Though Not Always Played By Teens): *August: Osage County, Billy Elliot, Cry-Baby, Grease, Gypsy, Hairspray, Legally Blonde, The Little Mermaid, Mamma Mia!, Mary Poppins, Next to Normal, Soul of Shaolin, Spelling Bee, Spring Awakening, 13, Top Girls, West Side Story, Wicked.*

All I Want To Do Is…DANCE! *Billy Elliot, A Chorus Line, Curtains, Spamalot.* Honorable mention: All I want to do is ROCK!: *Rock of Ages.*

Teen Sex Leads to Trouble: *August: Osage County, Cry-Baby, Equus, Grease, Jersey Boys, Mamma Mia!, Spring Awakening, West Side Story.*

Night of the Hunter: Shows starring guys named Hunter: Hunter Parrish in *Spring Awakening,* Hunter Bell in *[title of show].* Honorable mention: Hunter Foster in Off-Broadway's *Happiness.*

Fastest Quick-Changes: Twelve in 40 seconds: Arnie Burton and Cliff Saunders in *The 39 Steps.*

Stars Come Out: Joan Allen, Elizabeth Ashley, James Barbour, Stephanie J. Block, Matthew Broderick, Cedric the Entertainer, Stockard Channing, Brian Dennehy, Christine Ebersole, Raúl Esparza, Tovah Feldshuh, Will Ferrell, Jane Fonda, Sutton Foster, John Goodman, Richard Griffiths, Katie Holmes, Jeremy Irons, Bill Irwin, Brian d'Arcy James, Allison Janney, Elton John, Nathan Lane, Frank Langella, Angela Lansbury, Arthur Laurents, John Leguizamo, John Lithgow, David Mamet, Constantine Maroulis, Janet McTeer, Liza Minnelli, Elisabeth Moss, Haley Joel Osment, Mary-Louise Parker, Estelle Parsons, Dolly Parton, David Hyde Pierce, Jeremy Piven, Martha Plimpton, Daniel Radcliffe, Stephen

---

Broadway's Longest Runs

By number of performances. Asterisk (*) indicates show still running as of May 31, 2009. Totals are for original runs except where otherwise noted.

The Phantom of the Opera 8883
Cats 7485
Les Misérables 6680
A Chorus Line 6137
Oh! Calcutta! (Revival) 5959
Beauty and the Beast 5461
Chicago (Revival) 5200
Rent 5123
The Lion King 4832
Miss Saigon 4097
42nd Street 3486
Grease 3388
Fiddler on the Roof 3242
Life With Father 3224
Tobacco Road 3182
Mamma Mia! 3170
Hello, Dolly! 2844
My Fair Lady 2717
Hairspray 2642
The Producers 2502
Avenue Q 2418

Sondheim, Kristin Scott Thomas, Dianne Wiest.

Boo! Ghosts or Ghost References in Shows: *Blithe Spirit, Next to Normal* (the son), *Spring Awakening* (Wendla and Moritz in Act II), *Billy Elliot* (the mother), *Desire Under the Elms* (the previous wife, in the parlor), *The Lion King* (Mufasa), *Sunday in the Park With George* (Dot, in Act II). Honorable Mentions: *Phantom of the Opera, Rock of Ages* (the angel).

Hail to the Chief: Shows With Presidents as Main Characters: *November, You're Welcome America.* Honorable Mention for Having an actual President in the audience: *Joe Turner's Come and Gone.*

Awards They Should Give: #2 Best Special Effects. Our nominees: *Billy Elliot* (flying, giant puppets, dancing dresses), *Blithe Spirit* (ghostly manifestations), *Desire Under the Elms* (the suspended house), *Shrek the Musical* (the dragon), *A Tale of Two Cities* (the guillotine), *You're Welcome America* (Ferrell's parachute entrance), *Cirque Dreams* (jungle effects).

Oddest Program Credit: "Peanut Butter & Co. is the official peanut butter of *American Buffalo.*"

Going Green: Leading Characters Who Are, at Some Point, Green: Joining the ever-green Ephaba in *Wicked,* the Monster in *Young Frankenstein* and Nicky in *Avenue Q* were Shrek and Princess Fiona in *Shrek The Musical.* Honorable mention: the title character in Off-Broadway's *The Toxic Avenger.*

Rock Groups: Huge boulders formed the sets

---

for *Waiting for Godot* and *Desire Under the Elms.*

Awards They Should Give: #3 Best New Rendition of an Old Song in a Revival or Jukebox Musical. Our nominees: Karen Olivo's "America" in *West Side Story,* Craig Bierko's "Luck Be a Lady" in *Guys and Dolls,* the cast's title song in *White Christmas,* the cast's "Cum on Feel the Noize" in *Rock of Ages,* Liza and company's "Jubilee" in *Liza's at the Palace...,* the cast's title song in *9 to 5,* the cast's "Aquarius" in *Hair.*

I'm Flying: Shows in Which the Lead Character, at Some Point, Flies: *Billy Elliot, Boeing-Boeing, Cirque Dreams, Mary Poppins, 9 to 5, Spamalot, Wicked, Guys and Dolls* (the flight to Havana).

Tura! Tura! Tura!: The fictional Tura family was busy on Broadway this season, with Maria Tura and Josef Tura fleeing Nazis in *To Be or Not To Be* and Tessie Tura staying dressy in *Gypsy.*

Coups de Theatre: Angela Lansbury dances herself into a trance in *Blithe Spirit.* Dancing makes Billy fly in *Billy Elliot.* The whole Cabot homestead rises into the air in *Desire Under the Elms.* A single wad of cash changes hands many times under many circumstances in the revised "Runyonland" sequence of *Guys and Dolls.* Members of the "Tribe" invite the audience onto the stage to sing "Let the Sun Shine In" at the finale of *Hair.* Tovah Feldshuh's quick thinking narrowly averts Nazi detection of Jews hiding the basement in *Irena's Vow.* Alice Ripley tells the spirit of her dead son that she's literally willing to die to dance with him in *Next to Normal.* Liza Minnelli sings until she collapses into the arms of her backup singers in *Liza's at the Palace....* Frank Langella realizes that his duty to the Church will cost him his life in *A Man for All Seasons.* Janet McTeer exults in a moment of freedom in a rainstorm in *Mary Stuart.* Allison Janney fantasizes a big old-fashioned dance number when she realizes she is now "One of the Boys" in *9 to 5 the Musical.* Marin Ireland tears Thomas Sadoski a new one in the opening diatribe of *reasons to be pretty.* An unexpected burst of affection results in the song "Can't Fight This Feeling" in *Rock of Ages.* Christopher Sieber shows off the stagecraft that made him a convincing midget in "What's Up, Duloc?" from *Shrek the Musical.* James Barbour comforts a young woman as both of them approach the guillotine in the finale of *A Tale of Two Cities.* Zach Grenier takes us inside the mind of Ludwig van Beethoven as he composes one of the 33 variations in the show of the same name. The jeweled furniture appears in the climactic moment of *[title of show].* Nathan Lane and Bill Irwin try to help the beached John Goodman who has fallen and cannot get up in *Waiting for Godot.* Will Ferrell, playing President George W. Bush, ad-libs nicknames for random audience members in *You're Welcome America. A Final Night with George W. Bush.*

Accent on Youth

First Preview: April 7, 2009. Opened: April 29, 2009.
Still running as of May 31, 2009.

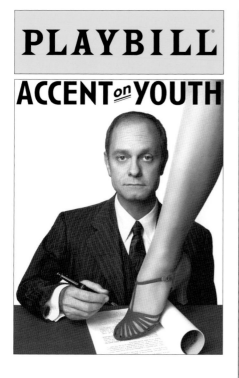

PLAYBILL

CAST
(in alphabetical order)

Miss Darling	LISA BANES
Genevieve Lang	ROSIE BENTON
Butch	CURT BOURIL
Dickie Reynolds	DAVID FURR
Linda Brown	MARY CATHERINE GARRISON
Frank Galloway	BYRON JENNINGS
Flogdell	CHARLES KIMBROUGH
Steven Gaye	DAVID HYDE PIERCE
Chuck	JOHN WERNKE

The action takes place in the New York duplex of
Steven Gaye over the course of a year.

Stage Manager ....DENISE YANEY

UNDERSTUDIES

For Frank Galloway and Flogdell:
ROSS BICKELL
For Chuck:
CURT BOURIL
For Miss Darling:
CYNTHIA DARLOW
For Steven Gaye and Butch:
JACK KOENIG
For Genevieve Lang and Linda Brown:
KAREN WALSH
For Dickie Reynolds:
JOHN WERNKE

MANHATTAN THEATRE CLUB
Samuel J. Friedman Theatre

ARTISTIC DIRECTOR	EXECUTIVE PRODUCER
Lynne Meadow	Barry Grove

BY SPECIAL ARRANGEMENT WITH

Daryl Roth   Ostar Productions   Rebecca Gold/Debbie Bisno

PRESENTS

ACCENT on YOUTH

BY

Samson Raphaelson

WITH

Lisa Banes   Rosie Benton   Curt Bouril
David Furr   Mary Catherine Garrison   Byron Jennings
Charles Kimbrough   David Hyde Pierce   John Wernke

SCENIC DESIGN	COSTUME DESIGN	LIGHTING DESIGN
John Lee Beatty	Jane Greenwood	Brian MacDevitt

ORIGINAL MUSIC & SOUND DESIGN	HAIR & WIG DESIGN	PRODUCTION STAGE MANAGER
Obadiah Eaves	Tom Watson	Roy Harris

DIRECTED BY

Daniel Sullivan

GENERAL MANAGER	ASSOCIATE ARTISTIC DIRECTOR
Florie Seery	Mandy Greenfield

DIRECTOR OF ARTISTIC DEVELOPMENT	DIRECTOR OF MARKETING	PRESS REPRESENTATIVE
Jerry Patch	Debra Waxman-Pilla	Boneau/Bryan-Brown

PRODUCTION MANAGER	DIRECTOR OF CASTING	DIRECTOR OF DEVELOPMENT
Kurt Gardner	Nancy Piccione	Jill Turner Lloyd

Manhattan Theatre Club wishes to express its appreciation to Theatre Development Fund for its support of this production.

4/29/09

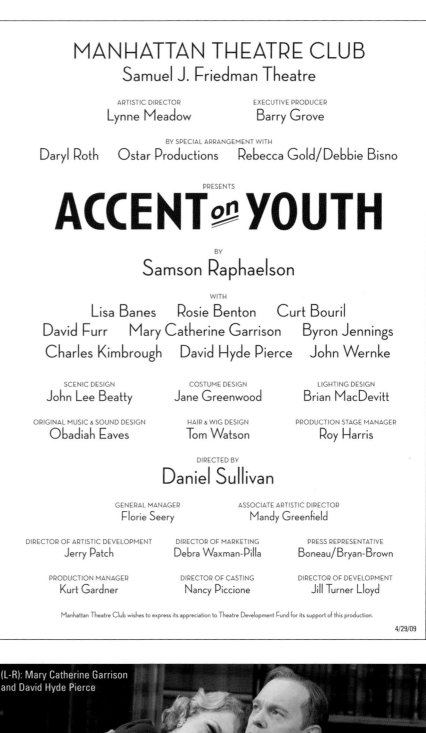

(L-R): Mary Catherine Garrison and David Hyde Pierce

Photo by Joan Marcus

Accent on Youth

Lisa Banes
Miss Darling

Rosie Benton
Genevieve Lang

Curt Bouril
Butch

David Furr
Dickie Reynolds

Mary Catherine Garrison
Linda Brown

David Hyde Pierce
Steven Gaye

Byron Jennings
Frank Galloway

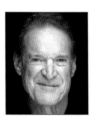
Charles Kimbrough
Flogdell

John Wernke
Chuck

Ross Bickell
u/s Frank Galloway, Flogdell

Cynthia Darlow
u/s Miss Darling

Jack Koenig
u/s Steven Gaye, Butch

Karen Walsh
u/s Genevieve Lang, Linda Brown

Samson Raphaelson
Playwright

Daniel Sullivan
Director

John Lee Beatty
Scenic Design

Jane Greenwood
Costume Design

Brian MacDevitt
Lighting Design

CREW
Front Row (L-R): Unknown, Louis Shapiro, Denise Yaney.
Back Row (L-R): Angela Simpson, Chris Wiggins, Jeff Dodson, Timothy Walters, Ian Harbor, Michael DiMarco.

Photos by Brian Mapp

Obadiah Eaves
Original Music & Sound Design

Tom Watson
Hair & Wig Design

Lynne Meadow
Artistic Director, Manhattan Theatre Club, Inc.

Barry Grove
Executive Producer, Manhattan Theatre Club, Inc.

Daryl Roth
Producer

Bill Haber,
Ostar Productions
Producer

BOX OFFICE
(L-R): Jeffrey Davis and Keith Stephenson

FRONT OF HOUSE STAFF
Sitting (L-R): Jackson Ero, Russ Ramsey, Ed Brashear, Richard Ponce, John Wyffels.
Standing (L-R): Dinah Glorioso, Patricia Polhill, Nilsa Nairn, Ramon Pesante, Amber Wilkerson.

Accent on Youth

(L-R): David Hyde Pierce and Charles Kimbrough

Accent on Youth
SCRAPBOOK

Correspondents: Roy Harris and Denise Yaney, Stage Managers

When we began rehearsal for Samson Raphaelson's 1934 comedy, *Accent on Youth*, on March 3, 2009, we were fairly certain we had something very special. A funny, touching play with a deep undercurrent of conflicted feelings about age, love, and sex, with as nearly perfect a cast as you could wish for: David Hyde Pierce as Steven Gaye, accomplished Broadway playwright, a quasi Noel Coward; Mary Catherine Garrison as his secretary, Linda Brown, who does a duckling-swan transformation between Acts I and II; Charles Kimbrough as Flogdell, Gaye's loyal butler; Rosie Benton as Genevieve Lang, a young, sexy, Broadway star; David Furr, Lisa Banes, and the hilarious Byron Jennings all playing actors in different stages of their careers, and John Wernke and Curt Bouril as part of the Princeton "glee club."

In addition, the Tony-Award winning design team of John Lee Beatty, Jane Greenwood, and Brian MacDevitt (who have among them a total of 38 Tony nominations, with four wins) and Obadiah Eaves's period-perfect music. And finally, the supremely gifted Tony Award-winning director, Daniel Sullivan. Our home: one of the loveliest jewel-box Broadway theat\res that ever existed: Manhattan Theatre Club's Friedman (neé the Biltmore).

Rehearsals were probably some of the best times any of us has ever had in a rehearsal room. Lots of hard work, many line kerfuffles, many run-thrus, and lots of hilarity. On the first day, Dan told us that playwright Raphaelson's advice on acting his play was "Don't rush the exposition. They aren't going anywhere," to which Dan added, "So the first act will be very stately."

A few days into rehearsal, DHP (as we affectionately referred to David Hyde Pierce) said with some frustration, "I don't know what I'm doing," to which Dan replied, "I don't either." Several days later as we were struggling with the beginning of the third act, Mr. Kimbrough with full force and belief said the following line: "I'm into my sixties, but I can still touch the floor with my testicles." The actual line is "I'm into my sixties, but I can still touch the floor with my knuckles." But we did admire the certainty with which he said the incorrect line.

Mary Catherine told us one day as we rehearsed the final scene that her subtext for her entrance in the final scene was "I may be naked but I'm a grown-up." Very near the end of the second week of rehearsal, as we did our first run, DHP commented at our act break, "It feels like we're doing the *Mahabharata*."

One happily unusual event during rehearsals was that we watched Ernst Lubitsch's film *Trouble in Paradise*, for two reasons: it was written by our playwright and it was very much of the period of the play. Miriam Hopkins, Kay Francis, and Herbert Marshall were hilarious. One day Dan told Rosie Benton, who, playing a flamboyant young actress, liked lolling on the couch in her two scenes, "You only get to lie on the couch once in the third act, so make your choice."

Once Mr. Kimbrough apologized for not speaking at the appropriate time, saying, "I was

1. Members of the cast take bows on opening night at the Friedman Theatre.
2. Cast member Charles Kimbrough at Espace restaurant for the opening night party.

lost in the dream of my own performance." One of our stage managers was heard to say late one afternoon, "I love the second act. There's so much good kissing."

When we moved into the theatre there were five days of tech rehearsals before our first audience. Everyone worked very hard. Lights, sound, and the gorgeous costumes and wigs began to come together to tell the play's story. And the good times continued too. "In a year and a half at the Shubert and a year and a half at the Hirschfeld," DHP said, "I was never lifted off my feet by the doorman."

We did twenty-four previews before opening. Afternoon rehearsals were for tightening the play and the performances. One day, Dan told Lisa Banes that she needed more comic energy in the first scene, to which DHP replied, "Asking Lisa for more comic energy is like asking Iran for more nuclear weapons." Another time, having decided to cut Mr. Kimbrough's large soup spoon at the top of the second act, Dan explained, "We have enough phallic metaphors in the play."

A few days before we froze the show, he said to the company at the beginning of notes, "I can tell when we're nearing the end because my actor notes are all about pronouns."

After we opened we began having brunch every Sunday before the matinee. These were hosted by our stage managers, Roy Harris and Denise Yaney, a tradition they began ten years ago when they were stage managing O'Neill's *A Moon for the Misbegotten* at the Walter Kerr. Over the next two months we had some delightful culinary fare. For instance, there were Denise's fabled deviled eggs and her Quiche by Deniche. Roy made his blueberry bread, pasta salad, broccoli cheese cornbread, and roast sweet

potato fries. Standby Cynthia Darlow, noted around the Rialto for her culinary skills, made her mascarpone tart and her sun-dried tomato-arugula-cheese pinwheels. Assistant house manager Richard Ponce brought in varieties of bagels with cream cheese nearly every week. David Furr contributed chocolate-covered biscotti. Margie Howard, our SM sub, brought in her coffee cake. There were quiche from ticket-taker Ed Brashear and granola yogurt parfait from usher Wendy Wright. Wardrobe supervisor Angie Simpson made her bean dip with Tostitos. Hair supervisor Natasha Steinhagen made her potato salad. The Sunday we hosted the company of *Exit the King*, we had carrot cake from stage manager Jim Woolley; brownies from Andrea Martin; Amy's Bread cinnamon buns from Erika Rolfsrud. We found that these Sunday events were a terrific way for the company to socialize. They were very successful.

Our one cavil about the whole *Accent on Youth* experience: it didn't last nearly long enough.

All My Sons

First Preview: September 18, 2008. Opened: October 16, 2008.
Closed January 11, 2009 after 32 Previews and 101 Performances.

PLAYBILL

ARTHUR MILLER'S ALL MY SONS

CAST
(in order of appearance)

Joe Keller .... JOHN LITHGOW
Dr. Jim Bayliss .... DAMIAN YOUNG
Frank Lubey .... JORDAN GELBER
Sue Bayliss .... BECKY ANN BAKER
Lydia Lubey .... DANIELLE FERLAND
Chris Keller .... PATRICK WILSON
Bert .... MICHAEL D'ADDARIO
Kate Keller .... DIANNE WIEST
Ann Deever .... KATIE HOLMES
George Deever .... CHRISTIAN CAMARGO
Neighbors .... SHERMAN HOWARD,
CLARK JACKSON, LIZBETH MACKAY,
CHRISTOPHER GREY MISA,
DANIELLE SKRAASTAD

UNDERSTUDIES
For Joe Keller, Dr. Jim Bayliss:
SHERMAN HOWARD
For Chris Keller, George Deever, Frank Lubey,
Dr. Jim Bayliss:
CLARK JACKSON
For Kate Keller, Sue Bayliss:
LIZBETH MACKAY
For Ann Deever, Lydia Lubey:
DANIELLE SKRAASTAD
For Bert:
CHRISTOPHER GREY MISA

GERALD SCHOENFELD THEATRE
236 West 45th Street
A Shubert Organization Theatre
Gerald Schoenfeld, *Chairman*   Philip J. Smith, *President*

Robert E. Wankel, *Executive Vice President*

ERIC FALKENSTEIN   OSTAR PRODUCTIONS
BARBARA H. FREITAG   STEPHANIE P. McCLELLAND
SCOTT DELMAN   ROY FURMAN   RUTH HENDEL
in association with
HAL LUFTIG   JANE BERGÈRE   JAMIE deROY
present

JOHN LITHGOW   **DIANNE WIEST**
PATRICK WILSON   **KATIE HOLMES**

in

ARTHUR MILLER'S **ALL MY SONS**

with

BECKY ANN BAKER   CHRISTIAN CAMARGO   MICHAEL D'ADDARIO
DANIELLE FERLAND   JORDAN GELBER   DAMIAN YOUNG

SHERMAN HOWARD   CLARK JACKSON
LIZBETH MACKAY   CHRISTOPHER GREY MISA   DANIELLE SKRAASTAD

Scenic & Costume Design **TOM PYE**	Lighting Design **PAUL ANDERSON**	Sound Design **CHRISTOPHER SHUTT & CAROLYN DOWNING**
Projection Design **FINN ROSS for MESMER**	Wig Design **PAUL HUNTLEY**	Associate Producer/Casting Director **CINDY TOLAN**
Production Stage Manager **ANDREA "SPOOK" TESTANI**	Technical Supervisor **NICK SCHWARTZ-HALL**	Press Representative **BONEAU/BRYAN-BROWN**
Associate Producers **A. ASNES/A. ZOTOVICH M. MILLS/L. STEVENS**	Company Manager **KIMBERLY KELLEY**	General Management **RICHARDS/CLIMAN, INC.**

Directed By
SIMON McBURNEY

Special thanks to Complicité (Simon McBurney: Artistic Director; Judith Dimant: Managing Director)

10/16/08

The cast in the opening scene.

Photo by Joan Marcus

All My Sons

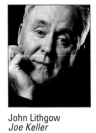
John Lithgow
Joe Keller

Dianne Wiest
Kate Keller

Patrick Wilson
Chris Keller

Katie Holmes
Ann Deever

Becky Ann Baker
Sue Bayliss

Christian Camargo
George Deever

Michael D'Addario
Bert

Danielle Ferland
Lydia Lubey

Jordan Gelber
Frank Lubey

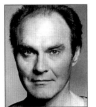
Damian Young
Dr. Jim Bayliss

Sherman Howard
Neighbor

Clark Jackson
Neighbor

Lizbeth Mackay
Neighbor

Christopher Grey
Misa
Neighbor

Danielle Skraastad
Neighbor

Arthur Miller
Playwright

Simon McBurney
Director

Tom Pye
Scenic Design/
Costume Design

Paul Huntley
Hair and Wig Design

David R. Richards and Tamar Haimes,
Richards/Climan, Inc.
General Manager

Eric Falkenstein
Producer

Bill Haber,
Ostar Productions
Producer

Barbara Heller
Freitag
Producer

Roy Furman
Producer

Ruth Hendel
Producer

Stephanie P.
McClelland
Producer

Hal Luftig
Associate Producer

Jane Bergère
Associate Producer

Jamie deRoy
Associate Producer

Lauren Stevens
Associate Producer

Adam Zotovich
Associate Producer

Andrew Asnes
Associate Producer

All My Sons

STAGE CREW
Front Row (L-R): Heidi Brown, Cletus Karamon, Erin Kennedy Lunsford, Katy Lathan, Drew Barr, Andrea "Spook" Testani, Rodney Giebler, Alex Lyu Volckhausen.

Middle Row (L-R): Glenn Ingram, Ned Hatton, Leslie Ann Kilian, George Sheer, Melissa Crawford, Dan Shaheen, Kim Kelley.

Back Row (holding umbrella): Tim McWilliams

FRONT OF HOUSE STAFF
Front Row (L-R): Francine Kramer, Emily Christenson, Anthony Martinez, Thomas Barry.

Middle Row (L-R): Denise Demirjian, Gillian Sheffler, Sheryl Goldberg.

Back Row: House Manager David Conte

STAFF FOR *ALL MY SONS*

GENERAL MANAGEMENT
RICHARDS/CLIMAN, INC.
David R. Richards   Tamar Haimes

COMPANY MANAGER
Kimberly Kelley

GENERAL PRESS REPRESENTATIVE
BONEAU/BRYAN-BROWN
Adrian Bryan-Brown   Jackie Green
Kelly Guiod

PRODUCTION STAGE	
MANAGER	Andrea "Spook" Testani
Stage Managers	Alex Lyu Volckhausen,
	Dan Shaheen
Associate Director	Drew Barr
Associate Set Design	Frank McCullough,
	Lauren Alvarez
UK Associate Set Design	James Humphrey
Associate Lighting Design	Lauren Phillips
Associate Costume Design	Amy Clark
Associate Projection Design	Brian Beasley
Fight Captain	Clark Jackson
Production Carpenter	Don Robinson
Production Electrician	Cletus Karamon
Production Propertyman	Scott Laule
Production Sound Operator	Ned Hatton
Projection Programmer	Peter Acken
Light Board Programmer	Keith Buchanan
Wardrobe Supervisor	Kay Grunder
Mr. Lithgow's Dresser	Patrick Bevilacqua
Dressers	Melissa Crawford,
	George Sheer
Hair Supervisor	Erin Kennedy Lunsford
Associate General Manager	John Gendron
General Management Associate	Jeromy Smith
General Management Assistant	Cesar Hawas
Director of Voice	Patsy Rodenburg
Casting Associate	Adam Caldwell
Casting Assistant	Nicole Becker

Production Assistants	Rachel Maier,
	Sarah Michele Penland
Child Wrangler	Katy Lathan
Consultant	Annie Castledine
Advertising	SpotCo/
	Drew Hodges, Jim Edwards,
	Tom Greenwald, Stephen Sosnowski,
	Timothy Falotico
Poster Photo	Andrew Eccles
Marketing	Type A Marketing/
	Anne Rippey, Janette Roush,
	Nick Pramik
Accountant	Fried & Kowgios CPA's LLP/
	Robert Fried, CPA
Production Comptroller	Elliott Aronstam, CPA
Banking	City National Bank
Insurance	DeWitt Stern Group/
	Joseph Bower
Sponsorship Consultant	Jed Bernstein
Marketing Associate	Joe McGowan
Marketing Associate/	
Asst. to Producer	Abigail Rose Solomon
Payroll Services	CSI/
	Lance Castellana, James Castellana,
	Norman Sewell
Production Photographer	Joan Marcus
Opening Night	
Coordination	The Lawrence Company Events/
	Michael P. Lawrence, Joanna B. Cepler
Theatre Displays	King Displays, Wayne Sapper
Concierge/Chauffeur Services	Get Services LLC

CREDITS
Scenery constructed by Showman Fabricators. Apple tree constructed by Susan Pitocchi Studio. Costumes constructed by Tricorne, Inc.; Barbara Matera Ltd.; Claudia Diaz Costumes; Cego Custom Shirts. Costumes supplied by Western Costume Company, Bra*Tenders. Lighting equipment supplied by PRG - 4th Phase. Projection supplied by New City Video & Staging, Inc. Sound equipment from Sound Associates. Natural herb cough drops courtesy of Ricola USA, Inc. Dental special effects by Marc J. Beshar, D.M.D.

SPECIAL THANKS
Jill Albert, Margaret Cotter, Jonathan Farber, M.P. Gad, Chad Gracia, Ralph Guild, R.J. Jean, Marsha & Henry Laufer, Mark & Marianna McCall, Rose Polidoro, J. Pullano, J. Rizzo, D. Ross, A.J. Sharyn, P. Siegal, N. & S. Sopkin, M. Weill, David Yazber, Robert Zimmerman

---

THE SHUBERT ORGANIZATION, INC.
Board of Directors

Gerald Schoenfeld Chairman	**Philip J. Smith** President
Wyche Fowler, Jr.	**John W. Kluge**
Lee J. Seidler	**Michael I. Sovern**

Stuart Subotnick

Robert E. Wankel
Executive Vice President

David Andrews Senior Vice President – Shubert Ticketing	**Elliot Greene** Senior Vice President – Finance
Juan Calvo Vice President and Controller	**John Darby** Vice President – Facilities
Peter Entin Vice President – Theatre Operations	**Charles Flateman** Vice President – Marketing
Anthony LaMattina Vice President – Audit & Production Finance	**Brian Mahoney** Vice President – Ticket Sales

D.S. Moynihan
Vice President – Creative Projects

Theatre Manager ....David M. Conte

All My Sons
SCRAPBOOK

Correspondent: Christian Camargo, "George Deever"

Memorable Opening Night Note: It was the day-after note from Rebecca Miller that trumped all others. To put it simply, we passed with flying colors.

Opening Night Gifts: From the comical Sherman Howard (a.k.a. ShoHo) notes of perversion, to the goodie box from Katie (one word...Prada) to the miniature apple trees from Patrick to the hand-drawn sketch by Mr. Lithgow—the opening night gifts were beyond amazing.

Most Exciting Celebrity Visitor: Goldie Hawn, no...Snake Plissken...no it was...Lauren Bacall...no...Dustin Hoffman…Bill Moyers,… Perhaps Lynn Redgrave? Or Marian Seldes? Definitely Oprah, or maybe Mr. Holmes…? OK, you get the point: pretty much everyone in the "Who's Who" came to this show. Not a bad spot to be in. If I were to have to single out one it would be Kirk Douglas rising to his feet at curtain and coming backstage to shake hands with every cast member big and small. A gentleman and hero.

Most Shows in Their Career: I think John Lithgow gets that one. Twenty Broadway shows...I'm exhausted just thinking about it.

Special Backstage Ritual: There's a strange Duck War going on. I don't know who started it (I think Dianne is the culprit), but there are these plastic ducks that show up in the strangest of places...

Favorite Moment During Each Performance: Bert (Michael D.). You just never knew where he's gunna land.

Favorite Off-Site Hangout: Angus McIndoe seems to rank up top.

Favorite Snack Food: Spook's banana bread! And Liz's brownies. Those will be two of the things I miss most.

Mascot: A Duck.

Favorite Therapy: Katie H. and I would say "Just tonight" before going on. Meaning we would give our best just for that night. Then the next day would come...and so on...we now have to say it before every go.

Memorable Ad-Libs: Joe: "I got a real flexible family...I mean...and business too." It got us wondering about the key-parties that would happen around the Keller household.
In Act II Patrick lifts the tree. One night he got it caught in the neighbor's gate, struggled a bit, then just lifted the whole thing off its hinges. He threw it all down, looked offstage to the neighbors, shrugged, and yelled, "Sorry!"

Memorable Stage Door Fan Encounter: This fan named Tom Cruise kept coming to the show and somehow getting backstage (apparently he knew someone). He would come to each of us and tell us how amazing we were, so after a few compliments we didn't mind so much. We actually began to miss him when he wasn't there.

Catchphrase Only the Company Would Recognize: "Don't pull a Lubey."

1. Curtain call on opening night.
2. Cast member Danielle Ferland at Espace restaurant for the opening night party.
3. Cast member Patrick Wilson (R) and wife Dagmara at the premiere.

Company In-Jokes: Anything Lubey-related.

Memorable Directorial Note: All of them. One? Okay: "Elan." Look it up, it's French.

Understudy Anecdote: Watching the understudies try to memorize their lines while performing in the initial previews. They had no time and were pulling double shifts to get it all together. Are they appreciated enough? Hmm....

Nicknames: "ShoHo," "Lubey" (Jordan Gelber), "Lord Lithgow," "Dumb Person" (That's Patrick. Well I was the only one who called him that but I really think he liked it), and "Ducky Diane" (actually no one called her that, but I feel everyone wants to) and "The Terrors" (the two Berts).

Ghostly Encounters Backstage: There's a ghost in the men's dressing room who keeps putting a half glass of water on Clark's table. Really. It's a ghost.

Superstitions That Turned Out To Be True: Dianne really is not from our solar system. She was dropped here quite by accident, but fortunately entertainment found her.

Coolest Thing About Being in This Show: Everyone in the cast and crew. There's not a more positive and inspiring group to be around.

American Buffalo

First Preview: October 31, 2008. Opened: November 17, 2008.
Closed November 24, 2008 after 20 Previews and 8 Performances.

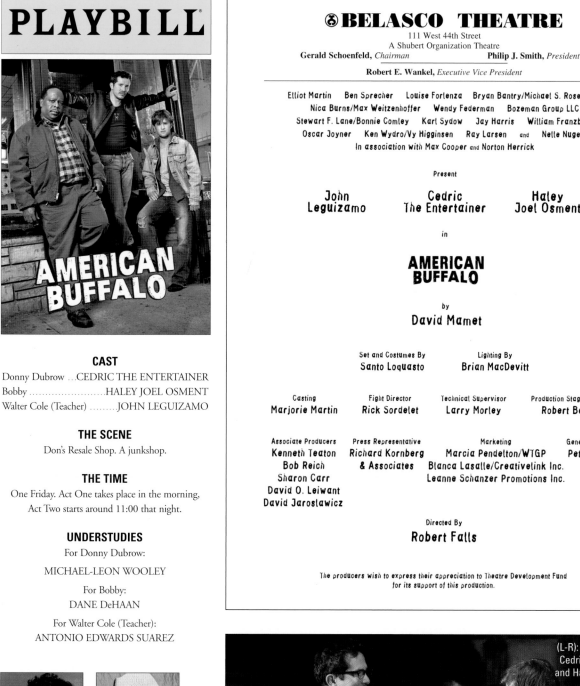

PLAYBILL

AMERICAN BUFFALO

CAST
Donny Dubrow ...CEDRIC THE ENTERTAINER
Bobby ....HALEY JOEL OSMENT
Walter Cole (Teacher) ....JOHN LEGUIZAMO

THE SCENE
Don's Resale Shop. A junkshop.

THE TIME
One Friday. Act One takes place in the morning,
Act Two starts around 11:00 that night.

UNDERSTUDIES
For Donny Dubrow:
MICHAEL-LEON WOOLEY

For Bobby:
DANE DeHAAN

For Walter Cole (Teacher):
ANTONIO EDWARDS SUAREZ

John Leguizamo
Walter Cole
(Teacher)

Cedric The
Entertainer
Donny Dubrow

ⓢ BELASCO THEATRE
111 West 44th Street
A Shubert Organization Theatre
Gerald Schoenfeld, *Chairman*   Philip J. Smith, *President*

Robert E. Wankel, *Executive Vice President*

Elliot Martin   Ben Sprecher   Louise Forlenza   Bryan Bantry/Michael S. Rosenberg
Nica Burns/Max Weitzenhoffer   Wendy Federman   Bozeman Group LLC
Stewart F. Lane/Bonnie Comley   Karl Sydow   Jay Harris   William Franzblau
Oscar Joyner   Ken Wydro/Vy Higginsen   Ray Larsen   and   Nette Nugent
In association with Max Cooper and Norton Herrick

Present

John   Cedric   Haley
Leguizamo   The Entertainer   Joel Osment

in

AMERICAN BUFFALO

by
David Mamet

Set and Costumes By   Lighting By
Santo Loquasto   Brian MacDevitt

Casting   Fight Director   Technical Supervisor   Production Stage Manager
Marjorie Martin   Rick Sordelet   Larry Morley   Robert Bennett

Associate Producers   Press Representative   Marketing   General Manager
Kenneth Teaton   Richard Kornberg   Marcia Pendelton/WTGP   Peter Bogyo
Bob Reich   & Associates   Blanca Lasalle/Creativelink Inc.
Sharon Carr   Leanne Schanzer Promotions Inc.
David O. Leiwant
David Jaroslawicz

Directed By
Robert Falls

*The producers wish to express their appreciation to Theatre Development Fund
for its support of this production.*

11/17/08

(L-R): John Leguizamo,
Cedric the Entertainer
and Haley Joel Osment

Photo by Joan Marcus

American Buffalo

Haley Joel Osment
Bobby

Dane DeHaan
Understudy for Bobby

Antonio Edwards Suarez
Understudy for Walter Cole

Michael-Leon Wooley
Understudy for Donny Dubrow

David Mamet
Playwright

Robert Falls
Director

Santo Loquasto
Set and Costume Design

Brian MacDevitt
Lighting Design

Rick Sordelet
Fight Director

Peter Bogyo
General Manager

Ben Sprecher
Producer

Wendy Federman
Producer

Stewart F. Lane and Bonnie Comley
Producer

Max Cooper
Producer

STAFF CREDITS FOR *AMERICAN BUFFALO*

GENERAL MANAGER
Peter Bogyo

COMPANY MANAGER
Lisa M. Poyer

GENERAL PRESS REPRESENTATIVE
Richard Kornberg & Associates
Richard Kornberg   Don Summa
Billy Zavelson   Alyssa Hart

TECHNICAL SUPERVISOR
Larry Morley

RAIN BY
Gregory Meeh
Jauchem and Meeh Special Effects

THE FOXBORO COMPANY, INC.
Nelle Nugent ....President and CEO
Kenneth Teaton ....SVP Production and Creative Affairs
Jeff Lock ....Executive Assistant
David Friedlander, Esq. ....Counsel

PRODUCTION STAGE MANAGER ....Robert Bennett
Stage Manager ....Denise Yaney
Assistant to General Manager ....Martin Giannini
Production Assistant ....Aaron Gonzalez
Production Intern ....Georgie Williams
Assistant Director ....Stephanie Yankwitt
Production Assistant to Elliot Martin ....Kate Kenny
Assistants to Ben Sprecher .....Jennifer Wills, Karen Derby
Associate Set Designer ....Jenny Sawyers
Assistant Set Designer ....Yoki Lai
Associate Costume Designer ....Mitchell Bloom
Associate Lighting Designer ....Jennifer Schriever
Sound Consultant ....Carl Casella
Associate Sound Consultant ....Wallace Flores
Dialect Coach ....Kate Wilson
Props Coordinator ....Kathy Fabian
Associate Props Coordinator ....Rose Howard
Prop Shoppers ....Jennifer Breen, Carrie Mossman,
Christina Gould

Flame Treatment ....Turning Star
Production Electrician ....Michael Pitzer
Wardrobe Supervisor ....Kathleen Gallagher
Dresser ....Kevin Andre Dickens
Production Legal
Counsel ....Robinson, Brog, Leinwand et al/
Richard Ticktin, Esq.
Insurance ....DeWitt Stern Group/Peter Shoemaker
Accountant ....Fried & Kowgios CPA's LLP/
Robert Fried, CPA
Controller ....Galbraith & Company, Inc./
Sarah Galbraith
Advertising ....Serino Coyne llc/
Sean Pomposello, Joaquin Esteva,
Miriam Naggar, Becca Goland-Van Ryn
Artwork Photography ....Justin Borucki Photography
Production Photography ....Carol Rosegg
Website Design and
Internet Marketing ....Bay Bridge Productions/
Laura Wagner, Jean Strong
Marketing......................Walk Tall Girl Productions/
Marcia Pendelton, Stephen Beasley,
Michelle Harris, Marc Rivas
Marketing ....Creative Link/
Blanca Lasalle, Javier Lopez
Marketing..............Leanne Schanzer Promotions, Inc./
Leanne Schanzer, Justin Schanzer,
Kara Laviola
Theatre Displays ....BAM Signs, Inc./
Adam Miller
Opening Night Coordination ....Broadway Parties/
Lisa Rice
Banking ....Commerce Bank/Barbara von Borstel
Payroll Service ....CSI, Castellana Services Inc.
Car Service ....Broadway Trans, Inc./Ralph Taliercio

CREDITS
Scenery built and painted by Great Lakes Scenic Studios Inc. Lighting equipment supplied by PRG Lighting. Sound equipment from Sound Associates, Inc. Flip Mino is the official camcorder of *American Buffalo*.

Peanut Butter & Co. is the official peanut butter of *American Buffalo*.

SPECIAL THANKS
Bay Street Theatre Co.

---

www.americanbuffalobroadway.com
www.youtube.com/americanbuffalo2008
www.myspace.com/americanbuffalobroadway

 THE SHUBERT ORGANIZATION, INC.
Board of Directors

| **Gerald Schoenfeld** | **Philip J. Smith** |
| Chairman | President |

| **Wyche Fowler, Jr.** | **John W. Kluge** |

| **Lee J. Seidler** | **Michael I. Sovern** |

Stuart Subotnick
Robert E. Wankel
Executive Vice President

David Andrews	**Elliot Greene**
Senior Vice President –	Senior Vice President –
Shubert Ticketing	Finance

Juan Calvo	**John Darby**
Vice President	Vice President –
and Controller	Facilities

Peter Entin	**Charles Flateman**
Vice President –	Vice President –
Theatre Operations	Marketing

Anthony LaMattina	**Brian Mahoney**
Vice President –	Vice President –
Audit & Production Finance	Ticket Sales

D.S. Moynihan
Vice President – Creative Projects

House Manager ....Carol Flemming
Carpenter ....George Dummitt
Electrician ....Matthew Maloney
Property Person ....Laura Koch

The American Plan

First Preview: January 2, 2009. Opened: January 22, 2009.
Closed March 22, 2009 after 22 Previews and 70 Performances.

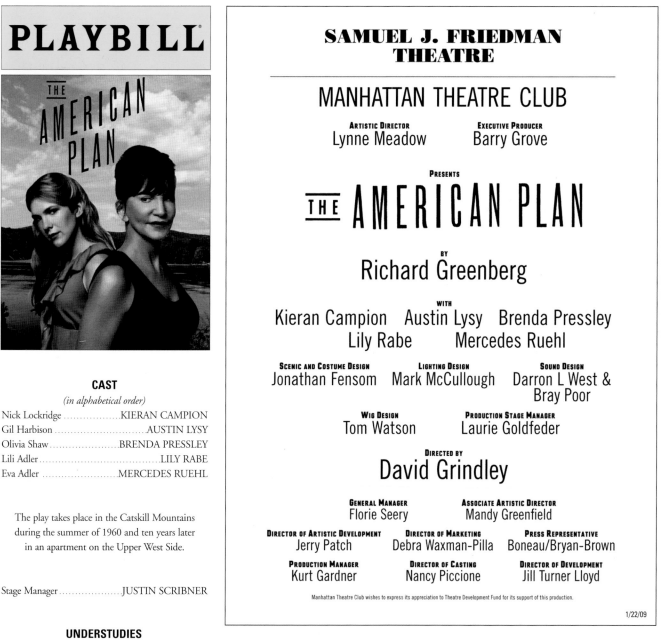

PLAYBILL

SAMUEL J. FRIEDMAN THEATRE

MANHATTAN THEATRE CLUB

ARTISTIC DIRECTOR
Lynne Meadow

EXECUTIVE PRODUCER
Barry Grove

PRESENTS

THE AMERICAN PLAN

BY

Richard Greenberg

WITH

**Kieran Campion   Austin Lysy   Brenda Pressley
Lily Rabe   Mercedes Ruehl**

SCENIC AND COSTUME DESIGN
Jonathan Fensom

LIGHTING DESIGN
Mark McCullough

SOUND DESIGN
**Darron L West &
Bray Poor**

WIG DESIGN
Tom Watson

PRODUCTION STAGE MANAGER
Laurie Goldfeder

DIRECTED BY
David Grindley

GENERAL MANAGER
Florie Seery

ASSOCIATE ARTISTIC DIRECTOR
Mandy Greenfield

DIRECTOR OF ARTISTIC DEVELOPMENT
Jerry Patch

DIRECTOR OF MARKETING
Debra Waxman-Pilla

PRESS REPRESENTATIVE
Boneau/Bryan-Brown

PRODUCTION MANAGER
Kurt Gardner

DIRECTOR OF CASTING
Nancy Piccione

DIRECTOR OF DEVELOPMENT
Jill Turner Lloyd

Manhattan Theatre Club wishes to express its appreciation to Theatre Development Fund for its support of this production.

1/22/09

CAST

(in alphabetical order)

Nick Lockridge .... KIERAN CAMPION
Gil Harbison .... AUSTIN LYSY
Olivia Shaw .... BRENDA PRESSLEY
Lili Adler .... LILY RABE
Eva Adler .... MERCEDES RUEHL

The play takes place in the Catskill Mountains
during the summer of 1960 and ten years later
in an apartment on the Upper West Side.

Stage Manager .... JUSTIN SCRIBNER

UNDERSTUDIES

For Lili Adler:
KATE ARRINGTON
For Olivia Shaw:
HARRIETT D. FOY
For Eva Adler:
PATRICIA HODGES
For Nick Lockridge, Gil Harbison:
JOHN WERNKE

(L-R): Lily Rabe, Mercedes Ruehl and Brenda Pressley.

Photo by Carol Rosegg

The American Plan

Kieran Campion
Nick Lockridge

Austin Lysy
Gil Harbison

Brenda Pressley
Olivia Shaw

Lily Rabe
Lili Adler

Mercedes Ruehl
Eva Adler

Kate Arrington
u/s Lili Adler

Harriett D. Foy
u/s Olivia Shaw

Patricia Hodges
u/s Eva Adler

John Wernke
*u/s Nick Lockridge,
Gil Harbison*

Richard Greenberg
Playwright

David Grindley
Director

Jonathan Fensom
*Scenic and
Costume Design*

Tom Watson
Wig Design

Justin Scribner
Stage Manager

Lynne Meadow
*Director/
Artistic Director,
Manhattan Theatre
Club, Inc.*

Barry Grove
*Executive Producer,
Manhattan Theatre
Club, Inc.*

Leah Curney
u/s Lili Adler

(L-R): Kieran Campion
as Nick Lockridge and
Austin Lysy as Gil
Harbison on Jonathan
Fensom's dockside set.

Photo by Carol Rosegg

The American Plan

MANHATTAN THEATRE CLUB STAFF

Artistic Director...........................Lynne Meadow
Executive Producer ....Barry Grove
General Manager ....Florie Seery
Associate Artistic Director ....Mandy Greenfield
Director of Artistic Development ......Jerry Patch
Artistic Consultant ....Daniel Sullivan
Director of Artistic Administration/
    Assistant to the Artistic Director ....Amy Gilkes Loe
Artistic Associate..........................Lisa McNulty
Artistic Assistant ....Kevin Emrick
Administrative Assistant ....Rebecca Stang
Assistant to the Executive Producer ......Emily Hammond
Director of Casting ....Nancy Piccione
Casting Associate ....Kelly Gillespie
Casting Assistant ....Drew Ross
Literary Manager/
    Sloan Project Manager ....Annie MacRae
Play Development Assistant ....Alex Barron
Director of Musical
    Development ....Clifford Lee Johnson III
Director of Development ....Jill Turner Lloyd
Director, Individual Giving....................Jon Haddorff
Director, Institutional Giving..............Roger Kingsepp
Director, Special Events ....Antonello Di Benedetto
Manager, Individual Giving ....Emily Fleisher
Manager, Institutional Giving ....Andrea Gorzell
Development Associate/
    Individual Giving ....Edward Allen
Development Associate/
    Institutional Giving ....Laurel Bear
Development Associate/
    Special Events ....Samantha Mascali
Development Associate/
    Database Coordinator ....Kelly Haydon
Patrons' Liaison ....Ryan Hudec
Director of Marketing ....Debra Waxman-Pilla
Assistant Director of Marketing ....Sunil Ayyagari
Marketing Associate ....Caitlin Baird
Director of Finance ....Jeffrey Bledsoe
Business Manager ....Holly Kinney
Human Resources Manager ....Darren Robertson
HR & Business Associate ....Adam Cook
Business Assistant ....Gillian Campbell
Receptionist/Studio Coordinator ....Christina Prints
IT Manager ....Mendy Sudranski
Associate General Manager ....Lindsey Brooks Sag
Company Manager/NY City Center ....Erin Moeller
General Management Assistant ....Ann Mundorff
Director of Subscriber Services ....Robert Allenberg
Associate Subscriber Services Manager ......Andrew Taylor
Subscriber Services
    Representatives ....Mark Bowers, Eric Gerdts,
        Matthew Praet, Rosanna Consalva Sarto
Director of Telesales and Telefunding ....George Tetlow
Assistant Manager ....Terrence Burnett
Telemarketing Staff ....Stephen Brown, Kel Haney,
        Kate Sessions
Director of Education ....David Shookhoff
Asst. Director of Education/
    Coordinator, Paul A. Kaplan Theatre
    Management Program ....Amy Harris
Education Assistant,
    TheatreLink Coordinator ....Julia Davis

Education Assistant...........................Kelli Bragdon
MTC Teaching Artists ....Michael Bernard,
    Chris Ceraso, Charlotte Colavin,
    Dominic Colon, Allison Daugherty,
    Gilbert Girion, Andy Goldberg,
    Elise Hernandez, Jeffrey Joseph,
    Julie Leedes, Kate Long, Louis D. Moreno,
    Andres Munar, Melissa Murray,
    Angela Pietropinto, Alexa Polmer,
    Alfonso Ramirez, Carmen Rivera,
    Judy Tate, Candido Tirado, Joe White
Theatre Management
    Interns ....Kristin Ciccone, Ashley Dickerson,
        E'bess Greer, Pamela Kierejczyk,
        Cerissa Kimball, David Norman,
        Thatcher Stevens, Kristi Taylor,
        Anna Frenkel, Amber Wilkerson
Randy Carrig Casting Intern ....Caroline Pugliese

Production Manager ....Kurt Gardner
Associate Production Manager ....Philip Naudé
Assistant Production Manager ....Kelsey Martinez
Properties Supervisor ....Scott Laule
Assistant Properties Supervisor ....Julia Sandy
Props Carpenter ....Peter Grimes
Costume Supervisor ....Erin Hennessy Dean

GENERAL PRESS REPRESENTATION
BONEAU/BRYAN-BROWN
Chris Boneau   Aaron Meier
Christine Olver

Script Readers ....John Baker, Kyle Frisina,
    Ben Gottlieb, Branden Jacobs-Jenkins,
    Liz Jones, Portia Krieger,
    Aaron Leichter, Stephen Sanders

SERVICES

Accountants ....ERE, LLP
Advertising ....SpotCo/Drew Hodges,
    Jim Edwards, Denise Ganjou, Kristen Rathbun
Web Design ....Calico Systems
Legal Counsel ....John Breglio, Carol M. Kaplan/
    Paul, Weiss, Rifkind,
    Wharton and Garrison LLP
Real Estate Counsel ....Marcus Attorneys
Labor Counsel ....Harry H. Weintraub/
    Glick and Weintraub, P.C.
Immigration Counsel ....Theodore Ruthizer/
    Kramer, Levin, Naftalis & Frankel, LLP
Sponsorship Consultant ....Above the Title Entertainment/
    Jed Bernstein
Insurance ....Dewitt Stern Group, Inc./
    Anthony Pittari
Maintenance ....Reliable Cleaning
Production Photographer ....Carol Rosegg
Event Photography ....Bruce Glikas
Cover Photo ....Henry Leutwyler
Cover Design ....SpotCo
Theatre Displays ....King Display

PRODUCTION STAFF FOR *THE AMERICAN PLAN*
Company Manager...........................Seth Shepsle
Production Stage Manager ....Laurie Goldfeder

Stage Manager ....Justin Scribner
Assistant Director ....Rachel Slaven
Dialect Consultant ....Kate Wilson
Fight Director ....Thomas Schall
Associate Scenic Designer ....Jesse Polshuck
Assistant Scenic Designer ....Christine Peters
Associate Costume Designer ....Patrick Bevilacqua
Assistant Lighting Designer ....Bradley King
Associate Sound Designer ....Matthew Hubbs
Hair/Make-Up Supervisor ....Kevin Phillips
Automation Operator ....Vaughn G. Preston
Lightboard Programmer ....Marc Polemeni
Dresser.....................................Virginia Neininger
Production Assistant ....Michael Alifanz

CREDITS

Scenery and automation by Showman Fabricators.
Costumes built by Jennifer Love Costumes. Lighting equipment provided by PRG Lighting. Sound equipment provided by Masque Sound. Natural herbal cough drops courtesy of Ricola USA. The services of Rachel Slaven were partially made possible through Theatre Ontario's Professional Theatre Training Program, funded by the Ontario Arts Council. Makeup provided by M•A•C.

MUSIC CREDITS

"Thrill on the Hill" written by Hank Ballard. Used by permission of Fort Knox Music Inc. c/o Carlin America, Inc. and Trio Music Company (BMI). The music for the lullaby "Nicht ist das gluck fur mich" was composed by Thomas Cabaniss.

For more information visit
www.ManhattanTheatreClub.org

**MANHATTAN THEATRE CLUB
SAMUEL J. FRIEDMAN THEATRE STAFF**

Theatre Manager ....Russ Ramsey
Assistant House Manager ....Richard Ponce
Box Office Treasurer ....David Dillon
Assistant Box Office
    Treasurers ....Tevy Bradley, Jeffrey Davis
Head Carpenter ....Chris Wiggins
Head Propertyman ....Timothy Walters
Sound Engineer ....Louis Shapiro
Master Electrician ....Jeff Dodson
Wardrobe Supervisor ....Angela Simpson
Apprentices ....Michael DiMarco, Ian Harbor
Chief Engineer ....Deosarran
Maintenance Engineers ....Ricky Deosarran,
    Maximo Perez
Security ....Initial Security
Lobby Refreshments ....Sweet Concessions

August: Osage County

First Preview: October 30, 2007. Opened: December 4, 2007.
Still running as of May 31, 2009.

☯ THE MUSIC BOX

239 W. 45th Street
A Shubert Organization Theatre
Gerald Schoenfeld, *Chairman*   Philip J. Smith, *President*
Robert E. Wankel, *Executive Vice President*

Jeffrey Richards   Jean Doumanian   Steve Traxler   Jerry Frankel
Ostar Productions   Jennifer Manocherian   The Weinstein Company
Debra Black/Daryl Roth   Ronald & Marc Frankel/Barbara Freitag
Rick Steiner/Staton Bell Group

PRESENT

The Steppenwolf Theatre Company production of

AUGUST: OSAGE COUNTY

BY

Tracy Letts

with

Robert Foxworth   Kimberly Guerrero   Brian Kerwin   Madeleine Martin
Mariann Mayberry   Michael McGuire   Amy Morton   Sally Murphy   Estelle Parsons
Molly Regan   Jim True-Frost   Troy West   Frank Wood

SCENIC DESIGN	COSTUME DESIGN	LIGHTING DESIGN	SOUND DESIGN
Todd Rosenthal	**Ana Kuzmanic**	**Ann G. Wrightson**	**Richard Woodbury**

ORIGINAL MUSIC	DRAMATURG	ORIGINAL CASTING
David Singer	**Edward Sobel**	**Erica Daniels**

NEW YORK CASTING	FIGHT CHOREOGRAPHER	DIALECT COACH
Stuart Howard, Amy Schecter & Paul Hardt	**Chuck Coyl**	**Cecilie O'Reilly**

PRODUCTION STAGE MANAGER	PRODUCTION SUPERVISOR	TECHNICAL SUPERVISOR
Deb Styer	**Jane Grey**	**Theatersmith, Inc./Smitty**

PRESS REPRESENTATIVE	GENERAL MANAGEMENT
Jeffrey Richards Associates	**Richards/Climan, Inc.**

DIRECTED BY

Anna D. Shapiro

"August: Osage County" was commissioned by Steppenwolf Theatre Company and the World Premiere was presented at Steppenwolf Theatre Company, Chicago, IL. Martha Lavey, Artistic Director and David Hawkanson, Executive Director

The Producers wish to express their appreciation to the Theatre Development Fund for its support of this production.

10/1/08

CAST

Beverly Weston	MICHAEL McGUIRE
Violet Weston	ESTELLE PARSONS
Barbara Fordham	AMY MORTON
Bill Fordham	FRANK WOOD
Jean Fordham	MADELEINE MARTIN
Ivy Weston	SALLY MURPHY
Karen Weston	MARIANN MAYBERRY
Mattie Fae Aiken	MOLLY REGAN
Charlie Aiken	ROBERT FOXWORTH
Little Charles	JIM TRUE-FROST
Johnna Monevata	KIMBERLY GUERRERO
Steve Heidebrecht	BRIAN KERWIN
Sheriff Deon Gilbeau	TROY WEST

SETTING

A large country home outside Pawhuska, Oklahoma,
60 miles northwest of Tulsa, Oklahoma.

UNDERSTUDIES/STANDBYS

For Charles, Beverly: STEPHEN PAYNE
For Violet, Mattie Fae: SUSANNE MARLEY
For Charles, Steve, Bill, Beverly,
Sheriff Deon Gilbeau: SCOTT JAECK
For Barbara, Karen, Ivy: DEE PELLETIER
For Jean: ANNE BERKOWITZ
For Johnna, Ivy, Karen:
KRISTINA VALADA-VIARS
For Bill, Steve, Little Charles, Sheriff Deon Gilbeau:
AARON SEROTSKY

Estelle Parsons (standing) with members of the ensemble.

Photo by Joan Marcus

August: Osage County

Robert Foxworth
Charlie

Kimberly Guerrero
Johnna Monevata

Brian Kerwin
Steve Heidebrecht

Madeleine Martin
Jean Fordham

Mariann Mayberry
Karen Weston

Michael McGuire
Beverly Weston

Amy Morton
Barbara Fordham

Sally Murphy
Ivy Weston

Estelle Parsons
Violet Weston

Molly Regan
Mattie Fae

Jim True-Frost
Little Charles

Troy West
Sheriff Deon Gilbeau

Frank Wood
Bill Fordham

Anne Berkowitz
Understudy for Jean

Scott Jaeck
Understudy for Steve, Bill, Sheriff, Charles, Beverly

Stephen Payne
Understudy for Charles, Beverly

Susanne Marley
Understudy for Violet, Mattie Fae

Dee Pelletier
Understudy for Barbara, Karen, Ivy

Aaron Serotsky
Understudy for Bill, Steve, Little Charles, Sheriff

Kristina Valada-Viars
Understudy for Johnna, Ivy, Karen

Tracy Letts
Playwright

Anna D. Shapiro
Director

Todd Rosenthal
Set Design

Ana Kuzmanic
Costume Design

Ann G. Wrightson
Lighting Design

Richard Woodbury
Sound Design

David Singer
Original Music

Chuck Coyl
Fight Choreographer

Christopher C. Smith, Smitty/ Theatersmith, Inc.
Technical Supervisor

David R. Richards and Tamar Haimes, Richards/Climan, Inc.
General Manager

Jeffrey Richards
Producer

Jean Doumanian
Producer

Steve Traxler
Producer

Jerry Frankel
Producer

August: Osage County

Bill Haber,
Ostar Productions
Producer

Jennifer
Manocherian
Producer

Bob Weinstein,
The Weinstein
Company
Producer

Harvey Weinstein,
The Weinstein
Company
Producer

Debra Black
Producer

Daryl Roth
Producer

Barbara Freitag
Producer

Rick Steiner
Producer

Dan Staton,
Staton Bell Group
Producer

Marc Bell,
Staton Bell Group
Producer

Martha Lavey
*Artistic Director,
Steppenwolf Theatre
Company*

David Hawkanson
*Executive Director,
Steppenwolf Theatre
Company*

ALUMNI:
2008 - 2009

Ian Barford
Little Charles

Deanna Dunagan
Violet Weston

Francis Guinan
Charlie Aiken

Munson Hicks
u/s Charles, Beverly

Jay Patterson
*u/s Charles, Steve,
Bill, Sheriff Deon
Gilbeau*

Jeff Perry
Bill Fordham

Molly Ranson
Jean Fordham

Rondi Reed
Mattie Fae Aiken

TRANSFER
STUDENTS:
2008 - 2009

Elizabeth Ashley
Mattie Fae Aiken

Guy Boyd
Charlie Aiken

Avia Bushyhead
*u/s Johnna, Ivy,
Karen*

John Cullum
Beverly Weston

Johanna Day
Barbara Fordham

Frank Deal
*u/s Bill, Steve,
Charles, Beverly,
Sheriff Deon Gilbeau*

Michael Milligan
Little Charles

Phylicia Rashad
Violet Weston

Drew Richardson
*u/s Barbara, Karen,
Ivy*

Samantha Ross
Johnna Monevata

Jeff Still
*u/s Charles, Steve,
Bill, Beverly, Sheriff
Deon Gilbeau*

Emily Walton
u/s Jean

Amy Warren
Karen Weston

August: Osage County

CREW
Front Row (L-R): Bill Rowland, Neil Rosenberg, Jane Grey, Cambra Overend, Valerie Spradling

Back Row (L-R): Kim Garnett, Rob Bevenger, Dennis Maher, Liam O'Brien

FRONT OF HOUSE STAFF
Front Row (L-R): Kenneth Kelly, Lottie Dennis, Jenna Scanlon

Middle Row (L-R): Joseph Amato, Jonathan Shulman, Joseph Lopez, Steven Staszewski, Dennis Scanlon

Back Row (L-R): Nicholas Stavola, Christopher Caron, Michael Composto

August: Osage County

SCRAPBOOK

Correspondents: Aaron Serotsky and Emily Walton, Understudies

Memorable Note: We received a lovely note from Natasha Richardson, expressing her admiration for the production and the performances. A classy lady, and a tragic loss for the theatre.

Anniversary Parties and/or Gifts: Just a spirited game of White Elephant at Christmas time. Gift highlights included: a Mr. T. talking key chain, a traveling brassiere case, and of course, a big shiny bottle of vodka that doubled as a disco ball.

Most Exciting Celebrity Visitor: This question was answered as I write these very words: Oprah (and Gayle!) are in the house on this Saturday

matinee in June. As to what she said, we'll have to get back to you.

"Easter Bonnet" and "Gypsy of the Year" Sketches: We've done two BC/EFA sketches, both written by Aaron Serotsky. An "Easter Bonnet" skit promoting the upcoming *August* middle school educational tour, and a "Gypsy" skit previewing next season's sequel, *February: Osage County*, which did feature a scantily clad Michael Milligan, a "Not-So-Little Charles."

Who Performed the Most Roles: We have four understudies who have each performed three different roles.

Special Backstage Rituals: Frank Wood bringing a dozen bagels, complete with flavored

cream cheeses, to EVERY SINGLE matinee.

Frank Wood and Mariann Mayberry squirting each other with water guns in the wings before a particularly emotional entrance. Mariann occasionally uses Kimberly Guerrero as a human shield.

The highly competitive and sometimes near-violent poker game that occurs in the third floor greenroom. And no, a straight does not beat a flush.

Stage Management quoting a different line from the show each night at the "places" call. And please remember we've had over six hundred performances. That's a lot of lines.

Favorite In-Theatre Gathering Place: The

August: Osage County
SCRAPBOOK

ever-glamorous theatre basement, or as we like to call it, The Grotto. We also have a lovely alley where we have hosted many a post-show gathering.

Favorite Off-Site Hangout: The play's too long to allow hanging out "off-site." Although, for special events, Brian Kerwin very generously opens his palatial Upper West Side home to food, friends, and frivolity.

Favorite Snack Foods: Our glorious stage managers provide an unending supply of mixed nuts and candy miniatures. An informal straw poll seems to find Snickers the popular favorite.

Mascot: Buster, the adorable canine son of our Production Stage Manager, Jane Grey. Though in recent months, he's been given some healthy competition by Che, the young revolutionary pug belonging to Ms. Elizabeth Ashley. They eye each other suspiciously from across the room.

Favorite Therapies: Ricola, Ben Gay, Throat-Coat Tea, massage, Pilates, plus wine, beer and mixed drinks.

Memorable Ad-Libs: Here are a few: all, of course, reported with the utmost respect. John Cullum, during one of his first performances as Beverly, in introducing Johnna to the household: Correct line: "You're welcome to use that American-made behemoth parked in the car port." As Mr. Cullum said it: "You're welcome to use that…(pause)…(pause)… blunderbuss parked out there in the car port."

Dee Pelletier, going on as Barbara one performance, brought a bit of existential flair to the proceedings as she described Aunt Mattie Fae's green bean casserole: Correct line: (It's good you made one too)… "hers is inedible." As Dee said it: (It's good you made one too)… "hers is inevitable."

And of course, who can forget Johanna Day as Barbara, calling to Johnna in the third act, as plates of fish have been thrown about the dining room, during a rather spirited exchange? Correct line: "Johnna?! Little spill in here!" As Johanna said it: "Little Johnna?! Spill in here!"

Audience Issue: We did once have an interruption during one of the most climactic moments of the play; the reveal of a major plot point in the third act. A commotion arose in the house, culminating in our Stage Manager making an announcement that an audience member was in some distress and needed medical attention. The two actresses, Johanna Day and Elizabeth Ashley, quietly exited stage right, after being beckoned offstage by Jane Grey. We took a brief pause as the patron was taken from the theater, and the actresses then returned, sat down, and immediately resumed devastating the lives of the characters on stage. Just another day in *Osage County*.

Memorable Fan Encounter: We do have a fan of John Cullum's, a woman, who has seen the show twelve times. Whether she stays for the entire performance every time, or only for John's fifteen minutes at the top of the show, we are not sure.

The cast and crew gathered at Sardi's restaurant August 13, 2008 to accept a Mayor's Proclamation in honor of the show's 300th performance.

Busiest Day at the Box Office: Hard to say, but possibly the day after we won five Tony Awards!

Who Wore the Least: Mariann Mayberry, as Karen, in her hot pink slip from Act III. And I do mean hot. Pink.

Catchphrases Only the Company Would Recognize: "Ladies on the Landing." "Rapprochement." "Please join us at Chitra's."

Memorable Directorial Note: Hands down, the day that Anna Shapiro said to John Cullum: "John, after you finish your scene (the first of the play), and therefore are done for the rest of the play, could you please not change into street clothes and then exit the theatre THROUGH THE HOUSE?? Thank you."

Company Legends: The Music Box mouse, who seems to choose only the quietest and most intimate moments in the play during which to cross stage, generally left to right. Needless to say, he/she tends to steal the scene in which he/she appears. The mouse also once leapt out of the candy jar in the stage management office as Anna Shapiro was reaching in for some candy, causing her to scream loudly…during a particularly quiet moment onstage.

Tales From the Put-in: While not actually occurring during a put-in, we decided at one point to change Amy Morton and Estelle Parsons' exit during the blackout at the end of Act II so that they exited on the other side of the stage. They insisted they didn't need to rehearse it beforehand, but when the moment arrived that night, Amy grabbed Estelle's hand at the blackout and confidently led her through the wrong room, then stopped in the middle of the stage. She decided to go one way, but Estelle didn't trust her and refused to follow, so she pulled the other way, and together they knocked

over a lamp on the stereo, ran into a pole, and generally made lots of noise stumbling and giggling, before finally finding their way offstage. Those of us backstage enjoyed watching the hysterics on the infrared monitor. PS: We have put 36 actors into this show since its arrival on Broadway!!!

Understudy Anecdote: Dee Pelletier, playing Barbara at the matinee and Ivy in the evening. On the same day. Kristina Valada-Viars, playing Johnna for the third act after Kim Guerrero played it for the first two.

Nicknames: "The House of Payne" (and no, it isn't what you think). "Doodle"—generally referring to anyone acting particularly adorable at that moment

Embarrassing Moments: Estelle Parsons, shimmying her very pants off, as she did her little Violet dance at the end of Act I. Literally…shimmying her pants off. When she came offstage, she asked the stage manager, "Do you think anyone noticed?"

Fan Club: It would be a stretch to say that we have an official fan club. However…we do have a very proud cast mother, Carol Milligan, who sends regular batches of homemade organic cookies direct from Westerville, Ohio. They often disappear by the end of Act II. There are also a couple of very passionate young men who do a lovely rendition of one of the Barbara/Violet scenes on YouTube.

Coolest Thing About Being in This Show: On Tony Night 2008 we hired about 18 pedicabs to take us from the Music Box to Radio City Music Hall—they were all lined up out in front of the theatre when our matinee came down that Sunday night, and all the drivers were wearing *August* t-shirts. We loaded up and then proceeded in a pedicab parade to the Tony Awards. How green is that?

Avenue Q

First Preview: July 10, 2003. Opened: July 31, 2003.
Still running as of May 31, 2009.

PLAYBILL

Avenue Q

CAST

(in order of appearance)

Princeton, Rod .... HOWIE MICHAEL SMITH
Brian .... NICHOLAS KOHN
Kate Monster, Lucy
   & others ...... CHRISTY CARLSON ROMANO
Nicky, Trekkie Monster,
   Bear & others .... CHRISTIAN ANDERSON
Christmas Eve .... ANN SANDERS
Gary Coleman .... CARLA RENATA
Mrs. T., Bear & others .... JENNIFER BARNHART
Ensemble .... MINGLIE CHEN,
                             JONATHAN ROOT

Place: an outer borough of New York City
Time: the present

UNDERSTUDIES

For Princeton, Rod/Brian/
Nicky, Trekkie Monster, Bear & others:
JONATHAN ROOT, MATT SCHREIBER
For Kate Monster, Lucy & others:
JENNIFER BARNHART, MINGLIE CHEN,
SHARON WHEATLEY
For Mrs. T., Bear & others:
MINGLIE CHEN, CARMEN RUBY FLOYD,
SHARON WHEATLEY
For Christmas Eve:
MINGLIE CHEN
For Gary Coleman:
CARMEN RUBY FLOYD

Continued on next page

☺ GOLDEN THEATRE
A Shubert Organization Theatre
Gerald Schoenfeld, *Chairman*   **Philip J. Smith,** *President*

Robert E. Wankel, *Executive Vice President*

Kevin McCollum   Robyn Goodman   Jeffrey Seller
Vineyard Theatre   and   The New Group
present

Avenue
Q
The Musical

Music and Lyrics by   Book by   Based on an Original Concept by
Robert Lopez and Jeff Marx   **Jeff Whitty**   **Robert Lopez and Jeff Marx**

with
Christy Carlson Romano
Christian Anderson, Jennifer Barnhart, Nicholas Kohn,
Carla Renata, Ann Sanders, Howie Michael Smith

Puppets Conceived and Designed by
Rick Lyon

Set Design	Costume Design	Lighting Design	Sound Design
Anna Louizos	**Mirena Rada**	**Howell Binkley**	**Acme Sound Partners**

Animation Design	Music Director and Incidental Music	Music Coordinator
Robert Lopez	**Gary Adler**	**Michael Keller**

General Manager	Technical Supervisor	Production Stage Manager
John Corker	**Brian Lynch**	**Beverly Jenkins**

Press Representative	Marketing	Casting	Associate Producers
Sam Rudy Media Relations	**Scott A. Moore**	**Cindy Tolan**	**Sonny Everett Walter Grossman Mort Swinsky**

Music Supervision, Arrangements
and Orchestrations by
Stephen Oremus

Choreographer
Ken Roberson

Directed by
Jason Moore

Avenue Q was supported by a residency and public staged reading at the
2002 O'Neill Music Theatre Conference of the Eugene O'Neill Theater Center, Waterford, CT

www.avenueq.com

10/1/08

(L-R): Rod, Howie Michael Smith, Lucy and Christy Carlson Romano.

Photo by Carol Rosegg

Avenue Q

SWINGS
CARMEN RUBY FLOYD, MATT SCHREIBER,
SHARON WHEATLEY

DANCE CAPTAIN
CHRISTINE DALY

BAND
Keyboard/Conductor:
GARY ADLER
Keyboard/Associate Conductor:
MARK HARTMAN
Reeds:
PATIENCE HIGGINS
Drums:
SCOTT NEUMANN
Bass:
MARYANN McSWEENEY
Guitars:
BRIAN KOONIN

PUPPET COACH
MATT SCHREIBER

Ann Sanders as
Christmas Eve.

Photo by Carol Rosegg

Christy Carlson Romano
Kate Monster, Lucy & others

Christian Anderson
Nicky, Trekkie Monster, Bear & others

Jennifer Barnhart
Mrs. T., Bear & others

Nicholas Kohn
Brian

Carla Renata
Gary Coleman

Ann Sanders
Christmas Eve

Howie Michael Smith
Princeton, Rod

Minglie Chen
Ensemble

Carmen Ruby Floyd
Swing

Jonathan Root
Ensemble

Matt Schreiber
Swing

Sharon Wheatley
Swing

  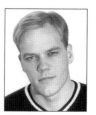

Robert Lopez and Jeff Marx
Music and Lyrics, Original Concept, Animation Design

Jeff Whitty
Book

Jason Moore
Director

Ken Roberson
Choreographer

Stephen Oremus
Music Supervision/ Arrangements/ Orchestrations

Rick Lyon
Puppet Design

Anna Louizos
Set Designer

Avenue Q

Mirena Rada
Costume Design

Howell Binkley
Lighting Designer

Tom Clark, Mark Menard and Nevin Steinberg,
Acme Sound Partners
Sound Designer

Gary Adler
*Musical Director/
Conductor/
Incidental Music*

Michael Keller
Music Coordinator

Brian Lynch/
Theatretech, Inc.
Technical Supervisor

John Corker
General Manager

Kevin McCollum
Producer

Robyn Goodman
Producer

Jeffrey Seller
Producer

Scott Elliott,
Founding Artistic
Director,
The New Group
Producer

Sonny Everett
Associate Producer

Mort Swinsky
Associate Producer

Avenue Q Alumni 2008-2009

Carey Anderson
*Kate Monster, Lucy
& others*

Steven Booth
Ensemble

Leo Daignault
Ensemble, Swing

Aymee Garcia
*Swing,
Dance Captain*

Heather Hawkins
*Mrs. T., Bear &
others*

Sala Iwamatsu
*Christmas Eve,
Mrs. T., Bear &
others*

Hazel Anne
Raymundo
Ensemble

Rashidra Scott
Gary Coleman

Sarah Stiles
*Kate Monster, Lucy
& others*

Jasmin Walker
Swing

Avenue Q Transfer Students 2008-2009

Angela Ai
*Christmas Eve,
Ensemble*

Carey Anderson
*Kate Monster, Lucy
& others*

Leo Daignault
Swing

Tonya Dixon
Gary Coleman

Heather Hawkins
*Mrs. T., Bear &
others*

Jed Resnick
*Princeton, Rod,
Ensemble*

Benjamin Schrader
Ensemble

Sarah Stiles
Swing

Jasmin Walker
Swing

Avenue Q

ELECTRICS AND SOUND
Front Row (L-R): Jennifer Lerner, Gretchen Metzloff, Sylvia Yoshioka, Elspeth Appleby

Back Row (L-R): Craig Caccamise, A.J. Giegerich, Joe Pfifferling

Photo by Robert Viagas

FRONT OF HOUSE STAFF
Front Row: Helen Bentley

Second Row (L-R): Patricia Byrne, Nilsa Nairn, Chip Jorgensen, Carolyne "Mrs. Jones" Jones-Barnes

Third Row (L-R): Veronica Morrissey, Shelia Miller, Mae Smith, Cookie Harlin, Felicia Masias, Scott Key, Peter Cooke

Back Row: Yuri Fernandez

MANAGEMENT
(L-R): Beverly Jenkins, Matt Schreiber, Nick Lugo, Christine Daly

Photos by Brian Mapp

CARPENTRY AND PROPS
Seated (L-R): Elise Viola, Jane Pien, Stephen McDonald

Standing (L-R): Tom Anderson, Justin Garvey

CREW
Front Row (L-R): Beverly Jenkins, Jennifer Lerner, Sylvia Yoshioka

Middle Row (L-R): Stephen McDonald, Gretchen Metzloff, Christine Daly, A.J. Giegerich, Elspeth Appleby, Kathy Guida, Jill Heller, Tom Anderson

Back Row (L-R): Nick Lugo, Matt Schreiber, Jane Pien, Charles Zarobinski, Craig Caccamise, Justin Garvey, Elise Viola, Joe Pfifferling

Avenue Q

WARDROBE
(L-R): Jill Heller and Kathy Guida

Photo by Brian Mapp

Avenue Q
SCRAPBOOK

①

③

x

1. The cast at the September 2008 "Broadway on Broadway" event.
2. Christy Carlson Romano poses with alter-ego Lucy T. Slut at a press conference welcoming the Disney star to the cast.
3. Producer Kevin McCollum speaks from the stage of the Golden Theatre at curtain call with the cast and alumni at the show's fifth anniversary, July 31, 2008.

Correspondent: Matt Schreiber, Swing

Most Roles in Show: Jen Barnhart definitely puppeteers the most characters in the show. At one point or another you can see her puppeteering Rod, Nicky, Trekkie Monster, Kate Monster, Lucy T. Slut, Mrs. T, a Bad Idea Bear and a Box puppet. That's at least eight characters, and I'm probably forgetting some. I would say that Christian Anderson, however, voices the most characters in the show. He provides the voices for Trekkie Monster, Nicky, a Bad Idea Bear, the Newcomer, and he also operates the giant Kate Monster head that comes over the set during the nightmare sequence.

Most Performances in This Show: Howie Michael Smith just celebrated his 1,000th performance... but I'm pretty sure Ann Sanders has got him beat and Jennifer Barnhart has everyone beat.

Special Backstage Rituals: At "places" for the top of the show, Nicholas Kohn likes to rub the boobs of the naked Lucy T. Slut puppet that is laying in the hospital bed. Carey Anderson usually stretches on the backstage steps and warms up. Christian Anderson farts. As the first bars of the theme song play, Jen Barnhart shouts, "Have a good show, everybody!!!"

Favorite Moments: Every night during "School For Monsters" Ann Sanders has a moment when Trekkie sings, "Now me have therapist, I work on this with her...." The audience can't really see what she is doing because her back is to them. She is doing what is fondly referred to as "Backting." During "Mixtape," when Kate asks Howie Michael Smith if they are going out on a date, Howie changes his reaction from performance to performance. We never know what he's going to do next!

In-Theatre Gathering Place: The Stage Management Office or Room 1.

Favorite Snack Foods: Chocolate, James Darrah's bird seed brittle, cake, anything that is edible.

Mascot: Christian Anderson's Brain

Favorite Therapy: We definitely go through a lot of Ricolas on a monthly basis. Mostly because of Christian.

Memorable Ad-Libs: Too many to list them all. A recent one came from Carla Renata (Gary Coleman). This occurred after Rod sings, "Canada." The cast is looking at him aghast, and the tension is broken by Gary who is supposed to say, "My Goodness will you look at the time, well I really should get moving...yes sir." This particular performance, Carla blanked on that line and said in lieu: "Ooooh...ooooh...I gotta get out of here."

At another special performance, Nicholas Kohn forgot an important entrance...which left Christian Anderson on stage as Nicky in ad-lib hell. Somewhere in his fear he created the following gems: "Hey Brian!!...can I have another beer? Thanks Brian....hmm...I wonder where Brian is!" He wasn't alone at least. Jen Barnhart was attached to him, but there was nothing she could really do but enjoy the ride.

Heaviest/Hottest Costume: That would have to be Ann Sanders (Christmas Eve). When her character is getting married she wears this big wedding dress that lights up. Two minutes after the wedding she has to put on this oversized furry Kate Monster head. The head on top of the wedding dress would have to be the heaviest costume in our show.

Who Wore the Least: Again, that would have to be Ann Sanders. At some point during the show she wears a red lace teddy...she does wear her show pants under it however.

Memorable Directorial Note: "Okay, let's take it from Porn!"

Company In-Jokes: "IRS...I thought you said UPS." "Goin' up to Room 11!" "Barrett's out!"

Understudy Anecdote: The hardest job in this show has to be that of the understudy. I know, because I am one. You constantly have to have every track accessible in your brain at a moment's notice, and it takes a rare breed to be capable of doing it. That being said, a special shout-out should be made to Jonathan Root. One week during flu season, he went on for all three lead male roles he covers in the show without forgetting a single line or a bit of blocking and pulling off great performances to boot.

Nicknames: "Sunshine and Rainbow Brite," "Crawl," "Idler" and "Mittens."

Ghostly Encounters Backstage: For years I would swear I could see a ghostly shadow looming around the ceiling of the backstage area, until I realized it was Tommy Anderson...our man on the fly rail. On a serious note, one of our beloved sub deck electricians, Bern Brannigan passed away this year. A few weeks after his funeral some strange unexplained electrical mishaps would happen backstage...like call boards resetting themselves in the middle of the show or going out entirely. We fondly blame these occurrences on the ghost of Bern.

Coolest Thing About Being in This Show: Two words: Puppet Sex.

z

Photos by Aubrey Reuben

z

Billy Elliot

First Preview: October 1, 2008. Opened: November 13, 2008.
Still running as of May 31, 2009.

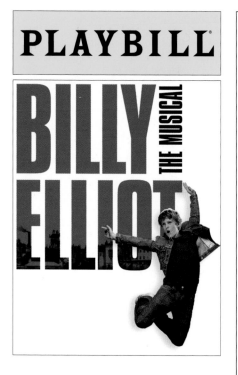

PLAYBILL

CAST

Billy...............................DAVID ALVAREZ,
TRENT KOWALIK,
KIRIL KULISH
Mrs. Wilkinson..................HAYDN GWYNNE
Dad.................................GREGORY JBARA
Grandma..........................CAROLE SHELLEY
Tony...............................SANTINO FONTANA
George.............................JOEL HATCH
Michael...........................DAVID BOLOGNA,
FRANK DOLCE
Debbie.............................ERIN WHYLAND
Small Boy.............MITCHELL MICHALISZYN,
MATTHEW MINDLER
Big Davey.........................DANIEL ORESKES
Lesley.....................STEPHANIE KURTZUBA
Scab/Posh Dad.....................DONNIE KEHR
Mum...............................LEAH HOCKING
Mr. Braithwaite..............THOMMIE RETTER
Older Billy/Scottish Dancer....STEPHEN HANNA
Posh Boy..........................KEEAN JOHNSON
Clipboard Woman................JAYNE PATERSON
"Expressing Yourself" Dancers .KEVIN BERNARD,
GRADY McLEOD BOWMAN,
JEFF KREADY, STEPHANIE KURTZUBA,
DAVID LARSEN,
DARRELL GRAND MOULTRIE,
JAMIE TORCELLINI, GRANT TURNER

⊛ IMPERIAL THEATRE
249 West 45th Street
A Shubert Organization Theatre
Gerald Schoenfeld, *Chairman*   Philip J. Smith, *President*

Robert E. Wankel, *Executive Vice President*

UNIVERSAL PICTURES STAGE PRODUCTIONS   WORKING TITLE FILMS   OLD VIC PRODUCTIONS
in association with WEINSTEIN LIVE ENTERTAINMENT present

BILLY ELLIOT THE MUSICAL
Based on the Universal Pictures/Studio Canal Film

HAYDN GWYNNE   GREGORY JBARA
CAROLE SHELLEY   SANTINO FONTANA

And Introducing
DAVID ALVAREZ   TRENT KOWALIK   KIRIL KULISH

With

DAVID BOLOGNA • FRANK DOLCE • STEPHEN HANNA • JOEL HATCH • LEAH HOCKING • THOMMIE RETTER • ERIN WHYLAND
JULIETTE ALLEN ANGELO • TOMMY BATCHELOR • KEVIN BERNARD • GRADY McLEOD BOWMAN • HEATHER ANN BURNS • MARIA CONNELLY
SAMANTHA CZULADA • KYLE DesCHAMPS • EBONI EDWARDS • BRIANNA FRAGOMENI • GREG GRAHAM • ERIC GUNHUS • MEG GUZULESCU
IZZY HANSON-JOHNSTON • KEEAN JOHNSON • DONNIE KEHR • CARA KJELLMAN • KARA KLEIN • DAVID KOCH • JEFF KREADY • AARON KABURICK
STEPHANIE KURTZUBA • DAVID LARSEN • CAROLINE LONDON • MERLE LOUISE • MARINA MICALIZZI • MITCHELL MICHALISZYN
MATTHEW MINDLER • DARRELL GRAND MOULTRIE • TESSA NETTING • DANIEL ORESKES • JAYNE PATERSON • LIZ PEARCE
CORRIEANNE STEIN • JAMIE TORCELLINI • GRANT TURNER • CASEY WHYLAND

Press Representative	General Management	Advertising
BARLOW • HARTMAN	NINA LANNAN ASSOCIATES/DEVIN KEUDELL	SPOTCO

Production Stage Manager	Music Contractor	Production Supervisors
BONNIE L. BECKER	MICHAEL KELLER	ARTHUR SICCARDI PATRICK SULLIVAN

Adult Casting Director	Children's Casting Director	Resident Director
TARA RUBIN CASTING	NORA BRENNAN	BT McNICHOLL

Associate Set Designer	Associate Costume Designer	Associate Lighting Designer (Programmer)	Associate Sound Designer
PAUL ATKINSON	CLAIRE MURPHY	VIC SMERDON	JOHN OWENS

Associate Choreographer	Assistant Choreographer	Hair, Wig and Make-Up Designer
KATHRYN DUNN	NIKKI BELSHER	CAMPBELL YOUNG

Musical Supervision and Orchestrations by	Music Director
MARTIN KOCH	DAVID CHASE

Costume Design by	Lighting Design by	Sound Design by
NICKY GILLIBRAND	RICK FISHER	PAUL ARDITTI

Executive Producers
DAVID FURNISH   ANGELA MORRISON

Produced by
TIM BEVAN   ERIC FELLNER   JON FINN   SALLY GREENE

Associate Director
JULIAN WEBBER

Set Design by
IAN MacNEIL

Choreography by
PETER DARLING

Directed by
STEPHEN DALDRY

Book and Lyrics by
LEE HALL

Music by
ELTON JOHN

PRESENTED BY FIDELITY INVESTMENTS

11/13/08

Trent Kowalik (center) as
Billy with the Ballet Girls.

Photo by Alastair Muir

Continued on next page

Continued on next page

Billy Elliot

MUSICAL NUMBERS

ACT 1

"The Stars Look Down" (The Eve of the Miners' Strike 1984) ....Full Company
"Shine" ....Mrs. Wilkinson, Ballet Girls, Billy
"We'd Go Dancing" ....Grandma, Men's Ensemble
"Solidarity" ....Full Company
"Expressing Yourself" ....Billy, Michael, Ensemble
"Dear Billy" (Mum's Letter) ....Billy, Mrs. Wilkinson, Mum
"Born to Boogie" ....Billy, Mrs. Wilkinson, Mr. Braithwaite
"Angry Dance" ....Billy, Men's Ensemble

ACT 2
Six Months Later

"Merry Christmas, Maggie Thatcher" ....Full Company
"Deep Into the Ground" ....Dad, Full Company
"He Could Go and He Could Shine" ....Dad, Tony, Ensemble
"Electricity" ....Billy
"Once We Were Kings" ....Full Company
"Dear Billy" (Billy's Reply) ....Billy, Mum
"Company Celebration" ....Full Company

ORCHESTRA

Conductor:
DAVID CHASE
Associate Conductor:
SHAWN GOUGH
Reeds:
ED SALKIN, RICK HECKMAN,
MIKE MIGLIORE, JAY BRANDFORD
Trumpets:
JAMES DELA GARZA, JOHN DENT,
ALEX HOLTON
Trombones:
DICK CLARK, JACK SCHATZ
French Horns:
ROGER WENDT, EVA CONTI
Keyboards:
JOSEPH JOUBERT, SHAWN GOUGH
Guitar:
JJ McGEEHAN
Bass:
RANDY LANDAU
Drums:
GARY SELIGSON
Percussion:
HOWARD JOINES
Music Coordinator:
MICHAEL KELLER

Kiril Kulish as Billy with the Police

Photos by David Scheinmann

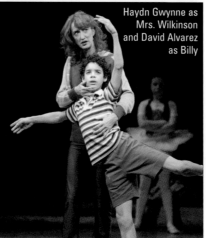

Haydn Gwynne as Mrs. Wilkinson and David Alvarez as Billy

ENSEMBLE

KEVIN BERNARD, GRADY McLEOD
BOWMAN, ERIC GUNHUS,
STEPHEN HANNA, LEAH HOCKING,
AARON KABURICK, DONNIE KEHR,
JEFF KREADY, STEPHANIE KURTZUBA,
DAVID LARSEN, MERLE LOUISE,
DARRELL GRAND MOULTRIE,
DANIEL ORESKES, JAYNE PATERSON,
THOMMIE RETTER, JAMIE TORCELLINI,
GRANT TURNER

BALLET GIRLS

JULIETTE ALLEN ANGELO,
HEATHER ANN BURNS, EBONI EDWARDS,
MEG GUZULESCU,
IZZY HANSON-JOHNSTON,
CAROLINE LONDON, MARINA MICALIZZI,
TESSA NETTING, CORRIEANNE STEIN,
CASEY WHYLAND

SWINGS

MARIA CONNELLY, SAMANTHA CZULADA,
KYLE DesCHAMPS, BRIANNA FRAGOMENI,
GREG GRAHAM, CARA KJELLMAN,
KARA KLEIN, DAVID KOCH, LIZ PEARCE

UNDERSTUDIES

For Billy:
TOMMY BATCHELOR
For Mrs. Wilkinson:
LEAH HOCKING, JAYNE PATERSON
For Dad:
DONNIE KEHR, DANIEL ORESKES
For Grandma:
MERLE LOUISE
For Tony:
JEFF KREADY, DAVID LARSEN
For George:
ERIC GUNHUS, JAMIE TORCELLINI
For Michael:
KEEAN JOHNSON
For Debbie:
MARIA CONNELLY

DANCE CAPTAIN

GREG GRAHAM

ASSISTANT DANCE CAPTAIN

CARA KJELLMAN

Haydn Gwynne is appearing with the permission of
Actors' Equity Association pursuant to an exchange
program between American Equity and UK Equity.

Billy Elliot

Haydn Gwynne
Mrs. Wilkinson

Gregory Jbara
Dad

Carole Shelley
Grandma

Santino Fontana
Tony

David Alvarez
Billy

Trent Kowalik
Billy

Kiril Kulish
Billy

David Bologna
Michael

Frank Dolce
Michael

Stephen Hanna
*Older Billy;
Scottish Dancer*

Joel Hatch
George

Leah Hocking
Mum

Thommie Retter
Mr. Braithwaite

Erin Whyland
Debbie

Juliette Allen Angelo
Ballet Girl

Tommy Batchelor
Tall Boy

Kevin Bernard
Ensemble

Grady McLeod
Bowman
Ensemble

Heather Ann Burns
Ballet Girl

Maria Connelly
Debbie Standby

Samantha Czulada
Swing

Kyle DesChamps
Swing

Eboni Edwards
Ballet Girl

Brianna Fragomeni
Swing

Greg Graham
*Swing/
Dance Captain*

Eric Gunhus
Ensemble

Meg Guzulescu
Ballet Girl

Izzy
Hanson-Johnston
Ballet Girl

Keean Johnson
Posh Boy

Aaron Kaburick
Ensemble

Donnie Kehr
*Scab/Posh Dad;
Ensemble*

Cara Kjellman
*Swing/
Asst. Dance Captain*

Kara Klein
Swing

David Koch
Swing

Jeff Kready
Ensemble

Billy Elliot

Stephanie Kurtzuba
Lesley; Ensemble

David Larsen
Ensemble

Caroline London
Ballet Girl

Merle Louise
Ensemble

Marina Micalizzi
Ballet Girl

Mitchell Michaliszyn
Small Boy

Matthew Mindler
Small Boy

Darrell Grand
Moultrie
Ensemble

Tessa Netting
Ballet Girl

Daniel Oreskes
Big Davey; Ensemble

Jayne Paterson
*Clipboard Woman;
Ensemble*

Liz Pearce
Swing

Corrieanne Stein
Ballet Girl

Jamie Torcellini
Ensemble

Grant Turner
Ensemble

Casey Whyland
Ballet Girl

Elton John
Music

Lee Hall
Book & Lyrics

Stephen Daldry
Director

Peter Darling
Choreographer

Ian MacNeil
Set Design

Nicky Gillibrand
Costume Design

Rick Fisher
Lighting Design

Paul Arditti
Sound Design

Martin Koch
*Musical Supervision
& Orchestrations*

Michael Keller
Music Coordinator

Tara Rubin Casting
Adult Casting

BT McNicholl
Resident Director

Arthur Siccardi
Theatrical Services,
Inc.
*Production
Supervisor*

TRANSFER
STUDENTS!

David Eggers
Swing

Blake Hammond
*Mr. Braithwaite,
Ensemble*

Joshua Horner
*"Expressing
Yourself" Dancer,
Ensemble*

Tanner Pflueger
Billy

Billy Elliot

COMPANY MANAGEMENT
(L-R): Carol Oune, Gregg Arst, Ashley Berman

STAGE MANAGEMENT
(L-R): Bonnie Becker (represented by puppet), Charles Underhill, Scott Rowen (represented by puppet), Mary Kathryn Flynt

CHILD GUARDIANS
(Clockwise): John Fahey, Bobby Wilson, John Funk, Emily Andres, Amanda Grundy

BOX OFFICE
(L-R): John Zameryka, Alexis G. Bond, Brian Goode, William Carrick

FRONT OF HOUSE STAFF
Front Row (L-R): Christopher Caoili, Frances Barbaretti, Joan Seymour, Joe Labitat

Back Row (L-R): Lois Fernandez, Ed Phillips, Dennis Norwood, Joseph Pullara, Crystal Walker, Adam Young

Photos by Brian Mapp

CREW
Front Row (L-R): Jay Satterwite, Mike Wojchik, Stephanie Vetter, Jay Brandford, Shawn Gough, Darryl Mull, Paul Ludick, Margo Lawless, Jeannie Naughton, Charlie Catanese, Margiann Flanagan

Middle Row (L-R): Kevin Kennedy, Richie Fullum, Brian Hutchinson, Justin Sanok, Pete Donovan, Kenneth Brown, Susan Corrado, Lyssa Everett, Tina Clifton, Nanette Golia, Terri Purcell, Michael Berglund

Back Row (L-R): Kevin Clifford, Chad Heulitt, Reg Vessey, Walter Bullard Jr., Paul Dean, Anthony Ferrer, Brad Robertson, Jay Gill, Lisa Preston, Jess Scoblick, Freddie Buckwalt

The Playbill Broadway Yearbook 2008-2009

Billy Elliot

STAFF FOR BILLY ELLIOT THE MUSICAL

GENERAL MANAGEMENT
NINA LANNAN ASSOCIATES
Devin Keudell

COMPANY MANAGER
Gregg Arst

Associate Company Manager .... Carol M. Oune
Assistant Company Manager .... Ashley Berman

GENERAL PRESS REPRESENTATIVE
BARLOW•HARTMAN
John Barlow   Michael Hartman
Juliana Hannett   Michelle Bergmann

CHILDREN'S CASTING
NORA BRENNAN

ADULT CASTING
TARA RUBIN CASTING
Tara Rubin CSA, Eric Woodall CSA
Dale Brown, Laura Schutzel CSA, Merri Sugarman CSA,
Rebecca Carfagna, Paige Blansfield

Production Stage Manager .... Bonnie L. Becker
Stage Manager .... Charles Underhill
Assistant Stage Managers .... Scott Rowen,
Mary Kathryn Flynt

Supervising Dialect Coach (UK) .... William Conacher
Resident Dialect Coach .... Ben Furey

Dance Captain .... Greg Graham
Assistant Dance Captain .... Cara Kjellman
Fight Captain .... Grady McLeod Bowman
Choreographic Supervision .... Ellen Kane
Staging and Dance Assistant .... Lee Proud

Associate Set Designer .... Paul Atkinson
Assistant Set Designer .... Jaimie Todd
Associate Costume Designer (UK) .... Claire Murphy
Associate Costume Designer (US) .... Brian Russman
Assistant Costume Designer (US) .... Rebecca Lustig

Assistant to Ms. Gillibrand .... Rachel Attridge
Associate Lighting Designer (UK) .... Vic Smerdon
Associate Lighting Designer (US) .... Daniel Walker
Assistant Lighting Designer (US) .... Kristina Kloss
Associate Sound Designer (UK) .... John Owens
Associate Sound Designer (US) .... Tony Smolenski IV
Moving Light Programmer (US) .... David Arch
Costume Shopper (UK) .... Bryony Fayers
Props Shoppers (UK) .... Kathy Anders, Lisa Buckley

Fight Director .... David S. Leong

Production Carpenter .... Gerard Griffin
Production Flyman .... Brian Hutchinson
Production Automation Carpenter ...... Charles Heulitt III
Production Electrician .... Jimmy Maloney, Jr.
Head Electrician .... Kevin Barry
Assistant Electrician .... Brad Robertson
Production Props Supervisor .... Joseph Harris, Jr.
Head Propmaster .... David Bornstein
Assistant Propmaster .... Reg Vessey
Production Sound .... Bob Biasetti
Special Effects Consultant .... Greg Meeh

Wardrobe Supervisor .... Terri Purcell
Associate Wardrobe Supervisor .... Nanette Golia
Dressers .... Michael Berglund, Kenneth Brown,
Charles Catanese, Lyssa Everett,
Margiann Flanagan, Jay Gill, Joby Horrigan,
Margo Lawless, Paul Ludick, Jeannie Naughton,
Duduzile Ndlovu-Mitall, David Oliver,
Lisa Preston, Jessica Scoblick, Pat Sullivan
Hair & Makeup Supervisor .... Susan Corrado
Assistant Hair Supervisor .... Monica Costea
Hair Dresser .... Cory McCutcheon
Head Children's Guardian .... Robert Wilson
Assistant Head Guardian .... Annie L. Grappone
Guardians .... Elizabeth Daniels, John V. Fahey,
John Funk, Amanda Grundy, Katherine Malak
Production Assistants .... Emily Andres,
Andrew Gottlieb, Alison M. Roberts
Rehearsal Pianists .... Joseph Joubert, Aron Accurso
Music Copying/Library Services (US) ..... Emily Grishman
Music Preparation

Children's Tutoring .... On Location Education/
Alan Simon, Jodi Green
Tutors .... Rachel Jeanty, Irene Karasik,
Alla Markova, Alana Serignese, Rachel Truman
Box Office Staff .... Bill Carrick, Paul Blaber,
Carlin Blum, Greer Bond, John Zameryka
Ballet Instructors .... Finis Jhung, Francois Perron
Acrobatic Instructor .... Hector Salazar
Physical Therapy .... PhysioArts/Jennifer Green
Company Physical Therapists .... Ryanne Glasper,
Suzanne Lynch
Orthopedic Consultant .... Dr. Phillip Bauman
Pediatric/ENT Consultant .... Dr. Barry Kohn
Health & Safety Consultants .... Eric D. Wallace,
Greg Petruska

Advertising .... SPOTCO/
Drew Hodges, Jim Edwards,
Tom Greenwald, Jim Aquino, Stacey Maya
Marketing .... Allied Live/
Laura Matalon, Tanya Grubich,
Daya Wolterstorff, Sara Rosenzweig
International Marketing Consultants .... AKA/
Adam Kenwright, Liz Furze, Richard Howle
Interactive Marketing Agency .... Situation Marketing/
Damian Bazadona, Lisa Cecchini,
Jackie Bodley, Jenn Elston
Production Videographer .... Suspension Productions/
Joe Locarro
Production Photographers .... David Scheinmann,
Carol Rosegg
Corporate Sponsorships .... Amy Willstatter's
Bridge to Hollywood LLC
Accountant .... FK Partners/Robert Fried
Comptroller .... Sarah Galbraith and Co./
Sarah Galbraith
Immigration .... Kramer Levin Naftalis & Frankel LLP/
Mark D. Koestler, Esq., Allison Gray, Esq.
Legal Counsel .... Loeb & Loeb/
Seth Gelblum
Franklin, Weinrib, Rudell & Vassallo, PC/
Elliot H. Brown
General Management Associates .... Adam Jackson,
Steve Dow, Libby Fox

Billy Elliot

General Management Interns ....Danielle Saks, Meghan Wilson, Casey Trascik
Production Supervisor Intern ....Lenora Hartley
Lighting Intern ....Trent Suidgeest
Sound Intern ....Rachel O'Connor
Press Associates ....Leslie Baden, Melissa Bixler, Tom D'Ambrosio, Bethany Larsen, Ryan Ratelle, Matt Shea, Wayne Wolfe
Children's Casting Assistant ....Jamie Tuss
Payroll Services ....Castellana Services, Inc.
Travel Agent ....Tzell Travel/ The "A" Team, Andi Henig
Housing ....Premier Relocation Solutions/ Christine Sodikoff
Banking ....Bank of America/Glen Rylko
Insurance ....AON/ Albert G. Ruben Insurance Services, Inc./ Susan M. Weiss
Structural Engineering
   Consultant ....McLaren Engineering Group/ Bill Gorlin
Demolition
   Services ....JRM Construction Management, LLC/ Philip R. Arnold, Jr.
Theatre Displays ....BAM Signs
Merchandising ....Encore Merchandising/ Joey Boyles
Opening Night
   Coordination ....The Lawrence Company Events, Inc./ Michael Lawrence
Directing Interns ....Steve Bebout, Mary Birnbaum, Katherine Carter

FOR UNIVERSAL PICTURES STAGE PRODUCTIONS

President and COO, Universal Studios..........Ron Meyer
Chairman ....Marc Shmuger
Co-Chairman ....David Linde
President of Production ....Donna Langley
Co-President of Production and EVP .....Jimmy Horowitz
President of Marketing and Distribution ..Adam Fogelson
President of Marketing ....Eddie Egan
SVP, Production Finance ....Arturo Barquet
Legal Affairs ....Keith Blau

FOR WORKING TITLE FILMS

Head of Marketing ....David Livingstone
Marketing Executive ....Susan Butterly
Vice President,
   Legal and Business Affairs ....Gráinne McKenna
President of Production (U.S.) ....Liza Chasin
Head of Film ....Debra Hayward
Head of Development ....Natascha Wharton
Head of Production ....Michelle Wright
Head of Legal and Business Affairs ....Sheeraz Shah
Finance Director ....Tim Easthill
Assistant to Eric Fellner ....Cara Shine
Assistant to Tim Bevan ....Chloe Dorigan
Assistant to Angela Morrison ....Tash Amis
Associate Producer.........................Marieke Spencer
Head of Finance, Billy Elliot ....Shefali Ghosh
Assistant to Jon Finn ....Katie Goodson-Thomas

FOR OLD VIC PRODUCTIONS

Chief Executive ....Sally Greene
Executive Producer ....Joseph Smith

Finance Director ....Vanessa Harrison
Administrator ....Becky Barber
Assistant to Sally Greene ....Emily Blacksell
Administrative Assistant ....Sophie Netchaef
Legal Representative ....David Friedlander

CREDITS

Scenery constructed and automation equipment provided by Hudson Scenic Studios, Inc. Back wall by Souvenir Scenic Studios, Ltd. Miners' banner by Alaister Brotchie. Flying by Foy. Lighting equipment from PRG Lighting. Sound equipment by Masque Sound. Puppets designed and contracted by the Wright Stuff Theatre of Puppets. Costumes constructed by Mark Costello, London; Tricorne NYC; Jennifer Love Costumes; Baracath Customwear; Douglas Earl Costumes; David Quinn. Custom knitwear by Maria Ficalora and Karen Eifert. Custom footwear by T.O. Dey and Capezio. Millinery and costume crafts by Rodney Gordon, Inc. Undergarments provided by Bra*Tenders. "Express" dress puppet frames and Maggie Thatcher tank by Sophie Jones. Dancing Dresses by Phil Reynolds Costumes, London. Ballet Girls clothing by Airy Fairy Costuming. Fabric painting and costume distressing by Nicola Killeen Textiles and Jeff Fender. Wigs made by Campbell Young Associates. Incidental and small props by the Spoon Group. Soft goods props by Mariah Hale. Musical instruments provided by Manny's Music, Pearl Drums, Mesa Boogie Guitar Amplifiers and Eden Electronics. Natural herb cough drops supplied by Ricola USA, Inc. Rehearsed at New 42nd Street Studios. Rehearsal scenery and props by the Technical Office Pty, Australia, and Adelaide Festival Centre Trust Workshops.

Billy Elliot on Broadway originally rehearsed at the Little Shubert Theatre, NYC; Ripley-Grier Studios, NYC; 3 Mills Studio, London.

Make-up Provided by
MAKE UP FOR EVER

To learn more about the production, please visit
www.BillyElliotBroadway.com

To become the next Billy Elliot, please visit
www.BeBilly.com

SPECIAL THANKS

The producers wish to thank the following partners for their generous support: HOTEL MELA, CAPEZIO, STEPS ON BROADWAY.

Special thanks to Cass Jones (technical director Aus.); Stephen Rebbeck (technical director UK); Dennis Crowley; Maggie Brohn; Mark Vogeley, Michael Stewart and staff of the Little Shubert Theatre; Stanislav Iavroski and the staff of Ripley-Grier Studios; Steve Roath and the staff of Chelsea Studios; Chuck Vassallo and the staff of the Professional Performing Arts School, New York City; American Ballet Theatre; Youth America Grand Prix (YAGP); Ann Willis Ratray (Acting Consultant); Joan Lader; Ray Hesselink; Tim Federle; Callie Carter; Sara Brians; Stacy Caddell; Fred Lassen; Dorothy Medico and Dorothy's School of Dance – Long Island; Laurie Rae Waugh of Acocella Group; Lisa Schuller of Halstead Property, LLC; Marie Claire Martineau of Maison International; the "Victoria Posse": Jackie Morgan, John Caswell, Tiffany Horton, Donald Ross, Peter Waterman, Gemma Thomas, Sarah Askew, Marian Lynch,

Sian Farley; Treagus Stoneman Associates, Ltd.; Louise Withers and Associates; David Blandon; Diane Dawson. With thanks to the National Coal Mining Museum for England, Wakefield, W. Yorkshire.

Working Title Films would like to thank Ron Meyer, Marc Shmuger, David Linde, Jimmy Horowitz, Donna Langley, Rick Finkelstein, Arturo Barquet, Allison Ganz, Stephanie Sperber, Stephanie Testa and Jonathan Treisman at Universal Pictures; Peter Bennett-Jones and Greg Brenman at Tiger Aspect Pictures; David Thompson at the BBC and Tessa Ross; Luke Lloyd Davies; Janine Shalom; all at Working Title Films for their continuing help and support; and especially to all the people who worked on the film Billy Elliot.

Old Vic Productions would like to thank Eric Fellner, Tim Bevan, Elton John, David Furnish, Lee Hall, Stephen Daldry, Peter Darling, Angela Morrison, Jon Finn and all at Working Title Films, Arthur Cohen, David Friedlander, Nick Simunek, Marieke Spencer, Jimmy Horowitz, John Barlow, Adam Kenwright, Janine Shalom, and most of all, to David, Kiril and Trent.

Elton John would like to thank Lee Hall, Stephen Daldry, David Furnish, Matt Still, Eric Fellner, Tim Bevan, Jon Finn, Sally Greene, Angela Morrison, Frank Presland, Keith Bradley, Clive Banks, Todd Interland, Davey Johnstone, Bob Birch, Guy Babylon, John Mahon, Nigel Olsen. And a special thanks to Liam, James and George for bringing Billy to life on stage.

Billy Elliot
SCRAPBOOK

Correspondent: Gregory Jbara, "Dad"

Most Exciting Celebrity Visitors: Vice President Joe Biden and his wife (on Valentine's Day). He shared a lovely anecdote about his love for his wife. Hillary Clinton, her daughter Chelsea and her mother came the Saturday evening after she was announced as Secretary of State. When Haydn Gwynne congratulated her on her new job she responded, "Yeah, well, we have a lot of work to do...." Lady Speaker of the House Nancy Pelosi and her husband Paul Pelosi were simply gracious. Robert De Niro brought his two sons backstage to meet the cast. Tyra Banks had the ballet girls in the palm of her hand after performing an African dance.

"Gypsy of the Year": The only cast member to appear at the "Gypsy of the Year" was Greg Jbara and his two sons, Zachary and Aidan, who assisted Seth Rudetsky in introducing the judges for the evening. And the only reason Zachary and Aidan were there was because their Mom, Julie, was trapped in Atlanta due to bad weather. Greg brought his sons onstage with him because he couldn't find a sitter at the last minute.

"Carols for a Cure" Carol: "Cold Christmas"

Actors Who Performed the Most Roles in This Show: Donnie Kehr or Stephen Hanna with four roles each. Honorable Mention: Thommie Retter changes his wig six times and each time using SPIRIT GUM!

Special Backstage Rituals: Just before Dad (Greg Jbara) takes Billy onstage toward the end of the opening number, "Stars Look Down," Greg, the ballet girls, the guardians and all stage hands en route do a "flutter of the fingers below the chin" as a high-sign before Greg drags Billy onstage.

Jeff Kready and Aaron Kaburick have a ritual they do every night. Before the curtain comes up for "Merry Christmas, Maggie Thatcher," they touch the "lucky" shoe that is hanging in the doorway of the set, upstage left. We're not sure why the shoe hangs there, but they touch it every night for luck. Our stage managers, Scott Rowen and Charlie Underhill often touch it for luck as well.

As recounted by Tessa Netting: SQUEEZING THE CHICKEN! This is an extremely important ritual with the ballet girls. Every night since the first preview we squeeze a little plastic chicken that is located in my "Stars Look Down" costume (before going downstairs I always do a chicken check with Jeannie to make sure it's in there, because one day it got lost and we had to squeeze Eboni). ANYWAY before EVERY show each ballet girl has their own special way of squeezing the chicken in a specific order and it gives us luck. Carole Shelley squeezes it too.

Favorite In-Theatre Gathering Place: Men's ensemble quick-change area near the wardrobe office, ballet girls' dressing room, sidewalk outside the 46th Street stage door between "half hour" and "places."

Photo by Aubrey Reuben

Photo by Elizabeth Pearce

Photo by Elizabeth Pearce

Photo by John Funk

Photo by Heidi Burns

Photo by Elizabeth Pearce

1. *Playbill Yearbook* correspondent Greg Jbara (top) at rehearsals with (L-R): David Alvarez, Haydn Gwynne, Kiril Kulish, Trent Kowalik, Carole Shelley and Santino Fontana.
2. Dance Captain Cara Kjellman, with Ballet Girls Izzy Hanson-Johnston and Eboni Edwards.
3. (L-R): Jayne Paterson, Tommy Batchelor, David Koch and BT McNicholl congratulate Greg Graham on getting the Gypsy Robe on opening night.
4. Music Director David Chase conducting during the sitzprobe, while director Stephen Daldry looks on in the background.
5. Company member Matthew Mindler warms up in his dressing room.
6. Brass player Alex Holton performs at the sitzprobe.

Billy Elliot

Scrapbook

1. Composer Elton John (top) with the ballet girls at the opening night cast party.
2. Frank Dolce and Elizabeth Daniels get dressed up for backstage trick-or-treating on Halloween.
3. Associate Director Julian Webber (striped shirt) at work with Joel Hatch, Erin Whyland and Izzy Hanson-Johnston.
4. Carole Shelley gets into character at the sitzprobe.
5. The sign we all had to pass each day.
6. The cast and crew welcome Sen. Hillary Clinton (C), soon to be named Secretary of State.

Favorite Off-Site Hangout: The kids love the park on 43rd Street. Adults like Chelsea Grill, La Esquina and cast members' apartments where libation is flowing.

Favorite Snack Foods: Anything chocolate, bagels on the weekends, birthday cakes, cookies or cupcakes, anything Kara Klein makes, David Koch's Rhubarb Crumble.

Favorite Therapy: Physio Arts and Pilates

Memorable Ad-Lib: This one totally broke the entire company during one of the most dramatic moments of the show. The line should be about a new "punch bag." For one glorious night it was about something no one had ever heard of: "You can't do that, man. I thought that was for a new bus pag."—Dan Oreskes

Record Number of Cell Phone Rings, Cell Phone Photos or Texting Incidents: At least 10.

Memorable Stage Door Fan Encounters: Have met *Billy Elliot* fans who have seen the show in London, Australia and on Broadway too many times to mention.

Fastest Costume Change: The Billys have about a 14-second costume change during "Solidarity." However, the entire male ensemble changes into police riot gear ONSTAGE in less than four bars of four.

Who Wore the Heaviest/Hottest Costume: The eight ensemble members who play the seven dancing dresses and one pair of dancing pants.

Who Wore the Least: Small boys in the boxing scene top of Act I.

Catchphrases Only the Company Would Recognize: An Australian "Yeeeaaahhh."

Company In-Jokes: "Puppet, puppet, no puppet, coconut."—Lee Proud (West End Dance Captain) during the first "Merry Christmas, Maggie Thatcher" rehearsal.

Onstage Finale Ritual: One nightly ritual that reminds me constantly how lucky we are to work with a group of kids is during the finale flaps. Every night the kids decide what the theme of that section is and begins chanting it onstage as we dance. Every night it infuses the company with a sense of joy and spontaneity. The company has been instructed to count out loud the eleven bars that lead into the shuffle ball change lines in the finale. The count changes nightly depending on the evening...for example: On the evening of Tuesday June 23 Trent Kowalik replaced Tommy Batchelor as "Billy" a third of the way into the second act due to Tommy feeling ill. During the finale, the chant was: "ONE BILLY SWITCHES...(five, six, seven, eight), TWO BILLY SWITCHES...(five, six seven, eight)," et cetera.

Ghostly Encounters Backstage: Countless spirit orbs appearing in the onstage photos with friends and family.

Coolest Thing About Being in This Show: You can't get a ticket. (Also happens to be the least cool thing about this show.)

Blithe Spirit

First Preview: February 26, 2009. Opened: March 15, 2009.
Still running as of May 31, 2009.

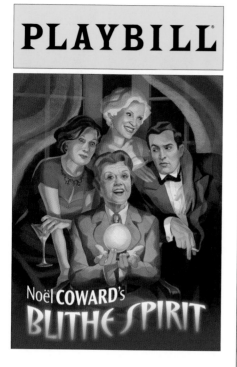

PLAYBILL®

Noël COWARD's
BLITHE SPIRIT

CAST

(in order of appearance)

Edith .... SUSAN LOUISE O'CONNOR
Ruth .... JAYNE ATKINSON
Charles .... RUPERT EVERETT
Dr. Bradman .... SIMON JONES
Mrs. Bradman .... DEBORAH RUSH
Madame Arcati .... ANGELA LANSBURY
Elvira .... CHRISTINE EBERSOLE

SETTING

The living room of the Condomine's house
in Kent, England

UNDERSTUDIES/STANDBYS

For Charles, Dr. Bradman:
MARK CAPRI
For Elvira, Ruth, Edith:
ELIZABETH NORMENT
For Madame Arcati, Mrs. Bradman:
SANDRA SHIPLEY

Rupert Everett is appearing with the permission of
Actors' Equity Association.

JEFFREY RICHARDS   JERRY FRANKEL   STEVE TRAXLER

SCOTT M. DELMAN   BAT-BARRY PRODUCTIONS   BROADWAY ACROSS AMERICA   KEN DAVENPORT

MICHAEL FILERMAN   FINN SCANLAN PRODUCTIONS   RONALD FRANKEL   JK PRODUCTIONS

KATHLEEN K. JOHNSON   PATTY ANN McKINNON   JUDITH RESNICK   TERRY SCHNUCK

JAMIE deROY/ALAN D. MARKS   ZEV BUFFMAN   BARBARA & BUDDY FREITAG/WENDY FEDERMAN

present

RUPERT EVERETT   CHRISTINE EBERSOLE   JAYNE ATKINSON

and

ANGELA LANSBURY

in

Noël COWARD's
BLITHE SPIRIT

with

SIMON JONES   DEBORAH RUSH   SUSAN LOUISE O'CONNOR

Scenic Design	*Costume Design*	*Lighting Design*	*Sound Design*
PETER J. DAVISON	MARTIN PAKLEDINAZ	BRIAN MacDEVITT	PETER FITZGERALD

Production Supervisor	*Wig and Hair Design*	*Casting*	*Production Management*
STEVEN ZWEIGBAUM	PAUL HUNTLEY	TELSEY+COMPANY	AURORA PRODUCTIONS

Press Representative	*Company Manager*	*General Management*
JEFFREY RICHARDS ASSOCIATES IRENE GANDY/ALANA KARPOFF	BRUCE KLINGER	RICHARDS/CLIMAN, INC.

Directed by

MICHAEL BLAKEMORE

The Producers wish to express their appreciation to the
Theatre Development Fund for its support of this production.

NOW **THAT'S**
BROADWAY!

3/15/09

(L-R): Deborah Rush, Rupert Everett,
Angela Lansbury, Jayne Atkinson
and Simon Jones

Photo by Robert J. Saferstein

Blithe Spirit

Angela Lansbury
Madame Arcati

Rupert Everett
Charles

Christine Ebersole
Elvira

Jayne Atkinson
Ruth

Simon Jones
Dr. Bradman

Deborah Rush
Mrs. Bradman

Susan Louise
O'Connor
Edith

Mark Capri
*u/s Charles,
Dr. Bradman*

Elizabeth Norment
u/s Elvira, Ruth, Edith

Sandra Shipley
*u/s Madame Arcati,
Mrs. Bradman*

Noël Coward
Playwright

Michael Blakemore
Director

Peter J. Davison
Scenic Design

Martin Pakledinaz
Costume Design

Brian MacDevitt
Lighting Design

Paul Huntley
Wig and Hair Design

David R. Richards and Tamar Haimes,
Richards/Climan, Inc.
General Manager

Bernard Telsey,
Telsey + Company
Casting

Jeffrey Richards
Producer

Jerry Frankel
Producer

Steve Traxler
Producer

Barry Weisbord,
Bat-Barry
Productions
Producer

Michael Filerman
Producer

Jeffrey Finn
Producer

Arlene Scanlan
Producer

Terry Schnuck
Producer

Jamie deRoy
Producer

Barbara Freitag
Producer

Wendy Federman
Producer

CREW
Front Row (L-R): Ed Chapman,
Karen L. Eifert, Rose Alaio,
Laura McGarty,
Steven Zweigbaum

Back Row (L-R): Thomas Manoy,
Scott Deverna, unknown,
unknown,
Cavan Jones, Robert Miller,
unknown, unknown, unknown

Photo by Brian Mapp

Blithe Spirit

FRONT OF HOUSE STAFF
Front Row (L-R): Mikael Page,
Evan Stern, Scott Key,
Melissa Maniglia

Second Row (L-R): Frank Sanabria,
Katherine Benoit, Alexis Stewart,
Stephen Ivelja

Third Row (L-R): Merida Colon,
Aspacia Savas, Maura Gaynor,
Thomas Barry

Back Row (L-R): Martin Cooper,
Paul Rodriguez, Brian Gaynair

Photo by Brian Mapp

STAFF FOR *NOËL COWARD'S BLITHE SPIRIT*

GENERAL MANAGEMENT
RICHARDS/CLIMAN, INC.
David R. Richards   Tamar Haimes

COMPANY MANAGER
BRUCE KLINGER

GENERAL PRESS REPRESENTATIVE
JEFFREY RICHARDS ASSOCIATES
IRENE GANDY
Alana Karpoff   Elon Rutberg   Shane Marshall Brown
Diana Rissetto

CASTING
TELSEY + COMPANY
Bernie Telsey CSA, Will Cantler CSA, David Vaccari CSA,
Bethany Knox CSA, Craig Burns CSA,
Tiffany Little Canfield CSA, Rachel Hoffman CSA,
Carrie Rosson CSA, Justin Huff CSA, Bess Fifer CSA,
Patrick Goodwin, Abbie Brady-Dalton

PRODUCTION MANAGEMENT
AURORA PRODUCTIONS INC.
Gene O'Donovan, W. Benjamin Heller II,
Bethany Weinstein, Amy Merlino Coey, Laura Archer,
Dana Hesch, Melissa Mazdra

PRODUCTION STAGE
   MANAGER ....STEVEN ZWEIGBAUM
Stage Manager ....Ara Marx
Associate Director ....Kim Weild
Associate Scenic Designer ....Ted LeFevre
Associate Costume Designer ....MaryAnn D. Smith
Assistant to the Costume Designer ....Noah Marin
Costume Intern ....Sophia Anastasiou
Makeup Design.................................Jason Hayes
Associate Lighting Designer ....Caroline Chao
Assistant Lighting Designer ....Peter Hoerburger
Assistant Sound Designer ....Megan Henninger
Associate General Manager .... John Gendron
General Management Associate ....Jeromy Smith
Production Assistant ....Sarah Michele Penland
Production Carpenter ....Jim Kane
Production Electrician ....Dan Coey
Production Props ....Peter Sarafin

Head Props ....Laura McGarty
Production Sound ....Ed Chapman
Wardrobe Supervisor ....Karen L. Eifert
Ms. Lansbury's Dresser ....Maeve Butler
Dressers ....Jill Frese, Geoffrey Polischuk
Hair Supervisor ....Erin Kennedy Lunsford
Associate to Mr. Richards ....Jeremy Scott Blaustein
Assistant to Mr. Richards ....Christopher Taggart
Assistant to Mr. Traxler ....Brandi Preston
General Management Assistant ....Cesar Hawas
Advertising ....Serino Coyne, Inc./
      Greg Corradetti, Tom Callahan,
      Robert Jones, Vanessa Javier
Interactive Marketing Agency ....Situation Marketing/
      Damian Bazadona, John Lanasa,
      Ryan Klink, Kristen Butler
Marketing Consultant ....Ken Davenport
Banking ....City National Bank/Michele Gibbons
Accountants ....Fried & Kowgios, CPA's LLP/
      Robert Fried, CPA
Comptroller ....Elliott Aronstam, CPA
Legal Counsel ....Lazarus & Harris LLP/
   Scott R. Lazarus, Esq., Robert C. Harris, Esq.
Payroll ....CSI/Lance Castellana
Production Photographer ....Robert J. Saferstein
Concierge/Chauffeur Services ....Get Services LLC
Company Mascots ....Lottie, Skye, Bob, Maud
Psychic Consultant ...Paula Roberts "The English Psychic"

Interlude music arranged and performed by
Lawrence Yurman and Christine Ebersole.

CREDITS
Scenery constructed by Showman Fabricators. Lighting
equipment from PRG Lighting. Sound equipment from
Sound Associates. Special effect furniture by Craig Grigg.
Flame retarding by Turning Star. Miss Lansbury's costumes
by Barbara Matera, Ltd. Miss Rush's costumes by Eric
Winterling, Inc. Miss Ebersole and Miss Atkinson's cos-
tumes by Euroco, Inc. Men's tailoring by Paul Chang
Custom Tailor, Chicago. Men's shirts by Anto Distinctive
Shirtmakers. Beading by Bessie Nelson Beading. Millinery
by Lynne Mackey Studio. Crafts by Arnold Levine, Inc.
Special jewelry by Lawrence Vrba, Ltd. Custom footwear by
LaDuca Shoes and Worldtone Dance. Special thanks to
Bra*Tenders, Early Halloween, Helen Uffner Vintage

Clothing, Illisa Vintage Lingerie, New York Vintage, Right
to the Moon Alice, Western Costume Company and
Duncan Quinn Tailoring. "Always" music and lyrics by
Irving Berlin. This selection is used by special arrangement
with The Rodgers & Hammerstein Organization on behalf
of the Estate of Irving Berlin, www.irvingberlin.com

www.BlitheOnBroadway.com

Boeing-Boeing

First Preview: April 19, 2008. Opened: May 4, 2008.
Closed January 4, 2009 after 17 Previews and 279 Performances.

PLAYBILL®

CAST
(in order of appearance)

Gloria ....PAIGE DAVIS
Bernard ....GREG GERMANN
Berthe ....CHRISTINE BARANSKI
Robert...............................MARK RYLANCE
Gabriella ....REBECCA GAYHEART
Gretchen...................................MISSI PYLE

SETTING
Bernard's apartment in Paris. One Saturday in April.
Early 1960s.

UNDERSTUDIES
For Bernard:
TOM GALANTICH
For Robert:
LIAM CRAIG
For Berthe:
PIPPA PEARTHREE
For Gabriella, Gloria, Gretchen:
JESSICA BOGART

CURTAIN-CALL CHOREOGRAPHY
KATHLEEN MARSHALL

Mark Rylance is appearing with the permission of
Actors' Equity Association.

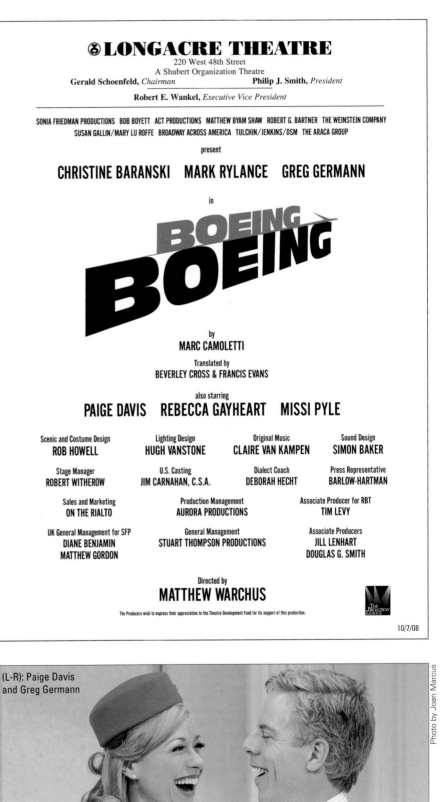

⑤ LONGACRE THEATRE
220 West 48th Street
A Shubert Organization Theatre

Gerald Schoenfeld, *Chairman*   Philip J. Smith, *President*

Robert E. Wankel, *Executive Vice President*

SONIA FRIEDMAN PRODUCTIONS   BOB BOYETT   ACT PRODUCTIONS   MATTHEW BYAM SHAW   ROBERT G. BARTNER   THE WEINSTEIN COMPANY
SUSAN GALLIN/MARY LU ROFFE   BROADWAY ACROSS AMERICA   TULCHIN/JENKINS/DSM   THE ARACA GROUP

present

CHRISTINE BARANSKI   MARK RYLANCE   GREG GERMANN

in

BOEING BOEING

by
MARC CAMOLETTI

Translated by
BEVERLEY CROSS & FRANCIS EVANS

also starring
PAIGE DAVIS   REBECCA GAYHEART   MISSI PYLE

Scenic and Costume Design	Lighting Design	Original Music	Sound Design
ROB HOWELL	HUGH VANSTONE	CLAIRE VAN KAMPEN	SIMON BAKER

Stage Manager	U.S. Casting	Dialect Coach	Press Representative
ROBERT WITHEROW	JIM CARNAHAN, C.S.A.	DEBORAH HECHT	BARLOW-HARTMAN

Sales and Marketing	Production Management	Associate Producer for RBT
ON THE RIALTO	AURORA PRODUCTIONS	TIM LEVY

UK General Management for SFP	General Management	Associate Producers
DIANE BENJAMIN MATTHEW GORDON	STUART THOMPSON PRODUCTIONS	JILL LENHART DOUGLAS G. SMITH

Directed by
MATTHEW WARCHUS

The Producers wish to express their appreciation to the Theatre Development Fund for its support of this production.

10/7/08

(L-R): Paige Davis
and Greg Germann

Photo by Joan Marcus

Boeing-Boeing

Christine Baranski
Berthe

Mark Rylance
Robert

Greg Germann
Bernard

Paige Davis
Gloria

Rebecca Gayheart
Gabriella

Missi Pyle
Gretchen

Jessica Bogart
Understudy for Gabriella, Gloria, Gretchen

Liam Craig
Understudy for Robert

Tom Galantich
Understudy for Bernard

Pippa Pearthree
Understudy for Berthe

Matthew Warchus
Director

Rob Howell
Scenic and Costume Design

Hugh Vanstone
Lighting Design

Simon Baker
Sound Design

Jim Carnahan
Casting

Stuart Thompson Productions
General Management

Sonia Friedman Productions
Producer

Bob Boyett
Producer

Bob Weinstein, The Weinstein Company
Producer

Harvey Weinstein, The Weinstein Company
Producer

Michael Jenkins, Tulchin/Jenkins/DSM
Producer

Kathryn Hahn
Gloria

Roxanna Hope
u/s Gabriella, Gloria, Gretchen

Mary McCormack
Gretchen

Ray Virta
u/s Bernard

Bradley Whitford
Bernard

CREW
Front Row (L-R): Kim Prentice, Barry Doss, Billy Barnes, Elisa Acevedo, Robert Witherow, Ric Rogers.

Back Row (L-R): John Lofgren, Wilbur Graham, Wayne Smith.

Photo by Ben Strothmann

Boeing-Boeing

FRONT OF HOUSE STAFF
Front Row (L-R):
Bob Reilly,
John Mallon,
Monica Caraballo,
Janet Kay.

Middle Row (L-R):
Jim McIntosh,
Dennis Norwood,
Paula Raymond,
Joe Biamonte,
Christina Gutierrez,
Kenny Weinstein.

Back Row (L-R):
Denise Eckels,
Marla Karaliolios.

DOORMAN
Enrico Bozzacco

PROPS ASSISTANT
Alan C. Edwards

STAFF FOR *BOEING-BOEING*

GENERAL MANAGEMENT
STUART THOMPSON PRODUCTIONS

Stuart Thompson	Caroline Prugh
James Triner	David Turner

COMPANY MANAGER
Cassidy J. Briggs

PRODUCTION MANAGEMENT
AURORA PRODUCTIONS INC.

Gene O'Donovan	W. Benjamin Heller II
Bethany Weinstein	Melissa Mazdra
Asia Evans	

PRESS REPRESENTATIVE
BARLOW•HARTMAN

Michael Hartman	John Barlow
Tom D'Ambrosio	Michelle Bergmann

Production Stage Manager	Robert Witherow
Stage Manager	Carolyn Kelson
Literal Translation by	Christopher Campbell
Associate Director	Mark Schneider
Associate Scenic Designer	Ted LeFevre
Associate Lighting Designer	Anthony Pearson
Associate Sound Designer	Christopher Cronin
Associate Costume Designer	Brian Russman
Hair Design	Larry Boyette
Makeup Design	Erica Whelan
Assistant to Ms. Marshall	Jennifer Savelli
Production Electrician	Dan Coey
Production Sound Operator	Wayne Smith
Production Properties	Peter Sarafin
Production Properties Assistant	Alan C. Edwards
Wardrobe Supervisor	Kimberly Prentice
Dressers	Barry Doss, Kathy Karadza
Hair Supervisor	Shanah-Ann Kendall
House Electrician	Richard Rogers
House Props	John P. Lofgren
House Carpenter	Wilber Graham, Jr.
Production Assistant	Caroline Andersen
Casting Associate	Kate Boka

UK Costume Supervisor	Irene Bohan
General Management Assistants	Megan Curren, Aaron Thompson
Management Intern	Geo Karapetyan
Banking	City National Bank/ Michele Gibbons
Payroll	Castellana Services, Inc.
Accountant	Fried & Kowgios CPA's LLP/ Robert Fried, CPA
Controller	J.S. Kubala
Insurance	DeWitt Stern Group
Legal Counsel	Lazarus & Harris/ Scott Lazarus, Esq., Robert Harris, Esq.
Advertising	SPOTCO/ Drew Hodges, Jim Edwards, Jim Aquino, Kyle Hall
Sales and Marketing	on the RIALTO/ Clint Bond Jr., Steven Rummer
Merchandise	The Araca Group
Production Photographer	Joan Marcus
Theatre Displays	King Displays

SONIA FRIEDMAN PRODUCTIONS

Producer	Sonia Friedman
Chief Executive Officer-NY	David Lazar
General Manager	Diane Benjamin
Creative Producer	Lisa Makin
Head of Production	Pam Skinner
Associate Producer	Matthew Gordon
Literary Associate	Jack Bradley
Production Assistant	Lucie Lovatt
Production Assistant	Martin Ball
Production Assistant	Jamie Hendry
Executive Assistant-NY	Dan Gallagher
Production Accountant	Melissa Hay
SFP Board	Helen Enright, Howard Panter, Rosemary Squire

For ACT PRODUCTIONS

Chairman	Roger Wingate
Director of Production	Nick Salmon
General Manager	Nia Janis
Assistant Producer	Imogen Kinchin

Makeup provided by
M•A•C Cosmetics

CREDITS

Scenery by Souvenir Scenic Studios Ltd. Lighting equipment from PRG Lighting. Sound equipment from Sound Associates. Costumes executed by Tricorne LLC. Millinery by Rodney Gordon Ltd. Custom footwear by Worldtone. Select vintage clothing by The Autumn Olive. Special thanks to Bra*Tenders for hosiery and undergarments. Souvenir merchandise designed and created by the Araca Group.

Opening Night party courtesy of Nikki Midtown. Opening Night party services: Reed Hatkoff at Really Spectacular Events.

 THE SHUBERT ORGANIZATION, INC.
Board of Directors

House Manager	Bob Reilly

Chicago

First Preview: October 23, 1996. Opened: November 14, 1996.
Still running as of May 31, 2009.

CHICAGO
THE MUSICAL

THE CAST

(in order of appearance)

Velma Kelly	BRENDA BRAXTON
Roxie Hart	MICHELLE DeJEAN
Fred Casely	GREGORY BUTLER
Sergeant Fogarty	ADAM ZOTOVICH
Amos Hart	KEVIN CHAMBERLIN
Liz	NICOLE BRIDGEWATER
Annie	DYLIS CROMAN
June	DONNA MARIE ASBURY
Hunyak	NILI BASSMAN
Mona	MARLA McREYNOLDS
Matron "Mama" Morton	CAROL WOODS
Billy Flynn	TOM WOPAT
Mary Sunshine	R. LOWE
Go-To-Hell Kitty	MELISSA RAE MAHON
Harry	SHAWN EMAMJOMEH
Doctor	JASON PATRICK SANDS
Aaron	DAN LoBUONO
The Judge	JASON PATRICK SANDS
Bailiff	JOE AARON REID
Martin Harrison	MICHAEL CUSUMANO
Court Clerk	JOE AARON REID
The Jury	SHAWN EMAMJOMEH

THE SCENE:

Chicago, Illinois. The late 1920s.

⑧ AMBASSADOR THEATRE

A Shubert Organization Theatre

Gerald Schoenfeld, *Chairman*   Philip J. Smith, *President*

Robert E. Wankel, *Executive Vice President*

Barry & Fran Weissler
in association with
Kardana/Hart Sharp Entertainment
present

**Michelle DeJean   Brenda Braxton
Tom Wopat
Kevin Chamberlin**

in

CHICAGO

Lyrics by   Music By   Book by
Fred Ebb   John Kander   Fred Ebb & Bob Fosse

Original Production Directed and Choreographed by **Bob Fosse**

Based on the play by Maurine Dallas Watkins

with

Carol Woods   R. Lowe

and

**Donna Marie Asbury   Nili Bassman   Nicole Bridgewater   Gregory Butler
Dylis Croman   Michael Cusumano   Shawn Emamjomeh
Gabriela Garcia   David Kent   Dan LoBuono   J. Loeffelholz
Melissa Rae Mahon   Marla McReynolds   Sharon Moore   Jill Nicklaus
Joe Aaron Reid   Jason Patrick Sands   Brian Spitulnik   Adam Zotovich**

Supervising Music Director	Music Director
Rob Fisher	**Leslie Stifelman**

Scenic Design	Costume Design	Lighting Design
John Lee Beatty	**William Ivey Long**	**Ken Billington**

Sound Design	Orchestrations	Dance Music Arrangements
Scott Lehrer	**Ralph Burns**	**Peter Howard**

Script Adaptation	Musical Coordinator	Hair Design
David Thompson	**Seymour Red Press**	**David Brian Brown**

Casting	Original Casting
Duncan Stewart	**Jay Binder**

Technical Supervisor	Dance Supervisor	Production Stage Manager
Arthur Siccardi	**Gary Chryst**	**David Hyslop**

Associate Producer	Presented in association with
Alecia Parker	**Live Nation**

General Manager	Press Representative
B.J. Holt	**Jeremy Shaffer** **The Publicity Office**

Based on the presentation by City Center's Encores!℠

Choreography by
Ann Reinking
in the style of Bob Fosse

Directed by
Walter Bobbie

Cast Recording on RCA Victor

10/1/08

Tom Wopat (center) as Billy Flynn with the ladies' Ensemble.

Photo by Paul Kolnik

Continued on next page

Chicago

MUSICAL NUMBERS

ACT I

ALL THAT JAZZ	Velma and Company
FUNNY HONEY	Roxie
CELL BLOCK TANGO	Velma and the Girls
WHEN YOU'RE GOOD TO MAMA	Matron
TAP DANCE	Roxie, Amos and Boys
ALL I CARE ABOUT	Billy and Girls
A LITTLE BIT OF GOOD	Mary Sunshine
WE BOTH REACHED FOR THE GUN	Billy, Roxie, Mary Sunshine and Company
ROXIE	Roxie and Boys
I CAN'T DO IT ALONE	Velma
MY OWN BEST FRIEND	Roxie and Velma

ACT II

ENTR'ACTE	The Band
I KNOW A GIRL	Velma
ME AND MY BABY	Roxie and Boys
MISTER CELLOPHANE	Amos
WHEN VELMA TAKES THE STAND	Velma and Boys
RAZZLE DAZZLE	Billy and Company
CLASS	Velma and Matron
NOWADAYS	Roxie and Velma
HOT HONEY RAG	Roxie and Velma
FINALE	Company

Michelle DeJean
as Roxie Hart

Photo by Paul Kolnik

UNDERSTUDIES

For Roxie Hart:
DYLIS CROMAN, MELISSA RAE MAHON
For Velma Kelly/Matron "Mama" Morton:
DONNA MARIE ASBURY,
NICOLE BRIDGEWATER
For Billy Flynn:
DAN LoBUONO, JASON PATRICK SANDS
For Amos Hart:
JASON PATRICK SANDS, ADAM ZOTOVICH
For Mary Sunshine:
J. LOEFFELHOLZ
For Fred Casely/"Me and My Baby":
DAVID KENT, JOE AARON REID,
BRIAN SPITULNIK

For all other roles:
GABRIELA GARCIA, DAVID KENT,
SHARON MOORE, JILL NICKLAUS,
BRIAN SPITULNIK

Dance Captains: Gregory Butler, Gabriela Garcia

"Tap Dance" specialty performed by
DAN LoBUONO, JOE AARON REID
and JASON PATRICK SANDS

"Me and My Baby" specialty performed by
MICHAEL CUSUMANO
and DAN LoBUONO

"Nowadays" whistle performed by
JASON PATRICK SANDS

Original Choreography for "Hot Honey Rag" by
BOB FOSSE

ORCHESTRA

Orchestra Conducted by
LESLIE STIFELMAN
Associate Conductor:
SCOTT CADY
Woodwinds:
SEYMOUR RED PRESS, JACK STUCKEY,
RICHARD CENTALONZA
Trumpets:
JOHN FROSK, DARRYL SHAW
Trombones:
DAVE BARGERON, BRUCE BONVISSUTO
Piano:
SCOTT CADY
Piano & Accordion:
JOHN JOHNSON
Banjo:
JAY BERLINER
Bass & Tuba:
RONALD RAFFIO
Violin:
MARSHALL COID
Drums & Percussion:
RONALD ZITO

Chicago

Michelle DeJean
Roxie Hart

Brenda Braxton
Velma Kelly

Tom Wopat
Billy Flynn

Kevin Chamberlin
Amos Hart

Carol Woods
Matron "Mama" Morton

R. Lowe
Mary Sunshine

Donna Marie Asbury
June

Nili Bassman
Hunyak

Nicole Bridgewater
Liz

Gregory Butler
Fred Casely/ Dance Captain

Dylis Croman
Annie

Michael Cusumano
Martin Harrison

Shawn Emamjomeh
Harry/The Jury

Gabriela Garcia
Swing/Dance Captain

David Kent
Swing

Dan LoBuono
Aaron

J. Loeffelholz
Standby Mary Sunshine

Melissa Rae Mahon
Go-To-Hell Kitty

Marla McReynolds
Mona

Sharon Moore
Swing

Jill Nicklaus
Swing

Joe Aaron Reid
Bailiff/Court Clerk

Jason Patrick Sands
Doctor/The Judge

Brian Spitulnik
Swing

Adam Zotovich
Sergeant Fogarty

John Kander & Fred Ebb
Music; Book/Lyrics

Bob Fosse
Book

Walter Bobbie
Director

Ann Reinking
Choreographer

John Lee Beatty
Set Design

William Ivey Long
Costume Designer

Ken Billington
Lighting Designer

Rob Fisher
Supervising Music Director

Seymour Red Press
Music Coordinator

Chicago

David Brian Brown
Wig/Hair Design

Duncan Stewart
Casting Director

Arthur Siccardi,
Theatrical Services
Inc.
Technical Supervisor

Barry & Fran Weissler
Producers

Morton Swinsky/
Kardana Productions
Producer

ALUMNI
2008-2009

Obba Babatundé
Billy Flynn

Eddie Bennett
Swing

Raymond Bokhour
Amos Hart

Bernard Dotson
*Doctor, The Judge,
"Tap Dance"
Specialty*

Nancy Lemenager
Velma Kelly

Kecia Lewis-Evans
*Matron "Mama"
Morton*

Bianca Marroquin
Roxie Hart

Jeff McCarthy
Billy Flynn

D. Micciche
Mary Sunshine

Josh Rhodes
*Doctor, The Judge,
"Tap Dance"
Specialty*

Eric Jordan Young
*Aaron, "Me and My
Baby" Specialty,
"Nowadays"
Whistle, "Tap
Dance" Specialty*

TRANSFER
STUDENTS
2008-2009

Raymond Bokhour
Amos Hart

Charlotte d'Amboise
Roxie Hart

Scott Davidson
Amos Hart

Bryn Dowling
Roxie Hart

LaVon Fisher-Wilson
*Matron "Mama"
Morton*

Melora Hardin
Roxie Hart

Tom Hewitt
Billy Flynn

James T. Lane
*Aaron, "Me and My
Baby" Specialty,
"Tap Dance"
Specialty*

Terra C. MacLeod
Velma Kelly

Bianca Marroquin
Roxie Hart

Jeff McCarthy
Billy Flynn

D. Micciche
Mary Sunshine

Brian O'Brien
*Bailiff, Court Clerk,
Fred Casely, "Tap
Dance" Specialty*

Sofia Vergara
*Matron "Mama"
Morton*

Amra-Faye Wright
Velma Kelly

Eric Jordan Young
*Aaron, "Me and My
Baby" Specialty,
"Tap Dance"
Specialty*

Chicago

ORCHESTRA
Front Row (L-R): Marshall Coid, David Grego.

Middle Row (L-R): Shawn Edmonds, Ken Hitchcock, Jeff Schiller, Dave Bargeron, Leslie Stifelman, John Johnson, Jay Berliner, Dan Gross.

Back Row (L-R): Bruce Bonvissuto, Rick Centalonza.

FRONT OF HOUSE STAFF
Front Row (L-R): Tyrone Hendrix (Ticket Taker), Leeann Kelley (Dewynters Staff), Rachel Zeolla (Dewynters Staff), Tasha Allen (Usher), Dorothea Bentley (Head Usher), Mary Simcoe (Usher), Carole Hollenbeck (Usher), Carol Bokun (Directress).

Middle Row (L-R): Jack Donaghy (Usher), Rita Sussman (Sound Associates Rep.), Timothy Newsome (Usher), Danielle Banyai (Usher), Marilyn Wasbotten (Usher), Lottie Dennis (Usher), Beatrice Carney (Usher), Jessica Porcelli (Theatre Refreshment Staff).

Back Row (L-R): Matt Kuehl (Dewynters Manager), Bobbi Parker (Usher), Christopher Holmes (Theatre Refreshment Staff).

STAGE MANAGEMENT
(L-R): Terry Witter (Stage Manager), David Hyslop (Production Stage Manager), Mindy Farbrother (Stage Manager).

Chicago

BOX OFFICE
(L-R): James Gatens (Treasurer), William Roeder (Assistant Treasurer), James Lyons (Assistant Treasurer).

HAIR AND WARDROBE
(L-R): Kevin Woodworth (Wardrobe Supervisor), Jo-Ann Bethell (Dresser), Justen Brosnan (Hair Supervisor), Paula Davis (Dresser).

Photos by Ben Strothmann

CREW
Front Row (L-R): Jenny Montgomery (Props), John Montgomery (Production Sound), Eileen MacDonald (Deck Sound), Jim Werner (Front Light).
Back Row (L-R): Luciana Fusco (Head Electrician), Joe Mooneyham (Production Carpenter), Bob Hale (Front Light), Billy Rowland (House Electrician).

STAFF FOR *CHICAGO*

GENERAL MANAGEMENT
B.J. Holt, General Manager
Nina Skriloff, International Manager

PRESS REPRESENTATIVE
THE PUBLICITY OFFICE
Jeremy Shaffer   Marc Thibodeau   Michael Borowski

Production Stage Manager	**David Hyslop**
Company Manager	**Hilary Hamilton**
Stage Managers	Terrence J. Witter, Mindy Farbrother
General Management Associate	Stephen Spadaro
Assistant Director	Jonathan Bernstein
Associate Lighting Designer	John McKernon
Assistant Choreographer	Debra McWaters
Assistant Set Designers	Eric Renschler, Shelley Barclay
Wardrobe Supervisor	Kevin Woodworth
Hair Supervisor	Scott Mortimer
Costume Assistant	Donald Sanders
Personal Asst. to Mr. Billington	Jon Kusner
Assistant to Mr. Lehrer	Thom Mohrman
Production Carpenter	Joseph Mooneyham
Production Electrician	James Fedigan
Head Electrician	Luciana Fusco
Front Lite Operator	Michael Guggino
Production Sound Engineer	John Montgomery
Production Props	Paula Zwicky
Dressers	Jo-Ann Bethell, Kathy Dacey, Paula Davis, Ronald Tagert, Eric Concklin
Banking	Chase Manhattan, Stephanie Dalton
Music Prep	Chelsea Music Services, Inc. Donald Oliver & Evan Morris
Payroll	Castellana Services, Inc.

Accountants	Rosenberg, Neuwirth & Kuchner Mark D'Ambrosi, Marina Flom
Insurance	Industrial Risk Specialists
Counsel	Seth Gelblum/Loeb & Loeb
Art Design	Spot Design
Advertising	SpotCo: Drew Hodges, Jim Edwards, Sara Fitzpatrick, Tom McCann, Josh Fraenkel
Education	Students Live/Amy Weinstein www.studentslive.net
Merchandising	Dewynters Advertising Inc.
Displays	King Display

NATIONAL ARTISTS MANAGEMENT CO.

Vice President of Marketing	Bob Bucci
Vice President of Business Affairs	Daniel M. Posener
Dramaturg/Creative Consultant	Jack DePalma
Chief Financial Officer	Bob Williams
Manager of Accounting/Admin.	Marian Albarracin
Assistant to Mrs. Weissler	Brett England
Assistant to the Weisslers	Suzanne Evans
Assistant to Ms. Parker	Emily Dimond
Director of Marketing	Ken Sperr
Promotions/Marketing Manager	Karen James
Receptionist	Michelle Coleman

SPECIAL THANKS
Additional legal services provided by Jay Goldberg, Esq. and Michael Berger, Esq. Emergen-C is the official health and energy drink mix of *Chicago*. Dry cleaning by Ernest Winzer Cleaners. Hosiery and undergarments provided by Bra*Tenders. Tuxedos by Brioni. Ike Behar tuxedo shirts provided by BBRAXTON Exceptional Grooming for Exceptional Men.

CREDITS
Lighting equipment by PRG Lighting. Scenery built and painted by Hudson Scenic Studios. Specialty Rigging by United Staging & Rigging. Sound equipment by PRG Audio. Shoulder holster courtesy of DeSantis Holster and Leather Goods Co. Period cameras and flash units by George Fenmore, Inc. Colibri lighters used. Bible courtesy of Chiarelli's Religious Goods, Inc. Black pencils by Dixon-Ticonderoga. Gavel courtesy of The Gavel Co. Zippo lighters used. Garcia y Vega cigars used. Hosiery by Donna Karan. Shoes by T.O. Dey. Orthopaedic Consultant, David S. Weiss, M.D.

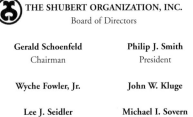

THE SHUBERT ORGANIZATION, INC.
Board of Directors

Gerald Schoenfeld Chairman	**Philip J. Smith** President
Wyche Fowler, Jr.	**John W. Kluge**
Lee J. Seidler	**Michael I. Sovern**

Stuart Subotnick

Robert E. Wankel
Executive Vice President

Peter Entin Vice President – Theatre Operations	**Elliot Greene** Vice President – Finance
David Andrews Vice President – Shubert Ticketing Services	**John Darby** Vice President – Facilities

D.S. Moynihan
Vice President – Creative Projects

House Manager	Patricia Berry

Chicago
SCRAPBOOK

Correspondent: Melissa Rae Mahon, "Go-To-Hell Kitty"

Anniversary Stats: We celebrated our 12th anniversary…and counting! And we are now the seventh-longest running Broadway show in history!

Memorable Fan Tribute: Donna Marie Asbury's number-one fan made a huge clock with show pictures of her on the face and different knives where the numbers should be!

Most Exciting Celebrity Visitors: Nicole Scherzinger from the Pussycat Dolls! Fierce! Captain C.B. "Sully" Sullenberger and crew from USAir Flight 1549.

"Easter Bonnet" Sketch: After a nine-year hiatus, *Chicago* performed in the "Easter Bonnet" this year. It was a sketch about "The six bitter musicals that closed in January, in their rendition of 'The Chopping Block Tango'!" written by Brian O'Brien and me. It was definitely an audience favorite (although, we were robbed of the awards by Jane Fonda and her crew from across the street). Highlights included hilarious monologues, fabulous home-made costume by Kevin Woodworth, set design by Joe Mooneyham, and an unforgettable bonnet design by Jo-Ann Bethell, Paula Zwicky and me. Our sketch had nine actors each paying

Cast members at "Easter Bonnet" with Yearbook correspondent Melissa Rae Mahon modeling the bonnet.

Celebrating the show's 12th anniversary and 5000th performance with a cake (L-R): Tom Hewitt, Raymond Bokhour, LaVon Fisher-Wilson, Bebe Neuwirth, Charlotte d'Amboise and Brenda Braxton.

tribute to a different show: James T. Lane (*Spamalot*), LaVon Fisher-Wilson (*Hairspray*), Donna Marie Asbury (the incinerating Patti LuPone), Amra-Faye Wright (Liza Minnelli), Brian Spitulnik (in drag for *Spring Awakening*), Jill Nicklaus (*Grease!*), Michael Cusumano (with puppet, *Avenue Q*), Brian O'Brien (*Young Frankenstein*), and me (bonnet model). Moral of the story? "Come to *Chicago*…we're hiring!"

Which Actor Performed the Most Roles in This Show: As always, our super swings, Gabriela Garcia, Sharon Moore, David Kent and Brian Spitulnik.

Special Backstage Rituals: Amra-Faye Wright, our fabulous Velma Kelly, started a new tradition of "drop and give me 20 pushups – at 'places'!" If it means we'll end up looking like her…20 it is. Also, lots of folks race to complete

the daily *New York Times* crossword puzzles. And there's the candy jar in the basement that we can't live without.

Favorite Moments During Each Performance: Well, personally I love going down the slide as "Go-To-Hell Kitty," and killing four people isn't so bad either! But we all love Charlotte d'Amboise's "Roxie" monologue. She's hilarious.

Favorite In-Theatre Gathering Place: I've heard a rumor that one can obtain a glass of wine in the girls' dressing room during "Hot Honey Rag!" Don't worry—we only have to bow!

Favorite Off-Site Hangout: Still Natsumi, so close you can't beat it.

Favorite Snack Foods: Bagel Sunday is always a hit. And Adam Zotovich's special delivery.

Mascots: We have a lot of dogs that visit backstage. Berger, Stevie, Ellie, Ruby, Mac, Marcus, Emmy, Quinn and Chloe.

Favorite Therapies: Tiger Balm all the way…and tequila.

Memorable Ad-Lib: LaVon Fisher-Wilson as Mama Morton: "Ya see, Sweetie, it's like this: Murder is like divorce. The reason don't count. It's the grounds. Temporary insanity, self defense, hittin' 'em in the head with a brick…."

Cell Phone Incidents: We wish Patti LuPone would come over to our theatre and kick some ass.

Memorable Press Encounters: High: We performed at the opening of Fleet Week on the new and improved Intrepid. Low: Spinning the Wheel of Fortune at Duane Reade, where the top prize was chapstick.

Memorable Fan Encounters: There will always be "crazy laughing man." He means well, but always laughs just before the punch line…he's psychic.

Which Orchestra Members Played the Most Instruments: Tony Award winner Seymour Red Press, Jack Stuckey, Richard Centalonza.

Sweethearts Within the Company: Michael

Cusumano and…fill in the blank. Everyone loves a little Mikey.

Catchphrases Only the Company Would Recognize: "This is some BBUUUULLLLL-SHIT!" "SHHHHH, Josh!"

Memorable Directorial Notes: "Let one cue kiss the ass of the one before!" "You want it? Come and get it!" OR "You want it? You can't have it!" "Pass the Ball!"

Company In-Joke: Bite the Jazz Apple

Company Legend: Greg Butler—living legend.

Nickname: Some people call Greg Butler "Mary Kate Olsen" because no one has ever seen him eat anything but a six-shot iced espresso!

Embarrassing Moment: Charlotte d'Amboise used to do this great bit during "Roxie." She jumped off the stage and went out into the audience to lovingly tease kids who were too young to be listening to her monologue. Normally she would get a running start, then dive and roll back onto the stage. Until one Sunday matinee when she dove, but crashed into the footlights. It was funny, but she was out for the rest of the day. Classic Charlotte. We love her.

Heaviest/Hottest Costume: No such thing in *Chicago*.

Who Looks the Best in the Least: Jason Patrick Sands.

Coolest Thing About Being in This Show: We embrace change. Improv is the best gift in a long-running show…keeps the creative juices flowing.

Other Memories This Year: B.J. Holt had a beautiful baby, Christina.
Luciana Fusco had a beautiful baby, Lina.
Solange Sandy had a beautiful baby, Nicholas.
Ray Bokhour had a beautiful baby, Phoebe.
Hilary Hamilton had a beautiful baby, Liam.
Adam Zotovich had a beautiful baby, Milana.
The company also bade a fond farewell to Michelle DeJean. She was a member of the *Chicago* family for more than 10 years—appearing first as a swing, then for years as Mona, and finally all over the country and on Broadway as Roxie Hart. We wish her Happy Trails!

Amra-Faye Wright and Jason Patrick Sands at the rechristening of the battleship Intrepid.

A Chorus Line

First Preview: September 18, 2006. Opened: October 5, 2006.
Closed August 17, 2008 after 18 Previews and 759 Performances.

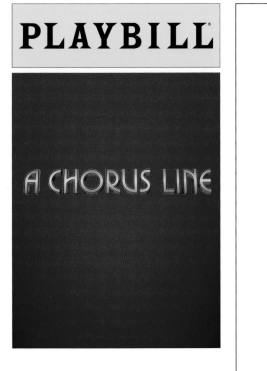

PLAYBILL

A CHORUS LINE

CAST

(in alphabetical order)

Larry	NICK ADAMS
Roy	TODD ANDERSON
Tricia	MICHELLE ARAVENA
Greg	TOMMY BERKLUND
Al	MIKE CANNON
Diana	NATALIE CORTEZ
Bebe	DENA DiGIACINTO
Tom	KURT DOMONEY
Butch	ERIC DySART
Val	JENIFER FOOTE
Cassie	JESSICA LEE GOLDYN
Sheila	DEIDRE GOODWIN
Paul	BRYAN KNOWLTON
Richie	JAMES T. LANE
Maggie	MELISSA LONE
Zach	MARIO LOPEZ
Connie	J. ELAINE MARCOS
Lois	COURTNEY LAINE MAZZA
Mark	PAUL McGILL
Judy	HEATHER PARCELLS
Don	ADAM PERRY
Mike	JEFFREY SCHECTER
Frank	ERIC SCIOTTO
Bobby	WILL TAYLOR
Kristine	KATHERINE TOKARZ

SWINGS

JOEY DUDDING, LYNDY FRANKLIN,
LORIN LATARRO, KIM SHRIVER,
DEONE ZANOTTO

Continued on next page

236 West 45th Street
A Shubert Organization Theatre

Gerald Schoenfeld, *Chairman*   **Philip J. Smith,** *President*

Robert E. Wankel, *Executive Vice President*

Vienna Waits Productions

presents

A CHORUS LINE

Conceived and Originally Choreographed and Directed by

Michael Bennett

Book by	Music by	Lyrics by
James Kirkwood &	**Marvin Hamlisch**	**Edward Kleban**
Nicholas Dante		

Originally Co-Choreographed by

Bob Avian

with

Nick Adams   Deanna Aguinaga   Todd Anderson   Michelle Aravena   Tommy Berklund
Mike Cannon   Natalie Cortez   Dena DiGiacinto   Kurt Domoney
Joey Dudding   Eric DySart   Jenifer Foote   Lyndy Franklin   Jessica Lee Goldyn
Deidre Goodwin   Bryan Knowlton   James T. Lane   Lorin Latarro   Melissa Lone
Mario Lopez   J. Elaine Marcos   Courtney Laine Mazza   Paul McGill   Heather Parcells
Adam Perry   Eric Sciotto   Jeffrey Schecter   Kim Shriver
Will Taylor   Katherine Tokarz   Deone Zanotto

Scenic Design by	Costume Design by	Lighting Design by	Sound Design by
Robin Wagner	**Theoni V. Aldredge**	**Tharon Musser**	**Acme Sound**
		Adapted by	**Partners**
		Natasha Katz	

Music Supervision by	Orchestrations by	Vocal Arrangements by
Patrick Vaccariello	**Jonathan Tunick**	**Don Pippin**
	Bill Byers & Hershy Kay	

Choreography Re-Staged by

Baayork Lee

Directed by

Bob Avian

The original production of A CHORUS LINE was produced by The Public Theater, in association with Plum Productions.

8/17/08

Mario Lopez (center) and the Ensemble perform the Finale.

Photo by Paul Kolnik

A Chorus Line

MUSICAL NUMBERS

I Hope I Get It	Company
I Can Do That	Mike
And	Bobby, Richie, Val, Judy
At the Ballet	Sheila, Bebe, Maggie
Sing!	Kristine, Al
Hello Twelve, Hello Thirteen, Hello Love	Company
Nothing	Diana
Dance: Ten; Looks: Three	Val
The Music and the Mirror	Cassie
One	Company
The Tap Combination	Company
What I Did for Love	Diana, Company
One: Reprise	Company

AN AUDITION

TIME: 1975
PLACE: A Broadway Theatre

"This show is dedicated to anyone who has ever danced in a chorus or marched in step…anywhere."
—Michael Bennett

ORCHESTRA

Conductor:
JIM LAEV
Associate Conductor/Keyboard 3:
MAGGIE TORRE
Assistant Conductor/Keyboard 2:
DAVID KREPPEL
Woodwind 1:
TED NASH
Woodwind 2:
LINO GOMEZ
Woodwind 3:
RICK HECKMAN
Woodwind 4:
JACQUELINE HENDERSON
Trumpet 1:
JOHN CHUDOBA
Trumpet 2:
SCOTT WENDHOLT

Trumpet 3:
JASON ASPINWALL
Trombone 1:
MICHAEL SELTZER
Trombone 2:
BEN HERRINGTON
Bass Trombone:
JACK SCHATZ
Bass:
BILL SLOAT
Keyboard 1:
ANN GERSCHEFSKI
Percussion:
DAN McMILLAN
Drums:
BRIAN BRAKE

Music Coordinator:
MICHAEL KELLER
Synthesizer Programmer:
BRUCE SAMUELS
Rehearsal Pianist:
JOHN O'NEILL

Music Copying:
EMILY GRISHMAN MUSIC PREPARATION/
KATHARINE EDMONDS, EMILY GRISHMAN

The line.

Photo by Paul Kolnik

Cast Continued

Vacation Swing: DEANNA AGUINAGA

Dance Captain: LYNDY FRANKLIN

UNDERSTUDIES

For Al:
TODD ANDERSON, KURT DOMONEY
For Bebe:
DEANNA AGUINAGA, MICHELLE ARAVENA,
LYNDY FRANKLIN,
COURTNEY LAINE MAZZA
For Bobby:
JOEY DUDDING, ERIC SCIOTTO
For Cassie:
LORIN LATARRO, DEONE ZANOTTO
For Connie:
MICHELLE ARAVENA, DEONE ZANOTTO
For Diana:
DEANNA AGUINAGA, MICHELLE ARAVENA,
COURTNEY LAINE MAZZA,
DEONE ZANOTTO
For Don:
KURT DOMONEY, ERIC SCIOTTO
For Greg:
TODD ANDERSON, JOEY DUDDING,
ERIC SCIOTTO
For Judy:
DEANNA AGUINAGA, JENIFER FOOTE,
LYNDY FRANKLIN, LORIN LATARRO,
KIM SHRIVER
For Kristine:
DEANNA AGUINAGA, LYNDY FRANKLIN,
COURTNEY LAINE MAZZA,
DEONE ZANOTTO
For Larry:
ERIC DySART, ERIC SCIOTTO
For Maggie:
MICHELLE ARAVENA, LYNDY FRANKLIN
For Mark:
KURT DOMONEY, JOEY DUDDING,
ERIC DySART
For Mike:
TODD ANDERSON, KURT DOMONEY
For Paul:
JOEY DUDDING, ERIC DySART
For Richie:
MIKE CANNON, ERIC DySART
For Sheila:
JENIFER FOOTE, LORIN LATARRO,
KIM SHRIVER
For Val:
COURTNEY LAINE MAZZA, KIM SHRIVER
For Zach:
TODD ANDERSON, TOMMY BERKLUND

A Chorus Line

Nick Adams
Larry

Tommy Berklund
Greg

Mike Cannon
Al

Natalie Cortez
Diana

Dena DiGiacinto
Bebe

Jenifer Foote
Val

Jessica Lee Goldyn
Cassie

Deidre Goodwin
Sheila

Bryan Knowlton
Paul

James T. Lane
Richie

Melissa Lone
Maggie

Mario Lopez
Zach

J. Elaine Marcos
Connie

Paul McGill
Mark

Heather Parcells
Judy

Adam Perry
Don

Jeffrey Schecter
Mike

Will Taylor
Bobby

Katherine Tokarz
Kristine

Deanna Aguinaga
Swing

Todd Anderson
Roy/Ensemble

Michelle Aravena
Tricia/Ensemble

Kurt Domoney
Tom

Joey Dudding
Swing

Eric DySart
Butch/Ensemble

Lyndy Franklin
Swing

Lorin Latarro
Swing

Courtney Laine Mazza
Lois/Ensemble

Eric Sciotto
Frank/Ensemble

Kim Shriver
Swing

Deone Zanotto
Swing

Michael Bennett
*Conception,
Original Director/
Choreographer*

Bob Avian
*Director and Original
Co-Choreographer*

Marvin Hamlisch
Music

Baayork Lee
*Choreography
Re-Staging*

A Chorus Line

Robin Wagner
Scenic Design

Natasha Katz
Lighting Design

Tom Clark, Mark Menard and Nevin Steinberg,
Acme Sound Partners
Sound Design

Patrick Vaccariello
Music Direction and Supervision

Michael Keller
Music Coordinator

Jonathan Tunick
Orchestrator

Jay Binder C.S.A.
Casting

Nikole Vallins
Casting

Alan Wasser
General Manager

Arthur Siccardi
Production Manager

John Breglio,
Vienna Waits
Productions
Producer

A CHORUS LINE ALUMNI 2008-2009

E. Clayton Cornelious
Butch

Charlotte d'Amboise
Cassie

Nadine Isenegger
Cassie (select performances), Lois

Kimberly Dawn
Neumann
Swing

Jessica Lea Patty
Swing

Jason Patrick Sands
Don

Grant Turner
Frank

Josh Walden
Vacation Swing

Kevin Worley
Al

BOX OFFICE
(L-R): Gary Powers, Vigi Cadunz and Manny Rivera.

DOORMAN
Lype O'Dell

COMPANY MANAGEMENT
(L-R): Michael Altbaum, Adam Miller

Photos by Ben Strothmann

A Chorus Line

FRONT OF HOUSE STAFF
Front Row (L-R): Annie Bree, Kathleen Spock, Yvet Valdoquiin, Nancy Barnicle, David M. Conte.

Middle Row (L-R): Roz Nyman, Jason Bratton, Sarah Ricker, Anthony Martinez.

Back Row (L-R): Bonny Hughes, Michelle Moyna, Emily Christensen, Geraldine White, Matt Blank.

ORCHESTRA
Sitting: Adam Kolker

Front Row (L-R): Scott Wendholt, John "Sunshine" Chudoba, Rick Shapiro, Mike Seltzer.

Middle Row (L-R): Rick Heckman, Ann Gerschefski, Tony Facanga, Maggie Torre, Jackie Henderson, Frank Lindquist, Alan Ferber, Jason Aspinwall.

Back Row (L-R): Brian Brake, Dan McMillan, Patrick Vaccariello.

CREW
(L-R): Kevin Kenneally, Tim McWilliams, Brian Hutchinson, Tim Semon, Laurie Goldfeder, Billy Barnes, Peter Guernsey, Brian Cook, Leslie Kilian, Beth Berkeley, Caitley Symons, Fritz Frizsell, Heidi Brown, Rory Powers, Scott Sanders, Eric Norris, Stephen Long, Libby Villanova, Hector Lugo, Shana Albery, Sarah Hench.

A Chorus Line

Scrapbook

Correspondent: Natalie Cortez, "Diana Morales"

The Final Performance: Going into that last day I didn't know what would happen, whether I would cry or feel happy. In the end it was both of those things. We had two shows that final Sunday, The matinee couldn't have been happier. I'd been with the show the entire two-year run and I was thinking, "Gosh, just one more time to go!" After all the injuries and pain and agonizing rehearsals, you do want it to come to an end to a certain extent.

At the last performance, Mike Cannon, who played Al, got us all together, and said, "Let's do OUR show and tell OUR story tonight." It was such a good thing to say. We were crying already, which was not good! But it gave us an excuse to really focus. The last performance was a complete validation, a chance for us to really put our mark on it in a way we hadn't ever been able to do. That was amazing.

Natalie Cortez

STAFF FOR *A CHORUS LINE*

GENERAL MANAGEMENT
ALAN WASSER ASSOCIATES
Alan Wasser   Allan Williams   Aaron Lustbader

GENERAL PRESS REPRESENTATIVE
BARLOW•HARTMAN
John Barlow   Michael Hartman
Wayne Wolfe   Melissa Bixler

CASTING
JAY BINDER CASTING
Jay Binder, C.S.A.
Jack Bowdan, C.S.A.   Mark Brandon   Sara Schatz
Nikole Vallins   Kate Sprance   Karen Young

PRODUCTION MANAGER
Arthur Siccardi

PRODUCTION STAGE MANAGER
Laurie Goldfeder

COMPANY MANAGER
Adam J. Miller

Stage Manager .... Justin Scribner
Assistant Stage Manager .... Kathryn L. McKee
Assistant Company Manager .... Michael Altbaum
Resident Choreographer .... Michael Gorman
Assistant Director .... Peter Pileski
Assistant Scenic Designer .... David Peterson
Associate Costume Designer .... Suzy Benzinger
Assistant Costume Designer .... Patrick Wiley
Wardrobe Consultant .... Alyce Gilbert
Associate Lighting Designer .... Yael Lubetzky
Assistant Lighting Designer .... Aaron Spivey
Assistant Sound Designer .... Michael Creason
Automated Lighting Programmer .... Matthew Hudson
Music Coordinator .... Michael Keller
Synthesizer Programmer .... Bruce Samuels
Production Carpenter .... Curtis Cowley
Head Carpenter .... Richard Fideli
Production Electrician .... Jimmy Fedigan
Head Electrician .... Eric Norris
Assistant Electrician .... Stephen R. Long
Production Sound Engineer .... Scott Sanders
Advance Sound .... John Dory
Wardrobe Supervisor .... Rory Powers
Prop Coordinator .... Heidi Brown
Dressers .... Shana Albery, Sarah Hench,
Hector Lugo, Patrick O'Neill,
Elizabeth Villanova, Kyle Wesson
House Electrician .... Leslie Ann Kilian
Follow Spot Operators .... Peter W. Guernsey,
Fritz Frizsell

Deck Sound .... Brian "Cookie" Cook, Beth Berkeley
House Props .... Laura Koch
House Carpenter .... Tim McWilliams
House Flyman .... Glenn Ingram

Advertising .... Serino Coyne/
Greg Corradetti, Andrea Prince, Ryan Greer

Website Design & Online Marketing
Strategy .... Situation Marketing LLC/
Damian Bazadona, Joey Oliva, Chris Powers

Marketing Services .... Type A Marketing
Legal Counsel .... Paul Weiss Rifkind Wharton
& Garrison, LLP/Deborah Hartnett
Accounting .... Rosenberg, Neuwirth & Kuchner/
Chris Cacace,
Mark D'Ambrosi
Production Associate .... Deborah Hartnett
Administrative Assistant to Mr. Breglio ... Helene Gaulrapp
Associate General Manager .... Aaron Lustbader
General Management Associates .... Jake Hirzel,
Thom Mitchell, Connie Yung
General Management Office .... Christopher Betz,
Christopher D'Angelo,
Jason Hewitt, Jennifer Mudge
Press Office Manager .... Bethany Larsen
Press Associates .... Leslie Baden, Michelle Bergmann,
Dennis Crowley, Tom D'Ambrosio,
Ryan Ratelle, Matt Shea
Production Assistant .... Annette Verga-Lagier
Production Photographer .... Paul Kolnik
Insurance .... Ventura Insurance Brokerage/
Janice Brown
Banking .... Commerce Bank/
Barbara von Borstel,
Ashley Elezi
Payroll .... Castellana Services, Inc.
Merchandising .... Max Merchandising/
Randi Grossman
Study Guide .... Peter Royston
Travel Services .... Road Rebel
Entertainment Touring
Assistants to Ms. Lee .... Steven Eng,
Cassey Kivnick
Opening Night Coordination .... Tobak Lawrence Co./
Suzanne Tobak, Michael P. Lawrence
Physical Therapist .... Performing Arts Physical Therapy
Orthopedic Consultant .... Philip Bauman M.D.
Group Sales .... Theatre Direct International/
Broadway.com/
1-800-BROADWAY

www.achorusline.com

CREDITS AND ACKNOWLEDGEMENTS
Scenery built and electrified by Hudson Scenic Studio Inc. Automation equipment provided by Hudson Scenic Studio, Inc. Electric truss built by Scenic Technologies. Lighting equipment provided by PRG Lighting. Sound equipment provided by PRG Audio. Finale costumes by Barbara Matera, Ltd. Costumes by Lynn Baccus; Euro Co Costumes, Inc.; Rick Kelly; D. Barak; Catherine Stribling. Leotards by Bal Togs Industries. Custom shirts by Cego Custom Shirts. Custom knitwear by C.C. Wei. Fabric dyeing and painting by the Craft Show. Footwear by T.O. Dey, J.C. Theatricals. Rehearsal hats by Arnold S. Levine, Inc. Ms. d'Amboise's hair by Paul Labrecque. Mike Costa's shirts provided by Lacoste. Men's socks provided by Gold Toe Brands, Inc. Finale top hats by Rodney Gordon, Inc. Finale shoes by Capezio. Ricola natural herb cough drops courtesy of Ricola USA, Inc. Emergen-C super energy booster provided by Alacer Corp. Cover photography by Walter Iooss. Rehearsed at 890 Broadway.

THE SHUBERT ORGANIZATION, INC.
Board of Directors

Gerald Schoenfeld	**Philip J. Smith**
Chairman	President
Wyche Fowler, Jr.	**John W. Kluge**
Lee J. Seidler	**Michael I. Sovern**

Stuart Subotnick

Robert E. Wankel
Executive Vice President

David Andrews	**Elliot Greene**
Senior Vice President – Shubert Ticketing	Senior Vice President – Finance
Juan Calvo	**John Darby**
Vice President and Controller	Vice President – Facilities
Peter Entin	**Charles Flateman**
Vice President – Theatre Operations	Vice President – Marketing
Anthony LaMattina	**Brian Mahoney**
Vice President – Audit & Production Finance	Vice President – Ticket Sales

D.S. Moynihan
Vice President – Creative Projects

Theatre Manager .... David M. Conte

A Chorus Line
SCRAPBOOK

Throughout the run whenever we danced the opening combination the audience would always go crazy because they love the show. But they didn't necessarily love US. To be honest, it was sometimes hard. We judged ourselves more than anybody out there could possibly have judged us. We always got big applause and big screams, but never big laughs, because a lot of these people had seen the show a hundred times.

But at the final performance we had OUR fans there. We found we had created a fan base of people who didn't listen to the original cast album; they just listened to US. It took the whole two years of the run to build a fan base of our own, but we had it, and it was remarkable and it was very comforting to us. They came to the final performance to celebrate US and OUR choices and OUR interpretations. That was incredible. We were prepared for the big applause and the big screams, but this time we also got big laughs! They liked the way WE told the story, which was definitely something special. They gave us standing ovations. It's hard to stand out there naked. But it was beautiful. It was like going to theatre church.

Special Note: We captured our feelings about being in *A Chorus Line* in a special way. Charlotte d'Amboise (Cassie) left the show a week before the closing. After her last performance we all met at Andy Blankenbuehler's studio and we did our own session tape, just like the one that the show is based on. We sat around for five hours with a big jug of wine like the original cast did, except we put ours on videotape. Jeff Schecter was in charge. We weren't looking back with longing; we were looking at our experience in the present. The experience benefited us a lot and helped us to get through the final week of performances. Hopefully something will be done with it, and that we'll eventually get to share it. We're really proud of what we did on *A Chorus Line.*

Correspondent: James T. Lane, "Richie"

The Final Performance: On the day of the last performance my mother locked herself out of my apartment, and I had to let her back in, so I arrived at the theatre all jittery and worrying that I hadn't eaten enough. But I wanted to be there for John Breglio's

James T. Lane

speech to the cast at 5:45 PM. I attempted to warm up, but I was too excited! We gathered on the stage and he stood right on the line and we just listened. He thanked us all for being there and quoted Diana Morales' line in "What I Did for Love" that "the gift was ours to borrow," meaning that *A Chorus Line* had been a gift to all of us from Michael Bennett and Baayork Lee and Bob Avian. He said this

closing was, like, "OK, now that you had this gift, it's back on the shelf for another generation." It was a nice start to the evening. The gift of dance is something we also get for a limited time. Some of us are lucky enough to be a member of Alvin Ailey or doing a musical like *A Chorus Line*, which is like the Olympic Gold Medal of musical theatre. But dancing is just another something that's ours to borrow. You pass it on and pass it on and pass it on.

After that, we started warming up together and sharing old stories. We have these rolling pins to warm up our backs and we were just rolling on them and talking about what it was going to be like not seeing each other anymore—or at least not until the next show. Places were called and Nick Adams, who played Larry, started cracking jokes as usual. He used to come up with a catchphrase for each performance, like Super Saturday or Wake 'Em Up Wednesday or Savor It Sunday. There were some obscene ones, but I won't repeat those. I don't remember if he named our final performance. And then we saw Baayork. She is the spirit of *A Chorus Line*, and we will never forget what she gave us. She always said that what you give to *A Chorus Line* you share with generations after you: "You have now been given the gift and you are now stamped as having had an *A Chorus Line* education. Go out into the world and spread the word."

So, for the last time, it was "curtain up," and the applause lasted for so long before even the first notes of the piano. It just roared. I felt my heart go up into my throat. And I said to myself, "No no no! We have to do this. We'll have plenty of time later for crazy emotional stuff."

How was the show that day? The performing level was so high it was like *A Chorus Line* Olympics. People were doing death-defying acts of performing, I don't know if it was really the night, or if I was just seeing everybody in a new light. Everything seemed like it was done to the nth degree. It was just mad. Shecky—Jeffrey Schecter, who plays Mike—has the first solo, "I Can Do That." His performance was perfect, every note, every turn, every acting intention. It was just magic. And he just flew when he did that Russian Split, and the energy just snowballed after that. "At the Ballet," "Sing"… it just grew by degrees.

My big moment comes in the Fourth Montage, which we called The Monster Montage. The audience started clapping at the start of it. I was in the huddle before "Gimme the Ball" and they were clapping so loud I couldn't hear the music. I leaped out of that circle and it was like floating on air. Throughout "Gimme the Ball" my feet never touched the ground. Nothing like that has ever happened in my life, that feeling of lightheadedness and ease on stage. All I remember is floating through the number. And then it was time for Jessica Lee Goldyn as Cassie. That's really where it became like the

Olympics because she is a gymnastic Cassie and her "Music and the Mirror" was amazing amazing amazing. There were some sniffles during "What I Did for Love." Some people just let it go. But I held on.

When the "curtain" came down, then people really let go. Mike Cannon, who plays Al, was sobbing. I was crying too, but there was such a sense of accomplishment! Two years, two months and two days of *A Chorus Line*! I really got my chops and cut my teeth on an amazing show with some amazing people.

Coming from this experience, I feel I could do anything. I guess I learned that the time is always now. There is no tomorrow. Tomorrow isn't promised to anybody, but today you've got to seize the moment because "in the moment" is where everything happens. And that's the truth.

I was reminded of the day I went to the open call for *A Chorus Line*. There were literally hundreds of people there and I almost left. But something said to me, "You're here. Why don't you stay and enjoy the moment?" I could have left. But I stayed. And I got the job.

Correspondent: Baayork Lee, Choreographer and Original 1975 Cast Member ("Connie Wong")

The Final Performance: For me, having come a full circle of 33 years with this show, it was phenomenal—more than I had ever dreamed. The only thing I can compare it to was the 1983 performance at which we broke the record to become the longest-running show in

Baayork Lee

Broadway history and casts from around the world joined us onstage. People wouldn't stop applauding and after the finale, when Michael Bennett was speaking to the audience, he called me out of the line and thanked me in front of all those people. I remember thinking, "This is a once-in-a-lifetime experience."

But here I was in 2008 at the final performance of the revival, and I found I was experiencing the same emotion, though for a very different reason. I've directed and/or choreographed the show about 40 times on tour and around the world, so when these big moments come I'm usually on the stage or backstage or in the back of the theatre taking notes. But at the closing night of the Broadway revival they gave me a seat in the center of the orchestra. And for the first time in all these years I could feel the energy and love for the show as a member of the audience. I never dreamed it could be like this. It was such a relief to just let myself go and enjoy Michael's brilliance. It's such a good show! When they finished "What I Did for Love" and the audience gave them a standing ovation, I joined right in. To experience a once-in-a-lifetime joy like that TWICE in one's life truly is a blessing.

Cirque Dreams: Jungle Fantasy

First Preview: June 16, 2008. Opened: June 26, 2008.
Closed: August 24, 2008 after 10 Previews and 70 Performances.

PLAYBILL®

THE ARTISTS
(in alphabetical order)

Contorting Lizard, Aerial Bird ....
    URANMANDAKH AMARSANAA (Mongolia)
Adventurer ....MARCELLO BALESTRACCI (USA)
Soultree Violinist ....JARED BURNETT (USA)
Jungleboy ....ZACHARY CARROLL (USA)
Mother Nature....................JILL DIANE (USA)
Bee, Ensemble............LAUREN DIBLASI (USA)
Frog Juggler ....RUSLAN DMYTRUK (Ukraine)
Bee, Ensemble ....IRYNA DMYTRUK (Ukraine)
Trapeze Owl ....IVAN DOTSENKO (Ukraine)
Balancing Giraffe,
    Snake Roller...VLADIMIR DOVGAN (Ukraine)
Monkey Foot Manipulator ....
    NATALIYA EGOROVA (Russia)
Unicorn, Ensemble ....JUDAH FRANK (USA)
Contorting Lizard,
    Aerial Bird ....
    BUYANKHISHIG GANBAATAR (Mongolia)
Contorting Lizard,
    Aerial Bird ......ERDENESUVD GANBAATAR
    (Mongolia)
Blackbird Hairialist ....
    STEFKA IORDANOVA (Bulgaria)
Vine Swinger ....DENYS KUCHER (Ukraine)
Vine Swinger..............VITALII LYKOV (Ukraine)
Percushroomist ....LEE MILLER (USA)
Contorting Lizard,
    Aerial Bird ....
    ODGEREL OYUNBAATAR (Mongolia)

Continued on next page

⌖ BROADWAY THEATRE
1681 Broadway
A Shubert Organization Theatre

Gerald Schoenfeld, *Chairman*   Philip J. Smith, *President*

Robert E. Wankel, *Executive Vice President*

A+ Theatricals, Broadway Across America, Cirque Productions, Adam Troy Epstein,
Fox Associates, New Space Entertainment, Albert Nocciolino,
Providence Performing Arts Center, Theatre League
presents

Cirque Dreams Jungle Fantasy

Music & Lyrics by
Jill Winters

Costume Design	*Additional Music by*	*Act Design*
Cirque Productions	**David Scott** **Keith Heffner**	**Neil Goldberg**
Lenora Taylor	**Billy Paul Williams** **Tony Aliperti**	**Heather Hoffman**
Santiago Rojo	**Lance Conque** **Christopher Pati**	**Iouri Klepatsky**

Scenic Design	*Lighting Design*	*Sound Design*
Jon Craine	**Kate Johnston**	**Craig Cassidy**

Executive Producers	*Animal Sculpture Designs*	*Production Design*	*Executive Producer*
Alan Wasser	**William Olson**	**Betsy Herst**	**James Geisler**
Allan Williams			

Press Representative	*Marketing*	*Production Management*
The Publicity Office	**Type A Marketing**	**Juniper Street Productions**

Choreographed by
Tara Jeanne Vallee

Created & Directed by
Neil Goldberg

6/26/08

Neil Goldberg
Creator, Director

Tara Jeanne Vallee
Choreographer

Jill Winters
Music & Lyrics

Alan Wasser
Executive Producer/ General Manager

Cirque Dreams: Jungle Fantasy

THE ADVENTURE

JUNGLE BY DAY

"A Bird Is Born" .... Emu, Jungleboys
"Eyes Wide Open" .... Mother Nature, Soultree, Percushroomist, Company
"Jungle Jumpin'" .... Adventurer, Company
"Hop Stretch" .... Mother Nature, Soultree, Ensemble
"Nature's Balance" .... Contorting Lizards
"Falling" .... Blackbird Hairialist, Jungleboys
"Swinging Vines" .... Vine Swingers
"You Can Grow Too" .... Mother Nature, Adventurer, Ensemble
"Froggling" .... Frog Juggler, Frogs
"Monkey Business" .... Adventurer, Monkey Manipulator
"Personality" .... Mother Nature, Emus
"Butterflying" .... Butterflyers, Ensemble
"Courage" .... Mother Nature, Soultree, Adventurer, Aerial Birds
"Amazing" .... Company

JUNGLE BY NIGHT

"Coloring Dreams" .... Company
"Rollin' Around" .... Snake Roller, Jungleboys, Adventurer
"Strange Things" .... Mother Nature, Company
"Owls on a Perch" .... Trapeze Owls, Soultree
"Take Credit" .... Mother Nature, Adventurer, Ensemble
"Jungle-ibrium" .... Balancing Giraffes, Ensemble
"How Do You Feel?" .... Mother Nature, Adventurer
"Roar" .... Jungle Kings
"Stampede" .... Jungle Kings, Company
"Jungle Fantasy Finale" .... Company

Cast Continued

Butterflyer,
    Jungle King .... SERGEY PARSHIN (Russia)
Jungle King, Ensemble .... PAVEL POZDNYAKOV
                                (Russia)
Jungleboy .... GLENN ROGERS (USA)
Butterflyer, Ensemble ... NAOMI SAMPSON (USA)
Emu, Ensemble ... KONSTANTIN SEROV (Russia)
Trapeze Owl .... CARLY SHERIDAN (Canada)
Jungle King, Monkey Manipulator ....
                        SERGUEI SLAVSKI (Russia)
Jungle King, Monkey Manipulator ....
            ALEXANDER TOLSTIKOV (Russia)
Balancing Giraffe .... ANATOLIY YENIY (Moldova)

Guy Kwan, John Paull III, Hillary Blanken,
Kevin Broomell, Ana Rose Greene,
Juniper Street Productions
Production Manager

CAST
Front Row (L-R):
Uranmandakh Amarsanaa,
Odgerel Oyunbaatar,
Buyankhishig Ganbaatar,
Erdenesuvd Ganbaatar.

Second Row (L-R):
Konstantin Serov,
Naomi Sampson, Elise Barbeau,
Sergey Parshin, Lauren DiBlasi,
Vladimir Dovgan, Serguei Slavski.

Back Row (L-R):
Jill Diane, Stefka Iordanova,
Anatoliy Yeniy, Veronique Rivet,
Ruslan Dmytruk, Vitalii Lykov,
Pavel Pozdnyakov, Denys Kucher,
Iryna Dmytruk, Jared Burnett,
Zachary Carroll, Glenn Rogers,
Alexander Tolstikov, Judah Frank,
Lee Miller, Marcello Balestracci,
Neil Goldberg.

Photo by Brian Mapp

Cirque Dreams: Jungle Fantasy

Butterflyers Naomi Sampson and Sergey Parshin

A scene from *Cirque Dreams.*

Photos by Carol Rosegg

Jungle-ibrium: Vladimir Dovgan and Anatoliy Yeniy

STAFF FOR *CIRQUE DREAMS: JUNGLE FANTASY*

GENERAL MANAGEMENT
ALAN WASSER ASSOCIATES
Alan Wasser   Allan Williams
Lane Marsh

GENERAL PRESS REPRESENTATIVE
THE PUBLICITY OFFICE
Marc Thibodeau   Michael S. Borowski
Jeremy Shaffer

PRODUCTION MANAGER
JUNIPER STREET PRODUCTIONS
Hillary Blanken   Guy Kwan
Kevin Broomell   Ana Rose Greene

MARKETING
TYPE A MARKETING
Anne Rippey   Erik Alden
Janette Roush   Nick Pramik
Maryanna Geller

Company Manager ....Lane Marsh

Assistant Company Manager ....Jake Hirzel
Stage Manager ....Tricia Tolivar

Production Carpenters ....Steve Gallo/Daniel Montes
Production Electrician ....Michael LoBue
Production Properties Supervisor ......Christopher Pantuso
Head Sound ....Tim Brannigan
Wardrobe Supervisor ....Erin Brooke Roth

Advertising ....Eliran Murphy Group, Ltd./
Barbara Eliran, Elizabeth Findlay,
Taryn O'Bra, Patrick Flood
Broadcast Media/TV Production ....Fresh Produce/
Frank Basile
Theatre Displays ....King Displays
Merchandising ....LTS Ent./Max Merchandising
Website Design ....Charles Forster
Legal Counsel ...Franklin, Weinrib, Rudell & Vassallo, PC/
Daniel M. Wasser
Accounting ....Rosenberg, Neuwirth & Kuchner
General Management Associates ....Jim Brandeberry,
Aaron Lustbader, Thom Mitchell,
Mark Shacket, Connie Yung

General Management Office ....Christopher Betz,
Dawn Kusinski, Patty Montesi,
Jennifer Mudge
Press Assistant ....Scott Sinclair
Insurance ....Ventura Insurance Brokerage, Inc./
Janice Brown
Banking....................................Commerce Bank
Payroll ....Castellana Services, Inc.
Travel Services ....Road Rebel
Group Sales ....Broadway InBound

www.CirqueDreamsBroadway.com

CREDITS AND ACKNOWLEDGEMENTS
Scenery by Scenic Arts Studios, Proof Productions and PRG
Scenic Technologies. Lighting by PRG Lighting. Sound by
Masque Sound. Softgoods by I. Weiss.

SPECIAL THANKS
Bloomingdale's, Bruce Kaiser, Bill Johnson, Harvey Gold,
Dan Epstein, Dan Daddona Studios, Music Mixing &
Mastering, Eben Jones.

Tracey C; Susan F; Jimmy G; Ross R; Frank B; Erik A; Jill
W; Dave S; Iouri K; Ava W; Joe J; Jennifer S., Meg G.

CIRQUE PRODUCTIONS STAFF
Founder, Artistic Director ....Neil Goldberg
Managing Director ....Jim Geisler
Assistant Artistic Director ....Heather Hoffman
Musical Director ....Jill Diane Winters
Directors Business Assistant ....Wendie Carper
Directors Personal Assistant ....Stacey Keller
Acrobatic Coach ....Iouri Klepatsky
Business Manager ....Gina Damato
Business Affairs & Logistics ....Brian Levitz
Corporate, Events & Sales Directors ....Andee Cohen,
Shirley Crane
Event Managers ....Nicholas Mitsis, Bill Olson
Marketing Coordinators ....David Stauffer,
Allison Goldberg
Production Manager ....James Queen
Production Designer ....Betsy Herst
Production Assistant ....Andrew Radowitz
Production Carpenter ....Daniel Montes
Carpentry ....Martin Lamberti, Arnie Braman
Wardrobe Managers ....Santiago Rojo, Lenora Taylor
Wardrobe Department .....Francisca Hortas, Keith Hall,

Jim Hardy, Robert Stanley,
Jenna Hockfert, Donna Dorvick,
Sima Bressler, Danielle Tabino,
Fabiana Foglia, Katonya Richmond
Dressers ....Thom Carlson, Holly Adelia Nissen,
Aaron Simms
Tour Sound Designer ....Joseph D. King
Illustration ....Nelli Leventhal
Accounting ....Jackie Engstrom
Insurance ....Ventura Insurance Brokerage, Inc.
CPA Firm ....Morrison, Brown, Argiz & Farra, LLP
Public Relations ....Terri Lynn, Superstars
Legal-Entertainment ....Toorock & Rosen, LLP
Legal-Corporate ....Moskowitz, Mandell & Salim, PA
Legal-Intellectual Property ....Lewis & Roca, LLP

AWA Touring Services ....Alison Spiriti, Matt Chinn,
Sean Mackey

Cry-Baby

First Preview: March 15, 2008. Opened: April 24, 2008.
Closed June 22, 2008 after 45 Previews and 68 Performances.

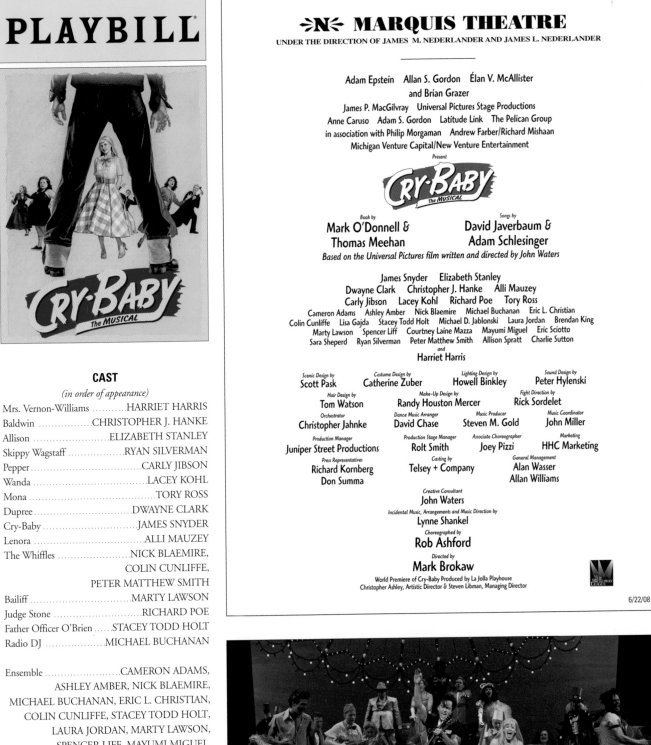

CAST
(in order of appearance)

Mrs. Vernon-Williams .... HARRIET HARRIS
Baldwin .... CHRISTOPHER J. HANKE
Allison .... ELIZABETH STANLEY
Skippy Wagstaff .... RYAN SILVERMAN
Pepper .... CARLY JIBSON
Wanda .... LACEY KOHL
Mona .... TORY ROSS
Dupree .... DWAYNE CLARK
Cry-Baby .... JAMES SNYDER
Lenora .... ALLI MAUZEY
The Whiffles .... NICK BLAEMIRE,
COLIN CUNLIFFE,
PETER MATTHEW SMITH
Bailiff .... MARTY LAWSON
Judge Stone .... RICHARD POE
Father Officer O'Brien ...... STACEY TODD HOLT
Radio DJ .... MICHAEL BUCHANAN

Ensemble .... CAMERON ADAMS,
ASHLEY AMBER, NICK BLAEMIRE,
MICHAEL BUCHANAN, ERIC L. CHRISTIAN,
COLIN CUNLIFFE, STACEY TODD HOLT,
LAURA JORDAN, MARTY LAWSON,
SPENCER LIFF, MAYUMI MIGUEL,
ERIC SCIOTTO, SARA SHEPERD,
RYAN SILVERMAN,
PETER MATTHEW SMITH,
ALLISON SPRATT, CHARLIE SUTTON

Continued on next page

⊁N⊰ MARQUIS THEATRE
UNDER THE DIRECTION OF JAMES M. NEDERLANDER AND JAMES L. NEDERLANDER

Adam Epstein   Allan S. Gordon   Élan V. McAllister
and Brian Grazer
James P. MacGilvray   Universal Pictures Stage Productions
Anne Caruso   Adam S. Gordon   Latitude Link   The Pelican Group
in association with Philip Morgaman   Andrew Farber/Richard Mishaan
Michigan Venture Capital/New Venture Entertainment
Present

Cry-Baby
The MUSICAL

Book by
Mark O'Donnell &
Thomas Meehan

Songs by
David Javerbaum &
Adam Schlesinger

Based on the Universal Pictures film written and directed by John Waters

James Snyder   Elizabeth Stanley
Dwayne Clark   Christopher J. Hanke   Alli Mauzey
Carly Jibson   Lacey Kohl   Richard Poe   Tory Ross
Cameron Adams   Ashley Amber   Nick Blaemire   Michael Buchanan   Eric L. Christian
Colin Cunliffe   Lisa Gajda   Stacey Todd Holt   Michael D. Jablonski   Laura Jordan   Brendan King
Marty Lawson   Spencer Liff   Courtney Laine Mazza   Mayumi Miguel   Eric Sciotto
Sara Sheperd   Ryan Silverman   Peter Matthew Smith   Allison Spratt   Charlie Sutton
and
Harriet Harris

Scenic Design by
Scott Pask

Costume Design by
Catherine Zuber

Lighting Design by
Howell Binkley

Sound Design by
Peter Hylenski

Hair Design by
Tom Watson

Make-Up Design by
Randy Houston Mercer

Fight Direction by
Rick Sordelet

Orchestrator
Christopher Jahnke

Dance Music Arranger
David Chase

Music Producer
Steven M. Gold

Music Coordinator
John Miller

Production Manager
Juniper Street Productions

Production Stage Manager
Rolt Smith

Associate Choreographer
Joey Pizzi

Marketing
HHC Marketing

Press Representatives
Richard Kornberg
Don Summa

Casting by
Telsey + Company

General Management
Alan Wasser
Allan Williams

Creative Consultant
John Waters

Incidental Music, Arrangements and Music Direction by
Lynne Shankel

Choreographed by
Rob Ashford

Directed by
Mark Brokaw

World Premiere of Cry-Baby Produced by La Jolla Playhouse
Christopher Ashley, Artistic Director & Steven Libman, Managing Director

6/22/08

James Snyder (center) with Elizabeth Stanley (in blue dress) and the Ensemble.

Cry-Baby

MUSICAL NUMBERS

ACT ONE

"The Anti-Polio Picnic" ....Mrs. Vernon-Williams, Allison, Baldwin and Ensemble
"Watch Your Ass" ....Pepper, Wanda, Mona, Dupree, Cry-Baby and Ensemble
"I'm Infected" ....Allison, Cry-Baby and Ensemble
"Squeaky Clean" ....Baldwin and the Whiffles
"Nobody Gets Me" ....Cry-Baby, Pepper, Wanda, Mona and Ensemble
"Nobody Gets Me" (Reprise) ....Allison
"Jukebox Jamboree" .... Dupree
"A Whole Lot Worse" ....Pepper, Wanda and Mona
"Screw Loose" ....Lenora
"Baby Baby Baby Baby Baby (Baby Baby)" ....Cry-Baby, Allison and Ensemble
"Girl, Can I Kiss You…?" ....Cry-Baby, Allison and Ensemble
"I'm Infected" (Reprise) ....Allison and Cry-Baby
"You Can't Beat the System" ....Full Company

ACT TWO

"Misery, Agony, Helplessness, Hopelessness, Heartache and Woe" ....Allison, Cry-Baby,
Dupree, Pepper, Wanda, Mona,
Mrs. Vernon-Williams and Ensemble
"All in My Head" ....Baldwin, Lenora and Ensemble
"Jailyard Jubilee" ....Dupree and Ensemble
"A Little Upset" ....Cry-Baby, Dupree, Allison and Ensemble
"I Did Something Wrong…Once" ....Mrs. Vernon-Williams
"Thanks for the Nifty Country!" ....Baldwin and the Whiffles
"This Amazing Offer" ....Baldwin and the Whiffles
"Do That Again" ....Cry-Baby and Allison
"Nothing Bad's Ever Gonna Happen Again" ....Full Company

MUSICIANS

Conductor:
LYNNE SHANKEL
Associate Conductor:
HENRY ARONSON
Keyboard 1:
LYNNE SHANKEL
Keyboard 2/Accordion:
HENRY ARONSON
Guitars:
JOHN BENTHAL, CHRIS BIESTERFELDT
Violin/Mandolin:
CENOVIA CUMMINS, MAXIM MOSTON
Violin/Viola:
ORLANDO WELLS
Cello:
SARAH SEIVER
Bass:
STEVE COUNT

Drums:
FRANK PAGANO
Reeds:
SCOTT KREITZER, CLIFF LYONS,
ROGER ROSENBERG
Trumpet:
BARRY DANIELIAN
Trombone:
DAN LEVINE
Percussion:
JOE MOWATT

Music Coordinator:
JOHN MILLER
Music Copying:
KAYE-HOUSTON MUSIC/
ANNE KAYE, DOUG HOUSTON
Synthesizer Programmer:
RANDY COHEN

SWINGS
LISA GAJDA, MICHAEL D. JABLONSKI,
BRENDAN KING, COURTNEY LAINE MAZZA

UNDERSTUDIES
For Cry-Baby:
RYAN SILVERMAN, ERIC SCIOTTO
For Allison:
ALLISON SPRATT, CAMERON ADAMS
For Mrs. Vernon-Williams:
LAURA JORDAN, TORY ROSS
For Judge Stone:
STACEY TODD HOLT,
PETER MATTHEW SMITH
For Baldwin:
COLIN CUNLIFFE,
PETER MATTHEW SMITH
For Pepper:
TORY ROSS, LISA GAJDA
For Mona:
LISA GAJDA
For Wanda:
ASHLEY AMBER, COURTNEY LAINE MAZZA
For Dupree:
ERIC L. CHRISTIAN, MICHAEL BUCHANAN
For Lenora:
ALLISON SPRATT,
COURTNEY LAINE MAZZA

Dance Captain ....SPENCER LIFF
Assistant
    Dance Captain ...COURTNEY LAINE MAZZA

Elizabeth Stanley (center)
with The Whiffles.

Photo by Joan Marcus

Cry-Baby

James Snyder
Cry-Baby

Elizabeth Stanley
Allison

Harriet Harris
Mrs. Vernon-Williams

Christopher J. Hanke
Baldwin

Alli Mauzey
Lenora

Dwayne Clark
Dupree

Carly Jibson
Pepper

Lacey Kohl
Wanda

Richard Poe
Judge Stone

Tory Ross
Mona

Cameron Adams
Ensemble

Ashley Amber
Ensemble

Nick Blaemire
Ensemble

Michael Buchanan
Ensemble

Eric L. Christian
Ensemble

Colin Cunliffe
Ensemble

Lisa Gajda
Swing

Stacey Todd Holt
Ensemble

Michael D. Jablonski
Swing

Laura Jordan
Ensemble

Brendan King
Swing/Fight Captain

Marty Lawson
Ensemble

Spencer Liff
Ensemble/Assistant Choreographer/ Dance Captain

Courtney Laine Mazza
Swing

Mayumi Miguel
Ensemble

Eric Sciotto
Ensemble

Sara Sheperd
Ensemble

Ryan Silverman
Ensemble

Peter Matthew Smith
Ensemble

Allison Spratt
Ensemble

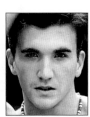
Charlie Sutton
Ensemble

Mark O'Donnell
Book

Thomas Meehan
Book

David Javerbaum
Songwriter

Adam Schlesinger
Songwriter

Cry-Baby

John Waters
Creative Consultant

Mark Brokaw
Director

Rob Ashford
Choreographer

Scott Pask
Scenic Designer

Howell Binkley
Lighting Designer

Catherine Zuber
Costume Designer

Peter Hylenski
Sound Designer

Tom Watson
Hair and Wig Design

Rick Sordelet
Fight Director

Christopher Jahnke
Orchestrations

John Miller
Music Coordinator

Guy Kwan, John Paull III, Hillary Blanken,
Kevin Broomell, Ana Rose Greene,
Juniper Street Productions
Production Manager

Richard Kornberg &
Associates
*Press
Representative*

Bernard Telsey,
Telsey + Company
Casting

Alan Wasser
General Manager

Adam Epstein
Producer

Allan S. Gordon
Producer

Élan V. McAllister
Producer

Brian Grazer
Producer

Christopher Ashley
*Artistic Director,
La Jolla Playhouse*

Ivor Royston,
The Pelican Group
Producer

Chester Gregory II
Dupree

BOX OFFICE
(L-R): Richard Thigpen and Larry Waxman.

Photo by Ben Strothmann

Cry-Baby

STAGE MANAGEMENT
(L-R): Jenny Slattery (Assistant Stage Manager), Rolt Smith (Production Stage Manager), Andrea O. Saraffian (Stage Manager).

STAGE CREW
Front Row (L-R): David Bornstein (Head Props), Hugh Hardyman (Carpenter), Jesse Stevens (Sound), David Dignazio (Head Sound).

Back Row (L-R): Pat Amari (Props), Matty Lynch (Head Carpenter), Scott Mecionis (Props), Dave Fulton (Carpenter), Rick Poulin (Electrician).

WARDROBE
Sitting (L-R): Philip Heckman, Tom Bertsch, Andrea Gonzalez.

Standing (L-R): Pamela Pierzina, Charlie Catanese, Del Miskie, Julie Hilimire, Christina Ainge, Michael Berglund, Kimberly Mark and John Webber.

HAIR
(L-R): Katie Beatty, Carla Muniz, Barry Lee Moe and Mitch Ely.

Cry-Baby

FRONT OF HOUSE STAFF
Front Row (L-R): Rosaire Lulu Caso (Chief Usher), Austin Nathaniel (Associate Manager).

Second Row: Michael Newsome, Daisy Irizarry, Karen Garcia-Ortiz, Peter Shayne.

Back Row: Phyllis Weinsaft, Hugh Dill, Mildred Dinato, Donna Flaherty, Nancy Diaz and Stanley Seidman.

ORCHESTRA
Front Row (L-R): Henry Aronson, Chris Biesterfeldt, Lynne Shankel, John Benthal.

Middle Row (L-R): Kenny Rampton, Frank Pagano, Roger Rosenberg, Dan Levine, Orlando Wells, Robert Moose.

Back Row (L-R): Justin Smith, Steve Count, Cliff Lyons, Joe Mowatt, Scott Kreitzer.

Not Pictured: Cenovia Cummins, Barry Danielian Max Moston and Sarah Seiver.

Photos by Ben Strothmann

ASSOCIATE COMPANY MANAGER
Christopher D'Angelo

DOORMAN
Rey Concepcion

THEATRE MANAGER
David Calhoun

Cry-Baby

GENERAL MANAGEMENT
ALAN WASSER ASSOCIATES
Alan Wasser   Allan Williams
Connie Chong

COMPANY MANAGER
Laura Kirspel

GENERAL PRESS REPRESENTATIVE
RICHARD KORNBERG & ASSOCIATES
Richard Kornberg   Don Summa
Alyssa Hart   Billy Zavelson

CASTING
TELSEY + COMPANY
Bernie Telsey CSA, Will Cantler CSA, David Vaccari CSA,
Bethany Knox CSA, Craig Burns CSA,
Tiffany Little Canfield CSA, Rachel Hoffman CSA,
Carrie Rosson CSA, Justin Huff CSA, Joe Langworth,
Bess Fifer CSA, Patrick Goodwin

PRODUCTION MANAGER
JUNIPER STREET PRODUCTIONS
Hillary Blanken   Guy Kwan
Kevin Broomell   Ana Rose Greene

Associate Company Manager	Christopher D'Angelo
Production Stage Manager	Rolt Smith
Stage Manager	Andrea O. Saraffian
Assistant Stage Manager	Jenny Slattery
Associate Director	Moritz von Stuelpnagel
Associate Choreographer	Joey Pizzi
Assistant Choreographer/Dance Captain	Spencer Liff
Assistant Choreographer	Christopher Bailey
Assistant Dance Captain	Courtney Laine Mazza
Fight Captain	Brendan King
Baton Sequences	Pamela Remler

Associate Scenic Designer	Orit Jacoby Carroll
Assistant Scenic Designer	Jeffrey A. Hinchee
Assistant Costume Designer	Holly Cain
Assistant Costume Designers	Lynn Bowling, Court Watson
Associate Lighting Designer	Ryan O'Gara
Assistant Lighting Designer	Carrie J. Wood
Associate Sound Designer	Keith Caggiano

Production Carpenter	Fred Gallo
Head Carpenter	Matthew Lynch
Flyman	Andrew D. Elman
Automation Carpenter	Hugh Hardyman
Assistant Carpenter	David Fulton
Production Electrician	Randall Zaibek
Head Electrician	Tom Ferguson
Automated Lights Programmer	Eric Norris
Production Properties Supervisor	Joseph Harris, Jr.
Head Props	Devin Biggart
Production Sound Engineer	David Dignazio
Assistant Sound	Jesse Stevens
Production Wardrobe Supervisor	Patrick Bevilacqua
Assistant Wardrobe Supervisor	Tom Bertsch
Dressers	Christina Ainge, Philip Heckman, John Webber, Michael Berglund, Charlie Catanese, Melissa Crawford, Julie Hilimire, Kimberly Mark, Del Miskie, Andrea Gonzalez, Pamela Kurz, Kimberly Prentice, Sarah Schaub, Chip White
Hair Supervisor	Katie Beatty
Hairdressers	Mitch Ely, Barry Lee Moe, Carla Muniz
Associate Conductor/Rehearsal Pianist	Henry Aronson
Music Preparation	Kaye-Houston Music Inc.
Synthesizer Programmer	Randy Cohen
Assistant Synth Programmer	Jim Mironchik
Assistant to John Miller	Charles Butler

Photo Illustration	Richie Fahey
Advertising	Serino Coyne Inc./ Nancy Coyne, Angelo Desimini, Sandy Block, Miriam Naggar
Marketing	HHC Marketing/ Hugh Hysell, Michael Redman
Website Design and Internet Marketing	Bay Bridge Productions/ Jean Strong, Laura Wagner
National Marketing/Sponsorship	Charlie Katz
Merchandising	Broadway NY Marketing Group LLC
Legal Counsel	Franklin, Weinrib, Rudell & Vassallo
Comptroller	Sarah Galbraith/ Sarah Galbraith Company
Accountants	Robert Fried CPA/ Fried & Kowgios CPAs LLP

General Management Office	Christopher Betz, Jake Hirzel, Dawn Kusinski, Patty Montesi, Jennifer Mudge
General Management Associates	Jim Brandeberry, Aaron Lustbader, Lane Marsh, Mark Shacket
Production Assistants	Ruth Zang, Colleen Danaher, Ginene Licata, Elise Hanley
Assistant to Mr. Epstein	Cameron Leel
Production Photographer	Joan Marcus
Insurance	DeWitt Stern Group/ Peter Shoemaker
Banking	Commerce Bank/ Barbara von Borstel, Olivia Cassin
Payroll	Castellana Services, Inc.
Travel Services	Tzell Travel Group/Andi Henig
Massage Therapy	Russell Beasley, LMT
Company Physical Therapists	PhysioArts
Orthopaedist	David S. Weiss, MD
Opening Night Coordination	Classic Entertainment Group
Rehearsal Studio	New 42nd Street Studios

GROUP SALES
Broadway.com/TDI
800-Broadway

www.crybabyonbroadway.com

myspace.com/crybabyonbroadway

CREDITS AND ACKNOWLEDGEMENTS

Scenery and scenic effects built and electrified by PRG Scenic Technologies, New Windsor, NY. Scenery painted by Scenic Arts Studios, Cornwall, NY. Show control and scenic motion control featuring Stage Command Systems by PRG Scenic Technologies. Additional scenery and props by La Jolla Playhouse. Softgoods built by I. Weiss and Sons, Inc., Long Island City, NY. Lighting equipment provided by PRG Lighting, North Bergen, NJ. Sound equipment provided by PRG Audio, Mt. Vernon, NY. Props built by Cigarbox Studios, Newburgh, NY; The Spoon Group, Rahway, NJ; and Portafiori Flowers, New York, NY. Costumes by Euro Co. Costumes; Jennifer Love Costumes; Carelli Costumes, Inc.; Timberlake Studios, Inc.; Claudia Diaz; Ed Dawson; Brian Hemesath; John Cowles; Arnold S. Levine, Inc.; Angels, the Costumiers; Worldtone Dance; and Hiatt Dance Boots. Natural herb cough drops courtesy of Ricola USA, Inc. Makeup provided by M•A•C. *Cry-Baby* exclusively uses Gibson & Epiphone guitars and Slingerland drums. Special thanks to Bra*Tenders for undergarments and hosiery.

Members of the ensemble perform Rob Ashford's Tony-nominated choreography

Photo by Joan Marcus

Curtains

First Preview: February 27, 2007. Opened: March 22, 2007.
Closed June 29, 2008 after 26 Previews and 511 Performances.

PLAYBILL®

CAST

(in order of appearance)

Jessica Cranshaw	PATTY GOBLE
Randy Dexter	JIM NEWMAN
Niki Harris	ERIN DAVIE
Bambi Bernét	MEGAN SIKORA
Bobby Pepper	NOAH RACEY
Johnny Harmon	MICHAEL X. MARTIN
Georgia Hendricks	KAREN ZIEMBA
Aaron Fox	JASON DANIELEY
Carmen Bernstein	DEBRA MONK
Oscar Shapiro	MICHAEL McCORMICK
Christopher Belling	EDWARD HIBBERT
Lieutenant Frank Cioffi	DAVID HYDE PIERCE
Mona Page	SHANNON LEWIS
Harv Fremont	AARON RAMEY
Roberta Wooster	JULIE TOLIVAR
Sidney Bernstein	GERRY VICHI
Detective O'Farrell	KEVIN BERNARD
Daryl Grady	JOHN BOLTON
Sasha Iljinsky	DAVID LOUD
Marjorie Cook	JENNIFER FRANKEL
Arlene Barucca	CALLIE CARTER
Roy Stetson	KEVIN BERNARD
Brick Hawvermale	SEAN McKNIGHT
Jan Setler	JENNIFER DUNNE
Connie Subbotin	PATTY GOBLE
Peg Prentice	BRITTANY MARCIN
Ronnie Driscoll	SEAN SAMUELS
Russ Cochran	MATT WALL

Continued on next page

❾ AL HIRSCHFELD THEATRE

A JUJAMCYN THEATRE

ROCCO LANDESMAN
President

PAUL LIBIN
Producing Director

JACK VIERTEL
Creative Director

JORDAN ROTH
Vice President

ROGER BERLIND   ROGER HORCHOW   DARYL ROTH
JANE BERGÈRE   TED HARTLEY   CENTER THEATRE GROUP

present

DAVID HYDE PIERCE *and* **DEBRA MONK**

in

CURTAINS

Book by
RUPERT HOLMES

Music by
JOHN KANDER

Lyrics by
FRED EBB

Original Book and Concept by
PETER STONE

Additional Lyrics by
JOHN KANDER *and* **RUPERT HOLMES**

Starring

KAREN ZIEMBA
JASON DANIELEY   ERIN DAVIE
and
EDWARD HIBBERT

Also Starring

JOHN BOLTON   MICHAEL X. MARTIN   MICHAEL McCORMICK
NOAH RACEY   MEGAN SIKORA   GERRY VICHI

with

KEVIN BERNARD   CALLIE CARTER   JENNIFER DUNNE
DAVID EGGERS   J. AUSTIN EYER   JENNIFER FRANKEL   PATTY GOBLE   LORIN LATARRO
SHANNON LEWIS   BRITTANY MARCIN   SEAN McKNIGHT   JIM NEWMAN   AARON RAMEY
SEAN SAMUELS   JULIE TOLIVAR   JEROME VIVONA   MATT WALL   STEPHANIE YOUELL

Set Design
ANNA LOUIZOS

Costume Design
WILLIAM IVEY LONG

Lighting Design
PETER KACZOROWSKI

Sound Design
BRIAN RONAN

Hair and Wig Design
PAUL HUNTLEY

Dance Arrangements
DAVID CHASE

Fight Direction
RICK SORDELET

Aerial Effects Design
PAUL RUBIN

Make-Up Design
ANGELINA AVALLONE

Associate Choreographer
JOANN M. HUNTER

Casting
JIM CARNAHAN, CSA

Production Supervisor
BEVERLEY RANDOLPH

Technical Supervisor
PETER FULBRIGHT

Music Coordinator
JOHN MONACO

General Management
101 PRODUCTIONS, LTD.

Marketing Services
LEANNE SCHANZER PROMOTIONS, INC.

Press Representative
BONEAU/BRYAN-BROWN

Associate Producers
BARBARA AND PETER FODOR

Orchestrations
WILLIAM DAVID BROHN

Music Director/Vocal Arrangements
DAVID LOUD

Choreography by
ROB ASHFORD

Directed by
SCOTT ELLIS

AMERICAN PREMIERE PRODUCED AT THE AHMANSON THEATRE BY CENTER THEATRE GROUP, LA'S THEATRE COMPANY

6/29/08

(L-R): Karen Ziemba, Debra Monk, David Hyde Pierce, Michael McCormick, Edward Hibbert and company.

Curtains

MUSICAL NUMBERS

ACT I

"Wide Open Spaces"	Randy, Niki, Jessica, Bobby, Ensemble
"What Kind of Man?"	Carmen, Oscar, Aaron, Georgia
"Thinking of Him"	Georgia, Aaron, Bobby
"The Woman's Dead"	Entire Company
"Show People"	Carmen, Cioffi, Entire Company
"Coffee Shop Nights"	Cioffi
"In the Same Boat 1"	Georgia, Niki, Bambi
"I Miss the Music"	Aaron
"Thataway!"	Georgia, Bobby, Ensemble

ACT II

"He Did It"	Entire Company
"In the Same Boat 2"	Bobby, Randy, Harv
"It's a Business"	Carmen, Stagehands
"Kansasland"	Randy, Niki, Harv, Bobby, Bambi, Ensemble
"Thinking of Him"/"I Miss the Music" (Reprise)	Aaron, Georgia
"A Tough Act to Follow"	Cioffi, Niki, Ensemble
"In the Same Boat 3"	Entire Company
"A Tough Act to Follow" (Reprise)	Entire Company

(Top-Bottom): Karen Ziemba, Noah Racey and company perform "Thataway!"

Photo by Joan Marcus

ORCHESTRA

Conductor: DAVID LOUD

Flute, Picc. Clarinet, Alto Sax:
ANDREW STERMAN
Oboe, Eng. Horn, Clarinet, Tenor Sax:
JULIE FERRARA
Clarinet, Alto Sax, Soprano Sax: OWEN KOTLER
Bassoon, Bass Clarinet, Baritone Sax, Flute, Clarinet:
MARK THRASHER
French Horn 1: R.J. KELLEY
French Horn 2: ANGELA CORDELL
Trumpet 1: MATT PETERSON
Trumpet 2: ANTHONY KADLECK
Trombone 1, House Contractor:
CHARLES GORDON
Bass Trombone, Tuba: JENNIFER WHARTON
Percussion: GREG LANDES
Drums: BRUCE DOCTOR
Acoustic Guitar, Electric Guitar, Banjo,
Classical Guitar: GREG UTZIG
Acoustic Bass: BILL ELLISON
Associate Music Director/Piano and Synthesizer:
SAM DAVIS

Musical Coordinator: JOHN MONACO
Music Copying Services: LARRY H. ABEL,
MUSIC PREPARATION INTERNATIONAL

Cast Continued

SWINGS

DAVID EGGERS, J. AUSTIN EYER,
LORIN LATARRO, JEROME VIVONA,
STEPHANIE YOUELL

UNDERSTUDIES

For Lieutenant Frank Cioffi & Christopher Belling:
KEVIN BERNARD
For Niki Harris:
STEPHANIE YOUELL
For Bambi Bernét:
LORIN LATARRO, SHANNON LEWIS
For Aaron Fox:
KEVIN BERNARD, AARON RAMEY
For Daryl Grady:
MICHAEL X. MARTIN, AARON RAMEY
For Carmen Bernstein:
JENNIFER FRANKEL, PATTY GOBLE
For Oscar Shapiro & Sidney Bernstein:
MICHAEL X. MARTIN, JEROME VIVONA
For Johnny Harmon:
JIM NEWMAN, JEROME VIVONA
For Bobby Pepper:
DAVID EGGERS
For Jessica Cranshaw:
JENNIFER FRANKEL, JULIE TOLIVAR
For Georgia Hendricks:
SHANNON LEWIS, JULIE TOLIVAR

Dance Captain:
DAVID EGGERS

SETTING

Act One
The Colonial Theatre in Boston, 1959, during the out-of-town tryout of the new musical, *Robbin' Hood!*

Act Two
The same, much later that night

Curtains

David Hyde Pierce
Lieutenant
Frank Cioffi

Debra Monk
Carmen Bernstein

Karen Ziemba
Georgia Hendricks

Jason Danieley
Aaron Fox

Erin Davie
Niki Harris

Edward Hibbert
Christopher Belling

John Bolton
Daryl Grady

Michael X. Martin
Johnny Harmon

Michael McCormick
Oscar Shapiro

Noah Racey
Bobby Pepper

Megan Sikora
Bambi Bernét

Gerry Vichi
Sidney Bernstein

Kevin Bernard
Roy Stetson,
Detective O'Farrell

Callie Carter
Arlene Barucca

Jennifer Dunne
Jan Setler

David Eggers
Swing,
Dance Captain

J. Austin Eyer
Swing

Jennifer Frankel
Marjorie Cook

Patty Goble
Jessica Cranshaw,
Connie Subbotin

Lorin Latarro
Swing

Shannon Lewis
Mona Page

Brittany Marcin
Peg Prentice

Sean McKnight
Brick Hawvermale

Jim Newman
Randy Dexter

Aaron Ramey
Harv Fremont

Sean Samuels
Ronnie Driscoll

Julie Tolivar
Roberta Wooster

Jerome Vivona
Swing

Matt Wall
Russ Cochran

Stephanie Youell
Swing

Beverley Randolph
Production
Supervisor

John Kander and Fred Ebb
Music, Additional Lyrics; Lyrics

Rupert Holmes
Book,
Additional Lyrics

Peter Stone
Original Book &
Concept

Curtains

Scott Ellis
Director

Rob Ashford
Choreographer

Anna Louizos
Set Design

William Ivey Long
Costume Design

Peter Kaczorowski
Lighting Design

Brian Ronan
Sound Design

William David Brohn
Orchestrations

Paul Huntley
Hair and Wig Design

Rick Sordelet
Fight Director

Paul Rubin
Aerial Effects Design

Angelina Avallone
Make-up Design

Joann M. Hunter
Associate Choreographer

Dave Solomon
Assistant Director

Teressa Esposito
Creative Associate to Mr. Holmes

Jim Carnahan, CSA
Casting

Roger Berlind
Producer

Wendy Orshan,
101 Productions, Ltd.
General Manager

Roger Horchow
Producer

Daryl Roth
Producer

Jane Bergère
Producer

Ted Hartley
Producer

Michael Ritchie
*Artistic Director,
Center Theatre
Group*

Charles Dillingham
*Managing Director,
Center Theatre
Group*

Gordon Davidson
*Founding Artistic
Director,
Center Theatre
Group*

Ward Billeisen
Brick Hawvermale

Joe Aaron Reid
Ronnie Driscoll

Christopher
Spaulding
Russ Cochran

Curtains

ORCHESTRA
Front Row (L-R): Dave Roth, Owen Kotler.

Back Row (L-R): Julie Ferrara, Greg Utzig, Jeremy Miloszewicz, Jennifer Wharton, Mark Thrasher, Charles Gordon, Bruce Doctor, Bill Ellison and Ken Hitchcock.

WARDROBE
Front Row (L-R): Frank Scaccia, Valerie Frith, Margo Lawless.

Back Row (L-R): Jason Blair, Theresa DiStasi, Misty Fernandez, David Mitchell, Alice Bee, Lisa Preston and Kay Gowenlock.

FRONT OF HOUSE STAFF
Front Row (L-R): Mary Marzan (Usher), Janice Rodriguez (Chief Usher), Jennifer DiDonato (Usher), Lorraine Feeks (Ticket Taker), Kerri Gillen (Usher), Julie Burnham (Director), Marisol Diaz (Usher), William Burke (Usher).

Second Row (L-R): Nicole Grillos (Usher), Henry Menendez (Usher), Tristan Blacer (Ticket Taker), Alex Gutierrez (Usher), Maura Leahy (Max Merchandising), Louis Mazza (Engineer).

Back Row (L-R): Jose Nunez (Porter), Albert Kim (Theatre Manager), Michael Yeshion (Bartender), Donald Royal (Usher), Roberto Ellington (Porter), Hollis Miller (Usher), Ron Marto (Security Guard), and Bart Ryan (Usher).

Curtains

HAIR
(L-R): Gay Boseker, Natasha Steinhagen, Larry Boyette and Brendan O'Neal.

DOORMAN
Neil Perez

PROPS
(L-R): Gene Manford, Sal Sclafani, Andy Trotto and Bob Adams.

COMPANY AND STAGE MANAGEMENT
(L-R): Kevin Bertolacci (Assistant Stage Manager), Scott Rollison (Stage Manager), Beverley Randolph (Production Supervisor/Production Stage Manager), Jerome Vivona (Assistant Stage Manager/Fight Captain) and Beverly Edwards (Company Manager).

CARPENTERS
Front Row (L-R): Erik Hansen, Joe Maher, Angelo Grasso, Paul Wimmer.

On Staircase (L-R): Richie Fullum, Morgan Shevett, Gabe Harris, Angelo Torre, Kevin Maher, Tom Lowery.

ELECTRICS AND SOUND
(L-R): Richard Mortell, Danny Ansbro, Cletus Karamon, Rob Dagna, Bonnie Runk, John Blixt, Dennis Short, Chris Sloan and Michele Gutierrez.

Curtains

Desire Under the Elms

First Preview: April 14, 2009. Opened: April 27, 2009.
Closed May 24, 2009 after 16 Previews and 32 Performances.

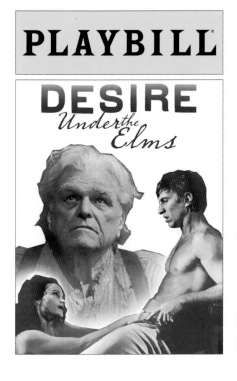

PLAYBILL

CAST

Eben Cabot ....PABLO SCHREIBER
Simeon Cabot ....DANIEL STEWART SHERMAN
Peter Cabot ....BORIS McGIVER
Ephraim Cabot ....BRIAN DENNEHY
Abbie Putnam ....CARLA GUGINO

SETTING

The Cabot farmhouse. New England. 1850

UNDERSTUDIES/STANDBYS

For Eben:
CHRISTIAN CONN
For Ephraim:
JOHN HENRY COX
For Abbie:
KELLY HUTCHINSON
For Simeon, Peter:
MICHAEL LAURENCE

ST. JAMES THEATRE
A JUJAMCYN THEATRE
ROCCO LANDESMAN
President

PAUL LIBIN
Producing Director

JACK VIERTEL
Creative Director

JORDAN ROTH
Vice President

Jeffrey Richards   Jerry Frankel   Steve Traxler
Bat-Barry Productions   Ronald Frankel   Norton Herrick
Judith Resnick   Daryl Roth   The Weinstein Company
Scott M. Delman/Alan D. Marks   Mort Swinsky/Michael Fuchs/Cindy & Jay Gutterman
Mark Johannes & Amy Danis/Jack Thomas   Morris Berchard/Eric Falkenstein
And
Jujamcyn Theaters
In Association With
Terri & Timothy Childs   Jam Theatricals   Jamie deRoy

Present

Brian   Carla   Pablo
Dennehy   Gugino   Schreiber

In

The Goodman Theatre production of

DESIRE
Under the Elms

By

Eugene O'Neill

With

Boris McGiver   Daniel Stewart Sherman

Scenic Design **Walt Spangler**	Costume Design **Ana Kuzmanic**	Lighting Design **Michael Philippi**	Original Music and Sound Design **Richard Woodbury**
Production Stage Manager **Robert Bennett**	Wig Design **Charles G. Lapointe**	Casting **Telsey + Company**	Technical Supervisor **Larry Morley**
Press Representative **Jeffrey Richards Associates**	Company Manager **Jolie Gabler**	Associate Producer **Broadway Across America**	General Manager **Richards/Climan, Inc.**

Directed By

Robert Falls

The producers wish to express their appreciation to
Theatre Development Fund for its support of this production.

NOW **THAT'S** BROADWAY!

4/27/09

(L-R): Pablo Schreiber, Brian Dennehy and Carla Gugino

Desire Under the Elms

Brian Dennehy
Ephraim Cabot

Carla Gugino
Abbie Putnam

Pablo Schreiber
Eben Cabot

Boris McGiver
Peter Cabot

Daniel Stewart
Sherman
Simeon Cabot

Christian Conn
u/s Eben

John Henry Cox
u/s Ephraim

Kelly Hutchinson
Abbie Standby

Michael Laurence
u/s Simeon, Peter

Eugene O'Neill
Playwright

Robert Falls
Director

Ana Kuzmanic
Costume Design

Richard Woodbury
*Original Music and
Sound Design*

Bernard Telsey,
Telsey + Company
Casting

David R. Richards and Tamar Haimes,
Richards/Climan Inc.
General Manager

Jeffrey Richards
Producer

Jerry Frankel
Producer

Steve Traxler
Producer

Barry Weisbord,
Bat-Barry
Productions
Producer

Ronald Frankel
Producer

Daryl Roth
Producer

Bob Weinstein,
The Weinstein
Company
Producer

Harvey Weinstein,
The Weinstein
Company
Producer

Morton Swinsky
Producer

Jay & Cindy Gutterman
Producers

Mark Johannes and
Amy Danis
Producers

Morris Berchard
Producer

Eric Falkenstein
Producer

Rocco Landesman,
President,
Jujamcyn Theaters
Producer

Jamie deRoy
Producer

Desire Under the Elms

SCRAPBOOK

Correspondent: Daniel Stewart Sherman, "Simeon Cabot"

Memorable Opening Night Card: "We are so lucky because we get paid to be 12 years old forever...but it's mostly bulls–t."

Opening Night Gifts: Pablo gave his "brothers" t-shirts saying, "Bacon's Good" for Daniel, and "Bacon's Bacon" for Boris. Carla gave everyone iPods with a playlist of music she put together representing the vibe of the story.

Celebrity Visits: Antonio Banderas and Melanie Griffith: They told us how honored they were to see our performances. Blythe Danner: She thinks it's tragic the show got zero Tony nominations.

Most Roles in the Show: Daniel Stewart Sherman was a walk-on fiddler; that makes two! Brian Dennehy has three, if you count the number of "rolls" he did in Chicago when he fell off the platform with the baby.

Backstage Rituals: Thumbs-up to props and stage manager at top of show. High-fiving Miss Gugino right before she gets pregnant. Watching Pablo cool off after running off to get the sheriff. Huggin' it out with Boris after we walk off.

Favorite Moment: Wondering if one of those friggin' chairs was gonna be in Brian's way at the end. He'd always give it a hearty kick if it was.

On-Site Gathering Place: Carla's room. She had all the stars...and it smelled good too!

Off-Site Gathering Places: Bar Centrale, Joe Allen, and Angus... Hell, it's right next door!

Favorite Snacks: Eclairs and leftover bacon. Cheesecake from Junior's. Carla's chocolate endeavors. Pablo's fetish with bear, deer and buffalo meat.

Mascot: Orville, the gutted pig. We had no choice; he was always hangin' around.

Therapies: What I like to call Carla's Potions—everything from 50 different teas, to throat drops that I think came from Argentina, to skin rubs that can change your singing voice from a baritone to a soprano in 17 minutes. And then there are Pablo's core workout DVDs. There are, like, 10 videos, and if you watch them all in the same day your life could end (but your body will be ripped) all for only $399.95! Call now!!

Ad-Lib: This award goes to the distinguished Boris. For some reason, which may never be explained (and, I hope, never will), instead of calling his father (Brian) an "old skinflint," Boris called him an old "c–ksucker"—and in a theatre where they do musicals!!! Outrageous! Ahhh... it was the best of times.

Cell Phone Rings: Our director had Miss Gugino record the message at top of show telling everyone to turn off their phones. She did it real sexy-like...and who isn't gonna respect THAT voice? I don't care if you're male or female.

Press Encounter: Classic Broadway! The two supporting actors are instructed to meet with the press...and then they wait for 45 minutes while everyone ELSE is interviewed, and then they are lucky enough to be in the group shots! Cast photos = yes. Our names on the posters in the lobby = no.

Stage Door Encounter: Pablo proceeds to tell Daniel (in front of everyone) to stop signing his name (Daniel's) over his butt (Pablo's) on the poster. Not sure what bothered Pablo more, that Daniel was signing his name there, or the fact that "Daniel Stewart Sherman" was able to fit over Pablo's butt.

Who Wore the Least: No contest: Pablo Schreiber, full birthday suit. Can't get THAT at Men's Wearhouse! "You're gonna like the way he looked... I guarantee it!!"

Company Catchphrase: "I-J-A-J!!!" (Don't ask... you will never find out.)

Memorable Directorial Note: (Well into the fourth day of tech:) "What do YOU think? ... cuz I haven't gotten there yet."

Nicknames: Brian—"The Old Man of the Sea." Carla—"The Flower Goddess." Pablo— "Mr. 12-Pak." Daniel—"Polar Bear." Boris—"The Court Jester."

Coolest Things About Being in This Show: Taking a bow when most shows go to intermission. Working with four extremely talented people every night. Performing a Eugene O'Neill play on a Broadway stage...and getting paid for all of it.

STAFF FOR *DESIRE UNDER THE ELMS*

GENERAL MANAGEMENT
RICHARDS/CLIMAN, INC.
David R. Richards   Tamar Haimes

COMPANY MANAGER
JOLIE GABLER

GENERAL PRESS REPRESENTATIVE
JEFFREY RICHARDS ASSOCIATES
IRENE GANDY
Alana Karpoff   Elon Rutberg
Shane Marshall Brown   Diana Rissetto

CASTING
TELSEY + COMPANY
Bernie Telsey CSA, Will Cantler CSA,
David Vaccari CSA, Bethany Knox CSA,
Craig Burns CSA, Tiffany Little Canfield CSA,
Rachel Hoffman CSA, Carrie Rosson CSA,
Justin Huff CSA, Bess Fifer CSA,
Patrick Goodwin, Abbie Brady-Dalton

FIGHT DIRECTOR
RICK SORDELET

DIALECT COACH
PATRICIA FLETCHER

TECHNICAL SUPERVISOR
LARRY MORLEY

PRODUCTION
STAGE MANAGER ....ROBERT BENNETT
Stage Manager ....Lois Griffing

Assistant Scenic Designers ....Ann Bartek,
                                                        Jisun Kim
Assistant Lighting Designer ....Paul Hackenmueller
Assistant Costume Designer ....Amelia Dombrowski
Assistant Sound Designers ....Erich Bechtel,
                                                        Nathaniel Hare
Associate General Manager ....John Gendron
General Management Associate ....John E. Gendron
General Management Assistant ....Cesar Hawas
Fight Captain ....Christian Conn
Production Assistants ....Conwell Worthington III,
                                                        Kristen Parker
Production Carpenter ....Todd Frank
Production Electrician ....Dan Coey
Production Sound ....Joanna Lynne Staub
Production Props ....Eric Castaldo
Lighting Programmer ....Ron Martin
Wardrobe Supervisor ....Rob Bevenger
Dressers ....Kathleen Gallagher, David Marquez
Hair Supervisor ....Justen Brosnan
Hair Assistant ....Hagen Linss
Associate to Mr. Richards ....Jeremy Scott Blaustein
Assistant to Mr. Richards ....Christopher Taggart
Assistant to Mr. Traxler ....Brandi Preston
Advertising ....SpotCo/Drew Hodges,
                                        Jim Edwards, Stephen Sosnowski,
                                                        Tim Falotico
Interactive Marketing Agency ....Situation Interactive/
                                        Damian Bazadona, John Lanasa,
                                                Ryan Klink, Kristen Butler
Banking ...............................J.P. Morgan Chase
Accountants ....Robert Fried, CPA
Comptroller ....Elliott Aronstam, CPA
Insurance ....DeWitt Stern Group
Legal Counsel ....Lazarus & Harris LLP./
                            Scott R. Lazarus, Esq., Robert C. Harris, Esq.

Payroll ....CSI/Lance Castellana
Production Photographer ....Liz Lauren
Company Mascots ....Lottie, Skye

CREDITS
Scenery constructed by Hudson Scenic. Lighting equipment from PRG Lighting. Sound equipment from Sound Associates. Costumes by Timberlake Studios.

MUSIC CREDITS
"Not Dark Yet" by Bob Dylan, ©1997 Special Rider Music. All rights reserved. International copyright secured. Reprinted by permission. "Fiddle Tune" by John Hartford.

Make-up provided by M•A•C

www.DesireonBroadway.com

JUJAMCYN THEATERS
ROCCO LANDESMAN
President
PAUL LIBIN   **JACK VIERTEL**   **JORDAN ROTH**
Producing Director   Creative Director   Vice President
DANIEL ADAMIAN   **JENNIFER HERSHEY**
General Manager   Director of Operations
MEREDITH VILLATORE   **JERRY ZAKS**
Chief Financial Officer   Resident Director

STAFF FOR THE ST. JAMES THEATRE
Manager ....Daniel Adamian
Associate Manager ....Hal Goldberg
Treasurer ....Vincent Sclafani
Carpenter ....Timothy McDonough Jr.
Propertyman ....Timothy McDonough
Electrician ....Albert Sayers

Dividing the Estate

First Preview: October 23, 2008. Opened: November 20, 2008.
Closed January 4, 2009 after 31 Previews and 50 Performances.

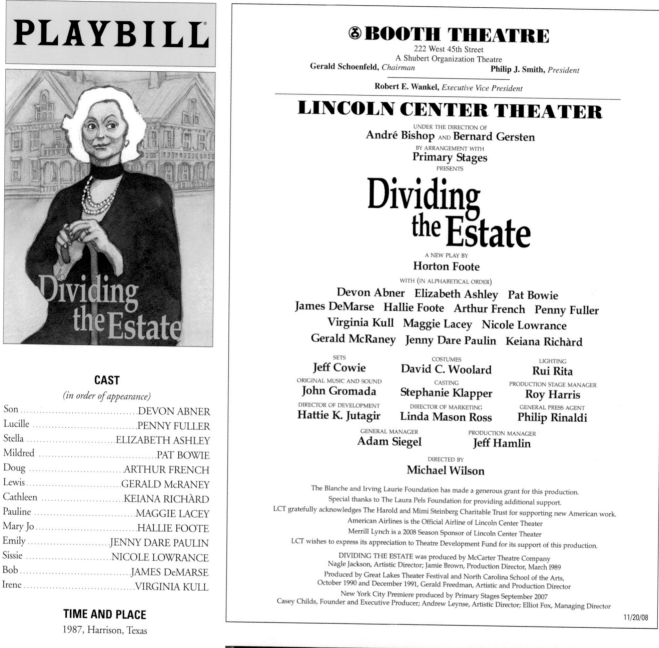

PLAYBILL

![Dividing the Estate]

Dividing the Estate

CAST

(in order of appearance)

Son	DEVON ABNER
Lucille	PENNY FULLER
Stella	ELIZABETH ASHLEY
Mildred	PAT BOWIE
Doug	ARTHUR FRENCH
Lewis	GERALD McRANEY
Cathleen	KEIANA RICHÀRD
Pauline	MAGGIE LACEY
Mary Jo	HALLIE FOOTE
Emily	JENNY DARE PAULIN
Sissie	NICOLE LOWRANCE
Bob	JAMES DeMARSE
Irene	VIRGINIA KULL

TIME AND PLACE

1987, Harrison, Texas

Asst. Stage Manager .....COLE P. BONENBERGER

UNDERSTUDIES

For Son: KEVIN O'ROURKE
For Bob: STEPHEN BRADBURY,
KEVIN O'ROURKE
For Lewis: STEPHEN BRADBURY
For Stella: JILL TANNER
For Lucille and Mary Jo: JENNIFER HARMON
For Mildred and Cathleen: KELLY TAFFE
For Doug: CHARLES TURNER
For Pauline and Irene: ANNIE PURCELL
For Emily and Sissie:
JENNIFER JOAN THOMPSON

The Playbill Broadway Yearbook 2008-2009

ⓢ BOOTH THEATRE
222 West 45th Street
A Shubert Organization Theatre

Gerald Schoenfeld, *Chairman*   Philip J. Smith, *President*

Robert E. Wankel, *Executive Vice President*

LINCOLN CENTER THEATER
UNDER THE DIRECTION OF
André Bishop AND Bernard Gersten
BY ARRANGEMENT WITH
Primary Stages
PRESENTS

Dividing the Estate

A NEW PLAY BY
Horton Foote

WITH (IN ALPHABETICAL ORDER)

Devon Abner   Elizabeth Ashley   Pat Bowie
James DeMarse   Hallie Foote   Arthur French   Penny Fuller
Virginia Kull   Maggie Lacey   Nicole Lowrance
Gerald McRaney   Jenny Dare Paulin   Keiana Richàrd

SETS	COSTUMES	LIGHTING
Jeff Cowie	**David C. Woolard**	**Rui Rita**
ORIGINAL MUSIC AND SOUND	CASTING	PRODUCTION STAGE MANAGER
John Gromada	**Stephanie Klapper**	**Roy Harris**
DIRECTOR OF DEVELOPMENT	DIRECTOR OF MARKETING	GENERAL PRESS AGENT
Hattie K. Jutagir	**Linda Mason Ross**	**Philip Rinaldi**
GENERAL MANAGER		PRODUCTION MANAGER
Adam Siegel		**Jeff Hamlin**

DIRECTED BY
Michael Wilson

The Blanche and Irving Laurie Foundation has made a generous grant for this production.
Special thanks to The Laura Pels Foundation for providing additional support.
LCT gratefully acknowledges The Harold and Mimi Steinberg Charitable Trust for supporting new American work.
American Airlines is the Official Airline of Lincoln Center Theater
Merrill Lynch is a 2008 Season Sponsor of Lincoln Center Theater
LCT wishes to express its appreciation to Theatre Development Fund for its support of this production.

DIVIDING THE ESTATE was produced by McCarter Theatre Company
Nagle Jackson, Artistic Director; Jamie Brown, Production Director, March 1989
Produced by Great Lakes Theater Festival and North Carolina School of the Arts,
October 1990 and December 1991, Gerald Freedman, Artistic and Production Director
New York City Premiere produced by Primary Stages September 2007
Casey Childs, Founder and Executive Producer; Andrew Leynse, Artistic Director; Elliot Fox, Managing Director

11/20/08

Photo by Joan Marcus

(L-R): Devon Abner, Elizabeth Ashley, Penny Fuller,
Maggie Lacey, James DeMarse, Hallie Foote,
Jenny Dare Paulin and Gerald McRaney

Dividing the Estate

Devon Abner
Son

Elizabeth Ashley
Stella

Pat Bowie
Mildred

James DeMarse
Bob

Hallie Foote
Mary Jo

Arthur French
Doug

Penny Fuller
Lucille

Virginia Kull
Irene

Maggie Lacey
Pauline

Nicole Lowrance
Sissie

Gerald McRaney
Lewis

Jenny Dare Paulin
Emily

Keiana Richàrd
Cathleen

Stephen Bradbury
Understudy

Jennifer Harmon
Understudy

Kevin O'Rourke
Understudy

Annie Purcell
Understudy

Kelly Taffe
Understudy

Jill Tanner
Understudy

Jennifer Joan Thompson
Understudy

Charles Turner
Understudy

Horton Foote
Playwright

Michael Wilson
Director

David C. Woolard
Costumes

John Gromada
Original Music and Sound

Paul Huntley
Wigs

André Bishop and Bernard Gersten, Lincoln Center Theater
Producer

Andrew Leynse
Artistic Director, Primary Stages

Elizabeth Ashley as Stella.

Photo by Joan Marcus

Dividing the Estate

Photos by Brian Mapp

RUNNING CREW
Front Row (L-R): Susan Goulet, Jimmy Keane, Jenny Scheer-Montgomery

Back Row (L-R): Graeme McDonnell, Francis Hauser, Kenneth McDonough, John Woytas

FRONT OF HOUSE STAFF
Front Row (L-R): Catherine Coscia (Head Usher), Marjorie Glover, Nadine Space

Middle Row (L-R): Daniel Rosario, Chrissie Collins (Director), Bernadette Bokun

Back Row (L-R): Marco Malgiolio, Timothy Wilhelm (Ticket-Taker)

STAGE MANAGEMENT
(L-R): Cole P. Bonenberger (Assistant Stage Manager), Marisa Levy (Production Assistant), Roy Harris (Production Stage Manager)

COSTUME DEPARTMENT
(L-R): Moira MacGregor-Conrad (Wardrobe Supervisor), James W. Swift, Catherine Dee

Dividing the Estate

ADMINISTRATIVE STAFF

GENERAL MANAGER ....ADAM SIEGEL
Associate General Manager ....Jessica Niebanck
General Management Assistant ....Meghan Lantzy
Facilities Manager ....Alex Mustelier
Assistant Facilities Manager ....Michael Assalone
GENERAL PRESS AGENT ....PHILIP RINALDI
Press Associate ....Barbara Carroll
PRODUCTION MANAGER ....JEFF HAMLIN
Associate Production Manager ....Paul Smithyman
DIRECTOR OF
   DEVELOPMENT ....HATTIE K. JUTAGIR
Associate Director of Development ......Rachel Norton
Manager of Special Events and
   Young Patron Program ....Karin Schall
Grants Writer ....Neal Brilliant
Manager, Patron Program ....Sheilaja Rao
Assistant to the
   Director of Development ....Raelyn Richards
Development Associate/
   Special Events ....Nicole Lindenbaum
Development Assistant/
   Patron Program ....Terra Gillespie
DIRECTOR OF FINANCE ....DAVID S. BROWN
Controller ....Susan Knox
Systems Manager ....Stacy Valentine
Finance Assistant ....Megan Wildebour
DIRECTOR OF MARKETING .LINDA MASON ROSS
Marketing Associate ....Kristin Miller
Marketing Assistant ....Ashley M. Dunn
DIRECTOR OF EDUCATION ....KATI KOERNER
Associate Director of Education ......Alexandra Lopez
Assistant to the
   Executive Producer ....Barbara Hourigan
Office Assistant ....Rhonda Lipscomb
Messenger ....Esau Burgess
Reception ....Brenden Rogers, Michelle Hamill

ARTISTIC STAFF

ASSOCIATE DIRECTORS ......GRACIELA DANIELE,
                          NICHOLAS HYTNER,
                          JACK O'BRIEN,
                          SUSAN STROMAN,
                          DANIEL SULLIVAN
RESIDENT DIRECTOR.............BARTLETT SHER
DRAMATURG and DIRECTOR,
   LCT DIRECTORS LAB ....ANNE CATTANEO
CASTING DIRECTOR ....DANIEL SWEE, CSA
MUSICAL THEATER
   ASSOCIATE PRODUCER ....IRA WEITZMAN
DIRECTOR OF LCT3 ....PAIGE EVANS
Artistic Administrator ....Julia Judge
Casting Associate ....Camille Hickman
Lab Assistant ....Kate Marvin

SPECIAL SERVICES

Advertising ....Serino-Coyne/
   Jim Russek, Roger Micone, Stephen Elms
Principal Poster Artist ....James McMullan
Poster Art for *Dividing the Estate* ....James McMullan

Counsel ....Peter L. Felcher, Esq.;
                    Charles H. Googe, Esq.;
             and Carol Kaplan, Esq. of
    Paul, Weiss, Rifkind, Wharton & Garrison
Immigration Counsel ....Theodore Ruthizer, Esq.;
                Mark D. Koestler, Esq.
   of Kramer, Levin, Naftalis & Frankel LLP
Labor Counsel ....Michael F. McGahan, Esq.
          of Epstein, Becker & Green P.C.
Auditor ....Douglas Burack, C.P.A.
               Lutz & Carr, L.L.P.
Insurance ....Jennifer Brown of
               DeWitt Stern Group
Photographer ....Joan Marcus
Travel ....Tygon Tours
Consulting Architect ....Hugh Hardy,
     H3 Hardy Collaboration Architecture
Construction Manager ....Yorke Construction
Payroll Service ....Castellana Services, Inc.

STAFF FOR *DIVIDING THE ESTATE*

COMPANY MANAGER........MATTHEW MARKOFF
Associate Director ....Maxwell Williams
Assistant to the Director ....Christy Pellegrini
Associate Set Designer ....David Barber
Associate Costume Designer ....Kevin Brainerd
Associate Lighting Designer ....Ben Krall
Asst. to Mr. Rita ....Carl Faber
Associate Sound Designer ....Christopher Cronin
Assistant Sound Designer ....Bridget O'Connor
Production Carpenter ....John Weingart
Production Electrician ....Graeme McDonnell
Production Propertyman ....Mark Dignam
Production Soundman ....Jenny Montgomery
Props ....Susan Barras
Fight Director ................................B.H. Barry
Wardrobe Supervisor ....Moira MacGregor-Conrad
Dressers ....Catherine Dee, James W. Swift
Hair Supervisor ....Cindy Demand
Casting Assistant ....Jennifer Pardilla
Assistant to Ms. Klapper and
   Ms. Pardilla..........................Carrie Virginia Lee
Production Assistant ....Marisa Levy

Wig and Hair Design
Paul Huntley

Technical Supervision by
William Nagle and Patrick Merryman

CREDITS

Scenery construction by Showman Fabricators. Costumes by Barbara Matera, Eric Winterling Costumes, Tricorne, Giliberto Designs and Timberlake Studios. Sound equipment by Masque Sound. Lighting equipment from PRG Lighting. Natural herb cough drops courtesy of Ricola USA, Inc.

Visit www.lct.org

PRIMARY STAGES STAFF

FOUNDER AND
   EXECUTIVE PRODUCER ....CASEY CHILDS
ARTISTIC DIRECTOR ....ANDREW LEYNSE
MANAGING DIRECTOR................ELLIOT FOX

ASSOCIATE ARTISTIC
   DIRECTOR ....MICHELLE BOSSY
Literary Manager and
   PSST Administrator ....Tessa LaNeve
Associate to the Artistic Director ....Lucy McMichael
DIRECTOR OF
   DEVELOPMENT ....JESSICA SADOWSKI COMAS
Development Associate ....Lindsay Hahnes
Government and Education Affairs ....Sue Breger
DIRECTOR OF MARKETING ....SHANTA MALI
Marketing Associate ....Aubry Nivens
Primary Services Manager ....Kara Hennessey
Public Relations ....Anne Einhorn
PRODUCTION
   SUPERVISOR ....PETER R. FEUCHTWANGER
BUSINESS MANAGER ....REUBEN SAUNDERS
IT and Rentals Manager ....David L. Goldsmith
Business Assistant ....Ingrid Bracey
General Press Representative ....O&M Co.:
      Rick Miramontez, Philip Carrubba

For groups of 20 or more:
Caryl Goldsmith Group Sales
(212) 889-4300

Dividing the Estate
SCRAPBOOK

1. Author Horton Foote arrives at what will turn out to be his final Broadway opening, with his daughter, actress Hallie Foote.
2. The cast takes bows on opening night.

Correspondent: Roy Harris, Stage Manager

The entire *Dividing the Estate* experience—from its Off-Broadway run at Primary Stages in the fall of 2007 to its final Broadway performance at the Booth Theatre on January 4, 2009—was one of the happiest theatre experiences for everyone involved. A cast that was as close to perfection as it gets. Michael Wilson, a director who understood the soul—and the comedy—of Horton Foote's great play. A design team that couldn't be bettered: beginning with Jeff Cowie's majestic set and including Rui Rita's pinpoint-precision lighting and David Woolard's costumes that both captured and lampooned simultaneously late 1980s southern fashion. The company felt it was in great hands with our house crew—Ken McDonough, Susan Goulet, Jimmy Keane—and production crew—electrician Graeme McDonnell, flyman Chris Wiggins, and sound op Jenny Montgomery—and the front-of-house led by theatre manager Lauri Wilson. A wonderful experience with one caveat: fate and the scary economic situation that made it impossible for us to play longer and deprived thousands of people from seeing the play.

Various off-stage rituals emerged, as they usually do from the exigencies of life. For instance, if you observed our stage right and upstage off-stage areas you might think we were performing in the North Pole. Everyone waiting to make their next entrance is wrapped in a blanket. We found early on in previews that we had to turn off the main upstage heat because of both clanging pipes and heat so intense that it felt like we were in a sauna back there. Hence, backstage was frigid. You might see Penny Fuller stage right wrapped in a blue blanket waiting to make her next entrance, or upstage Keiana Richàrd and Pat Bowie, both wrapped in blankets, getting ready to make numerous entrances and exits in the first scene as they set the table for dinner.

One of our favorite onstage incidents was the question: will one of the biscuits that Doug drops roll off into the front row tonight? Several times during the run, there were bets taken. Three biscuits made it into the laps of unsuspecting patrons.

Our favorite gathering place was the basement, which was permanently inhabited by Shubert Security and our great wardrobe team: Moira MacGregor-Conrad, Catherine (Cat) Dee, and James Swift. Often during performances, you might find one of our eight understudies down there going over lines, or having a snack, or just dishing the dish. On Sundays, it was the site of our weekly brunches, hosted by our stage managers: Roy Harris, Cole Bonenberger, and Marisa Levy. Because this is a company that likes to eat, and to eat with variety, we had some bonanza brunches. A few of the culinary delights were Gerald McRaney's Cajun cheese grits, Maggie Lacey's pumpkin bread (still warm when it arrived), one of many delicious and healthy salads from Jennifer Harmon, fresh fruit salad from Jill Tanner, egg soufflé from Annie Purcell, red beans and rice from Keiana Richàrd, Alabama blueberry bread from Roy Harris, cheese strata from Marisa Levy, Cajun cheesecake from Devon Abner, and many, many other treats. When we did our trim-the-tree brunch a few weeks before Christmas, wardrobe supervisor Moira MacGregor-Conrad and her sister, Fiona, made gorgeous Christmas cupcakes, displayed on a delightful revolving lazy Susan.

Three biggest laughs, every night, in the show: Mary Jo to Bob: "How much will I get?" Son to the entire family: "We can all live here together." And Mary Jo's final line, "I'm praying…. I'm praying."

Our company was a very verbally responsive bunch. Here are some responses that actors had to various notes from director Wilson during our preview period: "Oh, you mean, don't talk with my mouth full." "You want Attila the Hun, you'll get Attila the Hun." "Is 'more vocal energy' the same thing as louder?" "Somebody's gaslighting the perimeters of my internal monologue." "Oh, that's much too long a cross. I'll need a picnic lunch to accomplish it." "Next time I'll gimp up slower." The following exchange was heard in mid-rehearsals: "They've legalized gay marriage in Connecticut." "Yes, and the stock market's still falling."

A catchphrase only our company would recognize: "The mother-ship is hovering."

The coolest thing about being in *Dividing the Estate* is that nine of the 13 company members got a full-course meal—ham, beans, carrots, sweet potatoes with pecans and marshmallows, homemade iced tea and biscuits—on stage every night. This was especially good in our current economic crisis, because if you went out after the show, you only had to buy yourself something to drink. You were already sated!

We had a number of line-fumphers, as one does with any live theatrical experience. One of our favorites was Mildred's response to being asked by an offstage Lucille, where are you? Her response one night: "I'm in the kitchen…no, I'm in the living room. Oh, I don't know where I am." (She was actually in the living room.) Another favorite is when Lucille said to her sister Mary Jo, "I thought I'd clean one week and you'd do the cooking, and the next week I'd clean and you'd do the cooking…or, something like that."

But the offstage, in-the-wings conversations were the most memorable. For instance, just before the top of the first act one night, Ms. Ashley said to Gerald McRaney, "I may do the second act first and the first act second," to which he replied, "Shoot. I was just getting used to it the other way." Ms. Fuller was fond of reminding stage management, "What do you mean, don't complain? I'm an actor." And that old favorite from one actor to another: "What scene is this?"

After our Broadway run, most of the original company took the play to Hartford Stage Company, director Michael Wilson's home base. It had an additional six-week run.

Equus

First Preview: September 5, 2008. Opened: September 25, 2008.
Closed February 8, 2009 after 21 Previews and 156 Performances.

CAST
(in order of appearance)

Martin Dysart . . . . RICHARD GRIFFITHS
Alan Strang . . . . DANIEL RADCLIFFE
Nurse . . . . SANDRA SHIPLEY
Hesther Saloman . . . . KATE MULGREW
Frank Strang . . . . .T. RYDER SMITH
Dora Strang . . . . CAROLYN McCORMICK
The Young Horseman
   & Nugget . . . . LORENZO PISONI
Harry Dalton . . . . .GRAEME MALCOLM
Horses . . . . .COLLIN BAJA,
   TYRONE A. JACKSON, SPENCER LIFF,
   ADESOLA OSAKALUMI, MARC SPAULDING
Jill Mason . . . . .ANNA CAMP

The main action takes place in Rokeby Psychiatric
Hospital in southern England.

STANDBYS

For Martin Dysart: BILL BUELL
For Martin Dysart, Frank Strang, Harry Dalton:
PAUL O'BRIEN
For Alan Strang: PAUL DAVID STORY
For Hesther Saloman:
SANDRA SHIPLEY
For Jill Mason, Nurse: AMANDA QUAID
For Dora Strang, Nurse:
SUSAN PELLEGRINO
For The Young Horseman, Nugget:
SPENCER LIFF, ADESOLA OSAKALUMI
For Horses: KEVIN BOSEMAN

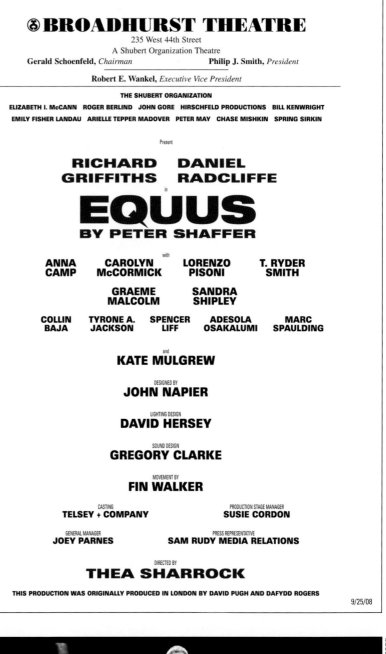

⊗ BROADHURST THEATRE
235 West 44th Street
A Shubert Organization Theatre

Gerald Schoenfeld, *Chairman*   Philip J. Smith, *President*

Robert E. Wankel, *Executive Vice President*

THE SHUBERT ORGANIZATION
ELIZABETH I. McCANN   ROGER BERLIND   JOHN GORE   HIRSCHFELD PRODUCTIONS   BILL KENWRIGHT
EMILY FISHER LANDAU   ARIELLE TEPPER MADOVER   PETER MAY   CHASE MISHKIN   SPRING SIRKIN

Present

RICHARD GRIFFITHS   DANIEL RADCLIFFE
in

EQUUS
BY PETER SHAFFER

with

ANNA CAMP   CAROLYN McCORMICK   LORENZO PISONI   T. RYDER SMITH

GRAEME MALCOLM   SANDRA SHIPLEY

COLLIN BAJA   TYRONE A. JACKSON   SPENCER LIFF   ADESOLA OSAKALUMI   MARC SPAULDING

and

KATE MULGREW

DESIGNED BY
JOHN NAPIER

LIGHTING DESIGN
DAVID HERSEY

SOUND DESIGN
GREGORY CLARKE

MOVEMENT BY
FIN WALKER

CASTING
TELSEY + COMPANY

PRODUCTION STAGE MANAGER
SUSIE CORDON

GENERAL MANAGER
JOEY PARNES

PRESS REPRESENTATIVE
SAM RUDY MEDIA RELATIONS

DIRECTED BY
THEA SHARROCK

THIS PRODUCTION WAS ORIGINALLY PRODUCED IN LONDON BY DAVID PUGH AND DAFYDD ROGERS

9/25/08

Photo by Carol Rosegg

(L-R): Richard Griffiths
and Daniel Radcliffe with
members of the cast.

Equus

Richard Griffiths
Martin Dysart

Daniel Radcliffe
Alan Strang

Kate Mulgrew
Hesther Saloman

Anna Camp
Jill Mason

Carolyn McCormick
Dora Strang

Lorenzo Pisoni
*The Young
Horseman & Nugget*

T. Ryder Smith
Frank Strang

Graeme Malcolm
Harry Dalton

Sandra Shipley
Nurse

Collin Baja
Horse

Tyrone A. Jackson
Horse

Spencer Liff
*Horse/
Assistant to the
Movement Director/
Dance Captain*

Adesola Osakalumi
Horse

Marc Spaulding
Horse

Kevin Boseman
Standby for Horses

Bill Buell
*Standby for
Martin Dysart*

Paul O'Brien
*Standby for
Martin Dysart,
Frank Strang,
Harry Dalton*

Susan Pellegrino
*Standby for
Dora Strang, Nurse*

Amanda Quaid
*Standby for
Jill Mason, Nurse*

Paul David Story
*Standby for
Alan Strang*

Peter Shaffer
Playwright

Thea Sharrock
Director

John Napier
Designer

David Hersey
Lighting Designer

Gregory Clarke
Sound Designer

Bernard Telsey,
Telsey + Company
Casting

Joey Parnes
General Manager

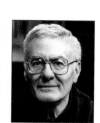
Gerald Schoenfeld,
Chairman,
The Shubert
Organization
Producer

Elizabeth I. McCann
Producer

Roger Berlind
Producer

Bill Kenwright
Producer

Arielle Tepper
Madover
Producer

Chase Mishkin
Producer

Spring Sirkin
Producer

Equus

2008-2009 AWARDS

TONY AWARD
Best Sound Design of a Play
(Gregory Clarke)

DRAMA DESK AWARD
Outstanding Lighting Design in a Play
(David Hersey)

1. Richard Griffiths as Dr. Martin Dysart.
2. Daniel Radcliffe as Alan Strang with Lorenzo Pisoni as Nugget.

STAFF FOR *EQUUS*

GENERAL MANAGEMENT
JOEY PARNES

John Johnson	S.D. Wagner
Leslie Glassburn	Kit Ingui

GENERAL PRESS REPRESENTATIVE
SAM RUDY MEDIA RELATIONS

Sam Rudy	Jim Randolph
Dale R. Heller	Robert Lasko

COMPANY MANAGER
KIM SELLON

CASTING
TELSEY + COMPANY
Bernie Telsey CSA, Will Cantler CSA, David Vaccari CSA,
Bethany Knox CSA, Craig Burns CSA,
Tiffany Little Canfield CSA, Rachel Hoffman CSA,
Carrie Rosson CSA, Justin Huff CSA,
Bess Fifer CSA, Patrick Goodwin

DIALECT & VOCAL COACH
DEBORAH HECHT

Production Stage Manager . . . . .Susie Cordon
Stage Manager .Allison Sommers
Assistant Stage Manager . . . . .Brian Rardin
Production Assistant . . . . .Cynthia Hennon
Associate Director . . . . .Rachel Russell
Assistant to the Director . . . . .Alicia Dhyana House
Assistant to the Movement Director/
Dance Captain . . . . .Spencer Liff
Associate Set Designer . . . . .Ray Huessy
Associate Lighting Designer . . . . .Ted Mather
Associate Costume Designer . . . . .Chloe Chapin
Production Carpenter . . . . .Larry Morley
Production Electrician . . . . .Steve Cochrane
Production Prop Supervisor . . . . .Mike Smanko
Production Sound Engineer . . . . .Beth Berkeley
Head Electrician . . . . .Jeff Turner

Moving Light Programmer . . . . .Rob Halliday
Wardrobe Supervisor . . . . .Dave Olin Rogers
Dressers . . . . .Sandy Binion, Geoffrey Polischuk
Advertising . . . . .Serino Coyne Inc./
Nancy Coyne, Greg Corradetti,
Natalie Serota, Danielle Boyle
Website Design . . . . .Dewynters
Legal Counsel . . . . .Lowenstein Sandler PC/
Franklin R. Weissberg
Accountants . . . . .Rosenberg, Neuwirth & Kuchner/
Mark A. D'Ambrosi, Patricia M. Pedersen
Banking . . . . .JP Morgan Chase Bank/
Stephanie Dalton
Insurance . . . . .DeWitt Stern/
Peter Shoemaker,
Stockbridge Group/Neil Goldstein
Payroll . . . . .Castellana Services Inc./
Lance Castellana, James Castellana,
Norman Sewell
Physical Therapist . . . . .Rhonda M. Barkow, PT, MS
Orthopedic Consultant . . . . .Phillip Bauman, MD
Security Services . . . . .SISS International
Housing Coordinator . . . . . . .Road Concierge/Lisa Morris
Opening Night Coordinator . . . .The Lawrence Company
Production Photographer . . . . .Carol Rosegg

CREDITS

Additional scenic elements by Hudson Scenic Studio, Inc.
Lighting equipment by PRG Lighting. Sound equipment
by Sound Associates. Horse costumes by Izquierdo.
Additional costumes by Timberlake Studios. Horse footwear
by Sharlot Batton of Montana Leatherworks. Makeup provided by M•A•C Cosmetics. Flying by Foy. Car service by
IBA Limousine. Natural herb cough drops courtesy of
Ricola USA. Emergen-C health and energy drink mix provided by Alacer Corporation. Souvenir merchandise
designed and created by Dewynters Ltd. Rehearsed at the
New 42nd Street Studios.

Equestrian costumes provided by Manhattan Saddlery.

SPECIAL THANKS

Cressida Shaffer; Lionshare Farm, Marcela Leone,
Ken Whelihan and all of the staff at Lionshare.

---

www.EquusOnBroadway.com

THE SHUBERT ORGANIZATION, INC.
Board of Directors

Gerald Schoenfeld	**Philip J. Smith**
Chairman	President
Wyche Fowler, Jr.	**John W. Kluge**
Lee J. Seidler	**Michael I. Sovern**

Stuart Subotnick

Robert E. Wankel
Executive Vice President

David Andrews	**Elliot Greene**
Senior Vice President –	Senior Vice President –
Shubert Ticketing	Finance
Juan Calvo	**John Darby**
Vice President	Vice President –
and Controller	Facilities
Peter Entin	**Charles Flateman**
Vice President –	Vice President –
Theatre Operations	Marketing
Anthony LaMattina	**Brian Mahoney**
Vice President –	Vice President –
Audit & Production Finance	Ticket Sales

D.S. Moynihan
Vice President – Creative Projects

House Manager . . . . .Hugh Barnett

Equus
SCRAPBOOK

THAT'S STRAW LAW

Richard & Jeffrey

Sir Peter

Richard White, Night Door

PORTRAITS BY GRAEME MALCOLM gramalcolm@yahoo.com

Tyrone

POST NO BILLS

WOP BOP WOP BOP WOP BOP WOP BOP

SPENCER

LORENZO & HAT

CHLOE

BUSTER THE SHOW DOG

SMANKO Props

kevin

SUSIE

Abreact?

HUGH BARNETT HOUSE MGT

PAUL O'BRIEN

SPASE

ALICIA HOUSE

THEA'S BOY BECKETT

P.D.S.

Allison and Brian

BETH BERKLEY Sound

Drawing by Chloe Chapin

BOOMER

Collage by Correspondent Allison Sommers, Stage Manager

Exit the King

First Preview: March 7, 2009. Opened: March 26, 2009.
Still running as of May 31, 2009.

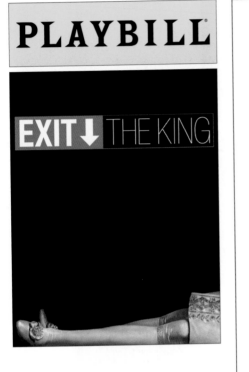

CAST
(in order of appearance)

The Guard ....BRIAN HUTCHISON
King Berenger ....GEOFFREY RUSH
Queen Marguerite ....SUSAN SARANDON
Juliette ....ANDREA MARTIN
The Doctor ....WILLIAM SADLER
Queen Marie ....LAUREN AMBROSE

TRUMPETER

SHANE ENDSLEY, SCOTT HARRELL

UNDERSTUDIES

For King Berenger, The Doctor:
MICHAEL HAMMOND
For King Berenger, The Guard:
DAVID MANIS
For Queen Marguerite, Queen Marie, Juliette:
ERIKA ROLFSRUD

Geoffrey Rush is appearing with the permission of
Actors' Equity Association.

⊛ ETHEL BARRYMORE THEATRE
243 West 47th Street
A Shubert Organization Theatre
Philip J. Smith, *Chairman*   **Robert E. Wankel,** *President*

STUART THOMPSON   ROBERT FOX   HOWARD PANTER
SCOTT RUDIN   TULCHIN/BARTNER   JON B. PLATT   JOHN FROST   THE WEINSTEIN COMPANY/ NORTON HERRICK
MICHAEL EDWARDS & CAROLE WINTER   DANIEL SPARROW/MIKE WALSH
THE SHUBERT ORGANIZATION

Present

GEOFFREY RUSH   SUSAN SARANDON

in

Written by
EUGENE IONESCO

Adapted by
NEIL ARMFIELD AND GEOFFREY RUSH

with
LAUREN AMBROSE

WILLIAM SADLER   BRIAN HUTCHISON
and
ANDREA MARTIN

Scenic and Costume Design
DALE FERGUSON

Lighting Design
DAMIEN COOPER

Sound Design
RUSSELL GOLDSMITH

Composer
JOHN RODGERS

Production Stage Manager
EVAN ENSIGN

Casting
DANIEL SWEE

Press Representative
BONEAU/BRYAN-BROWN

Production Management
AURORA PRODUCTIONS

General Management
STP/DANA SHERMAN

Associate Producer
RONNIE PLANALP

Directed by
NEIL ARMFIELD

BASED ON A PRODUCTION ORIGINALLY COMMISSIONED
AND PRODUCED BY COMPANY B AND MALTHOUSE MELBOURNE.

THE PRODUCERS WISH TO EXPRESS THEIR APPRECIATION TO THE THEATRE DEVELOPMENT FUND FOR ITS SUPPORT OF THIS PRODUCTION.

3/26/09

Photo by Joan Marcus

(L-R): Susan Sarandon, William Sadler, Geoffrey Rush, Lauren Ambrose and Andrea Martin

Exit the King

Geoffrey Rush
*King Berenger and
Co-Translator*

Susan Sarandon
Queen Marguerite

Lauren Ambrose
Queen Marie

Andrea Martin
Juliette

William Sadler
The Doctor

Brian Hutchison
The Guard

Michael Hammond
*u/s King Berenger,
The Doctor*

David Manis
*u/s King Berenger,
The Guard*

Erika Rolfsrud
*u/s Queen Marie,
Queen Marguerite,
Juliette*

Eugène Ionesco
Playwright

Neil Armfield
*Director and
Co-Translator*

Paul Huntley
*Wig Design
Consultant*

Stuart Thompson
Producer

Robert Fox
Producer

Scott Rudin
Producer

Jon B. Platt
Producer

BOX OFFICE
(L-R): Steven De Luca, Diane Heatherington

HOUSE MANAGER
Dan Landon

Photos by Samantha Souza

Bob Weinstein,
The Weinstein
Company
Producer

Harvey Weinstein,
The Weinstein
Company
Producer

Philip J. Smith,
Chairman,
The Shubert
Organization
Producer

Robert E. Wankel
President,
The Shubert
Organization
Producer

FRONT OF HOUSE STAFF
Front Row (L-R): John Dancy, George Nestor, Michael Reilly, John Cashman
Back Row (L-R): John Barbaretti, Kathy Reiter, Nathaniel West, Aileen Kilburn

Exit the King

(L-R): Lauren Ambrose and Geoffrey Rush

Photo by Joan Marcus

STAFF FOR *EXIT THE KING*

GENERAL MANAGEMENT
STUART THOMPSON PRODUCTIONS
Stuart Thompson   Dana Sherman
James Triner   David Turner   Caroline Prugh

COMPANY MANAGER
Adam J. Miller

PRODUCTION MANAGEMENT
AURORA PRODUCTIONS INC.
Gene O'Donovan   W. Benjamin Heller II
Bethany Weinstein
Amy Merlino Coey   Melissa Mazdra
Laura Archer   Dana Hesch

PRESS REPRESENTATIVE
BONEAU/BRYAN-BROWN
Chris Boneau   Susanne Tighe   Christine Olver

Production Stage Manager	Evan Ensign
Stage Manager	Jim Woolley
Associate Scenic Designer	Ted LeFevre
Associate Costume Designer	Barry Doss
Associate Lighting Designer	Dan Walker
Associate Sound Designer	Joanna Lynne Staub
Wig Design Consultant	Paul Huntley
Production Carpenter	Tony Menditto
Production Electrician	Michael Hyman
Production Props	Dylan Foley
Production Sound	Jason McKenna
Wardrobe Supervisor	Eileen Miller
Hair Supervisor	Ruth Carsch
Make-Up Supervisor	Barry Berger
Dresser	Barry Doss
Production Assistant	Bryan Rountree
General Management Assistants	Quinn Corbin, Megan Curren, Geo Karapetyan
General Management Intern	Brittany Levasseur
Casting Associate	Camille Hickman
Musicians' Consultant to STP	Michael Keller
Banking	City National Bank/ Michele Gibbons
Payroll	Castellana Services, Inc.
Accountant	Fried & Kowgios CPAs LLP/ Robert Fried, CPA
Controller	Joe Kubala
Insurance	Stockbridge Risk Management, Inc./ Neil Goldstein
Legal Counsel	Franklin, Weinrib, Rudell & Vasallo, P.C./ Elliot H. Brown
Advertising	SPOTCO/ Drew Hodges, Jim Edwards, Tom Greenwald, Jim Aquino, Stacey Maya
Production Photographer	Joan Marcus
Susan Sarandon's Headshot	Nigel Parry
Theatre Displays	King Displays, Inc.

For Company B

Board Chair	Louise Herron
Artistic Director	Neil Armfield AO
General Manager	Brenna Hobson
Associate Artist	Wayne Blair
Artistic Associate	Eamon Flack
Artistic Administrator	John Woodland
Head of Finance & Operations	Richard Drysdale

For more information on current and touring productions visit www.belvoir.com.au

For Malthouse Melbourne

Artistic Director	Michael Kantor
Executive Producer	Stephen Armstrong
Associate Producer & Business Manager	Catherine Jones

For more information on current and touring productions visit www.malthousemelbourne.com

For Ambassador Theatre Group

Chairman	Sir Eddie Kulukundis OBE
Deputy Chairman	Peter Beckwith OBE
Joint Chief Executive & Creative Director	Howard Panter
Joint Chief Executive	Rosemary Squire OBE
Chief Executive Officer – New York	David Lazar
Producer	Tali Pelman
Production Associate – New York	Dan Gallagher

This translation by Neil Armfield and Geoffrey Rush was commissioned and first produced by Company B and Malthouse Melbourne premiering on March 29, 2007 in the Merlyn Theatre, CUB Malthouse, Melbourne.

Company B and Malthouse Melbourne acknowledge Bille Brown, Julie Forsyth, Gillian Jones, Rebecca Massey, Phil Slater, David Woods, Millie Mullinar and Jenn Blake.

CREDITS
Scenic elements by Showman Fabricators and Scenic Art Studios. Lighting equipment from Hudson Sound & Light, LLC. Sound equipment from PRG Audio. Costumes by Carelli Costumes, Inc. Costumes by Tricorne, Inc. Tiaras and jewelery by Lawrence Vrba. Shoes by LaDuca. Fabric painting by Acanthus Finishes. Armour by Valentine Armouries. Hosiery and undergarments by Bra*Tenders. Makeup provided by M•A•C.

Australia transportation by Qantas

Rehearsed at the New 42nd Street Studios

Exit the King
SCRAPBOOK

(L-R): Cast members Andrea Martin, Susan Sarandon and William Sadler, director/adapter Neil Armfield and cast members Geoffrey Rush, Lauren Ambrose and Brian Hutchison at the opening night party at Sardi's restaurant.

Photo by Aubrey Reuben

Correspondent: Evan Ensign, Stage Manager
Opening Night Gifts: We got a lot of fantastic gifts for opening. Geoffrey gave Susan a giant wheel of Jarlsberg cheese. It's from a line in the show. We also had a great, impromptu gathering when director Neil Armfield visited on his way back to Australia.
Most Exciting Celebrity Visitors: Susan had all the visiting celebs sign a poster in her dressing room which was donated to BC/EFA to auction off. On a single night we had Jane Fonda, Lynn Redgrave, Angela Lansbury and Jane Powell backstage at the same time!
Special Backstage Ritual: No big rituals. Everyone just tried to connect right before the show started. Brian Hutchison (the Guard) had to walk by everyone when he entered and Geoffrey would always say, "Shake it and bake it, tin man."

Favorite Moment During Each Performance: Waiting to find out how stage management would announce who was playing trumpet that evening.
Favorite In-Theatre Gathering Place: We gathered regularly in Susan's dressing room.
Favorite Off-Site Hangout: Geoffrey could be found at Bar Centrale three or four nights a week.
Favorite Snack Food: Susan would bring us incredible chocolate from Pure Dark. We all weigh 100 pounds more than when we started. Except Lauren—she's allergic to chocolate.
Mascot: Penny (Susan's dog).
Favorite Therapies: B-12 shots, Ricola, Tavist-D and Throat-Coat Tea...but the most important was Red Bull. Susan got Red Bull (along with the special Red Bull fridge) donated! Regular, Sugar Free and Cola!!!!

Memorable Fan Encounters: When Bryan Rountree (Susan and Geoffrey's PA) would have his picture taken with Susan's dog. We figure they'll look back at the pictures years from now and have no idea who it is or why they have the picture.
We also had two fans who would get student rush seats, sit in the front row and wear crowns during the curtain call. They were great and had terrific laughs.
Fastest Costume Change: No quick changes in this show. Geoffrey had about seven minutes to make his costume change, which was the fastest one.
Heaviest/Hottest Costume: Brian Hutchison had to wear a full suit of armor and had to stand for the entire show.
Who Wore the Least: Everyone wore a lot of clothes in this show.
Catchphrases Only the Company Would Recognize: "I am so tired, so tired, so tired." Or "I am here. I exist."
Memorable Directorial Note: Many fun notes but mostly we knew he was happy when he would skip around the room!
Nicknames: Our day doorman called Geoffrey "Godfrey."
Coolest Thing About Being in This Show: We all had the best time!
Other Memories: Jim Woolley, our Assistant Stage Manager, would give Geoffrey a Broadway musical theatre quiz at every matinee (every show toward the end of the run). Geoffrey did extremely well, only missing a few. We think Geoffrey beats out Frank Langella and Alfred Molina as president of the "Girlie Man Club," a club of straight men who should be gay because they know obscure show tunes, can whip up a Thai meal in 10 minutes from leftovers in the fridge when they find out that company is coming, and know their Italian shoe brands.

CREW
Seated (L-R): Jim Woolley (Stage Manager), Enrique Vega (Hair), Bryan Rountree (Stage Manager), Jason McKenna (Sound), Barry Doss (Wardrobe), Evan Ensign (Production Stage Manager)

Standing (L-R): Mike Hyman (Electrician), Victor Verdejo (Carpenter), Al Galvez (Flyman - in back), Ruth Carsch (Hair), Philip Feller (Props), Francine Schwartz-Buryiak (Wardrobe), Adam Miller (Company Manager)

Photo by Samantha Souza

God of Carnage

First Preview: February 28, 2009. Opened: March 22, 2009.
Still running as of May 31, 2009.

PLAYBILL

CAST
(in alphabetical order)
Alan ....JEFF DANIELS
Annette ....HOPE DAVIS
Michael ....JAMES GANDOLFINI
Veronica ....MARCIA GAY HARDEN

STANDBYS
For Alan, Michael:
BRUCE McCARTY
For Annette, Veronica:
CHARLOTTE MAIER

2008-2009 AWARDS

TONY AWARDS
Best Play
(Yasmina Reza)
Best Direction of a Play
(Matthew Warchus)
Best Actress in a Play
(Marcia Gay Harden)

OUTER CRITICS CIRCLE AWARDS
Outstanding New Broadway Play
(Yasmina Reza)
Outstanding Actress in a Play
(Marcia Gay Harden)

DRAMA LEAGUE AWARD
Distinguished Production of a Play

⊗ BERNARD B. JACOBS THEATRE
242 West 45th Street
A Shubert Organization Theatre

Philip J. Smith, *Chairman*   Robert E. Wankel, *President*

Robert Fox   David Pugh & Dafydd Rogers   Stuart Thompson
Scott Rudin   Jon B. Platt   The Weinstein Company
The Shubert Organization

Present

Jeff Daniels
Hope Davis
James Gandolfini
Marcia Gay Harden

GOD OF CARNAGE

by

Yasmina Reza

translated by

Christopher Hampton

Scenic and Costume Design
Mark Thompson

Lighting Design
Hugh Vanstone

Music
Gary Yershon

Sound Design
Simon Baker/Christopher Cronin

Casting
Daniel Swee

Production Stage Manager
Jill Cordle

Press Representative
Boneau/Bryan-Brown

Production Management
Aurora Productions

General Management
STP / David Turner

Directed by
Matthew Warchus

The Producers wish to express their appreciation to
Theatre Development Fund for its support of this production.

NOW **THAT'S** BROADWAY!

3/22/09

(L-R): Marcia Gay Harden,
Hope Davis, Jeff Daniels
and James Gandolfini.

Photo by Joan Marcus

God of Carnage

Jeff Daniels
Alan

Hope Davis
Annette

James Gandolfini
Michael

Marcia Gay Harden
Veronica

Charlotte Maier
*Standby Annette,
Veronica*

Bruce McCarty
*Standby Alan,
Michael*

Yasmina Reza
Playwright

Christopher Hampton
Translator

Matthew Warchus
Director

Mark Thompson
*Set and Costume
Design*

Hugh Vanstone
Lighting Design

Simon Baker
Sound Design

Christopher Cronin
Sound Design

Beatrice Terry
Associate Director

Robert Fox
Producer

Stuart Thompson
Producer

Scott Rudin
Producer

Jon B. Platt
Producer

Bob Weinstein,
The Weinstein
Company
Producer

Harvey Weinstein,
The Weinstein
Company
Producer

Philip J. Smith,
Chairman,
The Shubert
Organization
Producer

Robert E. Wankel,
President,
The Shubert
Organization
Producer

MANAGEMENT AND CREW
Front Row (L-R): Randy Zaibek, Kenneth J. McGee,
Chris Morey, Jill Cordle

Back Row (L-R): Fred Ricci, Herb Messing, Chip White,
Michael Van Praagh

BOX OFFICE
(L-R): Jules Ochoa,
Michael Kohlbrenner

FRONT OF HOUSE STAFF
Front Row (L-R): Billy Mitchell, Patanne McEvoy, John
Minore, Eva Frances Laskow

Back Row (L-R): Rose Ann Cipriano, Al Peay

God of Carnage
Scrapbook

Correspondent: Ken McGee, ASM
Memorable Notes: Nice notes from Joanne Woodward and Tom Hanks.
Opening Night Gifts: Stuffed hamster and Marcia giving her own hand-thrown pottery.
"Easter Bonnet" Sketch: All four cast members were judges, so we didn't have a sketch.
Who Has Done the Most Shows: Jeff Daniels.
Special Backstage Ritual: Everybody hugs each other right before the curtain goes up.
Favorite Moment During Each Performance: When Hope's character vomits.
Favorite In-Theatre Gathering Place: Jeff's music room.
Favorite Off-Site Hangout: Bar Centrale.
Favorite Therapy: Massage between shows on Saturday.
Cell Phone Rings, Texting or Tweeting Incidents: During one performance, as Hope was saying one of her lines: "…there's nothing worse than a cell phone!" a cell phone rang loudly in the audience at that exact moment!
Busiest Day at the Box Office: Day after opening.

The cast takes a curtain call on opening night.

Memorable Press Encounter: Broadway Stars Vanity Fair photo shoot.
Favorite Snack Food: Altoids.

Sweethearts Within the Company: Everybody!
Coolest Thing About Being in This Show: That it's a huge hit!

STAFF FOR *GOD OF CARNAGE*

GENERAL MANAGEMENT
STUART THOMPSON PRODUCTIONS
Stuart Thompson   David Turner
James Triner   Dana Sherman   Caroline Prugh

COMPANY MANAGER
Chris Morey

PRODUCTION MANAGEMENT
AURORA PRODUCTIONS INC.
Gene O'Donovan   W. Benjamin Heller II
Bethany Weinstein   Melissa Mazdra
Amy Merlino Coey   Laura Archer   Dana Hesch

PRESS REPRESENTATIVE
BONEAU/BRYAN-BROWN
Chris Boneau   Susanne Tighe
Christine Olver   Kelly Guiod

Production Stage Manager ....Jill Cordle
Stage Manager ....Kenneth J. McGee
Associate Director ....Beatrice Terry
Associate Scenic Designer ....Nancy Thun
Associate Costume Designer ....Daryl A. Stone
Associate Lighting Designer ....Ted Mather
Vocal Coach ....Deborah Hecht
Makeup Consultant ....Judy Chin
Production Electrician ....Randall Zaibek
Production Properties Coordinator ....Denise J. Grillo
Production Sound ....Brien Brannigan
Wardrobe Supervisor ....Kay Grunder
Dresser ....Derek Moreno
Assistants to the Lighting Designer ....Zack Brown,
                                        Michael Megliola
Production Assistant ....Nathan K. Claus
RADA Trainee
    Assistant Director ....Caroline (CJay) Ranger
General Management Assistants ....Quinn M. Corbin,
                        Megan E. Curren, Geo Karapetyan

General Management Intern ....Brittany Levasseur
Casting Associate ....Camille Hickman
Assistant to Mr. Fox ....Sarah Richardson
Assistant to Mr. Rudin ....Kevin Graham-Caso
Assistant to Mr. Platt ....Terrie Lootens
Banking ....City National Bank/Michele Gibbons
Payroll ....Castellana Services, Inc.
Accountant ....Fried & Kowgios CPA's LLP/
                                        Robert Fried, CPA
Controller ....Joe Kubala
Insurance ....Stockbridge Risk Management/
                                            Neil Goldstein
Legal Counsel ....Davis Wright Tremaine LLP/
                        M. Graham Coleman, Robert Driscoll
Advertising ....Serino Coyne Inc./
                            Greg Corradetti, Robert Jones,
                        Sean Pomposello, Danielle Boyle
Interactive Marketing Agency ....Situation Interactive/
                            Tom O'Connor, Jenn Elston,
                                            John Lanasa
Production Photographer ....Joan Marcus
Hope Davis Headshot ....Brigitte Lacombe
Theatre Displays ....King Displays, Inc.
Transportation ....IBA Limousine Inc.

STAFF FOR DAVID PUGH LIMITED
Chairman ....Michael Medwin
Directors ....David Pugh, Dafydd Rogers,
                                            George Biggs
PA to the Directors ....Jane Allen
Accounts ....Nick Payne
Casting ....Sarah Bird
Dramaturg ....Ruth Little
Associate Producer ....Mark Jenkyns
Executive Store Manager ....Stewart Pugh

CREDITS
Scenery by Miraculous Engineering. Props by Luca Cristani. Floor by Hudson Scenic Studios, Inc. Lighting by Production Resource Group. Sound by Sound Associates. Special Effect Machine by Rorschach PropFX. Custom suit

for James Gandolfini by Giliberto Tailors. Makeup provided by M•A•C. BlackBerry devices courtesy of BlackBerry. English Harbour Rum courtesy of Antiqua Distillery Ltd. Eyeglasses by Julio Santiago at Artsee Eyewear. Special thanks to Bra*Tenders for hosiery and undergarments. Additional props courtesy of George Fenmore Inc. Rehearsed at Manhattan Theatre Club Creative Space.

Grease

First Preview: July 24, 2007. Opened: August 19, 2007.
Closed January 4, 2009 after 31 Previews and 554 Performances.

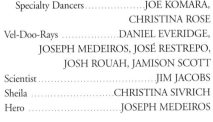

PLAYBILL

CAST

Danny Zuko	DEREK KEELING
Sandy Dumbrowski	ASHLEY SPENCER
Kenickie	ACE YOUNG
Sonny LaTierri	JOSÉ RESTREPO
Roger	WILL BLUM
Doody	RYAN PATRICK BINDER
Betty Rizzo	JANINE DiVITA
Marty	HELÉNE YORKE
Jan	LINDSAY MENDEZ
Frenchy	KIRSTEN WYATT
Patty Simcox	ALLISON FISCHER
Eugene Florczyk	JAMISON SCOTT
Miss Lynch	SUSAN BLOMMAERT
Vince Fontaine	DOMINIC V. FORTUNA
Cha-Cha DiGregorio	NATALIE HILL
Teen Angel	STEPHEN R. BUNTROCK

"Born to Hand-Jive"
Specialty Dancers .... JOE KOMARA,
CHRISTINA ROSE
Vel-Doo-Rays .... DANIEL EVERIDGE,
JOSEPH MEDEIROS, JOSÉ RESTREPO,
JOSH ROUAH, JAMISON SCOTT

Scientist	JIM JACOBS
Sheila	CHRISTINA SIVRICH
Hero	JOSEPH MEDEIROS

Ensemble .... NATALIE HILL, JOE KOMARA,
JOSEPH MEDEIROS, KEVEN QUILLON,
CHRISTINA ROSE, JOSH ROUAH,
ALLIE SCHULZ, CHRISTINA SIVRICH

Continued on next page

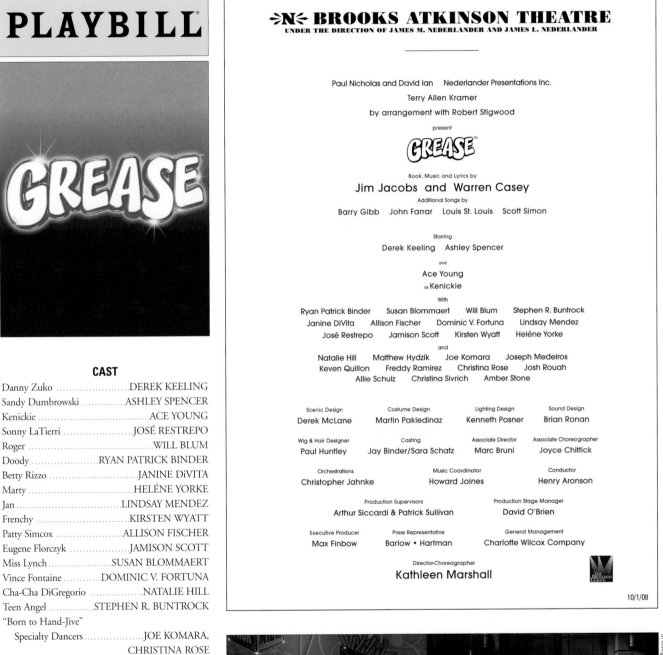

⇒N⇐ BROOKS ATKINSON THEATRE
UNDER THE DIRECTION OF JAMES M. NEDERLANDER AND JAMES L. NEDERLANDER

Paul Nicholas and David Ian   Nederlander Presentations Inc.

Terry Allen Kramer

by arrangement with Robert Stigwood

present

GREASE

Book, Music and Lyrics by

Jim Jacobs and Warren Casey

Additional Songs by

Barry Gibb   John Farrar   Louis St. Louis   Scott Simon

Starring

Derek Keeling   Ashley Spencer

and

Ace Young

as Kenickie

With

Ryan Patrick Binder   Susan Blommaert   Will Blum   Stephen R. Buntrock
Janine DiVita   Allison Fischer   Dominic V. Fortuna   Lindsay Mendez
José Restrepo   Jamison Scott   Kirsten Wyatt   Heléne Yorke

and

Natalie Hill   Matthew Hydzik   Joe Komara   Joseph Medeiros
Keven Quillon   Freddy Ramirez   Christina Rose   Josh Rouah
Allie Schulz   Christina Sivrich   Amber Stone

Scenic Design	Costume Design	Lighting Design	Sound Design
Derek McLane	Martin Pakledinaz	Kenneth Posner	Brian Ronan

Wig & Hair Designer	Casting	Associate Director	Associate Choreographer
Paul Huntley	Jay Binder/Sara Schatz	Marc Bruni	Joyce Chittick

Orchestrations	Music Coordinator	Conductor
Christopher Jahnke	Howard Joines	Henry Aronson

Production Supervisors	Production Stage Manager
Arthur Siccardi & Patrick Sullivan	David O'Brien

Executive Producer	Press Representative	General Management
Max Finbow	Barlow • Hartman	Charlotte Wilcox Company

Director-Choreographer

Kathleen Marshall

10/1/08

Ashley Spencer and Derek Keeling (center) sing "Summer Nights" with the Company.

Photo by Joan Marcus

Grease

SCENES AND MUSICAL NUMBERS

ACT I

Prologue

Scene 1: Rydell High, 1959
"Grease" ....Company

Scene 2: Cafeteria/School Steps
"Summer Nights" ....Danny, Sandy and Company

Scene 3: Locker Room
"Those Magic Changes" ....Doody and Company

Scene 4: Marty's Bedroom
"Freddy, My Love" ....Marty and Pink Ladies

Scene 5: Street Corner
"Greased Lightnin'" ....Kenickie and Guys

Scene 6: Rydell High
"Rydell Fight Song" ....Sandy and Patty

Scene 7: Bleachers
"Mooning" ....Roger and Jan
"Look at Me, I'm Sandra Dee" ....Rizzo
"We Go Together" ....T-Birds and Pink Ladies

ACT II

Scene 1: School Gym/Sandy's Room
"Shakin' at the High School Hop" ....Company
"It's Raining on Prom Night" ....Jan and Sandy
"Born to Hand-Jive" ....Vince and Company

Scene 2: School Steps
"Hopelessly Devoted to You" ....Sandy

Scene 3: Outside Burger Palace
"Beauty School Dropout" ....Teen Angel and Girls

Scene 4: Drive-In Movie
"Sandy" ....Danny

Scene 5: Jan's Rec Room
"Rock 'n' Roll Party Queen" ....Doody and Roger
"There Are Worse Things I Could Do" ....Rizzo
"Look at Me, I'm Sandra Dee" (Reprise) ....Sandy

Scene 6: Inside Burger Palace
"You're the One That I Want" ....Danny, Sandy and Company
"We Go Together" (Reprise) ....Company

"Grease" (Barry Gibb); ©1978 Crompton Songs (BMI). All rights reserved. Used by permission.

"Hopelessly Devoted to You" (John Farrar); ©1978 Unichappell-Stigwood Music (BMI), John Farrar Music (BMI) and Ensign Music Corporation (BMI). All rights on behalf of John Farrar Music (BMI) and Ensign Music Corporation (BMI). Administered by Unichappell-Stigwood Music Inc. (BMI). All rights reserved. Used by permission.

"Sandy" (Scott Simon, Louis St. Louis); ©1978 Ensign Music Corporation (BMI). All rights administered by Unichappell Music Inc. (BMI). All rights reserved. Used by permission.

"You're the One That I Want" (John Farrar); ©1978 Unichappell-Stigwood Music (BMI), John Farrar Music (BMI) and Ensign Music Corporation (BMI). All rights on behalf of John Farrar Music (BMI) and Ensign Music Corporation (BMI). Administered by Unichappell-Stigwood Music Inc. (BMI). All rights reserved. Used by permission.

Cast Continued

UNDERSTUDIES

For Danny, Teen Angel:
MATTHEW HYDZIK, JOSH ROUAH

For Sandy, Patty Simcox:
CHRISTINA ROSE, ALLIE SCHULZ

For Kenickie:
MATTHEW HYDZIK, JOSÉ RESTREPO

For Sonny LaTierri:
JOE KOMARA, KEVEN QUILLON

For Roger:
KEVEN QUILLON

For Doody:
JOSEPH MEDEIROS, KEVEN QUILLON

For Betty Rizzo:
NATALIE HILL, AMBER STONE

For Marty:
NATALIE HILL, CHRISTINA ROSE

For Jan, Frenchy:
CHRISTINA SIVRICH, AMBER STONE

For Eugene Florczyk:
JOE KOMARA, JOSEPH MEDEIROS

For Miss Lynch:
NATALIE HILL, CHRISTINA SIVRICH

For Vince Fontaine:
JOSH ROUAH, JAMISON SCOTT

For Cha-Cha DiGregorio:
ALLIE SCHULZ, AMBER STONE

For "Born to Hand-Jive" Dance Specialty:
MATTHEW HYDZIK, KEVEN QUILLON,
ALLIE SCHULZ, AMBER STONE

SWINGS

MATTHEW HYDZIK, FREDDY RAMIREZ,
AMBER STONE

DANCE CAPTAIN

AMBER STONE

BAND

Conductor/Synthesizer:
HENRY ARONSON

Associate Conductor/Piano/Synthesizer:
JOHN SAMORIAN

Drums:
JOHN CLANCY

Bass:
MICHAEL BLANCO

Guitars:
MICHAEL AARONS, JIM HERSHMAN

Tenor Sax/Woodwinds:
JOHN SCARPULLA

Woodwinds:
JACK BASHKOW

Music Coordinator:
HOWARD JOINES

Grease

Derek Keeling
Danny

Ashley Spencer
Sandy

Ace Young
Kenickie

Ryan Patrick Binder
Doody

Susan Blommaert
Miss Lynch

Will Blum
Roger

Stephen R. Buntrock
Teen Angel

Janine DiVita
Rizzo

Allison Fischer
Patty Simcox

Dominic V. Fortuna
Vince Fontaine

Lindsay Mendez
Jan

José Restrepo
Sonny

Jamison Scott
Eugene

Kirsten Wyatt
Frenchy

Heléne Yorke
Marty

Natalie Hill
Cha-Cha, Ensemble

Matthew Hydzik
Swing

Joe Komara
*Ensemble/Hand-Jive
Specialty Dancer*

Joseph Medeiros
Ensemble

Keven Quillon
Ensemble

Freddy Ramirez
Swing

Christina Rose
Ensemble

Josh Rouah
Ensemble

Allie Schulz
Ensemble

Christina Sivrich
Ensemble

Amber Stone
*Swing,
Dance Captain*

Jim Jacobs
*Book, Music and
Lyrics, On-Air Judge*

Warren Casey
*Book, Music and
Lyrics*

Kathleen Marshall
*Director and
Choreographer*

Derek McLane
Scenic Design

Martin Pakledinaz
Costume Design

Kenneth Posner
Lighting Designer

Brian Ronan
Sound Design

Paul Huntley
*Wig and Hair
Designer*

Joseph Dulude II
Make-Up Design

Grease

Jay Binder C.S.A.
Casting

Megan Larche
Casting

Henry Aronson
Conductor

Christopher Jahnke
Orchestrator

Howard Joines
Music Coordinator

Arthur Siccardi
*Production
Management*

Marc Bruni
Associate Director

Joyce Chittick
*Associate
Choreographer*

The Charlotte Wilcox
Company
General Manager

James L.
Nederlander,
Nederlander
Presentations Inc.
Producer

Terry Allen Kramer
Producer

GREASE
Alumni
2008-2009

Ashley Arcement
Swing

Jeb Brown
Vince Fontaine

Brian Crum
Swing

Max Crumm
Danny Zuko

Josh Franklin
*Vel-Doo-Ray,
Ensemble*

Cody Green
*"Born to Hand-Jive"
Dance Specialty*

Taylor Hicks
Teen Angel

Robyn Hurder
Marty

Lauralyn McClelland
Swing

Laura Osnes
Sandy Dumbrowski

Emily Padgett
Ensemble

Jenny Powers
Betty Rizzo

Matthew Saldívar
Kenickie

Brian Sears
*Hero, Vel-Doo-Ray,
Ensemble*

Anna Aimee White
*"Born to Hand-Jive"
Specialty Dancer,
Ensemble*

GREASE
Transfer Students
2008-2009

Ashley Arcement
Ensemble, Swing

Todd Buonopane
Roger, Vel-Doo-Ray

Holly Ann Butler
Swing

Xavier Cano
*Sonny LaTierri,
Vel-Doo-Ray*

Amanda Lea
LaVergne
*Cha-Cha DiGregorio,
Ensemble*

Mike McGowan
Vince Fontaine

Grease

Jason Wooten
Swing

WARDROBE AND HAIR
Front Row (Sitting, L-R):
Jack Curtin, Lisa Tucci.

Second Row (L-R):
Dana Calahan, Jorie Malan,
Cheryl Widner,
Theresa DiStasi,
Geoffrey Polischuk,
Karen L. Eifert,
Armando Licon,
Hilda Garcia-Suli.

Back Row (Standing, L-R):
Rosemary Keough,
Wendall Goings.

Photos by Ben Strothmann

PROPS
Front Row (Sitting, L-R): Billy Seelig, Steve DeVerna, Chuck Dague,
Jim Kane.

Back Row (Standing, L-R): Joseph DePaulo, Chris Pantuso.

CARPENTERS
(L-R): Tommy Lavaia, Mike Attianese, Ben Horrigan, Gerry Griffin,
Jerry Urcivoli, Jason Erny, Joe McCormick, Richie Fideli.

SOUND AND ELECTRICS
Front Row (L-R): Steve Clem, Manny Becker,
Susanne Williams, Michael "Jersey" Van Nest.

Back Row (L-R): Jeff Koger, Christopher
Robinson, Mike Farfalla.

Not Pictured: Brian GF McGarity.

FRONT OF HOUSE STAFF
Front Row (L-R): Joan Heller, Marie Gonzalez, Kimberlee Imperato.

Second Row (L-R): Kaitlin Dato, Jamie Zurich, Ilona Figueroa, Brenden Imperato, Brenda Schwarz.

Back Row (L-R): Susan Martin, Stephen Flaherty, Sam Figert, Robert Banyai.

Grease

STAGE MANAGEMENT
(L-R): David John O'Brien, Colleen Danaher, Stephen R. Gruse.

STAFF FOR *GREASE*

GENERAL MANAGEMENT
THE CHARLOTTE WILCOX COMPANY
Charlotte W. Wilcox

Matthew W. Krawiec   Dina S. Friedler
Steve Supeck   David Roth
Margaret Wilcox

GENERAL PRESS REPRESENTATIVE
BARLOW•HARTMAN

John Barlow   Michael Hartman
Ryan Ratelle   Melissa Bixler

COMPANY MANAGER
Alexandra Gushin Agosta

ASSISTANT COMPANY MANAGER
Michael Bolgar

CASTING
JAY BINDER CASTING
Jay Binder CSA
Jack Bowdan CSA, Mark Brandon, Sara Schatz
Assistants: Nikole Vallins, Kate Sprance, Karen Young

PRODUCTION STAGE MANAGER	DAVID JOHN O'BRIEN
Stage Manager	Stephen R. Gruse
Assistant Stage Manager	Colleen Danaher
Dance Captain	Amber Stone
Assistant Dance Captain	Keven Quillon
Assistant to the Director	Jenny Hogan
Associate Scenic Designer	Ted LeFevre
Assistant Scenic Designers	Anne Allen Goelz, Shoko Kambara
Assistant to the Scenic Designer	Erica Hemminger, Court Watson
Associate Costume Designer	Matthew Pachtman
Assistant Costume Designer	Sarah Sophia Turner
Assistant to the Costume Designer	Tescia Seufferlein
Associate Lighting Designer	Aaron Spivey
Assistant Lighting Designer	Kathleen Dobbins
Moving Light Programmer	David Arch
Assistant Sound Designer	Michael Creason

Production Electricians	James Fedigan, Randall Zaibek
Production Carpenter	Gerard Griffin
Production Flyman	Brian Hutchinson
Automation Carpenter	Benjamin Horrigan
Head Electrician	Brian GF McGarity
Production Sound Engineer	Michael Farfalla
Deck Sound	TJ McEvoy
Production Property Master	Christopher Pantuso
Wardrobe Supervisor	Lisa Tucci
Assistant Wardrobe Supervisor	Karen L. Eifert
Dressers	Elizabeth Cline, Hilda Garcia-Suli Wendall Goings, Rosemary Keough, Geoffrey Polischuk, Cheryl Widner
Stitcher	Dana Calaman
Associate Wig and Hair Designer	Giovanna Calabretta
Hair Supervisor	John "Jack" Curtin
Assistant Hair Supervisor	Armando Licon
Hair Dresser	Jorie Malan
Makeup Designer	Joe Dulude II
Associate Conductor	John Samorian
Synthesizer Programmer	Randy Cohen
Music Preparation Service	Mark Cumberland
Rehearsal Pianist	Chris Fenwick
Rehearsal Drummers	John Clancy, Joe Nero
Production Assistants	Sally Sibson, Jami Talbott
Music Department Intern	Eric Walton
Properties Intern	Christopher Digsby
Sound Intern	Kimberly Donowski
Assistant Synthesizer Programmer	Jim Mironchik
SDCF Observer	Jacob Toth
Legal Counsel	Franklin, Weinrib, Rudell & Vassallo, P.C., Elliot H. Brown, Esq., Daniel Wasser, Esq.
Accountants	Fried & Kowgios LLP, Robert Fried
Controller	Sarah Galbraith, Galbraith & Co Inc.
Advertising	Serino-Coyne, Angelo Desimini, Tom Callahan, Cara Christman, Matt Upshaw
Website Design	David Risley/Pygmalion Designs
Press Office Manager	Bethany Larson
Press Office Associates	Leslie Baden, Michelle Bergmann, Dennis Crowley, Tom D'Ambrosio, Matt Shea, Wayne Wolfe
Production Photography	Joan Marcus
Theatre Displays	King Displays, Inc.
Banking	JPMorgan Chase, Stephanie Dalton
Payroll Service	Castellana Services, Inc.
Opening Night Party Coordinator	Christopher Raphael, Cristina Baldacci/ The Really Spectacular Company, Inc.
Physical Therapy	PhysioArts
Massage Therapist	Russell Beasley, LMT
Company Orthopedist	David S. Weiss, MD
Merchandise	Rick Steiner and MCM Limelight
Insurance Consultant	Stockbridge Risk Management
Production Consultant	Christine D'Arienzo
Information Management Services	Marion Finkler Taylor
Travel Services	Andi Henig

CREDITS
Scenery by Hudson Scenic Studio, Inc. Automation by Hudson Scenic Studio, Inc. Costume construction by BaraCath Costumes; Barbara Matera Limited; Carelli Costumes, Inc.; Donna Langman Costumes; Eric Winterling, Inc.; Luigi's New York; Mardana; Maria Ficalora Knitwear, Ltd.; Paul Chang Custom Tailor; Seams Unlimited, Ltd.; Studio Rouge; Timberlake Studios, Inc.; and Tricorne, Inc. Custom fabric dyeing and printing by Gene Mignola, Inc., Jeff Fender. Millinery by Costume Armour, Lynne Mackey Studio, Arnold Levine, Marian "Killer" Hose and Leslie Norgate. Special thanks to Bra*Tenders for hosiery and undergarments. Custom footwear by LaDuca Shoes and Worldtone Dance. Lights by Hudson Sound & Light, LLC. Sound equipment by Production Resource Group. Properties by The Spoon Group. Custom car construction by Tom Carroll Scenery. Drums provided by Yamaha. Rehearsal piano provided by Baldwin. Guitars provided by Gibson. Guitar strings provided by D'Addario. Drop painted by Ryan Kravitz. Rehearsed at the New 42nd Street Studios. Natural herb cough drops courtesy of Ricola USA, Inc.

Makeup provided by M•A•C

STAFF FOR THE BROOKS ATKINSON THEATRE

House Manager	Susan Martin
Treasurer	Peter Attanasio
Assistant Treasurer	Anthony Giannone
House Carpenter	Thomas A. Lavaia
House Flyman	Joseph J. Maher
House Electrician	Manuel Becker
House Properties	Joseph P. DePaulo
Engineer	Kevin MacKay

Chairman	**James M. Nederlander**
President	**James L. Nederlander**

Executive Vice President
Nick Scandalios

Vice President
Corporate Development
Charlene S. Nederlander

Senior Vice President
Labor Relations
Herschel Waxman

Vice President
Jim Boese

Chief Financial Officer
Freida Sawyer Belviso

BOX OFFICE
(L-R): Robert Wilamowski, William O'Brien, Peter Attanasio.

Grease
SCRAPBOOK

Correspondent: Kirsten Wyatt, "Frenchy"

Memorable Opening Night Faxes: Our company received "Happy Opening" faxes from many other Broadway shows wishing us well. It's a wonderful tradition that really made us feel like a part of the community—especially with 14 Broadway debuts in our original company!

Opening Night Gift: My favorite was a fleece jacket with our Grease logo on it from Kathleen Marshall. If you ever walked backstage before the show, you were usually in a swarm of "*Grease* Fleece" because we all warmed up in them.

Most Exciting Celebrity Visitors: Olivia Newton-John, star of the *Grease* movie, watched our show one night, joined us on stage for the curtain call and then spoke about breast cancer awareness. It was an honor to meet such an icon and to see her really use her celebrity status to impact the world in a positive way.

I also got to meet Didi Conn, who played Frenchy in the movie. Not only did she look beautiful, but she was possibly one of the nicest people I've ever met.

Most Roles: My guess would be our swing and dance captain Amber Stone. She covered and performed each of the three ensemble women, one of the women in "Beauty School Dropout," Frenchy, Jan and occasionally had to play a boy in "Greased Lightning."

Most Shows in Their Career: I think Stephen Buntrock wins that category with *Grease* being his seventh Broadway show.

Special Backstage Ritual: We had a very special award called "The Buntrocky" which would be presented to an individual in the case of a major stage faux pas. I won't go into too many details but let's just say the ceremony included a mariachi band. The Buntrocky would be given in instances of missed entrances, wigs falling off in dance numbers and for someone (I won't name names) performing their big number in their socks because they forgot their shoes.

Favorite Moment: Our stage was set up so that most of the time there was no cross over available from stage right to stage left. This meant that we had to go down three flights of stairs on stage right, cross in the basement and then climb another three flights of stairs to finally arrive on stage left. Eventually Lindsay Mendez and I were granted the honor of crossing upstage of the scenery by our head carpenter, Tommy LaVaia. Tommy would escort us from stage right to behind the scenery, shine a flashlight for us so we could cross over and arrive safely on stage left. It was something he happily did for only the two of us every night and our knees thank him. I can honestly say there was something very special about the men and women of our *Grease* crew. We had a BLAST and I am so thankful to have worked with each and every one of them.

Cast members pose at the September "Broadway on Broadway" event in Times Square.

In-Theatre Gathering Places: We always gathered in one of two places: the stage managers' office or Dressing Room B3 which was the Teen Angel/Vince Fontaine dressing room. They had a TV with the Food Network and a couch.

Off-Site Hangout: Trecolori, the Italian restaurant right next door to the theater. It is this great little family run restaurant with FANTASTIC food and great service. They became a big part of our *Grease* family and I'd like to think we became part of theirs.

Favorite Snack Food: The hair room had good snacks. My favorite was when they had Dill Pickle Pringles. Delicious!! Don't knock it 'til you try it. And you could always walk into the Jan/Miss Lynch/Marty dressing room for a mid-show chocolate pick-me-up.

Mascot: Patty Simcox (a.k.a. Allison Fischer)

Favorite Therapies: We were big on Tiger Balm and foam rollers.

Memorable Ad-Lib: Ace Young going up on his lines and saying the first thing he could think of, which was, "It's all about me!"

Cell Phone Issues: I don't know about number of rings, but if we did hear cell phones it would consistently be in one spot. There was only one really quiet moment in *Grease*: when Rizzo tells Kenickie she thinks she's pregnant. She would tell him and he would be silent for a few seconds before he responded and then exited. I can think of at least three times when a phone rang during that silence. It's called vibrate, people!

Stage Door Fan Encounter: Many times in between our matinee and evening shows I would order food and just stay inside the theatre. One afternoon the doorman found me and said there was someone waiting outside to meet me. I walked out of the stage door and there was this tiny little 4-year-old girl all dressed up as Frenchy in a pink wig and in a homemade Pink Ladies Jacket. She and her parents had waited for me because Frenchy was her favorite. It was one of the cutest things I've ever seen.

Catchphrases Only the Company Would Recognize: "This is not a resting spot, people!"

Company In-Jokes: The Ratz, The Debbie and Duncan/Chip/Diddy Nightly Challenge.

Embarrassing Moments: In our show Marty's bedroom was a giant Barbie carrying case that the Pink Ladies would have to unlock and open and then we'd start the scene. One night, no matter how hard we tried, the unit would not unlock. We were furiously attempting to open it while trying to make it seem like nothing was wrong, but eventually the audience started laughing and we started laughing and everything kind of dissolved. Finally, the curtain was brought in, the problem was taken care of and we started over. I remember the audience yelling and clapping as the curtain rose. They love it when that stuff happens!

Coolest Thing About Being in This Show: Many times when I would talk to audience members at the stage door they'd tell me not only how much they loved *Grease* but that it was their first Broadway show. This was especially true of kids. I'd like to think that in some small way we were helping to create Broadway's next generation.

Guys and Dolls

First Preview: February 5, 2009. Opened: March 1, 2009.
Still running as of May 31, 2009.

PLAYBILL

CAST

(in order of appearance)

Nicely-Nicely Johnson	TITUSS BURGESS
Benny Southstreet	STEVE ROSEN
Rusty Charlie	SPENCER MOSES
Sarah Brown	KATE JENNINGS GRANT
Agatha	ANDREA CHAMBERLAIN
Martha	JESSICA RUSH
Calvin	WILLIAM RYALL
Arvide Abernathy	JIM ORTLIEB
Harry the Horse	JIM WALTON
Lt. Brannigan	ADAM LeFEVRE
Nathan Detroit	OLIVER PLATT
Angie the Ox	GRAHAM ROWAT
Society Max	JAMES HARKNESS
Liver Lips Louie	NICK ADAMS
Damon	RAYMOND DEL BARRIO
The Greek	JOSEPH MEDEIROS
Brandy Bottle Bates	RON TODOROWSKI
Scranton Slim	JOHN SELYA
Sky Masterson	CRAIG BIERKO
Mimi	LORIN LATARRO
Joey Biltmore	BRIAN SHEPARD
Adelaide	LAUREN GRAHAM
General Cartwright	MARY TESTA
Big Jule	GLENN FLESHLER
Carmen	KEARRAN GIOVANNI
Hot Box Girls	KEARRAN GIOVANNI, LORIN LATARRO, RHEA PATTERSON, JESSICA RUSH, JENNIFER SAVELLI, BROOKE WENDLE

Continued on next page

Continued on next page

≈N≈ NEDERLANDER THEATRE

UNDER THE DIRECTION OF
JAMES M. NEDERLANDER AND JAMES L. NEDERLANDER

HOWARD PANTER FOR AMBASSADOR THEATRE GROUP
NORTHWATER ENTERTAINMENT

TULCHIN/BARTNER
DARREN BAGERT

BILL KENWRIGHT
TOM GREGORY

NEDERLANDER PRESENTATIONS, INC.
INDEPENDENT PRESENTERS NETWORK

with
DAVID MIRVISH
OLYMPUS THEATRICALS

MICHAEL JENKINS/DALLAS SUMMER MUSICALS
SONIA FRIEDMAN PRODUCTIONS

present

**OLIVER PLATT
CRAIG BIERKO**

**LAUREN GRAHAM
KATE JENNINGS GRANT**

in

Guys AND DOLLS

A MUSICAL FABLE OF BROADWAY
BASED ON A STORY AND CHARACTERS OF DAMON RUNYON

Music and Lyrics by
FRANK LOESSER

Book by
JO SWERLING AND ABE BURROWS

With

TITUSS BURGESS
JIM ORTLIEB

GLENN FLESHLER
STEVE ROSEN

ADAM LEFEVRE
MARY TESTA

NICK ADAMS ANDREA CHAMBERLAIN RAYMOND DEL BARRIO MELISSA FAGAN KEARRAN GIOVANNI JAMES HARKNESS LORIN LATARRO
BENJAMIN MAGNUSON JOSEPH MEDEIROS SPENCER MOSES RHEA PATTERSON GRAHAM ROWAT JESSICA RUSH WILLIAM RYALL MARCOS SANTANA
JENNIFER SAVELLI JOHN SELYA BRIAN SHEPARD RON TODOROWSKI JIM WALTON BROOKE WENDLE

Scenery Design	Costume Design	Lighting Design	Sound Design
ROBERT BRILL	PAUL TAZEWELL	HOWELL BINKLEY	STEVE CANYON KENNEDY
Video Design	Hair & Wig Design	Fight Director	Casting
DUSTIN O'NEILL	CHARLES LAPOINTE	STEVE RANKIN	TARA RUBIN CASTING
Orchestrations	Dance Arrangements	Conductor	Music Coordinator
BRUCE COUGHLIN	JAMES LYNN ABBOTT	JEFFREY KLITZ	MICHAEL KELLER
Marketing Direction	Technical Supervision	Press Representative	Production Stage Manager
TYPE A MARKETING/ ANNE RIPPEY	DON S. GILMORE	BARLOW-HARTMAN	FRANK HARTENSTEIN

General Management
ALCHEMY PRODUCTION GROUP
CARL PASBJERG & FRANK SCARDINO

Associate Producers
JILL LENHART
PETER GODFREY

Executive Producer
DAVID LAZAR

Music Direction, Vocal Arrangements and Incidental Music
TED SPERLING

Choreography by
SERGIO TRUJILLO

Directed by
DES McANUFF

3/1/09

Oliver Platt (center) and Gamblers

Photo by Carol Rosegg

Guys and Dolls

MUSICAL NUMBERS

ACT I

Overture	The Orchestra
"Runyonland"	The Company
"Fugue for Tinhorns"	Nicely-Nicely, Benny and Rusty
"Follow the Fold"	Sarah, Arvide, Calvin, Martha and Agatha
"The Oldest Established"	Nicely-Nicely, Benny, Nathan and Crapshooters
"Follow the Fold" (Reprise)	Sarah, Arvide, Calvin, Martha and Agatha
"I'll Know"	Sarah and Sky
"A Bushel and a Peck"	Adelaide and the Hot Box Girls
"Adelaide's Lament"	Adelaide
"Guys and Dolls"	Nicely-Nicely and Benny
"Havana"	The Company
"If I Were a Bell"	Sarah
"My Time of Day"	Sky
"I've Never Been in Love Before"	Sky and Sarah

ACT II

Entr'acte	The Orchestra
"Take Back Your Mink"	Adelaide and the Hot Box Girls
"Adelaide's Lament" (Reprise)	Adelaide
"More I Cannot Wish You"	Arvide
"The Crapshooter's Dance"	The Crapshooters
"Luck Be a Lady"	Sky and the Crapshooters
"Sue Me"	Adelaide and Nathan
"Sit Down, You're Rockin' the Boat"	Nicely-Nicely and the Company
"Follow the Fold" (Reprise)	The Company
"Marry the Man Today"	Adelaide and Sarah
"Guys and Dolls" (Reprise)	The Company

ORCHESTRA

Conductor: JEFFREY KLITZ
Associate Conductor: JEFF MARDER
Concertmaster: CENOVIA CUMMINS
Violins: LORI MILLER, MING YEH
Cello 1: MAIRI DORMAN-PHANEUF
Cello 2: SARAH HEWITT-ROTH
Lead Trumpet: DON DOWNS
Trumpet: CJ CAMERIERI
Trombone: MIKE DAVIS
Bass Trombone/Tuba: MATT INGMAN
Reed 1: TOM MURRAY
Reed 2: KEN DUBISZ
Reed 3: MARK THRASHER
Keyboard: JEFF MARDER
Guitar/Banjo: GREG UTZIG
Bass: MARK VANDERPOEL
Drums: STEVE BARTOSIK
Percussion: JAVIER DIAZ
Music Coordinator: MICHAEL KELLER
Keyboard Programmer: RANDY COHEN

Cast Continued

SETTING

New York City in the time of Damon Runyon

ENSEMBLE

NICK ADAMS, ANDREA CHAMBERLAIN,
RAYMOND DEL BARRIO,
KEARRAN GIOVANNI, JAMES HARKNESS,
LORIN LATARRO, JOSEPH MEDEIROS,
SPENCER MOSES, RHEA PATTERSON,
GRAHAM ROWAT, JESSICA RUSH,
WILLIAM RYALL, JENNIFER SAVELLI,
JOHN SELYA, BRIAN SHEPARD,
RON TODOROWSKI, JIM WALTON,
BROOKE WENDLE

SWINGS

MELISSA FAGAN, BENJAMIN MAGNUSON,
MARCOS SANTANA

DANCE CAPTAIN

MARCOS SANTANA

UNDERSTUDIES

For Sky Masterson:
GRAHAM ROWAT

For Nathan Detroit:
ADAM LeFEVRE

For Nicely-Nicely Johnson:
JIM WALTON

For Arvide Abernathy:
WILLIAM RYALL

For Lt. Brannigan:
JIM WALTON

For Benny Southstreet:
BEN MAGNUSON

For Big Jule:
WILLIAM RYALL

For Sarah Brown:
JESSICA RUSH

For Adelaide:
ANDREA CHAMBERLAIN, LORIN LATARRO

For General Cartwright:
ANDREA CHAMBERLAIN

Lauren Graham,
as Miss Adelaide,
sings "Take Back
Your Mink."

Photo by Carol Rosegg

Guys and Dolls

Oliver Platt
Nathan Detroit

Lauren Graham
Miss Adelaide

Craig Bierko
Sky Masterson

Kate Jennings Grant
Sarah Brown

Tituss Burgess
Nicely-Nicely Johnson

Glenn Fleshler
Big Jule

Adam LeFevre
Lt. Brannigan

Jim Ortlieb
Arvide Abernathy

Steve Rosen
Benny Southstreet

Mary Testa
General Cartwright

Nick Adams
Liver Lips Louie, Ensemble

Andrea Chamberlain
Agatha, Ensemble

Raymond Del Barrio
Damon, Ensemble

Melissa Fagan
Swing

Kearran Giovanni
Carmen, Hot Box Girl, Ensemble

James Harkness
Society Max, Ensemble

Lorin Latarro
Mimi, Hot Box Girl, Ensemble

Benjamin Magnuson
Swing

Joseph Medeiros
The Greek, Ensemble

Spencer Moses
Rusty Charlie, Ensemble

Rhea Patterson
Hot Box Girl, Ensemble

Graham Rowat
Angie the Ox, Ensemble

Jessica Rush
Martha, Ensemble

William Ryall
Calvin, Ensemble

Marcos Santana
Swing/ Dance Captain

Jennifer Savelli
Hot Box Girl, Ensemble

John Selya
Scranton Slim, Ensemble

Brian Shepard
Joey Biltmore, Ensemble

Ron Todorowski
Brandy Bottle Bates, Ensemble

Jim Walton
Harry the Horse, Ensemble

Brooke Wendle
Hot Box Girl, Ensemble

Frank Loesser
Music and Lyrics

Des McAnuff
Director

Sergio Trujillo
Choreographer

Ted Sperling
Music Director, Vocal and Incidental Music Arrangements

Guys and Dolls

Robert Brill
Set Design

Paul Tazewell
Costume Design

Howell Binkley
Lighting Design

Steve Canyon
Kennedy
Sound Design

Steve Rankin
Fight Director

Tara Rubin Casting
Casting

Bruce Coughlin
Orchestrations

James Lynn Abbott
Dance Arrangements

Jeffrey Klitz
Conductor

Michael Keller
Music Coordinator

Bill Kenwright
Producer

Darren Bagert
Producer

James L.
Nederlander,
Nederlander
Presentations, Inc.
Producer

Michael A. Jenkins/
Dallas Summer
Musicals
Producer

Sonia Friedman
Productions
Producer

Alissa Zulvergold
Production Assistant

Barrett Martin
*Society Max,
Ensemble*

CAST AND CREW

Guys and Dolls

CREW
Front Row (L-R): Kelly Martindale (Production Stage Manager), Jason Bowles (Props), Tasha Cowd (Wardrobe), Kyle Wesson (Wardrobe), Michele Rutter (Hair Supervisor), Alex Lyu Volckhausen (Stage Manager), Andrew C. Gottlieb (ASM)

Back Row (L-R): Michael D. Hannah (Wardrobe), Dave Cohen (Carpenter), Frank (Wardrobe), John (Props), Maureen George (Wardrobe), Gus Poitras (Carpenter), Pamela Pierzina (Wardrobe), Dora Suarez (Wardrobe), Mary Kay Yezerski-Bondoc (Hair), Rick Caroto (Hair), Christel Murdoch (Wardrobe), Paul Wimmer (Carpenter), Chris Pantuso (Props), Jenny Slattery (ASM), Brett Bingman (Sound), Charlie Gravina (Carpenter)

ORCHESTRA
Kneeling (L-R): Lori Miller, Jeff Marder, Mark Thrasher

Standing (L-R): Steve Bartosik, Ming Yeh, Sarah Hewitt-Roth, Matt Ingman, Mairi Dorman-Phaneuf, Greg Thymius, Kory Grossman

Not pictured: Cenovia Cummins, C.J. Camerieri, Don Downs, Mike Davis, Ken Dubisz, Tom Murray, Greg Utzig, Mark Vanderpoel, Javier Diaz, Jeff Klitz

Photos by Samantha Souza

FRONT OF HOUSE STAFF
First Row (L-R): Sonny Curry, Marlon Pichardo, Louise Angelino (House Manager), Shannon Luker, Iris Cortes, Ralph Hendrix

Middle Row (L-R): Eddie Cuevas, Angel Diaz, Junesse Cartagena

Back Row (L-R): Brian Baeza, Terrence Cummiskey, Katie Spillane, Joaquin Quintana, Joe Santiago

BOX OFFICE
(L-R): Gary Kenny (Treasurer), Erich Stollberger, Christina Kenny

Guys and Dolls

STAFF FOR *GUYS AND DOLLS*

GENERAL MANAGEMENT
ALCHEMY PRODUCTION GROUP
Carl Pasbjerg   Frank P. Scardino

COMPANY MANAGER
JIM BRANDEBERRY

GENERAL PRESS REPRESENTATIVE
BARLOW•HARTMAN
John Barlow   Michael Hartman
Juliana Hannett   Michelle Bergmann

CASTING
TARA RUBIN CASTING
Tara Rubin CSA, Merri Sugarman CSA, Dale Brown,
Eric Woodall CSA, Laura Schutzel CSA,
Paige Blansfield, Rebecca Carfagna, Kaitlin Shaw

MAKE-UP DESIGNER
ANGELINA AVALLONE

VIDEO CONTENT PRODUCTION
THE ORACLE GROUP/Ari Novak

MARKETING
TYPE A MARKETING
Anne Rippey   Jeanette Roush   Nick Pramik

Associate General Manager ....Chris Morey
Production Stage Manager ....Frank Hartenstein
Stage Manager ....Kelly Martindale
Assistant Stage Manager ....Alex Lyu Volckhausen
Assistant Company Manager ....Sherra Johnston
Associate to the General Managers ....Tegan Meyer
Dance Captain ....Marcos Santana
Fight Captain ....Graham Rowat
Dialect Coach ....Stephen Gabis
Dramaturg ....James Magruder
Assistant Director ....Shelley Butler
Associate Choreographer ....Jane Lanier
Associate Scenic Designer ....Dustin O'Neill
Associate Costume Designer ....Nancy Palmatier
Associate Lighting Designer ....Mark Simpson
Associate Sound Designer ....Andrew Keister
Associate Hair Designer ....Leah Loukas
Assistant Set Designers ....Erica Hemminger,
Steven Kemp, Caleb Levengood,
Angrette McCloskey, Michael Locher,
Daniel Meeker
Assistant Costume Designers ....Michael Zecker,
Courtney Watson, Maria Zamansky,
Caitlin Hunt
Assistant Lighting Designer ....Christian DeAngelis
Moving Light Programmer ....David Arch
Video Programmer ....Thomas Hague
Sound Programmer ....Wallace Flores
Production Carpenter ....Fred Gallo
Head Carpenter ....Todd Frank
Assistant Carpenters ....Scott Poitras, David Cohen
Production Electrician ....James Fedigan
Head Electrician ....Eric Norris
Assistant Electricians ....Gary Fernandez,
Lorne MacDougall
Production Property Master ....Chris Pantuso

Assistant Property Master ....Jason Bowles
Head Sound Engineer ....Julie Randolph
Assistant Sound Engineer ....Brett Bingman
Sound Associate ....Stephanie Celustka
Wardrobe Supervisor ....Debbie Cheretun
Associate Wardrobe Supervisor ....Jim Hall
Dressers ....Don Bonilla, Fred Castner,
Suzanne Delahunt, Maureen George,
Betty Gillispie, Jim Hodun, Bob Kwiatkowski,
Pamela Pierzina, Kyle Wesson
Hair Supervisor ....Michele Rutter
Assistant Hair Supervisor ....Mary Kay Yezerski-Bondoc
Hair Stylist ....Rick Caroto
Music Copying ....Emily Grishman Music Preparation/
Emily Grishman, Katharine Edmonds
Asst. Keyboard Programmers ....Jim Mironenik,
Bryan Crook
Music Intern ....Oran Eldor
Production Assistants ....Jenny Slattery,
Andrew Gottlieb, Alissa Zulvergold
Executive Assistant to Des McAnuff ....Jay Turton
Physical Therapy ....Performing Arts Physical Therapy
Advertising...SpotCo/
Drew Hodges, Jim Edwards,
Tom Greenwald, Jim Aquino, Stacey Maya
Production Photographer ....Carol Rosegg
Accountant ....Fried & Kowgios LLC/Robert Fried
Controller ....Galbraith & Co/
Sarah Galbraith
Legal Counsel .....Franklin Weinrib Rudell & Vassallo PC/
Elliot Brown, Dan Wasser
SSDC Director Observer ....David Alpert
SDCF Choreographic Observer ....Kevin Hill
Scenic Design Intern ....Hannah Hogan
Associate Producer/Infinity Stages ....Adam Sansiveri
Payroll Services ....Castellana Services, Inc.
Banking ....TD Bank/Olivia Cassin
Insurance ....Dewitt Stern Inc./
Pete Shoemaker, Rebecca Alspector
Opening Night Coordination ....McNabb Roick/
Jim McNabb, Ty Kuppig
Theatre Displays ....King Displays, Inc.

CREDITS
Scenic Technologies. Sign-A-Rama. Lighting equipment
from Production Resource Group. Sound by Sound
Associates. Costumes by Matera, Tricorne. Overcoats by
Giliberto Designs, Inc. Millinery by Lynne Mackey Studio.
Keyboard by Yamaha.

THE AMBASSADOR THEATRE GROUP LTD.
Chairman ....Sir Eddie Kulukundis OBE
Deputy Chairman ....Peter Beckwith OBE
Joint Chief Executive &
    Creative Director ....Howard Panter
Joint Chief Executive ....Rosemary Squire OBE
Operations &
    Building Development Director ....David Blyth
Finance & Commercial Director ....Helen Enright
Executive Director ....Michael Lynas
Business Affairs Director ....Peter Kavanagh

AMBASSADOR THEATRE GROUP – New York
Chief Executive Officer ....David Lazar
Production Associate ....Dan Gallagher

TULCHIN/BARTNER PRODUCTIONS, LLC
Robert G. Bartner ....Producer
Norman Tulchin ....Producer
Steven Tulchin ....Producer
Lauren Doll ....Associate Producer
Mario Aiello ....General Manager
Sarah Nashman.....................Production Assistant
Anna Parrotta ....Assistant to the General Manager

GUYS AND DOLLS
Rehearsed at the New 42nd Street Studios.

Souvenir merchandise designed and created by
The Araca Group.

NEDERLANDER

Chairman ....James M. Nederlander
President ....James L. Nederlander

Executive Vice President
Nick Scandalios

Vice President   Senior Vice President
Corporate Development   Labor Relations
Charlene S. Nederlander   **Herschel Waxman**

Vice President   Chief Financial Officer
Jim Boese   **Freida Sawyer Belviso**

STAFF FOR THE NEDERLANDER THEATRE
House Manager ....Louise Angelino
Treasurer ....Gary Kenny
Assistant Treasurer ....Keshave Sattaur
House Carpenter ....Joseph Ferreri Sr.
Flyman ....Joseph Ferreri Jr.
House Electrician ....Richard Beck
House Properties ....William Wright

Photo by Carol Rosegg

(L-R): Craig Bierko and
Kate Jennings Grant

Gypsy

SCENES AND MUSICAL NUMBERS

ACT ONE

Overture		The Orchestra
Scene 1:	Vaudeville theatre stage. Seattle.	
	"May We Entertain You"	Baby June and Baby Louise
Scene 2:	Kitchen. Seattle.	
	"Some People"	Rose
Scene 3:	Road between Seattle and Los Angeles.	
	Reprise: "Some People"	Rose
Scene 4:	Backstage of vaudeville theatre. Los Angeles.	
	"Small World"	Rose and Herbie
Scene 5:	Stage of vaudeville theatre. Los Angeles.	
	"Baby June and Her Newsboys"	Baby June, Baby Louise and Newsboys
Scene 6:	Hotel room. Akron.	
	"Have an Eggroll, Mr. Goldstone"	Rose, Herbie, June, Mr. Goldstone and Boys
	"Little Lamb"	Louise
Scene 7:	Chinese restaurant. New York.	
	"You'll Never Get Away From Me"	Rose and Herbie
Scene 8:	Stage of Grantziger's Palace Theatre. New York.	
	"Dainty June and Her Farmboys"	Dainty June and Farmboys
Scene 9:	Mr. Grantziger's office.	
	"If Momma Was Married"	Louise and June
Scene 10:	Theatre alley. Buffalo.	
	"All I Need Is the Girl"	Tulsa and Louise
Scene 11:	Railway station. Omaha.	
	"Everything's Coming Up Roses"	Rose

ACT TWO

Entr'acte		The Orchestra
Scene 1:	Desert. Texas.	
	"Madame Rose's Toreadorables"	Louise and the Hollywood Blondes
	"Together Wherever We Go"	Rose, Herbie and Louise
Scene 2:	Backstage of a burlesque house. Wichita.	
	"You Gotta Get a Gimmick"	Mazeppa, Electra and Tessie Tura
Scene 3:	Backstage corridor. Wichita.	
Scene 4:	Backstage and onstage: Wichita, Detroit, Philadelphia and Minsky's Burlesque.	
	"The Strip"	Louise
Scene 5:	Louise's dressing room, Minsky's Burlesque.	
Scene 6:	Stage.	
	"Rose's Turn"	Rose

ORCHESTRA

Conductor: PATRICK VACCARIELLO
Violins: MARILYN REYNOLDS,
    FRITZ KRAKOWSKI, ERIC DEGIOIA,
    DANA IANCULOVICI
Violas: CRYSTAL GARNER, SALLY SHUMWAY
Cello: PETER PROSSER, VIVIAN ISRAEL
Bass: BRIAN CASSIER
Woodwinds: EDWARD SALKIN,
    ADAM KOLKER, DENNIS ANDERSON,
    RALPH OLSEN, JOHN WINDER

Trumpets: TONY KADLECK,
    JAMES DELAGARZA, KAMAU ADILIFU
Trombones: BRUCE EIDEM,
    WAYNE GOODMAN, ROBERT FOURNIER
French Horn: NANCY BILLMAN
Harp: SUSAN JOLLES
Keyboards: JEFFREY HARRIS
Drums: PAUL PIZZUTI
Percussion: THAD WHEELER
Music Coordinator: SEYMOUR RED PRESS

Cast Continued

Edna Mae	NANCY RENÉE BRAUN
Carol Ann	SARAH MARIE HICKS
Betsy Ann	BECKLEY ANDREWS
Cigar	BILL RAYMOND
Pastey	JIM BRACCHITTA
Tessie Tura	ALISON FRASER
Mazeppa	LENORA NEMETZ
Electra	MARILYN CASKEY
Renée	JESSICA RUSH
Phil	BRIAN REDDY
Bougeron-Cochon	BILL BATEMAN

STANDBYS

For Rose: LINDA BALGORD
Herbie: JIM BRACCHITTA, ANDREW BOYER
Louise: JESSICA RUSH, LISA ROHINSKY
Dainty June: MINDY DOUGHERTY,
    NICOLE MANGI
Tulsa: PEARCE WEGENER, MATTY PRICE
Tessie Tura: DOROTHY STANLEY
Mazeppa, Electra, Miss Cratchitt:
    DOROTHY STANLEY, JESSICA RUSH
Georgie: MATT GIBSON
Bougeron-Cochon: JOHN SCACCHETTI
Uncle Jocko: ANDREW BOYER, MATTY PRICE
Pastey: PEARCE WEGENER, MATT GIBSON
Baby Louise, Baby June:
    JACLYN TAYLOR RUGGIERO
Baby June: KATIE MICHA
Goldstone: ANDREW BOYER
Cigar, Pop, Weber: ANDREW BOYER,
    BILL BATEMAN
Phil: ANDREW BOYER, JOHN SCACCHETTI
Balloon Girl, Agnes: ALICIA SABLE
Military Boys: KYRIAN FRIEDENBERG
Newsboys: RIDER QUENTIN STANTON
Yonkers, L.A., Kansas: MATTY PRICE,
    MATT GIBSON
Renée, Waitress: NANCY RENÉE BRAUN,
    LISA ROHINSKY

Swings: MATT GIBSON, LISA ROHINSKY

Dance Captain: BILL BATEMAN

Leigh Ann Larkin and Caroline the Cow

Photo by Paul Kolnik

Gypsy

Patti LuPone
Rose

Boyd Gaines
Herbie

Laura Benanti
Louise

Leigh Ann Larkin
Dainty June

Tony Yazbeck
Tulsa

Marilyn Caskey
Electra

Alison Fraser
Tessie Tura

Lenora Nemetz
*Mazeppa,
Miss Cratchitt*

Bill Bateman
*Georgie,
Mr. Goldstone,
Bougeron-Cochon,
Dance Captain*

Jim Bracchitta
*Uncle Jocko, Pastey,
Standby Herbie*

Sami Gayle
Baby June

Katie Micha
*Baby Louise,
Standby Baby June*

Bill Raymond
Pop, Cigar

Brian Reddy
Weber, Phil

Andrew Boyer
*Standby Herbie,
Goldstone,
Uncle Jocko, Pop,
Cigar, Weber, Phil*

Dorothy Stanley
*Standby Electra,
Mazeppa,
Tessie Tura,
Miss Cratchitt*

Beckley Andrews
Betsy Ann, Ensemble

Nancy Renée Braun
Edna Mae, Ensemble

Jacob Clemente
Boy Scout, Ensemble

Mindy Dougherty
Geraldine

Kyrian Friedenberg
*Vladimir, Rich Boy,
Ensemble*

Sarah Marie Hicks
Carol Ann, Ensemble

Steve Konopelski
L.A., Ensemble

Matthew Lobenhofer
*Tap Dancer, Julius,
Ensemble*

Nicole Mangi
Agnes, Ensemble

Matty Price
East St. Louis

Jaclyn Taylor
Ruggiero
*Balloon Girl,
Ensemble*

Jessica Rush
Renée

Alicia Sable
*Marjorie May,
Ensemble*

John Scacchetti
Kansas, Ensemble

Geo Seery
Little Rock

Rider Quentin
Stanton
*Hopalong,
Military Boy,
Ensemble*

Pearce Wegener
*Driver, Yonkers,
Ensemble*

Matt Gibson
Swing

Lisa Rohinsky
Swing

Gypsy

Arthur Laurents
Book/Director

Jule Styne
Music

Stephen Sondheim
Lyrics

Gypsy Rose Lee

Jerome Robbins
*Original Direction/
Choreography*

Patrick Vaccariello
Music Director

Martin Pakledinaz
Costume Design

Howell Binkley
Lighting Design

Dan Moses Schreier
Sound Design

Jay Binder C.S.A.
Casting

Paul Huntley
Wig & Hair Design

Angelina Avallone
Make-up Design

John Kander
*Original Dance
Arrangements*

Seymour Red Press
Music Coordinator

Laura Green,
Richard Frankel
Productions
*General
Manangement*

Guy Kwan, John Paull III, Hillary Blanken,
Kevin Broomell, Ana Rose Greene,
Juniper Street Productions
Production Manager

Roger Berlind,
Berlind Productions
Producer

Marc Routh,
The Routh Frankel
Baruch Viertel Group
Producer

Richard Frankel,
The Routh Frankel
Baruch Viertel Group
Producer

Steven Baruch,
The Routh Frankel
Baruch Viertel Group
Producer

Tom Viertel,
The Routh Frankel
Baruch Viertel Group
Producer

Roy Furman
Producer

Debra Black
Producer

Ted Hartley
Producer

Roger Horchow,
Roger Horchow
Productions
Producer

Jack Viertel
Producer

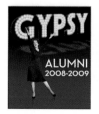

Andy Richardson
Boy Scout

Emma Rowley
Baby Louise

Mandy Bruno
*Renée, Waitress,
Standby for Louise,
Mazeppa, Electra,
Miss Cratchitt,
Tessie Tura*

Emma Zaks
*Geraldine,
Standby for Agnes,
Dainty June*

Gypsy

WARDROBE
Front Row (L-R): Kimberly Baird, Marisa Lerette, Renee Borys.

Middle Row (L-R): Tree Sarvay, Lyle Jones, Michael Louis.

Back Row (L-R): Danny Mura, Robert Guy, Kurt Kielmann.

LIGHTING AND SOUND
Front Row (L-R): Al Sayers, Sue Pelkofer, Sandy Paradise.

Middle Row (L-R): Bob Miller, David Gotwald, Joe Lenihan.

Back Row (L-R): Scott Silvian, Ron Martin.

CARPENTERS
Front Row (L-R): John Paull, Mark Hallisey.

Middle Row (L-R): Dave Brown, Tim McDonough, Jr, Ryan McDonough.

Back Row (L-R): Tom Fitzsimons, Tim McDonough.

FRONT OF HOUSE STAFF
Front Row (L-R): Margaret McElroy, Catherine Junior, Cynthia Lopiano, Barbara Carrol, Harry Joshi.

Second Row (L-R): Julia Furay, Leonard Bernfeld Baron, Jim Barry.

Third Row (L-R): Chadwick Vogel, Sherry Przybyszewski, Kaiser Akram, Russ Buenteo, Amanda Rose.

Back Row (L-R): Jacobo Medrano, Francisco Medina, Antoin Ramirez, Beau Bisson, Juan Luis Acevedo, Justin Karr.

Gypsy

BOX OFFICE
(L-R): Vincent Sclafani, Vincent Siniscalchi, Michael Milione.

HAIR
(L-R): Jeff Silverman, Danny Koye, Mia Neal, Carmel Vargyas (in photo), Nathaniel Hathaway, Vanessa Anderson.

PROPS
(L-R): Rich Anderson, Tom Thompson, "Chowsie."

STAGE MANAGEMENT
Front Row (L-R): Liza Vest, Christine Rudakewycz (Child Wrangler).

Back Row (L-R): Gary Mickelson, Craig Jacobs, Tom Capps.

DOORMAN
James Cline

STAFF FOR *GYPSY*

GENERAL MANAGEMENT
RICHARD FRANKEL PRODUCTIONS
Richard Frankel   Marc Routh   Laura Green
Rod Kaats   Joe Watson

COMPANY MANAGER
Sammy Ledbetter
Associate Company Manager ....Townsend Teague

GENERAL PRESS REPRESENTATIVE
BARLOW•HARTMAN
John Barlow   Michael Hartman
Ryan Ratelle   Melissa Bixler

CASTING
JAY BINDER CASTING
Jay Binder, CSA   Jack Bowdan, CSA
Mark Brandon   Sara Schatz
Nikole Vallins   Allison Estrin

TECHNICAL SUPERVISION
JUNIPER STREET PRODUCTIONS
Hillary Blanken   Kevin Broomell
Guy Kwan   Ana Rose Greene

Production Stage Manager ....**Gary Mickelson**
Stage Manager ....Tom Capps
Assistant Stage Manager ....Nancy Elizabeth Vest
Assistant Director ....Isaac Klein
Assistant Choreographer ....Roger Preston Smith
Associate Scenic Designer ....Jerome Martin

Photos by Ben Strothmann

Gypsy

Assistant Scenic Designer .... Adrienne Kapalko
Associate Costume Designer .... Martha Bromelmeier
Assistants to Martin Pakledinaz .... Sarah Cubbage,
　　　　　　　　　　　　　　　　　Tescia Seufferlein
Associate Lighting Designer .... Ryan O'Gara
Assistant Lighting Designer .... Amanda Zieve
Associate Sound Designer .... David Bullard
Assistant Sound Designer .... David Stollings
Associate Wig Designer .... Giovanna Calabretta
Company Management Intern .... Andrew Michaelson

Production Carpenter .... Jack Anderson
Head Carpenter .... John Paull
Assistant Carpenter .... Mark Hallisey
Automation Carpenter .... David Brown
Automation Flyman .... Timothy McDonough Jr.
Stage Carpenter .... Ryan McDonough
Production Electrician .... Dan Coey
Head Electrician .... Ron Martin
Assistant Electrician .... Sandy Paradise
Automated Light Programmer .... Timothy F. Rogers
Front Light Operators .... Sue Pelkofer, Bob Miller
Stage Sound Assistant .... Joe Lenihan
Head Sound Engineer .... David Gotwald
Assistant Sound Engineer .... Scott Silvian
Production Property Master .... Tim Abel
Head Property Master .... J. Marvin Crosland
Assistant Property Master .... Thomas G. Thomson
Stage Property Assistant .... Richard Anderson
Wardrobe Supervisor .... Robert Guy
Assistant Wardrobe Supervisor .... Kimberly Baird
Miss LuPone's Dresser .... Pat White
Dressers .... Renee Borys, Kurt Kielmann,
　　　　　　　　　　　　Michael Louis, Danny Mura,
　　　　　　　　Tree Sarvay, Estella Marie Simmons,
　　　　　　　　　　　　Arlene Watson, Lyle Jones
Hair & Wig Supervisor .... Nathaniel A. Hathaway
Assistant Hair & Wig Supervisor .... Carmel Vargyas
Hairdressers .... Vanessa Anderson, Danny Koye,
　　　　　　　　　　　　　　　　　　　Jeff Silverman
Production Assistants .... Emma Atherton, Elise Hanley,
　　　　　　　　　　　Laura Kimsey, Megan Loughran,
　　　　　　　　　　Laura Skolnik, Alissa Zulvergold
Children's Tutoring .... On Location Education,
　　　　　　　　　　　　　　　　　　　　Alan Simon
Children's Guardian .... Christine Rudakewycz

Music Director/Conductor .... Patrick Vaccariello
Music Coordinator .... Seymour Red Press
Associate Music Director/Conductor .... Jeffrey Harris
Special Keyboard Arrangements .... Danny Troob,
　　　　　　　　　　　　　　　　　　　Nathan Kelly
Synthesizer Programmer .... Randy Cohen
Music Preparation .... Anixter Rice Music Services
Rehearsal Pianist .... Jim Laev
Drummer .... Paul Pizzuti

Assistant to Stephen Sondheim .... Steven Clar
Assistant to Roger Berlind .... Jeffrey Hillock
Assistant to Steve Baruch .... Sonja Soper
Assistant to Tom Viertel .... Tania Senewiratne
Assistant to Roy Furman .... Eileen Williams
Assistant to Debra Black .... Rosemary Kenny
Assistant to Ted Hartley .... David Woodard
Assistant to Roger Horchow .... Donna Harper
Assistant to David Ian .... Alison Kelly

Assistant to Scott Rudin .... Adam Klaff
Assistant to Jack Viertel .... Joanna Gang

Advertising .... Serino Coyne, Inc./
　　　　　　　Sandy Block, Scott Johnson, Robert Jones
Promotions/Marketing .... Broadway Print & Mail
Merchandising .... Dewynters
Production Photography .... Paul Kolnik, Joan Marcus
Web Design .... Simma Park
Theatre Displays .... King Displays
Music Copying .... Anixter Rice Music Services
Insurance .... DeWitt Stern Group, Inc./
　　　　　　　　　Peter Shoemaker, Mary DeSpirt
Legal Counsel .... Patricia Crown, Esq.,
　　　　　　　　　　　　　Coblence & Associates
Banking .... Chase Manhattan Bank/Margaret Wong
Payroll Service .... Castellana Services, Inc.
Accounting .... Fried & Kowgios Partners, CPAs, LLP
New York Rehearsals .... New 42nd Street Studios
Group Sales .... Show Tix (212) 302-7000

RICHARD FRANKEL PRODUCTIONS STAFF
Finance Director .... **Michael Naumann**
Assistant to Richard Frankel .... Heidi Libby
Assistant to Marc Routh .... Katie Adams
Assistant to Laura Green .... Joshua A. Saletnik
Assistant Finance Director .... Susan Bartelt
Information Technology Manager .... Roddy Pimentel
Finance Assistants .... Heather Allen,
　　　　　　　　　　　　　　　　　　　Laura Burns
National Sales and Marketing Director ..Ronni Mandell
Director of Business Affairs .... **Michael Sinder**
Business Affairs Assistant .... Dario Dalla Lasta
Marketing Manager .... Melissa Marano
Promotions Manager .... Alana Karpoff
Office Manager .... **Lori Steiger-Perry**
Office Management Assistant .... Shannon O'Neil
Receptionists .... Christina Cataldo, Marcella Grimaux
Interns .... Amanda Ryan, Liz Halakan,
　　　　　　　　　　Meghan Hunter, Jenny Kanelos,
　　　　　　　Heather Caruso, Ashley Nelson, Claire Cook,
　　　　　　　Sebastian Peimonte, Shannon Tooley,
　　　　　　　　Corey Phillips, Ioanna Psaroudakis

Special thanks to Erik Preminger

The producers would like to acknowledge and thank the parents of each of the juvenile actors in *Gypsy*: Denise DeBella and Mike Stanton; Larissa & Douglas Friedenberg; Denise and Steve Johnson; Robin & Larry Klitzman; Angie & Lee Lobenhofer; Rita & Mike Richardson; Kathie & James Rowley.

Makeup provided by M•A•C Cosmetics

CREDITS AND ACKNOWLEDGEMENTS
Scenery and scenic effects built and electrified by PRG Scenic Technologies, New Windsor, NY and Black Walnut, Valley Cottage, NY. Scenery painted by Black Walnut, Valley Cottage, NY, and Scenic Art Studios, Cornwall, NY. Show control and scenic motion control featuring Stage Command Systems® by PRG Scenic Technologies, New Windsor, NY. Softgoods built by I. Weiss and Sons, Inc., Long Island City, NY. Lighting equipment provided by PRG Lighting, North Bergen, NJ. Sound equipment provided by PRG Audio, Mt. Vernon. NY. Furniture and

props executed by The Spoon Group, Rahway, NJ, and Joe Props, Kane, PA. Hauling by Clark Transfer, Inc. Ms. LuPone's costumes by Barbara Matera, Ltd. & Eric Winterling, Inc. Ms. Benanti's costumes by Eric Winterling, Inc. Costumes by Tricorne Inc., Paul Chang Custom Tailors, Izquierdo Studio, Krostyne Studio, Seams Unlimited. Millinery by Lynne Mackey Studio, Arnold S. Levine Inc., Rodney Gordon Inc., Carelli Costumes, Ellen Christine. Shoes by Worldtone Dance, Capezio Dance, LaDuca Shoes, JC Theatrical, Freeds, Celebrity Shoes. Fabric dyeing and printing by Gene Mignola Inc., Ellen Steingraeber & Izquierdo Studios. "Electra"-fication by Chic Silber. Special thanks to Helen Uffner Vintage Clothing, Early Halloween New York City, Odds Costumes Rental, New York Vintage, Right to the Moon Alice, Odds and Adds. Lozenges provided by Ricola. Limousine services provided by Nice Guys Limousine, Inc. Special thanks to Barbara Crompton, Staci Levine, Tanase Popa, Michael Zande. Natural herb cough drops courtesy of Ricola USA, Inc. Special thanks to Bra*Tenders for undergarments and hosiery. Fur by Sharnelle Furs, Ltd.

"Happy Birthday to You" (Mildred J. Hill, Patty Smith Hill); ©1935 (Renewed) Summy-Birchard Company (ASCAP). All rights reserved. Used by permission.

♪ JUJAMCYN THEATERS

ROCCO LANDESMAN
President

PAUL LIBIN　　**JACK VIERTEL**　　**JORDAN ROTH**
Producing Director　Creative Director　Vice President
DANIEL ADAMIAN　　　**JENNIFER HERSHEY**
General Manager　　　Director of Operations
MEREDITH VILLATORE　　　**JERRY ZAKS**
Chief Financial Officer　　　Resident Director

STAFF FOR THE ST. JAMES THEATRE
Manager .... Daniel Adamian
Associate Manager .... Hal Goldberg
Treasurer .... Vincent Sclafani
Carpenter .... Timothy McDonough
Propertyman .... Barnett Epstein
Electrician .... Albert Sayers

Laura Benanti as
Gypsy Rose Lee

Hair

Preview: March 6, 2009. Opened: March 31, 2009.
Still running as of May 31, 2009.

PLAYBILL

THE COMPANY

(in order of appearance)

Dionne .... SASHA ALLEN
Berger .... WILL SWENSON
Woof .... BRYCE RYNESS
Hud .... DARIUS NICHOLS
Claude .... GAVIN CREEL
Sheila .... CAISSIE LEVY
Jeanie .... KACIE SHEIK
Crissy .... ALLISON CASE
Mother .... MEGAN LAWRENCE
Dad .... ANDREW KOBER
Margaret Mead .... ANDREW KOBER
Hubert .... THEO STOCKMAN
Abraham Lincoln .... SAYCON SENGBLOH
Buddhadalirama .... MEGAN LAWRENCE
Tribe Members .... ATO BLANKSON-WOOD,
STEEL BURKHARDT, JACKIE BURNS,
LAUREN ELDER, ALLISON GUINN,
ANTHONY HOLLOCK, KAITLIN KIYAN,
NICOLE LEWIS, JOHN MOAURO,
BRANDON PEARSON, MEGAN REINKING,
PARIS REMILLARD, SAYCON SENGBLOH,
MAYA SHARPE, THEO STOCKMAN,
TOMMAR WILSON

Continued on next page

♪ AL HIRSCHFELD THEATRE

A JUJAMCYN THEATRE

ROCCO LANDESMAN
President

PAUL LIBIN
Producing Director

JACK VIERTEL
Creative Director

JORDAN ROTH
Vice President

THE PUBLIC THEATER
Oskar Eustis, Artistic Director   Andrew D. Hamingson, Executive Director
JEFFREY RICHARDS   JERRY FRANKEL
GARY GODDARD ENTERTAINMENT   KATHLEEN K. JOHNSON   NEDERLANDER PRODUCTIONS, INC.
FRAN KIRMSER PRODUCTIONS/JED BERNSTEIN   MARC FRANKEL   BROADWAY ACROSS AMERICA
BARBARA MANOCHERIAN/WENCARLAR PRODUCTIONS   JK PRODUCTIONS/TERRY SCHNUCK
ANDY SANDBERG   JAM THEATRICALS   THE WEINSTEIN COMPANY/NORTON HERRICK
JUJAMCYN THEATERS

JOEY PARNES Executive Producer

by special arrangement with
ELIZABETH IRELAND McCANN

present

HAIR

The American Tribal Love-Rock Musical

Book & Lyrics by
GEROME RAGNI & JAMES RADO

Music by
GALT MacDERMOT

with

**SASHA ALLEN   ALLISON CASE   GAVIN CREEL   CAISSIE LEVY
DARIUS NICHOLS   BRYCE RYNESS   KACIE SHEIK   WILL SWENSON**

and

ATO BLANKSON-WOOD   STEEL BURKHARDT   JACKIE BURNS   BRIANA CARLSON-GOODMAN
LAUREN ELDER   ALLISON GUINN   CHASTEN HARMON   ANTHONY HOLLOCK
JAY ARMSTRONG JOHNSON   KAITLIN KIYAN   ANDREW KOBER   JOSH LAMON
MEGAN LAWRENCE   NICOLE LEWIS   RYAN LINK   JOHN MOAURO   BRANDON PEARSON
MEGAN REINKING   PARIS REMILLARD   MICHAEL JAMES SCOTT   SAYCON SENGBLOH
MAYA SHARPE   THEO STOCKMAN   TOMMAR WILSON

Scenic Design	Costume Design	Lighting Design	Sound Design
SCOTT PASK	MICHAEL McDONALD	KEVIN ADAMS	ACME SOUND PARTNERS

Orchestrations	Music Director	Music Coordinator
GALT MacDERMOT	NADIA DIGIALLONARDO	SEYMOUR RED PRESS

Casting	Production Stage Manager	Wig Design
JORDAN THALER & HEIDI GRIFFITHS	NANCY HARRINGTON	GERARD KELLY

Press Representative	Associate Producer	Marketing	Sponsorship
O&M CO.	JENNY GERSTEN	ALLIED LIVE, INC.	ROSE POLIDORO

Associate Producers
ARIELLE TEPPER MADOVER   DEBBIE BISNO/REBECCA GOLD   CHRISTOPHER HART
APPLES AND ORANGES   TONY & RUTHE PONTURO   JOSEPH TRAINA

Choreography by
KAROLE ARMITAGE

Directed by
DIANE PAULUS

ORIGINALLY PRODUCED IN 1967 AND SUBSEQUENTLY REVIVED IN 2008 BY THE PUBLIC THEATER
THE PRODUCERS WISH TO EXPRESS THEIR APPRECIATION TO THEATRE DEVELOPMENT FUND FOR ITS SUPPORT OF THIS PRODUCTION.

3/31/09

(Center, L-R): Gavin Creel and Will Swenson with the Tribe

Photo by Joan Marcus

Hair

MUSICAL NUMBERS

ACT 1

"Aquarius" .... Dionne and Tribe
"Donna" .... Berger and Tribe
"Hashish" .... Tribe
"Sodomy" .... Woof and Tribe
"Colored Spade" .... Hud and Tribe
"Manchester, England" .... Claude and Tribe
"I'm Black" .... Hud, Woof, Berger, Claude and Tribe
"Ain't Got No" .... Woof, Hud, Dionne and Tribe
"Sheila Franklin" .... Tribe
"I Believe in Love" .... Sheila and Trio
"Ain't Got No" .... Tribe
"Air" .... Jeanie with Crissy and Dionne
"The Stone Age" .... Berger
"I Got Life" .... Claude and Tribe
"Initials" .... Tribe
"Going Down" .... Berger and Tribe
"Hair" .... Claude, Berger and Tribe
"My Conviction" .... Margaret Mead
"Easy to Be Hard" .... Sheila
"Don't Put It Down" .... Berger, Woof, Tommar
"Frank Mills" .... Crissy
"Hare Krishna" .... Tribe
"Where Do I Go" .... Claude and Tribe

ACT 2

"Electric Blues" .... Steel, Andrew, Megan L., Nicole
"Oh Great God of Power" .... Tribe
"Black Boys" .... Megan R., Jackie, Kaitlin, Darius, Brandon, Tommar
"White Boys" .... Dionne, Nicole, Saycon
"Walking in Space" .... Tribe
"Minuet" .... Orchestra
"Yes, I's Finished on Y'alls Farmlands" .... Darius, Ato, Brandon, Tommar
"Four Score and Seven Years Ago"/ "Abie Baby" .... Saycon, Ato, Darius, Brandon, Tommar
"Give Up All Desires" .... Buddhadalirama, Woof, Sheila, Crissy
"Three-Five-Zero-Zero" .... Tribe
"What a Piece of Work Is Man" .... Paris, Maya, Claude
"How Dare They Try" .... Tribe
"Good Morning Starshine" .... Sheila and Tribe
"Ain't Got No" (Reprise) .... Claude and Tribe
"The Flesh Failures" .... Claude, Sheila, Dionne, Woof
"Eyes Look Your Last" .... Tribe
"Let the Sun Shine In" .... Tribe

Sasha Allen (center) with the Tribe.

Photo by Joan Marcus

2008-2009 AWARDS

TONY AWARD
Best Revival of a Musical

DRAMA DESK AWARD
Outstanding Revival of a Musical

DRAMA LEAGUE AWARD
Distinguished Revival of a Musical

OUTER CRITICS CIRCLE AWARD
Outstanding Revival of a Musical

Hair

Sasha Allen
Dionne

Allison Case
Crissy

Gavin Creel
Claude

Caissie Levy
Sheila

Darius Nichols
Hud

Bryce Ryness
Woof

Kacie Sheik
Jeanie

Will Swenson
Berger

Ato Blankson-Wood
Tribe

Steel Burkhardt
Electric Blues Quartet, Tribe

Jackie Burns
Black Boys Trio, Tribe

Briana Carlson-Goodman
Swing

Lauren Elder
Tribe

Allison Guinn
Tribe

Chasten Harmon
Swing

Anthony Hollock
Tribe

Jay Armstrong Johnson
u/s Claude

Kaitlin Kiyan
Black Boys Trio, Tribe

Andrew Kober
Margaret Mead, Dad, Tribe

Josh Lamon
Swing

Megan Lawrence
Mother, Buddhadalirama, Tribe

Nicole Lewis
Aretha, White Boys Trio, Tribe

Ryan Link
u/s Berger

John Moauro
Tribe

Brandon Pearson
Tribe

Megan Reinking
Black Boys Trio, Tribe

Paris Remillard
What a Piece Duo, Tribe

Michael James Scott
Swing

Saycon Sengbloh
Abraham Lincoln, White Boys Trio, Tribe

Maya Sharpe
What a Piece Duo, Tribe

Theo Stockman
Principal, Hubert, Tribe

Tommar Wilson
Tribe

James Rado
Co-Creator

Gerome Ragni
Co-Creator

Galt MacDermot
Composer

Hair

Diane Paulus
Director

Karole Armitage
Choreographer

Scott Pask
Scenic Design

Kevin Adams
Lighting Design

Tom Clark, Mark Menard and Nevin Steinberg,
Acme Sound Partners
Sound Designer

Seymour Red Press
Music Coordinator

Heidi Griffiths and
Jordan Thaler
Casting

Oskar Eustis
*Artistic Director,
The Public Theater*

Andrew D.
Hamingson
*Executive Director,
The Public Theater*

Jeffrey Richards
Producer

Jerry Frankel
Producer

Garry Goddard,
Gary Goddard
Entertainment
Producer

Forbes Candlish,
Gary Goddard
Entertainment
Producer

James L.
Nederlander,
Nederlander
Presentations, Inc.
Producer

Barbara
Manocherian
Producer

Wendy Federman
*Producer,
WenCarLar*

Carl Moellenberg
*Producer,
WenCarLar*

Larry Hirschhorn
*Producer,
WenCarLar*

Terry Schnuck
Producer

Bob Weinstein,
The Weinstein
Company
Producer

Harvey Weinstein,
The Weinstein
Company
Producer

Rocco Landesman,
President,
Jujamcyn Theaters
Producer

Joey Parnes
Executive Producer

Elizabeth Ireland
McCann
Producer

Arielle Tepper
Madover
Associate Producer

Hair

CREW

Front Row (L-R): Martha Blake, Amelia Haywood, Shannon McDowell, Gayle Palmieri, Clarion Overmoyer, Cat Dee, Scott Sanders, Gloria Burke, Will Sweeney, Sal Sclafani

Middle Row (L-R): Gabe Harris, Joseph J. Maher, Danny Koye, Worth Strecker, John Robelen III, Tom Burke, Brian Dawson

Back Row (L-R): Rocco Williams, John Blixt, Jim Wilkinson

BAND

Front Row (L-R): Elaine Burt, Bernard Purdie, Steve Bargonetti, Allen Won, Vincent MacDermot

Back Row (L-R): Joe Cardello, Andy Schwartz, Chris Jaudes, Ronnie Buttacavoli, Wilbur Bascomb

COMPANY MANAGEMENT
(L-R): Kit Ingui (Assistant Company Manager), Kim Sellon (Company Manager), Leslie A. Glassburn (Associate Company Manager)

STAGE MANAGEMENT
(L-R): Nancy Harrington (Production Stage Manager), Julie Baldauff (Stage Manager), Elizabeth Miller (Assistant Stage Manager), Johnny Milani (Production Assistant)

Hair

Photo by Samantha Souza

STAFF FOR *HAIR*

GENERAL MANAGEMENT
Joey Parnes
John Johnson   S.D. Wagner

COMPANY MANAGER
Kim Sellon

FOR THE PUBLIC THEATER
Artistic Director .... Oskar Eustis
Executive Director .... Andrew D. Hamingson
Associate Producer .... Jenny Gersten
Director of Communications .... Candi Adams
Director of Marketing .... Ilene Rosen

PRESS REPRESENTATIVE
O&M Co.
Rick Miramontez
Molly Barnett   Philip Carrubba
Elizabeth Wagner

Production Stage Manager .... Nancy Harrington
Stage Manager .... Julie Baldauff
Assistant Stage Manager .... Elizabeth Miller
Associate Company Manager .... Leslie A. Glassburn
Assistant Company Manager .... Kit Ingui
Assistant Directors .... Allegra Libonati,
                                         Shira Milikowsky
Assistant Choreographer .... Christine O'Grady
Associate Set Designer .... Orit Jacoby Carroll
Assistant Set Designers .... Jeffrey Hinchee,
                                         Lauren Alvarez
Assistant to the Set Designer .... Warren Stiles
Mural Illustration .... Scott Pask with Amy Guip
Associate Lighting Designer .... Aaron Sporer
Assistant Lighting Designer .... Joel Silver
Associate Costume Designer .... Lisa Zinni
Assistant Costume Designer .... Chloe Chapin
Assistant to the Costume Designer ...... David Mendizabal
Costume Assistant .... Sydney Ledger
Assistant Sound Designer .... Alex Hawthorn
Production Carpenter .... Larry Morley
Production Electrician .... Steve Cochrane/
                                         Richard Mortell
Production Prop Supervisor .... Michael Smanko
Production Sound Engineer .... Scott Sanders
Head Electrician .... Brian Dawson
Moving Light Programmer .... Paul J. Sonnleitner
Monitor Mixer .... Jim Wilkinson
Wardrobe Supervisor .... John A. Robelen, III
Assistant Wardrobe Supervisor .... Martha Blake

Dressers .... Cat Dee, Amelia Haywood,
                    Shannon McDowell, Clarion Overmoyer,
                                         Gayle Palmieri
Hair/Wig Supervisor .... Gloria Burke
Hair Dresser .... Danny Koye
Production Assistant .... Johnny Milani
Music Consultant .... Tom Kitt
Music Copyist .... Rob Baumgardner
Associate to Jeffrey Richards .... Jeremy Scott Blaustein
Assistants to Jeffrey Richards .... Diana Rissetto,
                                      Christopher Taggart
Assistant to Jenny Gersten .... Eric Louie
Management Associate .... Madeline Felix
Casting Assistant .... Amber Wakefield
Casting Intern .... Ann Thayer
Advertising .... SpotCo/
                    Drew Hodges, Jim Edwards,
                    Stephen Sosnowski, Tim Falotico,
                                      Tom Greenwald
Interactive Marketing .... Situation Interactive/
                    Damian Bazadona, Jessica Dachille,
                    Jeremy Kraus, John Lanasa, Steve Rovery
Marketing .... Allied Live LLC/
                    Laura Matalon, Tanya Grubich,
                    Victoria Cairl, Meghan Zaneski
Sponsorship .... Rose Polidoro
Press Associates .... Jaron Caldwell, Amanda Dekker,
                    Jon Dimond, Yufen Kung, Richard Hillman
Press Interns .... Felicia Pollack,
                                      Mary Katherine Vigness
Legal Counsel .... Lazarus & Harris LLP/
                    Scott Lazarus, Esq., Robert Harris, Esq.
Public Theater Counsel .... Paul, Weiss, Rifkind,
                    Wharton & Garrison LLP/
                    Charles H. Googe Jr., Carolyn J. Casselman,
                                      Michael Bogner
Consulting Counsel .... Robinson Brog,
                    Leinwand Greene,
                    Genovese & Gluck PC/
                    Richard M. Ticktin, Esq., Roy A. Jacobs, Esq.
Accountants .... RNK/
                    Mark D'Ambrosi, Pat Pedersen, Ruthie Waugh
Banking .... JPMorgan Chase/
                    Stephanie Dalton, Stefanie Boger,
                                      Salvatore Romano
Insurance .... AON/Albert G Ruben/
                    George Walden, Claudia B. Kaufman
Payroll .... Castellana Services Inc/
                    Lance Castellana, James Castellana,
                                      Norman Sewell
Opening Night Coordinator ...... The Lawrence Company
Production Photographer .... Robert Saferstein

Music Advisor
Rob Fisher

CREDITS
Scenery and scenic effects built, painted and electrified by Showmotion, Inc., Norwalk, Connecticut. Set elements fabricated by Cigar Box Studios. Lighting equipment by PRG Lighting. Sound equipment by Sound Associates. Costumes executed by the Public Theater Costume Shop; John Kristiansen, New York Inc.; Tricorne LLC; Marc Happel; Giliberto Custom Tailors. Specialty costumes by Fritz Masten and Barbara Brust. Millinery by Lynne Mackey Studio & T. Michael Hall. Custom embroidery by Jason Hadley. Knitware by Clarion Overmoyer. Custom leatherwear by David Samuel Menkes. Select vintage clothing courtesy of Scaramouche. Military uniforms and accessories supplied by Kaufman's Army & Navy, NYC. Car service by IBA Limousine.

SPECIAL THANKS
Luke McDonough, Public Theater Costume Master; Jason Hadley, Costume Assistant: 40th Anniversary Concert; Theoni V. Aldredge; Tonne Goodman; Maj. Gabriel J. Zinni, USA; Mary Beth Regan; Grier Coleman; Anne Wingate & Kim Jones; Daybreak Vintage; Amy Carothers; Julian Christenberry; Jane Pfeffer; Don Frantz; Laurie Brown; Stuart Levy; Louise Foisy; Cynthia Ponce

Hair is supported, with love, by Levi's©.

Salon services, hair care and styling products provided by Bumble and bumble.

Synthesizers provided by Yamaha Corporation of America.

♪ JUJAMCYN THEATERS
ROCCO LANDESMAN
President
PAUL LIBIN   JACK VIERTEL   JORDAN ROTH
Producing Director   Creative Director   Vice President
DANIEL ADAMIAN   JENNIFER HERSHEY
General Manager   Director of Operations
MEREDITH VILLATORE   JERRY ZAKS
Chief Financial Officer   Resident Director

Staff for the Al Hirschfeld Theatre
Manager .... Albert T. Kim
Associate Manager .... Hal Goldberg
Treasurer .... Carmine La Mendola
Carpenter .... Joseph J. Maher, Jr.
Propertyman .... Sal Sclafani
Electrician .... Michele Gutierrez

Hair
SCRAPBOOK

1. Broadway Softball League Cheerleaders.

2. Some of our band (bottom to top): Allen Won, Vincent MacDermot, Elaine Burt, Christian Jaudes and Ronald Buttacavoli.

3. Andrew Kober getting into his Margaret Mead costume.

4. The entire cast!

5. Painting in our hallway.

Correspondent: Lauren Elder, "Tribe Member"

Memorable Opening Night Letter, Fax or Note: Geoffrey Rush wrote to "Go gaga at the go-go."

Opening Night Gifts: Everything! From *Hair* ID tags, to amazing cookies and brownies, poems, Miss Neisha's remix of "My Conviction," a disc of photos that tell our story since the 2007 concert, lots of LoVe!

Most Exciting Celebrity Visitors: Tom Brokaw gave us a history lesson on the sixties after the show one night. Aretha Franklin was pretty cool, too! She invited us all to the Ritz-Carlton for cocktails and snacks!

Gypsy Robe: Tommar Wilson got the Gypsy Robe and is in the process of adding an Afro hood with flowers and ribbons hanging off of it.

"Easter Bonnet" Sketch: Will Swenson and Tommar Wilson wrote it. It was called "Broadway Match.com," and hooked up different characters from other shows with hippies. It starred Briana Carlson-Goodman, Anthony Hollock, Ato Blankson-Wood, Andrew Kober, Steel Burkhardt, Jackie Burns, Johnny Milani, Gavin Creel, Sasha Allen, Allison Case and Darius Nichols.

Favorite Therapies: Definitely Ricolas, Throat Coat Lozenges (gross, but they work!), Gatorade, and hand sanitizer.

Most Roles in This Show: Well, everyone plays multiple roles, but I believe Theo Stockman played the most with the tribe, the principal, Hubert, a POW, and John Wilkes Booth.

Most Shows in Their Career: I think Tommar has the most, with six Broadway shows.

Favorite Moment: When Hubert takes a group photo of the hippies after "My Conviction." Every night we come up with a different theme for the picture. Past favorites include The Last Supper, Heat Exhaustion, and Hangin' Tough.

Most Memorable Ad-Libs: So many! We ad-lib all the time! But Will Swenson probably does the most, asking people for money, asking people why they're late, et cetera.

Web Buzz: It was great! Still is great! We really still can't believe how people have reacted to our show! We have an awesome website too, and love making silly videos to add to it.

Busiest Day at the Box Office: I think it was the day after we opened, we sold around $500,000 in tickets. It was really exciting!

Latest Audience Arrival: There have been a lot of late audience arrivals during Woof's speech, and Bryce Ryness is so incredible about acknowledging them in character, always welcoming them with love!

Fastest Costume Change: Megan Lawrence's change from Buddhadalirama to Mom right before "3500"—it's seconds!

Memorable Stage Door Fan Encounter: I had an audience member hug me and start crying, telling me how much the show meant to him, telling me that we were so free and fearless and he wanted to be like that.

Memorable Media Encounter: Performing on "Late Show with David Letterman"!

Heaviest/Hottest Costume: Probably Kacie Sheik as Jeanie, since she has to have a pregnant belly suit on under her costume.

Who Wore the Least: In the nude scene, almost everyone!

Catchphrases Only the Company Would Recognize: War is bad, man.

Orchestra Member Who Played the Most Instruments: Joe Cardello, our percussionist.

Orchestra Member Who Played the Most Consecutive Performances Without a Sub: This is a tie between Joe Cardello, Andy Schwartz, Vince MacDermot, Wilbur Bascomb, and Steve Bargonetti.

Memorable Directorial Note: Give me yummy butts! Kacie, show me your throbbing meat.

Coolest Thing About Being in This Show: Our tribe is really like a family. We really love each other, we love the show, and the audience feels that love. I think that is really cool. It is a magical experience every single night, and I wouldn't trade it for anything. LoVe!!!

Fan Club Info: www.hairbroadway.com

Hairspray

First Preview: July 18, 2002. Opened: August 15, 2002.
Closed January 4, 2009 after 31 Previews and 2642 Performances.

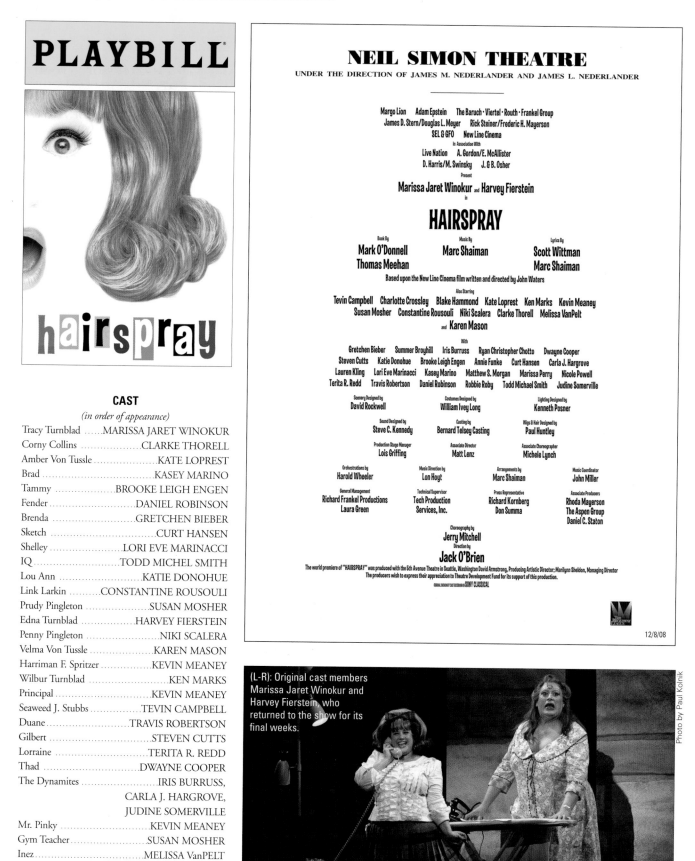

hairspray

CAST
(in order of appearance)

Tracy Turnblad	MARISSA JARET WINOKUR
Corny Collins	CLARKE THORELL
Amber Von Tussle	KATE LOPREST
Brad	KASEY MARINO
Tammy	BROOKE LEIGH ENGEN
Fender	DANIEL ROBINSON
Brenda	GRETCHEN BIEBER
Sketch	CURT HANSEN
Shelley	LORI EVE MARINACCI
IQ	TODD MICHEL SMITH
Lou Ann	KATIE DONOHUE
Link Larkin	CONSTANTINE ROUSOULI
Prudy Pingleton	SUSAN MOSHER
Edna Turnblad	HARVEY FIERSTEIN
Penny Pingleton	NIKI SCALERA
Velma Von Tussle	KAREN MASON
Harriman F. Spritzer	KEVIN MEANEY
Wilbur Turnblad	KEN MARKS
Principal	KEVIN MEANEY
Seaweed J. Stubbs	TEVIN CAMPBELL
Duane	TRAVIS ROBERTSON
Gilbert	STEVEN CUTTS
Lorraine	TERITA R. REDD
Thad	DWAYNE COOPER
The Dynamites	IRIS BURRUSS, CARLA J. HARGROVE, JUDINE SOMERVILLE
Mr. Pinky	KEVIN MEANEY
Gym Teacher	SUSAN MOSHER
Inez	MELISSA VanPELT

Continued on next page

NEIL SIMON THEATRE
UNDER THE DIRECTION OF JAMES M. NEDERLANDER AND JAMES L. NEDERLANDER

Margo Lion   Adam Epstein   The Baruch · Viertel · Routh · Frankel Group
James D. Stern/Douglas L. Meyer   Rick Steiner/Frederic H. Mayerson
SEL & GFO   New Line Cinema
In Association With
Live Nation   A. Gordon/E. McAllister
D. Harris/M. Swinsky   J. & B. Osher
Present

Marissa Jaret Winokur and Harvey Fierstein
in

HAIRSPRAY

Book By	Music By	Lyrics By
Mark O'Donnell	Marc Shaiman	Scott Wittman
Thomas Meehan		Marc Shaiman

Based upon the New Line Cinema film written and directed by John Waters

Also Starring
Tevin Campbell   Charlotte Crossley   Blake Hammond   Kate Loprest   Ken Marks   Kevin Meaney
Susan Mosher   Constantine Rousouli   Niki Scalera   Clarke Thorell   Melissa VanPelt
and   Karen Mason

With
Gretchen Bieber   Summer Broyhill   Iris Burruss   Ryan Christopher Chotto   Dwayne Cooper
Steven Cutts   Katie Donohue   Brooke Leigh Engen   Annie Funke   Curt Hansen   Carla J. Hargrove
Lauren Kling   Lori Eve Marinacci   Kasey Marino   Matthew S. Morgan   Marissa Perry   Nicole Powell
Terita R. Redd   Travis Robertson   Daniel Robinson   Robbie Roby   Todd Michael Smith   Judine Somerville

Scenery Designed by	Costumes Designed by	Lighting Designed by
David Rockwell	William Ivey Long	Kenneth Posner

Sound Designed by	Casting by	Wigs & Hair Designed by
Steve C. Kennedy	Bernard Telsey Casting	Paul Huntley

Production Stage Manager	Associate Director	Associate Choreographer
Lois Griffing	Matt Lenz	Michele Lynch

Orchestrations by	Music Direction by	Arrangements by	Music Coordinator
Harold Wheeler	Lon Hoyt	Marc Shaiman	John Miller

General Management	Technical Supervisor	Press Representative	Associate Producers
Richard Frankel Productions Laura Green	Tech Production Services, Inc.	Richard Kornberg Don Summa	Rhoda Mayerson The Aspen Group Daniel C. Staton

Choreography by
Jerry Mitchell
Direction by
Jack O'Brien

The world premiere of "HAIRSPRAY" was produced with the 5th Avenue Theatre in Seattle, Washington David Armstrong, Producing Artistic Director; Marilynn Sheldon, Managing Director
The producers wish to express their appreciation to Theatre Development Fund for its support of this production.
ORIGINAL BROADWAY CAST RECORDING ON SONY CLASSICAL

12/8/08

(L-R): Original cast members Marissa Jaret Winokur and Harvey Fierstein, who returned to the show for its final weeks.

Photo by Paul Kolnik

Hairspray

Chris Langdon

BOX OFFICE
(L-R): Marc Needleman, Anne

Front Row (L-R): Dawn Edmonds (Elevator Operator), Janine Peterson (Elevator Operator)

Back Row (L-R): Jose Lopez (Porter), James Mosaphir (Stage Door)

HAIR ROOM
(Clockwise, from Front): Mark Manalansan, Alex Bartlett, Jason Shur, Isabelle Decauwert, John Roberson

WARDROBE
First Row (L-R): Sue Cerceo, Mindy Eng

Second Row (L-R): Dora Suarez, Liz Goodrum, Joseph Phillip Armon

Back Row (L-R): Tanya Blue, Laura Horner, Kate McAleer, David Ruble

STAGE CREW
Front Row (L-R): Brian Kelly, Michael Bennet, Arthur Lutz

Back Row (L-R): Richie Kirby, Michael Pilipski, Lorena Sullivan, Istvan Tamas, Danny Viscardo, Brian Munroe, Gerald Stein

ELECTRICIANS
Front Row: Jessica Morton

Back Row (L-R): Stephen Vessa, Mark Hannan, John Kelly, Jim Travers, Sr., unknown.

Hairspray

Hairspray
SCRAPBOOK

CLOSING NIGHT
1. Original cast member Harvey Fierstein (red fringed dress) addresses the audience and the gathered creators and returned original cast members after the final performance.
2. Former cast member Linda Hart and director Jack O'Brien at the closing-night party.
3. Former cast member Laura Bell Bundy.
4. The farewell cake.
5. Former cast members Jackie Hoffman and David Greenspan.
6. Composer Marc Shaiman.
7. Former cast member Annie Golden.

Correspondent: Judine Somerville, "The Dynamites"

Memorable Fan Letter: It was a picture of the three of us who play the Dynamites, and the caption read, "I am dynamite like the Dynamites."

Sixth Anniversary Party: Held at the club Sportlight. Lots of the *Hairspray* Family were in attendance. Lots of good food, energy, people and memories. OH WHAT A NIGHT!

Most Exciting Celebrity Visitor: Tom Cruise. He attended the *'Spray* on three occasions, but we did not get to meet him. He sent cake from Magnolia Bakery and candy from Dylan's Candy Bar in NYC.

Most Performances in This Show: Todd Michel Smith and Judine Somerville were the two original cast members who were there at the final curtain on January 4, 2009, well over 1500 performances each.

In-Theatre Gathering Place: Harvey's dressing room was definitely the place to gather for food, fun, and the latest "411." I loved working with him. Ya know, us Brooklyn gals must stick together!

Off-Site Gathering Place: The place where the cast hung the most was Sosa Borella.

Heaviest/Hottest Costume: Harvey Fierstein's fat suit weighed in at 35-40 lbs....yikes.

Company Catchphrase: Catchphrase for the Dorm (also known as the ladies' ensemble room) was a short, catchy jingle involving the sound-man, thought up by Terita Redd: "Judine got caught by the microphone Bandit...caught, caught by the microphone Bandit...yeah yeah yeah...."

Coolest Things About Being in This Show: There are a lot of cool things about being in the *'Spray*. The coolest is being part of one of the most amazing, exhilarating, magical musicals. It not only changed lives but saved lives. And people walked away not only singing the songs but they knew that hope was alive and that anything is possible. I would like to add how amazing it was to be a part of such a wonderful family. To all of the *Hairspray* Family and the brilliant creative staff...thank you for saving my life and giving me life and wings TO FLY!

Hedda Gabler

First Preview: January 6, 2009. Opened: January 25, 2009.
Closed March 29, 2009 after 21 Previews and 74 Performances.

CAST
(in order of speaking)

Miss Juliane Tesman,
    Jørgen Tesman's Aunt ....HELEN CAREY
Berte, the Tesman's maid ....LOIS MARKLE
Jørgen Tesman ....MICHAEL CERVERIS
Mrs. Hedda Tesman,
    his wife ....MARY-LOUISE PARKER
Mrs. Thea Elvsted ....ANA REEDER
Judge Brack ....PETER STORMARE
Ejlert Løvborg ....PAUL SPARKS

UNDERSTUDIES

For Mrs. Hedda Tesman, Mrs. Thea Elvsted:
OPAL ALLADIN
For Jørgen Tesman, Ejlert Løvborg:
PETER BRADBURY
For Miss Juliane Tesman, Berte:
LUCY MARTIN
For Judge Brack:
RAY VIRTA

Production Stage Manager:
JAMES FITZSIMMONS
Stage Manager:
BRYCE McDONALD

AMERICAN AIRLINES THEATRE

ROUNDABOUTTHEATRECOMPANY

Todd Haimes, Artistic Director
Harold Wolpert, Managing Director
Julia C. Levy, Executive Director

Presents

Mary-Louise Parker

Michael Cerveris   Paul Sparks   Peter Stormare

in

HEDDA GABLER

By

Henrik Ibsen

New Adaptation by

Christopher Shinn

Literal Translation by
Anne-Charlotte Harvey

with

Lois Markle   Ana Reeder

and

Helen Carey

Set Design	Costume Design	Lighting Design	Sound Design	Original Music
Hildegard Bechtler	Ann Roth	Natasha Katz	John Gromada	PJ Harvey

Makeup & Hair Design	Wig Design	Production Stage Manager
Ivana Primorac	Peter Owen	James FitzSimmons

Casting	General Manager	Technical Supervisor	Press Representative
Jim Carnahan C.S.A. & Stephen Kopel	Rebecca Habel	Steve Beers	Boneau/Bryan-Brown

Director of Marketing & Sales Promotion	Founding Director	Associate Artistic Director
David B. Steffen	Gene Feist	Scott Ellis

Directed by

Ian Rickson

Roundabout Theatre Company is a member of the League of Resident Theatres.
www.roundabouttheatre.org

1/19/09

(L-R): Michael Cerveris, Peter Stormare (background), Mary-Louise Parker

Photo by Nigel Parry / CPi

Impressionism
SCRAPBOOK

Correspondent: Michael J. Passaro, Production Stage Manager

An Impression of *Impressionism*

"You don't get it when it's right in front of you. You have to step back. Up close, they're just splotches of paint. They're not water lilies until you stand in the right place."

One of the many pearls of wisdom that are found in *Impressionism*, though I must admit, this one always seemed rather ho-hum to me. Especially in comparison with the other, subtler life-lessons that Michael Jacobs ribbons through his play. Maybe those endless undergrad art-history classes made the sentiment so obvious; perhaps the eight-a-week dulled its resonance. But as I write this a few days after our closing—and allow myself to "step back" from the experience—those words keep coming back to me. Their obviousness has given way to an uncanny prescience and a warm glow that seems just right.

The white heat of a Broadway production schedule demands ritual. Throw together a bunch of loosely-connected people, disparate personalities, different disciplines, and force them to become a company. Now! Make a show! How? Routine. The math helps: four weeks rehearsal, six days a week, five-and-ten minute breaks every 55 or 80 minutes, meal break every five hours, 10/12 tech rehearsals, half-hour, 15, 5, *places*! The prescribed numbers beg for an antidote; they soon give way to softer patterns, which quickly form the bits-and-pieces that are remembered long after the final final curtain.

Such as:

Saturday afternoons in the rehearsal room—did we really end each week with a little pat-on-the-back (and a little drink!) to congratulate ourselves for so beautifully navigating the tricky waters of the rehearsal process? I think we did!

We staged the last scene for the first time. Joan and Jeremy were stunning. And Jack said, "Jesus wept!" And then we all wept!

Bill Haber, our first day in the theatre, reminding us of all the famous footsteps we were lucky enough to follow onto the stage of the Plymouth/Schoenfeld. Marsha turning to me—a quiet gasp, hand to mouth, tears in her eyes—when Bill mentioned *Plaza Suite*. A memory. Were it that every producer began tech rehearsals in such an honorable fashion.

Marsha and Joan—so early to the theatre to prepare for the show, soak themselves in the atmosphere. No matter when I arrived they were always ahead of me. "Even from here, there they are!" I can still hear them chattering and clattering as I climbed up all of those flights for our nightly talks.

Steve Lukens, our company manager, without fail standing guard at the call board each night during half-hour.

Warm-up with Margarita, Aaron, Michael T.—before every show, those crazy sounds, the funny jokes, the gossip.

André's preparation on stage right before his first scene; the slow, steady breathing, the sound of his necklace gently brushing the floor as he stretched.

1. (L-R): Joan Allen, Jeremy Irons, Marsha Mason, André De Shields, Michael T. Weiss, Margarita Levieva, Aaron Lazar. (Front): Hadley Delany in rehearsal at New 42nd Street Studios.
2. Irons with director Jack O'Brien.
3. Lazar and Levieva at Sardi's restaurant for the opening night party.

Michael and Aaron waiting for their entrance into Scene 8—writing snappy new dialogue…just…to fill the…seemingly endless pauses in…"Does…anyone…ever…stop by…once in a while….just…to look…at…the mermaid?"

Did you know that metal coffee mugs make for a wonderful massage? "Did you know that?" Jeremy did. Diane and I always looked forward to that massage at the calling desk, sometimes before Scene 3, usually before Scene 8. Double fisted—one mug in each hand. Indeed, Jeremy was always full of "many delightful surprises!"

Diane always put my script on the desk before each show I called—opened to the first page, waiting for me to show up and start. I won't soon forget that.

The Delany family. All of them. Only Hadley had a part in the show, but if we were lucky, we had visits from Forbes, Margot and especially the youngest, Seth, who loved running around the basement whenever he wasn't napping. A first-time family adventure into the world of Broadway and we wouldn't have had it any other way! "I certainly hope you like it better than nothing happening at all."

Thursday afternoons with the understudies—Henny, Stevie Ray, Lizzie, Neal, Harold, and Caroline. Heaven.

Saturday night on Broadway!

Sunday Brunch!

Arriving at the theatre before preset—always a cold, empty space. Watching the crew go through their checks, sensing the rhythm of the other routines simultaneously bubbling throughout the building, the company getting ready to put on a show. It doesn't make any difference how long the show plays—the rituals segue to memories—it just happens. In fact, I'd venture a guess and say that a short run only makes them more concentrated, more saturated —those "splotches of paint" are more colorful, the resulting water lilies even more spectacular.

"We were trapped in a place where we thought nothing was going to happen."

"And something did."

Something always does….

In the Heights

First Preview: February 14, 2008. Opened: March 9, 2008.
Still running as of May 31, 2009.

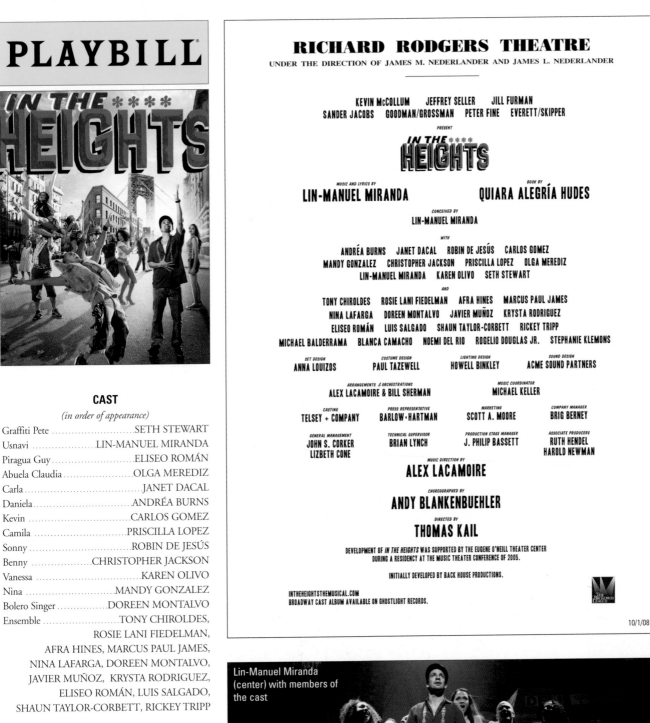

RICHARD RODGERS THEATRE

UNDER THE DIRECTION OF JAMES M. NEDERLANDER AND JAMES L. NEDERLANDER

KEVIN McCOLLUM   JEFFREY SELLER   JILL FURMAN
SANDER JACOBS   GOODMAN/GROSSMAN   PETER FINE   EVERETT/SKIPPER

PRESENT

IN THE HEIGHTS

MUSIC AND LYRICS BY
LIN-MANUEL MIRANDA

BOOK BY
QUIARA ALEGRÍA HUDES

CONCEIVED BY
LIN-MANUEL MIRANDA

WITH

ANDRÉA BURNS   JANET DACAL   ROBIN DE JESÚS   CARLOS GOMEZ
MANDY GONZALEZ   CHRISTOPHER JACKSON   PRISCILLA LOPEZ   OLGA MEREDIZ
LIN-MANUEL MIRANDA   KAREN OLIVO   SETH STEWART

AND

TONY CHIROLDES   ROSIE LANI FIEDELMAN   AFRA HINES   MARCUS PAUL JAMES
NINA LAFARGA   DOREEN MONTALVO   JAVIER MUÑOZ   KRYSTA RODRIGUEZ
ELISEO ROMÁN   LUIS SALGADO   SHAUN TAYLOR-CORBETT   RICKEY TRIPP
MICHAEL BALDERRAMA   BLANCA CAMACHO   NOEMI DEL RIO   ROGELIO DOUGLAS JR.   STEPHANIE KLEMONS

SET DESIGN
ANNA LOUIZOS

COSTUME DESIGN
PAUL TAZEWELL

LIGHTING DESIGN
HOWELL BINKLEY

SOUND DESIGN
ACME SOUND PARTNERS

ARRANGEMENTS & ORCHESTRATIONS
ALEX LACAMOIRE & BILL SHERMAN

MUSIC COORDINATOR
MICHAEL KELLER

CASTING
TELSEY + COMPANY

PRESS REPRESENTATIVE
BARLOW•HARTMAN

MARKETING
SCOTT A. MOORE

COMPANY MANAGER
BRIG BERNEY

GENERAL MANAGEMENT
**JOHN S. CORKER
LIZBETH CONE**

TECHNICAL SUPERVISOR
BRIAN LYNCH

PRODUCTION STAGE MANAGER
J. PHILIP BASSETT

ASSOCIATE PRODUCERS
**RUTH HENDEL
HAROLD NEWMAN**

MUSIC DIRECTION BY
ALEX LACAMOIRE

CHOREOGRAPHED BY
ANDY BLANKENBUEHLER

DIRECTED BY
THOMAS KAIL

DEVELOPMENT OF *IN THE HEIGHTS* WAS SUPPORTED BY THE EUGENE O'NEILL THEATER CENTER
DURING A RESIDENCY AT THE MUSIC THEATER CONFERENCE OF 2005.

INITIALLY DEVELOPED BY BACK HOUSE PRODUCTIONS.

INTHEHEIGHTSTHEMUSICAL.COM
BROADWAY CAST ALBUM AVAILABLE ON GHOSTLIGHT RECORDS.

10/1/08

CAST

(in order of appearance)

Graffiti Pete	SETH STEWART
Usnavi	LIN-MANUEL MIRANDA
Piragua Guy	ELISEO ROMÁN
Abuela Claudia	OLGA MEREDIZ
Carla	JANET DACAL
Daniela	ANDRÉA BURNS
Kevin	CARLOS GOMEZ
Camila	PRISCILLA LOPEZ
Sonny	ROBIN DE JESÚS
Benny	CHRISTOPHER JACKSON
Vanessa	KAREN OLIVO
Nina	MANDY GONZALEZ
Bolero Singer	DOREEN MONTALVO
Ensemble	TONY CHIROLDES,

ROSIE LANI FIEDELMAN,
AFRA HINES, MARCUS PAUL JAMES,
NINA LAFARGA, DOREEN MONTALVO,
JAVIER MUÑOZ, KRYSTA RODRIGUEZ,
ELISEO ROMÁN, LUIS SALGADO,
SHAUN TAYLOR-CORBETT, RICKEY TRIPP

SWINGS

MICHAEL BALDERRAMA,
BLANCA CAMACHO, NOEMI DEL RIO
ROGELIO DOUGLAS JR.,
STEPHANIE KLEMONS

Lin-Manuel Miranda (center) with members of the cast

Photo by Joan Marcus

Continued on next page

In the Heights

MUSICAL NUMBERS

ACT I

"In the Heights"	Usnavi, Company
"Breathe"	Nina, Company
"Benny's Dispatch"	Benny, Nina
"It Won't Be Long Now"	Vanessa, Usnavi, Sonny
"Inutil"	Kevin
"No Me Diga"	Daniela, Carla, Vanessa, Nina
"96,000"	Usnavi, Benny, Sonny, Vanessa, Daniela, Carla, Company
"Paciencia y Fe" ("Patience and Faith")	Abuela Claudia, Company
"When You're Home"	Nina, Benny, Company
"Piragua"	Piragua Guy
"Siempre" ("Always")	Camila
"The Club/Fireworks"	Company

ACT II

"Sunrise"	Nina, Benny, Company
"Hundreds of Stories"	Abuela Claudia, Usnavi
"Enough"	Camila
"Carnaval del Barrio"	Daniela, Company
"Atencion"	Kevin
"Alabanza"	Usnavi, Nina, Company
"Everything I Know"	Nina
"No Me Diga (Reprise)"	Daniela, Carla, Vanessa
"Piragua (Reprise)"	Piragua Guy
"Champagne"	Vanessa, Usnavi
"When the Sun Goes Down"	Nina, Benny
"Finale"	Usnavi, Company

(L-R): Marcy Harriell, Andréa Burns, Mandy Gonzalez and Janet Dacal

Photo by Joan Marcus

UNDERSTUDIES

For Usnavi:
MICHAEL BALDERRAMA, JAVIER MUÑOZ, SHAUN TAYLOR-CORBETT
For Abuela Claudia, Camila, Daniela:
BLANCA CAMACHO, DOREEN MONTALVO
For Nina:
JANET DACAL, NINA LAFARGA, KRYSTA RODRIGUEZ
For Benny:
ROGELIO DOUGLAS JR., MARCUS PAUL JAMES
For Kevin:
TONY CHIROLDES, ELISEO ROMÁN
For Vanessa:
JANET DACAL, KRYSTA RODRIGUEZ
For Carla:
STEPHANIE KLEMONS, KRYSTA RODRIGUEZ
For Sonny:
JAVIER MUÑOZ, SHAUN TAYLOR-CORBETT
For Graffiti Pete:
MICHAEL BALDERRAMA, RICKEY TRIPP
For Piragua Guy:
TONY CHIROLDES, SHAUN TAYLOR-CORBETT

Dance Captain:
MICHAEL BALDERRAMA
Assistant Dance Captain:
STEPHANIE KLEMONS

BAND

Conductor / Keyboard 1:
ALEX LACAMOIRE
Associate Conductor / Keyboard 2:
ZACHARY DIETZ
Lead Trumpet:
RAUL AGRAZ
Trumpet:
TREVOR NEUMANN
Trombones:
JOE FIEDLER, RYAN KEBERLE
Reeds:
DAVE RICHARDS, KRISTY NORTER
Drums:
ANDRES FORERO
Percussion:
DOUG HINRICHS, WILSON TORRES
Bass:
IRIO O'FARRILL
Guitar:
MANNY MOREIRA

In the Heights

Andréa Burns
Daniela

Janet Dacal
Carla

Robin De Jesús
Sonny

Carlos Gomez
Kevin

Mandy Gonzalez
Nina

Christopher Jackson
Benny

Priscilla Lopez
Camila

Olga Merediz
Abuela Claudia

Karen Olivo
Vanessa

Seth Stewart
Graffiti Pete

Tony Chiroldes
Ensemble

Rosie Lani Fiedelman
Ensemble

Afra Hines
Ensemble

Marcus Paul James
Ensemble

Nina Lafarga
Ensemble

Doreen Montalvo
Bolero Singer/
Ensemble

Javier Muñoz
Ensemble

Krysta Rodriguez
Ensemble

Eliseo Román
Piragua Guy/
Ensemble

Luis Salgado
Ensemble;
Latin Assistant
Choreographer

Shaun Taylor-Corbett
Ensemble

Rickey Tripp
Ensemble

Michael Balderrama
Swing;
Dance Captain/
Fight Captain

Blanca Camacho
Swing

Noemi Del Rio
Swing

Rogelio Douglas Jr.
Swing

Stephanie Klemons
Swing

Lin-Manuel Miranda
Usnavi;
Music and Lyrics;
Original Concept

Quiara Alegría Hudes
Book

Thomas Kail
Director

Andy
Blankenbuehler
Choreographer

Alex Lacamoire
Music Director,
Arranger,
Orchestrator

Anna Louizos
Set Designer

Paul Tazewell
Costume Designer

Howell Binkley
Lighting Designer

In the Heights

Tom Clark, Mark Menard and Nevin Steinberg,
Acme Sound Partners
Sound Designer

Bill Sherman
Arranger/
Orchestrator

Michael Keller
Music Coordinator

Bernard Telsey,
Telsey + Company
Casting

John S. Corker
General Manager

Brian Lynch/
Theatretech, Inc.
Technical Supervisor

Casey Hushion
Assistant Director

Kevin McCollum
Producer

Jeffrey Seller
Producer

Jill Furman
Producer

Robyn Goodman,
Goodman/Grossman
Producer

Sonny Everett,
Everett/Skipper
Producer

Ruth Hendel
Associate Producer

Joshua Henry
Benny, Ensemble

Antuan Raimone
Ensemble, Swing

Marcos Santana
Swing

Danny Bolero
Ensemble

Dwayne Clark
Ensemble

Marcy Harriell
Vanessa

Joshua Henry
Benny, Ensemble,
Swing

José-Luis Lopez
Swing

Javier Muñoz
Usnavi

Rick Negron
Kevin

Dawn Noel Pignuola
Swing

Antuan Raimone
Swing

Jon Rua
Swing

Gabrielle Ruiz
Ensemble

Marcos Santana
Swing

Elise Santora
Swing

In the Heights

CREW
Front Row (L-R): Jamie Stewart, Heather Hogan, J. Day

Second Row (L-R): Jason Wilkosz, David Speer, Justin Rathbun, Ronnie Knox

Third Row (L-R): Amber Wedin, Leslie Moulton, Jennifer Hohn

Back Row (L-R): Brig Berney, Alon Ben-David

Photos by Brian Mapp

BOX OFFICE
(L-R): Kathleen Cadunz, Saheed Baksh, Corinne Dorso

FRONT OF HOUSE STAFF
Front Row (L-R): Barbara Rodell, Carmen Frank, Giovanny Lopez, Beverly Thornton, Joseph Melchiorre, John Hollingsworth, Matt Rodriguez, Dorothy Darby

Back Row (L-R): Fran Eppy, Maureen Dabreo, Christopher Langdon, Timothy Pettolina (House Manager), Hank Sanders, Jacqueline Corrigan, Lori Miata, Sonia Torres

In the Heights

STAFF FOR *IN THE HEIGHTS*

GENERAL MANAGEMENT
John S. Corker
Lizbeth Cone

GENERAL PRESS REPRESENTATIVES
BARLOW•HARTMAN
Michael Hartman	John Barlow
Wayne Wolfe	Melissa Bixler

DIRECTOR OF MARKETING
Scott A. Moore

CASTING
TELSEY + COMPANY
Bernie Telsey CSA, Will Cantler CSA, David Vaccari CSA,
Bethany Knox CSA, Craig Burns CSA,
Tiffany Little Canfield CSA, Rachel Hoffman CSA,
Carrie Rosson CSA, Justin Huff CSA, Joe Langworth,
Bess Fifer CSA, Patrick Goodwin

COMPANY MANAGER	Brig Berney
TECHNICAL SUPERVISION	Brian Lynch/ Theatretech, Inc.
PRODUCTION STAGE MANGER	J. Philip Bassett
WIG DESIGNER	Charles LaPointe
Assistant Director	Casey Hushion
Associate Choreographer	Joey Dowling
Fight Director	Ron Piretti
Dance Captain/Fight Captain	Michael Balderrama
Stage Manager	Amber Wedin
Assistant Stage Manager	Heather Hogan
Latin Assistant Choreographer	Luis Salgado
Assistant Dance Captain	Stephanie Klemons
Associate Scenic Designers	Donyale Werle, Todd Potter
Assistant Scenic Designers	Hilary Noxon, Heather Dunbar
Associate Costume Designer	Michael Zecker
Assistant Costume Designer	Caitlin Hunt
Associate Lighting Designer	Mark Simpson
Assistant Lighting Designers	Greg Bloxham, Ryan O'Gara
Associate Sound Designer	Sten Severson
Moving Light Programmer	David Arch
Advance Carpenter	McBrien Dunbar
Advance Flyman	Cheyenne Benson
Production Electrician	Keith Buchanan
Head Electrician	Christopher Kurtz
Production Sound	Dan Robillard
Production Propmaster	George Wagner
Head Propmaster	David Speer
Follow Spot Operator	Jason Wilkosz
Sound Engineer	Justin Rathbun
Wardrobe Supervisor	Rick Kelly
Hair Supervisor	Jamie Stewart
Dressers	Alon Ben-David, Gary Biangone, Moira MacGregor-Conrad, Leslie Moulton
Rehearsal Pianists	Zachary Dietz, Cian McCarthy Kat Sherrell
Musical Coordinator	Michael Keller
Copyist	Emily Grishman Music Preparation/ Emily Grishman, Katharine Edmonds
Keyboard Programming	Randy Cohen
Rehearsal Drummer	Doug Hinrichs

Music Assistant	Colleen Darnell
Management Assistant	Andy Jones
Production Assistants	Jess Slocum, Mark Barna
Executive Assistant to Messrs. McCollum & Seller	Ryan Hill
Assistant to Messrs. McCollum & Seller	Caitlyn Thomson
Assistant to Mr. Corker	Kim Marie Vasquez
Legal Counsel	Levine Plotkin Menin, LLP/ Loren Plotkin, Susan Mindell, Conrad Rippy, Cris Criswell
Advertising	SpotCo/Drew Hodges, Jim Edwards, Peter Milano, Pete Duffy, Tom Greenwald
Accountant	FK Partners/Robert Fried
Controller	Sarah Galbraith and Co.
Insurance	D.R. Reiff & Associates
Banking	Signature Bank/ Margaret Monigan, Mary Ann Fanelli
Payroll	Castellana Services
Merchandise	Marquee Merchandise LLC/ Matt Murphy
Travel Arrangements	Tzell Travel
Flier Distribution	Laura Cosentino/Roselily
Website/Internet Marketing	SpotCo/ Sara Fitzpatrick, Matt Wilstein
Production Photographer	Joan Marcus
Physical Therapy	Mark Hunter Hall
Merchandising	George Fenmore/ More Merchandising International

THE PRODUCING OFFICE
Kevin McCollum	Jeffrey Seller
John S. Corker	Debra Nir
Caitlyn Thomson	

SPECIAL THANKS
Luis Miranda; John Buzzetti; Mark Sendroff;
Nick Lugo; LaVie Productions/R. Erin Craig,
Off-Broadway General Manager

CREDITS
Scenery constructed by Centerline Studio, Inc. Lighting equipment from PRG Lighting. Sound equipment from PRG Audio. New York Daily News, L.P., used with permission. Chain motors from Show Motion. Trucking by Clark Transfer, Inc. Percussion equipment and drum programming by Dan McMillan. Latin percussion supplied by Pearl Drum Company. Andres Patrick Forero plays Yamaha Drum heads, Sabian cymbals, Vic Firth sticks and Reunion Blues, exclusively. Wireless handsets by Verizon. Costumes built by Donna Langman Costumes; Tricorne, Inc.; Paul Chang Custom Taylor. Millinery by Lynne Mackey Studio. Hosiery and undergarments from Bra*Tenders. Natural herb cough drops courtesy of Ricola USA, Inc. Goya products furnished by Goya Foods, Inc. Lottery items courtesy of NY State Lottery. Cell phones courtesy of Motorola. Cups, straws and stirrers courtesy of Solo, Inc. Mars Inc. products used. Adams gum and Cadbury chocolates used. Werthers Original courtesy of Storck USA. MASTERFOODS USA products used. Unilever N.A. products used. Kraft Foods products used. Massimo-Zanetti beverages used. Country Club cola products and Iberia Food products courtesy of Luis Botero, North Shore Bottling Company, Brooklyn, NY. Beauty salon supplies provided by Ray Beauty Supply. Piragua Cart, artificial food props, other props provided by John Creech

Design and Production. Local trucking provided by Prop Transport. Flicker candles provided by Clara Sherman, Kinnelon, NJ. Car service counter, bodega counter provided by Blackthorne Studio. Various bodega prop dressing courtesy of Rock Ice Café and Catering, Dunellen, NY. Food display hanging racks courtesy of Green Acres Health Food Store, Piscataway, NJ. Additional set and hand props courtesy of George Fenmore, Inc. Steel security gates by Steelcraft Folding Gate Corp. Raul Agraz and Trevor Neumann exclusively use Cannonball trumpets.

Bolero singer is Doreen Montalvo. Radio voices by Joshua Henry, Eliseo Román and Daphne Rubin-Vega

Smoke, haze and strobe lights are used
in this production.

In the Heights rehearsed at
The New 42nd Street Studios.

NEDERLANDER
Chairman	**James M. Nederlander**
President	**James L. Nederlander**

Executive Vice President
Nick Scandalios

Vice President Corporate Development **Charlene S. Nederlander**	Senior Vice President Labor Relations **Herschel Waxman**
Vice President **Jim Boese**	Chief Financial Officer **Freida Sawyer Belviso**

HOUSE STAFF FOR
THE RICHARD RODGERS THEATRE
House Manager	Timothy Pettolina
Box Office Treasurer	Fred Santore Jr.
Assistant Treasurer	Daniel Nitopi
Electrician	Steve Carver
Carpenter	Kevin Camus
Propertymaster	Stephen F. DeVerna
Engineer	Sean Quinn

Priscilla Lopez and Rick Negron

In the Heights
Scrapbook

Photos by Aubrey Reuben

1. Composer and star Lin-Manuel Miranda (center) takes his last curtain call in the show on February 15, 2009, with (L-R) Priscilla Lopez, Marcy Harriell, Christopher Jackson and Mandy Gonzalez.
2. (L-R) Gonzalez and Jackson at "Broadway on Broadway" in Times Square September 14, 2008.

Correspondent: Javier Muñoz, "Usnavi"

Most Exciting Celebrity Visitor: Diana Ross, who walked into the stage manager's office after the show and said "I'm Home!!"!

"Easter Bonnet" Sketch: This year I was given the opportunity to host along with Karen Olivo and we were both incredibly nervous. I'm not sure how we did but we cracked each other up the entire time!!

Special Backstage Rituals: There's an endless amount of backstage rituals so just a few are Olga and I holding hands and saying "I love you" to each other right before the start of the show off stage right; Eliseo, Afra and I group-hugging after the opening number stage left; general craziness during "Dispatch" and "Paciencia y Fe" stage left involving everyone who is there, which always makes me wish I had a video camera backstage!

Favorite Moment During Each Performance: This is easy! During "Alabanza," Usnavi doesn't sing but the entire company builds the chorus, slowly voice by voice and I breathe deep, listening to the cast SING!! It's so beautiful it blows me away every single show.

Favorite In-Theatre Gathering Place: The basement, where we gather before every single show at five minutes to curtain to grab hands and form a prayer circle. It's the one chance we all get to see each other for the night and connect.

Favorite Off-Site Hangouts: There are a few: Bamboo 52, Bourbon Street and Havana Central.

Favorite Snack Food: Amazing cookies baked by Grace, who is a friend of one of our musicians.

Mascot: Don't really have one but I have a pet fish, a beta named Punk, in my dressing room!

Favorite Therapies: Ricola, physical therapy and Tequila Sundays!!

Cell Phone Rings, Cell Phone Photos,

Tweeting or Texting Incidents During a Performance: There are more little red cell phone lights going off in the theatre than you'd guess and they're always distracting and annoying.

Memorable Press Encounter: The Houston affiliate for ABC came and interviewed me and I gave them a tour; they were exceptionally sweet and kind and very excited about the show. That was a very cool interview.

Memorable Stage Door Fan Encounter: One teenager asked me to sign his shaved head with a sharpie and I did, but I kept imagining his mother's reaction! Honestly though, anytime young people are at the stage door it's pretty amazing. They always say they are very inspired by what they've just seen and all I can think and hope is that they do something great with that inspiration.

Latest Audience Arrival: I do recall a couple right down front walking out before the end of the show, right after I say the line "Tell the whole block I'm staying." Perhaps they wished for a different ending? Or perhaps one of them had diarrhea? I'll never know, LOL.

Fastest Costume Change: The ensemble members in "Paciencia y Fe" who change from head to toe three times! It's crazy!!

Busiest Day at the Box Office: The day we won our Tony for Best Musical! HOLLA!

Who Wore the Least: I'd say just about all the ensemble women are pretty scantily dressed. They might as well be doing "Broadway Bares"!

Catchphrases Only the Company Would Recognize: "You're a…." "Saturday night on Broadway, they ain't ready!" "On the wings of love." "The thing with the thing." "You ain't got no friends!" "OKRRRRRR!"

Company In-Jokes: If there is a fire you should leave the theatre…and head to the Marriott for drinks.

Best In-House Parody Lyrics: In place of "In the Heights, I've got today!" sing "In my tights, I've got mamey!" (Pronounced "Mah-MAY—it's a fruit.)

Understudy Anecdote: When you've forgotten who your next dance partner is during a huge group number just look around with eyes that say "Are you my mommy?" and sure enough your next partner/mommy will find you.

Nicknames: "PLO," "Rosie the Rock," "K-Rod," "Chocolate Thunder," "Brother Jackson," "El Passión," "Superman," "Little Bro," "The Monster."

Sweethearts Within the Company: We're all in love with this show and truly love each other as family; corny but true.

Embarrassing Moments: Enduring several severe colds that caused my voice to crack show after show and saying to myself, "Yes, audience, you paid hundreds of dollars to be here and listen to me sing like Peter Brady!"

Coolest Thing About Being in This Show: What isn't cool about being in *In the Heights*?

Also: I would like to add one more memory. Just after we won the Tony in 2008, and the entire original cast was still in the show, I had a moment where during the curtain call, in my old ensemble track, I looked around the stage, taking in every cast member's face and all the energy of the audience, and I locked that feeling and that image in my memory because I knew this was the end of our journey together and that everything would change. Which of course is what happened; Karen left for *West Side* fame, Lin left, I moved up, change happened, and will continue to. This story will go on inspiring more and more people, way beyond us. But that one moment lives in my mind forever. This particular group of people, of hearts and minds, that made history together, made dreams come true and have changed the world for the better.

Irena's Vow

First Preview: March 10, 2009. Opened: March 29, 2009.
Still running as of May 31, 2009.

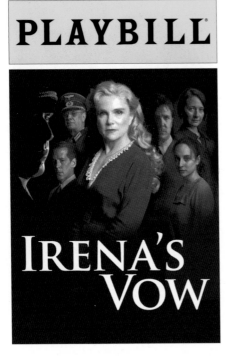

CAST
(in order of appearance)

Irena Gut Opdyke .... TOVAH FELDSHUH
Major Rugemer .... THOMAS RYAN
Schultz .... STEVEN HAUCK
Ida Hallar .... MAJA C. WAMPUSZYC
Lazar Hallar .... GENE SILVERS
Fanka Silberman .... TRACEE CHIMO
Sturmbannführer Rokita .... JOHN STANISCI
Helen/Rokita's Secretary .... SANDI CARROLL
The Visitor/Polish Worker .... SCOTT KLAVAN
Mayor of Jerusalem/
     SS Officer .... PETER REZNIKOFF

UNDERSTUDIES AND STANDBYS

For Ida, Fanka, Helen/Rokita's Secretary:
HEATHER KENZIE
For Rugemer, Schultz, Mayor/Officer:
PAUL O'BRIEN
For Rokita, Lazar, The Visitor/Polish Worker:
KEVIN O'DONNELL

Standby for Irena Gut Opdyke: TINA BENKO

Setting: An American high school, 1988
Occupied Poland, 1939–1945
Jerusalem, 1988

Playwright's Dedication:
For Irena

— Dan Gordon

☾ WALTER KERR THEATRE
A JUJAMCYN THEATRE
ROCCO LANDESMAN
President

PAUL LIBIN
Producing Director

JACK VIERTEL
Creative Director

JORDAN ROTH
Vice President

POWER PRODUCTIONS/STAN RAIFF   DARYL ROTH   DEBRA BLACK   JAMES L. NEDERLANDER/TERRY ALLEN KRAMER   PETER FINE

PRESENT

AN INVICTUS THEATER COMPANY / THE DIRECTORS COMPANY PRODUCTION

TOVAH FELDSHUH
IN
IRENA'S VOW

A NEW PLAY BY
DAN GORDON

WITH
SANDI CARROLL   TRACEE CHIMO   STEVEN HAUCK
SCOTT KLAVAN   PETER REZNIKOFF   THOMAS RYAN
GENE SILVERS   JOHN STANISCI   MAJA C. WAMPUSZYC

SCENIC DESIGN	COSTUME DESIGN	LIGHTING DESIGN	PROJECTION DESIGN
KEVIN JUDGE	ASTRID BRUCKER	DAVID CASTANEDA	ALEX KOCH

ORIGINAL MUSIC AND SOUND DESIGN
QUENTIN CHIAPPETTA

WIG AND HAIR DESIGN
LEAH J. LOUKAS

PRODUCTION STAGE MANAGER
ALAN FOX

TECHNICAL SUPERVISION
ARTHUR SICCARDI
PATRICK SULLIVAN

PRESS REPRESENTATIVE
O&M CO.

MARKETING
HHC MARKETING

ASSOCIATE PRODUCERS
R. ERIN CRAIG
ALEXANDER FRASER
ROZ GOLDBERG

GENERAL MANAGER
LEONARD SOLOWAY

DIRECTED BY
MICHAEL PARVA

THE PRODUCERS WISH TO EXPRESS THEIR APPRECIATION TO THE THEATRE DEVELOPMENT FUND
FOR ITS SUPPORT OF THIS PRODUCTION.

3/29/09

(L-R): Maja Wampuszyc,
Tracee Chimo,
Tovah Feldshuh (kneeling),
Gene Silvers

Photo by Carol Rosegg

Irena's Vow

Tovah Feldshuh
Irena Gut Opdyke

Sandi Carroll
Helen/
Rokita's Secretary

Tracee Chimo
Fanka Silberman

Steven Hauck
Schultz

Scott Klavan
The Visitor/
Polish Worker

Peter Reznikoff
Mayor of Jerusalem/
SS Officer

Thomas Ryan
Major Rugemer
and co-founder
Invictus Theater

Gene Silvers
Lazar Hallar

John Stanisci
Sturmbannführer
Rokita
and co-founder
Invictus Theater

Maja C. Wampuszyc
Ida Hallar

Tina Benko
Standby for
Irena Gut Opdyke

Heather Kenzie
u/s Ida, Fanka,
Helen/
Rokita's Secretary

Paul O'Brien
u/s Rugemer,
Schultz,
Mayor/Officer

Kevin O'Donnell
u/s Rokita, Lazar,
The Visitor/
Polish Worker

Dan Gordon
Playwright

Michael Parva
Director
and Artistic Director,
The Directors
Company

Arthur Siccardi
Theatrical Services,
Inc.
Production
Supervisor

Hugh Hysell
HHC Marketing
Marketing

Daryl Roth
Producer

Debra Black
Producer

James L.
Nederlander
Producer

Terry Allen Kramer
Producer

Alexander Fraser
Associate Producer

Irena Gut Opdyke
(May 15, 1918 -
May 17, 2003)

PRODUCTION STAGE MANAGER
Alan Fox

DOORMAN
John Raymond Barker

FRONT OF HOUSE STAFF
(L-R): Adam Ferguson, T.J. D'Angelo, Juliette Cipriatti, Leo Linton

BOX OFFICE
(L-R): Harry Jaffie, Michael Loiacono

Photos by Brian Mapp

Irving Berlin's White Christmas

First Preview: November 14, 2008. Opened: November 23, 2008.
Closed January 4, 2009 after 12 Previews and 53 Performances.

PLAYBILL

CAST
(in order of appearance)

Bob Wallace .... STEPHEN BOGARDUS
Phil Davis .... JEFFRY DENMAN
Ralph Sheldrake .... PETER REARDON
General Henry Waverly .... CHARLES DEAN
Ed Sullivan Announcer ... SHEFFIELD CHASTAIN
Rita .... ANNE HORAK
Rhoda .... KATHERINE TOKARZ
Tessie .... AMY JUSTMAN
Betty Haynes .... KERRY O'MALLEY
Judy Haynes .... MEREDITH PATTERSON
Jimmy .... JARRAN MUSE
Quintet ..... CLIFF BEMIS, DREW HUMPHREY,
WENDY JAMES, AMY JUSTMAN,
KEVIN WORLEY
Mr. Snoring Man .... CLIFF BEMIS
Mrs. Snoring Man .... WENDY JAMES
Train Conductor .... DREW HUMPHREY
Martha Watson .... SUSAN MANSUR
Susan Waverly .... MELODY HOLLIS
Ezekiel Foster .... CLIFF BEMIS
Mike Nulty .... SHEFFIELD CHASTAIN
Sheldrake's Secretary .... WENDY JAMES
Regency Room
    Announcer .... SHEFFIELD CHASTAIN
Regency Room Dancers ... STEPHEN CARRASCO,
CHAD SEIB, KEVIN WORLEY

⇥N⇤ MARQUIS THEATRE
UNDER THE DIRECTION OF JAMES M. NEDERLANDER AND JAMES L. NEDERLANDER

Kevin McCollum   John Gore   Tom McGrath   Paul Blake   The Producing Office
Dan Markley   Sonny Everett   Broadway Across America

in association with
Paramount Pictures

present

Irving Berlin's WHITE CHRISTMAS

Based upon the Paramount Pictures film written for the screen by
Norman Krasna, Norman Panama, and Melvin Frank

Music and Lyrics by
Irving Berlin

Book by
David Ives and Paul Blake

starring

Stephen Bogardus   Kerry O'Malley
Jeffry Denman   Meredith Patterson

and

Charles Dean   Susan Mansur   Peter Reardon
Cliff Bemis   Sheffield Chastain   Melody Hollis

with

Phillip Attmore   Jacob ben Widmar   Sara Brians   Stephen Carrasco   Margot de la Barre   Mary Giattino
Anne Horak   Drew Humphrey   Wendy James   Amy Justman   Matthew Kirk   Sae La Chin
Richie Mastascusa   Jarran Muse   Alessa Neeck   Shannon O'Bryan   Con O'Shea-Creal   Athena Ripka
Kiira Schmidt   Chad Seib   Kelly Sheehan   Katherine Tokarz   Kevin Worley

Set Design	Costume Design	Lighting Design	Sound Design
Anna Louizos	**Carrie Robbins**	**Ken Billington**	**Acme Sound Partners**
Orchestrations	Vocal and Dance Arrangements	Music Coordinator	Marketing
Larry Blank	**Bruce Pomahac**	**Seymour Red Press**	**Scott A. Moore**
Technical Supervisor	Production Stage Manager	Associate Choreographer	Press Representative
Brian Lynch	**Michael J. Passaro**	**Kelli Barclay**	**Boneau/Bryan-Brown**
Casting	General Management	Associate Director	Associate Producers
Jay Binder	**John S. Corker**	**Marc Bruni**	**Richard A. Smith**
Nikole Vallins	**Barbara Crompton**		**Douglas L. Meyer/James D. Stern**

Music Supervisor
Rob Berman

Choreographer
Randy Skinner

Directed by
Walter Bobbie

11/23/08

The Finale

Continued on next page

Irving Berlin's White Christmas

SCENES

ACT ONE

Prologue	An Army Camp in Europe, Christmas Eve, 1944
Scene One	The Ed Sullivan Show, 1954
Scene Two	Bob and Phil's Dressing Room; Betty and Judy's Dressing Room
Scene Three	Jimmy's Back Room
Scene Four	A Train
Scene Five	The Front Desk at the Columbia Inn
Scene Six	The Barn Theatre
Scene Seven	The Front Porch of the Inn
Scene Eight	Sheldrake's Office; Martha's Switchboard
Scene Nine	The Barn Theatre

ACT TWO

Scene One	The Barn Theatre
Scene Two	Betty's Bedroom
Scene Three	The Barn Theatre
Scene Four	The Regency Room
Scene Five	The Ed Sullivan Show
Scene Six	The Front Desk at the Columbia Inn
Scene Seven	The Barn Theatre, Christmas Eve

MUSICAL NUMBERS

ACT ONE

Overture

"Happy Holiday"	Bob and Phil
"White Christmas"	Bob, Phil, Sheldrake and Ensemble
"Let Yourself Go"	Bob, Phil and Ensemble
"Love and the Weather"	Bob and Betty
"Sisters"	Betty and Judy
"The Best Things Happen While You're Dancing"	Phil, Judy and Quintet
"Snow"	Bob, Phil, Betty, Judy, Mr. Snoring Man, Mrs. Snoring Man and Ensemble
"What Can You Do With a General?"	Martha, Bob and Phil
"Let Me Sing and I'm Happy"	Martha and Ensemble
"Count Your Blessings Instead of Sheep"	Bob and Betty
"Blue Skies"	Bob and Ensemble

ACT TWO

Entr'acte

"I Love a Piano"	Phil, Judy and Ensemble
"Falling Out of Love Can Be Fun"	Martha, Betty and Judy
"Sisters" (Reprise)	Bob and Phil
"Love, You Didn't Do Right By Me/How Deep Is the Ocean"	Betty and Bob
"We'll Follow the Old Man"	Bob and Male Ensemble
"Let Me Sing and I'm Happy" (Reprise)	Susan
"How Deep Is the Ocean" (Reprise)	Bob and Betty
"We'll Follow the Old Man" (Reprise)	Bob, Phil, Sheldrake and Male Ensemble
"White Christmas" (Reprise)	Bob and Company
Finale: "I've Got My Love to Keep Me Warm"	Full Company

Cast Continued

ENSEMBLE

PHILLIP ATTMORE, STEPHEN CARRASCO, MARGOT DE LA BARRE, ANNE HORAK, DREW HUMPHREY, WENDY JAMES, AMY JUSTMAN, MATTHEW KIRK, SAE LA CHIN, JARRAN MUSE, ALESSA NEECK, SHANNON O'BRYAN, CON O'SHEA-CREAL, KIIRA SCHMIDT, CHAD SEIB, KELLY SHEEHAN, KATHERINE TOKARZ, KEVIN WORLEY

UNDERSTUDIES

For Bob Wallace: PETER REARDON
For Betty Haynes: AMY JUSTMAN
For Phil Davis: KEVIN WORLEY
For Judy Haynes: SHANNON O'BRYAN
For General Waverly: CLIFF BEMIS
For Susan Waverly: ATHENA RIPKA
For Ralph Sheldrake: SHEFFIELD CHASTAIN
For Martha Watson: WENDY JAMES
For Ezekiel Foster/Mr. Snoring Man: DREW HUMPHREY
For Mike Nulty/Ed Sullivan Announcer: JACOB ben WIDMAR

SWINGS

JACOB ben WIDMAR, SARA BRIANS, MARY GIATTINO, RICHIE MASTASCUSA

ASSISTANT CHOREOGRAPHERS

Dance Captain: SARA BRIANS
Assistant Dance Captain: MARY GIATTINO

MUSIC DIRECTOR

ROB BERMAN

Associate Music Director: DAVID GURSKY

ORCHESTRA

Violins: MARILYN REYNOLDS, PAUL WOODIEL, ROBIN ZEH, MARY WHITAKER, SUSAN FRENCH
Trumpets: CHRIS JAUDES, RONALD BUTTACAVOLI, ELAINE BURT
Keyboards: DAVID GURSKY (Associate Conductor), MICAH YOUNG
Celli: MAIRI DORMAN, DANNY MILLER
Woodwinds: STEVE KENYON, TODD GROVES, DAVID YOUNG, ALLEN WON, MARK THRASHER
Trombones: LARRY FARRELL, CLINT SHARMAN, JEFF NELSON
French Horn: DAVID BYRD-MARROW
Percussion: BILL HAYES
Bass: LOU BRUNO
Drums: RICH ROSENZWEIG

Irving Berlin's White Christmas

Stephen Bogardus
Bob Wallace

Kerry O'Malley
Betty Haynes

Jeffry Denman
Phil Davis

Meredith Patterson
Judy Haynes

Charles Dean
General Henry Waverly

Susan Mansur
Martha Watson

Peter Reardon
Ralph Sheldrake

Cliff Bemis
Ezekiel Foster/ Mr. Snoring Man

Sheffield Chastain
Mike Nulty/ Ed Sullivan Announcer

Melody Hollis
Susan Waverly

Phillip Attmore
Ensemble

Jacob ben Widmar
Swing

Sara Brians
Assistant Choreographer, Dance Captain, Swing

Stephen Carrasco
Ensemble

Margot De La Barre
Ensemble

Mary Giattino
Assistant Choreographer, Assistant Dance Captain, Swing

Anne Horak
Ensemble

Drew Humphrey
Ensemble

Wendy James
Mrs. Snoring Man

Amy Justman
Ensemble

Matthew Kirk
Ensemble

Sae La Chin
Ensemble

Richie Mastascusa
Swing

Jarran Muse
Ensemble

Alessa Neeck
Ensemble

Shannon M. O'Bryan
Ensemble

Con O'Shea-Creal
Ensemble

Athena Ripka
Understudy for Susan

Kiira Schmidt
Ensemble

Chad Seib
Ensemble

Kelly Sheehan
Ensemble

Katherine Tokarz
Ensemble

Kevin Worley
Ensemble

Irving Berlin
Music & Lyrics

David Ives
Book

Irving Berlin's White Christmas

Walter Bobbie
Director

Randy Skinner
Choreographer

Anna Louizos
Set Designer

Carrie Robbins
Costume Designer

Ken Billington
Lighting Designer

Tom Clark, Mark Menard and Nevin Steinberg,
Acme Sound Partners
Sound Design

Larry Blank
Orchestrations

Rob Berman
Music Supervisor

Marc Bruni
Associate Director

Jay Binder CSA
Casting

Nikole Vallins
Casting

Brian Lynch/
Theatretech, Inc.
Technical Supervisor

John S. Corker
General Manager

Kevin McCollum
Producer

Jeffrey Seller,
The Producing Office
Producer

Sonny Everett
Co-Producer

Douglas L. Meyer
Associate Producer

Photo by Brian Mapp

STAGE MANAGEMENT
(L-R): Jim Athens, Michael J. Passaro, Jay McLeod

Photo by Joan Marcus

Meredith Patterson and Jeffry Denman lead the chorus in "I Love a Piano"

Irving Berlin's White Christmas

Photo by Jay McLeod

ORCHESTRA
Conductor and Music Supervisor Rob Berman (center as Santa) and the Orchestra

Photos by Brian Mapp

COMPANY MANAGEMENT
(L-R): Barbara Crompton, Andy Jones

WARDROBE DEPARTMENT
Front Row (L-R): Kimberly Mark Sirota, Liz Brady, Del Miskie
Back Row (L-R): Jessica Worsnop, Michael Grawler, Soomi Marano, Jason Bishop, Jeffery Johnson, Chad Jason, Ricky Yates, Olivia Booth
Not pictured: Bill Hubner, Tracy Diebold

HAIR DEPARTMENT
(L-R): Joe Whitmeyer, Elisa Acevedo

FRONT OF HOUSE STAFF

Irving Berlin's White Christmas

STAFF FOR *IRVING BERLIN'S WHITE CHRISTMAS*

GENERAL MANAGEMENT
John S. Corker
Barbara Crompton

MARKETING
Scott A. Moore

CASTING
JAY BINDER CASTING
Jay Binder CSA   Jack Bowdan CSA
Mark Brandon, Sara Schatz, Nikole Vallins
Kate Sprance, Karen Young

BAY AREA CASTING CONSULTANTS
Meryl Shaw   Greg Hubbard

PRESS REPRESENTATIVE
BONEAU/BRYAN-BROWN
Chris Boneau   Joe Perrotta
Kelly Guiod

ASSOCIATE DIRECTOR
Marc Bruni

ASSOCIATE CHOREOGRAPHER
Kelli Barclay

COMPANY MANAGER
Barbara Crompton

PRODUCTION
STAGE MANAGER ....MICHAEL J. PASSARO
Technical Supervisor ....Brian Lynch/Theatretech, Inc.
Stage Manager ....Jay McLeod
Associate Company Manager ....Andrew Jones
Assistant Stage Manager ....Jim Athens
Associate Music Director....................David Gursky
Additional Orchestrations ....Peter Myers
Assistant Director ....David Ruttura
Directing Assistant ....Ross Evans
Assistant Choreographer/Dance Captain ....Sara Brians
Assistant Choreographer/
    Assistant Dance Captain ....Mary Giattino
Executive Assistant to Mr. McCollum
    and Mr. Seller ....Caitlyn Thomson
Assistant to Mr. Blake ....Michael Bosner
Assistant to the
    General Manager ....Kim Marie Vasquez
Management Associate ....Jen Collins
Marketing Assistant ....Samara Harand
Production Assistants ....Thomas Recktenwald,
                        Conwell Worthington III
Associate Set Designer ....Todd Potter
Automated Lighting Programmer ....Jason Badger
Associate Lighting Designers ....Ed McCarthy,
                        Jim Milkey
Moving Light Programmer ....Jason Badger
Associate Sound Designer ....Nick Borisjuk
Production Carpenter ....Lehan Sullivan
Head Carpenter ....Joe Valentino
Flyman ....Jeremy Palmer
Automation ....Kenny Brock, Chris Doornbos
Production Electrician ....Manuel Becker
Head Electrician ....Jack Culver

Assistant Electricians ......James Crayton, Chris Robinson
Sound Engineer ....Brad Gyorgak
Assistant Sound Engineer ....Elizabeth Coleman
Production Properties Master ....George Wagner
Prop Master ....David Speer
Production Wardrobe Supervisor ....Lee Austin
Wardrobe Supervisor ....Jessica Worsnop
Assistant Wardrobe ....Ricky Yates
Principal Wigs
    Designed by ....Paul Huntley Enterprises, Inc.
Ensemble Wigs
    Designed by ....Howard Leonard/Wigboys, Inc.
Production Hair Supervisor ....Elisa Acevedo
Children's Guardian ....Allison Mosier
Education Service ....On Location Education
NYC Studio Teacher ....Amy Wolk
Music Preparation ....Chelsea Music Service/
                        Paul Holderbaum
Synthesizer Programmer ....Bruce Samuels
Rehearsal Pianist ....Paul Masse, Matthew Perri
Advertising ....Spotco/
                        Drew Hodges, Jim Edwards,
                        Jim Aquino, Stacey Maya
Broadway Web Design &
    Internet Marketing ....Sara Fitz, Matt Wilstein,
                        Marc Mettler, Christina Sees
Merchandise ....Max Merchandising, LLC/
                        Randi Grossman, Meridith Maskara
Legal Counsel ....Levine Plotkin & Menin LLP/
                        Loren H. Plotkin, Esq., Susan Mindell, Esq.
Accounting ....FK Partners/Robert Fried
Bookkeeper ....Galbraith and Company/
                        Sarah Galbraith
Insurance ...........................D.R. Reiff & Associates/
                        Sonny Everett, Dennis Reiff
Banking ....JP Morgan Chase
Payroll ....CSI Payroll Services, Inc./Lance Castellana

THE PRODUCING OFFICE
Kevin McCollum   Jeffrey Seller
John S. Corker   Debra Nir   Scott A. Moore
Caitlyn Thomson

CREDITS
Scenery built by Hudson Scenic. Certain scenery built by Centerline. Drops painted by Scenic Art Studios, Inc. Certain scenery and scenic effects built, painted, electrified and automated by ShowMotion Inc. Lighting equipment by PRG Lighting. Sound equipment by PRG Audio. Women's clothing by Parsons-Meares Ltd. Jimmy's Sequence by CMC & Design. Men's custom tailoring by Scafati. Additional tailoring by Saint Laurie Merchant Tailors. Custom knitwear by Maria Ficalora. Oxydol ensembles by Martin Izquierdo Studio. Dance shoes by Capezio, NYC; Worldtone Dance Shoes. Millinery by Arnold S. Levine, Inc.; Studio Rouge; Timberlake Studios. Sisters' shoes by Phil LaDuca NYC. Principal wigs by Paul Huntley Enterprises, Inc. Ensemble wigs built by Wigboys, Inc. Snow effects by Snowmasters Inc. Chain motors from ShowMotion, Inc. Radios from Production Radio Rentals. Quick-Ice packs provided by Medi-Ice. Spike tape provided by Garden Hardware.

SPECIAL THANKS
Mary Ellin Barrett, Linda Emmet, Elizabeth Peters, Ted Chapin, Victoria Traube, Bert Fink, Neil Mazzella, William

M. Mensching, Joseph Forbes, Roger Gray, Darren DeVerna, David Strang, Eric Pearce, Kevin Branch, Kevin Collins of Capezio NYC, Ricola natural herb cough drops courtesy of Ricola USA, Inc., Linda at Medi. Emergen-C products courtesy of Alacer Corporation. Special thanks to Actors' Equity Association and SSD&C for their special consideration on this production.

Performance rights to *Irving Berlin's White Christmas* are licensed by R&H Theatricals: www.rnhtheatricals.com.

NEDERLANDER

Chairman	**James M. Nederlander**
President	**James L. Nederlander**

Executive Vice President
Nick Scandalios

Vice President	Senior Vice President
Corporate Development	Labor Relations
Charlene S. Nederlander	**Herschel Waxman**

Vice President	Chief Financial Officer
Jim Boese	**Freida Sawyer Belviso**

STAFF FOR THE MARQUIS THEATRE
Manager ....David Calhoun
Associate Manager ....Austin Nathaniel
Treasurer ....Rick Waxman
Assistant Treasurer ....John Rooney
Carpenter ....Joseph P. Valentino
Electrician ....James Mayo
Property Man ....Scott Mecionis

DOORMAN
Juan "Cisco" Garcia

Irving Berlin's White Christmas
SCRAPBOOK

Correspondent: Kerry O'Malley, "Betty Haynes"

Memorable Gifts: Athena Ripka (our "Susan Waverly" understudy, who performed the role five times on Broadway) gave wonderful date books to the whole company, reminding us to count our blessings. Also, Chad Jason, Stephen Bogardus' dresser, made mini versions of Meredith's and my finale costumes.

Most Exciting Celebrity Visitor and What They Did/Said: Robert DeNiro came with his family. Jeffry, Stephen, Meredith and I got to meet them and take a photo. That was pretty thrilling! We also got to meet Aretha Franklin and Gavin DeGraw at the NYSE Christmas Tree Lighting ceremony. I was particularly excited to meet Leonard Lopate of WNYC! And Tommy Tune came backstage!

Mascot: Swing Jacob ben Widmar

Special Backstage Rituals: 1. Katherine Tokarz set up a "sweatshop" at her dressing table station to sew warmup "onesies" for the cast. They are adorable.
2. Meredith does a ballet barre every night before the show, so the crew installed a barre for her on the back of the dressing room set! So thoughtful! And she has taught some great stretches to prop man David Speer, which he thinks will enhance his marathon career—he is an avid runner.
3. Katherine and Anne ("Rhoda" and "Rita") do a "box hug" before the show every night.

Favorite Moments During Each Performance: 1. I love doing "Love, You Didn't Do Right By Me" for many reasons. I get paid to listen to Stephen Bogardus' effortless, gorgeous, haunting rendition of "How Deep Is the Ocean" every night while I dance with three beautiful men (Kevin Worley, Stephen Carrasco and Chad Seib, choreographed by Randy Skinner) while wearing one of the most beautiful dresses to ever grace a stage (designed by Carrie Robbins), singing a stunning song in a sensational orchestration by Larry Blank, played by the best band on Broadway under the expert and loving guidance of Rob Berman, on a magnificent set designed by Anna Louizos. It is a sequence in the show that is breathtaking to look at and deeply emotionally satisfying and musically thrilling, and I am aware of its beauty at every second.
2. I have watched "Let Yourself Go" practically every show in the four years I have done the show. Usually I watch with Judy and the Ed Sullivan Announcer—Michael Thomas Holmes my first three years and Sheffield Chastain on Broadway. Several traditions started with Michael Thomas Holmes (Boston 2005, St. Paul 2006, Boston 2007, St. Paul 2008)—one of which is meowing a good number of lyrics in the show (which Liz Brady, my dresser, and Elisa Acevedo, our hairdresser, now do with me throughout the show). We also shout "Tequila!" at a certain point, and sing "aqua rimba" instead of "hot marimba"—a particularly memorable misheard lyric (I think inspired by the color of the suits—Michael asked me, "What is an aqua rimba?" and after

Katherine Tokarz and Anne Horak do the "Box Hug."

howling with laughter we sang it every show from then on). I feed off of the energy of the dancers in that number and it gets me in the right mood to start the show.
3. Watching Susan Mansur perform "Let Me Sing and I'm Happy"—every night it was a little different, and she always tried to make us laugh. I loved to watch Rob Berman's face in the pit when she did something new and unexpected—always delightful.
4. During the overture there are three consecutive rising trumpet calls. The first year in San Francisco, BDJ and Jeffry Denman would sing "Eat at McDonald's...Eat at McDonald's...Eat at McDonald's where you can get a shake...and fries." Jeffry has continued spreading the good word and now we've got pretty much everyone on stage right singing it. Even the stage managers sometimes sing it when they're calling the show.
5. From prop man David Speer: "Kevin Worley doing his best to butch up his Train entrance while wearing a sweater that a blind, 89-year-old auntie from the Ozarks knit him for Christmas...his fifth Christmas."
6. A little thing we call "O'Malley Crossing"— this comes in two parts. First, as stage manager Jay McLeod describes: "After Kerry O'Malley as Betty finishes her reconciliation scene with Bob (under the Christmas Tree in the barn), Kerry has a very fast change into the finale "Red" dress. After the blackout, Kerry had to run offstage, down the spiral stairs stage right, through the basement and then up the spiral stairs on stage left to her dressing room. It was an exhausting path to take (especially on two-show days, during our nine-performance weeks) ... I noticed this and changed the path so that Kerry could just simply cross the stage behind the big red barn curtain during the "in one" (General's speech) scene. With much more "free time" now Kerry was able to remove her shoes and run across the stage while quietly giggling and ass-slapping each of the crew and cast members who would line up nightly to do the changeover and prepare the next scene upstage of the red barn curtain." Part two—after I made

it to the hallway, whoever was in the hallway would line up shouting "Ding-ding-ding-ding O'Malley Crossing!!" like at an intersection when a train is coming through. It was funny every single time.
7. At the end of Act I, the General throws a huge amount of paper into the air. When the curtain comes down prop man David Speer gets a lot of help picking it all up—Melody, Alison, Jay and Jim helped every show. There were always yucks to be had...with Bogie, all the while, crossing the stage and firing off a few zingers.
8. I love "Blue Skies" because it gives everyone a chance to really show off—the dancers get variations that are sometimes solos, duos, trios, etc. and the band members get to really rock out. Walter Bobbie and Randy Skinner gave everyone a chance to shine, and I watch it every night.

Favorite In-Theatre Gathering Place: I have a whole "craft services" type setup in my dressing room. I have the biggest dress in the show ("Big Red," my finale costume) and also somehow managed to score the biggest dressing room! It's the star suite that has also housed Julie Andrews, Bernadette Peters, Liza Minnelli, Sutton Foster, Reba McEntire and many other wonderful leading ladies. It's great because I have an inner dressing room and an outer sitting room. I was a presenter at the International Emmys this year and was given a Nespresso Lattissima machine as a gift, so I set it up and people got to have espressos, cappucinos and macchiattos whenever they wanted. I am a big Nespresso fan now! I love to bake, so I would bake cakes or cookies, or just put out all sorts of munchies.

"Kerry's Cafe"

Soon people started contributing food— especially Christmas cookies from their relatives, all sorts of yumminess.

Favorite Off-Site Hangout: Bourbon Street, on 46th between Eighth and Ninth Avenues.

Favorite Snack Foods: The Nespresso machine was a big hit, particularly the caramel flavor, and the peanut-butter-filled pretzels always went quickly. I put out mostly sweets, and Meredith usually had healthy food—fruit and nuts. Meredith always had sliced apples with peanut butter at intermission to help give her the energy to get through "I Love a Piano."

Favorite Therapies: We learned late in the game that physical therapy was necessary for the company—the ensemble is climbing up and down spiral staircases throughout the show, as well as tapping their hearts out. I also had a foot massager in my room (quite popular) and there is a massage chair in the greenroom.

Memorable Ad-Libs: Stephen Bogardus has had some funny lyric moments. My favorite is when he sang an alternate lyric in "Sisters." The lyric is "She wore the dress and I stayed home." He sang "She wrote the book and I called home." What makes it particularly funny, though, is that Kate Baldwin heard about it (she played Betty in San Francisco in 2005, Detroit 2006, Toronto 2007) and everyone in her company had a great laugh about it—until she went on that night and sang the same thing! I wasn't there to witness it, but I imagine it was pretty hilarious. Stephen has also flubbed the introduction to Susan Mansur's character, Martha Watson, twice. The line is "Martha the Megaphone Watson" which one night became "Martha the Mega. . .watt Watson" and another night became "Martha the Megatone Watson"—best part was watching how hard he tried not to laugh about it throughout her whole song.

Memorable Press Encounters: Joe Perrotta, our press representative extraordinaire, had us doing every single press opportunity possible. We rang the closing bell of the New York Stock Exchange. We sang at the Christmas Tree Lighting of the NYSE, did the Macy's Thanksgiving Day Parade.

We did the "Broadway on Broadway" concert, and did "Good Morning America," which was a particularly challenging one. We were performing on a tiny, cramped stage in the middle of Times Square at the crack of dawn in the middle of two nine-show weeks on our "day off." Traffic was whizzing by, the stage was slippery, it was crazy! And yet, it turned out wonderfully and we all had a lot of fun doing it and were happy for the national TV exposure for our show. My friends were joking that they fully expected us to be parachuting into Times Square in our red finale costumes on New Year's Eve when the ball dropped, we were so ever-present on the scene.

Memorable Stage Door Fan Encounter: Melody Hollis, who plays Susan Waverly, has a nice story: "When I was five years old my only goal was: to meet Sutton Foster. So we went to see *Thoroughly Modern Millie*. After the show we went to the stage door to get her autograph. Everyone that was in the show asked if I wanted their autograph and I said, "No, I want Sutton Foster's." So, we finally gave up but we gave the stage doorman a picture that I drew for her. Three years later I was eight, and it was my first year of *White Christmas*. The only day off we had we went to see a show. *Drowsy Chaperone*!! We had a backstage pass to see Sutton! After the show we bolted to see her and the best thing she said, "Hey, maybe one day you will be on Broadway and you will be in this dressing room in this theatre, Melody!" Two years later here I am! Not in her dressing room but in the theatre. But the VERY best part is that on opening night at the party she came over to me and said, "Hi, I'm Sutton Foster and you did a great job!" So,

Richie Mastascusa models the Gypsy Robe with Ricky Jay Yates

I told her the story and she went, "Wow!" and so did I!

Fastest Costume Change: This is a tie! Both are 43 seconds long, but Meredith wins for difficulty! Meredith's change into her "Sisters" dress after "I Love a Piano" is insanely fast. She changes out of a bodice, pants, shoes that are rigged with tap mikes, and earrings into her "Sisters" dress with new earrings. There are three people (Del Miskie, Liz Brady and Soomi Marano) helping her make the change. My change into "Sisters" after "Love and the Weather" is a close second but has fewer pieces and requires only two people to help (Del Miskie and Liz Brady).

Other Stories and Memories: 1. Peter Reardon, who plays Sheldrake, is a fellow New Englander and would make me laugh every night with his Boston accent on "Their jokes are lousy" and many other backstage comments made in a silly Pepperidge Farm accent. He would enter after "Love, You Didn't Do Right by Me" wearing a white shirt and plaid jacket (as prop man David Speer asks, "Who knew anyone looked so good in plaid?"). For most of the first week of previews I noticed that the second button on his shirt was never done and asked him why. He said he hadn't noticed, which began a nightly button parade he did for me. Every night he put something different on that button — be it a Swarovski crystal stolen from the "Blue Skies" sparkly tights stash, or pieces of Rita and Rhoda's tree costumes that had fallen on the floor. He began scavenging for things to put on the button, and I began to look forward to it every night, wondering what would be there. One night he did all three buttons! Best of all, though, was when, on the final game of the NFL regular season, he put a tiny New England Patriots logo on that button. My eyes lit up with utter delight—I almost broke, but held it together, until we got to the wings and I giggled like a little kid. I will love him forever for that one.

2. I do a "spit take" in the scene at Jimmy's nightclub—a comic bit which I have never been required to do in a show before. My first year doing the show I asked comic genius Michael Thomas Holmes to help me with it. We went

into a rehearsal room with cups of water and he just kept asking me ridiculous questions (most of which can not be repeated here) so that I would have an honest reaction to the outrageous question and get a really good spray of spit. It was possibly the most hilarious rehearsal I have ever had, and I still break into laughter about some of the questions he asked me. It's a pretty great bit, and also Athena Ripka's favorite moment in the show. What can I say? Spit takes are funny!

3. Jeffry Denman has done a series of rap videos starting in St. Paul in 2006. The first, with Kevin Worley, was a takeoff on "Saturday Night Live's" Lazy Sunday, which became "Lazy Tuesday." In Boston 2007, it was "The Real Phil Davis" and this year's ("Without WC") was particularly fun, inspired by the Dark Knight, about how Broadway desperately needed a Christmas show and we at *White Christmas* were prepared to save Broadway from a year without a Christmas show. It's great, great fun! They are all available for viewing on YouTube by searching Jeffry's name. He had an ace team of collaborators in Kevin Worley, Drew Humphrey, and Erin Denman (nee Crouch).

4. Richie Mastascusa was the recipient of our Gypsy Robe, and he was so moved and excited at the ceremony, it was such an emotional event to witness. Ricky Jay Yates designed a beautiful sleeve with a quilted snow scene. Each cast member signed a snowflake and they were all attached to the sleeve. It was very magical.

Singing in the Macy's Thanksgiving Day Parade, 2008.

5. We got a Broadway Bear for the BC/EFA auction that is held every year, and they chose to do Betty's "Big Red" dress. Robert (Robbie) Manning at Parsons-Meares, who also built the real gown in the show, built her dress and Paul Huntley did her wig, all based on Carrie Robbins' original design. We hope she raises tons of money at the auction. She was named "Beary O'Malley"—this was one of the greatest thrills for me! She's gorgeous!

6. Rob Berman, our conductor and musical supervisor of all the companies, left us for a few days while he went to visit the Detroit and St. Paul companies. When he returned, at the moment he puts on his Santa suit for his bow, he turned to discover that the entire band had put on Santa hats! What did I say? We have the best band on Broadway!

Photos courtesy Kerry O'Malley

Jersey Boys

First Preview: October 4, 2005. Opened: November 6, 2005.
Still running as of May 31, 2009.

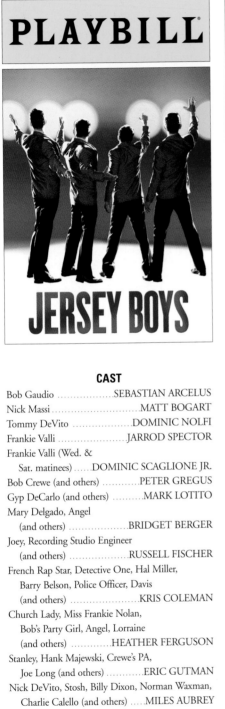

CAST

Bob Gaudio	SEBASTIAN ARCELUS
Nick Massi	MATT BOGART
Tommy DeVito	DOMINIC NOLFI
Frankie Valli	JARROD SPECTOR
Frankie Valli (Wed. & Sat. matinees)	DOMINIC SCAGLIONE JR.
Bob Crewe (and others)	PETER GREGUS
Gyp DeCarlo (and others)	MARK LOTITO
Mary Delgado, Angel (and others)	BRIDGET BERGER
Joey, Recording Studio Engineer (and others)	RUSSELL FISCHER
French Rap Star, Detective One, Hal Miller, Barry Belson, Police Officer, Davis (and others)	KRIS COLEMAN
Church Lady, Miss Frankie Nolan, Bob's Party Girl, Angel, Lorraine (and others)	HEATHER FERGUSON
Stanley, Hank Majewski, Crewe's PA, Joe Long (and others)	ERIC GUTMAN
Nick DeVito, Stosh, Billy Dixon, Norman Waxman, Charlie Calello (and others)	MILES AUBREY
Frankie's Mother, Nick's Date, Angel, Francine (and others)	SARA SCHMIDT
Thugs	KEN DOW, JOE PAYNE

Continued on next page

(L-R): Matt Bogart, Jarrod Spector, Sebastian Arcelus and Dominic Nolfi.

Photo by Joan Marcus

Jersey Boys

MUSICAL NUMBERS

ACT ONE

"Ces Soirées-La (Oh What a Night)" – Paris, 2000 ....French Rap Star, Backup Group
"Silhouettes" ....Tommy DeVito, Nick Massi, Nick DeVito, Frankie Castelluccio
"You're the Apple of My Eye" ....Tommy DeVito, Nick Massi, Nick DeVito
"I Can't Give You Anything But Love" ....Frankie Castelluccio
"Earth Angel" ....Tommy DeVito, Full Company
"Sunday Kind of Love" ....Frankie Valli, Tommy DeVito, Nick Massi, Nick's Date
"My Mother's Eyes" ....Frankie Valli
"I Go Ape" ....The Four Lovers
"(Who Wears) Short Shorts" ....The Royal Teens
"I'm in the Mood for Love/Moody's Mood for Love" ....Frankie Valli
"Cry for Me" ....Bob Gaudio, Frankie Valli, Tommy DeVito, Nick Massi
"An Angel Cried" ....Hal Miller and The Rays
"I Still Care" ....Miss Frankie Nolan and The Romans
"Trance" ....Billy Dixon and The Topix
"Sherry" ....The Four Seasons
"Big Girls Don't Cry" ....The Four Seasons
"Walk Like a Man" ....The Four Seasons
"December, 1963 (Oh What a Night)" ....Bob Gaudio, Full Company
"My Boyfriend's Back" ....The Angels
"My Eyes Adored You" ....Frankie Valli, Mary Delgado, The Four Seasons
"Dawn (Go Away)" ....The Four Seasons
"Walk Like a Man" (reprise) ....Full Company

ACT TWO

"Big Man in Town" ....The Four Seasons
"Beggin'" ....The Four Seasons
"Stay" ....Bob Gaudio, Frankie Valli, Nick Massi
"Let's Hang On (To What We've Got)" ....Bob Gaudio, Frankie Valli
"Opus 17 (Don't You Worry 'Bout Me)" ....Bob Gaudio, Frankie Valli and
The New Seasons
"Bye Bye Baby" ....Frankie Valli and The Four Seasons
"C'mon Marianne" ....Frankie Valli and The Four Seasons
"Can't Take My Eyes Off You" ....Frankie Valli
"Working My Way Back to You" ....Frankie Valli and The Four Seasons
"Fallen Angel" ....Frankie Valli
"Rag Doll" ....The Four Seasons
"Who Loves You" ....The Four Seasons, Full Company

Cast Continued

SWINGS
DOUGLAS CRAWFORD, KATIE O'TOOLE,
ERIC SCHNEIDER, JAKE SPECK

Dance Captain: PETER GREGUS
Assistant Dance Captain: KATIE O'TOOLE

UNDERSTUDIES
For Tommy DeVito, Bob Gaudio:
ERIC GUTMAN, JAKE SPECK
For Nick Massi:
MILES AUBREY, DOUGLAS CRAWFORD,
JAKE SPECK
For Frankie Valli:
RUSSELL FISCHER,
DOMINIC SCAGLIONE JR.,
ERIC SCHNEIDER
For Gyp DeCarlo:
MILES AUBREY, DOUGLAS CRAWFORD
For Bob Crewe:
ERIC GUTMAN, DOUGLAS CRAWFORD

ORCHESTRA
Conductor: ADAM BEN-DAVID
Associate Conductor: DEBORAH N. HURWITZ
Keyboards: DEBORAH N. HURWITZ,
STEPHEN "HOOPS" SNYDER
Guitars: JOE PAYNE
Bass: KEN DOW
Drums: KEVIN DOW
Reeds: MATT HONG, BEN KONO
Trumpet: DAVID SPIER

Music Coordinator: JOHN MILLER

SCRAPBOOK

Correspondent: Andrew Rannells, "Bob Gaudio"
Anniversary Parties and/or Gifts: A transistor radio with "Jersey Boys" stamped on the side.
Most Exciting Celebrity Visitor and What They Did/Said: Tom Cruise. Bill Clinton... he used the bathroom backstage.
Actor Who Performed the Most Roles in This Show: Heather Ferguson...so many....
Actor Who Has Done the Most Shows: Outside of *Jersey Boys*? Mark Lotito.
Special Backstage Rituals: "Riding the Snake."
Favorite Moment During Each Performance (On Stage or Off): The Finale.... seriously.
Favorite In-Theatre Gathering Place: Stage management office
Favorite Snack Foods: Bowl Appétite! (disgustingly delicious)
Mascot: Skaggs
Memorable Ad-Lib: "Bang!" in lieu of an actual gunshot
Record Number of Cell Phone Rings, Cell Phone Photos or Texting Incidents During a Performance: How about a fist fight after "Walk Like a Man"? Does that count?
Memorable Press Encounter: Aggressive Australian Woman
What Did You Think of the Web Buzz on Your Show: Generous
Latest Audience Arrival: Intermission
Fastest Costume Change: Bridget Berger...10 seconds
Busiest Day at the Box Office: Every day, sucka!
Who Wore the Least: All of the ladies
Catchphrases Only the Company Would Recognize: "Ride the Snake"
Sweethearts Within the Company: Unrequited? Everyone and Matt Bogart
Memorable Directorial Note: "You are not James Dean."

Jersey Boys

Sebastian Arcelus
Bob Gaudio

Matt Bogart
Nick Massi

Dominic Nolfi
Tommy DeVito

Jarrod Spector
Frankie Valli

Peter Gregus
Bob Crewe and others

Mark Lotito
Gyp DeCarlo and others

Miles Aubrey
Norm Waxman and others

Bridget Berger
Mary Delgado and others

Kris Coleman
Hal Miller and others

Douglas Crawford
Swing

Ken Dow
Thug, Bass

Heather Ferguson
Lorraine and others

Russell Fischer
Joey, Recording Studio Engineer and others

Eric Gutman
Hank Majewski and others

Katie O'Toole
Swing

Joe Payne
Thug, Guitars

Dominic Scaglione Jr.
Frankie Valli on Wed. & Sat. mats.

Sara Schmidt
Francine and others

Eric Schneider
Swing

Jake Speck
Swing

Marshall Brickman
Book

Rick Elice
Book

Bob Gaudio
Composer

Bob Crewe
Lyricist

Des McAnuff
Director

Sergio Trujillo
Choreographer

Ron Melrose
Music Direction, Vocal Arrangements and Incidental Music

Klara Zieglerova
Scenic Design

Jess Goldstein
Costume Design

Howell Binkley
Lighting Design

Steve Canyon Kennedy
Sound Design

Steve Rankin
Fight Director

Steve Orich
Orchestrations

John Miller
Music Coordinator

Adam Ben-David
Conductor

Jersey Boys

Tara Rubin Casting
East Coast Casting

Sharon Bialy and Sherry Thomas
West Coast Casting

Stephen Gabis
Dialect Coach

Michael David,
Dodger Theatricals
Producer

Edward Strong,
Dodger Theatricals
Producer

Rocco Landesman,
Dodger Theatricals
Producer

Kevin and Tamara Kinsella
Producers

Ivor Royston,
The Pelican Group
Producer

Ralph Bryan,
Latitude Link
Producer

Rick Steiner
Producer

John and Bonnie
Osher
Producers

Dan Staton
Producer

Marc Bell
Producer

Frederic H.
Mayerson
Producer

Lauren Mitchell
Associate Producer

Rhoda Mayerson
Associate Producer

Joop van den Ende,
Stage Entertainment
Producer

Christopher Ashley
*Artistic Director
La Jolla Playhouse*

JERSEY BOYS
ALUMNI
2008-2009

Travis Cloer
*Joey, Recording
Studio Engineer
(and others)*

Cory Grant
*Frankie Valli
on Wed. & Sat. mats.*

Christian Hoff
Tommy DeVito

Donnie Kehr
*Nick DeVito,
Stosh, Billy Dixon,
Norman Waxman,
Charlie Calello (and
others)*

Rebecca Kupka
Swing

John Leone
Nick Massi, Swing

Michael Longoria
Frankie Valli

J. Robert Spencer
Nick Massi

JERSEY BOYS
TRANSFER STUDENTS
2008-2009

Cory Grant
*Frankie Valli on Wed.
& Sat. mats.*

John Hickman
Swing

Michelle Knight
Swing

Andrew Rannells
Bob Gaudio

Jersey Boys

Matthew Scott
Stanley, Hank Majewski, Crewe's PA, Joe Long (and others)

Taylor Sternberg
Swing

ELECTRICS DEPARTMENT
Front Row (L-R):
Jan Nebozenko, David Shepherd,
Dave Karlson, Brian Aman (standing)
Back Row (L-R):
Robert Fehribach, Michael Bogden,
Gary Marlin, Sean Fedigan

FRONT OF HOUSE STAFF
Front Row (L-R):
Rose Balsamo, Caroline Siewert

Back Row (L-R):
Amy Marquez, Russell Saylor
Barbara Hill, Anne Cavanaugh (Ticket Taker)
Carmella Galante (Ticket Taker)
Sally Lettieri, Robert Fowler

PROPS DEPARTMENT
(L-R): Ken Harris, Kyp Seiferth, John Tomson, Scott Mulrain

Not pictured: Emiliano Pares

CARPENTRY DEPARTMENT
(L-R): Greg Burton, Alex Gutierrez, Peter Wright, Ron Fucarino

Not pictured: Mike Kelly

Jersey Boys

HAIR DEPARTMENT
(L-R): Patricia Peek, Frederick Waggoner, Hazel Higgins

HOUSE MANAGERS
(L-R): Matt Fox, Justin Karr

STAGE DOOR
Christine Ehren, Gustavo Catuy

Photos by Brian Mapp

STAGE AND COMPANY MANAGEMENT
(L-R): Brendan Fay, Michelle Reupert, Robbie Young, Tim Sulka (Associate Company Manager), Sandy Carlson (Company Manager)

WARDROBE DEPARTMENT
(L-R): Janet Anderson, Nancy Ronan, Nick Staub, Aaron Simms

STAFF FOR *JERSEY BOYS*

GENERAL PRESS REPRESENTATION
BONEAU/BRYAN-BROWN
Adrian Bryan-Brown   Susanne Tighe
Heath Schwartz

COMPANY MANAGER
Sandra Carlson

PRODUCTION STAGE
    MANAGER ....MICHELLE BOSCH
Stage Manager ....Jason Brouillard
Assistant Stage Manager ....Michelle Reupert
Senior Associate General Manager ......Jennifer F. Vaughan
Associate General Manager ....Flora Johnstone
Assistant General Manager ....Dean A. Carpenter
Assistant Production Supervisor ....Jeff Parvin
Associate Company Manager ....Tim Sulka
Technical Supervision ....Tech Production Services/
    Peter Fulbright, Mary Duffe,
    Colleen Houlehen, Lauren A. Duffy
Music Technical Design ....Deborah N. Hurwitz
Musician Swing ....Steve Gibb
Assistant Directors...................Holly-Anne Ruggiero,
    West Hyler, Daisy Walker
Second Assistant Director.....................Alex Timbers
Associate Choreographer ....Kelly Devine

Assistant Choreographers ....Danny Austin,
    Caitlin Carter
Associate Music Supervisor ....Michael Rafter
Dialect Coach ....Stephen Gabis
Fight Captain ....Peter Gregus
Associate Scenic Designers ....Nancy Thun, Todd Ivins
Assistant Scenic Designers ....Sonoka Gozelski,
    Matthew Myhrum
Associate Costume Designer ....Alejo Vietti
Assistant Costume Designers ....China Lee,
    Elizabeth Flauto
Associate Lighting Designer................Patricia Nichols
Assistant Lighting Designer.............Sarah E. C. Maines
Associate Sound Designer ....Andrew Keister
Associate Projection Designer ....Jason Thompson
Assistant Projection Designer ....Chris Kateff
Story Board Artist ....Don Hudson
Casting Directors ....Tara Rubin, CSA;
    Merri Sugarman, CSA
Casting Associates ....Eric Woodall, CSA;
    Laura Schutzel, CSA
Casting Assistants ....Rebecca Carfagna,
    Paige Blansfield, Dale Brown
Automated Lighting Programmer ....Hillary Knox
Projection Programming ....Paul Vershbow
Set Model Builder ....Anne Goelz
Costume Intern ....Jessica Reed
Production Carpenter ....Michael W. Kelly

Deck Automation ....Greg Burton
Fly Automation ....Ron Fucarino
Flyman ....Peter Wright
Production Electrician ....James Fedigan
Head Electrician ....Brian Aman
Assistant Electrician ....Gary L. Marlin
Follow Spot Operator ....Sean Fedigan
Production Sound Engineer ....Andrew Keister
Head Sound Engineer ....Julie M. Randolph
Production Props ....Emiliano Pares
Assistant Props............................Kenneth Harris Jr.
Production Wardrobe Supervisor ....Lee J. Austin
Assistant Wardrobe Supervisor ....Nancy Ronan
Wardrobe Department ......Davis Duffield, Kelly Kinsella,
    Shaun Ozminski, Michelle Sesco,
    Nicholas Staub, Ricky Yates
Hair Supervisor ....Amy Neswald
Hair Assistant ....Frederick G. Waggoner
Hair Department ....Hazel Higgins
Assistant to John Miller......................Charles Butler
Synthesizer Programming ....Deborah N. Hurwitz,
    Steve Orich
Music Copying ....Anixter Rice Music Service
Music Production Assistant ....Alexandra Melrose
Production Assistants ....Kerry McGrath,
    Michelle Reupert, Bryan Rountree,
    Deborah Wolfson
Dramaturg ....Allison Horsley

Jersey Boys

Associates to Messrs. Michael David
and Ed Strong ....Pamela Lloyd, James Love
Advertising ....Serino Coyne, Inc./
Scott Johnson, Sandy Block, Jean Leonard
Marketing ....Dodger Marketing/
Gordon Kelly, Jessica Ludwig
Promotions ....HHC Marketing/
Hugh Hysell, Michael Redman
Banking ....Commerce Bank/Barbara von Borstel
Payroll ....Castellana Services Inc./
Lance Castellana, Norman Seawell, James Castellana
Accountants ....Schall and Ashenfarb, C.P.A.
Finance Director ....Paula Maldonado
Insurance ....AON/Albert G. Rubin Insurance Services/
George Walden, Claudia Kaufman
Counsel ....Nan Bases, Esq.
Special Events ....John L. Haber
Travel Arrangements ....The "A" Team at Tzell Travel/
Andi Henig
MIS Services ....Rivera Technics: Sam Rivera
Web Design ....Curious Minds Media, Inc.
Production Photographer ....Joan Marcus
Theatre Displays ....King Displays

DODGERS
DODGER THEATRICALS
Richard Biederman, Michael Bolgar, Sandra Carlson, Dean A. Carpenter, Michael David, Anne Ezell, Lauren Freed, John L. Haber, Richard Hester, Flora Johnstone, Gordon Kelly, Abigail Kornet, Pamela Lloyd, James Elliot Love, Jessica Ludwig, Paula Maldonado, Lauren Mitchell, Sally Campbell Morse, Jeff Parvin, Samuel Rivera, R. Doug Rodgers, Maureen Rooney, Bill Schaeffer, Andrew Serna, Bridget A. Stegall, Edward Strong, Tim Sulka, Jennifer F. Vaughan, Laurinda Wilson, Josh Zeigler, Ashley Zimmerman

LA JOLLA PLAYHOUSE
Artistic Director ....Christopher Ashley
Managing Director ....Steven B. Libman
Associate Artistic Director ....Shirley Fishman
Director Emeritus ....Des McAnuff
General Manager ....Debby Buchholz
Associate General Manager ....Jenny Case
Director of Marketing ....Joan Cumming
Director of Development ....Ellen Kulik
Director of Finance ....John T. O'Dea
Director of Education & Outreach ......Steve McCormick
Production Manager ....Peter J. Davis
Associate Production Manager ....Linda S. Cooper
Technical Director ....Brian Busch
Associate Technical Directors ....Chris Borreson,
Chris Kennedy
Costume Shop Manager ....Susan Makkoo
Sound Supervisor ....Peter Hashagen
Lighting Supervisor ....Mike Doyle
Prop Master ....Debra Hatch
Charge Scenic Artist ....Mark Jensen
Theatre Operations Manager ....Ned Collins

Dodger Group Sales 1-877-5DODGER
Exclusive Tour Direction ....Steven Schnepp/
Broadway Booking Office NYC

CREDITS
Scenery, show control and automation by ShowMotion, Inc., Norwalk, CT. Lighting equipment from PRG Lighting. Sound equipment by Masque Sound. Projection equipment by Sound Associates. Selected men's clothing custom made by Saint Laurie Merchant Tailors, New York City. Costumes executed by Carelli Costumes, Studio Rouge, Carmen Gee, John Kristiansen New York, Inc. Selected menswear by Carlos Campos. Props provided by The Spoon Group, Downtime Productions, Tessa Dunning. Select guitars provided by Gibson Guitars. Laundry services provided by Ernest Winzer Theatrical Cleaners. Additional set and hand props courtesy of George Fenmore, Inc. Rosebud matches by Diamond Brands, Inc., Zippo lighters used. Rehearsed at the New 42nd Street Studios. Natural herb cough drops courtesy of Ricola USA, Inc. Emergen-C by Alacer Corporation. PLAYBILL® cover photo by Chris Callis.

www.jerseyboysinfo.com

Scenic drops adapted from *George Tice: Urban Landscapes*/W.W. Norton. Other photographs featured are from *George Tice: Selected Photographs 1953–1999*/David R. Godine. (Photographs courtesy of the Peter Fetterman Gallery/Santa Monica.)

SONG CREDITS
"Ces Soirees-La ("Oh What a Night")" (Bob Gaudio, Judy Parker, Yannick Zolo, Edmond David Bacri). Jobete Music Company Inc., Seasons Music Company (ASCAP). "Silhouettes" (Bob Crewe, Frank Slay, Jr.), Regent Music Corporation (BMI). "You're the Apple of My Eye" (Otis Blackwell), EMI Unart Catalog Inc. (BMI). "I Can't Give You Anything But Love" (Dorothy Fields, Jimmy McHugh), EMI April Music Inc., Aldi Music Company, Cotton Club Publishing (ASCAP). "Earth Angel" (Jesse Belvin, Curtis Williams, Gaynel Hodge), Embassy Music Corporation (BMI). "Sunday Kind of Love" (Barbara Belle, Anita Leanord Nye, Stan Rhodes, Louis Prima), LGL Music Inc./Larry Spier, Inc. (ASCAP). "My Mother's Eyes" (Abel Baer, L. Wolfe Gilbert), Abel Baer Music Company, EMI Feist Catalog Inc. (ASCAP). "I Go Ape" (Bob Crewe, Frank Slay, Jr.), MPL Music Publishing Inc. (ASCAP). "(Who Wears) Short Shorts" (Bob Gaudio, Bill Crandall, Tom Austin, Bill Dalton), EMI Longitude Music, Admiration Music Inc., Third Story Music Inc., and New Seasons Music (BMI). "I'm in the Mood for Love" (Dorothy Fields, Jimmy McHugh), Famous Music Corporation (ASCAP). "Moody's Mood for Love" (James Moody, Dorothy Fields, Jimmy McHugh), Famous Music Corporation (ASCAP). "Cry for Me" (Bob Gaudio), EMI Longitude Music, Seasons Four Music (BMI). "An Angel Cried" (Bob Gaudio), EMI Longitude Music (BMI). "I Still Care" (Bob Gaudio), Hearts Delight Music, Seasons Four Music (BMI). "Trance" (Bob Gaudio), Hearts Delight Music, Seasons Four Music (BMI). "Sherry" (Bob Gaudio), MPL Music Publishing Inc. (ASCAP). "Big Girls Don't Cry" (Bob Gaudio, Bob Crewe), MPL Music Publishing Inc. (ASCAP). "Walk Like a Man" (Bob Crewe, Bob Gaudio), Gavadima Music, MPL Communications Inc. (ASCAP). "December, 1963 (Oh What a Night)" (Bob Gaudio, Judy Parker), Jobete Music Company Inc, Seasons Music Company (ASCAP). "My Boyfriend's Back" (Robert Feldman, Gerald Goldstein, Richard Gottehrer), EMI Blackwood Music Inc. (BMI). "My Eyes Adored You" (Bob Crewe, Kenny Nolan), Jobete Music Company Inc, Kenny Nolan Publishing (ASCAP), Stone Diamond Music

Corporation, Tannyboy Music (BMI). "Dawn, Go Away" (Bob Gaudio, Sandy Linzer), EMI Full Keel Music, Gavadima Music, Stebojen Music Company (ASCAP). "Big Man in Town" (Bob Gaudio), EMI Longitude Music (BMI), Gavadima Music (ASCAP). "Beggin'" (Bob Gaudio, Peggy Farina), EMI Longitude Music, Seasons Four Music (BMI). "Stay" (Maurice Williams), Cherio Corporation (BMI). "Let's Hang On (To What We've Got)" (Bob Crewe, Denny Randell, Sandy Linzer), EMI Longitude Music, Screen Gems-EMI Music Inc., Seasons Four Music (BMI). "Opus 17 (Don't You Worry 'Bout Me)" (Denny Randell, Sandy Linzer) Screen Gems-EMI Music Inc, Seasons Four Music (BMI). "Everybody Knows My Name" (Bob Gaudio, Bob Crewe), EMI Longitude Music, Seasons Four Music (BMI). "Bye Bye Baby" (Bob Crewe, Bob Gaudio), EMI Longitude Music, Seasons Four Music (BMI). "C'mon Marianne" (L. Russell Brown, Ray Bloodworth), EMI Longitude Music and Seasons Four Music (BMI). "Can't Take My Eyes Off You" (Bob Gaudio, Bob Crewe), EMI Longitude Music, Seasons Four Music (BMI). "Working My Way Back to You" (Denny Randell, Sandy Linzer), Screen Gems–EMI Music Inc, Seasons Four Music (BMI). "Fallen Angel" (Guy Fletcher, Doug Flett), Chrysalis Music (ASCAP). "Rag Doll" (Bob Crewe, Bob Gaudio), EMI Longitude Music (BMI), Gavadima Music (ASCAP). "Who Loves You?" (Bob Gaudio, Judy Parker), Jobete Music Company Inc, Seasons Music Company (ASCAP).

SPECIAL THANKS
Peter Bennett, Elliot Groffman, Karen Pals, Janine Smalls, Chad Woerner of La Jolla Playhouse, Alma Malabanan-McGrath and Edward Stallsworth of the New 42nd Street Studios, David Solomon of the Roundabout Theatre Company, Dan Whitten. The authors, director, cast and company of *Jersey Boys* would like to express their love and thanks to Jordan Ressler.

IN MEMORY
It is difficult to imagine producing anything without the presence of beloved Dodger producing associate James Elliot Love. Friend to everyone he met, James stood at the heart of all that is good about the theatrical community. He will be missed, but his spirit abides.

Grammy Award-winning cast album now available on Rhino Records.

JUJAMCYN THEATERS

ROCCO LANDESMAN
President

PAUL LIBIN **JACK VIERTEL** **JORDAN ROTH**
Producing Director Creative Director Vice President

DANIEL ADAMIAN   **JENNIFER HERSHEY**
General Manager   Director of Operations

MEREDITH VILLATORE   **JERRY ZAKS**
Chief Financial Officer   Resident Director

STAFF FOR THE AUGUST WILSON THEATRE
Manager ....Matt Fox
Treasurer ....Nick Russo
Associate Manager ....Justin L. Karr
Carpenter ....Dan Dour
Propertyman ....Scott Mulrain
Electrician ....Robert Fehribach
Engineer ....Ralph Santos

Joe Turner's Come and Gone

First Preview: March 19, 2009. Opened: April 16, 2009.
Still running as of May 31, 2009.

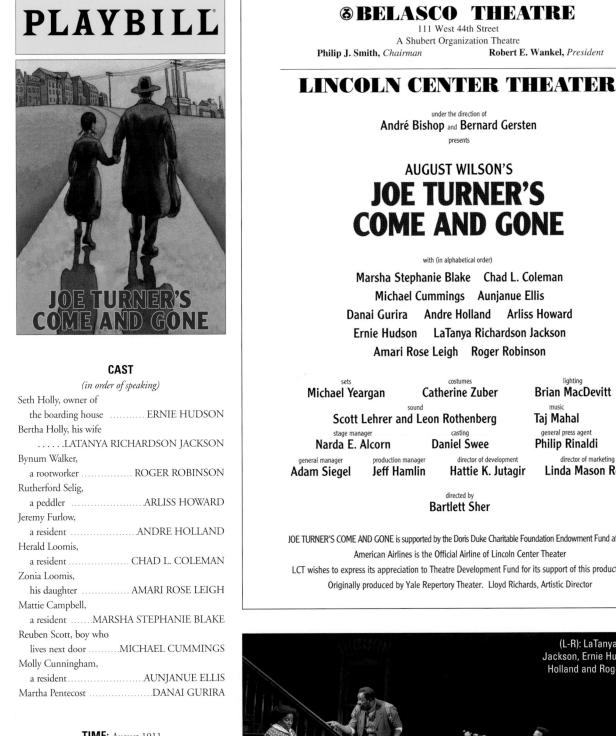

PLAYBILL®

JOE TURNER'S COME AND GONE

CAST

(in order of speaking)

Seth Holly, owner of
the boarding house .... ERNIE HUDSON
Bertha Holly, his wife
.....LATANYA RICHARDSON JACKSON
Bynum Walker,
a rootworker .... ROGER ROBINSON
Rutherford Selig,
a peddler .... ARLISS HOWARD
Jeremy Furlow,
a resident .... ANDRE HOLLAND
Herald Loomis,
a resident .... CHAD L. COLEMAN
Zonia Loomis,
his daughter .... AMARI ROSE LEIGH
Mattie Campbell,
a resident ...... MARSHA STEPHANIE BLAKE
Reuben Scott, boy who
lives next door .... MICHAEL CUMMINGS
Molly Cunningham,
a resident .... AUNJANUE ELLIS
Martha Pentecost .... DANAI GURIRA

TIME: August 1911
PLACE: A boardinghouse in Pittsburgh

Assistant Stage Manager ..... MICHAEL P. ZALESKI

Continued on next page

The Playbill Broadway Yearbook 2008-2009

⊗ BELASCO THEATRE
111 West 44th Street
A Shubert Organization Theatre

Philip J. Smith, *Chairman*   Robert E. Wankel, *President*

LINCOLN CENTER THEATER

under the direction of
André Bishop and **Bernard Gersten**

presents

AUGUST WILSON'S

JOE TURNER'S COME AND GONE

with (in alphabetical order)

Marsha Stephanie Blake   Chad L. Coleman
Michael Cummings   Aunjanue Ellis
Danai Gurira   Andre Holland   Arliss Howard
Ernie Hudson   LaTanya Richardson Jackson
Amari Rose Leigh   Roger Robinson

sets	costumes	lighting
Michael Yeargan	**Catherine Zuber**	**Brian MacDevitt**

sound
Scott Lehrer and Leon Rothenberg

music
Taj Mahal

stage manager	casting	general press agent
Narda E. Alcorn	**Daniel Swee**	**Philip Rinaldi**

general manager	production manager	director of development	director of marketing
Adam Siegel	**Jeff Hamlin**	**Hattie K. Jutagir**	**Linda Mason Ross**

directed by
Bartlett Sher

JOE TURNER'S COME AND GONE is supported by the Doris Duke Charitable Foundation Endowment Fund at LCT

American Airlines is the Official Airline of Lincoln Center Theater

LCT wishes to express its appreciation to Theatre Development Fund for its support of this production

Originally produced by Yale Repertory Theater. Lloyd Richards, Artistic Director

4/16/09

(L-R): LaTanya Richardson
Jackson, Ernie Hudson, Andre
Holland and Roger Robinson,

Photo by T. Charles Erickson

Joe Turner's Come and Gone

It is August in Pittsburgh, 1911. The sun falls out of heaven like a stone. The fires of the steel mill rage with a combined sense of industry and progress. Barges loaded with coal and iron ore trudge up the river to the mill towns that dot the Monongahela and return with fresh, hard, gleaming steel. The city flexes its muscles. Men throw countless bridges across the rivers, lay roads and carve tunnels through the hills sprouting with houses. From the deep and the near South the sons and daughters of newly freed African slaves wander into the city. Isolated, cut off from memory, having forgotten the names of the gods and only guessing at their faces, they arrive dazed and stunned, their hearts kicking in their chests with a song worth singing. They arrive carrying Bibles and guitars, their pockets lined with dust and fresh hope, marked men and women seeking to scrape from the narrow, crooked cobbles and the fiery blasts of the coke furnace a way of bludgeoning and shaping the malleable parts of themselves into a new identity as free men of definite and sincere worth.

Foreigners in a strange land, they carry as part and parcel of their baggage a long line of separation and dispersement which informs their sensibilities and marks their conduct as they search for ways to reconnect, to reassemble, to give clear and luminous meaning to the song which is both a wail and a whelp of joy.

— August Wilson

Cast Continued

UNDERSTUDIES

For Seth Holly and Bynum Walker:
MICHAEL ROGERS
For Bertha Holly:
BRENDA THOMAS DENMARK
For Rutherford Selig:
CHRISTOPHER McHALE
For Herald Loomis and Jeremy Furlow:
NYAMBI NYAMBI
For Zonia Loomis:
OLIVIA FORD
For Mattie Campbell, Molly Cunningham
and Martha Pentecost:
AFTON C. WILLIAMSON
For Reuben Scott:
ELON VAN BUCKLEY

Marsha Stephanie
Blake
Mattie Campbell

Chad L. Coleman
Herald Loomis

Michael Cummings
Reuben Scott

Aunjanue Ellis
Molly Cunningham

Danai Gurira
Martha Pentecost

Andre Holland
Jeremy Furlow

Arliss Howard
Rutherford Selig

Ernie Hudson
Seth Holly

LaTanya Richardson
Jackson
Bertha Holly

Amari Rose Leigh
Zonia Loomis

Roger Robinson
Bynum Walker

Brenda Thomas
Denmark
Understudy

Olivia Ford
Understudy

Christopher McHale
Understudy

Nyambi Nyambi
Understudy

Michael Rogers
Understudy

Elon Van Buckley
Understudy

Afton C. Williamson
Understudy

August Wilson
Playwright

Bartlett Sher
Director

Michael Yeargan
Sets

Joe Turner's Come and Gone

Catherine Zuber
Costumes

Brian MacDevitt
Lighting

Scott Lehrer
Sound

William Berloni
Animal Trainer

André Bishop and Bernard Gersten,
Lincoln Center Theater
Producer

RUNNING CREW
Front Row (L-R): Matthew Maloney, Jr.,
Yolanda Ramsey (Hair Supervisor),
Mark Hannon, Wayne Smith (Production
Soundman), Laura Koch (House Property
Person), George Dummitt (House
Carpenter)

Back Row (L-R): John Alban,
Ritchie Anderson, Graeme McDonnell
(Production Electrician),
Matthew Maloney (House Electrician)

FRONT OF HOUSE STAFF
Front Row (L-R): Pamela Gittlitz,
Eugenia Raines, Kathy Dunn

Back Row (L-R): Carole Hollenbeck,
Patricia Murphy, Joseph Pittman,
Michelle Moyna, Dexter Luke

Photos by Brian Mapp

BOX OFFICE
(L-R): Gerard O'Brien, Augie Pugliese

WARDROBE
(L-R): Tina Marie Clifton (Dresser), Moira MacGregor-Conrad
(Wardrobe Supervisor), Kevin Andre Dickens (Dresser)

STAGE MANAGEMENT
(L-R): Narda E. Alcorn (Stage Manager),
Michael P. Zaleski (Asst. Stage Manager)

Joe Turner's Come and Gone

ADMINISTRATIVE STAFF

GENERAL MANAGER ....ADAM SIEGEL
  Associate General Manager ....Jessica Niebanck
  General Management Assistant ....Meghan Lantzy
  Facilities Manager ....Alex Mustelier
  Associate Facilities Manager ....Michael Assalone
GENERAL PRESS AGENT ....PHILIP RINALDI
  Press Associate ....Barbara Carroll
PRODUCTION MANAGER ....JEFF HAMLIN
  Associate Production Manager ....Paul Smithyman
DIRECTOR OF
  DEVELOPMENT ....HATTIE K. JUTAGIR
  Associate Director of Development .....Rachel Norton
  Manager of Special Events and
    Young Patron Program ....Karin Schall
  Grants Writer ....Neal Brilliant
  Manager, Patron Program ....Sheilaja Rao
  Assistant to the
    Director of Development ....Raelyn Lagerstrom
  Development Associate/
    Special Events ....Nicole Lindenbaum
  Development Assistant/
    Patron Program ....Terra Gillespie
DIRECTOR OF FINANCE..........DAVID S. BROWN
  Controller ....Susan Knox
  Systems Manager ....Stacy Valentine
  Finance Assistant ....Megan Wildebour
DIRECTOR OF
  MARKETING ....LINDA MASON ROSS
  Marketing Associate ....Kristin Miller
  Marketing Assistant ....Ashley M. Dunn
DIRECTOR OF EDUCATION ....KATI KOERNER
  Associate Director of Education ....Alexandra Lopez
  Assistant to the Executive Producer .....Barbara Hourigan
  Office Manager ....Brian Hashimoto
  Office Assistant ....Rhonda Lipscomb
  Messenger ....Esau Burgess
  Reception ....Brenden Rogers, Michelle Metcalf

ARTISTIC STAFF

ASSOCIATE DIRECTORS ......GRACIELA DANIELE,
                   NICHOLAS HYTNER,
                   JACK O'BRIEN,
                   SUSAN STROMAN,
                   DANIEL SULLIVAN
RESIDENT DIRECTOR.............BARTLETT SHER
DRAMATURG and DIRECTOR,
  LCT DIRECTORS LAB ....ANNE CATTANEO
CASTING DIRECTOR ....DANIEL SWEE, CSA
MUSICAL THEATER
  ASSOCIATE PRODUCER ....IRA WEITZMAN
DIRECTOR OF LCT3 ....PAIGE EVANS
  Artistic Administrator ....Julia Judge
  Casting Associate ....Camille Hickman
  Lab Assistant ....Kate Marvin

SPECIAL SERVICES

Advertising. ....Serino-Coyne/Jim Russek,
        Roger Micone, Becca Goland-Van Ryn
Principal Poster Artist ....James McMullan
Poster Artwork for
  Joe Turner's Come and Gone ....James McMullan

Counsel ....Peter L. Felcher, Esq.;
                   Charles H. Googe, Esq.;
         and Carol Kaplan, Esq. of
     Paul, Weiss, Rifkind, Wharton & Garrison
Immigration Counsel ....Theodore Ruthizer, Esq.;
                Mark D. Koestler, Esq.
    of Kramer, Levin, Naftalis & Frankel LLP
Labor Counsel ....Michael F. McGahan, Esq.
        of Epstein, Becker & Green, P.C.
Auditor ....Douglas Burack, C.P.A.
                Lutz & Carr, L.L.P.
Insurance ....Jennifer Brown of
                DeWitt Stern Group
Photographer ....T. Charles Erickson
Video Services ....Fresh Produce Productions/
                Frank Basile
Travel ....Tygon Tours
Consulting Architect ....Hugh Hardy,
    H3 Hardy Collaboration Architecture
Construction Manager ....Yorke Construction
Payroll Service ....Castellana Services, Inc.
Merchandising ....Marquee Merchandise, LLC/
                Matt Murphy

STAFF FOR *JOE TURNER'S COME AND GONE*

COMPANY MANAGER........MATTHEW MARKOFF
Assistant Director ....Lileana Blain-Cruz
Associate Set Designer ....Mikiko Suzuki McAdams
Assistant Costume Designers ....Nicole Moody,
                David Newell
Associate Lighting Designer ....Jennifer Schriever
Assistant Lighting Designer ....Rebecca Eichorn
Assistant to the Lighting Designer ....Zach Blane
Associate Sound Designer ....David Thomas
Assistant Sound Designer ....Ashley Hanson
Production Carpenter ....John Weingart
Production Electrician ....Graeme McDonnell
Production Propertyman ....Mark Dignam
Production Soundman ....Wayne Smith
Hair and Make-Up Design ....Jon Carter
Specialty Make-Up ....Lou Zakarian
Movement ....Dianne McIntyre
Movement Assistant ....Shireen Dickson
Props ....Susan Barras
Wardrobe Supervisor ....Moira MacGregor-Conrad
Dressers................................Tina Marie Clifton,
              Kevin Andre Dickens
Hair Supervisor ....Yolanda Ramsey
Assistant to Mr. Sher ....Sarna Lapine
Production Assistant ....Rosy Garner
Costume Shopper ....Lindsey Jones
Children's Guardian ....Brooke Engen
Children's Tutoring ....On Location Education
Animal Handler...........................Monica Schaffer

Vocal Coach ....Deborah Hecht

Technical Supervision by
William Nagle and Patrick Merryman

Animal Training by
William Berloni Theatrical Animals, Inc.

CREDITS

Scenery construction by PRG Scenic Technologies, a division of Production Resource Group, L.L.C. and Great Lakes Scenic Studio. Show control and scenic motion control featuring Stage Command Systems® by PRG Scenic Technologies, a division of Production Resource Group, L.L.C., New Windsor, NY. Costumes by Euro Co., Jennifer Love Costumes, John Cowles and Angels the Costumiers. Millinery by Arnold S. Levin. Additional props by Costume Armour. Sound equipment by Sound Associates. Lighting equipment from PRG Lighting. Natural herb cough drops courtesy of Ricola USA, Inc.

SONG CREDITS

"Kulanjan," "Tunkaranke," "Queen Bee," and "Guede Man Na" all arranged from the traditional by Taj Mahal and Toumani Diabate; "From the Depth of Silence" and "Kisetsu" by Somei Santoh; "Kothbiro" arranged from the traditional by Ayub Ogada; "Country Blues No. 1" by Taj Mahal.

SPECIAL THANKS

Jacqui Malone, Peter John Still

Visit www.lct.org
For groups of 20 or more:
Caryl Goldsmith Group Sales
(212) 889-4300

House Manager ....Carol Flemming
Carpenter ....George Dummitt
Electrician ....Matthew Maloney
Property Person ....Laura Koch

Joe Turner's Come and Gone
SCRAPBOOK

Correspondent: Michael P. Zaleski, Assistant Stage Manager

Opening Night Gifts: The amazing Lincoln Center Tiffany key rings, tote bags and t-shirts with our show logo, copies of our beautiful set renderings, and lots of champagne!

Most Exciting Celebrity Visitors: President Barack Obama and First Lady Michelle Obama; Denzel Washington, James Earl Jones.

Most Roles in This Show: Afton Williamson— she understudies Mattie, Molly and Martha.

Most Shows in Their Career: Roger Robinson.

Special Backstage Rituals: Before every show, the kids come to Laura's office to spend some quality time with Eugene and Eugenia (our pigeons).

Favorite Moments During Each Performance: Any time with food. Between the grits, biscuits, fried chicken, rice and green beans, there's really no reason to eat before the show.

Favorite In-Theatre Gathering Place: The greenroom, although trying to fit nine people into the stage management office is always interesting!

Favorite Off-Site Hangout: Café Un Deux Trois

Favorite Snack Food: Fried Chicken. As she clears the table after "Sunday Dinner" onstage, Marsha Stephanie has a knack for wrapping up her piece of chicken so that she can grab it right when the curtain comes in for intermission.

Mascot: Eugenia the pigeon.

Favorite Therapy: Ricola! And Purell (you know...for the Swine Flu...and the pigeons).

Memorable Ad-Lib: During a rehearsal in previews when Amari, one of our kids, stood in for Aunjanue for Molly's first entrance.

Memorable Stage Door Fan Encounter: During one show, a fan dressed as a Ghostbuster (with props and all) waited outside the stage door for Ernie from intermission through the end of the show.

Fastest Costume Change: Either Ernie's change into his Sunday Suit or Aunjanue's change into her Sunday Dinner dress.

Heaviest/Hottest Costume: Chad Coleman in his black coat and hat.

Who Wore the Least: Chad Coleman with his shirt half off.

Catchphrase Only the Company Would Recognize: "Where the door go?"

Memorable Directorial Note: "The first act needs more work than A.I.G."

Company In-Jokes: Every night, Roger and Rich (one of our prop men) call each other new names...Hephaestus, Obediah and Llewelyn were some of the best.

Understudy Anecdote: Our understudy rehearsals can be pretty schizophrenic since most of our understudies cover two characters or more. We never have the time for them to work their way through the play as just one character. The second they exit as one character, it's time to run back onstage to pick up as someone else.

1. Cast members LaTanya Richardson Jackson and Ernie Hudson at the opening night party at the Millennium Broadway.
2. Cast member Roger Robinson at the opening night party.
3. Constanza Romero, widow of author August Wilson, with director Bartlett Sher at the Belasco.
4. President Barack Obama (R) with First Lady Michelle Obama (2nd from L between unidentified audience members) attends the show on May 30, 2009.

Sweethearts Within the Company: Our kids—even though they didn't actually kiss until our final dress.

Embarrassing Moment: During the Juba one night, one of the ladies' skirts came unhooked and fell down. She grabbed it and had to hold it up in back through the whole dance and the rest of the act.

Ghostly Encounters Backstage: At the Belasco? Lots! We've had sightings by the cast, crew and folks in the audience. There are two ghosts haunting the theatre – Mr. Belasco and Blanche Bates. During tech, there were sightings of a woman in a blue dress up in the balcony. We've actually had a few times when props or costume pieces had mysteriously moved during the show.

Superstitions That Turned Out To Be True: Pigeon poop is, in fact, good luck. We've also had to send folks outside for whistling backstage and saying "tomorrow" three times in a row.

Coolest Thing About Being in This Show: Being able to watch the show every night.

2008-2009 AWARDS

TONY AWARDS
Best Featured Actor in a Play
(Roger Robinson)
Best Lighting Design of a Play
(Brian MacDevitt)

ACTORS' EQUITY ASSOCIATION
Richard Seff Award
(Roger Robinson)

THEATRE WORLD AWARD
First Major New York Stage Appearance
(Chad L. Coleman)

Photos by Aubrey Reuben

Photo by Owen Iverson

Legally Blonde

First Preview: April 3, 2007. Opened: April 29, 2007.
Closed October 19, 2008 after 30 Previews and 595 Performances.

PLAYBILL

CAST

Elle Woods	BAILEY HANKS
Warner Huntington III	RICHARD H. BLAKE
Vivienne Kensington	KATE SHINDLE
Emmett Forrest	CHRISTIAN BORLE
Professor Callahan	MICHAEL RUPERT
Paulette	ORFEH
Serena	TRACY JAI EDWARDS
Margot	KATE ROCKWELL
Pilar	ASMERET GHEBREMICHAEL
Shandi/Brooke Wyndham	NICOLETTE HART
Kate/Chutney	STEPHANIE FITTRO
Leilani	AUTUMN HURLBERT
Cece/District Attorney	EMILY PADGETT
Kristine	APRIL BERRY
Gabby/Stenographer	BETH CURRY
Veronica/Enid	LUCIA SPINA
Store Manager/Judge	AMBER EFÉ
Courtney/Mom/Whitney	CARA MASSEY
Grandmaster Chad/Dewey/Kyle	BRYAN WEST
Dad/Winthrop/Reporter	KEVIN PARISEAU
Pforzheimer	JASON GILLMAN
Lowell/Carlos	KYLE BROWN
Padamadan/Nikos	MANUEL HERRERA
Aaron	BARRY ANDERSON
Bruiser	CHICO
Rufus	CHLOE
Beer Bash Dancers	MANUEL HERRERA, NICK KENKEL

Harvard Students, Marching Band, Cheerleaders,
   Inmates, Salespeople ....BARRY
ANDERSON, APRIL BERRY, KYLE BROWN,

Continued on next page

Continued on next page

⇒N⇐ **PALACE THEATRE**
UNDER THE DIRECTION OF
STEWART F. LANE, JAMES M. NEDERLANDER AND JAMES L. NEDERLANDER

Hal Luftig   Fox Theatricals   Dori Berinstein

James L. Nederlander   Independent Presenters Network   Roy Furman   Amanda Lipitz
      Broadway Asia   Barbara Whitman   FWPM Group   Hendel/Wiesenfeld
   Goldberg/Binder   Stern/Meyer   Lane/Comley   Bartner-Jenkins/Nocciolino
                 and Warren Trepp

In Association with MGM ON STAGE   Darcie Denkert and Dean Stolber

Present

LEGALLY BLONDE *The Musical*™

Music and Lyrics by
LAURENCE O'KEEFE and **NELL BENJAMIN**   Book by
HEATHER HACH

BASED UPON THE NOVEL BY AMANDA BROWN
and THE METRO-GOLDWYN-MAYER MOTION PICTURE

Starring

BAILEY HANKS

CHRISTIAN BORLE   ORFEH

RICHARD H. BLAKE   KATE SHINDLE   NICOLETTE HART

and **MICHAEL RUPERT**

With

TRACY JAI EDWARDS   ASMERET GHEBREMICHAEL   KATE ROCKWELL   LUCIA SPINA
BARRY ANDERSON   APRIL BERRY   KYLE BROWN   LINDSAY NICOLE CHAMBERS   BETH CURRY   AMBER EFÉ
TIFFANY ENGEN   STEPHANIE FITTRO   JOSH FRANKLIN   JASON GILLMAN   ROD HARRELSON   ERIC HATCH
MANUEL HERRERA   AUTUMN HURLBERT   NICK KENKEL   CARA MASSEY   RUSTY MOWERY
EMILY PADGETT   KEVIN PARISEAU   JODY REYNARD   DANI SPIELER   BRYAN WEST

Produced for Fox Theatricals by
KRISTIN CASKEY and **MIKE ISAACSON**

Scenic Design	Costume Design	Lighting Design	Sound Design
DAVID ROCKWELL	GREGG BARNES	KEN POSNER & PAUL MILLER	ACME SOUND PARTNERS

Casting	Hair Design	Associate Director	Associate Choreographer
TELSEY + COMPANY	DAVID BRIAN BROWN	MARC BRUNI	DENIS JONES

Technical Supervisor	Animal Trainer	Production Stage Manager
SMITTY/ THEATERSMITH, INC.	WILLIAM BERLONI	KRISTEN HARRIS

Press Representative	Associate Producers	General Management
BARLOW•HARTMAN	PMC PRODUCTIONS YASUHIRO KAWANA ANDREW ASNES/ADAM ZOTOVICH	NLA/MAGGIE BROHN

Music Director/Conductor	Orchestrations	Arrangements	Music Contractor
JAMES SAMPLINER	CHRISTOPHER JAHNKE	LAURENCE O'KEEFE & JAMES SAMPLINER	MICHAEL KELLER

Directed and Choreographed by
JERRY MITCHELL

10/1/08

Bailey Hanks as
Elle Woods (center)
with the Delta Nus.

Legally Blonde

SCENES AND MUSICAL NUMBERS

ACT I

Scene 1: UCLA Delta Nu Sorority House/Mall/Elle's Door
"Omigod You Guys" ....Margot, Serena, Pilar, Delta Nu's, Elle, Shopgirl, Manager
Scene 2: Restaurant
"Serious" ....Warner, Elle
Scene 3: Delta Nu Sorority House/Golf Course/Harvard Law School Admissions Office
"Daughter of Delta Nu" ....Margot, Serena, Pilar, Kate, Delta Nu's
"What You Want" ....Elle, Margot, Serena, Pilar, Kate, Mom, Dad, Grandmaster Chad,
Winthrop, Pforzheimer, Lowell, Delta Nu's and Company
Scene 4: Harvard Yard
"The Harvard Variations" ....Emmett, Aaron, Enid, Padamadan and Harvard Students
Scene 5: Callahan's Classroom
"Blood in the Water" ....Callahan and Company
Scene 6: Harvard Yard
"Positive" ....Elle, Margot, Serena, Pilar, Greek Chorus
Scene 7: The Hair Affair
"Ireland" ....Paulette
"Ireland" (Reprise) ....Paulette
Scene 8: Harvard Party
"Serious" (Reprise) ....Elle, Warner
Scene 9: Harvard Yard/Elle's Room/Callahan's Classroom
"Chip on My Shoulder" ....Emmett, Elle, Greek Chorus, Company
Scene 10: Dewey's Trailer
Scene 11: Harvard Hallway
"So Much Better" ....Elle, Greek Chorus and Company

ACT II

Scene 1: Conference Room of Stidwell, Zyskowski, Fox & Callahan/Women's Prison
"Whipped Into Shape" ....Brooke, Callahan and Company
Scene 2: Hansen-Harkness Department Store
"Take It Like a Man" ....Elle, Emmett, Salespersons
Scene 3: The Hair Affair
"Bend and Snap" ....Elle, Paulette, Serena, Margot, Pilar, Salonfolk
Scene 4: Courtroom
"There! Right There!" ....Elle, Callahan, Emmett, Brooke, Vivienne, Warner,
Enid, Judge, Nikos, Carlos and Company
Scene 5: Callahan's Office/Elle's Door
"Legally Blonde" ....Elle, Emmett
Scene 6: The Hair Affair
"Legally Blonde Remix" ....Vivienne, Enid, Elle, Company
Scene 7: Courtroom/Bathroom of the Wyndham Mansion
"Omigod You Guys" (Reprise) ....Elle and Company
Scene 8: Harvard Law Graduation
"Find My Way/Finale" ....Elle, Paulette and Company

Cast Continued

BETH CURRY, AMBER EFÉ,
STEPHANIE FITTRO, JOSH FRANKLIN,
JASON GILLMAN, MANUEL HERRERA,
NICK KENKEL, CARA MASSEY,
RUSTY MOWERY, EMILY PADGETT,
KEVIN PARISEAU, BRYAN WEST

UNDERSTUDIES

For Elle Woods: AUTUMN HURLBERT,
KATE ROCKWELL
For Emmett Forrest: BARRY ANDERSON,
JOSH FRANKLIN
For Professor Callahan: JOSH FRANKLIN,
KEVIN PARISEAU
For Paulette: AMBER EFÉ, CARA MASSEY
For Warner Huntington III: JASON GILLMAN,
BRYAN WEST
For Vivienne Kensington: TRACY JAI EDWARDS,
CARA MASSEY
For Brooke Wyndham/Shandi: BETH CURRY,
ASMERET GHEBREMICHAEL,
EMILY PADGETT
For Serena: LINDSAY NICOLE CHAMBERS,
TIFFANY ENGEN
For Margot: BETH CURRY, TIFFANY ENGEN,
AUTUMN HURLBERT, EMILY PADGETT
For Pilar: BETH CURRY, TIFFANY ENGEN,
EMILY PADGETT
For Enid: LINDSAY NICOLE CHAMBERS,
CARA MASSEY

SWINGS

LINDSAY NICOLE CHAMBERS,
TIFFANY ENGEN, ROD HARRELSON,
ERIC HATCH, JODY REYNARD,
DANI SPIELER

DANCE CAPTAINS

RUSTY MOWERY, TIFFANY ENGEN

SETTING

In and around the Delta Nu house,
Southern California.
In and around the Harvard Law campus,
Cambridge, Massachusetts.

ORCHESTRA

Conductor: JAMES SAMPLINER
Associate Conductor: MATT GALLAGHER
Concertmaster: ENTCHO TODOROV
Viola: TODD LOW
Cello: ANJA WOOD
Lead Trumpet: DAVE TRIGG
Trumpet: BUD BURRIDGE
Trombone: KEITH O'QUINN

Reed 1: CHUCK WILSON
Reed 2: DAN WILLIS
Reed 3: CHAD SMITH
French Horn: ROGER WENDT
Drums: GREG JOSEPH
Bass: MARK VANDERPOEL
Keyboard 1: JAMES SAMPLINER
Keyboards: CHARLIE ALTERMAN,
MATT GALLAGHER

Guitars: JOHN PUTNAM,
JAKE EZRA SCHWARTZ
Percussion: PABLO RIEPPI
Music Coordinator: MICHAEL KELLER
Copyist: EMILY GRISHMAN
MUSIC PREPARATION —
EMILY GRISHMAN/
KATHARINE EDMONDS
Synthesizer Programming: LELAND MUSIC CO.

Legally Blonde

Bailey Hanks
Elle Woods

Christian Borle
Emmett

Orfeh
Paulette

Michael Rupert
Callahan

Richard H. Blake
Warner Huntington III

Kate Shindle
Vivienne

Nicolette Hart
Brooke Wyndham

Barry Anderson
Aaron, Ensemble

April Berry
Ensemble

Kyle Brown
Lowell/Carlos

Lindsay Nicole
Chambers
Swing

Beth Curry
Ensemble

Tracy Jai Edwards
Serena

Amber Efé
Ensemble

Tiffany Engen
*Swing/Assistant
Dance Captain*

Stephanie Fittro
Kate/Chutney

Josh Franklin
Ensemble

Asmeret
Ghebremichael
Pilar

Jason Gillman
Pforzheimer

Rod Harrelson
Swing

Eric Hatch
Swing

Manuel Herrera
Nikos/Padamadan

Autumn Hurlbert
Leilani

Nick Kenkel
*Ensemble/Assistant
Choreographer*

Cara Massey
Ensemble

Rusty Mowery
*Dance Captain/
Ensemble*

Emily Padgett
*DA Joyce Riley/
Ensemble*

Kevin Pariseau
Ensemble

Jody Reynard
Swing

Kate Rockwell
Margot

Dani Spieler
Swing

Lucia Spina
Enid

Bryan West
*Kyle/Dewey/
Grandmaster Chad*

Heather Hach
Book Writer

Laurence O'Keefe
Music and Lyrics

Legally Blonde

Nell Benjamin
Music and Lyrics

Jerry Mitchell
Director/
Choreographer

David Rockwell
Scenic Designer

Gregg Barnes
Costume Design

Kenneth Posner
Lighting Designer

Paul Miller
Lighting Designer

David Brian Brown
Wig/Hair Design

Tom Clark, Mark Menard and Nevin Steinberg,
Acme Sound Partners
Sound Designer

Justen M. Brosnan
Makeup Design

Bernard Telsey,
Telsey + Company
Casting

James Sampliner
Music Director/
Conductor/
Co-Arranger

Christopher Jahnke
Orchestrations

Michael Keller
Music Coordinator

Smitty/
Theatersmith, Inc/
Christopher C. Smith
Technical Supervisor

William Berloni
Animal Trainer

Marc Bruni
Associate Director

Denis Jones
Associate
Choreographer

Nina Lannan
Associates
General
Management

Hal Luftig
Producer

Dori Berinstein
Producer

James L.
Nederlander
Producer

Roy Furman
Producer

Amanda Lipitz
Producer

Simone Genatt-Haft,
Broadway Asia
Producer

Marc Routh,
Broadway Asia
Producer

Barbara Whitman
Producer

Barbara Freitag,
FWPM Group
Producer

Jennifer Maloney,
FWPM Group
Producer

Ruth Hendel,
Hendel/Wiesenfeld
Producer

Hal Goldberg,
Goldberg/Binder
Producer

Douglas L. Meyer,
Stern/Meyer
Producer

Stewart F. Lane and
Bonnie Comley
Producer

Michael A. Jenkins,
Bartner-Jenkins/
Nocciolino
Producer

Yasuhiro Kawana
Associate Producer

Legally Blonde

Adam Zotovich
Associate Producer

Andrew Asnes
Associate Producer

Nathan Balser
Ensemble

Laura Bell Bundy
Elle Woods

Paul Canaan
Ensemble

Ven Daniel
*Grandmaster Chad/
Dewey/Kyle,
Ensemble*

Gaelen Gilliland
*Courtney/Mom/
Whitney, Ensemble*

Becky Gulsvig
Leilani, Ensemble

Natalie Joy Johnson
Veronica/Enid

Andy Karl
*Grandmaster Chad/
Dewey/Kyle,
Ensemble*

Michelle Kittrell
Cece/
*District Attorney,
Ensemble,
Dance Captain*

Matthew Risch
*Lowell/Carlos,
Ensemble*

Bryce Ryness
Ensemble

Casey Leigh
Thompson
*Gabby/Stenographer,
Ensemble, Swing*

FRONT OF HOUSE STAFF
Front Row (L-R): Estello Genesoni,
Verne Shayne, Kelly Collins

Second Row (L-R):
Rebecca Segarra, Ani Kehr,
Robert Collins, Colleen Keenan

Third Row (L-R): Sandy Darbasie,
Adriana Casablanca, Lynette Meyers,
Bill Mullen, Gloria Hill, Dixon Rosario,
Disting Birona, Lorraine O'Sullivan

Back Row (L-R): Val Ramos,
Juliar Pazmino, Rachel Bentley,
Scott Muso, Jennifer Butt

Photos by Ben Strothmann

CONCESSIONS
(L-R):
Shrondia Curry,
Shantell Cargle,
Christina
Weathersby,
Rohan Redwood

MERCHANDISING
(L-R): Jen Zappola, Vic Romero

Legally Blonde

GENERAL MANAGER
NINA LANNAN ASSOCIATES
Maggie Brohn

Company Manager
Paul Morer

Assistant Company Manager .... Katherine McNamee

GENERAL PRESS REPRESENTATIVE
Barlow•Hartman

Michael Hartman	John Barlow
Leslie Baden	Matt Shea

CASTING
TELSEY + COMPANY
Bernie Telsey CSA, Will Cantler CSA, David Vaccari CSA,
Bethany Knox CSA, Craig Burns CSA,
Tiffany Little Canfield CSA, Rachel Hoffman CSA,
Carrie Rosson CSA, Justin Huff CSA,
Bess Fifer CSA, Patrick Goodwin

Associate Director	Marc Bruni
Associate Choreographer	Denis Jones
Assistant Choreographer	Nick Kenkel
PRODUCTION STAGE MANAGER	Kristen Harris
Stage Manager	Kimberly Russell
Assistant Stage Managers	Kelly Stillwell, Chris Jamros
Dance Captains	Rusty Mowery, Tiffany Engen
Assistant to David Rockwell	Barry Richards
Associate Designer	Richard Jaris
Assistant Designers	Todd Ivins, Gaetane Bertol, Brian Drucker, Rob Bissinger, Larry Brown, Corrine Merrill
Modelmakers	Joannie Schlaffer, Rachael Short-Janocko, Morgan Moore, Tomo Tanaka
Set Design Graphics	Alexi Logothetis, Charles Rush, Jerry Sabatini, Matthew Goodrich
Associate Costume Designer	Sky Switser
Assistant Costume Designer	Matthew R Pachtman
Costume Assistants	Sarah Sophia Turner, Jeriana Hochberg
Costume Interns	Nina Damato, Sydney Gallas
Assistant Lighting Designer	Jonathan Spencer
Advance Sound	Dan Robillard
Assistant Sound Designer	Jeffrey Yoshi Lee
Automated Lighting Programmer	Timothy F. Rogers
Dialect Coach	Stephen Gabis
Fight Director	Thomas Schall

MAKEUP DESIGN .... JUSTEN M. BROSNAN

Production Carpenter	Donald J. Oberpriller
Fly Automation Carpenter	Robert M. Hentze
Production Flyman	Robert W. Kelly
Carpenters	Joel Brandwine, Jeff Lunsford
Production Electricians	James J. Fedigan, Randall Zaibek
Head Electrician	Dan Coey
Assistant Electricians	Eric Abbott, Lorne MacDougall
Production Sound	Mike Wojchik
Production Properties	Timothy M. Abel
Head Properties	Ken Keneally
Assistant Properties	Rob Conover
Wardrobe Supervisor	Dolly Williams
Assistant Wardrobe Supervisor	Fred Castner

Star Dresser	Laura Ellington
Dressers	Grant Barrett, Tina Clifton, Tasha Cowd, Gina Gornik, Michael Harrell, James Hodun, Jeff Johnson, Melanie McClintock, Jeff McGovney, Marcia McIntosh, Christel Murdock, Jack Scott, Pamela Sorensen, Veneda Truesdale, Marcia VanKuiKen
Hair Supervisor	Enrique Vega
Assistant Hair Supervisor	Joseph Whitmeyer
Hair Dressers	Joel Hawkins, Jacqueline Pietro
Additional Arrangements	Alex Lacamoire
Rehearsal Musicians	Matt Gallagher, Brian Hertz
Production Assistants	Caroline Andersen, Christopher Munnell
Dog Trainer	William Berloni
Dog Handlers	Kylen Kline, AJ Sullivan
Assistant Trainer	Dorothy Berloni
Company Physical Therapist	Sean Gallagher, PAPT

Advertising	Serino Coyne, Inc./ Sandy Block, Stephen Elms, Becca Goland-Van Ryn, Roger Micone
Website Design/ Online Marketing Strategy	Situation Marketing LLC/ Damian Bazadona, Chris Powers, Ian Bennett, Jimmy Lee
Marketing Director	Adam Jay
Comptroller	Tabitha Falcone/ Sarah Galbraith Company
Accountants	Robert Fried CPA, Fried & Kowgios CPAs LLP
General Management Associate	Libby Fox
General Management Interns	Zarinah Washington, Danielle Saks
Press Associates	Michelle Bergmann, Tom D'Ambrosio, Juliana Hannett, Ryan Ratelle, Wayne Wolfe
Press Office Manager	Bethany Larsen
Production Photographer	Paul Kolnik
Additional Photography	Bruce Glikas
Insurance	Albert G. Ruben Company Inc./ Claudia Kaufman
Banking	City National Bank, Gregg Santos
Payroll	Castellana Services, Inc.
Merchandising	Max Merchandising, Randi Grossman
Travel Agent	Tzell Travel/The "A" Team, Andi Henig
Legal Counsel	Franklin, Weinrib, Rudell & Vassallo, P.C./ Elliot H. Brown, Daniel M. Wasser, Matthew C. Lefferts
Associate to Mr. Luftig	Brian Smith
Assistant to Ms. Caskey	Megan Larche
Assistant to Mr. Isaacson	Jamie Griser
SSDC Observer	Christine O'Grady
Music Intern	Evan Jay Newman

GROUP SALES
Theatre Direct/Showtix
1-800-BROADWAY

www.legallyblondethemusical.com

ACKNOWLEDGEMENTS
The producers wish to thank the following partners for their generous support: VISA, TIFFANY & CO., VAVOOM

PROFESSIONAL HAIRCARE and ELLE MAGAZINE.
Other products graciously provided by the following partners: Puma, Juicy Couture, UPS, Manhattan Portage, Nanette Lepore. Handbags provided by Lana Marks; Mobile phones provided by Verizon Wireless; iPods and Elle Woods' computer provided by Apple; Sound effects by Tivo, Inc.; some jeans provided by Rich & Skinny Jeans; and Elle's dorm room furnished by Pottery Barn Teen.

CREDITS
Scenery constructed and automation equipment provided by Showmotion Inc. Scenic drops painted by Scenic Arts Studio. Costumes constructed by Barbara Matera Ltd., Carelli Costumes, Donna Langman, John David Ridge, Tricorne and D.D. Dolan. Custom millinery by Lynne Mackey Studio, Killer. Custom shoes by Capri Shoes, J.C. Theatrical, LaDuca Productions and T.O. Dey. Custom painting by Jeff Fender, screenprinting by Steven Gillespie and knitting by C.C. Wei. Undergarments provided by Bra*Tenders. Lighting equipment by PRG Lighting. Sound equipment supplied by Sound Associates. Props provided by Spoon Group, Beyond Imagination, Jennie Marino/Moonboots. Special assistant with hand prop construction Meghan Abel. Receptors provided by Muse Research. Guitar amps by Mega Boogie. Pianos provided by Yamaha Musical Theatre Corp. Dogs adopted from Associated Humane Society of New Jersey, Four Paws Rescue of New Jersey, the Connecticut Humane Society and Bulldog Rescue of Connecticut. Rehearsed at the New 42nd Street Studios. Natural herb cough drops supplied by Ricola USA Inc. Makeup provided by M•A•C Cosmetics.

SPECIAL THANKS
Michael Harrell, Rosemary Phelps, Cory Ching, Dr. Wayne Goldberg, Rachel Pachtman, Tom LaMere, Stephanie Steele, Stewart Adelson, Joe Ortmeyer, Marc Platt, Karen McCullah, Kirsten Smith, Gail Cannold, Sue Spiegel, Ken Marsolais, Mitchell Cannold, Bairbre Finn. San Francisco Business Agent FX Crowley. Our production team would like to thank the San Francisco crew for their terrific work.

NEDERLANDER

Chairman	**James M. Nederlander**
President	**James L. Nederlander**

Executive Vice President
Nick Scandalios

Vice President	Senior Vice President
Corporate Development	Labor Relations
Charlene S. Nederlander	**Herschel Waxman**

Vice President	Chief Financial Officer
Jim Boese	**Freida Sawyer Belviso**

STAFF FOR THE PALACE THEATRE

Theatre Manager	Dixon Rosario
Treasurer	Cissy Caspare
Assistant Treasurer	Anne T. Wilson
Carpenter	Thomas K. Phillips
Flyman	Robert W. Kelly
Electrician	Eddie Webber
Propertymaster	Steve Camus
Engineer	Rob O'Conner
Chief Usher	Gloria Hill

Legally Blonde
SCRAPBOOK

Correspondent: Asmeret Ghebremichael, "Pilar"

Memorable Fan Gifts: A word puzzle and chocolates from Timothy, a 4-year-old from Los Angeles whose parents met at the Palace Theatre. *Legally Blonde* was the first Broadway show he'd ever seen, and he's since been back twice.

Opening Night Gift: An engraved Tiffany & Co. charm from Jerry Mitchell.

Most Exciting Celebrity Visitor and What He Did/Said: Robert DeNiro...he didn't have to do or say much, he's Robert DeNiro!!!

Actor Who Performed the Most Roles in This Show: My guess is Tiffany Engen, the super swing. She has played male characters in our show, aside from almost every female role.

Who Has Done the Most Shows in Their Career: I'm guessing Michael Rupert, who celebrated 40 years on Broadway. Richard Blake has also been on Broadway since he was 12 or 13.

Special Backstage Rituals: Singing alternate notes and lyrics to the onstage music, high-fives with our crew.

Favorite Moment During Each Performance: "Bend and Snap" is my favorite part of the show each day.

Favorite In-Theatre Gathering Place: We tend to congregate in the "Quad," which is the area near stage management's office. I also hang out in Elle's dressing room a lot.

Favorite Off-Site Hangout: Langan's, Trecolori.

Favorite Snack Foods: Salt and vinegar potato chips!!!

Mascot: Anything pink.

Favorite Therapies: Massage, Emergen-C.

Memorable Ad-Lib: Noah Weisberg going up on his solo during "The Harvard Variations" and basically rewriting his lines. He talked about having things to be proud of, and he somehow managed to keep the whole thing in time!! I'll never forget that.

Record Number of Cell Phone Rings or Texting Incidents During a Performance: Not sure, but there were definitely more texts and calls being made backstage than in the audience.

Memorable Press Encounter: Singing "Omigod You Guys" for the news on our first day back to work after the 2007 strike.

Stage Door Fan Encounter: Meeting a fan who remembered me from *Wicked*, because he called me the wrong name back then and felt really embarrassed about it. Needless to say, he didn't get an autograph, but we laughed about it when he came back to *Blonde*!

What Did You Think of the Web Buzz on Your Show: I thought it was very helpful! We attracted a lot of kids who wouldn't normally be into Broadway shows.

Latest Audience Arrival: Intermission.

Fastest Costume Change: My change at the beginning of "What You Want."

Busiest Day at the Box Office: Any day between Christmas and New Year's Day.

Heaviest/Hottest Costumes: The marching band costumes are heavy and hot.

Who Wore the Least: Elle in her bunny suit!

Catchphrases Only the Company Would Recognize: "Dog Show!" "Jumpoff." I can't write the other one :-)

Sweethearts Within the Company: Andy Karl and Orfeh were the top sweethearts!

Orchestra Member Who Played the Most Instruments: Pablo Rieppi, our fantastic percussionist. I'm not sure how many different instruments he played, but he played at least three.

Orchestra Member Who Played the Most Consecutive Performances Without a Sub: Probably our conductor, James Sampliner. I don't know for sure, because all the subs were at the show the day I tried to ask the band :-)

Memorable Directorial Note: Jerry gave me the note to "show my beautiful ass" to the audience

Bailey Hanks poses for news photographers outside the Palace Theatre after winning the role of Elle Woods on a TV reality show.

as much as possible during "Spring Break Cabo."

Company In-Jokes: Picking themes for each performance: supermodel day, paddle turn day, et cetera.

Company Legend: Michael Rupert.

Embarrassing Moment: Laura Bell losing her wig during "Bend and Snap" and then thanking the audience for attending "*Legally Bald.*"

Coolest Thing About Being in This Show: Getting the chance to tape the show for MTV!!

Fan Club Website: There is a fan page for me on Facebook.

CREW
Front Row (L-R): Fred Castner, Dolly Williams, Jack Scott, Chasity Neutze.

Second Row (L-R): Jeff Johnson, Pam Sorensen, Jeff McGovney, Marcia McIntosh, Laura Bell Bundy.

Third Row (L-R): Eugene Nicks, Grant Barrett, Tasha Cowd, Michael Harrell, John Cooper.

Back Row (L-R): Ken Keneally, Seth Sklar-Heyn, Christel Murdock, Tina Clifton, Joel Hawkins, Melanie McClintock, Gina Gornik, Joe Whitmeyer, Veneda Truesdale, Enrique Vega.

The Lion King

First Preview: October 15, 1997. Opened: November 13, 1997.
Still running as of May 31, 2009.

PLAYBILL

THE LION KING

CAST

(in order of appearance)

RAFIKI ....Tshidi Manye
MUFASA ....Nathaniel Stampley
SARABI ....Jean Michelle Grier
ZAZU ....Jeff Binder
SCAR ....Derek Smith
YOUNG SIMBA................Clifford Lee Dickson
    (Tues., Wed., Sat. Mat., Sun. Eve.)
YOUNG SIMBA ....Jerome Stephens, Jr.
    (Thurs., Fri., Sat. Eve., Sun. Mat.)
YOUNG NALA ....Nia Imani Hunter
    (Wed., Thurs., Sat. Mat., Sun. Mat.)
YOUNG NALA ....Cypress Eden Smith
    (Tues., Fri., Sat. Eve., Sun. Eve.)
SHENZI ....Jacquelyn Renae Hodges
BANZAI ....James Brown-Orleans
ED ....Enrique Segura
TIMON ....Danny Rutigliano
PUMBAA ....Tom Alan Robbins
SIMBA ....Dashaun Young
NALA ....Kissy Simmons
ENSEMBLE SINGERS ....Alvin Crawford,
    Lindiwe Dlamini, Bongi Duma,
    Jean Michelle Grier, Christine Horn, Joel Karie,
    Ron Kunene, Sheryl McCallum, S'bu Ngema,
    Mpume Sikakane, L. Steven Taylor,
    Kenny Redell Williams
ENSEMBLE DANCERS ....Kylin Brady,
    Camille M. Brown, Michelle Brugal,
    Gabriel Croom, Christopher Freeman,
    Nicole Adell Johnson, Geoff Myers,

Continued on next page

MINSKOFF THEATRE

UNDER THE DIRECTION OF
JAMES M. NEDERLANDER, JAMES L. NEDERLANDER,
SARA MINSKOFF ALLAN AND THE MINSKOFF FAMILY

Disney
PRESENTS

THE LION KING

Music & Lyrics by
ELTON JOHN & TIM RICE

Additional Music & Lyrics by
LEBO M, MARK MANCINA, JAY RIFKIN, JULIE TAYMOR, HANS ZIMMER

Book by
ROGER ALLERS & IRENE MECCHI

Starring
DEREK SMITH   NATHANIEL STAMPLEY   TSHIDI MANYE
JEFF BINDER   TOM ALAN ROBBINS   DANNY RUTIGLIANO
DASHAUN YOUNG   KISSY SIMMONS
JAMES BROWN-ORLEANS   JACQUELYN RENAE HODGES   ENRIQUE SEGURA
CLIFFORD LEE DICKSON   NIA IMANI HUNTER   CYPRESS EDEN SMITH   JEROME STEPHENS, JR.

SEAN BRADFORD KYLIN BRADY CAMILLE M. BROWN MICHELLE BRUGAL ALVIN CRAWFORD GABRIEL CROOM
GARLAND DAYS LINDIWE DLAMINI BONGI DUMA ANGELICA EDWARDS JIM FERRIS CHRISTOPHER FREEMAN
JEAN MICHELLE GRIER CHRISTINE HORN KENNY INGRAM TONY JAMES NICOLE ADELL JOHNSON DENNIS JOHNSTON
JOEL KARIE RON KUNENE SHERYL McCALLUM WILLIA-NOEL MONTAGUE GEOFF MYERS S'BU NGEMA
SELLOANE A. NKHELA BRANDON CHRISTOPHER O'NEAL DAWN NOEL PIGNUOLA LaQUET SHARNELL
MPUME SIKAKANE SOPHIA STEPHENS JEREMIAH TATUM L. STEVEN TAYLOR RYAN BROOKE TAYLOR
TORYA THOM CHRISTOPHER WARREN KENNY REDELL WILLIAMS

Adapted from the screenplay by
IRENE MECCHI & JONATHAN ROBERTS & LINDA WOOLVERTON

Produced by
PETER SCHNEIDER & THOMAS SCHUMACHER

Scenic Design	*Costume Design*	*Lighting Design*	*Mask & Puppet Design*
RICHARD HUDSON	JULIE TAYMOR	DONALD HOLDER	JULIE TAYMOR & MICHAEL CURRY

Sound Design	*Hair & Makeup Design*	*Associate Director*	*Production Dance Supervisor*
STEVE CANYON KENNEDY	MICHAEL WARD	JOHN STEFANIUK	MAREY GRIFFITH

Associate Producer	*Technical Director*	*Production Stage Manager*	*Production Supervisor*
ANNE QUART	DAVID BENKEN	RON VODICKA	DOC ZORTHIAN

Music Supervisor	*Music Director*	*Associate Music Producer*	*Music Coordinator*	*Orchestrators*
CLEMENT ISHMAEL	KARL JURMAN	ROBERT ELHAI	MICHAEL KELLER	ROBERT ELHAI DAVID METZGER BRUCE FOWLER

Music Produced for the Stage & Additional Score by	*Additional Vocal Score, Vocal Arrangements & Choral Director*	*Casting*
MARK MANCINA	LEBO M	BINDER CASTING/ MARK BRANDON

Choreography by
GARTH FAGAN

Directed by
JULIE TAYMOR

©Disney

Disney
ON BROADW.

10/1/08

The cast performs "The Circle of Life."

Photo by Joan Marcus

The Lion King

SCENES AND MUSICAL NUMBERS

ACT ONE

Scene 1　Pride Rock
　　　　"Circle of Life" with "Nants' Ingonyama" ....Rafiki, Ensemble
Scene 2　Scar's Cave
Scene 3　Rafiki's Tree
Scene 4　The Pridelands
　　　　"The Morning Report" ....Zazu, Young Simba, Mufasa
Scene 5　Scar's Cave
Scene 6　The Pridelands
　　　　"I Just Can't Wait to Be King" ....Young Simba, Young Nala, Zazu, Ensemble
Scene 7　Elephant Graveyard
　　　　"Chow Down" ....Shenzi, Banzai, Ed
Scene 8　Under the Stars
　　　　"They Live in You" ....Mufasa, Ensemble
Scene 9　Elephant Graveyard
　　　　"Be Prepared" ....Scar, Shenzi, Banzai, Ed, Ensemble
Scene 10　The Gorge
Scene 11　Pride Rock
　　　　"Be Prepared" (Reprise) ....Scar, Ensemble
Scene 12　Rafiki's Tree
Scene 13　The Desert/The Jungle
　　　　"Hakuna Matata" ....Timon, Pumbaa, Young Simba, Simba, Ensemble

ACT TWO

Entr'acte　"One by One" ....Ensemble
Scene 1　Scar's Cave
　　　　"The Madness of King Scar" ....Scar, Zazu, Banzai, Shenzi, Ed, Nala
Scene 2　The Pridelands
　　　　"Shadowland" ....Nala, Rafiki, Ensemble
Scene 3　The Jungle
Scene 4　Under the Stars
　　　　"Endless Night" ....Simba, Ensemble
Scene 5　Rafiki's Tree
Scene 6　The Jungle
　　　　"Can You Feel the Love Tonight" ....Timon, Pumbaa, Simba, Nala, Ensemble
　　　　"He Lives in You" (Reprise) ....Rafiki, Simba, Ensemble
Scene 7　Pride Rock
　　　　"King of Pride Rock"/"Circle of Life" (Reprise) ....Ensemble

SONG CREDITS

All songs by Elton John (music) and Tim Rice (lyrics) except as follows:

"Circle of Life" by Elton John (music) and Tim Rice (lyrics)
with **"Nants' Ingonyama"** by Hans Zimmer and Lebo M
"He Lives in You" (**"They Live in You"**): Music and lyrics by Mark Mancina, Jay Rifkin, and Lebo M
"One by One": Music and lyrics by Lebo M
"Shadowland": Music by Lebo M and Hans Zimmer, lyrics by Mark Mancina and Lebo M
"Endless Night": Music by Lebo M, Hans Zimmer, and Jay Rifkin, lyrics by Julie Taymor
"King of Pride Rock": Music by Hans Zimmer, lyrics by Lebo M.

ADDITIONAL SCORE

Grasslands chant and Lioness chant by Lebo M; Rafiki's chants by Tsidii Le Loka.

Brandon Christopher O'Neal, Dawn Noel Pignuola,
LaQuet Sharnell, Jeremiah Tatum,
Ryan Brooke Taylor

SWINGS AND UNDERSTUDIES

RAFIKI: Angelica Edwards, Sheryl McCallum,
　Selloane A. Nkhela, Mpume Sikakane
MUFASA: Alvin Crawford, L. Steven Taylor
SARABI: Camille M. Brown, Sheryl McCallum
ZAZU: Jim Ferris, Enrique Segura,
　Thom Christopher Warren
SCAR: Jeff Binder, Thom Christopher Warren
SHENZI: Angelica Edwards, Sophia Stephens
BANZAI: Garland Days, Kenny Ingram,
　Kenny Redell Williams
ED: Gabriel Croom, Kenny Ingram,
　Dennis Johnston
TIMON: Jim Ferris, Enrique Segura
PUMBAA: Jim Ferris, Thom Christopher Warren
SIMBA: Sean Bradford, Dennis Johnston, Joel Karie
NALA: Nicole Adell Johnson, Selloane A. Nkhela,
　Sophia Stephens

SWINGS: Sean Bradford, Garland Days,
Angelica Edwards, Kenny Ingram, Tony James,
Dennis Johnston, Willia-Noel Montague,
Sophia Stephens, Torya

DANCE CAPTAINS

Garland Days, Willia-Noel Montague

SPECIALTIES

CIRCLE OF LIFE VOCALS: Bongi Duma,
　S'bu Ngema
MOUSE SHADOW PUPPET: Joel Karie
ANT HILL LADY: Michelle Brugal
GUINEA FOWL: Ryan Brooke Taylor
BUZZARD POLE: Christopher Freeman
GAZELLE WHEEL: LaQuet Sharnell
BUTTERFLIES: LaQuet Sharnell
GAZELLE: Brandon Christopher O'Neal
LIONESS CHANT VOCAL: S'bu Ngema
ACROBATIC TRICKSTER: Jeremiah Tatum
STILT GIRAFFE CROSS: Gabriel Croom
GIRAFFE SHADOW PUPPETS:
　Kenny Redell Williams,
　Brandon Christopher O'Neal
CHEETAH: Dawn Noel Pignuola
SCAR SHADOW PUPPETS:
　Brandon Christopher O'Neal,
　Ryan Brooke Taylor, Kenny Redell Williams
SIMBA SHADOW PUPPETS:
　Christopher Freeman, Geoff Myers,
　Jeremiah Tatum

Continued on next page

The Lion King

Cast Continued

ONE BY ONE VOCAL: Bongi Duma,
    Selloane A. Nkhela
ONE BY ONE DANCE: Bongi Duma,
    Ron Kunene, S'bu Ngema
FIREFLIES: Camille M. Brown
PUMBAA POLE PUPPET: Kenny Redell Williams
NALA POLE PUPPET: Dawn Noel Pignuola
FLOOR DANCERS: Michelle Brugal,
    Ryan Brooke Taylor
FLYING DANCERS: Gabriel Croom,
    Brandon Christopher O'Neal,
    Dawn Noel Pignuola, LaQuet Sharnell
LIONESS/HYENA SHADOW PUPPETS:
    Lindiwe Dlamini, Christine Horn, Ron Kunene,
    Sheryl McCallum, Mpume Sikakane

Bongi Duma, Tshidi Manye, S'bu Ngema,
Selloane A. Nkhela and Mpume Sikakane are
appearing with the permission of Actors' Equity
Association.

ORCHESTRA
CONDUCTOR: Karl Jurman
KEYBOARD SYNTHESIZER/
    ASSOCIATE CONDUCTOR: Cherie Rosen
SYNTHESIZERS: Ted Baker, Paul Ascenzo
WOOD FLUTE SOLOIST/FLUTE/PICCOLO:
    David Weiss
CONCERTMASTER: Francisca Mendoza
VIOLINS: Krystof Witek, Avril Brown
VIOLIN/VIOLA: Ralph Farris
CELLOS: Eliana Mendoza, Bruce Wang
FLUTE/CLARINET/BASS CLARINET:
    Robert DeBellis
FRENCH HORNS: Patrick Milando,
    Alexandra Cook, Greg Smith
TROMBONE: Rock Ciccarone
BASS TROMBONE/TUBA: George Flynn
UPRIGHT AND ELECTRIC BASSES:
    Tom Barney
DRUMS/ASSISTANT CONDUCTOR:
    Tommy Igoe
GUITAR: Kevin Kuhn
PERCUSSION/ASSISTANT CONDUCTOR:
    Rolando Morales-Matos
MALLETS/PERCUSSION: Valerie Dee Naranjo,
    Tom Brett
PERCUSSION: Junior "Gabu" Wedderburn
MUSIC COORDINATOR: Michael Keller

Based on the Disney film *The Lion King*
Directed by Roger Allers and Rob Minkoff
Produced by Don Hahn
**Special thanks to all the artists and staff
of Walt Disney Feature Animation**

Derek Smith
Scar

Nathaniel Stampley
Mufasa

Tshidi Manye
Rafiki

Jeff Binder
Zazu

Tom Alan Robbins
Pumbaa

Danny Rutigliano
Timon

Dashuan Young
Simba

Kissy Simmons
Nala

James
Brown-Orleans
Banzai

Jacquelyn Renae
Hodges
Shenzi

Enrique Segura
Ed

Clifford Lee Dickson
Young Simba

Nia Imani Hunter
Young Nala

Cypress Eden Smith
Young Nala

Jerome Stephens, Jr.
Young Simba

Sean Bradford
Swing

Kylin Brady
Ensemble

Camille M. Brown
Ensemble

Michelle Brugal
Ensemble

Alvin Crawford
Ensemble

The Lion King

Gabriel Croom
Ensemble

Garland Days
Swing,
Dance Captain

Lindiwe Dlamini
Ensemble

Bongi Duma
Ensemble

Angelica Edwards
Swing

Jim Ferris
Standby Zazu, Timon,
Pumbaa

Christopher Freeman
Ensemble

Jean Michelle Grier
Sarabi/Ensemble

Christine Horn
Ensemble

Kenny Ingram
Swing

Tony James
Swing

Nicole Adell Johnson
Ensemble

Dennis Johnston
Swing

Joel Karie
Ensemble

Ron Kunene
Ensemble

Sheryl McCallum
Ensemble

Willia-Noel
Montague
Swing,
Dance Captain

Geoff Myers
Ensemble

S'Bu Ngema
Ensemble

Selloane A. Nkhela
Ensemble

Brandon Christopher
O'Neal
Ensemble

Dawn Noel Pignuola
Ensemble

LaQuet Sharnell
Ensemble

Mpume Sikakane
Ensemble

Sophia Stephens
Swing

Jeremiah Tatum
Ensemble

L. Steven Taylor
Ensemble

Ryan Brooke Taylor
Ensemble

Torya
Swing

Thom Christopher
Warren
Standby Zazu, Scar,
Pumbaa

Kenny Redell
Williams
Ensemble

Sir Elton John
Music

Tim Rice
Lyrics

Roger Allers
Book

Irene Mecchi
Book

The Lion King

Julie Taymor
Director, Costume Design, Mask/Puppet Co-Design, Additional Lyrics

Garth Fagan
Choreographer

Lebo M
Additional Music & Lyrics, Additional Vocal Score, Vocal Arrangements, Choral Director

Mark Mancina
Additional Music & Lyrics, Music Produced for the Stage, Additional Score

Hans Zimmer
Additional Music & Lyrics

Jay Rifkin
Additional Music & Lyrics

Richard Hudson
Scenic Design

Donald Holder
Lighting Design

Michael Curry
Mask & Puppet Design

Steve Canyon Kennedy
Sound Design

Mark Brandon, Binder Casting
Casting

David Benken
Technical Director

John Stefaniuk
Associate Director

Karl Jurman
Music Director/Conductor

Jen Bender
Resident Director

Ruthlyn Salomons
Resident Dance Supervisor

Robert Elhai
Associate Music Producer, Orchestrator

Michael Keller
Music Coordinator

Thomas Schumacher,
Disney Theatrical Productions

ALUMNI 2008-2009

Guy V. Barfield II
Young Simba

John E. Brady
Pumbaa

Michelle Aguilar Camaya
Butterflies, Ensemble Dancer, Flying Dancer, Gazelle Wheel

Ian Yuri Gardner
Swing

Stephanie Guiland-Brown
Ensemble Dancer

Bonita J. Hamilton
Shenzi

Michael Alexander Henry
Ensemble Singer

Meena T. Jahi
Ensemble Singer, Lioness/Hyena Shadow Puppets

Cornelius Jones, Jr.
Swing

Gregory A. King
Buzzard Pole, Ensemble Dancer, Simba Shadow Puppets

Jack Koenig
u/s Mufasa, Scar

Lisa Lewis
Cheetah, Ensemble Dancer, Flying Dancer, Nala Pole Puppet

Shavar McIntosh
Young Simba

Ray Mercer
Acrobatic Trickster, Ensemble Dancer, Simba Shadow Puppets

Jennifer Harrison Newman
Swing

The Lion King

Wallace Smith
Simba

Halle Vargas Sullivan
Young Nala

NicKayla Tucker
Young Nala

Phillip W. Turner
*Ensemble Dancer,
Simba Shadow
Puppets*

Rema Webb
*Ensemble Singer,
Lioness/Hyena
Shadow Puppets*

Lisa Nicole
Wilkerson
*Ensemble Singer,
Lioness/Hyena
Shadow Puppets*

Sant'gria Bello
*Ensemble Dancer,
Floor Dancer,
Guinea Fowl,
Scar Shadow
Puppets*

Ta'Rea Campbell
Nala

Charity de Loera
*Ensemble Dancer,
Gazelle Wheel*

Stephanie
Guiland-Brown
Ensemble Dancer

Jeremy Gumbs
Young Simba

Bonita J. Hamilton
Shenzi

Chantylla Johnson
Young Nala

Lisa Lewis
*Cheetah,
Ensemble Dancer,
Floor Dancer,
Flying Dancer,
Nala Pole Puppet*

Ray Mercer
*Acrobatic Trickster,
Ensemble Dancer,
Simba Shadow
Puppets*

Theresa Nguyen
*Cheetah,
Ensemble Dancer,
Flying Dancer
Nala Pole Puppet*

Phillip W. Turner
*Ensemble Dancer,
Simba Shadow
Puppets*

Natalie Turner
Swing

Rema Webb
*Ensemble Singer,
Lioness/Hyena
Shadow Puppets*

Lisa Nicole
Wilkerson
*Ensemble Singer,
Lioness/Hyena
Shadow Puppets*

Staff for *THE LION KING* Worldwide

Associate Producer ....Anne Quart
Production Supervisor ....Doc Zorthian
Production Administrator ....Myriah Perkins
Associate Director ....John Stefaniuk
Production Dance Supervisor ....Marey Griffith
Music Supervisor ....Clement Ishmael
Dance Supervisor ....Celise Hicks
Associate Scenic Designer ....Peter Eastman
Associate Costume Designer ....Mary Nemecek Peterson
Associate Mask & Puppet Designer ....Louis Troisi
Associate Sound Designer ....John Shivers
Associate Hair & Makeup Designer ....Carole Hancock
Associate Lighting Designer ....Jeanne Koenig
Assistant Lighting Designer ....Marty Vreeland
Assistant Sound Designer ....Shane Cook
Automated Lighting Programmer ....Aland Henderson
Production Coordinator ....Tara Engler
Management Assistant ....Elizabeth Fine

DISNEY ON BROADWAY PUBLICITY
Senior Publicist ....Dennis Crowley
Publicist ....Adriana Douzos

Staff for *THE LION KING* New York

Company Manager ....THOMAS SCHLENK
Assistant Company Manager ....Michael Height
Production Stage Manager ....Ron Vodicka
Resident Director ....Jen Bender
Resident Dance Supervisor ....Ruthlyn Salomons

Musical Director/Conductor ....Karl Jurman

Stage Managers ....Carmen I. Abrazado,
                    Narda E. Alcorn, Antonia Gianino,
                                  Jimmie Lee Smith
Dance Captains ......Garland Days, Willia-Noel Montague
Fight Captain ....Ryan Brooke Taylor
Assistant Choreographers ....Norwood J. Pennewell,
                                      Natalie Rogers
Fight Consultant ....Rick Sordelet
South African Dialect Coach ....Ron Kunene
Casting Associates ....Jack Bowdan, C.S.A.;
                      Mark Brandon; Sara Schatz
Casting Assistants ....Allison Estrin, Nikole Vallins
Corporate Counsel ....Michael Rosenfeld
Physical Therapy ....Neuro Tour Physical Therapy/
                                      Sarah Bingham
Consulting Orthopedist ....Philip Roth, M.D.
Child Wrangler ....Niki White
Executive Travel ....Robert Arnao, Patt McRory
Production Travel ....Jill Citron
Web Design Consultant ....Joshua Noah
Advertising ....Serino/Coyne Inc.
Interactive Marketing ....Situation Marketing/
          Damian Bazadona, Lisa Cecchini, Jenn Elston

Production Carpenter ....Drew Siccardi
Head Carpenter ....Michael Trotto
House Carpenter ....Patrick Sullivan
Assistant Carpenters ....Kirk Bender, Michael Phillips
Automation Carpenters ....Aldo "Butch" Servilio,
                                    George Zegarsky

Carpenters ....Giuseppe Iannello, Daniel Macormack,
                    Terry McGarty, Duane Mirro
Flying Supervision ....Dave Hearn
Production Flymen ....Kraig Bender, Dylan Trotto
House Flyman ....Richard McQuail
Production Electrician ....James Maloney
House Electrician ....Michael Lynch
Board Operator ....Edward Greenberg
House Assistant Electrician ....Stephen Speer
Automated Lighting Technician ....Sean Strohmeyer
Key Spot Operator ....Doug Graf
Assistant Electricians ....William Brennan,
                    David Holliman, Joseph P. Lynch,
                                  Thomas Richards
Production Propman ....Victor Amerling
House Propman ....Frank Ferrante
Props ....Matthew Lavaia, Michael Lavaia,
                                    Robert McCauley
Head Sound ....Alain Van Achte
Sound Assistants ....Donald McKennan, Scott Scheidt
Production Wardrobe Supervisor ....Kjeld Andersen
Assistant Wardrobe Supervisor ....Cynthia Boardman
Puppet Supervisor ....Anne Salt
Puppet Dayworkers ....Islah Abdul-Rahiim,
                                      Ilya Vett
Mask/Puppet Studio ....Jeff Curry
Dressers ....Meredith Chase-Boyd,
            Andy Cook, Tom Daniel, Donna Doiron,
    April Fernandez-Taylor, Michelle Gore-Butterfield,
        Douglas Hamilton, Mark Houston,
    Sara Jablon, Mark Lauer, Dawn Reynolds,
        Kathryn Rohe, Sarah Stith,

The Lion King

Sheila Terrell, Dave Tisue,
Steven Washington, Walter Weiner
Stitcher ....Janeth Iverson
Production Hair Supervisor ....Jon Jordan
Assistant Hair Supervisor ....Adenike Wright
Production Makeup Supervisor ....Elizabeth Cohen
Assistant Makeup Supervisor ....Marian Torre
Makeup Artist ....Rebecca Kuzma

Music Development ....Nick Glennie-Smith
Music Preparation ....Donald Oliver and Evan Morris/
Chelsea Music Service, Inc.
Synthesizer Programmer ....Ted Baker
Orchestral Synthesizer Programmer ......Christopher Ward
Electronic Drum Programmer ....Tommy Igoe
Addt'l Percussion Arrangements ....Valerie Dee Naranjo
Music Assistant ....Elizabeth J. Falcone
Personal Assistant to Elton John ....Bob Halley
Assistant to Tim Rice ....Eileen Heinink
Assistant to Mark Mancina ....Chuck Choi

Associate Scenic Designer ....Jonathan Fensom
Assistant Scenic Designer ....Michael Fagin
Lighting Design Assistant ....Karen Spahn
Automated Lighting Tracker ....Lara Bohon
Projection Designer ....Geoff Puckett
Projection Art ....Caterina Bertolotto
Assistant Sound Designer ....Kai Harada
Assistant Costume Designer ....Tracy Dorman
Stunt Consultant ....Peter Moore
Children's Tutoring ....On Location Education
Production Photography ....Joan Marcus,
Marc Bryan-Brown
Associate Producer 1996–1998 ....Donald Frantz
Project Manager 1996–1998 ....Nina Essman
Associate Producer 1998–2002 ....Ken Denison
Associate Producer 2000-2003 ....Pam Young
Associate Producer 2002-2007 ....Todd Lacy
Associate Producer 2003-2008 ....Aubrey Lynch
Original Music Director ....Joseph Church

Disney's *The Lion King* is a registered trademark owned by
The Walt Disney Company and used under special license
by Disney Theatrical Productions.

HOUSE STAFF FOR THE MINSKOFF THEATRE
House Manager ....Victor Irving
Treasurer ....Nicholas Loiacono
Assistant Treasurer ....Cheryl Loiacono

CREDITS
Scenery built and mechanized by Hudson Scenic Studio,
Inc. Additional scenery by Chicago Scenic Studios, Inc.;
Edge & Co., Inc.; Michael Hagen, Inc.; Piper Productions,
Inc.; Scenic Technologies, Inc.; I. Weiss & Sons, Inc.
Lighting by Westsun, vari*lite® automated lighting
provided by Vari-Lite, Inc. Props by John Creech Design &
Production. Sound equipment by Pro-Mix, Inc. Additional
sound equipment by Walt Disney Imagineering. Rehearsal
Scenery by Brooklyn Scenic & Theatrical. Costumes
executed by Barbara Matera Ltd., Parsons-Meares Ltd.,
Donna Langman, Eric Winterling, Danielle Gisiger, Suzie
Elder. Millinery by Rodney Gordon, Janet Linville, Arnold
Levine. Ricola provided by Ricola, Inc. Shibori dyeing by
Joan Morris. Custom dyeing and painting by Joni Johns,
Mary Macy, Parsons-Meares Ltd., Gene Mignola.

Additional Painting by J. Michelle Hill. Knitwear by Maria
Ficalora. Footwear by Sharlot Battin, Robert W. Jones,
Capezio, Vasilli Shoes. Costume Development by
Constance Hoffman. Special Projects by Angela M. Kahler.
Custom fabrics developed by Gary Graham and Helen
Quinn. Puppet Construction by Michael Curry Design, Inc.
and Vee Corporation. Shadow puppetry by Steven Kaplan.
Pumbaa Puppet Construction by Andrew Benepe. Flying by
Foy. Trucking by Clark Transfer. Wigs created by Wig
Workshop of London. Marimbas by De Morrow
Instruments, Ltd. Latin Percussion by LP Music Group.
Drumset by DrumWorkshop. Cymbals by Zildjian. Bass
equipment by Eden Electronics.

SONG EXCERPTS (used by permission):
"Supercalifragilisticexpialidocious" written by Richard M.
Sherman and Robert B. Sherman; "Five Foot Two, Eyes of
Blue" written by Sam Lewis, Joe Young, and Ray
Henderson; "The Lion Sleeps Tonight" written by Hugo
Peretti, George David Weiss, Luigi Creatore and Solomon
Linda.

NEDERLANDER

Chairman .... **James M. Nederlander**
President .... **James L. Nederlander**

Executive Vice President
Nick Scandalios

Vice President	Senior Vice President
Corporate Development	Labor Relations
Charlene S. Nederlander	**Herschel Waxman**

| Vice President | Chief Financial Officer |
| **Jim Boese** | **Freida Sawyer Belviso** |

DISNEY THEATRICAL PRODUCTIONS
President ....Thomas Schumacher
EVP & Managing Director ....David Schrader
SVP & General Manager ....Alan Levey

Senior Vice President, Creative Affairs .....Michele Steckler
Senior Vice President, International ....Ron Kollen
Vice President, Operations ....Dana Amendola
Vice President, Labor Relations ....Allan Frost
Vice President, Worldwide Publicity
& Communications ....Joe Quenqua
Vice President, Domestic Touring ....Jack Eldon
Vice President, Theatrical Licensing ....Steve Fickinger
Vice President, Human Resources ....June Heindel
Director, Domestic Touring ....Michael Buchanan
Director, Casting & Development ....Jennifer Rudin, CSA
Director, Publicity & Communications ......Jay Carducci
Manager, Labor Relations ....Stephanie Cheek
Manager, Human Resources ....Jewel Neal
Manager, Publicity ....Ashok Sinha
Manager, Information Systems ....Scott Benedict
Senior Computer Support Analyst ....Kevin A. McGuire
Senior IT Support Analyst ....Andy Singh
IT/Business Analyst ....William Boudiette

Production
Executive Music Producer ....Chris Montan
Vice President, Physical Production ....John Tiggeloven

Director, International ....Michael Cassel
Senior Manager, Safety ....Canara Price
Manager, Physical Production ....Karl Chmielewski
Dramaturg & Literary Manager ....Ken Cerniglia

Marketing
Vice President, Broadway ....Andrew Flatt
Vice President, International ....Fiona Thomas
Director, Broadway ....Kyle Young
Director, Broadway ....Michele Groner
Director, Education & Outreach ....Peter Avery
Website Manager ....Eric W. Kratzer
Media Asset Manager ....Cara L. Moccia
Assistant Manager, Promotions ....Craig Buckley
Assistant Manager, Advertising ....Lauren Daghini

Sales
Director, National Sales ....Bryan Dockett
Manager,
New Business Development ....Jacob Lloyd Kimbro
Manager, Sales & Ticketing ....Nick Falzon
Manager, Group Sales ....Juil Kim

Business and Legal Affairs
Senior Vice President ....Jonathan Olson
Vice President ....Robbin Kelley
Executive Director ....Harry S. Gold
Senior Counsel ....Seth Stuhl
Paralegal/Contract Administration ....Colleen Lober

Finance
VP Finance & Business Development ....Mario Iannetta
Director ....Joe McClafferty
Senior Manager, Finance ....Dana James
Manager, Finance ....John Fajardo
Manager, Production Accounting ....Liza Breslin
Production Accountants ......Joy Sims Brown, Nick Judge,
Barbara Toben
Assistant Production Accountant ....Isander Rojas
Senior Sales Analyst ....Liz Jurist Schwarzwalder
Senior Business Planner ....Shaan Akbar

Administrative Staff
Shillae Anderson, Dusty Bennett, Sarah Bills, Lindsay
Braverman, Amy Caldamone, Jessica Doina, Cristi Finn,
Dayle Gruet, Gregory Hanoian, Abbie Harrison, Wilfredo
Hernandez Jr., Connie Jasper, Tom Kingsley, Cyntia Leo,
Lisa Mitchell, Ryan Pears, Roberta Risafi, Colleen Rosati,
David Scott, Benjy Shaw, Colleen Verbus, Kyle Wilson,
Jason Zammit

DISNEY THEATRICAL MERCHANDISE
Vice President ....Steven Downing
Operations Manager ....Shawn Baker
Merchandise Manager ....Neil Markman
Associate Buyer ....Violet Burlaza
Assistant Manager, Inventory ....Suzanne Jakel
Retail Supervisor ....Alyssa Somers
On-Site Retail Manager ....Anjie Maraj
On-Site Assistant Retail Manager ....Jana Cristiano

Disney Theatrical Productions • 1450 Broadway
New York, NY 10018

guestmail@disneytheatrical.com

The Little Mermaid

First Preview: November 3, 2007. Opened: January 10, 2008.
Still running as of May 31, 2009.

PLAYBILL

Disney's THE LITTLE MERMAID

CAST OF CHARACTERS

(in order of appearance)

Pilot	MERWIN FOARD
Prince Eric	SEAN PALMER
Grimsby	JONATHAN FREEMAN
King Triton	NORM LEWIS
Mersisters	CATHRYN BASILE, CICILY DANIELS, MICHELLE LOOKADOO, ZAKIYA YOUNG MIZEN, CHELSEA MORGAN STOCK, KAY TRINIDAD
Sebastian	ROGELIO DOUGLAS JR.
Ariel	SIERRA BOGGESS
Flounder	TREVOR BRAUN (Wed. mat., Sat. mat., Sun. mat.) BRIAN D'ADDARIO (Tues. eve., Wed. eve., Thurs. eve., Fri. eve., Sat. eve.)
Scuttle	EDDIE KORBICH
Gulls	JOE ABRAHAM, ENRIQUE BROWN, RHETT GEORGE
Ursula	FAITH PRINCE
Flotsam	TYLER MAYNARD
Jetsam	ERIC LaJUAN SUMMERS
Carlotta	MEREDITH INGLESBY
Chef Louis	JIMMY SMAGULA

⋙N⋘ LUNT–FONTANNE THEATRE

UNDER THE DIRECTION OF
JAMES M. NEDERLANDER AND JAMES L. NEDERLANDER

Disney Theatrical Productions
under the direction of
Thomas Schumacher
presents

Disney's **THE LITTLE MERMAID**

Music	Lyrics	Book
ALAN MENKEN	HOWARD ASHMAN & GLENN SLATER	DOUG WRIGHT

Based on the Hans Christian Andersen story and the Disney film produced by Howard Ashman & John Musker
and written & directed by John Musker & Ron Clements.

Starring

SIERRA BOGGESS   SEAN PALMER

NORM LEWIS   ROGELIO DOUGLAS JR.   EDDIE KORBICH   JONATHAN FREEMAN
TYLER MAYNARD   ERIC LaJUAN SUMMERS   JIMMY SMAGULA
TREVOR BRAUN   BRIAN D'ADDARIO
and
FAITH PRINCE
as Ursula

JOE ABRAHAM   JULIE BARNES   CATHRYN BASILE   ENRIQUE BROWN   JAMES BROWN III   CICILY DANIELS
J. AUSTIN EYER   MERWIN FOARD   LYNDY FRANKLIN   RHETT GEORGE   AMY HALL   BEN HARTLEY
MEREDITH INGLESBY   MICHELLE LOOKADOO   ALAN MINGO, JR.   ZAKIYA YOUNG MIZEN   JC MONTGOMERY
MICHELLE PRUIETT   BRET SHUFORD   JASON SNOW   CHELSEA MORGAN STOCK   EPHRAIM M. SYKES   KAY TRINIDAD

Scenic Design	Costume Design	Lighting Design
GEORGE TSYPIN	TATIANA NOGINOVA	NATASHA KATZ

Sound Design	Hair Design	Makeup Design	Projection & Video Design
JOHN SHIVERS	DAVID BRIAN BROWN	ANGELINA AVALLONE	SVEN ORTEL

Dance Arrangements	Music Coordinator	Fight Director	Casting
DAVID CHASE	MICHAEL KELLER	RICK SORDELET	TARA RUBIN CASTING

Associate Producer	Associate Director	Associate Choreographer
TODD LACY	BRIAN HILL	TARA YOUNG

Technical Director	Production Supervisor
DAVID BENKEN	CLIFFORD SCHWARTZ

Orchestrations by
DANNY TROOB

Music Director
Incidental Music & Vocal Arrangements by
MICHAEL KOSARIN

Choreography by
STEPHEN MEAR

Directed by
FRANCESCA ZAMBELLO

4/6/09

(L-R): Sean Palmer and Sierra Boggess during "Kiss the Girl."

Photo by Joan Marcus

Continued on next page

The Little Mermaid

MUSICAL NUMBERS

ACT I

Overture
"Fathoms Below"† .... Pilot, Sailors, Prince Eric, Grimsby
"Daughters of Triton"* .... Mersisters
"The World Above" .... Ariel
"Human Stuff" .... Scuttle, Gulls
"I Want the Good Times Back" .... Ursula, Flotsam, Jetsam, Eels
"Part of Your World"* .... Ariel
"Storm at Sea"
"Part of Your World" (Reprise)* .... Ariel
"She's in Love" .... Mersisters, Flounder
"Her Voice" .... Prince Eric
"The World Above" (Reprise) .... King Triton
"Under the Sea"* .... Sebastian, Sea Creatures
"Sweet Child" .... Flotsam, Jetsam
"Poor Unfortunate Souls"* .... Ursula

ACT II

Entr'acte
"Positoovity" .... Scuttle, Gulls
"Beyond My Wildest Dreams" .... Ariel, Carlotta, Maids
"Les Poissons"* .... Chef Louis
"Les Poissons" (Reprise) .... Chef Louis, Chefs
"One Step Closer" .... Prince Eric
"I Want the Good Times Back" (Reprise) .... Ursula, Flotsam, Jetsam
"Kiss the Girl"* .... Sebastian, Animals
"Sweet Child" (Reprise) .... Flotsam, Jetsam
"If Only" .... Ariel, Prince Eric, Sebastian, King Triton
"The Contest" .... Grimsby, Princesses
"Poor Unfortunate Souls" (Reprise) .... Ursula
"If Only" (Reprise) .... King Triton, Ariel
"Finale"† .... Prince Eric, Ariel, Ensemble

Music by Alan Menken
* Lyrics by Howard Ashman
† Lyrics by Howard Ashman and Glenn Slater
All other lyrics by Glenn Slater

ORCHESTRA

Conductor: MICHAEL KOSARIN
Associate Conductor: GREG ANTHONY

Concertmaster: SUZANNE ORNSTEIN
Violin: MINEKO YAJIMA
Cello 1: ROGER SHELL
Cello 2: DEBORAH ASSAEL-MIGLIORE
Lead Trumpet: NICHOLAS MARCHIONE
Trumpet: FRANK GREENE
Trombone: GARY GRIMALDI
Bass Trombone/Tuba: JEFF CASWELL
Reed 1: STEVE KENYON

Reed 2: DAVID YOUNG
Reed 3: MARC PHANEUF
French Horn: ZOHAR SCHONDORF
Keyboard 1: ARON ACCURSO
Keyboard 2: GREG ANTHONY
Keyboard 3: ANDREW GROBENGIESER
Bass: RICHARD SARPOLA
Drums: JOHN REDSECKER
Percussion: JOE PASSARO

Electronic Music Design: ANDREW BARRETT
Music Coordinator: MICHAEL KELLER

Cast Continued

ENSEMBLE

JOE ABRAHAM; CATHRYN BASILE;
ENRIQUE BROWN; CICILY DANIELS;
MERWIN FOARD; RHETT GEORGE;
AMY HALL; BEN HARTLEY;
MEREDITH INGLESBY;
MICHELLE LOOKADOO; ALAN MINGO, JR.;
ZAKIYA YOUNG MIZEN; JC MONTGOMERY;
BRET SHUFORD;
CHELSEA MORGAN STOCK;
EPHRAIM M. SYKES; KAY TRINIDAD

SWINGS

JULIE BARNES, JAMES BROWN III,
J. AUSTIN EYER, LYNDY FRANKLIN,
MICHELLE PRUIETT, JASON SNOW

DANCE CAPTAINS

JAMES BROWN III, JASON SNOW

UNDERSTUDIES

Ariel:
MICHELLE LOOKADOO, MICHELLE
PRUIETT, CHELSEA MORGAN STOCK
Ursula:
CICILY DANIELS, MEREDITH INGLESBY
Prince Eric:
J. AUSTIN EYER, BRET SHUFORD
King Triton:
MERWIN FOARD, JC MONTGOMERY
Sebastian:
RHETT GEORGE, ALAN MINGO, JR.
Scuttle:
JOE ABRAHAM, JASON SNOW
Grimsby:
MERWIN FOARD, JC MONTGOMERY
Flotsam:
BRET SHUFORD, JASON SNOW
Jetsam:
JAMES BROWN III, J. AUSTIN EYER
Chef Louis:
JOE ABRAHAM, MERWIN FOARD

Faith Prince
as Ursula

Photo by Joan Marcus

The Little Mermaid

Sierra Boggess
Ariel

Faith Prince
Ursula

Sean Palmer
Prince Eric

Norm Lewis
King Triton

Rogelio Douglas Jr.
Sebastian

Eddie Korbich
Scuttle

Jonathan Freeman
Grimsby

Tyler Maynard
Flotsam

Eric LaJuan
Summers
Jetsam

Jimmy Smagula
Chef Louis

Trevor Braun
Flounder at certain performances

Brian D'Addario
Flounder at certain performances

Joe Abraham
Ensemble

Julie Barnes
Swing

Cathryn Basile
Ensemble

Enrique Brown
Ensemble

James Brown III
*Swing/
Dance Captain*

Cicily Daniels
Ensemble

J. Austin Eyer
Swing

Merwin Foard
Pilot/Ensemble

Lyndy Franklin
Swing

Rhett George
Ensemble

Amy Hall
Ensemble

Ben Hartley
Ensemble

Meredith Inglesby
Carlotta/Ensemble

Michelle Lookadoo
Ensemble

Alan Mingo, Jr.
Ensemble

Zakiya Young Mizen
Ensemble

JC Montgomery
Ensemble

Michelle Pruiett
Swing

Bret Shuford
Ensemble

Jason Snow
Swing

Chelsea Morgan
Stock
Ensemble

Ephraim M. Sykes
Ensemble

Kay Trinidad
Ensemble

The Little Mermaid

Alan Menken
Composer

Howard Ashman
Lyrics

Glenn Slater
Lyrics

Doug Wright
Book

Francesca Zambello
Director

Stephen Mear
Choreographer

George Tsypin
Scenic Design

Tatiana Noginova
Costume Design

Natasha Katz
Lighting Design

John H. Shivers
Sound Design

Danny Troob
Orchestrator

Michael Kosarin
*Music Direction/
Vocal and Incidental
Music Arrangements*

David Brian Brown
Wig/Hair Design

Angelina Avallone
Make-up Design

Sven Ortel
*Projection & Video
Design*

Michael Keller
Music Coordinator

Rick Sordelet
Fight Director

Pichón Baldinu
Aerial Design

Tara Rubin Casting
Casting

Brian Hill
Associate Director

Tara Young
*Associate
Choreographer*

David Benken
Technical Director

Clifford Schwartz
*Production
Supervisor*

Andrew Barrett
*Electronic Music
Design*

Thomas Schumacher
*Disney Theatrical
Productions*

ALUMNI
2008-2009

Adrian Bailey
Ensemble

Derrick Baskin
Jetsam

Heidi Blickenstaff
Ursula

Tituss Burgess
Sebastian

Robert Creighton
*Chef Louis,
Ensemble, Gull*

John Treacy Egan
Chef Louis

Tim Federle
*Ensemble, Gull,
Swing*

Bahiyah Sayyed
Gaines
Ensemble

Joanne Manning
*Dance Captain,
Swing*

The Little Mermaid

Courtney Laine
Mazza
Swing

Betsy Morgan
Swing

Arbender J.
Robinson
Ensemble, Gull

Sherie Rene Scott
Ursula

Price Waldman
Ensemble, Swing

Daniel J. Watts
Ensemble

TRANSFER STUDENTS
2008-2009

Megan Campanile
Ensemble, Mersister

Robert Creighton
Chef Louis

Tyrone A. Jackson
Ensemble

Staff for *THE LITTLE MERMAID*

COMPANY MANAGER ....EDUARDO CASTRO
Production Manager ....Jane Abramson
Assistant Company Manager ....Margie McGlone
Production Supervisor ....Clifford Schwartz
Stage Manager ....Theresa Bailey
Assistant Stage Managers ....Robert M. Armitage,
　　　　Alexis Shorter, Matthew Aaron Stern
Dance Captains ....James Brown III, Jason Snow
Fight Captain ....James Brown III
Assistant to the Associate Producer ....Kerry McGrath
Production Assistants ....Steven Malone,
　　　Jennifer Noterman, Thomas Recktenwald,
　　　　　　　　　　　　　　Marielle Solan

DISNEY ON BROADWAY PUBLICITY

Senior Publicist ....Dennis Crowley
Publicist ....Adriana Douzos

---

Associate Scenic Designer ....Peter Eastman
Assistant Scenic Designer ....Denny Moyes
Scenic Design Assistants ....Gaetane Bertol,
　　　　　　Larry Brown, Kelly Hanson,
　　　　　Niki Hernandez-Adams,
　　　Nathan Heverin, Rachel Short Janocko,
　　　Jee an Jung, Mimi Lien,
　　Frank McCullough, Arnulfo Maldonado,
　　　　Robert Pyzocha, Chisato Uno
Sculptor ....Arturs Virtmanis
Associate Costume Designer ....Tracy Christensen
Assistant Costume Designers ....Brian J. Bustos,
　　　　　　　　　　　　　　　Amy Clark

Costume Shoppers ....Leon Dobkowski, Vanessa Leuck
Associate Lighting Designer ....Yael Lubetzky
Lighting Design Assistant ....Craig Stelzenmuller
Automated Lighting Programmer ....Aland Henderson
Automated Lighting Tracker ....Joel Shier
Assistant to the Lighting Designer ....Richard Swan
Associate Sound Designer ....David Patridge
Associate Hair Designer ....Jonathan Carter
Assistant Hair Designer ....Thomas Augustine
Projection Design Assistants ....Peter Acken,
　　　　　　　　　　　　　　　Katy Tucker
Associate Aerial Designer ....Angela Phillips
Magic/Illusion Designer ....Joe Eddie Fairchild
Associate to Technical Director ....Rose Palombo
Production Carpenter ....Stephen Detmer
Head Carpenter ....Patrick Eviston
Fly Automation ....Jeff Zink
Deck Automation ....Michael L. Shepp, Jr.
Rigger ....Rick Howard
Production Electrician ....Rick Baxter
Head Electrician ....Joseph Pearson
Assistant Electrician ....Damian Caza-Cleypool
Moving Light Technician ....Jesse Hancox
Production Props ....Jerry L. Marshall
Assistant Props ....Steven E. Wood
Production Sound Engineer ....David Patridge
Head Sound ....George Huckins
Deck Sound ....Scott Anderson
Wardrobe Supervisor ....Nancy Schaefer
Assistant Wardrobe Supervisor ....Edmund Harrison
Wardrobe Staff ....Rachael Garrett, Sue Hamilton,
　　　　Melanie Hansen, Barbara Hladsky,

Franklin Hollenbeck, Greg Holtz,
Teresia Larsen, Terry LaVada,
Robert J. Malkmus III, Paul Riner,
Erin Brooke Roth, Eric Rudy,
Rita Santi, Rodd Sovar, Claire Verlaet
Hair Supervisor ....Wanda Gregory
Assistant Hair Supervisor ....Lisa Fraley
Hairdressers ....Joshua First, Jennifer Pendergraft
Make-Up Supervisor ....Tiffany Hicks
Assistant Make-Up Supervisor ....Jorge Vargas
Associate Music Director ....Greg Anthony
Additional Orchestrations ....Larry Hochman,
　　　　　　　　　　　　　　Michael Starobin
Music Preparation ....Anixter Rice Music Service
Electronic Music Design ....Andrew Barrett,
　　　　　　　　　for Lionella Productions, Ltd.
Electronic Music Design Assistant ....Jeff Marder
Associate to Mr. Menken ....Rick Kunis
Rehearsal Drummer ....John Redsecker
Rehearsal Pianists .....Aron Accurso, Brent-Alan Huffman,
　　　　　　Andrew Grobengieser, Brian Hertz
Children's Vocal Coach ....Marianne Challis
Chaperone ....John Mara
Children's Tutoring ....On Location Education/
　　　　　　　　　　　　　　　Serena Stanley

CASTING
TARA RUBIN CASTING
Tara Rubin, CSA, Eric Woodall, CSA
Laura Schutzel, CSA, Merri Sugarman, CSA
Rebecca Carfagna, Paige Blansfield, Dale Brown

The Little Mermaid

AERIAL DESIGNER ....PICHÓN BALDINU

DIALOGUE &
  VOCAL COACH ....DEBORAH HECHT

Advertising ....Serino Coyne, Inc.
Interactive Marketing ....Situation Marketing/
  Damian Bazadona, Lisa Cecchini,
  Jenn Elston
Web Design Consultant ....Joshua Noah
Logo Art ....Scott Thornley + Company
Production Photography ....Joan Marcus
Acoustic Consultant ....Paul Scarbrough, A'Kustiks
Structural Engineering Consultant ....Bill Gorlin,
  McLaren, P.C.
Executive Travel ....Robert Arnao, Patricia McRory
Production Travel ....Jill L. Citron
Payroll Managers ....Anthony DeLuca, Cathy Guerra
Counsel – Immigration ....Michael Rosenfeld
Physical Therapy ....The Green Room P.T./Heidi Green
Consulting Orthopedic Surgeon ....Dr. Phillip Bauman

CREDITS

Scenery by Showman Fabricators, Inc.; Show Canada Industries; Adirondack Studios, Inc.; The Paragon Innovation Group, Inc.; Proof Productions. Automation of scenery and rigging by Showman Fabricators, Inc., Long Island City, NY featuring Raynok Motion Control. Lighting equipment by PRG Lighting. Projection equipment by PRG Lighting. Sound equipment by Sound Associates Inc. Costume construction by Parsons-Meares Ltd.; Barbara Matera, Ltd.; Eric Winterling, Inc.; Tricorne, Inc.; Martin Izquierdo Studio. Custom millinery provided by Lynne Mackey Studio; Rodney Gordon; Arnold S. Levine, Inc.; Marian Jean Hose. Custom fabric dyeing and printing by Gene Mignola, Hochi Asiatico, Martin Izquierdo Studio, Olympus Flag and Banner. Costume painting by Hochi Asiatico, Virginia Clow, Claudia Dzundza, Martin Izquierdo Studio, Mary Macy, Parmelee Welles Tolkan, Margaret Peot. Custom footwear by Capri Shoes by Oscar Navarro; Handmade Shoes by Fred Longtin; LaDuca Shoes; Pluma Shoes by Walter Raimundo; Capezio. Custom jewelry and crafts by Arnold S. Levine, Inc.; Marian Jean Hose; Martin Izquierdo Studios; Gaetane Bertol; Larry Vrba. Undergarments by Bra*Tenders; On Stage Dancewear. Ursula mechanics by Jon Gellman Effects. Mermaid tails by Michael Curry Design, Inc. Eel electrics by Birtek Specialty Lighting. Knitwear provided by Karen Eifert and Maria Ficalora Knitwear, Ltd. Wigs by Bob Kelly Wigs; Ray Marston Wigs; Victoria Wood. Props by Arnold S. Levine, Inc.; Jerard Studio; Michael Curry Design, Inc.; The Paragon Innovation Group, Inc.; Provost Displays; I.C.B.A; Puppet Heap; Rabbit's Choice; Vogue Too; Zoë Morsette. Ricola natural herb cough drops courtesy of Ricola USA, Inc. Emergen-C health and energy drink mix provided by Alacer Corp.

Makeup Provided By M•A•C.

Gliding By Heelys®.

THE LITTLE MERMAID originally premiered at the Ellie Caulkins Opera House, Denver Center for the Performing Arts, Colorado.

THE LITTLE MERMAID
rehearsed at the New 42nd Street Studios.

SPECIAL THANKS

Kate Boucher, Ian Galloway and Dan Murtha of Bolt Action Five, Michael Curry, Jackie Galloway, Helen Goddard, Green Hippo, Nichol Hignite, Courtney Hoffman, Diana Kuriyama, Anna Ledwich, Calvin Klein Inc., Jim Haag/Vendura, Larry Sonn, Georgia Stitt, Crystal Thompson, Walt Disney Imagineering R&D.

DISNEY THEATRICAL PRODUCTIONS

President ....Thomas Schumacher
EVP & Managing Director ....David Schrader
SVP, Creative Affairs ....Michele Steckler
Senior Vice President, International ....Ron Kollen
Vice President, Operations ....Dana Amendola
Vice President, Labor Relations ....Allan Frost
Vice President, Worldwide Publicity
  & Communications ....Joe Quenqua
Vice President, Domestic Touring ....Jack Eldon
Vice President, Theatrical Licensing ....Steve Fickinger
Vice President, Human Resources ....June Heindel
Director, Domestic Touring ....Michael Buchanan
Director, Casting & Development ...Jennifer Rudin, CSA
Director, Publicity & Communications ....Jay Carducci
Manager, Labor Relations ....Stephanie Cheek
Manager, Human Resources ....Jewel Neal
Manager, Publicity ....Ashok Sinha
Manager, Information Systems ....Scott Benedict
Senior Computer Support Analyst ....Kevin A. McGuire
Senior IT Support Analyst ....Andy Singh
IT/Business Analyst ....William Boudiette

Production

Executive Music Producer ....Chris Montan
Vice President, Physical Production ....John Tiggeloven
Director, International ....Michael Cassel
Senior Manager, Safety ....Canara Price
Manager, Physical Production ....Karl Chmielewski
Dramaturg & Literary Manager ....Ken Cerniglia

Marketing

Vice President, Broadway ....Andrew Flatt
Vice President, International ....Fiona Thomas
Director, Broadway ....Kyle Young
Director, Broadway ....Michele Groner
Director, Education & Outreach ....Peter Avery
Website Manager ....Eric W. Kratzer
Assistant Manager, Marketing ....Lauren Daghini

Sales

Director, National Sales ....Bryan Dockett
Manager,
  New Business Development ....Jacob Lloyd Kimbro
Manager, Sales & Ticketing ....Nick Falzon
Manager, Group Sales ....Juil Kim

Business and Legal Affairs

Senior Vice President ....Jonathan Olson
Vice President ....Robbin Kelley
Senior Counsel ....Seth Stuhl
Attorney ....Daniel M. Posener
Paralegal/Contract Administration ....Colleen Lober

Finance

VP Finance & Business Development ....Mario Iannetta
Director ....Joe McClafferty
Senior Manager, Finance ....Dana James
Manager, Finance ....John Fajardo
Manager, Production Accounting ....Liza Breslin
Production Accountants ....Joy Sims Brown,
  Nick Judge, Barbara Toben
Assistant Production Accountant ....Isander Rojas
Senior Sales Analyst ....Liz Jurist Schwarzwalder
Senior Business Planner ....Shaan Akbar

Administrative Staff

Dusty Bennett, Sarah Bills, Dayle Bland, Lindsay Braverman, Amy Caldamone, Alana Degner, Michael Dei Cas, Jessica Doina, Cristi Finn, Gregory Hanoian, Abbie Harrison, Tom Kingsley, Cyntia Leo, Lisa Mitchell, Ryan Pears, Roberta Risafi, Colleen Rosati, David Scott, Benjy Shaw, Christina Tuchman, Colleen Verbus, Kyle Wilson, Jason Zammit

DISNEY THEATRICAL MERCHANDISE

Vice President ....Steven Downing
Operations Manager ....Shawn Baker
Merchandise Manager ....Neil Markman
Associate Buyer ....Violet Burlaza
Assistant Manager, Inventory ....Suzanne Jakel
Retail Supervisor ....Alyssa Somers
On-Site Retail Manager ....Jeff Knizner
On-Site Assistant Retail Manager ....Mark Murynec

Disney Theatrical Productions
c/o New Amsterdam Theatre
214 W. 42nd St.
New York, NY 10036

guestmail@disneytheatrical.com

Chairman ....**James M. Nederlander**
President ....**James L. Nederlander**

Executive Vice President
Nick Scandalios

Vice President	Senior Vice President
Corporate Development	Labor Relations
Charlene S. Nederlander	**Herschel Waxman**

| Vice President | Chief Financial Officer |
| **Jim Boese** | **Freida Sawyer Belviso** |

STAFF FOR THE LUNT-FONTANNE

House Manager ....Tracey Malinowski
Treasurer ....Joe Olcese
Assistant Treasurer ....Gregg Collichio
House Carpenter ....Terry Taylor
House Electrician ....Dennis Boyle
House Propertyman ....Andrew Bentz
House Flyman ....Matt Walters
House Engineers ....Robert MacMahon,
  Joseph Riccio III

The Little Mermaid
SCRAPBOOK

Photo by Aubrey Reuben

Photo by Tomas Vrzala

Sierra Boggess at the 2008 "Broadway on Broadway" event.

Trevor Braun wows the crowd at the 2009 "Easter Bonnet" competition with his rendition of "And I Am Telling You I'm Not Going."

Correspondent: Tyler Maynard, "Flotsam"

Memorable Fan Letter: I believe Sherie Rene Scott got a letter that said something to the effect that thanks to the show's soundtrack, a 3-year-old was able to poo-poo on the potty. Seriously.

Anniversary Parties and/or Gifts: When Faith Prince joined the show there was a champagne party for her. There was a cake that was supposed to look like "Ursula" and her tentacles. It was indeed delicious.

Most Exciting Celebrity Visitors: Three-way tie. 1. When Posh Spice and Becks came with the boys, she said referring to "Sebastian" the crab character, "Wasn't the lobster wonderful?" 2. Brangelina. They just stood there. That was enough for me. 3. Jen and Violet Garner. The whole show I pretended I was a spy and I was just wearing the green wig as my alias to assist Sydney Bristow...and her child.

"Easter Bonnet" and "Gypsy of the Year" Sketches: The highlight of the year's sketches was Trevor Braun singing "And I Am Telling You I'm Not Going." I think it was what got the ball rolling to get him into *Billy Elliot*. Talented and funny kid, that one.

Actor Who Performed the Most Roles in This Show: That's a tie between Jason Snow and Austin Eyer. They covered 12 roles, including Prince Eric, Flotsam and Jetsam, and Scuttle.

Who Has Done the Most Shows: I believe that one has to go to Eddie Korbich. That man is Old School all the way.

Mascots: Lorelai and Rory Gilmore.

Special Backstage Rituals: Ask Eddie Korbich.

He wrote the book on rituals.

Favorite Snack Foods: Wanda's famous firecrackers and the candy bowl in the hair room.

Favorite Therapy: HEIDI GREEN!!! ALL THE WAY!! And the lovely staff at Physio Arts.

Memorable Ad-Lib: In Denver, Sherie's pod came into the finale, then turned right back and went off stage. She grabbed the shell (her life force) and threw it at "Ariel" and said, "Here, you do it" and that was the finale. We were still working out the kinks.

Memorable Stage Door Fan Encounters: I liked being confused for "Prince Eric" at the stage door. "Scuttle," not so much.

What Did You Think of the Web Buzz on Your Show: I didn't think about it at all until the tween sensation Drew Seeley showed up.

Latest Audience Arrival: Let's just say "Ariel" had legs.

Fastest Costume Change: Michelle Lookadoo from a piece of sexy sea coral to the "Ariel" double.

Heaviest/Hottest Costumes: Heaviest: "Ursula"/"Carlotta." Hottest: "Flotsam and Jetsam"/"Sebastian"

Who Wore the Least: Oddly enough, the virginal heroine, Ariel.

Catchphrases Only the Company Would Recognize: "HEEP! BOAT GONE YONDA!"

Sweethearts Within the Company: None actually—not that I didn't give it the old college try.

Company Legend: Adrian Bailey.

Memorable Directorial Note: When we were

trying out in Denver, we had a big speech from our director Francesca on being ambassadors for Disney. We all wanted to get pins that said "Ambassador." Never did though.

Tale From the Put-In: There was this time where they called the whole company to the stage to watch what was called the Zip Fish, which was added later in the run. It was supposed to quickly zip across stage. It took a nose dive and then dragged slowly offstage like a corpse. We watched that happen three times.

Understudy Anecdote: Austin Eyer was on for the Blowfish in Act I, and Prince Eric in Act II. That's talent. Enough said.

Nicknames: Mine was "Villy," short for "villain," I believe. But there were many—some I cannot say.

Embarrassing Moments: I had a back injury recently and had two ice packs shoved between my back and my tail harness during "Good Times Back." Let's just say that ice packs slide easily out of green trashbag-like costumes. Faith Prince almost took a tumble over the packs.

Ghostly Encounters Backstage: Mrs. Potts (from *Beauty and the Beast*) hit me with her spout. She wanted her room back.

Superstitions That Turned Out To Be True: I said the name of the Scottish Play backstage. An hour later, I fell hard from a slip on the Heelys. What are the rules to reverse that curse again?

The Coolest Thing About Being in This Show: The word cool does not really go well with my show. I was hot the whole time. Ask Ariel, I bet she thinks it's the coolest.

Liza's at the Palace...

Opened: December 3, 2008.
Closed January 4, 2009 after 22 Performances.

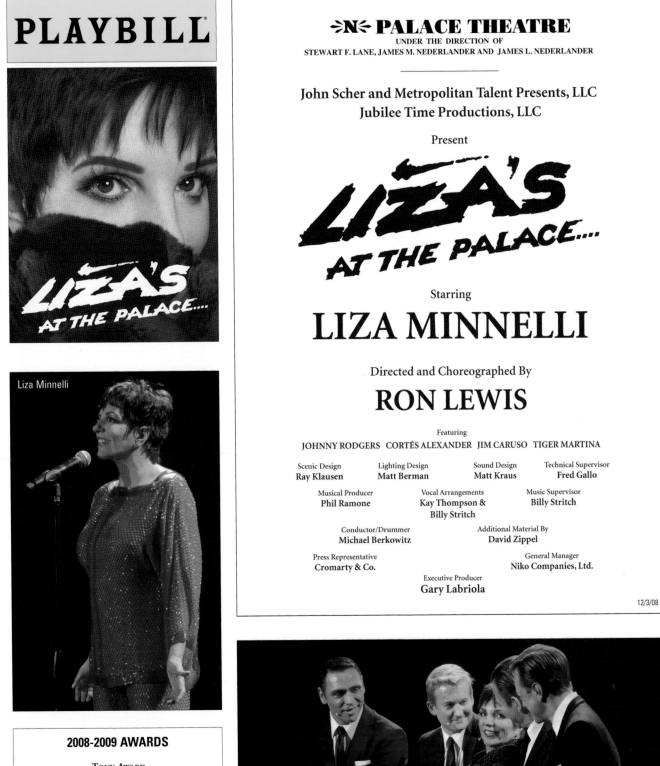

PLAYBILL

AT THE PALACE....

Liza Minnelli

2008-2009 AWARDS

TONY AWARD
Best Special Theatrical Event

DRAMA DESK AWARD
Special Award
(Liza Minnelli)

≫N≪ **PALACE THEATRE**
UNDER THE DIRECTION OF
STEWART F. LANE, JAMES M. NEDERLANDER AND JAMES L. NEDERLANDER

John Scher and Metropolitan Talent Presents, LLC
Jubilee Time Productions, LLC

Present

LIZA'S
AT THE PALACE....

Starring

LIZA MINNELLI

Directed and Choreographed By

RON LEWIS

Featuring
JOHNNY RODGERS   CORTÉS ALEXANDER   JIM CARUSO   TIGER MARTINA

Scenic Design	Lighting Design	Sound Design	Technical Supervisor
Ray Klausen	Matt Berman	Matt Kraus	Fred Gallo

Musical Producer	Vocal Arrangements	Music Supervisor
Phil Ramone	Kay Thompson & Billy Stritch	Billy Stritch

Conductor/Drummer	Additional Material By
Michael Berkowitz	David Zippel

Press Representative	General Manager
Cromarty & Co.	Niko Companies, Ltd.

Executive Producer
Gary Labriola

12/3/08

(L-R): Tiger Martina, Johnny Rodgers, Liza Minnelli, Cortés Alexander and Jim Caruso

Photos by Eric Antoniou

Liza's at the Palace...

MUSICAL NUMBERS

ACT I

"Teach Me Tonight"
(Music by Gene DePaul; lyrics by Sammy Cahn)

"I Would Never Leave You"
(By Billy Stritch, Johnny Rodgers and Brian Lane Green)

"If You Hadn't, But You Did"
(Music by Jule Styne; lyrics by Betty Comden and Adolph Green)

"What Makes a Man a Man?"
(Music and lyrics by Charles Aznavour)

"My Own Best Friend"
(Music by John Kander; lyrics by Fred Ebb)

"Maybe This Time"
(Music by John Kander; lyrics by Fred Ebb)

"He's Funny That Way"
(Music by Neil Moret; lyrics by Richard Whiting)

"Palace Medley"
New introduction by David Zippel, John Kander and Billy Stritch; original song by Roger Edens; "Shine on Harvest Moon" by N. Bayes, J. Norworth, N. Graw; "Some of These Days" by S. Brooks; "My Man" by M. Yvain, A. Willemetz, J. Charles; "I Don't Care" by H. Sutton, R. Grant, J. Lennox

"Cabaret"
(Music by John Kander; lyrics by Fred Ebb)

ACT II

"And the World Goes 'Round"
(Music by John Kander; lyrics by Fred Ebb)

"Hello, Hello"
(Music and lyrics by Kay Thompson)

"Jubilee Time"
(Music and lyrics by Kay Thompson)

"Basin Street Blues"
(Music by Spencer Williams, with special verse by Kay Thompson)

"Clap Yo' Hands"
(Music by George Gershwin; lyrics by Ira Gershwin)

"Liza (All the Clouds'll Roll Away)"
(Music by George Gershwin; lyrics by Ira Gershwin/Gus Kahn)

"I Love a Violin"
(Music and lyrics by Kay Thompson)

"Mammy"
(Music by Walter Donaldson; lyrics by Sam M. Lewis and Joe Young)

"Theme from *New York, New York*"
(Music by John Kander; lyrics by Fred Ebb)

"I'll Be Seeing You"
(Music by Sammy Fain; lyrics by Irving Kahal)

MUSICAL NUMBERS ARRANGED AND ORCHESTRATED BY

RALPH BURNS, NED GINSBURG, MARVIN HAMLISCH, SONNY KOMPANEK, DON SEBESKY, ARTIE SCHROEK, BILLY STRITCH AND TORRIE ZITO

ORCHESTRA

Conductor/Drummer:
MICHAEL BERKOWITZ
Pianist/Musical Supervisor:
BILLY STRITCH
Keyboards:
RICK CUTLER
Percussion:
DAVID NYBERG
Trombone:
DAN LEVINE
Guitar:
BILL WASHER
Bass:
CHIP JACKSON
Trumpet:
ROSS KONIKOFF, DAVE TRIGG
Alto Sax:
CHUCK WILSON
Bari Sax:
ED XIQUES
Tenor Sax:
FRANK PEROWSKY
Musical Contractor:
ROSS KONIKOFF

Mr. Berkowitz uses DW drums and hardware exclusively.

Piano by STEINWAY & SONS.

Photo by Eric Antoniou

Liza Minnelli

Liza's at the Palace...

Liza Minnelli

Ron Lewis
*Director/
Choreographer*

Johnny Rodgers

Cortés Alexander

Jim Caruso

Tiger Martina

Billy Stritch
*Pianist and
Musical Supervisor*

David Zippel
Additional Material

Manny Kladitis,
Niko Companies, Ltd.
*General
Management*

PERSONAL ASSISTANT TO LIZA MINNELLI
Lisa Zay

STAGE CREW

LIGHTING AND SOUND
(L-R): Matt Kraus (Sound Designer/Audio Mixer) and
Matt Berman (Lighting Designer/PSM)

SOUND AND LIGHTING
(L-R): Ty Lackey (Monitor Engineer) and
Thomas Thoon (Head Frontlight Operator)

STAGE MANAGEMENT
(L-R): Matt Berman (Prod. Stage Manager)
and Rocky Noel (Asst. Stage Manager)

ORCHESTRA
Front Row (L-R): Bill Washer, Frank Perowsky,
Ross Konikoff, Dan Levine, Mike Berkowitz

Back Row (L-R): Rick Cutler, Dave Trigg, Chuck
Wilson, Billy Stritch, Chip Jackson, Ed Xiques,
David Nyberg

Liza's at the Palace...

STAFF FOR *LIZA'S AT THE PALACE...*

GENERAL MANAGEMENT
Niko Companies, Ltd.
www.nikocompanies.com

GENERAL PRESS REPRESENTATIVE
CROMARTY & COMPANY
Peter Cromarty/Alice Cromarty
www.cromarty.com

PRODUCTION STAGE MANAGER
Matt Berman

COMPANY MANAGER ....Petrina Moritz
Assistant Choreographer/Dance Captain .....Tiger Martina
Assistant Stage Manager ....Rocky Noel
Assistant Scenic Designer ....Robert F. Wolin
Assistant Sound Designer ....Bob Hanlon
Production Carpenter ....Peter Johnson
Production Electrician ....Jon Lawson
Head Front Light ....Thomas Thoon
Lighting Programmer ....Brendon Boyd
Monitor Engineer ....Ty Lackey
Production Sound Engineer ....Matt Kraus
Teleprompter Operator ....Gary D. Labriola
Wardrobe Supervisor ....Kathy Guida
Ms. Minnelli's Dresser ....Casey Paul
Music Preparation ....Donald Oliver, Paul Holderbaum/
Chelsea Music
Photographer, PLAYBILL Cover ....Daniela Frederici
Photography ....Rick Day, Daniela Frederici,
Bill Westmoreland
Accountant...........................Rosenberg, Neuwirth,
& Kuchner, CPAs/
Mark D'Ambrosi, Jana Jevnikar
Banking ....HSBC/
Lisa Buffa
Press Assistants ....Felicia Velasco, John Ward
Theatre Displays ....King Displays, Inc./
Ken Lubin
Payroll Services ....Castellana Services, Inc./
Lance Castellana
Marketing ....HHC Marketing/
Hugh Hysell, Matt Sicoli, Nicole Pando

MUSICIANS
Music Contractor ....Ross Konikoff
Drums ....Michael Berkowitz

Keyboards ....Rick Cutler
Bass ....Chip Jackson
Trumpet ....Ross Konikoff
David Trigg
Trombone ....Dan Levine
Percussion ....David Nyberg
Guitar ....Bill Washer
Saxophone ....Frank Perowsky
Chuck Wilson
Ed Xiques

STAFF FOR LIZA MINNELLI
Personal Assistant to Liza Minnelli ....Lisa Zay
Assistant to Ms. Minnelli ....Phyllis Little
Business Manager ....Starr & Company
Attorney ....Allen H. Arrow, Esq.
Law Firm ....Shukat Arrow Hafer Weber & Herbsman
Booking Agent ....DearLab Productions/
Gary Labriola
Manager ....Gary Labriola
Travel Coordinator ....Anna Cruz
President of Liza's Official Fan Club ....Scott Schechter/
www.officializaminnelli.com
Souvenir Program Editor ....Jim Caruso

STAFF FOR METROPOLITAN TALENT PRESENTS
Co-Chief Executive Officer ....John Scher
Co-Chief Executive Officer ....Al Cafaro
Chief Financial Officer ....Errol Antzis
Senior Producer ....Ian Noble
Associate Producer ....Jeanne Bohorquez
Booking Coordinator ....Stacy Reader
Marketing Director ....Brian O'Boyle
Marketing Manager ....Dana Wise
New Media Director ....Howard Brooks
New Media Coordinator ....Nadine Dunn
Ticketing Director ....Scott Campbell
Assistant to John Scher ....Diana Guthey
Accountant..........................GoldBiz Management/
Ed Gold
Design Services.....................The CH Major Group/
Chris Major, Regis Albrecht
Insurance Services ....Family Financial Group/
Butch Franklin, Carolyn Norton
Marketing Consultant ...Marketing Entertainment Group/
Keith Hurd
Marketing Consultant ....HHC Marketing/
Hugh Hysell, Matt Sicoli,
Nicole Pando

Publicity ....On Tour PR/
Renee Pfefer

CREDITS
Liza's costumes are original Halstons. Liza's costumes for the show executed by Donna Langman Costumes New York. Lighting equipment provided by PRG-Scenic Technologies. Scenery fabrication by PRG-Scenic Technologies, a division of Production Resource Group, LLC, New Windsor, NY. Show control and scenic motion control featuring stage command systems® by Scenic Technologies, a division of Production Resource Group, LLC, New Windsor, NY. Sound equipment provided by Sound Associates, Inc. Instrument rentals provided by Studio Instrument Rentals.

ACKNOWLEDGEMENTS & SPECIAL THANKS
Sam Harris, Sam Irvin, John Kander & Fred Ebb
To my dear friend Michael Feinstein, without whom none of this would have been possible.

In loving memory of Bill "Pappy" Lavorgna

Chairman ....**James M. Nederlander**	
President ....**James L. Nederlander**	

Executive Vice President
Nick Scandalios

Vice President	Senior Vice President
Corporate Development	Labor Relations
Charlene S. Nederlander	**Herschel Waxman**

Vice President	Chief Financial Officer
Jim Boese	**Freida Sawyer Belviso**

STAFF FOR THE PALACE THEATRE
Theatre Manager ....Dixon Rosario
Treasurer ....Cissy Caspare
Assistant Treasurer ....Anne T. Wilson
Carpenter ....Thomas K. Phillips
Flyman ....Robert W. Kelly
Electrician ....Eddie Webber
Propertymaster ....Steve Camus
Engineer ....Rob O'Conner
Chief Usher ....Gloria Hill

WARDROBE SUPERVISOR
Kathy Guida

GENERAL MANAGEMENT
Manny Kladitis

Casey Paul (Ms. Minnelli's Dresser) embraces a friend, Annette McLaughlin.

Photos by Peter Cromarty

Liza's at the Palace...
SCRAPBOOK

Correspondent: Jim Caruso, "Dick Williams"

Opening Night Gifts: Liza gave "The Williams Brothers" fluffy backstage robes and incredible sterling Elsa Peretti cufflinks engraved with the name of the specific Williams Brother we're playing. I play Dick Williams, so my cufflinks say "Dick," which is fairly hilarious. We gave Liza and Ron Lewis (our director) a fabulous photo from our rehearsal period, when Ron was standing in for Liza, doing one of those iconic 'boys posing around the leading lady' moments!

Who Has Done the Most Shows in Their Career: Perhaps Liza.

Most Exciting Celebrity Visitor: Mayor Bloomberg said to Liza, "You ARE New York, New York!"

Special Backstage Ritual: Prayer circle before each and every show.

Favorite Off-Site Hangouts: Joe Allen and Bar Centrale!

Favorite Snack Food: On opening night, our pal and ex-Williams Brother Clarke Thorell sent us a veritable mountain of chocolate candy, which gets us through matinee days.

Memorable Press Encounter: Peddling our show and stationary bikes for Broadway Cares/Equity Fights AIDS and Duracell—in order to store enough energy to light up the 2009 sign in Times Square on New Years Eve!

Catchphrases Only the Company Would Recognize: "We killed 'em in Antwerp!" "We'll always have Uruguay...." "Let's do this one for Donny and Marie!"

Memorable Directorial Note: "Shit—anyone knows that...."

Nicknames: "Liza May/Lucie Menucie." "Carusie." "Tezzie." "JohnnyRodgie." "Tigee." "Stritchee."

1. Liza Minnelli and her artistic crew take bows on opening night at the Palace Theatre.
2. Music director Billy Stritch in rehearsal.
3. Minnelli signs copies of the show's CD for fans at Barnes & Noble bookstore.
4. (L-R): Backup singers/dancers Cortés Alexander, Johnny Rodgers, "Yearbook" correspondent Jim Caruso and Tiger Martina prepare to perform with Minnelli at the signing.
5. The backup singers work with Minnelli at Chelsea Rehearsal Studios.
6. Director/choreographer Ron Lewis in rehearsal.

Mamma Mia!

First Preview: October 5, 2001. Opened: October 18, 2001.
Still running as of May 31, 2009.

PLAYBILL®

A NEW MUSICAL BASED ON THE SONGS OF ABBA

MAMMA MIA!

CAST
(in order of speaking)

Sophie Sheridan	ALLISON CASE
Ali	AMINA ROBINSON
Lisa	SAMANTHA EGGERS
Tanya	JUDY McLANE
Rosie	GINA FERRALL
Donna Sheridan	CAROLEE CARMELLO
Sky	CHRIS PELUSO
Pepper	BEN GETTINGER
Eddie	RAYMOND J. LEE
Harry Bright	BEN LIVINGSTON
Bill Austin	PEARCE BUNTING
Sam Carmichael	SEAN ALLAN KRILL
Father Alexandrios	BRYAN SCOTT JOHNSON

THE ENSEMBLE

BRENT BLACK, TIMOTHY BOOTH,
ISAAC CALPITO, ALLYSON CARR,
MEGHANN DREYFUSS, LORI HALEY FOX,
HEIDI GODT, FRANKIE JAMES GRANDE,
COREY GREENAN,
BRYAN SCOTT JOHNSON,
MONICA KAPOOR, CORINNE MELANÇON,
COURTNEY REED, GERARD SALVADOR,
TRACI VICTORIA, LEAH ZEPEL

WINTER GARDEN
1634 Broadway
A Shubert Organization Theatre
Gerald Schoenfeld, *Chairman*   Philip J. Smith, *President*
Robert E. Wankel, *Executive Vice President*

JUDY CRAYMER, RICHARD EAST AND BJÖRN ULVAEUS
FOR LITTLESTAR IN ASSOCIATION WITH UNIVERSAL

PRESENT

MAMMA MIA!

MUSIC AND LYRICS BY
BENNY ANDERSSON
BJÖRN ULVAEUS
AND SOME SONGS WITH STIG ANDERSON

BOOK BY CATHERINE JOHNSON

PRODUCTION DESIGNED BY
MARK THOMPSON

LIGHTING DESIGNED BY
HOWARD HARRISON

SOUND DESIGNED BY
**ANDREW BRUCE &
BOBBY AITKEN**

MUSICAL SUPERVISOR, ADDITIONAL MATERIAL
& ARRANGEMENTS
MARTIN KOCH

CHOREOGRAPHY
ANTHONY VAN LAAST

DIRECTED BY
PHYLLIDA LLOYD

10/1/08

(L-R): Judy McLane, Carolee Carmello and Gina Ferrall

Photo by Joan Marcus

Continued on next page

Mamma Mia!

MUSICAL NUMBERS

(in alphabetical order)

CHIQUITITA
DANCING QUEEN
DOES YOUR MOTHER KNOW
GIMME! GIMME! GIMME!
HONEY, HONEY
I DO, I DO, I DO, I DO, I DO
I HAVE A DREAM
KNOWING ME, KNOWING YOU
LAY ALL YOUR LOVE ON ME
MAMMA MIA
MONEY, MONEY, MONEY
ONE OF US
OUR LAST SUMMER
SLIPPING THROUGH MY FINGERS
S.O.S.
SUPER TROUPER
TAKE A CHANCE ON ME
THANK YOU FOR THE MUSIC
THE NAME OF THE GAME
THE WINNER TAKES IT ALL
UNDER ATTACK
VOULEZ-VOUS

Cast Continued

UNDERSTUDIES
For Sophie Sheridan:
MEGHANN DREYFUSS, SAMANTHA EGGERS
For Ali:
COURTNEY REED, TRACI VICTORIA,
LEAH ZEPEL
For Lisa:
LANENE CHARTERS, MONICA KAPOOR,
COURTNEY REED, LEAH ZEPEL
For Tanya:
LORI HALEY FOX, HEIDI GODT,
CORINNE MELANÇON
For Rosie:
LORI HALEY FOX, HEIDI GODT
For Donna Sheridan:
LORI HALEY FOX, HEIDI GODT,
CORINNE MELANÇON
For Sky:
COREY GREENAN, RYAN SANDER
For Pepper:
ISAAC CALPITO, GERARD SALVADOR
For Eddie:
MATTHEW FARVER,
FRANKIE JAMES GRANDE, RYAN SANDER

For Harry Bright:
TIMOTHY BOOTH,
BRYAN SCOTT JOHNSON
For Bill Austin:
BRENT BLACK, TIMOTHY BOOTH,
BRYAN SCOTT JOHNSON
For Sam Carmichael:
BRENT BLACK, TIMOTHY BOOTH
For Father Alexandrios:
BRENT BLACK, TIMOTHY BOOTH,
MATTHEW FARVER

SWINGS
LANENE CHARTERS, MATTHEW FARVER,
RYAN SANDER, COLLETTE SIMMONS

DANCE CAPTAIN
JANET ROTHERMEL

On a Greek Island, a wedding is about to take place...

PROLOGUE
Three months before the wedding

ACT ONE
The day before the wedding

ACT TWO
The day of the wedding

THE BAND
Music Director/Conductor/Keyboard 1:
WENDY BOBBITT CAVETT
Associate Music Director/Keyboard 3:
ROB PREUSS
Keyboard 2:
STEVE MARZULLO
Keyboard 4:
MYLES CHASE
Guitar 1:
DOUG QUINN
Guitar 2:
JEFF CAMPBELL
Bass:
PAUL ADAMY
Drums:
RAY MARCHICA
Percussion:
DAVID NYBERG
Music Coordinator:
MICHAEL KELLER
Synthesizer Programmer:
NICHOLAS GILPIN

Photo by Brian Mapp

CAST AND STAGE MANAGEMENT
On Floor (L-R): Courtney Reed, Amina Robinson, Ian Paget, Judy McLane

Seated (L-R): Collette Simmons, Carolee Carmello, Dean R. Greer, Timothy Booth, Heidi Godt, Corinne Melançon, Sharone Sayegh, Ben Livingston, Allyson Carr, Brandi Burkhardt, Corey Greenan, Tony Gonzalez, Ben Gettinger, Sherry Cohen, Andrew Fenton, Lanene Charters

Standing (L-R): Gina Ferrall, Bryan Scott Johnson, Robin Levine, Matthew Farver, Raymond J. Lee, Traci Victoria, Lori Haley Fox, Elizabeth Share, Mark Dancewicz

Mamma Mia!

 Carolee Carmello
Donna Sheridan

 Allison Case
Sophie Sheridan

 Gina Ferrall
Rosie

 Judy McLane
Tanya

 Sean Allan Krill
Sam Carmichael

 Pearce Bunting
Bill Austin

 Ben Livingston
Harry Bright

 Chris Peluso
Sky

 Samantha Eggers
Lisa

 Amina Robinson
Ali

 Ben Gettinger
Pepper

 Raymond J. Lee
Eddie

 Brent Black
Ensemble

 Timothy Booth
Ensemble

 Isaac Calpito
Ensemble

 Allyson Carr
Ensemble

 Lanene Charters
Swing

 Meghann Dreyfuss
Ensemble

 Matthew Farver
Swing

 Lori Haley Fox
Ensemble

 Heidi Godt
Ensemble

 Frankie James Grande
Ensemble

 Corey Greenan
Ensemble

 Bryan Scott Johnson
Father Alexandrios, Ensemble

 Monica Kapoor
Ensemble

 Corinne Melançon
Ensemble

 Courtney Reed
Ensemble

 Janet Rothermel
Dance Captain

 Gerard Salvador
Ensemble

 Ryan Sander
Assistant Dance Captain, Swing

 Collette Simmons
Swing

 Traci Victoria
Ensemble

 Leah Zepel
Ensemble

Björn Ulvaeus
Music & Lyrics

Benny Andersson
Music & Lyrics

Mamma Mia!

Catherine Johnson
Book

Phyllida Lloyd
Director

Anthony Van Laast,
MBE
Choreographer

Mark Thompson
Production Designer

Howard Harrison
Lighting Designer

Andrew Bruce
Sound Designer

Bobby Aitken
Sound Designer

Martin Koch
Musical Supervisor

David Holcenberg
*Associate Music
Supervisor*

Nichola Treherne
*Associate
Choreographer*

Martha Banta
Resident Director

Tara Rubin Casting
Casting

David Grindrod
Casting Consultant

Arthur Siccardi
Theatrical Services,
Inc.
Production Manager

Judy Craymer
Producer

Richard East
Producer

Nina Lannan
Associates
*General
Management/
Executive Producer*

ALUMNI
2008-2009

Carey Anderson
Sophie Sheridan

Jon-Erik Goldberg
Swing

Andy Kelso
Sky

Veronica J. Kuehn
Ali

Robin Levine
Ensemble, Swing

Carrie Manolakos
Sophie Sheridan

Steve Morgan
Ensemble

Michael Pemberton
Bill Austin

Joi Danielle Price
Ensemble

Britt Shubow
Ensemble

Chistopher Shyer
Sam Carmichael

TRANSFER
STUDENTS
2008-2009

Brandi Burkhardt
Sophie Sheridan

Mark Dancewicz
Ensemble

Annie Edgerton
Ensemble

Jon-Erik Goldberg
Pepper, Swing

Tony Gonzalez
*Dance Captain,
Ensemble, Swing*

Mamma Mia!

Robin Levine
Ensemble, Swing

Ian Paget
Ensemble

Michael Pemberton
Bill Austin

Joi Danielle Price
Swing

Sharone Sayegh
Ensemble

Elizabeth Share
Ensemble

CREW
Front Row (L-R): Vickey Walker, Glenn Russo, Irene L. Bunis, Michael Maloney

Second Row (L-R): Pitsch Karrer, Chasity Neutze, Robert Krauss, Carey Bertini, Steven Cozzi, Mai-Linh Lofgren, Reginald Carter, Francis Lofgren

Back Row (L-R): Richard Carney, Aarne Lofgren, Art Soyk, Craig Cassidy, Andy Sather, Don Lawrence, Stephen Burns, Leon Stieb

Photos by Brian Mapp

FRONT OF HOUSE STAFF
Front Row (L-R): Ken Costigan, Craig Dawson, John Mitchell

Back Row (L-R): Michael Bosch, Sabiel Almonte, Dennis Marion, Robin Steinthal, Manuel Levine

BAND
Front Row (L-R): Ray Marchica, Jeff Campbell

Back Row (L-R): Paul Adamy, Wendy Bobbitt Cavett, Myles Chase

---

In loving memory of Daniel McDonald, a cast member of the *Mamma Mia!* Broadway Company 2004-2005.

LITTLESTAR SERVICES LIMITED

Directors ....Judy Craymer
Richard East
Benny Andersson
Björn Ulvaeus
International Executive Producer ....Andrew Treagus
Business & Finance Director ....Ashley Grisdale
Administrator ....Peter Austin
PA to Judy Craymer...........................Katie Wolfryd
Marketing & Communications Manager ....Claire Teare
Marketing & Communications
    Coordinator ....Liz McGinity
Head of Accounts ....Jo Reedman

Accountant ....Sheila Egbujie
Accountant ....Kerri Jordan
Administrative Assistant ....Matthew Willis
Receptionist ....Kimberley Wallwork
Legal Services ....Barry Shaw
Howard Jones at Sheridans
Production Insurance Services ....Walton & Parkinson Ltd.
Business Manager for Benny Andersson and
    Björn Ulvaeus & Scandinavian Press ......Görel Hanser

NINA LANNAN ASSOCIATES

GENERAL MANAGERS ....DEVIN M. KEUDELL,
AMY JACOBS
ASSOCIATE GENERAL MANAGER/
    COMPANY MANAGER ....RINA L. SALTZMAN
Assistant Company Manager ....Liza Garcia

Management Associate ....Katherine McNamee

ANDREW TREAGUS ASSOCIATES LIMITED

GENERAL MANAGER ....JULIAN STONEMAN
Production Administrator ....Daniel Sparrow
PA to Andrew Treagus ....Jacki Harding
Production Coordinator ....Stella Warshaw
International Travel Manager ....Caroline Dulin
International Travel Manager ....Maria Persson
Production Assistant &
    PA to Julian Stoneman ....Ffion Jones
Administrative Assistant ....James Mullan

PRODUCTION TEAM

ASSOCIATE
    CHOREOGRAPHER ....NICHOLA TREHERNE

Mamma Mia!

DANCE SUPERVISOR ....JANET ROTHERMEL
RESIDENT DIRECTOR ....MARTHA BANTA
ASSOCIATE
   MUSIC SUPERVISOR ......DAVID HOLCENBERG
ASSOCIATE
   SCENIC DESIGNER (US) ....NANCY THUN
ASSOCIATE
   SCENIC DESIGNER (UK) .....JONATHAN ALLEN
ASSOCIATE
   COSTUME DESIGNERS ....LUCY GAIGER
                         SCOTT TRAUGOTT
ASSOCIATE HAIR DESIGNER ..JOSH MARQUETTE
ASSOCIATE
   LIGHTING DESIGNERS ....DAVID HOLMES
                         ED MCCARTHY
                         ANDREW VOLLER
ASSOCIATE
   SOUND DESIGNERS ....BRIAN BEASLEY
                         DAVID PATRIDGE
MUSICAL TRANSCRIPTION ......ANDERS NEGLIN
CASTING CONSULTANT ....DAVID GRINDROD

CASTING
TARA RUBIN CASTING
Tara Rubin CSA
Eric Woodall, CSA; Laura Schutzel, CSA;
Merri Sugarman, CSA;
Rebecca Carfagna; Paige Blansfield; Dale Brown

PRESS REPRESENTATIVE
BONEAU/BRYAN-BROWN
Adrian Bryan-Brown   Joe Perrotta
Kelly Guiod

MARKETING U.S.
TMG – THE MARKETING GROUP
TANYA GRUBICH   LAURA MATALON
Victoria Cairl

**MUSIC PUBLISHED BY EMI GROVE PARK MUSIC,
INC. AND EMI WATERFORD MUSIC, INC.**

STAFF FOR *MAMMA MIA!*
PRODUCTION
   STAGE MANAGER ....ANDREW FENTON
Stage Managers...............Sherry Cohen, Dean R. Greer
Assistant Dance Captain ....Ryan Sander

PRODUCTION MANAGER.....ARTHUR SICCARDI

Head Carpenter ....Chris Nass
Assistant Carpenters ....Stephen Burns,
                         Clark Middleton
Production Electrician ....Rick Baxter
Head Electrician ....Don Lawrence
Assistant Electrician ....Andy Sather
Vari*Lite Programmer ....Andrew Voller
Production Sound ....David Patridge
Head Sound ....Craig Cassidy
Assistant Sound................................Pitsch Karrer
Production Properties ....Simon E.R. Evans
Head Properties ....Gregory Martin
Wardrobe Supervisor ....Irene L. Bunis
Assistant Wardrobe ....Ron Glow
Dressers ....Carey Bertini, Jim Collum,
                Lauren Kievit, Trevor McGinness,

          Elvia Pineda, Eric Pregent,
          Christine Richmond, I Wang
Hair Supervisor ....Sandy Schlender
Assistant Hair Supervisor ....Vickey Walker
Assistant Lighting Designer ....Jeffrey Lowney
Assistant Costume Designer ....Angela Kahler
House Crew ....Richard Carney, Reginald Carter,
     Gregory Chabay, Mai-Linh Lofgren DeVirgilio,
          Meredith Kievit, Aarne Lofgren,
          Francis Lofgren, John Maloney,
          Glenn Russo, Dennis Wiener
Rehearsal Pianist ....Sue Anschutz
Box Office ....Mary Cleary, Lee Cobb,
         Steve Cobb, James Drury, Sue Giebler,
         Bob McCaffrey, Ron Schroeder
Casting Directors ....Tara Rubin CSA, Eric Woodall
Casting Associates ....Laura Schutzel, Merri Sugarman
Casting Assistants ....Rebecca Carfagna, Jeff Siebert,
                        Paige Blansfield
Canadian Casting ....Stephanie Gorin Casting, C.D.C.
Associate to Casting Consultant ....Stephen Crockett
London Casting Assistant ....James Orange
Legal Counsel (U.S.) ....Lazarus & Harris LLP
                      Scott Lazarus, Esq.
                      Robert Harris, Esq.
Immigration Counsel ....Mark D. Koestler/
         Kramer Levin Naftalis & Frankel LLP
Accounting ....Rosenberg, Neuwirth and Kuchner/
               Chris Cacace, In Woo
Advertising ....Serino Coyne, Inc./
         Nancy Coyne, Greg Corradetti,
         Ryan Greer, Caroline Lenher,
             Ruth Rosenberg
Press Office Staff ....Chris Boneau, Ian Bjorklund,
         Jim Byk, Brandi Cornwell,
         Jackie Green, Juliana Hannett,
         Linnae Hodzic, Jessica Johnson,
         Amy Kass, Kevin Jones,
         Aaron Meier, Christine Olver,
         Matthew Polk, Matt Ross,
         Heath Schwartz, Susanne Tighe
Production Photographer ....Joan Marcus
Merchandising ....Max Merchandise, LLC/
             Randi Grossman, Victor Romero
Theater Displays ....King Display
Insurance ....Dewitt, Stern/
             Walton & Parkinson Ltd.
Orthopedic Consultant ....Dr. Philip Baumann
Banking .............................J.P. Morgan Trust
Travel Agent ....Tzell Travel
Original Logo Design ....© Littlestar Services Limited

CREDITS AND ACKNOWLEDGMENTS
Scenery constructed and painted by Hudson Scenic Studio,
Inc. and Hamilton Scenic Specialty. Computer motion
control and automation by Feller Precision, Inc.
SHOWTRAK computer motion control for scenery and
rigging. Sound equipment supplied by Masque Sound.
Lighting equipment supplied by Fourth Phase and
Vari*Lite, Inc. Soft goods by I. Weiss and Sons. Costumes
by Barbara Matera, Ltd., Tricorne New York City and
Carelli Costumes, Inc. Additional costume work by Allan
Alberts Productions. Millinery by Lynn Mackey. Wet suits
by Aquatic Fabricators of South Florida. Custom men's
shirts by Cego. Custom knitting by C.C. Wei. Custom
fabric printing and dyeing by Dye-namix and Gene

Mignola. Shoes by Native Leather, Rilleau Leather and T. O.
Dey. Gloves by Cornelia James - London. Hair color by
Redken. Properties by Paragon Theme and Prop
Fabrication. Cough drops provided by Ricola U.S.A.
Physical therapy provided by Sean Gallagher.

Mamma Mia! was originally produced in London by
LITTLESTAR SERVICES LIMITED on April 6, 1999.

Experience *Mamma Mia!* in these cities:
London/Prince of Wales Theatre/mamma-mia.com
Broadway/Winter Garden Theatre/telecharge.com
Las Vegas/Mandalay Bay Theatre/mandalaybay.com
North American Tour/ticketmaster.com
International Tour/mamma-mia.com

For more information on the above
and our other productions in
Berlin, Barcelona and Nagoya
visit and book at:
www.mamma-mia.com

*Mamma Mia! How Can I Resist You? The Inside Story of
Mamma Mia! and the songs of ABBA* available now.
Order at: www.barnesandnoble.com

For more information and tour schedules visit:
www.mamma-mia.com

THE SHUBERT ORGANIZATION, INC.
Board of Directors

Mamma Mia!
SCRAPBOOK

Correspondent: Sean Allan Krill, "Sam Carmichael"

Memorable Note or Fan Letter: I got the sweetest note from an 8-year-old girl named Lily Schmidt. She handwrote it and decorated it with her own illustrations, and sent it to the theatre. I was so touched with the time and effort put into it. I keep it in my dressing room. Also, a few months ago I received a pencil drawn portrait of myself from a very talented woman named Monica del Haya. It was a very good likeness, and I was very flattered.

Anniversary Party: Just after I joined the cast, the show celebrated its seventh anniversary at Lucky Strike—we were the first party in the new space and it was a blast. I bowled terribly though. Maybe it was the vodka?

Most Exciting Celebrity Visitor: Harvey Fierstein was our celebrity guest judge for our Holiday Dressing Room Door Contest. He made me laugh when he was assessing Chris Peluso's door: once Chris—who plays Sky in the show—was done explaining his door, Harvey paused for a moment and then said, "It's a good thing you're pretty."

"Gypsy of the Year" Sketch: Created by Robert Horn, Frankie James Grande & Ray Lee, it was basically a TKTS booth agent explaining to tourists how every show on Broadway has been "*Mamma Mia*-fied" to fight the recession. So each show, including *Little Mermaid* and *Equus*, contains an ABBA song and a mega-mix for a finale. Very funny.

"Easter Bonnet" Sketch: Created by Gerard Salvador & Frankie James Grande, it used Miranda (of YouTube fame) singing "The Rose" with choreography by Monica Kapoor.

Most Roles in This Show: As far as roles in the show, since I've joined, that would have to be Lori Haley Fox. She is what we call a triple Dynamo cover, so I've seen her play Tanya, Rosie, and played opposite her Donna. But the swings definitely have performed the most tracks in the show—it's amazing to watch them get plugged into a spot and make it work so effortlessly. Our swings are Lanene Charters, Matt Farver, Ryan Sander and Collette Simmons.

Most Shows in Career: I would think it would be between Brent Black and Meghann Dreyfuss who have been with this production since opening night on Broadway back in 2001—and Lori Haley Fox who has been with the show on and off since its inception in London, on the tours, and here on Broadway. Hmmm, maybe I need to get those three to duke it out and count to see who wins?

Special Backstage Rituals: For me? I always sing along with Carolee Carmello on the "AHAAAAAAA, ah ah ah AAAAAAAAAAAAAH, ALL THE THINGS I COULD DO" part of "Money Money Money" just before the Dads Arrival scene. I also hum along onstage while Carolee's singing (and I'm frozen) during "Mamma Mia." There you have it: my extensive *Mamma Mia!* warm-up.

1. Harvey Fierstein (L) assessing Chris Peluso's door during the Holiday Door Contest.
2. "Yearbook" correspondent Sean Allan Krill with Allison Case at the seventh anniversary party.

Photos courtesy Sean Allan Krill

Favorite Moment: On stage: Listening to Carolee sing the end of "Winner"—AT ME. She sings the heck out of it, and I have the best seat in the house. Off stage: Sitting upstage of the set with Brandi during "Our Last Summer." It's always been one of my favorite parts of the show because I get some QT with my Sophie.

Favorite In-Theatre Gathering Place: People always seem to end up in either the boys' dressing room or Amina & Samantha's room (Ali & Lisa). Ryan Sander calls my dressing room Café Krill. I drink a lot of coffee.

Favorite Off-Site Hangout: Definitely Harmony View kitty-corner across the street. It's been renamed Emmett O'Lunneys, but everyone still just calls it Harmony. Often post-show you hear the one-word query, "Harmony?"

Favorite Snack Food: Carolee brings snacks for the company almost every Saturday matinee. Yummm.

Mascot: Does the mermaid on the Starbucks logo count?

Favorite Therapy: PT every Friday to anyone who needs it to help with the aching bodies sometimes caused by our raked stage.

Memorable Ad-Libs. Oh my. Two of my favorites ever: Carolee, during the wedding says to me, "Don't go getting all self-righteous on me." Instead she said, "Don't go getting all self-involved on me!" And then recently, during 'Dads' Arrival' Ben Livingston, as Harry, is supposed to say, "Now who says I'm an unadventurous old stick-in-the-mud?" and instead he said, "Now who says I'm an...

uninteresting... old... fart." Took me a long time to recover from that one.

Cell Phone Rings, Cell Phone Photos or Texting Incidents: We don't have a lot of cellphone rings during the show, but wow are there a lot of cameras that come out during the bows and the finale. Flash flash flash. I like to yell jokingly, "Tag me!"

Memorable Stage Door Fan Encounters: People are always so sweet at the door. I think the most touching thing is when people who barely speak English take the time and make the effort to say a kind word. In my experience trying to speak outside my native language, that is very impressive to me.

Fastest Costume Change: It's either Carolee's quick change into the wedding dress, or Brandi's quick change into her party outfit for the bachelorette party at the end of Act 1. In Carolee's case, it's a complete quick change: old dress off and then zipped into the wedding

Mamma Mia!
SCRAPBOOK

dress in a matter of seconds. In Brandi's case, she's underdressed the party outfit underneath what she wears during "Lay All Your Love" so she just has to rip off the top layer.

Busiest Day at the Box Office: I'm not sure—but I was walking into work yesterday and there was a line from the box office at 51st all the way down the block and across 50th Street!

Heaviest/Hottest Costume: Has to be the jumpsuits—they're HEAVY.

Who Wore the Least: Definitely Chris Peluso. He gets down to a tiny little swimsuit during "Lay All Your Love."

Catchphrases Only the Company Would Recognize: We always say 'the jetty' which is the hydraulic boardwalk-y looking dock thing in our set. I don't know if there are a lot of people who use the word "jetty" in their daily life. Also we call the costumes that the ensemble wears to do the scene changes "Greek Grannies."

Orchestra Member Who Played the Most Instruments: Our percussionist David Nyberg plays a LOT of different instruments during the course of the show. He's surrounded by all kinds of things: timpani, xylophones, shakers, cymbals, chimes, bells... I can't even count. It's very impressive to watch him play the show—it's like a percussion ballet down there. They should sell tickets.

Orchestra Member Who Played the Most Consecutive Performances Without a Sub: Doug Quinn, our guitarist, rarely misses a show.

Best In-House Parody Lyrics: The show is chock-full o' clever people who are always making up lyrics. I've often heard the first line of "Lay All Your Love" ("I wasn't jealous before we met") sung as "I was in jail just before we met...." And, instead of "Chiquitita tell me what's wrong" there's always the ever popular "Chicken Pita, tell me what's wrong...."

Memorable Directorial Note: My shirt had come unbuttoned during "S.O.S." and I got this note: "Sean, could you please make sure your shirt is buttoned up one more button. Sam shouldn't have more cleavage then Donna."

Embarrassing Moments: Once during the "Gimme! Gimme! Gimme!" scene between Sophie and myself, I gestured out to the "island" and instead of saying, "This used to be such a quiet little island." I said, "This used to be such a quiet little audience." Oops.

Ghostly Encounters Backstage: Once when I had just joined the company some dust drifted down from the rafters and I sneezed. Someone said something like, "Barbara dust?" Took me awhile to get it but I finally realized they meant Barbra Streisand...as in *Funny Girl*, which played at this theatre...and I thought, Wow. Cool.

Coolest Thing About Being in This Show: I still, to this day, love the music. Also, I love the looks on people's faces when I come out in that jumpsuit and they see the codpiece. It's priceless.

1. The unveiling of the *Mamma Mia* portrait at Tony's di Napoli. (L-R): Ben, Brandi, Chris, Judy, Sean, Carolee, Gina and Pearce.
2. The Daddies pose for Polaroids for BC/EFA collection.
3. "Crazy" Pearce gives an impromptu mandolin concert backstage.
4. Ray Lee (Eddie) heading down to start Act II.

Mary Poppins

MUSICAL NUMBERS

Mary Poppins takes place in and around the Banks' household somewhere in London at the turn of the last century.

ACT I

"Chim Chim Cher-ee" † .... Bert
"Cherry Tree Lane" (Part 1)* .... George and Winifred Banks,
Jane and Michael, Mrs. Brill, and Robertson Ay
"The Perfect Nanny" .... Jane and Michael
"Cherry Tree Lane" (Part 2) .... George and Winifred Banks, Jane, and Michael,
Mrs. Brill, and Robertson Ay
"Practically Perfect"* .... Mary Poppins, Jane, and Michael
"Jolly Holiday" † .... Bert, Mary Poppins, Jane, Michael, Neleus, and the Statues
"Cherry Tree Lane" (Reprise),
  "Being Mrs. Banks,"*
  "Jolly Holiday" (Reprise) .... George, Winifred, Jane, and Michael
"A Spoonful of Sugar" .... Mary Poppins, Jane, Michael, Robertson Ay, and Winifred
"Precision and Order"* .... Bank Chairman and the Bank Clerks
"A Man Has Dreams" † .... George Banks
"Feed the Birds" .... Bird Woman and Mary Poppins
"Supercalifragilisticexpialidocious" † .... Mary Poppins, Mrs. Corry, Bert, Jane,
Michael, Fannie, Annie, and Customers
"Temper, Temper"* .... Valentine, William, Mr. Punch, the Glamorous Doll, and other Toys
"Chim Chim Cher-ee" (Reprise) .... Bert and Mary Poppins

ACT II

"Cherry Tree Lane" (Reprise) .... Mrs. Brill, Michael, Jane, Winifred, Robertson Ay, and George
"Brimstone and Treacle" (Part 1)* .... Miss Andrew
"Let's Go Fly a Kite" .... Bert, Park Keeper, Jane, and Michael
"Cherry Tree Lane" (Reprise),
  "Being Mrs. Banks" (Reprise) .... George and Winifred
"Brimstone and Treacle" (Part 2) .... Mary Poppins and Miss Andrew
"Practically Perfect" (Reprise) .... Jane, Michael, and Mary Poppins
"Chim Chim Cher-ee" (Reprise) .... Bert
"Step in Time" † .... Bert, Mary Poppins, Jane, Michael, and the Sweeps
"A Man Has Dreams,"
  "A Spoonful of Sugar" (Reprise) .... George and Bert
"Anything Can Happen"* .... Jane, Michael, Mary Poppins, and the Company
"A Spoonful of Sugar" (Reprise) .... Mary Poppins
"A Shooting Star" † .... Orchestra

* New Songs   † Adapted Songs

SONG CREDITS

"The Perfect Nanny," "A Spoonful of Sugar," "Feed the Birds," "Let's Go Fly a Kite"
written by Richard M. Sherman and Robert B. Sherman.

"Chim Chim Cher-ee," "Jolly Holiday," "A Man Has Dreams," "Supercalifragilisticexpialidocious,"
"Step in Time" written by Richard M. Sherman and Robert B. Sherman,
with new material by George Stiles and Anthony Drewe.

"Cherry Tree Lane," "Practically Perfect," "Being Mrs. Banks," "Precision and Order," "Temper, Temper,"
"Brimstone and Treacle," "Anything Can Happen" written by George Stiles and Anthony Drewe.

Cast Continued

Glamorous Doll .... CATHERINE WALKER
Jack-In-A-Box .... SEAN McCOURT
Miss Andrew .... RUTH GOTTSCHALL

ENSEMBLE

AARON J. ALBANO, KRISTIN CARBONE,
BARRETT DAVIS, NICOLAS DROMARD,
JAMES HINDMAN, BRIAN LETENDRE,
TONY MANSKER, SEAN McCOURT,
JEFF METZLER, VASTHY E. MOMPOINT,
KATHLEEN NANNI, MEGAN OSTERHAUS,
T. OLIVER REID, JANELLE ANNE ROBINSON,
NICK SANCHEZ, LAURA SCHUTTER,
JESSICA SHERIDAN, COREY SKAGGS,
SHEKITRA STARKE, STEPHAN STUBBINS,
CATHERINE WALKER

SWINGS

PAM BRADLEY, KATHY CALAHAN,
BRIAN COLLIER, SUZANNE HYLENSKI,
ROMMY SANDHU,
JONATHAN RICHARD SANDLER

Statues, bank clerks, customers, toys, chimney
sweeps, lamp lighters and inhabitants of
Cherry Tree Lane played by members of the
company.

Scarlett Strallen is appearing with the permission of
Actors' Equity Association pursuant to an exchange
program between American Equity and UK Equity.

UNDERSTUDIES

Mary Poppins: KRISTIN CARBONE,
  MEGAN OSTERHAUS,
  CATHERINE WALKER
Bert: NICOLAS DROMARD, MATT LOEHR,
  TONY MANSKER
George Banks: JAMES HINDMAN,
  SEAN McCOURT
Winifred Banks: KRISTIN CARBONE,
  MEGAN OSTERHAUS, LAURA SCHUTTER
Mrs. Brill: ANN ARVIA, PAM BRADLEY
Robertson Ay: AARON J. ALBANO,
  BRIAN COLLIER
Bird Woman: JANELLE ANNE ROBINSON,
  JESSICA SHERIDAN
Miss Andrew/Queen Victoria/Miss Smythe:
  ANN ARVIA, JANELLE ANNE ROBINSON,
  JESSICA SHERIDAN
Admiral Boom/Bank Chairman:
  JAMES HINDMAN, SEAN McCOURT,
  COREY SKAGGS

Continued on next page

Mary Poppins

Cast Continued

Mrs. Corry: PAM BRADLEY, KATHY CALAHAN,
  MEGAN OSTERHAUS
Katie Nanna: PAM BRADLEY,
  KATHY CALAHAN, SUZANNE HYLENSKI
Miss Lark: PAM BRADLEY, KATHY CALAHAN,
  LAURA SCHUTTER
Neleus: BRIAN COLLIER, BARRETT DAVIS,
  NICOLAS DROMARD
Von Hussler: ROMMY SANDHU,
  COREY SKAGGS
Jack-in-a-Box: NICOLAS DROMARD,
  ROMMY SANDHU,
  JONATHAN RICHARD SANDLER
Northbrook: JAMES HINDMAN,
  JONATHAN RICHARD SANDLER,
  COREY SKAGGS
Policeman/Mr. Punch: NICOLAS DROMARD,
  SEAN McCOURT, ROMMY SANDHU
Park Keeper: NICOLAS DROMARD,
  TONY MANSKER, COREY SKAGGS
William: BRIAN COLLIER,
  NICOLAS DROMARD, ROMMY SANDHU,
  JONATHAN RICHARD SANDLER
Valentine: BRIAN COLLIER,
  NICOLAS DROMARD,
  STEPHAN STUBBINS
Glamorous Doll: KATHY CALAHAN,
  SUZANNE HYLENSKI

DANCE CAPTAINS

BRIAN COLLIER, SUZANNE HYLENSKI

ORCHESTRA

Conductor: BRAD HAAK
Associate Conductor/2nd Keyboard:
  DALE RIELING
Assistant Conductor/Piano: MILTON GRANGER
Bass: PETER DONOVAN
Drums: DAVE RATAJCZAK
Percussion: DANIEL HASKINS
Guitar/Banjo/E-Bow: NATE BROWN
Horns: RUSSELL RIZNER,
  LAWRENCE DiBELLO
Trumpets: JASON COVEY, JOHN SHEPPARD
Trombone/Euphonium: MARC DONATELLE
Bass Trombone/Tuba: RANDY ANDOS
Clarinet: PAUL GARMENT
Oboe/English Horn: ALEXANDRA KNOLL
Flutes: BRIAN MILLER
Cello: STEPHANIE CUMMINS
Music Contractor: DAVID LAI

Scarlett Strallen
Mary Poppins

Adam Fiorentino
Bert

Daniel Jenkins
George Banks

Rebecca Luker
Winifred Banks

Jane Carr
Mrs. Brill

Ann Arvia
Bird Woman

Mark Price
Robertson Ay

Ruth Gottschall
*Miss Andrew,
Queen Victoria,
Miss Smythe*

Jeff Steitzer
*Admiral Boom,
Bank Chairman*

Alexandra Berro
*Jane Banks
at certain
performances*

Kelsey Fowler
*Jane Banks
at certain
performances*

Matthew Gumley
*Michael Banks
at certain
performances*

Cassady Leonard
*Jane Banks
at certain
performances*

Neil McCaffrey
*Michael Banks
at certain
performances*

Zach Rand
*Michael Banks
at certain
performances*

Nicolas Dromard
*Northbrook,
Ensemble*

James Hindman
*Park Keeper,
Mr. Punch, Ensemble*

Brian Letendre
Neleus, Ensemble

Sean McCourt
*Von Hussler,
Ensemble*

Janelle Anne
Robinson
*Mrs. Corry,
Ensemble*

Mary Poppins

Jessica Sheridan
Miss Lark, Ensemble

Corey Skaggs
Policeman, Ensemble

Aaron J. Albano
Ensemble

Pam Bradley
Swing

Kathy Calahan
Swing

Kristin Carbone
Ensemble

Brian Collier
Swing, Dance Captain

Barrett Davis
Ensemble

Suzanne Hylenski
Swing, Dance Captain

Tony Mansker
Ensemble

Jeff Metzler
Ensemble

Vasthy E. Mompoint
Fannie, Ensemble

Kathleen Nanni
Ensemble

Megan Osterhaus
Katie Nanna, Annie, Ensemble

T. Oliver Reid
William, Ensemble

Nick Sanchez
Valentine, Ensemble

Rommy Sandhu
Swing

Jonathan Richard Sandler
Swing

Laura Schutter
Ensemble

Shekitra Starke
Ensemble

Stephan Stubbins
Ensemble

Catherine Walker
Glamorous Doll, Ensemble

P.L. Travers
Author of Mary Poppins

Cameron Mackintosh
Producer & Co-Creator

Thomas Schumacher
Producer and President, Disney Theatrical Group

Richard M. Sherman and Robert B. Sherman
Original Music & Lyrics

Julian Fellowes
Book

George Stiles
New Songs, Additional Music, Dance & Vocal Arrangements

Anthony Drewe
New Songs & Additional Lyrics

Richard Eyre
Director

Matthew Bourne
Co-Director & Choreographer

Bob Crowley
Scenic and Costume Design

Stephen Mear
Co-Choreographer

Howard Harrison
Lighting Designer

Mary Poppins

Steve Canyon Kennedy
Broadway Sound Designer

William David Brohn
Orchestrations

David Caddick
Music Supervisor

Brad Haak
Music Director

Naomi Donne
Makeup Designer

Angela Cobbin
Wig Creator

Geoffrey Garratt
Associate Choreographer

Anthony Lyn
Associate Director

Tom Kosis
Resident Choreographer

David Benken
Technical Director

Tara Rubin Casting
Casting

Nicole Bocchi
Jane Banks

Ashley Brown
Mary Poppins

Kate Chapman
Miss Lark, Ensemble

Lila Coogan
Jane Banks

Eric Hatch
Ensemble

Stephanie Kurtzuba
Swing

Gavin Lee
Bert

Jacob Levine
Michael Banks

Daniel Marconi
Michael Banks

Cass Morgan
Bird Woman

Jayne Paterson
Ensemble

Dominic Roberts
Valentine, Ensemble

Chad Seib
William, Ensemble

David Baum
Ensemble

Catherine Brunell
Annie, Ensemble

Kate Chapman
Mrs. Corry, Ensemble

Alison Jaye Horowitz
Jane Banks

Nick Kepley
Neleus, Ensemble

Melissa Lone
Ensemble

Dennis Moench
Valentine, Ensemble

Amber Owens
Fannie, Ensemble

Chad Seib
Ensemble, Swing

Mary Poppins

Marlon Sherman
Michael Banks

Sam Strasfeld
*Northbrook,
Ensemble*

SCRAPBOOK

Correspondent: Jonathan Sandler, Swing
Milestone Party: We celebrated the 1000th performance with a big party, hosted by leading lady Scarlett Strallen, with delicious gourmet cuisine prepared by our very own Mr. Banks, Dan Jenkins.
Celebrity Visitor: Kathie Lee Gifford visited and conducted the finale, after some coaching from our MD Brad Haak. The next morning on TV she recounted how fun the experience was and emphatically exclaimed, "Brad Haak is HOT!!!"
Memorable Fax: A little girl wrote a fan letter to the kids that read, "I like Jane and the boy with Jane singing." The nameless boy she refers to is Michael Banks, the child co-star of the show. :)
"Easter Bonnet" Sketch: Kathy Calahan and Tony Mansker wrote and choreographed this year's sketch, about putting tap numbers into inappropriate shows for tapping e.g. *West Side Story, South Pacific, Jersey Boys* and *Wicked*.
Actors Who Performed the Most Roles in This Show: Our dance captains and swings compete for that title. They are on for opposite gender tracks (boys on for girls and vice versa) on a regular basis and often perform 2-3 tracks in one show.
Special Backstage Ritual: We all hit our sweep brushes together every night before "Step in Time."
In-Theatre Gathering Place: Jane Carr's dressing room on Sunday matinees for Tea Club.
Off-Site Hangout: Schnipper's and Sunrise Deli.
Favorite Snack Foods: Skittles, Cheez-Its, and Firecrackers (a secret recipe to enhance Saltines).
Mascot: Willoughby (a dog puppet).
Favorite Therapy: Pam Bradley's AMAZING massages.
Fastest Costume Change: From colorful "Jolly Holiday" back into blacks for the Rainy Cross.
Who Wore the Least: The statues in "Jolly Holiday."
Catchphrases Only the Company Would

Adam Fiorentino and Scarlett Strallen at Sardi's restaurant October 17, 2008, being introduced to the press as the Broadway company's new stars.

Recognize: "I'm late for the Windy Cross!"
Embarrassing Moment: Holding the final pose of "Supercal Reprise" for what seemed like an eternity during a technical malfunction. The audience thought we wanted them to shout "encore!" Finally Gavin Lee broke the freeze and filled them in.
Ghostly Encounters: Olive, our resident Ziegfeld Girl in spirit, likes to make the chimneys malfunction. Recent noteworthy visits: She sabotaged our automation of "Jolly Holiday" one day this year, so NOTHING moved on the deck...no sliders crossing, no flower pots growing, no statue plinths moving on or off.
Superstition That Turned Out To Be True: If a swing brings a project to work, thinking he/she has time to kill, he/she will certainly be on at last moment.
Other Memory: Ten people out sick...six swings covering them.
Çoolest Things About Being in This Show: The AMAZING cast and crew, and seeing the reactions of children in the audience.

THE ORIGINAL FILM SCREENPLAY
FOR WALT DISNEY'S *MARY POPPINS*
BY BILL WALSH * DON DA GRADI

DESIGN CONSULTANT
TONY WALTON

STAFF FOR *MARY POPPINS*

COMPANY MANAGER	DAVE EHLE
Assistant Company Manager	Laura Eichholz
Management Assistant	Verity Van Tassel
Show Accountant	Joy Brown
Production Stage Manager	Mark Dobrow
Stage Manager	Jason Trubitt
Assistant Stage Managers	Valerie Lau-Kee Lai, Alexis R. Prussack, Michael Wilhoite
Dance Captains	Brian Collier, Suzanne Hylenski
Production Assistants	Sarah Bierenbaum, Will O'Hare, Thomas Recktenwald

DISNEY ON BROADWAY PUBLICITY

Senior Publicist	Dennis Crowley
Publicist	Adriana Douzos
Associate Scenic Designer	Bryan Johnson
Scenic Design Associate	Rosalind Coombes
US Scenic Assistants	Dan Kuchar, Rachael Short-Janocko, Frank McCullough
UK Scenic Assistants	Al Turner, Charles Quiggin, Adam Wiltshire
Associate Costume Designer	Christine Rowland
Associate Costume Designer	Mitchell Bloom
Assistant Costume Designer	Patrick Wiley
Assistant Costume Designer	Rick Kelly
Associate Lighting Designer	Daniel Walker
Assistant Lighting Designer	Kristina Kloss
Lighting Programmer	Rob Halliday
Associate Sound Designer	John Shivers
Wig Creator	Angela Cobbin
Illusions Designer	Jim Steinmeyer
Technical Director	David Benken
Scenic Production Supervisor	Patrick Eviston
Assistant Technical Supervisor	Rosemarie Palombo
Production Carpenter	Drew Siccardi
Production Flyman	Michael Corbett
Foy Flying Operator	Raymond King
Automation	Steve Stackle, David Helck
Carpenters	Eddie Ackerman, Frank Alter, Brett Daley, Tony Goncalves, Gary Matarazzo
Production Electrician	James Maloney
Key Spot Operator	Joseph P. Garvey
Lighting Console Operator	Carlos Martinez
Pyro Operator	Kevin Strohmeyer
Automated Lighting Technician	Andy Catron
Assistant Electricians	Gregory Dunkin, Al Manganaro, Chris Passalacqua
Production Propman	Victor Amerling
Assistant Propman	Tim Abel
Props	Joe Bivone, John Saye, John Taccone, Gary Wilner
Production Sound Engineer	Andrew Keister

Mary Poppins

Sound Engineer .... Kurt Fischer
Sound Engineer .... Marie Renee Foucher
Sound Assistant .... Bill Romanello, Karen Zabinski
Production Wardrobe Supervisor .... Helen Toth
Assistant Wardrobe Supervisor .... Abbey Rayburn
Dressers .... Richard Byron, Vivienne Crawford,
Catherine Dee, Marjorie Denton,
Russell Easley, Ron Fleming,
Maya Hardin, Ginny Hounsell,
Kyle LaColla, Janet Netzke,
Tom Reiter, Elisa Richards,
Gary Seibert, Jean Steinlein
Production Hair Supervisor .... Gary Martori
Hair Dept Assistants .... Chris Calabrese,
Wanda Gregory, Kelly Reed
Production Makeup Supervisor .... Angela Johnson
Makeup Artist .... Amy Porter
Child Guardian .... Christina Huschle
UK Prop Coordinators .... Kathy Anders, Lisa Buckley
UK Wig Shop Assistant .... Beatrix Archer

Music Copyist .... Emily Grishman Music Preparation –
Emily Grishman/
Katharine Edmonds
Keyboard Programming .... Stuart Andrews

MUSIC COORDINATOR .... DAVID LAI

DIALECT & VOCAL COACH .... DEBORAH HECHT

Associate General Manager .... Alan Wasser
Production Co-Counsel .... F. Richard Pappas
Casting Directors .... Tara Rubin, Eric Woodall
Children's Tutoring .... On Location Education,
Muriel Kester
Physical Therapy .... Physioarts
Advertising .... Serino Coyne, Inc
Interactive Marketing .... Situation Marketing/
Damian Bazadona, Lisa Cecchini,
Jenn Elston
Web Design Consultant .... Joshua Noah
Production Photography .... Joan Marcus
Production Travel .... Jill L. Citron
Payroll Managers .... Anthony DeLuca, Cathy Guerra
Corporate Counsel .... Michael Rosenfeld

CREDITS

Scenery by Hudson Scenic, Inc.; Adirondack Studios, Inc.;
Proof Productions, Inc.; Scenic Technologies, a division of
Production Resource Group, LLC, New Windsor NY.
Drops by Scenic Arts. Automation by Hudson Scenic, Inc.
Lighting equipment by Hudson Sound & Light, LLC.
Lighting truss by Showman Fabricators, Inc. Sound
Equipment by Masque Sound. Projection equipment by
Sound Associates Inc. Magic props by William Kennedy of
Magic Effects. Props by The Spoon Group, LLC;
Moonboots Productions Inc.; Russell Beck Studio Ltd.
Costumes by Barbara Matera Ltd.; Parsons-Meares, Ltd.;
Eric Winterling; Werner Russold; Studio Rouge; Seamless
Costumes. Millinery by Rodney Gordon, Arnold Levine,
Lynne Mackey Studio. Shoes by T.O. Dey. Shirts by Cego.
Puppets by Puppet Heap. Flying by Foy. Ricola cough drops
courtesy of Ricola USA, Inc. Emergen-C super energy
booster provided by Alcer Corp. Makeup provided by
M•A•C.

MARY POPPINS rehearsed at the
New 42nd Street Studios.

THANKS

Thanks to Marcus Hall Props, Claire Sanderson, James Ince
and Sons, Great British Lighting, Bed Bazaar, The Wakefield
Brush Company, Heron and Driver, Ivo and Kay Covney,
Mike and Rosi Compton, Bebe Barrett, Charles Quiggin,
Nicola Kileen Textiles, Carl Roberts Shaw, David Scotcher
Interiors, Original Club Fenders Ltd., Lauren Pattison,
Robert Tatad.

FOR CAMERON MACKINTOSH LIMITED

Directors .... Nicholas Allott, Richard Johnston
Deputy Managing Director .... Robert Noble
Executive Producer & Casting Director ..... Trevor Jackson
Technical Director .... Nicholas Harris
Financial Controller .... Richard Knibb
Associate Producer .... Darinka Nenadovic
Sales & Marketing Manager .... David Dolman
Head of Musical Development .... Stephen Metcalfe
Production Associate .... Shidan Majidi

DISNEY THEATRICAL PRODUCTIONS

President .... Thomas Schumacher
EVP & Managing Director .... David Schrader
SVP & General Manager .... Alan Levey

Senior Vice President, Creative Affairs ..... Michele Steckler
Senior Vice President, International .... Ron Kollen
Vice President, Operations .... Dana Amendola
Vice President, Labor Relations .... Allan Frost
Vice President, Worldwide Publicity &
Communications .... Joe Quenqua
Vice President, Domestic Touring .... Jack Eldon
Vice President, Theatrical Licensing .... Steve Fickinger
Vice President, Human Resources .... June Heindel
Director, Domestic Touring .... Michael Buchanan
Director, Casting & Development .... Jennifer Rudin, CSA
Director, Publicity & Communications ...... Jay Carducci
Manager, Labor Relations .... Stephanie Cheek
Manager, Human Resources .... Jewel Neal
Manager, Publicity .... Ashok Sinha
Manager, Information Systems .... Scott Benedict
Senior Computer Support Analyst .... Kevin A. McGuire
Senior IT Support Analyst .... Andy Singh
IT/Business Analyst .... William Boudiette

Production

Executive Music Producer .... Chris Montan
Vice President, Physical Production .... John Tiggeloven
Director, International .... Michael Cassel
Senior Manager, Safety .... Canara Price
Manager, Physical Production .... Karl Chmielewski
Dramaturg & Literary Manager .... Ken Cerniglia

Marketing

Vice President, Broadway .... Andrew Flatt
Vice President, International .... Fiona Thomas
Director, Broadway .... Kyle Young
Director, Broadway .... Michele Groner
Director, Education & Outreach .... Peter Avery
Website Manager .... Eric W. Kratzer
Media Asset Manager .... Cara L. Moccia
Assistant Manager, Marketing .... Lauren Daghini

Sales

Director, National Sales .... Bryan Dockett
New Business Development
Manager .... Jacob Lloyd Kimbro
Manager, Sales & Ticketing .... Nick Falzon
Manager, Group Sales .... Juil Kim

Business and Legal Affairs

Senior Vice President .... Jonathan Olson
Vice President .... Robbin Kelley
Executive Director .... Harry S. Gold
Senior Counsel .... Seth Stuhl
Paralegal/Contract Administration .... Colleen Lober

Finance

VP Finance & Business Development .... Mario Iannetta
Director .... Joe McClafferty
Senior Manager, Finance .... Dana James
Manager, Finance .... John Fajardo
Manager, Production Accounting .... Liza Breslin
Production Accountants .... Joy Sims Brown, Nick Judge
Assistant Production Accountant .... Isander Rojas
Senior Business Planner .... Shaan Akbar
Senior Sales Analyst .... Liz Jurist Schwarzwalder

Administrative Staff

Shillae Anderson, Dusty Bennett, Sarah Bills, Dayle Bland,
Lindsay Braverman, Amy Caldamone, Michael Dei Cas,
Jessica Doina, Cristi Finn, Gregory Hanoian,
Abbie Harrison, Connie Jasper, Tom Kingsley, Cyntia Leo,
Lisa Mitchell, Ryan Pears, Roberta Risafi, Colleen Rosati,
David Scott, Benjy Shaw, Colleen Verbus, Kyle Wilson,
Jason Zammit

DISNEY THEATRICAL MERCHANDISE

Vice President .... Steven Downing
Operations Manager .... Shawn Baker
Merchandise Manager .... Neil Markman
Associate Buyer .... Violet Burlaza
Assistant Manager, Inventory .... Suzanne Jakel
Retail Supervisor .... Alyssa Somers
On-Site Retail Manager .... Seth Augspurger
On-Site Assistant Retail Manager .... Scott Koonce

Disney Theatrical Productions • 1450 Broadway
New York, NY 10018

guestmail@disneytheatrical.com

STAFF FOR THE NEW AMSTERDAM THEATRE

Theatre Manager .... John M. Loiacono
Guest Services Manager .... Kenneth Miller
Box Office Treasurer .... Andrew Grennan
Assistant Treasurer .... Anthony Oliva
Chief Engineer .... Frank Gibbons
Engineer .... Dan Milan
Security Manager .... Carl Lembo
Head Usher .... Susan Linder
Lobby Refreshments .... Sweet Concessions
Special thanks .... Sgt. Arthur J. Smarsch,
Det. Adam D'Amico

Mary Stuart

First Preview: March 30, 2009. Opened: April 19, 2009.
Still running as of May 31, 2009.

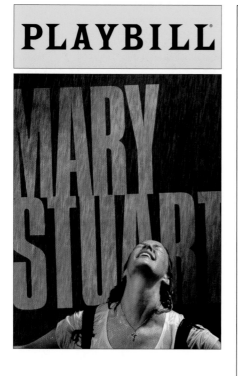

CAST
(in order of speaking)

Hanna Kennedy, *Mary's nurse* ....MARIA TUCCI
Sir Amias Paulet,
  Mary's jailer.........MICHAEL COUNTRYMAN
Mary Stuart, *Queen of Scotland*.....JANET McTEER
Mortimer,
  Paulet's nephew..........CHANDLER WILLIAMS
Lord Burleigh ....NICHOLAS WOODESON
Elizabeth, *Queen of England* ....HARRIET WALTER
Count Aubespine,
  French Ambassador...........MICHAEL RUDKO
Earl of Shrewsbury ....BRIAN MURRAY
Earl of Leicester ......JOHN BENJAMIN HICKEY
O'Kelly, *Mortimer's friend* ....ADAM GREER
Sir William Davison ....ROBERT STANTON
Melvil, *Mary's house steward* ...MICHAEL RUDKO
Courtiers, Officers and others ......TONY CARLIN,
  GUY PAUL, ADAM GREER

The action takes place between Fotheringhay Castle
and Elizabeth's Court.

2008-2009 AWARDS

TONY AWARD
Best Costume Design of a Play
(Anthony Ward)

DRAMA DESK AWARD
Outstanding Actress in a Play
(Janet McTeer)

⊛ BROADHURST THEATRE
235 West 44th Street
A Shubert Organization Theatre

Philip J. Smith, *Chairman*   **Robert E. Wankel,** *President*

Arielle Tepper Madover   Debra Black   Neal Street Productions/Matthew Byam Shaw
Scott M. Delman   Barbara Whitman   Jean Doumanian/Ruth Hendel
David Binder/CarlWend Productions/Spring Sirkin
Daryl Roth/James L. Nederlander/Chase Mishkin

present

The Donmar Warehouse Production

Janet McTeer   Harriet Walter

in

SCHILLER'S

MARY STUART

A new version by Peter Oswald

Jacqueline Antaramian   Tony Carlin   Michael Countryman
Monique Fowler   Adam Greer   John Benjamin Hickey
Guy Paul   Michael Rudko   Robert Stanton   Maria Tucci
Chandler Williams   Nicholas Woodeson

and

Brian Murray

Scenic and Costume Designer **Anthony Ward**

Lighting Designer **Hugh Vanstone**

Sound Designer **Paul Arditti**

Casting	UK Casting	Technical Supervisor	Production Stage Manager
Daniel Swee, CSA	**Anne McNulty**	**Aurora Productions**	**Barclay Stiff**
Marketing Director	Press Representative		General Management
Eric Schnall	**Boneau/Bryan-Brown**		**101 Productions, Ltd.**

Directed by

Phyllida Lloyd

Mary Stuart opened at The Donmar Warehouse on July 20, 2005.
Arielle Tepper Madover, Act Productions, Neal Street Productions, Matthew Byam Shaw transferred
The Donmar Warehouse Production to the Apollo Theatre, Opening Night October 19, 2005.
The producers wish to express their appreciation to Theatre Development Fund for its support of this production.

Original Production Sponsor
BARCLAYS CAPITAL

4/19/09

Photo by Joan Marcus

(L-R): Chandler Williams, Nicholas Woodeson, Tony Carlin, John Benjamin Hickey, Harriet Walter,
Robert Stanton, Adam Greer, Brian Murray, Guy Paul and Michael Countryman

Mary Stuart

Cast Continued

UNDERSTUDIES

For Aubespine/Melvil/O'Kelly/Courtier/Officer/
Earl of Leicester:
TONY CARLIN
For Elizabeth/Hanna Kennedy:
MONIQUE FOWLER
For Mortimer/Davison:
ADAM GREER
For Lord Burleigh/Paulet:
GUY PAUL
For Earl of Shrewsbury:
MICHAEL RUDKO
For Mary/Hanna Kennedy:
JACQUELINE ANTARAMIAN

Janet McTeer and Harriet Walter are appearing with
the permission of Actors' Equity Association.

Janet McTeer as imprisoned Mary Stuart, savoring a rare sojourn outdoors, where it is raining.

Photo by Joan Marcus

WARDROBE CREW
(L-R): Kristen Gardner, Kelly Saxon, Mickey Abbate

Photo by Barclay Stiff

Janet McTeer
Mary Stuart

Harriet Walter
Elizabeth

Brian Murray
Earl of Shrewsbury

Jacqueline Antaramian
u/s Mary, Hanna Kennedy

Tony Carlin
Courtier, Officer and Others

Michael Countryman
Sir Amias Paulet

Monique Fowler
u/s Elizabeth, Hanna Kennedy

Adam Greer
O'Kelly, Courtier, Officer and Others

John Benjamin Hickey
Earl of Leicester

Guy Paul
Courtier, Officer and Others

Michael Rudko
Count Aubespine/ Melvil

Robert Stanton
Sir William Davison

Maria Tucci
Hanna Kennedy

Chandler Williams
Mortimer

Nicholas Woodeson
Lord Burleigh

Friedrich Schiller
Playwright

Phyllida Lloyd
Director

Anthony Ward
Scenic and Costume Designer

Hugh Vanstone
Lighting Designer

Paul Arditti
Sound Designer

Mary Stuart

Seth Sklar-Heyn
Assistant Director

Arielle Tepper
Madover
Producer

Debra Black
Producer

Barbara Whitman
Producer

Jean Doumanian
Producer

Ruth Hendel
Producer

Carl Moellenberg,
Carlwend
Productions
Producer

Wendy Federman,
Carlwend
Productions
Producer

Spring Sirkin
Producer

Daryl Roth
Producer

James L.
Nederlander
Producer

Chase Mishkin
Producer

Michael Grandage,
Artistic Director,
The Donmar
Warehouse
Originating Theatre

FRONT OF HOUSE STAFF
Front Row (L-R): Julie Lugo, Debbie Eng, Karen Diaz, William Browne

Second Row (L-R): Lisa Boyd, Gillian Sheffler, Hugh Lynch, Doreen Barnard (Bartender)

Back Row: Tony Lopez

STAGE AND COMPANY MANAGEMENT
(L-R): Sean Free (Company Manager), Barclay Stiff (Production Stage Manager), Brandon Kahn (Stage Manager)

Photos by Barclay Stiff

HAIR SUPERVISOR
Carmel Vargyas

BOX OFFICE
(L-R): Clifford Cobb (Head Treasurer), Noreen Morgan (Assistant Treasurer) and Mike Lynch (Assistant Treasurer)

DOORMAN
Richard White

Mary Stuart

CREW
(L-R): Tim McWilliams, Bill Lewis, Charlie DeVerna, Ron Vitelli, Tom Lawrey, Brian Bullard, Andrew Meeker

STAFF FOR MARY STUART

GENERAL MANAGEMENT
101 PRODUCTIONS, LTD.
Wendy Orshan   Jeffrey Wilson
David Auster
Elie Landau

COMPANY MANAGER
Sean Free

GENERAL PRESS REPRESENTATIVE
BONEAU/BRYAN-BROWN
Adrian Bryan-Brown   Jim Byk
Rachel Stange

U.S. TECHNICAL SUPERVISION
AURORA PRODUCTIONS
Gene O'Donovan   W. Benjamin Heller II
Bethany Weinstein   Amy Merlino Coey
Melissa Mazdra   Laura Archer   Dana Hesch

HAIR DESIGNER
Campbell Young

Production Stage Manager	Barclay Stiff
Stage Manager	Brandon Kahn
Assistant Director	Seth Sklar-Heyn
Dialect Coach	Kate Wilson
Fight Director	Tom Schall
Associate Scenic Designer	Christine Peters
Associate Costume Designer	Daryl Stone
UK Costume Associate	Stephanie Arditti
Associate Lighting Designers	Philip Rosenberg, Jake DeGroot
Assistants to Lighting Designer	Zack Brown, Mike Megliola
Associate Sound Designer	Jeremy J. Lee
Associate Hair Designer	Luc Verschueren
Casting Associate	Camille Hickman

Production Electrician	Jon Lawson
Moving Light Programmer	Mike Hill
Production Sound	William Lewis
Production Props	Andrew Meeker
Prop Shopper	Denise J. Grillo
House Carpenter	Brian McGarty
House Electrician	Charlie DeVerna
House Flyman	Brian Bullard
House Properties	Ron Vitelli
Wardrobe Supervisor	Kelly Saxon
Dressers	Mickey Abbate, Kristen Gardner
Hair Supervisor	Carmel Vargyas

Production Assistant	Eileen Kelly
Assistant to Ms. Madover	Holly Ferguson

Legal Counsel	Lazarus & Harris, LLP/ Scott R. Lazarus, Esq., Robert C. Harris, Esq.,
Accountant	Fried & Kowgios
Comptroller	Galbraith & Co Inc./ Tabitha Falcone
Advertising	SPOTCO/ Drew Hodges, Jim Edwards, Tom Greenwald Y Darius Suyama, Pete Duffy
101 Productions, Ltd. Staff	Denys Baker, Mark Barna, Beth Blitzer, Katharine Croke, Clinton Kennedy, Michael Rudd, Mary Six Rupert, Samara Ungar, Hannah Wachtel
101 Productions, Ltd. Intern	Samara Harand
Banking	City National Bank/ Anne McSweeney
Insurance	Ventura Brokerage, Inc./ Christine Sadofsky
Immigration	Traffic Control Group/ David King Visa Consultants/Lisa Carr
Theatre Displays	King Displays, Inc.
Payroll Services	Castellana Services, Inc.
Production Photographer	Joan Marcus
Website Design	Dotmeta/Yujin Asai
Opening Night Coordinator	The Lawrence Company/ Michael P. Lawrence

FOR THE DONMAR WAREHOUSE

Artistic Director	Michael Grandage
Executive Producer	James Bierman
Acting General Manager	Patrick Gracey
PA to the Executive	Miriam Green
Casting and Creative Associate	Anne McNulty
Resident Casting Assistant	Vicky Richardson
Development Director	Kate Mitchell
Development Manager	Deborah Lewis
Development Officer	Rosie Dalling
Development Administrator	Nicola Stockley
Marketing Manager	Jonathan Aplin
Press Representative	Kate Morley for Blueprint PR
Marketing & Press Assistant	Kim Savage
Office Administrator	Frankie Bridges
General Assistant	Lara DeLaney
Deputy Production Manager	Kate West
Head of Wardrobe	Tansy Blaik-Kelly
Deputy Head of Wardrobe	Morag Pirrie
Associate Directors	Douglas Hodge, Jamie Lloyd

Associate Director USA	Seth Sklar-Heyn
Resident Assistant Director	Paul Hart
Education Associates	Dominic Francis, Sophie Watkiss

CREDITS
Scenery by Souvenir Scenery UK and Showman Fabricators. Lighting by PRG. Sound equipment by Masque Sound. Rain effect by Showman Fabricators and Water Sculptures, UK. Mr. Murray's suit by Gilberto Tailors. Wigs made by Campbell Young. Millinery by Arnold Levine.

SPECIAL THANKS
Coffee makers generously provided by Keurig.

Mary Stuart rehearsed at the
New 42nd Street Studios

www.marystuartonbroadway.com

THE SHUBERT ORGANIZATION, INC.
Board of Directors

Philip J. Smith Chairman	**Robert E. Wankel** President
Wyche Fowler, Jr.	**John W. Kluge**
Lee J. Seidler	**Michael I. Sovern**

Stuart Subotnick

Elliot Greene Chief Financial Officer	**David Andrews** Senior Vice President – Shubert Ticketing
Juan Calvo Vice President and Controller	**John Darby** Vice President – Facilities
Peter Entin Vice President – Theatre Operations	**Charles Flateman** Vice President – Marketing
Anthony LaMattina Vice President – Audit & Production Finance	**Brian Mahoney** Vice President – Ticket Sales

D.S. Moynihan
Vice President – Creative Projects

House Manager	Hugh Barnett

Mary Stuart
SCRAPBOOK

Correspondent: Barclay Stiff, Stage Manager

Favorite Moment During Each Performance: There were several brilliant moments in *Mary Stuart*. One of the best was the rain sequence that starts Act III. It was a spectacular moment seeing a heavy rainstorm fill the entire stage. Janet and Maria were the lucky (or unlucky) ones that had to run into the pouring rain and perform an intense 14-minute scene. They would get drenched from head to toe nightly. Thankfully the water was warm!

In-Theatre Gathering Place: Janet's dressing room was the most popular place that the company liked to hang out. It was on stage level and was very convenient for the cast to retreat to during the show. Janet was always so welcoming and truly loved catching up with everyone in the company.

Off-Site Hangout: The cast were frequent customers at Angus McIndoe across the street. Our director Phyllida Lloyd always joked that we should just schedule all of our notes sessions at the bar.

Favorite Snack Foods: Jolly Ranchers and Mini Twix were quite popular. So much so we decided to try to go two weeks without them. We failed miserably!

Mascot: Bothwell, the stuffed hamster. This show would not have worked without his guidance and support.

Favorite Therapy: Altoids and Ricola were in constant supply. The cast also fell in love with the Keurig single-brew coffee makers. Having several coffee/tea options proved to be quite popular with the cast and crew.

Record Number of Cell Phone Rings: *Mary Stuart* had to be the quietest show of the season. We had several intimate scenes that were so quiet that you could hear a pin drop. Any noise NOT from the show was painful and drove the cast crazy. Cell phone rings were the absolute worst. The most memorable one occurred as Mary (Janet) was confessing her sins just before she would go to her death. Janet patiently waited for the SIX rings to finish. She never skipped a beat. A total pro!

Fastest Costume Change: Tony Carlin had the most costume changes in the show. All of them were pretty quick.

Busiest Day at the Box Office: The day after our opening night. We received some really great reviews!

Who Wore the Heaviest/Hottest Costumes: Janet and Harriet wore full period costumes. They deserve a medal for putting up with the oversized dresses and tight, tight, tight corsets. They looked amazing!

Company In-Jokes: "Top that, Jane Fonda!"

Coolest Thing About Being in This Show: Having a 200-year-old play profoundly resonate with a NYC audience in 2009. This is a credit to the amazing ensemble of actors and Phyllida Lloyd's razor sharp direction. It truly does not get much better than that!

1. Curtain call on opening night.
2. Harriet Walter having fun during a photo shoot.
3. Janet McTeer and Walter horse around while trying on gowns for the Tony Awards.
4. Cast member Nicholas Woodeson at the opening night party at Tavern on the Green.
5. Director Phyllida Lloyd at the Broadhurst Theatre for the premiere.

Monty Python's Spamalot

First Preview: February 14, 2005. Opened: March 17, 2005.
Closed January 11, 2009 after 34 Previews and 1575 Performances.

PLAYBILL

CAST OF CHARACTERS

(in order of appearance)

Historian, Not Dead Fred, French Guard,
Minstrel, Prince Herbert ....TOM DECKMAN
Mayor, Patsy, Guard 2 ....DAVID HIBBARD
King Arthur ....MICHAEL SIBERRY
Sir Robin, Guard 1,
Brother Maynard ....CLAY AIKEN
Sir Lancelot, The French Taunter, Knight of Ni,
Tim the Enchanter ....RICK HOLMES
Sir Dennis Galahad, The Black Knight,
Prince Herbert's Father ....BRADLEY DEAN
Dennis's Mother, Sir Bedevere,
Concorde ....WALLY DUNN
The Lady of the Lake ....MERLE DANDRIDGE
Sir Not Appearing, Monk ......PATRICK WETZEL
Nun ....MATTHEW CROWLE
God ....JOHN CLEESE
French Guards ....THOMAS CANNIZZARO,
GAVIN LODGE
Minstrels............EMILY HSU, GAVIN LODGE,
BRIAN J. MARCUM
Sir Bors ....BRIAN J. MARCUM

ENSEMBLE

THOMAS CANNIZZARO,
MATTHEW CROWLE, NIKKI DELLA PENTA,
ANDREW FITCH, JENNY HILL, EMILY HSU,
BETH JOHNSON, GAVIN LODGE,
BRIAN J. MARCUM, ARIEL REID,
VANESSA SONON, PATRICK WETZEL

Continued on next page

The Playbill Broadway Yearbook 2008-2009

SAM S. SHUBERT THEATRE

225 West 44th Street
A Shubert Organization Theatre

Gerald Schoenfeld, *Chairman*   Philip J. Smith, *President*

Robert E. Wankel, *Executive Vice President*

Boyett Ostar Productions The Shubert Organization
Arielle Tepper Stephanie McClelland/Lawrence Horowitz Elan V. McAllister/Allan S. Gordon
Independent Presenters Network Roy Furman GRS Associates
Jam Theatricals TGA Entertainment Live Nation
present

Monty Python's

SPAMALOT

Book & Lyrics by   Music by
Eric Idle   John Du Prez & Eric Idle

A new musical lovingly ripped off from the motion picture
"Monty Python and the Holy Grail"
from the original screenplay by
Graham Chapman, John Cleese, Terry Gilliam, Eric Idle, Terry Jones, Michael Palin
starring

Michael Siberry   Merle Dandridge
Clay Aiken

also starring

Tom Deckman   Rick Holmes   Bradley Dean   Wally Dunn   David Hibbard

with

Piper Lindsay Arpan Thomas Cannizzaro Matthew Crowle Nikki Della Penta Mika Duncan
Andrew Fitch Jenny Hill Emily Hsu Beth Johnson Kristie Kerwin Gavin Lodge Brian J. Marcum
Michael O'Donnell Ariel Reid Pamela Remler Vanessa Sonon Rick Spaans Patrick Wetzel Lee A. Wilkins

Set & Costume Design by **Tim Hatley**	Lighting Design by **Hugh Vanstone**

Sound Design by **Acme Sound Partners**	Hair & Wig Design by **David Brian Brown**	Special Effects Design by **Gregory Meeh**	Projection Design by **Elaine J. McCarthy**
Music Director/Vocal Arrangements **Todd Ellison**	Orchestrations by **Larry Hochman**	Music Arrangements by **Glen Kelly**	Music Coordinator **Michael Keller**
Associate Directors **Peter Lawrence** **BT McNicholl**	Associate Choreographer **Darlene Wilson**	Dance Supervisor **Scott Taylor**	Production Stage Manager **Frank Lombardi**
Casting **Tara Rubin Casting**	Press Representative **Boneau/Bryan-Brown**	Marketing **HHC Marketing**	
General Management **101 Productions, Ltd.**	Production Management **Gene O'Donovan**	Associate Producers **Randi Grossman** **Tisch/Avnet Financial**	

Choreography by
Casey Nicholaw

Directed by
Mike Nichols

GRAMMY® - WINNING CAST ALBUM
AVAILABLE ON DECCA BROADWAY

10/1/08

(L-R): Clay Aiken, Rick Holmes, Bradley Dean, Wally Dunn and Michael Siberry sing "All for One."

Photo by Joan Marcus

217

Monty Python's Spamalot

SCENES & MUSICAL NUMBERS

ACT I

Overture
Scene 1: The Mighty Portcullis
Scene 2: Moose Village
    "Fisch Schlapping Song" ....Historian, Mayor, Villagers
Scene 3: Mud Castle
    "King Arthur's Song" ....King Arthur, Patsy
Scene 4: Plague Village
    "I Am Not Dead Yet" ....Not Dead Fred, Lance, Robin and Bodies
Scene 5: Mud Village
Scene 6: The Lady of the Lake and The Laker Girls
    "Come With Me" ....King Arthur, Lady of the Lake and Laker Girls
    "The Song That Goes Like This" ....Sir Galahad and Lady of the Lake
Scene 7: The Knights
    "All for One" ....King Arthur, Patsy, Sir Robin, Sir Lancelot,
                                    Sir Galahad and Sir Bedevere
Scene 8: Camelot
    "Knights of the Round Table" ....Lady of the Lake, King Arthur, Patsy,
                               Sir Robin, Sir Lancelot, Sir Galahad,
                           Sir Bedevere and The Camelot Dancers
    "The Song That Goes Like This (Reprise)" ....Lady of the Lake
Scene 9: The Feet of God
Scene 10: Find Your Grail
    "Find Your Grail" ....Lady of the Lake, King Arthur, Patsy, Sir Robin,
                            Sir Lancelot, Sir Galahad, Sir Bedevere,
                                   Knights and Grail Girls
Scene 11: The French Castle
    "Run Away" ....French Taunters, King Arthur, Patsy, Sir Robin,
                            Sir Lancelot, Sir Galahad, Sir Bedevere,
                            French Guards and French Citizens

ACT II

Scene 1: The Mighty Portcullis
Scene 2: A Very Expensive Forest
    "Always Look on the Bright Side of Life" ....Patsy, King Arthur, Knights and
                                        The Knights of Ni
Scene 3: Sir Robin and His Minstrels
    "Brave Sir Robin" ....Sir Robin and Minstrels
Scene 4: The Black Knight
Scene 5: Another Part of the Very Expensive Forest
    "You Won't Succeed on Broadway" ....Sir Robin and Ensemble
Scene 6: A Hole in the Universe
    "The Diva's Lament" ....Lady of the Lake
Scene 7: Prince Herbert's Chamber
    "Where Are You?" ....Prince Herbert
    "Here Are You" ....Prince Herbert
    "His Name Is Lancelot" ....Sir Lancelot, Prince Herbert and Ensemble
Scene 8: Yet Another Part of the Very Expensive Forest
    "I'm All Alone" ....King Arthur, Patsy and Knights
    "The Song That Goes Like This (Reprise)" ....Lady of the Lake and King Arthur
Scene 9: The Killer Rabbit
    "The Holy Grail" ....King Arthur, Patsy, Sir Robin, Sir Lancelot,
                            Sir Galahad, Sir Bedevere and Knights
Finale
    "Find Your Grail Finale - Medley" ....The Company

---

Cast Continued

STANDBYS
MIKA DUNCAN, MICHAEL O'DONNELL

UNDERSTUDIES
THOMAS CANNIZZARO,
MATTHEW CROWLE, JENNY HILL,
EMILY HSU, GAVIN LODGE,
VANESSA SONON, LEE A. WILKINS

SWINGS
PIPER LINDSAY ARPAN, KRISTIE KERWIN,
PAMELA REMLER, RICK SPAANS,
LEE A. WILKINS

DANCE CAPTAINS
LEE A. WILKINS, BETH JOHNSON

ORCHESTRA
Conductor: TODD ELLISON
Associate Conductor: ANTONY GERALIS
Assistant Conductor: RANDY COHEN
Concertmaster: ANN LABIN
Violins: MAURA GIANNINI, MING YEH
Viola: RICHARD BRICE
Cello: DIANE BARERE
Reeds: KEN DYBISZ, ALDEN BANTA
Lead Trumpet: CRAIG JOHNSON
Trumpet: ANTHONY GORRUSO
Trombone: TIM ALBRIGHT
French Horn: THERESA MACDONNELL
Keyboard 1: RANDY COHEN
Keyboard 2 and Accordion: ANTONY GERALIS
Guitars: SCOTT KUNEY
Bass: DAVE KUHN
Drums: SEAN McDANIEL
Percussion: DAVE MANCUSO

Music Coordinator: MICHAEL KELLER
Music Copying:
EMILY GRISHMAN MUSIC PREPARATION/
EMILY GRISHMAN, KATHARINE EDMONDS

Photo by Joan Marcus

(L-R): Bradley Dean as Sir Galahad and Merle Dandridge as The Lady of the Lake.

Monty Python's Spamalot

Michael Siberry
King Arthur

Merle Dandridge
The Lady of the Lake

Clay Aiken
*Sir Robin, Guard 1,
Brother Maynard*

Tom Deckman
*Historian,
Not Dead Fred,
French Guard,
Minstrel,
Prince Herbert*

Rick Holmes
*Sir Lancelot,
The French Taunter,
Knight of Ni,
Tim the Enchanter*

Bradley Dean
*Sir Dennis Galahad,
The Black Knight,
Prince Herbert's
Father*

Wally Dunn
*Dennis's Mother,
Sir Bedevere,
Concorde*

David Hibbard
*Mayor, Patsy,
Guard 2*

Piper Lindsay Arpan
Swing

Thomas Cannizzaro
*French Guard,
Ensemble,
Fight Captain*

John Cleese
God

Matthew Crowle
Nun, Ensemble

Nikki Della Penta
Ensemble

Mika Duncan
*Standby for Arthur,
Lancelot, Galahad,
Robin, Bedevere*

Andrew Fitch
Ensemble

Jenny Hill
Ensemble

Emily Hsu
Minstrel, Ensemble

Beth Johnson
*Ensemble, Assistant
Dance Captain*

Kristie Kerwin
Swing

Gavin Lodge
*French Guard,
Minstrel, Ensemble*

Brian J. Marcum
*Minstrel, Sir Bors,
Ensemble*

Michael O'Donnell
Standby

Ariel Reid
Ensemble

Pamela Remler
Swing

Vanessa Sonon
Ensemble

Rick Spaans
Swing

Patrick Wetzel
*Sir Not Appearing,
Monk, Ensemble*

Lee A. Wilkins
*Swing,
Dance Captain*

Ed Nelson
Company Manager

Eric Idle and John Du Prez
Book, Lyrics and Music; Composer

Mike Nichols
Director

Casey Nicholaw
Choreographer

Tim Hatley
*Set & Costume
Design*

Hugh Vanstone
Lighting Design

Monty Python's Spamalot

Tom Clark, Mark Menard and Nevin Steinberg,
Acme Sound Partners
Sound Design

David Brian Brown
Wig & Hair Design

Gregory Meeh
*Special Effects
Design*

Todd Ellison
*Musical Director/
Vocal Arranger*

Larry Hochman
Orchestrations

Michael Keller
Music Coordinator

Peter Lawrence
Associate Director

BT McNicholl
Associate Director

Tara Rubin Casting
Casting

Bill Haber,
OSTAR Enterprises
Producer

Bob Boyett
Producer

Gerald Schoenfeld,
Chairman,
The Shubert
Organization
Producer

Philip J. Smith,
President,
The Shubert
Organization
Producer

Arielle Tepper
Producer

Stephanie P.
McClelland
Producer

Lawrence Horowitz,
M.D.
Producer

Elan V. McAllister
Producer

Allan S. Gordon
Producer

Roy Furman
Producer

Morton Swinsky,
GRS Associates
Producer

Arny Granat,
Jam Theatricals Ltd.
Producer

Steve Traxler,
Jam Theatricals Ltd.
Producer

Steve Tisch,
Tisch-Avnet Financial
Associate Producer

Jon Avnet,
Tisch-Avnet Financial
Associate Producer

Jonathan Brody
*French Guard,
Ensemble*

Callie Carter
*Swing,
Dance Captain*

Stephen Collins
King Arthur

Kevin Covert
*Sir Not Appearing,
Monk, Ensemble*

Jennifer Frankel
Ensemble

Lisa Gajda
Ensemble

Jonathan Hadary
King Arthur

Anthony Holds
Standby

Drew Lachey
*Mayor, Patsy,
Guard 2*

Monty Python's Spamalot

Marin Mazzie
The Lady of the Lake

Abbey O'Brien
Ensemble

Robert Petkoff
*Sir Robin, Guard 1,
Brother Maynard*

Steve Rosen
*Dennis's Mother,
Sir Bedevere,
Concorde*

Billy Sprague, Jr.
Swing

Hannah Waddingham
The Lady of the Lake

Brandi Wooten
Ensemble

Callie Carter
*Minstrel, Ensemble,
Dance Captain*

Kevin Crewell
*Sir Not Appearing,
Monk, Ensemble*

Jennifer Frankel
Ensemble

Stephanie Gibson
Ensemble

Martin Moran
*Sir Robin, Guard 1,
Brother Maynard*

Beth Johnson Nicely
*Ensemble,
Dance Captain*

Billy Sprague, Jr.
*Swing,
Dance Captain*

FRONT OF HOUSE STAFF
Front Row (L-R): Joanne Blessington, Aspacia Savas, Giovanni LaDuke, Merida Colon, Katherine Benoit, Erin O'Donnell

Second Row (L-R): Delia Pozo, Frank Sanabria, Stephen Ivelja, Tomas Ortiz, Linda Engh, Elvis Caban, Paul Rodriguez

Third Row (L-R): Mickey Fisher, Michael DiLiberto, Farin Schlussel, Gem Trotta, Brian Gaynair

Back Row (L-R): Roberto Aruajo, Melissa Maniglia, Gino Gianoli, Kayeryna Shyrkavets

Monty Python's Spamalot
SCRAPBOOK

The cast warms up for the September 2008 "Broadway on Broadway" event.

Correspondent: Thomas Cannizzaro, "French Guard, Ensemble, Etc."

Most Exciting Celebrity Visitor: Robin Williams said, "You are all so @#%!ing funny! Every last one o' you mother!#@$%#$."

"Gypsy of the Year" Sketch: Pam Remler, our original Dance Captain/Swing, put it together. It was a wonderful gathering of *Spamalot* performers from four different companies!

Most Roles in This Show: Our male standbys performed five roles each.

Most Performances in This Show: Thomas Cannizzaro: 1474.5, with one month to go.

Special Backstage Rituals: Beth's lingerie pose for Emily.

Favorite Moment During Each Performance: Ni Knight Improv: "I'm the real father of Sarah Palin's daughter's baby."

Favorite In-Theatre Gathering Place: Stage Managers' office. As long as Frank approved it!

Favorite Off-Site Hangout: Rick Holmes chooses Café Un Deux Trois.

Favorite Snack Foods: Buckeyes and doughnuts.

Mascots: Monty, Shubert, Madison, Buster, Stewy, Razor (all adopted during the run).

Favorite Therapy: Big Black Dong (nickname for foam roller).

Memorable Ad-Lib: "I use it to cover a rash."—Wally Dunn

Memorable Press Encounter: Promosexual!

Memorable Stage Door Fan Encounter: Shockwave and Darryl!

What Did You Think of the Web Buzz on Your Show: There was BUZZ?!

Latest Audience Arrival: January 12th's audience.

Fastest Costume Changes: Mayor of Finland to Patsy. Also, Rick Spaans into costume when Thomas left after the second number for the birth of his daughter.

Company Legend: BT.

Heaviest/Hottest Costumes: Female ensemble as the Ni Knights.

Who Wore the Least: Female ensemble as showgirls.

Catchphrase Only the Company Would Recognize: "Minots!"

Sweethearts Within the Company: Monk and Nun.

Best In-House Parody Lyrics: "Try your luck at the rest stop."

Memorable Directorial Note: "He's a Necrophiliac." Killing Babies.

Nicknames: "Dolores," "Droppo," "Boo"

Ghostly Encounters Backstage: Eric Idle in the last year.

Coolest Thing About Being in This Show: It's Monty Python!

Other Memories: Saturday Night on Broadway Sparkle Award, a.k.a. the SNOB. Four years, three Tonys, six kings, five ladies, countless knights and girls. It was a long, wonderful ride. We will all miss it dearly!

STAFF FOR *SPAMALOT*

GENERAL MANAGEMENT
101 PRODUCTIONS, LTD.
Wendy Orshan Jeffrey M. Wilson
David Auster

COMPANY MANAGER
Edward Nelson

GENERAL PRESS REPRESENTATIVE
BONEAU/BRYAN-BROWN
Adrian Bryan-Brown   Jackie Green
Aaron Meier   Christine Olver

CASTING
TARA RUBIN CASTING
Tara Rubin, CSA, Eric Woodall, CSA
Laura Schutzel, CSA, Merri Sugarman, CSA
Rebecca Carfagna, Paige Blansfield, Dale Brown

PRODUCTION MANAGEMENT
AURORA PRODUCTIONS, INC.
Gene O'Donovan
W. Benjamin Heller II   Bethany Weinstein
Melissa Mazdra   Hilary Austin

Fight Director ....**David DeBesse**

Make-Up Designer ....**Joseph A. Campayno**

Production Stage Manager ....Frank Lombardi
Stage Manager ....Jim Woolley
Stage Managers ....Allison Lee, Kenneth J. McGee
Associate Company Manager ....Katharine Croke
Dance Supervisor ....Scott Taylor
Dance Captain ....Lee A. Wilkins
Assistant Dance Captain ....Beth Johnson
Fight Captain ....Thomas Cannizzaro
Assistant to Mike Nichols ....Colleen O'Donnell
Associate Scenic Designer ....Paul Weimer
Assistant Scenic Designers ....Raul Abrego,
Derek Stenborg

Monty Python's Spamalot

UK Assistant Designer ....Andy Edwards
Associate Costume Designer ....Scott Traugott
Costume Associate ....Ilona Somogyi
Assistant Costume Designers ....Cory Ching,
Robert J. Martin
Costume Assistant ....Jessica Wegener
Magic Consultant ....Marshall Magoon
Puppetry Consultant ....Michael Curry
Associate Lighting Designer ....Philip S. Rosenberg
Assistant Lighting Designer ....John Viesta
Moving Light Programmer.....................Laura Frank
Assistant Sound Designer ....Sten Severson
Associate Special Effects Designer ....Vivien Leone
Associate Projection Designer ....Gareth Smith
Assistant Projection Designers ....Ariel Sachter-Zeltzer,
Jake Pinholster
Projection Programmers......................Randy Briggs,
Paul Vershbow
Projection Illustrator ....Julianne Kroboth
Production Carpenter ....Hank Hale
Assistant Carpenters...................Adam Bair, Erik Yans
Production Electrician ....Michael S. LoBue
Head Electrician ....Michael Hyman
Assistant Electricians ....Karen Z. Hyman, Neal Schatz
Production Props Supervisor ....Will Sweeney
Assistant Props ....James Cariot
Props Shopper..............................Maggie Kuypers
Sound ....John Dory
Assistant Sound ....Jim Wilkinson
Wardrobe Supervisor ....Linda Lee
Assistant Wardrobe Supervisor ....Sonya Wysocki
Dressers ....Jenny Barnes, Carli Beardsley,
Meredith Benson, Douglas Earl,
Dan Foss, Stephanie Luette,
Shannon McDowell, Shannon D. Quinones,
Andrea Roberts, James A. Roy
Hair Supervisor ....Michele Rutter
Assistant Hair Supervisor ....Mary Kay Yeserski-Bondoc
Hairdresser ....Ron Mack
Hair and Makeup Stylist ....Lisa Weiss
Vocal Coach ....Kate Wilson
Rehearsal Pianists ....Sue Anderson, Glen Kelly,
Antony Geralis
Rehearsal Drummer ....Sean McDaniel
Electronic Music Programming ....James Abbott
Production Associate ....Lisa Gilbar
Production Assistants ....Chad Lewis,
Mary Kathryn Flynt
Associate Producer
for Ostar Enterprises ....Rachel Neuburger
Executive Assistant to Mr. Haber ....Theresa Pisanelli
Assistant to Mr. Haber ....Kristen Jackson
Assistant to Mr. Boyett ....Diane Murphy
Assistant to Messrs. Granat & Traxler ....Katrine Heintz
Legal Counsel ....Lazarus & Harris LLP
Scott Lazarus, Esq.
Robert C. Harris, Esq.
Accountant ....Rosenberg, Neuwirth, & Kuchner, CPAs
Christopher Cacace
Comptroller ....Jana Jevnikar
Advertising ....Serino Coyne
Angelo Desimini, Tom Callahan, Steve Knight
Marketing ....HHC Marketing/
Hugh Hysell, Matt Sicoli,
Candice Beckmann

Marketing Assistants ....Michael Redman,
Nicole Pando, James Hewson,
Kayla Kuzbel, Brad Renner
101 Productions Director of Finance/
Marketing ....Elie Landau
101 Productions, Ltd. Staff ....Denys Baker,
Mark Barna, Beth Blitzer,
Danielle Fazio, Clifton Kennedy,
Heidi Neven, Julie Anne Nolan,
Mary Six Rupert, Samara Ungar,
Hannah Wachtel
Press Associates ....Chris Boneau, Jim Byk,
Brandi Cornwell, Matt Polk,
Susanne Tighe
Press Assistants ....Ian Bjorklund, Kelly Guiod,
Jessica Johnson, Kevin Jones,
Amy Kass, Joe Perrotta,
Linnae Petruzzelli, Matt Ross,
Heath Schwartz
Banking ....City National Bank/Anne McSweeney
Insurance ....DeWitt Stern, Inc./Jennifer Brown
Travel ....Altour International, Inc./Melissa Casal
Housing ....Road Rebel Entertainment Touring
Alison Muffitt
Opening Night Coordinator ....Tobak-Dantchik
Suzanne Tobak, Michael Lawrence
Physical Therapy ....PhysioArts/Jennifer Green
Orthopedist ....David S. Weiss, M.D.
Immigration ....Traffic Control Group, Inc./
David King
Theatre Displays ....King Displays, Inc.
Merchandising ....Max Merchandising, LLC/
Shopalot, LLC
Merchandise Manager ....David Eck
Production Photographer ....Joan Marcus
Payroll Services ....Castellana Services, Inc.

Finnish program by Michael Palin.

www.MontyPythonsSpamalot.com

CREDITS

Scenery and scenic automation by Hudson Scenic Studio,
Inc. Additional scenery by Scenic Art Studios, Inc., Chicago
Scenic Studios, Hawkeye Scenic Studios. Lighting equip-
ment from Fourth Phase. Sound equipment from PRG
Audio. Costumes executed by Barbara Matera Ltd.; Carelli
Costumes; Euro Co Costumes; Parsons-Meares, Ltd.;
Tricorne, Inc. Additional costumes by Costume Armour,
Inc., John Kristiansen; Western Costumes. Shoes by T.O.
Dey; LaDuca Shoes NYC; Capri Shoes; Capezio. Millinery
by Lynne Mackey Studio, Rodney Gordon. Hair by Ray
Marston Wig Studio Ltd., Bob Kelly Wig Creations.
Selected makeup furnished by M•A•C. Props by The Spoon
Group LLC; The Rabbit's Choice; Cigar Box Studios, Inc.;
Costume Armour, Inc.; Jerard Studio; Gilbert Center;
Margaret Cusack; Elizabeth Debbout; Erin Edmister;
George Fenmore. Some specialty props and costumes
furnished by Museum Replicas Inc. Piano from Ortigara's
Musicville, Inc. Spamahorn created and provided by
Dominic Derasse. Video projection system provided by
Scharff-Weisberg, Inc. Video projection services by
Vermillion Border Productions. Flying by Foy. Black Knight
illusion executed by Entertainment Design & Fabrication.
Spam cam and film furnished by Polaroid. Lozenges
by Ricola.

SPAM® is a registered trademark of
Hormel Foods LLC.

Air travel consideration furnished by Orbitz®.

All songs published by Rutsongs Music & Ocean Music
Ltd., ©2004. All rights Reserved, except songs from Monty
Python & the Holy Grail, published by EMI/Python
(Monty) Pictures as follows: "Finland," music and lyrics by
Michael Palin; "Knights of the Round Table," music by Neil
Innes, lyrics by Graham Chapman and John Cleese; "Brave
Sir Robin," music by Neil Innes, lyrics by Eric Idle; and
"Always Look on the Bright Side of Life," music and lyrics
by Eric Idle from Life of Brian, published by Python
(Monty) Pictures.

SPAMALOT
rehearsed at New 42nd Street Studios

SPECIAL THANKS
Bill Link, Devin Burgess,
Veronica DeMartini, John Malakoff

Exclusive stock and amateur stage performing rights are represented by Theatrical Rights Worldwide, 1359 Broadway,
Suite 914, New York, NY 10018, www.theatricalrights.com.

Next to Normal

First Preview: March 27, 2009. Opened: April 15, 2009.
Still running as of May 31, 2009.

PLAYBILL®

next to normal

CAST

(in alphabetical order)

Henry .... ADAM CHANLER-BERAT
Natalie .... JENNIFER DAMIANO
Dr. Madden/Dr. Fine .... LOUIS HOBSON
Diana .... ALICE RIPLEY
Dan .... J. ROBERT SPENCER
Gabe .... AARON TVEIT

UNDERSTUDIES

For Dan, Dr. Madden/Dr. Fine: MICHAEL BERRY
For Natalie: MEGHANN FAHY
For Diana: JESSICA PHILLIPS
For Gabe, Henry: TIM YOUNG

BAND

Conductor/Piano: CHARLIE ALTERMAN
Violin/Keyboard: YUIKO KAMAKARI
Cello: BENJAMIN KALB
Guitars: ERIC DAVIS
Bass: MICHAEL BLANCO
Drums/Percussion: DAMIEN BASSMAN

Drum and Additional Percussion Arrangements by
DAMIEN BASSMAN

Additional Guitar Arrangements by
MICHAEL AARONS

Music Coordinator: MICHAEL KELLER
Copyist: EMILY GRISHMAN
MUSIC PREPARATION

☽ BOOTH THEATRE

222 West 45th Street
A Shubert Organization Theatre

Philip J. Smith, *Chairman*   **Robert E. Wankel,** *President*

DAVID STONE
JAMES L. NEDERLANDER   BARBARA WHITMAN   PATRICK CATULLO
SECOND STAGE THEATRE
Carole Rothman   Ellen Richard

present

ALICE RIPLEY   J. ROBERT SPENCER

next to normal

music by
TOM KITT

book and lyrics by
BRIAN YORKEY

also starring

AARON TVEIT
JENNIFER DAMIANO
ADAM CHANLER-BERAT   LOUIS HOBSON

MICHAEL BERRY   MEGHANN FAHY   JESSICA PHILLIPS   TIM YOUNG

| set design by | costume design by | lighting design by | sound design by |
| MARK WENDLAND | JEFF MAHSHIE | KEVIN ADAMS | BRIAN RONAN |

orchestrations by
MICHAEL STAROBIN and TOM KITT

| vocal arrangements | music director | music coordinator |
| ANNMARIE MILAZZO | CHARLIE ALTERMAN | MICHAEL KELLER |

| casting | press representative |
| TELSEY + COMPANY | BARLOW • HARTMAN |

| production stage manager | company manager | technical supervisor | general management |
| JUDITH SCHOENFELD | MARC BORSAK | LARRY MORLEY | 321 THEATRICAL MANAGEMENT |

musical staging by
SERGIO TRUJILLO

directed by
MICHAEL GREIF

The World Premiere of **next to normal** was presented by Second Stage Theatre on February 13, 2008.
next to normal was subsequently presented at Arena Stage, Washington D.C. in November 2008.
The producers wish to express their appreciation to Theatre Development Fund for its support of this production.
Original Broadway Cast Recording on GHOSTLIGHT RECORDS

4/15/09

(L-R): Alice Ripley,
Aaron Tveit and
J. Robert Spencer

Photo by Joan Marcus

Next to Normal

Alice Ripley
Diana

J. Robert Spencer
Dan

Aaron Tveit
Gabe

Jennifer Damiano
Natalie

Adam Chanler-Berat
Henry

Louis Hobson
Dr. Madden/Dr. Fine

Michael Berry
*u/s Dan,
Dr. Madden/Dr. Fine*

Meghann Fahy
u/s Natalie

Jessica Phillips
*u/s Diana,
Dance Captain*

Timothy Young
u/s Gabe/Henry

Tom Kitt
*Composer/
Co-Orchestrator*

Brian Yorkey
Librettist/Lyricist

Michael Greif
Director

Sergio Trujillo
Musical Staging

Mark Wendland
Set Design

Kevin Adams
Lighting Design

Brian Ronan
Sound Design

Michael Starobin
Co-Orchestrator

AnnMarie Milazzo
Vocal Arrangements

Michael Keller
Music Coordinator

Bernard Telsey,
Telsey + Company
Casting

Marcia Goldberg, Nancy Nagel Gibbs and
Nina Essman,
321 Theatrical Management
General Management

David Stone
Producer

James L.
Nederlander
Producer

Barbara Whitman
Producer

Carole Rothman,
Artistic Director,
Second Stage
Theatre
Producer

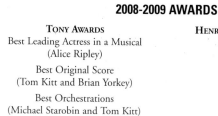

2008-2009 AWARDS

TONY AWARDS
Best Leading Actress in a Musical
(Alice Ripley)

Best Original Score
(Tom Kitt and Brian Yorkey)

Best Orchestrations
(Michael Starobin and Tom Kitt)

HENRY HEWES DESIGN AWARD
Scenic Design
(Mark Wendland)

Next to Normal

CREW
Front Row (L-R): Robert Witherow, Sally E. Sibson, Sara Jayne Darneille, Christopher Sloan, Susan Goulet, Judith Schoenfeld

Back Row (L-R): Vangeli Kaseluris, Jenny Scheer-Montgomery, Kyle LaColla, Elizabeth Berkeley, Angelo Grasso, Kenneth McDonough, Timmy McWilliams

BAND
Front Row: Charlie Alterman

Back Row (L-R): Yuiko Kamakari, Damien Bassman, Mark Vanderpoel

Next to Normal

(L-R): Jennifer Damiano, Aaron Tveit and Adam Chanler-Berat

Photo by Joan Marcus

Next to Normal
SCRAPBOOK

Correspondent: Adam Chanler-Berat, "Henry"

Memorable Opening Night Message: An Al Hirschfeld-esque cartoon of the cast and the creative team given as a gift by two lovely women Rita Kitt (Tom Kitt's wife) and Laura Pietropinto (Assistant Director)—they are sisters, by the way!

Memorable Opening Night Gifts: It's a tie between Sally (one of our assistant stage managers)'s cookies and beautiful framed sheet music from Tom and Brian (our writers).

Most Exciting Celebrity Visitors: Out of who's come so far...Nicole Kidman and Keith Urban were out in the audience crying their eyes out! They sent a beautiful bouquet of flowers with a note confirming that they had in fact cried through pretty much all of Act II, Wooohooo!!! That's a good thing here at *Next to Normal*.

Who Got the Gypsy Robe: We don't have an ensemble; there are only six of us here. So we participated in a new tradition called "break a leg." In this tradition, on opening night, the youngest member of the company breaks a prosthetic leg on the set. Jenn had trouble breaking it. Her face got really red.

Actor Who Performed the Most Roles in This Show: Louis Hobson! He plays the over-prescribing Doctor Fine and the sexy, hypnotic Doctor Madden. At the stage door he is often asked if he has a private practice.

Who Has Done the Most Shows in Their Career: The Ripley. Or Michael Greif. They'll have to duke it out.

Special Backstage Ritual: Is acting stupid and immature a backstage ritual?

Favorite Moment During Each Performance (On Stage or Off): It changes every week. But today, the song "A Promise." When Henry gets to tell Natalie that he can't function without her. So beautifully romantic.

Favorite In-Theatre Gathering Place: Duh. Louis and my dressing room! Well known for the home of crazy make-'em-ups.

Favorite Off-Site Hangout: Jenn and Meghann (her understudy)'s apartment. It has the largest balcony in all of NYC. Swear.

Favorite Snack Food: During the show? Pretzels and peanut butter for me. Swedish Fish or Sour Patch Kids for Jenn.

Favorite Therapy: Water, Ricola, Dr. Kessler's vapors, Throat-Coat Tea, Neti Pot. Vocal health is expensive. Hah.

Memorable Ad-Lib: Louis went to "the white room" during one of his Dr. Fine rants. He said something like "Take the round yellow ones with the trapezoidal white ones...If a tree... is leaving...to go...."

Cell Phone Incidents: We have really respectful audiences. But when they do forget to turn their phones off, they ring at the most inappropriate times (like during "A Light in the Dark" and "He's Not Here.")

Memorable Stage Door Fan Encounter: A girl ran up to me and said "You are INCREDIBLY sexy. Here is my number. I'm going to Canal Bar tonight. I want to see you there." I never expected that Henry would bring that out of a woman.

Fastest Costume Change: From "Psychopharmacologist" into "Perfect for You." Jeff Mahshie, our costume designer, rigged the outfit I wear so that I can tear it off and throw on my polo. It caused problems when we were at Second Stage, but I've gotten used to it.

Busiest Day at the Box Office: Apparently every morning at 5 AM! That's when our fans start lining up for rush tickets! Someone should be out there selling blankets and pillows. They'd make a fortune.

Who Wore the Heaviest/Hottest Costume: Probably Bobby. He has like five layers of wool! Thanks Jeff....

Catchphrases Only the Company Would Recognize: "Get ova heeere." "Now please, Louis." "Jennifaaa DAAAAMIIIano." "Who wants Carrot Top at their sweet seventeen? This sucks. I'm leaving." "It's the winter wind it's faaaaaa." "The Espresso Machine."

Which Orchestra Member Played the Most Instruments: Well, Yuiko plays Violin and Keyboard 2. But Damien has like 40 things up there that he bangs on. So? You pick.

Memorable Directorial Note: "Ish?" as Michael sticks out his arm and rotates his hand back and forth.

Nickname: Alice called Michael Greif "Papa Curly" for a while.

Embarrassing Moments: 1) Jenn fell backstage in "Wish I Were Here" after she takes her pill and runs off. I heard a thump from onstage. I couldn't help but laugh. 2) Jenn and I have a saliva trail after our kiss in "Hey 3"... she's gonna kill me for saying that. 3) I have this weird burp thing that happens every show while I'm at the dinner table watching Dan sing "He's Not Here" to Diana. I think it's the odd twist I'm doing with my body.

Ghostly Encounters Backstage: We're pretty sure the Booth is haunted. But as far as we know, they are friendly.

Superstitions That Turned Out To Be True: What could go wrong, will go wrong, eventually.

Coolest Thing About Being in This Show: We get to be bad-asses eight shows a week.

Also: Charlie Alterman, our Music Director, does THE BEST Liza Minnelli impression I have ever heard. In a perfect world, they'll meet and do a cabaret show together.

1. (L-R): Author Brian Yorkey; actors J. Robert Spencer, Jennifer Damiano, Alice Ripley and Aaron Tveit; composer Tom Kitt, producer David Stone, actor Louis Hobson and director Michael Greif at the Edison Ballroom for the cast party.
2. Damiano and Ripley on opening night.
3. (L-R): Damiano, *Yearbook* correspondent Adam Chanler-Berat and Hobson at Barnes & Noble Lincoln Center for a CD signing.
4. Kitt (center) with (L) son Michael and (R) wife Rita arrives at the Booth Theatre for the opening.

9 to 5: The Musical

First Preview: April 7, 2009. Opened: April 30, 2009.
Still running as of May 31, 2009.

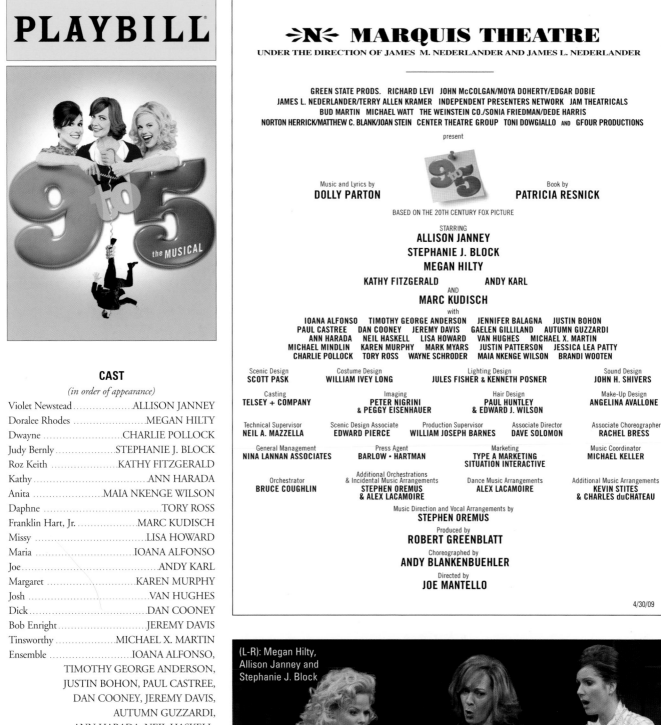

PLAYBILL

CAST
(in order of appearance)

Violet Newstead	ALLISON JANNEY
Doralee Rhodes	MEGAN HILTY
Dwayne	CHARLIE POLLOCK
Judy Bernly	STEPHANIE J. BLOCK
Roz Keith	KATHY FITZGERALD
Kathy	ANN HARADA
Anita	MAIA NKENGE WILSON
Daphne	TORY ROSS
Franklin Hart, Jr.	MARC KUDISCH
Missy	LISA HOWARD
Maria	IOANA ALFONSO
Joe	ANDY KARL
Margaret	KAREN MURPHY
Josh	VAN HUGHES
Dick	DAN COONEY
Bob Enright	JEREMY DAVIS
Tinsworthy	MICHAEL X. MARTIN

Ensemble ....IOANA ALFONSO,
TIMOTHY GEORGE ANDERSON,
JUSTIN BOHON, PAUL CASTREE,
DAN COONEY, JEREMY DAVIS,
AUTUMN GUZZARDI,
ANN HARADA, NEIL HASKELL,
LISA HOWARD, VAN HUGHES,
MICHAEL X. MARTIN, MICHAEL MINDLIN,
KAREN MURPHY, JESSICA LEA PATTY,
CHARLIE POLLOCK, TORY ROSS,
WAYNE SCHRODER,
MAIA NKENGE WILSON,
BRANDI WOOTEN

Continued on next page

⇒N⇐ MARQUIS THEATRE

UNDER THE DIRECTION OF JAMES M. NEDERLANDER AND JAMES L. NEDERLANDER

GREEN STATE PRODS.   RICHARD LEVI   JOHN McCOLGAN/MOYA DOHERTY/EDGAR DOBIE
JAMES L. NEDERLANDER/TERRY ALLEN KRAMER   INDEPENDENT PRESENTERS NETWORK   JAM THEATRICALS
BUD MARTIN   MICHAEL WATT   THE WEINSTEIN CO./SONIA FRIEDMAN/DEDE HARRIS
NORTON HERRICK/MATTHEW C. BLANK/JOAN STEIN   CENTER THEATRE GROUP   TONI DOWGIALLO AND GFOUR PRODUCTIONS

present

9 to 5

Music and Lyrics by
DOLLY PARTON

Book by
PATRICIA RESNICK

BASED ON THE 20TH CENTURY FOX PICTURE

STARRING
ALLISON JANNEY
STEPHANIE J. BLOCK
MEGAN HILTY

KATHY FITZGERALD   **ANDY KARL**
AND
MARC KUDISCH

with

IOANA ALFONSO   TIMOTHY GEORGE ANDERSON   JENNIFER BALAGNA   JUSTIN BOHON
PAUL CASTREE   DAN COONEY   JEREMY DAVIS   GAELEN GILLILAND   AUTUMN GUZZARDI
ANN HARADA   NEIL HASKELL   LISA HOWARD   VAN HUGHES   MICHAEL X. MARTIN
MICHAEL MINDLIN   KAREN MURPHY   MARK MYARS   JUSTIN PATTERSON   JESSICA LEA PATTY
CHARLIE POLLOCK   TORY ROSS   WAYNE SCHRODER   MAIA NKENGE WILSON   BRANDI WOOTEN

Scenic Design	Costume Design	Lighting Design	Sound Design
SCOTT PASK	WILLIAM IVEY LONG	JULES FISHER & KENNETH POSNER	JOHN H. SHIVERS

Casting	Imaging	Hair Design	Make-Up Design
TELSEY + COMPANY	PETER NIGRINI & PEGGY EISENHAUER	PAUL HUNTLEY & EDWARD J. WILSON	ANGELINA AVALLONE

Technical Supervisor	Scenic Design Associate	Production Supervisor	Associate Director	Associate Choreographer
NEIL A. MAZZELLA	EDWARD PIERCE	WILLIAM JOSEPH BARNES	DAVE SOLOMON	RACHEL BRESS

General Management	Press Agent	Marketing	Music Coordinator
NINA LANNAN ASSOCIATES	BARLOW • HARTMAN	TYPE A MARKETING SITUATION INTERACTIVE	MICHAEL KELLER

Orchestrator	Additional Orchestrations & Incidental Music Arrangements	Dance Music Arrangements	Additional Music Arrangements
BRUCE COUGHLIN	STEPHEN OREMUS & ALEX LACAMOIRE	ALEX LACAMOIRE	KEVIN STITES & CHARLES duCHATEAU

Music Direction and Vocal Arrangements by
STEPHEN OREMUS

Produced by
ROBERT GREENBLATT

Choreographed by
ANDY BLANKENBUEHLER

Directed by
JOE MANTELLO

4/30/09

(L-R): Megan Hilty, Allison Janney and Stephanie J. Block

Photo by Joan Marcus

9 to 5: The Musical

MUSICAL NUMBERS

ACT ONE

"9 to 5" .... Violet, Doralee, Dwayne, Judy and Ensemble
"Around Here" .... Violet and Ensemble
"Here for You" .... Hart
"I Just Might" .... Judy, Doralee, Violet
"Backwoods Barbie" .... Doralee
"The Dance of Death" .... Judy, Hart and Ensemble
"Cowgirl's Revenge" .... Doralee, Hart and Ensemble
"Potion Notion" .... Violet, Hart and Ensemble
"Joy to the Girls" .... Judy, Doralee, Violet, Hart and Ensemble
"Heart to Hart" .... Roz and Ensemble
"Shine Like the Sun" .... Doralee, Judy, Violet

ACT TWO

Entr'acte .... Orchestra
"One of the Boys" .... Violet and Boys
"5 to 9" .... Roz
"Always a Woman" .... Hart and Men's Ensemble
"Change It" .... Doralee, Violet, Judy and Ensemble
"Let Love Grow" .... Joe, Violet
"Get Out and Stay Out" .... Judy
Finale: "9 to 5" .... The Company

Cast members performing the title song.

ORCHESTRA

Conductor:
STEPHEN OREMUS
Associate Conductor:
MATT GALLAGHER
Keyboard 1:
STEPHEN OREMUS
Keyboard 2 and Organ:
MATT GALLAGHER
Keyboard 3:
JODIE MOORE (Assistant Conductor)
Guitars:
MICHAEL AARONS, JAKE EZRA SCHWARTZ
Guitars/Pedal Steel:
JOHN PUTNAM
Bass:
DAVE PHILLIPS
Drums:
SEAN MCDANIEL
Percussion:
DAVE MANCUSO

Reeds:
VINCENT DELLA ROCCA, AARON HEICK,
DAVE RIEKENBERG
Trumpets:
BOB MILLIKEN, BRIAN PARESCHI
Trombones:
KEITH O'QUINN, JENNIFER WHARTON
Violins:
SUZY PERELMAN, CHRIS CARDONA
Cello:
AMY RALSKE
Music Coordinator:
MICHAEL KELLER
Keyboard Programming:
RANDY COHEN
Music Copying:
EMILY GRISHMAN MUSIC PREPARATION–
EMILY GRISHMAN/KATHARINE EDMONDS

Cast Continued

SWINGS

JENNIFER BALAGNA, MARK MYARS,
JUSTIN PATTERSON

Dance Captain:
MARK MYARS
Assistant Dance Captain:
JENNIFER BALAGNA

UNDERSTUDIES

Violet:
ANN HARADA, LISA HOWARD
Judy:
GAELEN GILLILAND, JESSICA LEA PATTY,
TORY ROSS
Doralee:
GAELEN GILLILAND, AUTUMN GUZZARDI
Hart:
MICHAEL X. MARTIN, WAYNE SCHRODER
Roz:
ANN HARADA, KAREN MURPHY, TORY
ROSS
Joe:
PAUL CASTREE, JUSTIN PATTERSON
Dwayne:
JUSTIN BOHON, JUSTIN PATTERSON
Dick:
JEREMY DAVIS, WAYNE SCHRODER
Josh:
JUSTIN BOHON, MICHAEL MINDLIN
Kathy:
TORY ROSS, MAIA NKENGE WILSON
Margaret:
TORY ROSS, GAELEN GILLILAND
Maria:
JESSICA LEA PATTY, JENNIFER BALAGNA
Missy:
BRANDI WOOTEN, GAELEN GILLILAND
Tinsworthy:
DAN COONEY, WAYNE SCHRODER

TIME

Photos by Joan Marcus

Marc Kudisch as
Franklin Hart, Jr.

9 to 5: The Musical

Allison Janney
Violet Newstead

Stephanie J. Block
Judy Bernly

Megan Hilty
Doralee Rhodes

Marc Kudisch
Franklin Hart, Jr.

Andy Karl
Joe

Kathy Fitzgerald
Roz Keith

Ioana Alfonso
Maria/Ensemble

Timothy George
Anderson
Ensemble

Jennifer Balagna
*Swing, Assistant
Dance Captain*

Justin Bohon
Ensemble

Paul Castree
Ensemble

Dan Cooney
Dick

Jeremy Davis
*Bob Enright/
Ensemble*

Gaelen Gilliland
u/s Judy, Doralee

Autumn Guzzardi
Ensemble

Ann Harada
Kathy/Ensemble

Neil Haskell
Ensemble

Lisa Howard
Missy/Ensemble

Van Hughes
Josh/Ensemble

Michael X. Martin
Tinsworthy/Ensemble

Michael Mindlin
Ensemble

Karen Murphy
Margaret/Ensemble

Mark Myars
*Swing;
Dance Captain*

Justin Patterson
Swing

Jessica Lea Patty
Ensemble

Charlie Pollock
Dwayne/Ensemble

Tory Ross
Daphne/Ensemble

Wayne Schroder
Ensemble

Maia Nkenge Wilson
Anita/Ensemble

Brandi Wooten
Ensemble

Dolly Parton
*Composer and
Lyricist*

Patricia Resnick
Book

Joe Mantello
Director

Andy
Blankenbuehler
Choreographer

Scott Pask
Scenic Designer

9 to 5: The Musical

William Ivey Long
Costume Designer

Kenneth Posner
Lighting Designer

Jules Fisher and Peggy Eisenhauer
Lighting Designer/Imaging

John H. Shivers
Sound Designer

Stephen Oremus
Music Director, Additional Orchestrations, Vocal and Incidental Music Arrangements

Bruce Coughlin
Orchestrations

Alex Lacamoire
Dance Arrangements/ Additional Orchestrations

Michael Keller
Music Coordinator

Bernard Telsey, Telsey + Company
Casting

Paul Huntley
Wig and Hair Designer

Angelina Avallone
Make-up Designer

Neil A. Mazzella/ Hudson Theatrical Associates
Technical Supervision

Dave Solomon
Associate Director

William Joseph Barnes
Production Supervisor

Nina Lannan Associates
General Management

John McColgan
Producer

Moya Doherty
Producer

Edgar Dobie
Producer

James L. Nederlander
Producer

Terry Allen Kramer
Producer

Arny Granat, Jam Theatricals
Producer

Steve Traxler, Jam Theatricals
Producer

Bob Weinstein, The Weinstein Company
Producer

Harvey Weinstein, The Weinstein Company
Producer

Sonia Friedman Productions Ltd.
Producer

Dede Harris
Producer

Michael Ritchie
Artistic Director, Center Theatre Group

Charles Dillingham
Managing Director, Center Theatre Group

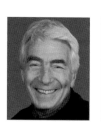
Gordon Davidson
Founding Artistic Director, Center Theatre Group

2008-2009 AWARD

DRAMA DESK AWARD
Outstanding Actress in a Musical
(Allison Janney)

Photo by Brian Mapp

BOX OFFICE
(L-R): Rick Waxman, Mike Kane, John Rooney

9 to 5: The Musical

FRONT OF HOUSE STAFF
Front Row (L-R): Frank Feliciano,
Dorothy Marguette

Second Row (L-R): Charlie Spencer,
Jamie Lee Fitze, Odalis Concepcion

Third Row (L-R): Frank Tupper, Phyllis Weinsaft,
Hugh Dill

Fourth Row (L-R): Stanley Seidman, unknown,
Nancy Diaz, John Clark

Back Row (L-R): Daisy Irizarry, David Cox,
Omar Aguilar, Rosaire Caso

HAIR AND WARDROBE
Front Row (L-R): Samantha Lawrence,
Tree Sarvay, Steven Kirkham, Charlene Belmond

Middle Row (L-R): Laura Beattie, Ed Wilson,
Deirdre LaBarre

Back Row (L-R): Tanya Guercy-Blue,
Maggie Horkey, Stephanie Luette,
Therese Ducey, Douglas Petitjean

Photos by Brian Mapp

MANAGEMENT
Front Row (L-R): Chris Zaccardi, William Joseph Barnes, Kathryn L. McKee,
Adam Jackson

Back Row (L-R): Timothy R. Semon, Kimberly Kelley

CREW
Front Row (L-R): Pat Amari, Scott Mecionis, Michael Bernstein, Stephen Reid,
Mark Diaz, Eileen MacDonald, unknown

Back Row (L-R): Joseph Valentino, Russ Mecionis, Dan Robillard,
Dan Tramontozzi

9 to 5: The Musical

STAFF FOR *9 to 5 THE MUSICAL*

GENERAL MANAGER
NINA LANNAN ASSOCIATES
Nina Lannan   Maggie Brohn

COMPANY MANAGER
Kimberly Kelley

Associate Company Manager ....Adam Jackson

GENERAL PRESS REPRESENTATIVE
BARLOW•HARTMAN
Michael Hartman   John Barlow
Wayne Wolfe   Melissa Bixler

CASTING
TELSEY + COMPANY
Bernie Telsey CSA, Will Cantler CSA, David Vaccari CSA,
Bethany Knox CSA, Craig Burns CSA,
Tiffany Little Canfield CSA, Rachel Hoffman CSA,
Carrie Rosson CSA, Justin Huff CSA, Bess Fifer CSA,
Patrick Goodwin, Abbie Brady-Dalton

Associate Director ....Dave Solomon
Associate Choreographer ....Rachel Bress

Production Supervisor ....William Joseph Barnes
Production Stage Manager
  (Pre-Production) ....C. Randall White
Stage Manager ....Timothy R. Semon
Assistant Stage Managers ....Chris Zaccardi,
  Kathryn L. McKee
Production Assistants.....................Christopher Paul,
  Raynelle Wright, Stuart Shefter,
  McKenzie Murphy
Assistant Producer ....Brian Salb
Dance Captain ....Mark Myars
Assistant Dance Captain ....Jennifer Balagna
Associate Technical Supervisors ....Irene Wang,
  Frank Illo
Associate Scenic Designer ....Nick Francone
Assistant Scenic Designers ....Orit Jacoby Carroll,
  Frank McCullough, Lauren Alvarez,
  Jeffrey Hinchee
Associate Costume Designer ....Scott Traugott
Assistant Costume Designer ....Robert J. Martin
Costume Design Assistant ....Brenda Abbandandolo
Associate Wig and Hair Designer .....Giovanna Calabretta
Associate Lighting Designer ....Philip Rosenberg
Assistant Lighting Designer ....Aaron Spivey, Carl Faber
Automated Lighting Programmer ....David Arch
Associate Sound Designer/
  Production Sound Engineer ....David Patridge
Imaging Associate ....C. Andrew Bauer
Imaging Assistant ....Dan Scully
LED Image Wall
  Programmer ....Laura Frank for Luminous FX LLC
Additional Character &
  Castle Animation ....Illum Productions
  Creative Director: Jerry Chambless
  Animation Director: Joseph Merideth
Production Carpenter ....Donald J. Oberpriller
Carpenters ....Eric "Speed" Smith, Chad Hershey,
  Mark Diaz
Production Electrician ....Gregory Husinko

Head Electrician ....Eric Abbott
Assistant Electrician/Vari*Lite Tech ....Derek Healy
Head of Sound ....Dan Tramontozzi
Assistant Sound ....Dan Robillard
Production Properties ....Timothy M. Abel
Head Properties ....Michael Bernstein
Assistant Properties ....Ken Keneally
Wardrobe Supervisor ....Douglas Petitjean
Assistant Wardrobe Supervisor ....Deirdre LaBarre
Dressers ....Laura Beattie, Tracey Diebold,
  Adam Girardet, Kay Gowenlock,
  Timothy Greer, Barry Hoff, Maggie Horkey,
  Samantha Lawrence, John Rinaldi,
  Tree Sarvay, Kelly Smith, Ron Tagert
Hair Supervisor ....Edward J. Wilson
Assistant Hair Supervisor ....Steven Kirkham
Hairdressers ....Charlene Belmond, Therese Ducey
Rehearsal Musicians ....Jodie Moore, Sean McDaniel
Music Assistant ....Colleen Darnall
Advertising ....Spotco/Drew Hodges, Jim Edwards,
  Tom Greenwald, Tom McCann,
  Josh Fraenkel
Marketing ....Type A Marketing/
  Anne Rippey, Janette Roush, Nick Pramik
Interactive Marketing ....Situation Interactive/
  Damian Bazadona, John Lanasa,
  Rebecca Spears, Maris Smith
Comptroller.............................Sarah Galbraith/
  Sarah Galbraith Company
Accountant ....Robert Fried CPA/
  Fried & Kowgios CPAs LLP
General Management Associates ....Steve Dow,
  David Roth, Libby Fox
General Management Interns ....Mattea Cogliano,
  Erica Ruff
Press Associates ....Leslie Baden,
  Michelle Bergmann, Tom D'Ambrosio,
  Juliana Hannett, Matt Shea
Production Photographer ....Joan Marcus
Insurance ....DeWitt Stern
Banking ....City National Bank, Michele Gibbons
Payroll............................Castellana Services, Inc.
Associate to William Ivey Long ....Donald Sanders
Orthopaedic Medical Coverage ......David S. Weiss, M.D.
Company Physical Therapist ....PhysioArts
Merchandising ....The Araca Group
Travel Agent ....Tzell Travel/
  The "A" Team, Andi Henig
Concierge/Chauffeur ....get services llc
Legal Counsel ....Carolyn J. Casselman/
  Paul, Weiss, Rifkind, Wharton & Garrison

www.9to5themusical.com

Special Thanks to
Linda Wallem

ACKNOWLEDGEMENTS
Scenery and automation constructed by Hudson Scenic Studios and PRG Scenic Technologies. Flying by Foy. Costumes by Scafati Inc., Carelli Costumes, Tricorne, John David Ridge, EuroCo Costumes, Valentina, Jennifer Love Costumes, Maria Ficalora Custom Knitwear, Muto-Little, Giliberto Designs Inc. Shoes by T.O. Dey and Capezio. Undergarments provided by Bra*Tenders. Lighting equipment by PRG Lighting. Sound equipment supplied by

Sound Associates. Props provided by Spoon Group and Proof Productions, Inc. Special effects equipment by Jauchem & Meeh Inc. Trucking by Clark Transfers. Graphic arts and special assistance by Megan Abel. Video Wall by XL Video. Keyboards provided by Yamaha. "Days of Our Lives" text courtesy of Corday Productions, Inc., Sony Pictures Television.

SPECIAL THANKS
Peter Chernin, John Breglio,
Caroline Andersen, Ellen Campion

American premiere produced at
The Ahmanson Theatre by Center Theatre Group,
L.A. Theatre Company

9 to 5 (The Movie)
Story by Patricia Resnick

Screenplay by
Colin Higgins and Patricia Resnick

Produced by
Jane Fonda and Bruce Gilbert

Directed by Colin Higgins

Rehearsed at the New 42nd Street Studios

| Chairman ....**James M. Nederlander** |
| President ....**James L. Nederlander** |

Executive Vice President
Nick Scandalios

Vice President	Senior Vice President
Corporate Development	Labor Relations
Charlene S. Nederlander	**Herschel Waxman**

| Vice President | Chief Financial Officer |
| **Jim Boese** | **Freida Sawyer Belviso** |

STAFF FOR THE MARQUIS THEATRE
Manager..............................David Calhoun
Associate Manager ....Austin Nathaniel
Treasurer ....Rick Waxman
Assistant Treasurer ....John Rooney
Carpenter ....Joseph P. Valentino
Electrician ....James Mayo
Property Man ....Scott Mecionis

Marc Kudisch
and Megan Hilty

Photo by Joan Marcus

9 to 5: The Musical
SCRAPBOOK

Correspondent: Tory Ross, "Daphne"

Opening Night Gifts: We had some amazing opening night gifts, but the most useful turned out to be personalized stationery from our director, Joe Mantello. Of course, the memo pads were personalized with our office characters' names. The inter-office memos that are circulated on a nightly basis are HILARIOUS. Bob Enright is a male slut. In a close second place was the porn I gave everyone. I found an adult film from the early 80's called "*8 to 4*," which closely resembles *9 to 5*. I encouraged everyone to watch it, not necessarily for the sexy bits, but for the body hair and the scene work. The copy machine scene alone is worth it.

Most Exciting Celebrity Visitors: Hands down... this would be having Dolly, Jane, Lily and Dabney backstage after our opening in L.A.

Gypsy Robe: There was a lot of in-house buzz about our Gypsy Robe before the ceremony, as no one could figure out if it was going to be Michael X. Martin or Paul Castree. They might as well be the Lunts of contemporary American musical theatre. Paul ended up getting it and started his speech with his signature catchphrase... "two things...".

Role That Has Been Played By the Most Actors: Though we've only been open a short time, we've had the most extraordinary turnover in one of our featured dancing tracks. Brendan King, who did the L.A. run of the show, booked a lead in *Cirque de Soleil* during tech, and he was replaced by Neil Haskell (of "So You Think You Can Dance" fame). Poor Neil dislocated his shoulder, so the track was temporarily filled by our dance-captain-extraordinaire Mark Myars and currently is being played by Spencer Liff. It's pretty amazing that four of Broadway's most incredible dancers have played our office maintenance man (who later in the show gets promoted to Tinsworthy's henchman).

Special Backstage Rituals: Every night before the show, we gather in a circle in our pajamas, hold hands, and pass energy. Yeah...it's very freshman-year-musical-theatre-y and we don't care. Then, whomever gets squeezed by both hands at the same time gets tickled/molested and picks a word of the day, which we all proudly yell after a huddle. Then we usually get shushed by our stage managers after which they escort Kathy Fitzgerald from the stage. It's awesome. There's also the SR positivity circle, which involves some sort of weird, atonal singing as the curtain rises, but is honestly a bit of a mystery to me as I have to enter at the top of the show. My favorite ritual was Dolly, Judy (her assistant) and Danny (her bodyguard) giving us high fives as we exited the stage after every single preview. Every single one.

Favorite Moment: It's a tie on this one. Our first favorite is singing the backup vocals to "Shine Like the Sun" on SL at the end of Act I with some of the best singers on Broadway. Dolly joined us one night, so now we can all say we've sung with Dolly Parton. The other occurs in Allison's dressing room after the hospital scene and before "Shine Like the Sun." We all

1. Dolly Parton and the creative team at our first sitzprobe in L.A., one of the most incredible moments of all of our lives.
2. Dolly at the piano with Luka Blankenbuehler, son of choreographer Andy Blankenbuehler.
3. Allison Janney backstage getting into her Snow White costume.

congregate and listen as Justin Bohon reads aloud from Dolly's autobiography: "Dolly: My Life and Other Unfinished Business." Her story is incredible: inspiring, self-deprecating, witty, smart and perfect. Just like her. Justin also does character voices and sings... so it's performance art. We're already a third of the way through it!

Favorite In-Theatre Gathering Place: Allison's dressing room. In addition to story-time (see above), we also have Saturday night dance party in which we dance around in our pajamas to very loud hip-hop music at the five minute call, and we enjoy the bar we got her in L.A. She's incredibly generous, so as a bit of a thank-you, I found a vintage bar on Craigslist that the crew refinished and we decoupaged with pictures from the show. It's pretty spectacular.

Favorite Off-Site Hangout: Dolly threw us a party at the restaurant Vynl, which infamously has a bathroom that is dedicated to her, complete with a Dolly tiled-wall and a Dolly dolly. I think it also plays Dolly music, but every time I

go there, it's occupied, so I have to go into Elvis'. Boo. She was also kind enough to do photo-ops with cast/crew/orchestra members in the bathroom throughout the party.

Favorite Snack Food: When the going got rough during tech in L.A., Dolly would drop off baskets filled with Moon Pies and Goo Goo Clusters which are two of her favorite Southern treats. When she discovered that we all shared her sweet-tooth, she started making us Dolly fudge (peanut butter and chocolate) on her tour bus, in the microwave (!) that is probably the best fudge I've ever had in my life. She explained that she gets insomnia and it helped her pass the time.

Most Memorable Ad-Lib: All three of our leading ladies have come up with some doozies, but the winner goes to Megan Hilty. During a scene in which Doralee is trying to stop Mr. Hart from calling the police, Marc went to the phone and found the cord already detached from the wall. She said, "Well, it's already unplugged, so neen-

9 to 5: The Musical
SCRAPBOOK

er, neener, neener." Yeah. Neener neener neener. She's confessed she's never said that before in her life. We all laughed for a week.

Catchphrases Only the Company Would Recognize: "No snacks!" "T-Tats." "You're a catchphrase." "Delicate." And "Two things...".

Treasures That Got Cut: "Tattletales." It was a fan-favorite. And I'm not just saying that because I had a solo in it and we got to eat Jell-o on the cafeteria set.

Memorable Directorial Notes: There was a lot going on in LA, so during down moments of tech, Joe would walk around and check out our 1979 "looks," i.e. hair and outfit and such. On one particular day, he nixed Ann's "tomato soup can" hospital wig and walked by Justin Bohon (who was outfitted as an injured high school football player, complete with "Magnum PI"-esque wig and moustache) and just said, "No." It was a brilliant moment.

Company In-Jokes: We're the bastards at the family reunion.

Nicknames: We don't have nicknames. We have character names. Every single person in the office plays a specific character with a sordid past. The office politics, gossip and backstory runs deep!

Coolest Thing About Being in this Show: Becoming BFFs with Dolly...and the amazing, ridiculously talented, fun, kooky, warm, loving cast, creative team, crew, management, orchestra and house crew this project brought together. We have a blast EVERY NIGHT at work and I think the audience can feel it.

Character Names (Some Real, Some Made Up by the Cast):

"Maria Delgado" - Ioana Alfonso
"Charles Johnson" - Timothy Anderson
"Tina Tatts" - Jennifer Balagna
"Judy Bernly" - Stephanie J. Block
"Milton J. Bradley" - Justin Bohon
"Belinda Pitt" - Rachel Bress
"Jerry Balls" - Paul Castree
"Dick Bernly" - Dan Cooney
"Bob Enright" - Jeremy Davis
"Roz Keith" - Kathy Fitzgerald
"Debbie Dey" - Gaelen Gilliland
"Heather Fairfax" - Autumn Guzzardi
"Kathy Henry Hwang" - Ann Harada
"Chip Nutts" - Neil Haskell
"Doralee Rhodes" - Megan Hilty
"Delta Bea Marshall" - Lisa Howard
"Kirk Savoy" - Van Hughes
"Violet Newstead" - Allison Janney
"Joe Reif" - Andy Karl
"Skippy Enright" - Brendan King
"Franklin Hart, Jr." - Marc Kudisch
"Braider McGuiness" - Spencer Liff
"Mr. Tinsworthy" - Michael X. Martin
"Peter 'Piss Boi' Benson" - Michael Mindlin
"Margaret Pomerance" - Karen Murphy
"A.J. Jones" - Mark Myars
"Ted Steele" - Justin Patterson
"Mercedes La-a Harris" - Jessica Lea Patty
"Rick 'Magnum' Wyland" - Charlie Pollock
"Daphne Rutebegah" - Wayne Schroder
"Anita Betta Jobbe" - Maia Nkenge Wilson
"Lori Balls" - Brandi Wooten

1. Dolly (center) with the orchestra at the recording session for the cast album.
2. Original film stars (L-R): Jane Fonda, Dolly Parton and Lily Tomlin attend the debut.
3. (L-R): Stephanie J. Block, Megan Hilty and Allison Janney congratulate Paul Castree on getting the Gypsy Robe, which he's wearing.
4. Dolly and Megan Hilty at the recording session.
5. (L-R): Jen Balagna, Tim Anderson, Neil Haskell, Michael Mindlin and Dolly Parton in the Dolly-themed bathroom at Vynl.

The Norman Conquests

First Preview: April 7, 2009. Opened: April 23, 2009.
Still running as of May 31, 2009.

THE NORMAN CONQUESTS

TABLE MANNERS • LIVING TOGETHER •
ROUND AND ROUND THE GARDEN

CAST
(in alphabetical order)

Ruth	AMELIA BULLMORE
Annie	JESSICA HYNES
Norman	STEPHEN MANGAN
Tom	BEN MILES
Reg	PAUL RITTER
Sarah	AMANDA ROOT

The actors in *The Norman Conquests* are appearing with the permission of Actors' Equity Association.

UNDERSTUDIES

For Annie: CASSIE BECK
For Norman: PETER BRADBURY
For Ruth/Sarah: ANGELA PIERCE
For Tom/Reg: TONY WARD

TABLE MANNERS

The action takes place in the dining room of a
Victorian house in England
during a weekend in July.

Act I	Act II
Scene I: Saturday, 6pm	Scene I: Sunday, 8pm
Scene II: Sunday, 9am	Scene II: Monday, 8am

Continued on next page

The Playbill Broadway Yearbook 2008-2009

◯ CIRCLE IN THE SQUARE

UNDER THE DIRECTION OF
THEODORE MANN and PAUL LIBIN
SUSAN FRANKEL, General Manager

Sonia Friedman Productions
Steven Baruch   Marc Routh   Richard Frankel   Tom Viertel
Dede Harris   Tulchin/Bartner/Lauren Doll
Jamie deRoy   Eric Falkenstein   Harriet Newman Leve   Probo Productions
Douglas G. Smith   Michael Filerman/Jennifer Manocherian   Richard Winkler

In association with
Dan Frishwasser   Pam Laudenslager/Remmel T. Dickinson
Jane Dubin/True Love Productions   Barbara Manocherian/Jennifer Isaacson

Present

The Old Vic Theatre Company
Production of

THE NORMAN CONQUESTS

by

Alan Ayckbourn

Starring

Amelia Bullmore   Jessica Hynes   Stephen Mangan
Ben Miles   Paul Ritter   Amanda Root

Scenery and Costumes Designed by	Lighting Designed by	Music by
Rob Howell	**David Howe**	**Gary Yershon**

Sound Designed by	Original Casting by	Production Stage Manager
Simon Baker	**Gabrielle Dawes, CDG**	**Ira Mont**

US General Management	UK General Management	Production Manager	Press Representative
Frankel Green Theatrical Management	**Diane Benjamin for SFP**	**Aurora Productions**	**Boneau/ Bryan-Brown**

Directed by

Matthew Warchus

This production was first performed as a trilogy on October 6, 2008
produced by The Old Vic Theatre Company
(Artistic Director Kevin Spacey, Chair Sally Greene, Producers John Richardson and Kate Pakenham)

THE OLD VIC

4/23/09

(Clockwise): Stephen Mangan (standing), Ben Miles, Amanda Root, Jessica Hynes, Amelia Bullmore and Paul Ritter in *Table Manners*

Photo by Joan Marcus

The Norman Conquests

(L-R): Paul Ritter, Stephen Mangan, Jessica Hynes, Ben Miles and Amelia Bullmore in *Round and Round the Garden*

Photo by Richard Termine

Cast Continued

LIVING TOGETHER

The action takes place in the sitting room of a
Victorian house in England
during a weekend in July.

Act I	Act II
Scene I: Saturday, 6:30pm	Scene I: Sunday, 9pm
Scene II: Saturday, 8pm	Scene II: Monday, 8am

ROUND AND ROUND THE GARDEN

The action takes place in the garden of a
Victorian house in England
during a weekend in July.

Act I	Act II
Scene I: Saturday, 5:30pm	Scene I: Sunday, 11am
Scene II: Saturday, 9pm	Scene II: Monday, 9am

Amelia Bullmore
Ruth

Jessica Hynes
Annie

Stephen Mangan
Norman

Ben Miles
Tom

Paul Ritter
Reg

Amanda Root
Sarah

Cassie Beck
u/s Annie

Peter Bradbury
u/s Norman

Angela Pierce
u/s Ruth, Sarah

Tony Ward
u/s Tom, Reg

Alan Ayckbourn
Playwright

Matthew Warchus
Director

Rob Howell
*Scenery and
Costume Design*

David Howe
Lighting Designer

**Simon Baker for
Autograph**
Sound Designer

**Kevin Spacey,
Artistic Director,
The Old Vic**
Original Producer

**Laura Green,
Frankel Green
Theatrical
Management**
*General
Management*

**Sonia Friedman
Productions Ltd.**
Producer

Steven Baruch
Producer

Marc Routh
Producer

Richard Frankel
*Producer,
General
Management*

The Norman Conquests
SCRAPBOOK

Correspondent: Ira Mont, PSM
Opening Night Gifts: We loved the big baskets from Frankel Green Theatrical Management.
Most Exciting Celebrity Visitor: Estelle Parsons ("Sarah" in the original Broadway production) loved it!
Favorite In-Theatre Gathering Place: Greenroom
Special Backstage Ritual: Working on the 1000-piece jigsaw puzzle in the greenroom.
Favorite Off-Site Hangout: Gallagher's (Leo's side).
Favorite Therapies: PG Tips and lemon-ginger tea.
Most Cell Phone Rings, Cell Phone Photos or Texting Incidents During a Single Performance: Four
Coolest Thing About Being in This Show: Three shows in one.

Photo by Aubrey Reuben

Cast members (L-R): Stephen Mangan, Amelia Bullmore, Jessica Hynes and Paul Ritter at Arena for the opening night party.

Tom Viertel
Producer

Dede Harris
Producer

Lauren Doll
Producer

Color Photos by Brian Mapp

Jamie deRoy
Producer

Eric Falkenstein
Producer

Harriet Newman Leve
Producer

CREW
Seated (L-R): Andrew Michaelson, Jessica Worsnop, Sue Stepnik, Julia P. Jones, Townsend Teague

Standing (L-R): Jim Bay, Stewart Wagner, Ira Mont, Bobby Clifton, Tony Menditto, Joe Caputo, Owen Parmele

Michael Filerman
Producer

Jennifer Manocherian
Producer

Barbara Manocherian
Producer

FRONT OF HOUSE STAFF
Front Row (L-R): Cristina Marie, Amy Wolk, Sophie Koufakis, Denise Demirjian

Middle Row (L-R): Roxanne Gayol, Katherine Maldonado, Xavier Young, Rosetta M. Jlelaty, Michael Trupia

Back Row (L-R): Patricia Kennedy, Patricia Cuocci, Laurel Brevoort, Georgia Keghlian, Travis Libin

BOX OFFICE
(L-R): Michael McCarthy, Cheryl Dennis, Michael Kumor

The Norman Conquests

STAFF FOR *THE NORMAN CONQUESTS*

GENERAL MANAGEMENT
FRANKEL GREEN THEATRICAL MANAGEMENT
Richard Frankel   Laura Green   Joe Watson
Leslie Ledbetter

COMPANY MANAGER
Kathy Lowe
Associate Company Manager ....Townsend Teague

GENERAL PRESS REPRESENTATIVE
BONEAU/BRYAN-BROWN
Adrian Bryan-Brown   Jim Byk
Aaron Meier   Rachel Stange

New York Casting by Jim Carnahan, C.S.A.

Production Stage Manager ....Ira Mont
Stage Manager ....Julia P. Jones
Associate Director ....Annabel Bolton
Assistant Director ....Mark Schneider
Production Manager ....Aurora Productions/
Gene O'Donovan, Ben Heller,
Bethany Weinstein
Video Designer ....Duncan McLean
Dialect Consultant ....Elizabeth A. Smith
Associate Set Designer ....Paul Weimer
Associate Costume Designer ....Daryl Stone
Associate Lighting Designer ....Vivien Leone
Associate Sound Designer ....Christopher Cronin
Management Assistant ....Andrew Michaelson

Production Assistant ....Nathan K. Claus
Wardrobe Supervisor ....Sue Stepnik
Dressers ....Bobby Clifton, Jessica Worsnop

Asst. to Ms. Friedman ....Lucie Lovatt
Asst. to Mr. Routh ....Katie Adams
Asst. to Mr. Baruch ....Sonja Soper
Asst. to Mr. Viertel ....Tania Senewiratne
Asst. to Ms. Harris ....Matthew Parent
Asst. to Mr. Bartner ....Sarah Nashman
Advertising ....Spotco, Inc./
Drew Hodges, Tom Greenwald,
Jim Edwards, Jim Aquino, Stacey Maya
Promotions/Marketing ....Broadway Print and Mail
Insurance ....De Witt Stern Group
Legal ....Patricia Crown, Coblence and Associates
Banking....................................JPMorgan Chase
Payroll Service ....Castellana Service, Inc.
Accounting ....Fried and Kowgios Partners, LLP
Travel Agencies ....JMC Travel, Road Rebel

FRANKEL GREEN THEATRICAL MANAGEMENT STAFF
Finance Director ....Michael Naumann
Assistant to Mr. Frankel ....Heidi Libby
Assistant to Ms. Green ....Joshua A. Saletnik
Assistant Finance Director ....Sue Bartelt
Finance Associate ....Heather Allen
IT Manager ....Roddy Pimentel
Sales & Marketing Director ....Ronni Mandell
Director of Business Affairs ....Michael Sinder
Business Affairs Assistant ....Dario Dallalasta
Booking ....On the Road Booking, LLC/
Simma Levine, President
Office Manager ....Emily Wright
Receptionists ....Christina Cataldo, Allison Raines
Interns....................Carrie Brinker, Burke Campbell,
Caitlin Fahey, Stephanie Halbedel,
Beky Hughston, Collin Kim, Sue Lippa,
Katie Pope, Bailie Slevin

SONIA FRIEDMAN PRODUCTIONS
Producer ....Sonia Friedman
General Manager ....Diane Benjamin
Creative Producer ....Lisa Makin
Head of Production ....Pam Skinner
Associate Producer ....Sharon Duckworth
Literary Associate ....Jack Bradley
Production Assistant ....Lucie Lovatt
Production Assistant ....Martin Ball
Production Accountant ....Melissa Hay
Chief Executive Officer-NY ....David Lazar
Executive Assistant-NY ....Dan Gallagher
SFP Board ....Helen Enright, Howard Panter,
Rosemary Squire

CREDITS AND ACKNOWLEDGEMENTS
Set construction by Souvenir Scenic Studios. U.S. scenic by Showmotion, Inc. Costumes made by Kevin Matthias and Kathy Pedersen. Lighting equipment provided by PRG Lighting. Sound and video equipment provided by Sound Associates, Inc.

SPECIAL THANKS
Jane Semark, Lorna Earl,
Anna Maria Casson
and the staff at The Old Vic Theatre.
Makeup provided by M•A•C

MUSIC CREDITS
"Here Comes the Sun" performed by Nina Simone courtesy of the RCA Records label by arrangement with Sony Music Entertainment. "Here Comes the Sun" performed by Steve Harley & Cockney Rebel. Courtesy of EMI Records Ltd.

Under license from EMI Film & Television Music.

THE OLD VIC
Chief Executive ....Sally Greene
Artistic Director ....Kevin Spacey
Producers ....Kate Pakenham, John Richardson
Development Director ....Vivien Wallace
General Manager, OVTC ....Ros Brooke-Taylor
Production Manager ....Dominic Fraser
Finance Director ....Vanessa Harrison
Marketing Director ....Catrin John
Manager, American Associates &
New Voices Network ....Rachael Stevens
Head of Development, American Associates
of The Old Vic ....Amanda Woods
U.S. Legal Counsel ....David Friedlander
Associates ....Edward Hall, David Liddiment,
Matthew Warchus, Anthony Page

○ CIRCLE IN THE SQUARE THEATRE
Under the direction of
Theodore Mann and Paul Libin
Susan Frankel, General Manager
House Manager ....Cheryl Dennis
Head Carpenter ....Anthony Menditto
Head Electrician ....Stewart Wagner
Prop Master..........................Owen E. Parmele
FOH Sound Engineer ....Jim Bay
Box Office Treasurer ....Michael G. McCarthy
Administrative Assistant ....Courtney Kochuba
Assistant to Paul Libin ....Clark Mims Tedesco
Assistant to Theodore Mann ....Eric P. Vitale

○ CIRCLE IN THE SQUARE THEATRE SCHOOL
President ....Paul Libin
Artistic Director ....Theodore Mann
Theatre School Director ....E. Colin O'Leary
Arts Education/Development ....Jonathan Mann
Administrative Assistant ....David Pleva
Administrative Assistant ....Rachel Kincaid

GOVERNMENT, FOUNDATION & PATRON SUPPORT
Stephen & Mary Birch Foundation; Jewels of Charity; Thomas L. Kelly Foundation; Blanche & Irving Laurie Foundation; Frederick Loewe Foundation; Edith Meiser Foundation; Newman's Own, Inc.; NYC Department of Cultural Affairs; Patrick J. Patek Scholarship Fund; Jerome Robbins Foundation; Ross Family Fund; Martin E. Segal; Vera Stern; Geraldine Stutz Foundation; John Veitch Bequest; Arthur N. Wiener Trust.

Pal Joey

First Preview: November 14, 2008. Opened: December 18, 2008.
Closed March 1, 2009 after 37 Previews and 85 Performances.

PLAYBILL

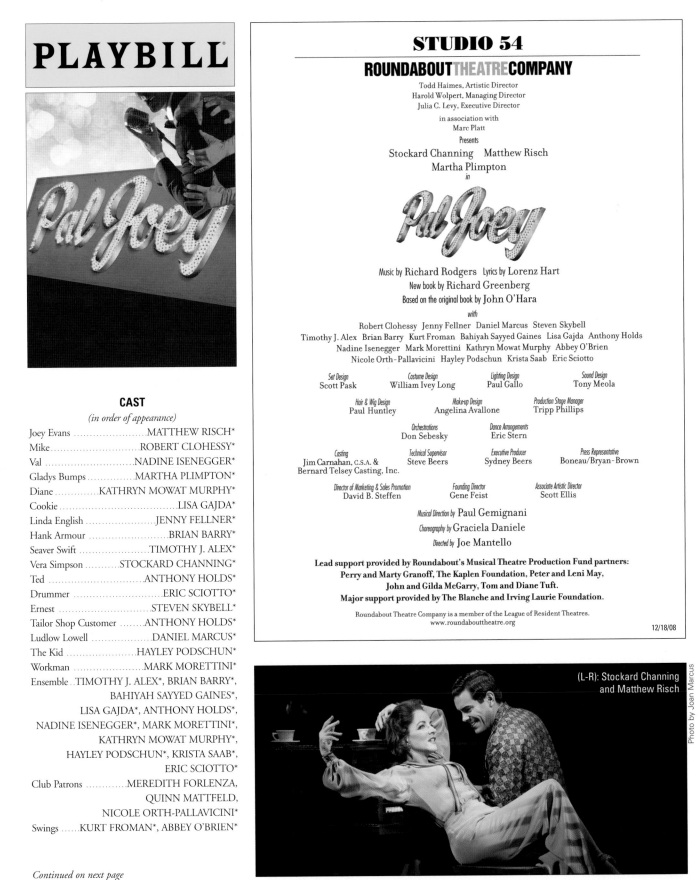

CAST
(in order of appearance)

Joey Evans	MATTHEW RISCH*
Mike	ROBERT CLOHESSY*
Val	NADINE ISENEGGER*
Gladys Bumps	MARTHA PLIMPTON*
Diane	KATHRYN MOWAT MURPHY*
Cookie	LISA GAJDA*
Linda English	JENNY FELLNER*
Hank Armour	BRIAN BARRY*
Seaver Swift	TIMOTHY J. ALEX*
Vera Simpson	STOCKARD CHANNING*
Ted	ANTHONY HOLDS*
Drummer	ERIC SCIOTTO*
Ernest	STEVEN SKYBELL*
Tailor Shop Customer	ANTHONY HOLDS*
Ludlow Lowell	DANIEL MARCUS*
The Kid	HAYLEY PODSCHUN*
Workman	MARK MORETTINI*

Ensemble TIMOTHY J. ALEX*, BRIAN BARRY*,
BAHIYAH SAYYED GAINES*,
LISA GAJDA*, ANTHONY HOLDS*,
NADINE ISENEGGER*, MARK MORETTINI*,
KATHRYN MOWAT MURPHY*,
HAYLEY PODSCHUN*, KRISTA SAAB*,
ERIC SCIOTTO*

Club Patrons MEREDITH FORLENZA,
QUINN MATTFELD,
NICOLE ORTH-PALLAVICINI*
Swings KURT FROMAN*, ABBEY O'BRIEN*

STUDIO 54

ROUNDABOUTTHEATRECOMPANY

Todd Haimes, Artistic Director
Harold Wolpert, Managing Director
Julia C. Levy, Executive Director

in association with
Marc Platt

Presents

Stockard Channing   Matthew Risch
Martha Plimpton

in

Pal Joey

Music by Richard Rodgers   Lyrics by Lorenz Hart
New book by Richard Greenberg
Based on the original book by John O'Hara

with

Robert Clohessy   Jenny Fellner   Daniel Marcus   Steven Skybell
Timothy J. Alex   Brian Barry   Kurt Froman   Bahiyah Sayyed Gaines   Lisa Gajda   Anthony Holds
Nadine Isenegger   Mark Morettini   Kathryn Mowat Murphy   Abbey O'Brien
Nicole Orth-Pallavicini   Hayley Podschun   Krista Saab   Eric Sciotto

Set Design Scott Pask	*Costume Design* William Ivey Long	*Lighting Design* Paul Gallo	*Sound Design* Tony Meola
Hair & Wig Design Paul Huntley	*Make-up Design* Angelina Avallone	*Production Stage Manager* Tripp Phillips	
	Orchestrations Don Sebesky	*Dance Arrangements* Eric Stern	
Casting Jim Carnahan, C.S.A. & Bernard Telsey Casting, Inc.	*Technical Supervisor* Steve Beers	*Executive Producer* Sydney Beers	*Press Representative* Boneau/Bryan-Brown
Director of Marketing & Sales Promotion David B. Steffen	*Founding Director* Gene Feist	*Associate Artistic Director* Scott Ellis	

Musical Direction by Paul Gemignani
Choreography by Graciela Daniele
Directed by Joe Mantello

Lead support provided by Roundabout's Musical Theatre Production Fund partners:
Perry and Marty Granoff, The Kaplen Foundation, Peter and Leni May,
John and Gilda McGarry, Tom and Diane Tuft.
Major support provided by The Blanche and Irving Laurie Foundation.

Roundabout Theatre Company is a member of the League of Resident Theatres.
www.roundabouttheatre.org

12/18/08

(L-R): Stockard Channing
and Matthew Risch

Photo by Joan Marcus

Continued on next page

Pal Joey

MUSICAL NUMBERS

Time: The late 1930s

Place: Chicago

ACT I

Overture ....Orchestra

SCENE 1: **A cheap club on the South Side of Chicago**

"Chicago" ....Joey

"You Mustn't Kick It Around" ....Joey, Gladys & Girls

SCENE 2: **A coffee shop**

"I Could Write a Book" ....Joey & Linda

SCENE 3: **The club**

"Chicago" (Reprise) ....Girls

"That Terrific Rainbow" ....Gladys & Girls

SCENE 4: **The Simpson living room**

"What Is a Man?" ....Vera

SCENE 5: **Linda's house**

"Are You My Love?" ....Joey & Linda

"Happy Hunting Horn" ....Joey & Girls

SCENE 6: **The club**

"Happy Hunting Horn" (Continued) ....Joey & Girls

SCENE 7: **Vera's bedroom**

"Bewitched, Bothered and Bewildered" ....Vera

SCENE 8: **A men's tailor shop**

"Bewitched, Bothered and Bewildered" (Reprise) ....Vera

"Pal Joey (What Do I Care for a Dame?)" ....Joey

SCENE 9: **Ballet**

"Chez Joey" ....Joey & Company

ACT II

SCENE 1: **The club**

"The Flower Garden of My Heart" ....Ludlow Lowell, Gladys & Girls

SCENE 2: **Joey's apartment**

"In Our Little Den of Iniquity" ....Joey & Vera

SCENE 3: **The club**

"Zip" ....Gladys

SCENE 4: **Backstage: Joey's dressing room**

"Plant You Now, Dig You Later" ....Girls

SCENE 5: **The tailor shop**

"Do It the Hard Way" ....Joey & Linda

SCENE 6: **The club**

"Zip" (Reprise) ....Val

"I Still Believe in You" ....Linda

SCENE 7: **The Simpson living room**

"Bewitched, Bothered and Bewildered" (Reprise) ....Vera

SCENE 8: **The tailor shop**

"Take Him" ....Linda & Vera

SCENE 9: **The street**

"I'm Talkin' to My Pal" ....Joey

"I Still Believe in You" (Reprise) ....Linda

"I Could Write a Book" (Reprise) ....Joey

Cast Continued

UNDERSTUDIES

For Joey Evans: ERIC SCIOTTO*

For Vera Simpson:
    NICOLE ORTH-PALLAVICINI*

For Gladys Bumps: LISA GAJDA*

For Linda English, Val: HAYLEY PODSCHUN*

For Mike, Ernest: MARK MORETTINI*

For Ludlow Lowell: ANTHONY HOLDS*.

Dance Captain: BRIAN BARRY*

Production Stage Manager: TRIPP PHILLIPS*
Stage Manager: JASON HINDELANG*

*Members of Actors' Equity Association, the union
of professional actors and stage managers in the
United States.

ORCHESTRA

Conductor: PAUL GEMIGNANI
Associate Conductor: ANNBRITT duCHATEAU
Assistant Conductor: LARRY LELLI
Violins: SYLVIA D'AVANZO (Concertmistress),
    MATTHEW LEHMANN
Viola: RICHARD BRICE
Cello: ROGER SHELL
Woodwinds: ERIC WEIDMAN,
    SCOTT SHACHTER, TOM CHRISTENSEN,
    DON McGEEN
Trumpets: DOMINIC DERASSE,
    MIKE PONELLA
Trombone: ROBERT SUTTMANN
French Horn: RON SELL
Keyboards: ANNBRITT duCHATEAU
Bass: JOHN BEAL
Drums/Percussion: LARRY LELLI
Synthesizer Programmer: RANDY COHEN
In-House Contractor: RON SELL
Music Copying:
    EMILY GRISHMAN MUSIC PREPARATION–
    KATHARINE EDMONDS/
    EMILY GRISHMAN

Pal Joey

Stockard Channing
Vera Simpson

Matthew Risch
Joey Evans

Martha Plimpton
Gladys Bumps

Robert Clohessy
Mike

Jenny Fellner
Linda English

Daniel Marcus
Ludlow Lowell

Steven Skybell
Ernest

Timothy J. Alex
*Seaver Swift,
Ensemble*

Brian Barry
*Hank Armour,
Ensemble*

Kurt Froman
Swing

Bahiyah Sayyed
Gaines
Ensemble

Lisa Gajda
Cookie, Ensemble

Anthony Holds
*Ted, Tailor Shop
Customer, Ensemble*

Nadine Isenegger
Val, Ensemble

Mark Morettini
Workman, Ensemble

Kathryn Mowat
Murphy
Diane, Ensemble

Abbey O'Brien
Swing

Nicole Orth-
Pallavicini
Club Patron

Hayley Podschun
The Kid, Ensemble

Krista Saab
Ensemble

Eric Sciotto
Drummer, Ensemble

Richard Rodgers
Music; 1902-1979

Lorenz Hart
Lyrics; 1895-1943

Richard Greenberg
New Book

John O'Hara
Original Book

Joe Mantello
Director

Graciela Daniele
Choreography

Paul Gemignani
Musical Director

Scott Pask
Set Design

William Ivey Long
Costume Design

Paul Gallo
Lighting Design

Tony Meola
Sound Design

Paul Huntley
Hair and Wig Design

Angelina Avallone
Make-up Design

Don Sebesky
Orchestrations

Pal Joey

Dave Solomon
Associate Director

Jim Carnahan
Casting

Bernard Telsey,
Telsey + Company
Casting

Marc Platt
Producer

Gene Feist
*Founding Director,
Roundabout Theatre
Company*

Todd Haimes
*Artistic Director,
Roundabout Theatre
Company*

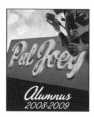

Christian Hoff
Joey Evans

ROUNDABOUT THEATRE COMPANY STAFF

ARTISTIC DIRECTOR	**TODD HAIMES**
MANAGING DIRECTOR	**HAROLD WOLPERT**
EXECUTIVE DIRECTOR	**JULIA C. LEVY**
ASSOCIATE ARTISTIC DIRECTOR	**SCOTT ELLIS**

ARTISTIC STAFF

DIRECTOR OF ARTISTIC DEVELOPMENT/
DIRECTOR OF CASTING ....**Jim Carnahan**

Artistic Consultant ....Robyn Goodman
Resident Director ....Doug Hughes
Associate Artists ....Scott Elliott, Bill Irwin,
Joe Mantello, Mark Brokaw,
Kathleen Marshall
Literary Manager ....Jill Rafson
Casting Director ....Carrie Gardner
Casting Associate ....Kate Boka
Casting Associate ....Stephen Kopel
Artistic Associate ....Erica Rotstein
Literary Associate ....Josh Fiedler
Casting Interns ....Kyle Bosley, Jillian Cimini,
Erin Drake, Andrew Femenella,
Lauren Lewis, Quinn Meyers

EDUCATION STAFF

EDUCATION DIRECTOR ....**Greg McCaslin**

Director of Instruction and
Curriculum Development ....Reneé Flemings
Education Program Manager ....Jennifer DiBella
Program Associate for
School-Based Programs ....Amanda Hinkle
Education Associate
for Theatre-Based Programs ....Jay Gerlach
Education Coordinator ....Aliza Greenberg
Education Dramaturg ....Ted Sod
Teaching Artists ....Phil Alexander, Cynthia Babak,
Victor Barbella, LaTonya Borsay,
Rob Bronstein, Lori Brown-Niang,
Miss Stella, Hamilton Clancy,
Joe Doran, Katie Down, Amy Fortoul,
Tony Freeman, Sheri Graubert,

Matthew Gregory, Adam Gwon,
Karla Hendrick, Jim Jack, Lisa Renee Jordan,
Alvin Keith, Jonathan Lang, Rebecca Lord,
Tami Mansfield, Erin McCready,
Jordana Oberman, Evan O'Brient,
Deirdre O'Connor, Andrew Ondrecjak,
Laura Poe, Alexa Polmer-Spencer,
Nicole Press, Jennifer Rathbone,
Leah Reddy, Amanda Rehbein,
Taylor Ruckel, Chris Rummel,
Cassy Rush, Drew Sachs, Nick Simone,
Derek Straat, Daniel Robert Sullivan,
Vickie Tanner, Olivia Tsang,
Cristina Vaccaro, Jennifer Varbalow,
Leese Walker, Eric Wallach, Gail Winar
Education Interns ....Sara Curtin, Steven Tarca

ADMINISTRATIVE STAFF

GENERAL MANAGER ....**Sydney Beers**

Associate Managing Director ....Greg Backstrom
General Manager,
American Airlines Theatre ....Rebecca Habel
General Manager, Steinberg Center ....Rachel Ayers
General Counsel ....Nancy Hirschmann
Human Resources Manager ....Stephen Deutsch
MIS Director ....Jeff Goodman
Operations Manager ....Valerie D. Simmons
Associate General Manager ....Maggie Cantrick
Office Manager ....Scott Kelly
MIS Database Administrator ....Micah Kraybill
MIS Associate ....Dylan Norden
Assistant to the Managing Director ....Rebecca Skoff
Receptionists ....Dee Beider, Raquel Castillo,
Elisa Papa, Allison Patrick,
Monica Sidorchuk
Messenger ....Darnell Franklin
Management Intern ....Kara Kaufman
General Management Intern ....Laura Stuart

FINANCE STAFF

DIRECTOR OF FINANCE ....**Susan Neiman**

Assistant Controller ....John LaBarbera
Accounts Payable Administrator ....Frank Surdi
Financial Associate ....Yonit Kafka
Business Office Assistant ....Joshua Cohen
Business Interns ....Aaron Esman,
Jonathan Herger, Jaclyn Verbitski

DEVELOPMENT STAFF

Director, Institutional Giving ....Julie K. D'Andrea
Director, Special Events ....Steve Schaeffer
Director, Major Gifts ....Joy Pak
Director, Patron Programs ....Amber Jo Manuel
Manager, Donor Information Systems ....Lise Speidel
Manager, Patron Programs ....Eric Scott
Telefundraising Manager ....Gavin Brown
Manager, Corporate Relations ....Roxana Petzold
Patron Programs Associate ....Marisa Perry
Special Events Associate ....Ashley Firestone
Patrons Services Assistant ....David Pittman
Institutional Giving Associate ....Nick Nolte
Development Assistants ....Daniel Curley,
Nicholas Lalla
Assistant to the Executive Director ....David Jones, Jr.
Special Events Intern ....Kristy Cummings
Major Gifts Intern ....Jaimie Geddes
Development Intern ....Nick Luckenbaugh

MARKETING STAFF

DIRECTOR OF MARKETING
AND SALES PROMOTION ....**David B. Steffen**

Associate Director of Marketing ....Wendy Hutton
Marketing/Publications Manager .....Margaret Casagrande
Marketing Manager ....Stefanie Schussel
Marketing Associate ....Shannon Marcotte
Website Consultant ....Keith Powell Beyland
DIRECTOR OF TELESALES
SPECIAL PROMOTIONS ....**Marco Frezza**

Telesales Manager ....Anthony Merced
Telesales Office Coordinator ....Patrick Pastor
Marketing Interns ....Ashleigh Awusie, Candace Simon

Pal Joey

TICKET SERVICES STAFF

DIRECTOR OF
SALES OPERATIONS ....**Charlie Garbowski, Jr.**

Ticket Services Manager ....Ellen Holt
Subscription Manager ....Ethan Ubell
Box Office Managers ....Edward P. Osborne,
    Andrew Clements, Jaime Perlman
Group Sales Manager ....Jeff Monteith
Assistant Box Office Managers ....Krystin MacRitchie,
    Robert Morgan, Nicole Nicholson
Customer Services Coordinator ....Thomas Walsh
Assistant Ticket Services Managers ....Robert Kane,
    Bill Klemm, Carlos Morris
Ticket Services ....Solangel Bido, Lauren Cartelli,
    Joseph Clark, Barbara Dente, Nisha Dhruna,
    Adam Elsberry, Lindsay Ericson, Scott Falkowski,
    Catherine Fitzpatrick, James Graham, Kara Harrington,
    Tova Heller, Nicki Ishmael, Kate Longosky,
    Elisa Mala, Mead Margulies, Chuck Migliaccio,
    Adam Owens, Kayrose Pagan, Thomas Protulipac,
    Jessica Pruett-Barnett, Kaia Rafoss, Josh Rozett,
    Kenneth Senn, Heather Siebert, Nalene Singh,
    Lillian Soto, Hannah Weitzman

SERVICES

Counsel ....Paul, Weiss, Rifkind,
    Wharton and Garrison LLP,
    Charles H. Googe Jr., Carol M. Kaplan
Counsel ....Rosenberg & Estis
Counsel ....Andrew Lance,
    Gibson, Dunn, & Crutcher, LLP
Counsel ....Harry H. Weintraub,
    Glick and Weintraub, P.C.
Counsel ....Stroock & Stroock & Lavan LLP
Immigration Counsel ....Mark D. Koestler and
    Theodore Ruthizer
Government
   Relations ....Law Offices of Claudia Wagner LLC
House Physicians ....Dr. Theodore Tyberg,
    Dr. Lawrence Katz
House Dentist ....Neil Kanner, D.M.D.
Insurance ....DeWitt Stern Group, Inc.
Accountant ....Lutz & Carr CPAs, LLP
Advertising ....Spotco/
    Drew Hodges, Jim Edwards,
    Tom Greenwald, Kyle Hall,
    Beth Watson
Sponsorship ....Allied Live/
    Tanya Grubich, Laura Matalon,
    Meghan Zaneski
Interactive Marketing................Situation Marketing/
    Damian Bazadona, John Lanasa,
    Ryan Klink, Kristen Butler
Events Photography ....Anita and Steve Shevett
Production Photographer ....Joan Marcus
Theatre Displays ....King Displays, Wayne Sapper
Lobby Refreshments ....Sweet Concessions
Merchandising ....Marquee Merchandise, LLC/
    Matt Murphy

MANAGING DIRECTOR
   EMERITUS ....Ellen Richard

Roundabout Theatre Company
231 West 39th Street, New York, NY 10018
(212) 719-9393.

GENERAL PRESS REPRESENTATIVES
BONEAU/BRYAN-BROWN
Adrian Bryan-Brown
Matt Polk   Jessica Johnson   Amy Kass

STAFF FOR PAL JOEY

Company Manager ....Denise Cooper
Production Stage Manager ....Tripp Phillips
Stage Manager ....Jason Hindelang
Associate Director ....Dave Solomon
Associate Choreographer ....Maddie Kelly
Dance Captain ....Brian Barry
Associate Set Designers ....Orit Jacoby Carroll,
    Frank McCullough
Assistant Set Designers ....Lauren Alvarez,
    Jeff Hinchee
Associate Costume Designer ....Tom Beall
Assistant to the Costume Designer ....Donald Sanders
Costume Assistant ....Cathy Parrott
Associate Lighting Designer ....Paul Toben
Assistant Lighting Designers ....Sarah Jakubasz,
    Joel E. Silver
Assistant to Paul Gallo ....Jeremy Cunningham
Associate Sound Designer ....Zachary Williamson
Associate Wig and Hair Designer .....Giovanna Calabretta
Associate Music Director ....Annbritt duChateau
Rehearsal Pianist ....Paul Ford
Rehearsal Drummer ....Larry Lelli
Assistant Synthesizer Programmers ....Bryan Crook,
    Jim Mironchik
Production Carpenter ....Dan Hoffman
Automation Carpenter ....Paul Ashton
Flyman ....Steve Jones
Deck Carpenter ....Peter Ruen
Production Electrician ....Josh Weitzman
Assistant Production Electrician ....John Wooding
Automated Lighting Programmer ....Timothy F. Rogers
Conventional Lighting Programmer ....Sue Pelkoffer
Follow Spot Operators ....Dorian Fuchs,
    Jocelyn Smith, John Wooding
Production Properties ....Kathy Fabian/
    Propstar Inc.
Associate Props Coordinators ....Carrie Mossman,
    Scott Keclik
Propstar Artisans ....Rose Howard,
    Christina Gould, Edward Morris,
    Heather Sehrt
Propstar Shoppers ....Timothy Ferro,
    Tessa Dunning, Sarah Bird,
    Sid King, Jennifer Lutz
House Properties ....Lawrence Jennino
Properties Running Crew ....Dan Mendeloff,
    Jean Scheller
Local One IATSE Apprentice ....Dan Schultheis
Wardrobe Supervisor ....Nadine Hettel
Dressers ....Tara Delahunt, Joe Godwin,
    Victoria Grecki, Gina Gornik,
    Christel Murdock, Mary Ann Oberpriller
Hair and Wig Supervisor ....Ruth G. Carsch
Hair Assistant ....Enrique Vega
Assistant Make-up Artist ....Benedetta Celada
Production Sound Engineer ....Jordan Pankin
Deck Sound ....Aaron Straus
Production Assistants ....John Bantay,
    Brian D. Gold, Alissa R. Zulvergold
Costume Intern ....Jeanette Lee Porter

Company Manager Intern ....Chris Minnick
Scenery Fabrication ....Scenic Technologies,
    a division of Production Resource Group, LLC,
    New Windsor, NY
Show Control and Scenic Motion
   Control featuring Stage
   Command Systems ....Scenic Technologies,
    a division of Production Resource Group, LLC
Audio Equipment ....PRG Audio
Lighting Equipment ....PRG Lighting
Costumes by ....Carelli Costumes,
    Euroco Costumes, Jennifer Love Costumes,
    Joseph Scafati, Tricorne LLC
Shoes by ....Worldtone, LaDuca, Capezio
Fur by ....Fur and Furgery
Undergarments by ....Bra*Tenders
Milliner ....Rodney Gordon
Specialty Prop Construction ....Daedalus Design
    and Production Inc.,
    Cigar Box Studios,
    Aardvark Interiors,
    The Piano Exchange,
    Anything But Costumes,
    Tom Carroll Scenery,
    Costume Armour,
    Ferrous Research and Design
Specialty Soft Goods Construction ....Anne Guay,
    Mary Wilson
Custom Upholstery ....Mimi Sason
Flame Treatment ....Turning Star Inc.
Physical Therapist ....PhysioArts

Make-up Provided by M•A•C

STUDIO 54 THEATRE STAFF

Theatre Manager ....Matthew Armstrong
Box Office Manager ....Jaime Perlman
House Manager ....LaConya Robinson
Associate House Manager ....Jack Watanachaiyot
House Staff ....Justin Brown, Elicia Edwards,
    Linda Gjonbalaj, Hajjah Karriem,
    Jennifer Kneeland, Jonathan Martinez,
    Essence Mason, Nicole Ramirez,
    Delila Rivera, Diana Trent,
    Stella Varriale, Nick Wheatley
House Carpenter ....Dan Hoffman
House Electrician ....Josh Weitzman
House Properties ....Lawrence Jennino
Security ....Gotham Security
Maintenance ....Ralph Mohan, Maman Garba
Lobby Refreshments by ....Sweet Concessions

FOR THE RODGERS & HAMMERSTEIN
ORGANIZATION

President & Executive Director ....Ted Chapin
Senior Vice President & General Manager ......Bill Gaden
Senior Vice President &
   General Counsel ....Victoria G. Traube
Senior Vice President/Communications ....Bert Fink
Director of Music ....Bruce Pomahac

Performance rights to Pal Joey are licensed by R&H
Theatricals: www.rnhtheatricals.com.

Pal Joey
SCRAPBOOK

Photos by Alissa Zulvergold

1. Eric Sciotto receiving the Gypsy Robe from Richie Mastascusa (*White Christmas*).
2. (L-R): Kathryn Mowat Murphy, Lisa Gajda, Hayley Podschun, Krista Saab, Martha Plimpton, and Nadine Isenegger backstage on closing night.
3. (L-R): Krista Saab, Bahiyah Sayyed Gaines, Kathryn Mowat Murphy, Lisa Gajda, Hayley Podschun, and Nadine Isenegger on closing night.
4. The stage management team: John Bantay (ASM), "Yearbook" Correspondent Alissa Zulvergold (PA), Tripp Phillips (PSM), Jason Hindelang (SM), and Dave Solomon (Asst. Director).
5. Podschun, Zulvergold and Isenegger prepare for the final performance.

The Phantom of the Opera

First Preview: January 9, 1988. Opened: January 26, 1988.
Still running as of May 31, 2009.

PLAYBILL®

CAST

The Phantom of the Opera .HOWARD McGILLIN
Christine Daaé ....MARNI RAAB
Christine Daaé ....ELIZABETH LOYACANO
(Tues. and Thurs. eve. performances)
Raoul,
    Vicomte de Chagny ..TIM MARTIN GLEASON
Carlotta Giudicelli ....PATRICIA PHILLIPS
Monsieur André ....GEORGE LEE ANDREWS
Monsieur Firmin ....DAVID CRYER
Madame Giry.......................REBECCA JUDD
Ubaldo Piangi ....EVAN HARRINGTON
Meg Giry ....POLLY BAIRD
Monsieur Reyer/
    Hairdresser ("Il Muto") ....GEOFF PACKARD
Auctioneer ....JOHN KUETHER
Jeweler (Il Muto) ....FRANK MASTRONE
Monsieur Lefèvre/Firechief ..KENNETH KANTOR
Joseph Buquet ....RICHARD POOLE
Don Attilio ("Il Muto") ....JOHN KUETHER
Passarino ("Don Juan Triumphant")...JEREMY STOLLE
Slave Master ("Hannibal") ......DANIEL RYCHLEC
Flunky/Stage Hand/
    Solo Dancer ("Il Muto") ....JACK HAYES
Page ("Don Juan Triumphant") ....KRIS KOOP
Porter/Fireman ....CHRIS BOHANNON
Spanish Lady
    ("Don Juan Triumphant") ....SALLY WILLIAMS
Wardrobe Mistress/Confidante
    ("Il Muto") ....RAYANNE GONZALES
Princess ("Hannibal") ....SUSAN OWEN
Madame Firmin ....MELODY RUBIE

Innkeeper's Wife ("Don Juan
    Triumphant") .WREN MARIE HARRINGTON
Marksman ....PAUL A. SCHAEFER
The Ballet Chorus of
    the Opéra Populaire ....DARA ADLER,
                                AMANDA EDGE,
                        GIANNA LOUNGWAY,
                            MABEL MODRONO,
                    CARLY BLAKE SEBOUHIAN,
                            DIANNA WARREN
Ballet Swing ....LAURIE V. LANGDON
Swings ....SCOTT MIKITA, JAMES ROMICK,
                            JULIE SCHMIDT

Continued on next page

ⓈMAJESTIC THEATRE
247 West 44th Street
A Shubert Organization Theatre
Gerald Schoenfeld, *Chairman*   **Philip J. Smith,** *President*

Robert E. Wankel, *Executive Vice President*

CAMERON MACKINTOSH and
THE REALLY USEFUL THEATRE COMPANY, INC.
present

The
PHANTOM
of the
OPERA.

starring
HOWARD McGILLIN
MARNI RAAB
TIM MARTIN GLEASON

GEORGE LEE ANDREWS DAVID CRYER PATRICIA PHILLIPS
REBECCA JUDD EVAN HARRINGTON POLLY BAIRD

At certain performances
ELIZABETH LOYACANO
plays the role of 'Christine'

Music by
ANDREW LLOYD WEBBER
Lyrics by CHARLES HART
Additional lyrics by RICHARD STILGOE
Book by RICHARD STILGOE & ANDREW LLOYD WEBBER
Based on the novel 'Le Fantôme de L'Opéra' by GASTON LEROUX
Production Design by MARIA BJÖRNSON Lighting by ANDREW BRIDGE
Sound Design by MICK POTTER Original Sound Design by MARTIN LEVAN
Musical Supervision & Direction DAVID CADDICK Musical Director KRISTEN BLODGETTE
Production Supervisor PETER von MAYRHAUSER
Orchestrations by DAVID CULLEN & ANDREW LLOYD WEBBER
Casting by TARA RUBIN CASTING Original Casting by JOHNSON-LIFF ASSOCIATES
General Management ALAN WASSER ASSOCIATES

Musical Staging & Choreography by GILLIAN LYNNE
Directed by HAROLD PRINCE

10/1/08

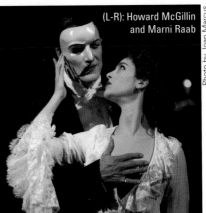

(L-R): Howard McGillin
and Marni Raab

Photo by Joan Marcus

The Phantom of the Opera

MUSICAL NUMBERS

PROLOGUE
The stage of the Paris Opéra House, 1911

OVERTURE

ACT ONE—PARIS 1881

Scene 1—The dress rehearsal of "Hannibal"
"Think of Me" ....Carlotta, Christine, Raoul
Scene 2—After the Gala
"Angel of Music" ....Christine and Meg
Scene 3—Christine's dressing room
"Little Lotte/The Mirror" (Angel of Music) ....Raoul, Christine, Phantom
Scene 4—The Labyrinth underground
"The Phantom of the Opera" ....Phantom and Christine
Scene 5—Beyond the lake
"The Music of the Night" ....Phantom
Scene 6—Beyond the lake, the next morning
"I Remember/Stranger Than You Dreamt It" ....Christine and Phantom
Scene 7—Backstage
"Magical Lasso" ....Buquet, Meg, Madame Giry and Ballet Girls
Scene 8—The Managers' office
"Notes/Prima Donna" ....Firmin, André, Raoul, Carlotta, Giry, Meg,
Piangi and Phantom
Scene 9—A performance of "Il Muto"
"Poor Fool, He Makes Me Laugh" ....Carlotta and Company
Scene 10—The roof of the Opéra House
"Why Have You Brought Me Here/Raoul, I've Been There" ....Raoul and Christine
"All I Ask of You" ....Raoul and Christine
"All I Ask of You" (Reprise) ....Phantom

ENTR'ACTE

ACT TWO—SIX MONTHS LATER

Scene 1—The staircase of the Opéra House, New Year's Eve
"Masquerade/Why So Silent" ....Full Company
Scene 2—Backstage
Scene 3—The Managers' office
"Notes/Twisted Every Way" ....André, Firmin, Carlotta, Piangi, Raoul,
Christine, Giry and Phantom
Scene 4—A rehearsal for "Don Juan Triumphant"
Scene 5—A graveyard in Peros
"Wishing You Were Somehow Here Again" ....Christine
"Wandering Child/Bravo, Bravo" ....Phantom, Christine and Raoul
Scene 6—The Opéra House stage before the Premiere
Scene 7—"Don Juan Triumphant"
"The Point of No Return" ....Phantom and Christine
Scene 8—The Labyrinth underground
"Down Once More/Track Down This Murderer" ....Full Company
Scene 9—Beyond the lake

Cast Continued

UNDERSTUDIES
For the Phantom: TIM MARTIN GLEASON,
    JAMES ROMICK, JEREMY STOLLE
For Christine: SUSAN OWEN
For Raoul: GEOFF PACKARD, JAMES ROMICK,
    PAUL A. SCHAEFER, JEREMY STOLLE
For Firmin: KENNETH KANTOR,
    JOHN KUETHER, JAMES ROMICK
For André: SCOTT MIKITA, RICHARD POOLE,
    JAMES ROMICK
For Carlotta: WREN MARIE HARRINGTON,
    KRIS KOOP, JULIE SCHMIDT
For Mme. Giry: KRIS KOOP, JULIE SCHMIDT,
    SALLY WILLIAMS
For Piangi: CHRIS BOHANNON,
    FRANK MASTRONE
For Meg Giry: AMANDA EDGE,
    MABEL MODRONO,
    CARLY BLAKE SEBOUHIAN
For Slavemaster: JACK HAYES
For Solo Dancer ("Il Muto"): DANIEL RYCHLEC
Dance Captain: LAURIE V. LANGDON
Assistant Dance Captain: DARA ADLER

ORCHESTRA
Conductors: DAVID CADDICK,
    KRISTEN BLODGETTE, DAVID LAI,
    TIM STELLA, NORMAN WEISS
Violins: JOYCE HAMMANN (Concert Master),
    ALVIN E. ROGERS, CLAIRE CHAN,
    KURT COBLE, JAN MULLEN, KAREN MILNE
Violas: STEPHANIE FRICKER,
    VERONICA SALAS
Cellos: TED ACKERMAN, KARL BENNION
Bass: MELISSA SLOCUM
Harp: HENRY FANELLI
Flute: SHERYL HENZE
Flute/Clarinet: ED MATTHEW
Oboe: MELANIE FELD
Clarinet: MATTHEW GOODMAN
Bassoon: ATSUKO SATO
Trumpets: LOWELL HERSHEY,
    FRANCIS BONNY
Bass Trombone: WILLIAM WHITAKER
French Horns: DANIEL CULPEPPER,
    PETER REIT, DAVID SMITH
Percussion: ERIC COHEN, JAN HAGIWARA
Keyboards: TIM STELLA, NORMAN WEISS

The Phantom of the Opera

Howard McGillin
The Phantom of the Opera

Marni Raab
Christine Daaé

Tim Martin Gleason
Raoul, Vicomte de Chagny

George Lee Andrews
Monsieur André

David Cryer
Monsieur Firmin

Patricia Phillips
Carlotta Giudicelli

Rebecca Judd
Madame Giry

Evan Harrington
Ubaldo Piangi

Polly Baird
Meg Giry

Elizabeth Loyacano
Christine Daaé at certain performances

Dara Adler
Assistant Dance Captain/ Ballet Chorus

Amanda Edge
Ballet Chorus, Meg Giry at certain performances

Chris Bohannon
Porter/Fireman

Rayanne Gonzales
Wardrobe Mistress/ Confidante

Jack Hayes
Flunky/Stagehand/ Solo Dancer

Wren Marie Harrington
Innkeeper's Wife

Kenneth Kantor
Monsieur Lefèvre/ Firechief

Kris Koop
Page

John Kuether
Auctioneer/ Don Attilio

Laurie V. Langdon
Dance Captain/ Ballet Swing

Gianna Loungway
Ballet Chorus

Frank Mastrone
Jeweler

Scott Mikita
Swing

Mabel Modrono
Ballet Chorus

Susan Owen
Princess

Geoff Packard
Monsieur Reyer/ Hairdresser

Richard Poole
Joseph Buquet

James Romick
Swing

Melody Rubie
Madame Firmin

Daniel Rychlec
Slave Master

Paul A. Schaefer
Marksman

Julie Schmidt
Swing

Carly Blake Sebouhian
Ballet Chorus

Jeremy Stolle
Passarino

Dianna Warren
Ballet Chorus

The Phantom of the Opera

HAIR, WARDROBE AND MAKEUP
Front Row (L-R): Elena Pellicciario, Pearleta N. Price, Thelma L. Pollard, Marylou Rios, Alexa Burt

Middle Row (L-R): Michael Jacobs, Margie Marchionni, Rosemary Taylor, Ann McDaniel, Erna Dias

Back Row (L-R): Sarah Stamp, Erika Smith, Andrew Nelson, Ron Blakely, Katie Kurz, Annette Lovece

Not pictured: Julie Ratcliffe, Leone Gagliardi

CREW
(L-R): Daryl Miller, Matt Mezick, Ray Pesce, Jack Farmer, Frank Dwyer, Brian Colonna, Robert Wallace, John Hulbert, Pat Alapan, Eric Carney

Not pictured: "Innumerable and all working!"

ORCHESTRA
Front Row (L-R): Ted Ackerman, Atsuko Sato, Jill Collura, Melanie Feld, Henry Fanelli

Back Row (L-R): Kristen Blodgette, John Ostrowski, Sheryl Henze, Bill Whitaker, Lowell Hershey, Joyce Hammann, Matt Goodman, Norman Weiss, Karl Bennion

Not pictured: Francis Bonny, Claire Chan, Kurt Coble, Eric Cohen, Daniel Culpepper, Stephanie Fricker, Jan Hagiwara, David Lai, Ed Matthew, Karen Milne, Jan Mullen, Peter Reit, Alvin E. Rogers, Veronica Salas, Melissa Slocum, David Smith, Tim Stella

MANAGEMENT
Front Row (L-R): Steve Greer (Company Manager), Bethe Ward (Stage Manager), Brian Westmoreland (Assistant Stage Manager), Craig Jacobs (Production Stage Manager)

Back Row (L-R): Laurie V. Langdon (Dance Captain), Josh Blye (Assistant Stage Manager), Cathy Kwon (Assistant Company Manager)

Not pictured: Brendan Smith (Stage Manager)

FRONT OF HOUSE STAFF
Front Row (L-R): Lucia Cappelletti, Danielle Berarducci, Cynthia Carlin, Marcia Rodriguez, Karen Starken, Dorothy Curich, Sylvia Bailey

Middle Row (L-R): Roseyls Aquino, Bobby Arajuo, Perry Dell'Aquila, James Muro, Joan Thorn, Sergio Solorzano, Troy Scarborough, Angelique James

Back Row (L-R): Devin Harjes, Grace Price

The Phantom of the Opera

STAFF FOR *THE PHANTOM OF THE OPERA*

General Manager
ALAN WASSER ASSOCIATES
Alan Wasser   Allan Williams

General Press Representative
THE PUBLICITY OFFICE
Marc Thibodeau   Michael S. Borowski
Jeremy Shaffer

Assistant to Mr. Prince
RUTH MITCHELL

Production Supervisor
PETER von MAYRHAUSER

Production Dance Supervisor
DENNY BERRY

Associate Musical Supervisor
KRISTEN BLODGETTE

Casting
TARA RUBIN CASTING

Technical Production Manager ....JAKE BELL
Company Manager ....STEVE GREER
Production Stage Manager ....CRAIG JACOBS
Stage Managers ....Bethe Ward, Brendan Smith
Assistant Company Manager ....Cathy Kwon

U.S. Design Staff
Associate Scenic Designer ....DANA KENN
Associate Costume Designer ....SAM FLEMING
Associate Lighting Designer ....DEBRA DUMAS
Associate Sound Designer ....PAUL GATEHOUSE
Sculptures Consultant ....Stephen Pyle
Pro Tools Programmer ....Lee McCutcheon

Casting Associates ....Eric Woodall, CSA;
Laura Schutzel, CSA;
Merri Sugarman, CSA
Casting Assistants........................Rebecca Carfagna,
Paige Blansfield, Dale Brown
Dance Captain ....Laurie V. Langdon
Production Carpenter ....Joseph Patria
Production Electrician ....Robert Fehribach
Production Propertyman ....Timothy Abel
Production Sound Engineer ....Shannon Slaton
Production Wig Supervisor ....Leone Gagliardi
Production Make-up Supervisor ....Thelma Pollard
Make-up Assistants ....Pearleta N. Price,
Shazia J. Saleem
Head Carpenter ....Russell Tiberio III
Automation Carpenters ....Santos Sanchez,
Michael Girman
Assistant Carpenter ....Giancarlo Cottignoli
Flyman ....Daryl Miller
Head Electrician ....Alan Lampel
Assistant Electrician ....JR Beket
Head Props ....Matthew Mezick
Asst. Props/Boat Captain ....Joe Caruso
Sound Operator ....John Trace
Wardrobe Supervisor ....Scott Westervelt
Assistant Wardrobe Supervisor ....Robert Strong Miller

Hair Supervisor ....Leone Gagliardi
Hairdressers ....Charise Champion,
Kathleen A. Kurz, Erika Smith,
Sarah Stamp

Conductor ....David Lai
Associate Conductor ....Tim Stella
Assistant Conductor ....Norman Weiss
Musical Preparation
Supervisor (U.S.) ....Chelsea Music Service, Inc.
Synthesizer Consultant ....Stuart Andrews

Assistants to the Gen. Mgr. ....Christopher Betz,
Jake Hirzel, Patty Montesi, Jennifer Mudge

Legal Counsel ....F. Richard Pappas
Accounting ....Rosenberg, Neuwirth and Kutchner
Christopher A. Cacace
Logo Design and Graphics ....Dewynters Plc
London
Merchandising ....Dewynters Advertising Inc.
Advertising ....Serino Coyne Inc.,
Greg Corradetti, Andrea Prince,
Danielle Boyle
Marketing Direction ....Type A Marketing
Anne Rippey
Director of Ticket Services ....Janette Roush
Displays ....King Displays, Wayne Sapper
Insurance (U.S.) ....DeWitt Stern Group
Peter K. Shoemaker
Insurance (U.K.) ....Walton & Parkinson Limited
Richard Walton
Banking ....Commerce Bank/Barbara von Borstel
Payroll Service ....Castellana Services, Inc.

Original Production Photographer ....Clive Barda
Additional Photography ....Joan Marcus,
Bob Marshak, Peter Cunningham
House Manager ....Peter Kulok

CREDITS AND ACKNOWLEDGMENTS
Scenic construction and boat automation by
Hudson Scenic Studios.
Scenery automation by Jeremiah J. Harris Associates,
Inc./East Coast Theatre Supply, Inc. Scenery painted by
Nolan Scenery Studios. Set and hand properties by McHugh
Rollins Associates, Inc. Sculptural elements by Costume
Armour. "Opera Ball" newell post statues and elephant by
Nino Novellino of Costume Armour. Proscenium sculptures
by Stephen Pyle. Draperies by I. Weiss and Sons, Inc. Soft
goods provided by Quartet Theatrical Draperies. Safety
systems by Foy Lighting equipment and special lighting
effects by Four Star Lighting, Inc. Sound equipment and
technical service provided by Masque Sound and Recording
Corp. Special effects designed and executed by Theatre
Magic, Inc., Richard Huggins, President. Costumes
executed by Barbara Matera, Ltd. Costumes for "Hannibal"
and "Masquerade" executed by Parsons/Meares, Ltd. Men's
costumes by Vincent Costumes, Inc. Costume crafts for
"Hannibal" and "Masquerade" by Janet Harper and
Frederick Nihda. Fabric painting by Mary Macy. Additional
costumes by Carelli Costumes, Inc. Costume accessories by
Barak Stribling. Hats by Woody Shelp. Millinery and masks
by Rodney Gordon. Footwear by Sharlot Battin of Montana
Leatherworks, Ltd. Shoes by JC Theatrical and Costume
Footwear and Taffy's N.Y. Jewelry by Miriam Haskell Jewels.

Eyeglasses by H.L. Purdy. Wigs by The Wig Party. Garcia y
Vega cigars used. Makeup consultant Kris Evans. Emergen-
C super energy booster provided by Alacer Corp.

Champagne courtesy of
Champagne G.H. Mumm

Furs by Christie Bros.

Shoes supplied by Peter Fox Limited

"The Phantom" character make-up created and
designed by Christopher Tucker

Magic Consultant—Paul Daniels

CAMERON MACKINTOSH, INC.
Managing Director ....Nicholas Allott
Production Associate ....Shidan Majidi

THE REALLY USEFUL COMPANY INC.
Public Relations ....BROWN LLOYD JAMES/
PETER BROWN

THE REALLY USEFUL GROUP
Directors ....LORD LLOYD WEBBER
LADY LLOYD WEBBER
ANDRÉ PTASZYNSKI
JONATHAN HULL
HOWARD WITTS
MARK WORDSWORTH

THE SHUBERT ORGANIZATION, INC.
Board of Directors

Gerald Schoenfeld
Chairman

Philip J. Smith
President

Wyche Fowler, Jr.

John W. Kluge

Lee J. Seidler

Michael I. Sovern

Stuart Subotnick

Robert E. Wankel
Executive Vice President

David Andrews
Senior Vice President –
Shubert Ticketing

Elliot Greene
Senior Vice President –
Finance

Juan Calvo
Vice President
and Controller

John Darby
Vice President –
Facilities

Peter Entin
Vice President –
Theatre Operations

Charles Flateman
Vice President –
Marketing

Anthony LaMattina
Vice President –
Audit & Production Finance

Brian Mahoney
Vice President –
Ticket Sales

D.S. Moynihan
Vice President – Creative Projects

The Phantom of the Opera
SCRAPBOOK

Correspondent: Kris Koop Ouellette, "Page"
The Phantom of the Opera celebrated the beginning of its 21st year on Broadway in January 2009. That's eight shows a week, 52 weeks a year of bringing audiences to their feet at the curtain call…whether the crowd is seeing the show for the first time or the 40th. While economic troubles plagued Broadway, *Phantom* producers sank three-quarters of a million dollars into a state-of-the-art sound system to ensure that audiences would leave the theatre understanding how this great show keeps going and going and going.

How Do You Keep It Fresh After All These Years? Besides frequently rehearsing with the original creative team—Director Harold Prince, Choreographer Gillian Lynne and Musical Supervisor David Caddick and Associate Kristen Blodgette AND getting the occasional visit from Lord Andrew Lloyd Webber and Sir Cameron Mackintosh—we gain inspiration from our only remaining original company member, George Lee Andrews ("Mssr. André"), who has been honored in "The Guinness Book of World Records" as the actor with the longest run on Broadway in a single show. George answers the question without hesitation: "I try to approach each show as a NEW one. That's how I (try to) stay fresh. But that means the weeks, months and years fly by, and I'm not carrying all of those other shows on my shoulders. I'm always surprised when people tell me how long they've been in the company, because it seems to me like they just got here."
Patricia Phillips ("Carlotta") has starred in the Broadway production of *The Phantom of the Opera* for almost four years, on and off. In the midst of a full production schedule, she squeezed in a critically acclaimed solo spot in *Jerry Springer, The Opera* in 2008, all the while raising her beautiful (and hilarious) son, David. Patricia has this way of keeping her performance fresh: "I love singing the role of Carlotta—so even though it's hard getting to work every day, the moment I begin singing, I am transported and I just LOVE what I do!"
Patricia also finds time to invest herself in company activities outside of the performance schedule. She attended the 21st Birthday Party and enjoyed "great pizza and beer!!" Patricia joined fellow cast members Geoff Packard, Rayanne Gonzales, Evan Harrington, Elizabeth Loyacano, and Paul Schaefer in a gorgeous rendition of "Away in a Manger" (arranged by Packard) for the Broadway Cares/Equity Fights AIDS fundraising effort, "Carols for a Cure." Their rendition was even performed on "Good Morning America." In all of her spare time (???), Patricia has converted her star dressing room into a favorite gathering place for herself and her *Phantom* pals. The room has many titles, depending on the crowd around her. The Pink Palace, The Diva Lounge, and her personal fave: Diva Daycare!
Satomi Hofmann joined the company this past year as a vacation swing, meaning that she is responsible for knowing EVERY vocal part and

(L-R): Tim Martin Gleason, Howard McGillin and Marni Raab with a cake celebrating the show's twenty-first anniversary.

EVERY piece of choreography, ALL staging and backstage moves (including wardrobe and hair changes) for EVERY ensemble woman in the show. It's quite an investment of time and talent, and she's made a great impression on the company! She describes the 21st Birthday Party: "I was a bit nervous, being new, but everyone was incredibly gracious and friendly, and George Lee Andrews even welcomed me and fellow newbie Cristin Hubbard in his speech to the company. After that, I felt almost immediately a part of the *Phantom* family."

Personally, What Is the Hardest Thing About This Job? For Satomi: "Not stepping on the skirt of the actress in front of me!" It seems like a bit of a theme in the swing-world…Satomi describes an event on her opening night in the show: "My first night in, I wore this enormous hat during 'Masquerade.' Well, I ended up on the wrong stair and every time I turned my head, I was essentially sawing Ken Kantor in half with the brim of my hat, all the while with him giggling behind me every time I hit him."
We should now introduce our favorite category in the "Playbill Broadway Yearbook":

Most Memorable Onstage F*@&-Ups From This Past Year…Your Personal Recollection: (We'll just do two, but there were more. Trust us.) Ken Kantor recalls a particular performance with such brilliant clarity, it makes it difficult to imagine this happened to a man with such an amazing memory! (Read "amazing" with just a hint of sarcasm….)
Ken says: "I came out to start 'LeFèvre' and as I walked in, I blanked out. I got to my spot and couldn't think of a thing. I'm sure I stood there

for about 20 seconds doing absolutely nothing. Finally, from the furthest upstage spot, Frank Mastrone took pity on me and started shouting 'Rehearsals!' 'Rehearsals!!!' 'Rehearsals!!!!' to help get me off the dime. But my mind was paralyzed and this didn't prompt me into 'Rehearsals, as you can see are underway…'. Finally David Cryer, whom I am told hasn't ad-libbed onstage in 17 years, shouted out 'Well, why are we here?' I looked at him as if he were the town fool and thought, 'That's not your line….' Well somehow that internal thought was distracting enough to push me into saying my proper line. I'm told that I became so amused at all that had happened that I finished the rest of the scene with a dopey grin on my face. When the scene FINALLY ended, I fell into the arms of Brendan Smith (who was calling the show) and who was crying with laughter at the Stage Manager's console. Ah, such helpful support from management."
Even Ken admits that his off-moment can't compare to David Gaschen's stellar exit. Kris Koop describes: "In the role of 'Piangi,' Gaschen wears an enormous fat-suit, a costume adorned with a giant medallion across his stomach and a tremendously heavy cape that trails him by a good five feet. David is known for cracking us all up both onstage and off, but this night may go down in history for the best screw-up ever. 'Piangi' is supposed to storm off haughtily after Carlotta makes her Diva exit in tears, stopping for just a moment to turn and spit the line 'Amateurs!' at the managers, and then depart with pompous dignity. But, oh….
It started off so well! David flung his cape

behind him as directed and began to exit Stage Left. But just before he got to his mark, his feet became entangled in the cape. His heavily padded body just HURLED to the floor in a face-plant so spectacular, the rest of us just froze, staring. Seriously FROZE. So when David realized that no one was coming to his rescue, he began to roll from side to side on the giant medallion on his stomach, his hands still trapped at his sides inside the cape, his face still stuck to the floor. Still, nobody moved for what felt like an eternity as we watched our dear friend try to flip himself over, like a turtle stuck on its back. Finally David struggled to his knees but could get up no further…so, of course, he turned his head and croaked 'AMATEURS.' Then he rose to his feet and marched into the wings with his head held high. The audience howled, but no louder than the rest of us. Tears were streaming down our faces while most of the cast turned upstage to try to conceal our laughter. It didn't work at all. Bravo to the actors who had to continue with the somber scene as though that hadn't just happened. The rest of us exited as quickly as our staging allowed and we haven't stopped laughing yet!"

Back to Ken! He was in attendance at the 21st Birthday Party, and discovered a wonderful way to personalize the event: "It was actually rather low-key... just the family. As you know, Sally Williams has left the company. Well, she was at the party and we presented her with a brass plaque I had made to commemorate her stoop as 'Sally's Stoop—A place for a weary company member to rest their weary ass.' That plaque is now hanging over her stoop." Which leads to the question…

How Do People With Such an Amazing Job Become Weary? "The stairs… Miles and miles and miles of stairs…."

So How Do YOU Keep It Fresh?: "Surprising the musicians during the intermission with a remote control whoopee cushion. They really screamed with laughter and begged to use it on David Lai in the pit."

What Is the Favorite Gathering Place For You and Your Phantom Pals? It seems to be unanimous among all of our contributors. Ken and Satomi say, "Well, it still has to be the 'Raoul Bar' on Saturday night, where we gather to sample different beverages. Everyone eventually brings something in to share and it's a wonderful chance to spend time with fellow cast members and to try new things!" And "Munching cookies in the Wig Room." And "Shorty's after Raoul Bar."

Janet Saia is the female swing in the Broadway company of *Phantom*: "working at the Majestic for six wonderful years." A professional singer for over 19 years, Janet describes the best part and the worst part of her difficult job: "I have a friend that is coming on Friday to see the show for the first time. Coming to NYC and seeing *Phantom* is on her 'bucket list.' The knowledge that I am in an experience that people hold up as one of the greatest forms of joy they could

have in their last days is the best reward of the job to me." And still… "There are days when, as an understudy, I am called in the afternoon to perform a challenging role that evening. Sometimes I get the call when I'm least expecting it and have to draw the energies physically and mentally to prepare for that level of performance. I have a bag of tricks that does wonders (which includes) Bikram Yoga between shows on Wednesday!" She also found inspiration from "our visiting PSM, Michael Passaro's songs on Saturday night intercom announcements, including excerpts from 'Y.M.C.A.'! Also his long-time habit of saying 'It's Saturday Night on Broadway and the call is PLACES!'"

What's Your Favorite Thing About Raoul Bar? "When they are serving Girl Scout Cookie Cocktails! It's at the end of the week on Saturday night and as many people as you could cram into a single tiny dressing room gather together and enjoy a taste treat created by Jeremy Stolle, ex-bartender extraordinaire. We can just be ourselves and celebrate life!" Just as long as nobody gets "Bo-hammered," right? (inside joke…)

Craig Jacobs is our wonderful Stage Manager, who spent a little time across the street with the Broadway production of *Gypsy* in the midst of his 12-year stint (and counting) at *Phantom*. They needed the expertise his 40 years stage-managing provides! Craig still made it to the 21st Birthday Party, however, and fondly recalls one particular part of the evening: "I always look forward to George Lee Andrews' toast… always encompassing the joy of performing on a nightly basis." Now back in his freezing-cold office at the Majestic, Craig describes the most rewarding things about working on *Phantom*: "The way the audience loves the show, and Hal Prince and HIS support to the company…always keeping an eye on the show to keep it at its best. And never forget the great support of the entire cast,

crew and front of house for BC/EFA. So how does Craig keep his show fresh? "Candy consumption and baked goods served on top of the Xerox machine, followed by The Vodka Cure 10:45 PM at Angus…."

Favorite Backstage Quote: Koop recalls everyone stopping in their tracks when we heard the following announcement: "Everyone please stay in costume. The LORD would like to speak with you onstage after the curtain call…."

Other Phantom News: Actress Polly Baird ("Meg Giry" on Broadway and on tour) was named "New Yorker of the Week" by news channel NY1 for her visitation work in local hospitals with her beautiful dog, Lexi. Lexi was selected from her litter because of her gentle demeanor and loving nature and the team underwent special training for their task. The duo's weekly visit is such a highlight in the lives of many of these critically ill children! Polly fondly recalls: "One little boy, who has spent his entire life in hospitals, was given the amazing news that the heart he needed for transplant had finally become available, and his life-saving surgery would be tomorrow. The young man, fully understanding the gravity of his situation, asked the surgeon to postpone because "tomorrow is when Lexi visits!"

Our gorgeous "Christine," Marni Raab, made *New York Post*'s Page Six when Spanish tennis hottie, Rafael Nadal enjoyed her beauty and her performance so much, he couldn't stop raving about her…Does this make the score "Love"? Both the Broadway cast of *Phantom* and the London cast were featured on CBS' "The Morning Show" on Halloween. Our incredible Phantom, Howard McGillin, sang "Music of the Night" so gorgeously at 9:30 in the morning—in full costume and makeup—and Raoul and Christine from the London company ventured to the actual setting of our story: The Paris Opera House. They made us all wilt as they sang "All I Ask of You" on the Grand Staircase, for the first time in history!

Everybody Wants To Be a Director! This (left) is the adorable Benjamin Schultz Greer, son of our Company Manager Steve Greer and Harris Schultz. After his nap, he'll set his sights high on taking over Broadway, taking notes from the best (right)…his stylish Poppy Prince!

The Philanthropist

First Preview: April 10, 2009. Opened: April 26, 2009.
Still running as of May 31, 2009.

PLAYBILL

THE PHILANTHROPIST

CAST
(in order of speaking)

John ....TATE ELLINGTON
Philip ....MATTHEW BRODERICK
Donald ....STEVEN WEBER
Celia ....ANNA MADELEY
Braham ....JONATHAN CAKE
Araminta ....JENNIFER MUDGE
Elizabeth ....SAMANTHA SOULE

TIME AND PLACE

The play is set in the rooms of an English university
professor in 1970.

ACT I	ACT II
Scene 1: A day in late October	Scene 1: The next morning
Scene 2: A week later	Scene 2: Later that day
Scene 3: After dinner	Scene 3: A few hours later. Evening

UNDERSTUDIES

For Celia, Elizabeth, Araminta:
JANIE BROOKSHIRE
For John, Braham:
MATTHIEU CORNILLON
For Don, Philip:
QUENTIN MARÉ

Production Stage Manager: ARTHUR GAFFIN
Stage Manager: JAMIE GREATHOUSE

AMERICAN AIRLINES THEATRE

ROUNDABOUTTHEATRECOMPANY

Todd Haimes, Artistic Director
Harold Wolpert, Managing Director
Julia C. Levy, Executive Director

Presents

Matthew Broderick

Jonathan Cake   Anna Madeley   Steven Weber

in

THE PHILANTHROPIST

By
Christopher Hampton

with
Tate Ellington   Jennifer Mudge   Samantha Soule

Set Design Tim Shortall	*Costume Design* Tobin Ost	*Lighting Design* Rick Fisher	*Sound Design* Gregory Clarke
Dialect Coach Gillian Lane-Plescia	*Production Stage Manager* Arthur Gaffin		*Casting* Carrie Gardner
Production Management Aurora Productions	*General Manager* Rebecca Habel		*Press Representative* Boneau/Bryan-Brown
Director of Marketing & Sales Promotion David B. Steffen	*Founding Director* Gene Feist		*Associate Artistic Director* Scott Ellis

Directed by
David Grindley

The Donmar Warehouse produced a production of *The Philanthropist* in 2005, directed by David Grindley
Michael Grandage, Artistic Director   James Bierman, Executive Producer

Roundabout Theatre Company is a member of the League of Resident Theatres.
www.roundabouttheatre.org

4/26/09

(L-R):
Matthew Broderick
and Steven Weber

Photo by Joan Marcus

The Philanthropist

Matthew Broderick
Philip

Jonathan Cake
Braham

Anna Madeley
Celia

Steven Weber
Don

Tate Ellington
John

Jennifer Mudge
Araminta

Samantha Soule
Liz

Janie Brookshire
u/s Celia, Elizabeth, Araminta

Matthieu Cornillon
u/s John, Braham

Quentin Maré
u/s Don, Philip

Christopher Hampton
Playwright

David Grindley
Director

Tobin Ost
Costume Design

Jim Carnahan
Casting

Gene Feist
Founding Director, Roundabout Theatre Company

Todd Haimes
Artistic Director, Roundabout Theatre Company

Photos by Brian Mapp

HAIR AND WIG SUPERVISOR
Manuela Laporte

STAGE AND COMPANY MANAGEMENT
(L-R): Jamie Greathouse, Arthur Gaffin, Carly DiFulvio

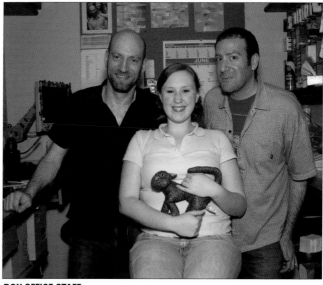

BOX OFFICE STAFF
(L-R): Robert Morgan, Heather Siebert, Mead Margulies

The Philanthropist
SCRAPBOOK

Correspondent: Steven Weber, "Donald"

Memorable Opening Night Letter: My friend Diedrich wrote me to say, "Don't suck!" It's a long way from "Have a great show," but it's in the same neighborhood.

Opening Night Gifts: Mainly flowers and booze. Matthew gave everyone a bottle of good scotch. We do a lot of drinking of fake booze on stage, so every night we make a point of following it with the real thing. Several characters have a lot of time between one scene and the next, and that's when the imbibing begins.

Most Exciting Celebrity Visitors: Laura Linney, Rachel Weisz. Sarah Jessica Parker, of course! Jerry Stiller came opening night, as did Tyne Daly. We've seen lots of cool English people, too, along with playwright Kenny Lonerghan and composer Scott Whitman, who's a good friend of Matthew's. One night I walked out of my dressing room and there, coming toward me as if hovering on a mist, was Marian Seldes, whom I know a little bit from a "Wings" episode we did together. She came toward me and lightly caressed my cheek with the back of her hand and whispered like a risen saint, "That was *wonderful!*" It was so moving, and everybody who ran into her had the same reaction. It was like she blessed the actors with her presence.

Who Has Done the Most Shows in Their Career: It's a toss-up between Matthew Broderick and Jonathan Cake, our wonderful English actor who plays the annoying and virile (or annoyingly virile) Braham. He's probably done dozens and dozens.

Special Backstage Rituals: I always greet the audience unseen from the wings, stage right, in English accent. If I try to ignore the audience, it creates a tension that can distract. I say, "Hello! Welcome! Turn your goddam phones off, open your minds, laugh and have fun!" My friend Tate Ellington (who plays "John" in the show) and I bump fists and give a hug. I go over my lines quickly in a very fast monologue, then Mr. Broderick comes sauntering stage left where we enter and he and I usually crack feeble jokes in English accents. Sometimes we start doing other accents, like the one Peter Sellers used in *Dr. Strangelove*. Then we're ready.

Favorite Moment During Each Performance: It's a small, small thing: There is a party sequence and we're all sitting abreast of one another when Jonathan Cake's character very brusquely insults Jenny Mudge's character. It's just this quick evisceration and it leaves her speechless. The whole thing can't be five seconds long, but it never fails to move me. Even if the show isn't going so great that night, that weird little moment invariably pulls me right back into what we're doing. In that moment Jenny's character becomes vulnerable and exposed and so alive—and yet she does it with a smile. It's as beautiful as anything I've ever seen, and I look forward to it every night.

Favorite In-Theatre Gathering Place: After the play starts Jenny goes up to to Sam Soule's (who plays the silent "Liz") room and they start sipping various libations while crocheting. Then

everybody comes back down and the girls congregate in Jennifer Mudge's dressing room and do a post-mortem. Sometimes we wind up in Matthew's dressing room, drinking. What a shock.

Favorite Off-Site Hangout: We've been making Café Un Deux Trois into our sanitorium away from home. We're fed steady amounts of scotch and vodka interspersed with french fries and raw meat. José the maitre d' greets us warmly and looks at us with a mixture of joy and pity as the actors come rolling in for their shots.

Favorite Snack Food: Everybody's a bit of a chocolate maven. Our SM, Artie Gaffin, keeps a cache of sweets at his station where he presses all the buttons.

Favorite Therapy: It's such a low-impact show; we're not screaming and we're not singing. I'd say we rely on alcohol, chocolate and crochet therapy.

Cell Phone Issues: In spite of our very pointed announcements at the beginning of both the first and second act, they continue to go off just enough to prove that there are people out there in the world who have no sense of responsibility when going to the theatre. And then there's the crumpling of candy wrappers. Some entrepreneurial person should create special theatre wrapping that's quiet.

Heaviest/Hottest Costume: Jonathan Cake wears a very foppish 1970s three-piece corduroy suit—not very forgiving material. He gets a laugh every night when he stands up and has to adjust his pants because they've become all bunched up at the crotch. A scream.

Who Wore the Least: Jennifer Mudge, who wears just a shirt at one point. Very fetching.

Catchphrases Only the Company Would Recognize: Just the word "Hello," but done in a chirpy, singing English accent: "hah-loow." It's funny to hear tough stagehands and grips saying it. It's very useful: It says everything is fine and horrible at the same time. It's the English equivalent of the American southern "bless her heart!"

Superstitions: Somebody probably did say "Macbeth" backstage, which accounts for our reviews. I will say that I whistle freely backstage because I don't believe in that superstition. It may have meant something years ago when the rigging people were all ex-sailors and used whis-

1. The cast takes a curtain call on opening night.
2. Star Matthew Broderick with his wife, actress Sarah Jessica Parker, at B.B. King Blues Club for the cast party.

tles to signal one another. But that era is long over. I hope.

Coolest Thing About Being in This Show: Ours is such a talky play that you wind up sitting still for long periods of time, which gives you a chance to take in the audience and the American Airlines Theatre itself (or have an embolism). Even if you're having a bad time on stage, it's always a clearly special and unique experience to look out at our beautiful and well-constructed theatre. It's like being in a cathedral, a very welcoming space. It's never anything less than special performing on that stage. It's strangely therapeutic.

Actor Grousing: Our reviews were across-the-board bad, really. And all utterly, phenomenally unfair and inaccurate. This is a play that really does have so much to offer, but it's not for everyone. It's not *Mamma Mia!*; it's about fucked-up English people who can't communicate. The reviewers seemed to find that very disturbing, but I think it's because they were just seeing themselves on the stage. It's a show about people who live in an insular world of academia who can't cope with the outside world, so they become critics of the outside world. Did it cut too close to home? My beef is that a play of such depth and complexity got so marginalized.

reasons to be pretty

First Preview: March 13, 2009. Opened: April 2, 2009.
Still running as of May 31, 2009.

PLAYBILL

reasons to be pretty

CAST
(in order of appearance)

Greg ....THOMAS SADOSKI
Steph ....MARIN IRELAND
Kent.............................STEVEN PASQUALE
Carly ....PIPER PERABO

The outlying suburbs. Not long ago.

UNDERSTUDIES
For Carly/Steph:
ANNE BOWLES
For Greg/Kent:
MICHAEL D. DEMPSEY

---

⑧LYCEUM THEATRE
149 West 45th Street
A Shubert Organization Theatre

Philip J. Smith, *Chairman*　　　Robert E. Wankel, *President*

Jeffrey Richards　Jerry Frankel
Gary Goddard Entertainment　Ted Snowdon
Doug Nevin/Erica Lynn Schwartz　Ronald Frankel/Bat-Barry Productions
Kathleen Seidel　Kelpie Arts, LLC　Jam Theatricals
Rachel Helson/Heather Provost

present

MCC Theater's

reasons to be pretty

Written by
Neil LaBute

with

Marin Ireland　Steven Pasquale　Piper Perabo　Thomas Sadoski

Scenic Design	Costume Design	Lighting Design	Sound & Music Design
David Gallo	**Sarah J. Holden**	**David Weiner**	**Rob Milburn & Michael Bodeen**

Casting	Technical Supervision	Production Stage Manager
Telsey + Company	**Hudson Theatrical Associates**	**Christine Lemme**

Fight Direction	Press Representative	General Manager
Manny Siverio	**O&M Co.**	**Daniel Kuney**

Directed by
Terry Kinney

World Premiere at MCC Theater June 2, 2008
Artistic Directors: Robert LuPone & Bernard Telsey
Associate Artistic Director: William Cantler
Executive Director: Blake West

We wish to express our appreciation to
Theatre Development Fund for its support of this production.

NOW **THAT'S** BROADWAY!

4/2/09

2008-2009 AWARDS

DRAMA DESK AWARD
Outstanding Featured Actor
in a Play
(Pablo Schreiber, Off-Broadway cast)

THEATRE WORLD AWARD
First Major New York Stage Appearance
(Marin Ireland)

(L-R): Marin Ireland
and Thomas Sadoski

Photo by Robert J. Saferstein

reasons to be pretty

Marin Ireland
Steph

Steven Pasquale
Kent

Piper Perabo
Carly

Thomas Sadoski
Greg

Anne Bowles
*Understudy
Carly/Steph*

Michael D. Dempsey
*Understudy
Greg/Kent*

Neil LaBute
Playwright

Terry Kinney
Director

David Gallo
Scenic Design

Bernard Telsey,
Telsey + Company
Casting

Daniel Kuney
General Manager

Jeffrey Richards
Producer

Jerry Frankel
Producer

Garry Goddard,
Gary Goddard
Entertainment
Producer

Forbes Candlish,
Gary Goddard
Entertainment
Producer

Ted Snowdon
Producer

Doug Nevin
Producer

Erica Lynn Schwartz
Producer

Barry Weisbord,
Bat-Barry
Productions
Producer

Valerie Gordon-Johnson and Doug Johnson,
Kelpie Arts, LLC
Co-Producer

Arny Granat,
Jam Theatricals
Producer

Steve Traxler,
Jam Theatricals
Producer

Rachel Helson
Producer

FRONT OF HOUSE STAFF
House Manager Joann Swanson (standing center) with the Lyceum Theatre ushers

Heather Provost
Producer

Robert LuPone,
Artistic Director,
MCC Theater
Producer

Blake West,
Executive Director,
MCC Theater
Producer

reasons to be pretty

WARDROBE
(L-R): Susan Checklick, Buster, Sandy Binion

Photos by Brian Mapp

BOX OFFICE
(L-R): Edvige Cadunz, Mike Cadunz, Jennifer Holze

SOUND AND LIGHTING
(L-R): Wallace Flores, Jonathan Cohen, Brian GF McGarity

PRODUCTION
(L-R): BD White, Sam Ellis, Buster

STAGE DOOR
(L-R): Roger Baron, Buster, John Donovan

MERCHANDISE
(L-R): Ginno Murphy, Christine Penzynski, Vinnie Gautieri

PROPS
(L-R): John Lofgren, Leah Nelson

COMPANY MANAGER, GENERAL MANAGER, STAGE MANAGEMENT
(L-R): Chris D'Angelo, Daniel Kuney, Christine Lemme, Matthew Farrell, Alexis Qualls

reasons to be pretty

Steven Pasquale as Kent

Photo by Robert J. Saferstein

reasons to be pretty
SCRAPBOOK

Correspondent: Christine Lemme, PSM

Opening Night Gifts: Marin found a variety of postcards that replace other words with "fuck" and she had simple silver key chains inscribed with "rtbp."

Most Exciting Celebrity Visitors and What They Did/Said: Bill Irwin, and he said "Thank you."

Most Roles in This Show: Anne Bowles, our female understudy, because she also plays Kent and Greg for our male understudy, Michael. Her Kent kicks ass.

Who Has Done the Most Shows: Our second props guy John Lofgren.

Special Backstage Rituals: Thai food Wednesdays.

Favorite Moment During Each Performance: Marin taking tiny steps setting herself at the top of the play. Tom nearly spewing his drink in the Mall—joke!

Favorite In-Theatre Gathering Place: Marin's dressing room

Favorite Off-Site Hangouts: Rosie's, Un Deux Trois, Bar Centrale

Favorite Snack Foods: Pretzels, Twizzlers, vodka, and baked goods from the Moms: Perabo, Ireland, Bowles.

Mascot: The cats keep us going as a majority (except for Steven and Jonathan, who wish they were kabobs). So they are Minnow, Mr. Beast, Zelda, Sweeney, Creepy, Little, Stinker and Miles.

Favorite Therapies: There's some arnica, some tiger balm and some Jameson's floating around.

Memorable Ad-Lib: It was non-verbal. The baseball mitt bounced off Steven and the proscenium and hit a patron in the head. Tom went to the edge of the stage and pointed at the guy and got him to throw the mitt back onstage so he could exit with it. The audience LOVED it.

Record Number of Cell Phone Rings, Cell Cell Phone Incidents During a Performance: One performance we had so many that we couldn't count them. This was very special as they would also make that Morse Code noise in the speakers! The actors went up because of it. The floor mics were removed and another system was set up and the problem, while it has not evaporated, is not a fifth character.

Latest Audience Arrival: A patron was seated five minutes before the intermission.

Fastest Costume Change: All Tom does is change clothes.

Hottest Costume: We are interpreting "hot" as Marin's asymmetrical sequined skirt.

Understudy Anecdote: Something about correctional institutions....

Sweethearts Within the Company: Sandy and Buster. (He doesn't get extra food at our theatre.)

Memorable Directorial Note: "Like the sound of a cheetah." "More Kowalski less Pasqualski."

Company In-Jokes: Treating each other like shit. (It's a LaBute play.)

Company Legends: The bruise in a perfect thumbprint.

Catchphrase Only the Company Would

1. (L-R): Bernard Telsey, Robert LuPone, director Terry Kinney, playwright Neil LaBute, Will Cantler and Blake West at Roundabout Studios rehearsal.
2. Cast member Marin Ireland at the 2009 Tony Awards.
3. Director Terry Kinney at Roundabout Studios.
4. The cast takes a curtain call on opening night at the Lyceum Theatre.

Recognize: "Say goodbye to your friends and get in the car."

Nicknames: "Marin Urine," "Rue," "Mom."

Embarrassing Moments: Tom exited the stage still having his phone conversation in the Mall cause he didn't have his keys.

Ghostly Encounters Backstage: The cast all claims John Barrymore speaks to them even though he doesn't.

Superstitions That Turned Out To Be True: Tom has so many superstitions there isn't

enough room to list them all. It's been difficult keeping the people in the theatre from mentioning The Scottish Play since it was recently in our theatre.

Coolest Thing About Being in This Show: The cast says, "Macking on the chicks." But really it's being part of such a great community. Getting opening night faxes from other shows and then doing that for those that followed us. Taking part in fundraising for "Easter Bonnet." All of it.

Photos by Aubrey Reuben

Rent

First Preview: April 16, 1996. Opened: April 29, 1996.
Closed: September 7, 2008 after 16 Previews and 5123 Performances.

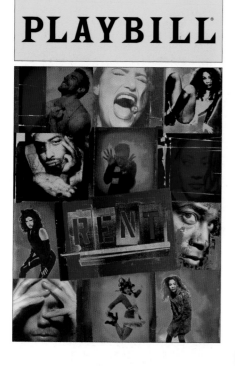

CAST

(in order of appearance)

Roger Davis	WILL CHASE
Mark Cohen	ADAM KANTOR
Tom Collins	MICHAEL MCELROY
Benjamin Coffin III	RODNEY HICKS
Joanne Jefferson	TRACIE THOMS
Angel Schunard	JUSTIN JOHNSTON
Mimi Marquez	RENÉE ELISE GOLDSBERRY
Maureen Johnson	EDEN ESPINOSA
Mark's mom and others	TRACY MCDOWELL

Christmas caroler, Mr. Jefferson,
a pastor, and others......MARCUS PAUL JAMES

Mrs. Jefferson, woman with bags,
and others......GWEN STEWART

Gordon, The Man, Mr. Grey,
and others......JAY WILKISON

Steve, man with squeegee, a waiter,
and others......TELLY LEUNG

Paul, a cop, and others......SHAUN EARL

Alexi Darling, Roger's mom,
and others......ANDREA GOSS

N **NEDERLANDER THEATRE**

UNDER THE DIRECTION OF
JAMES M. NEDERLANDER AND JAMES L. NEDERLANDER

Jeffrey Seller   Kevin McCollum   Allan S. Gordon
and New York Theatre Workshop

present

RENT

Book, Music and Lyrics by
Jonathan Larson

Will Chase   Shaun Earl   Eden Espinosa   Renée Elise Goldsberry
Andrea Goss   Rodney Hicks   Marcus Paul James
Justin Johnston   Adam Kantor   Telly Leung   Tracy McDowell
Michael McElroy   Gwen Stewart   Tracie Thoms   Jay Wilkison
Karmine Alers   Crystal Monée Hall   Trisha Jeffrey
Owen Johnston II   Destan Owens   Todd E. Pettiford   Kyle Post

Set Design	Costume Design	Lighting Design	Sound Design
Paul Clay	Angela Wendt	Blake Burba	Kurt Fischer

Original Concept/Additional Lyrics	Musical Arrangements	Dramaturg
Billy Aronson	Steve Skinner	Lynn M. Thomson

Casting	Publicity
Telsey + Company	Richard Kornberg/Don Summa

Music Director	Production Stage Manager
David Truskinoff	John Vivian

General Manager	Technical Supervision
John Corker	Unitech Productions, Inc.

Music Supervision and Additional Arrangements	Choreography
Tim Weil	Marlies Yearby

Director
Michael Greif

Original cast recording available on DreamWorks Records' CD's and cassettes

9/7/08

Will Chase
Roger

Shaun Earl
Ensemble

Eden Espinosa
Maureen

Renée Elise Goldsberry
Mimi

Continued on next page

Rent

MUSICAL NUMBERS

ACT ONE

Tune Up/Voice Mail #1	Mark, Roger, Mrs. Cohen, Collins, Benny
Rent	The Company
You Okay Honey?…	Angel, Collins
One Song Glory	Roger
Light My Candle	Roger, Mimi
Voice Mail #2	Mr. & Mrs. Jefferson
Today 4 U	Angel
You'll See	Benny, Mark, Collins, Roger, Angel
Tango: Maureen	Mark, Joanne
Life Support	Paul, Gordon, The Company
Out Tonight	Mimi
Another Day	Roger, Mimi, The Company
Will I?	Steve, The Company
On the Street	The Company
Santa Fe	Collins and The Company
I'll Cover You	Angel, Collins
We're Okay	Joanne
Christmas Bells	The Company
Over the Moon	Maureen
La Vie Boheme/I Should Tell You	The Company

ACT TWO

Seasons of Love	The Company
Happy New Year/Voice Mail #3	Mimi, Roger, Mark, Maureen, Joanne, Collins, Angel, Mrs. Cohen, Alexi Darling, Benny, The Man
Take Me or Leave Me	Maureen, Joanne
Without You	Roger, Mimi
Voice Mail #4	Alexi Darling
Contact	The Company
I'll Cover You: Reprise	Collins, The Company
Halloween	Mark
Goodbye, Love	Mark, Mimi, Roger, Maureen, Joanne, Collins, Benny
What You Own	Pastor, Mark, Collins, Benny, Roger
Voice Mail #5	Roger's Mom, Mimi's Mom, Mr. Jefferson, Mrs. Cohen
Your Eyes/Finale	Roger, The Company

UNDERSTUDIES

For Roger:
OWEN JOHNSTON II, KYLE POST,
JAY WILKISON
For Mark:
KYLE POST, JAY WILKISON
For Tom Collins:
MARCUS PAUL JAMES, DESTAN OWENS,
TODD E. PETTIFORD
For Benjamin:
MARCUS PAUL JAMES, TODD E. PETTIFORD
For Joanne:
CRYSTAL MONÉE HALL, TRISHA JEFFREY,
GWEN STEWART
For Angel:
SHAUN EARL, OWEN JOHNSTON II,
TELLY LEUNG
For Mimi:
KARMINE ALERS, TRISHA JEFFREY
For Maureen:
KARMINE ALERS, TRACY MCDOWELL

SWINGS

KARMINE ALERS, CRYSTAL MONÉE HALL,
TRISHA JEFFREY, OWEN JOHNSTON II,
DESTAN OWENS, TODD E. PETTIFORD,
KYLE POST

DANCE CAPTAIN

OWEN JOHNSTON II

THE BAND

Conductor, Keyboards:
DAVID TRUSKINOFF
Bass:
STEVE MACK
Guitar:
BOBBY BAXMEYER
Drums:
JEFF POTTER
Keyboards, Guitar:
JOHN KORBA

FILM BY

TONY GERBER

Andrea Goss
Ensemble

Rodney Hicks
Benny

Marcus Paul James
Ensemble

Justin Johnston
Angel

Rent

Adam Kantor
Mark

Telly Leung
Ensemble

Tracy McDowell
Ensemble

Michael McElroy
Collins

Gwen Stewart
Ensemble

Tracie Thoms
Joanne

Jay Wilkison
Ensemble

Karmine Alers
Understudy

Crystal Monée Hall
Understudy

Trisha Jeffrey
Understudy

Owen Johnston II
Understudy

Destan Owens
Understudy

Todd E. Pettiford
Understudy

Kyle Post
Understudy

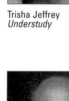
Jonathan Larson
Book, Music, Lyrics

Michael Greif
Director

Marlies Yearby
Choreography

David Truskinoff
*Music Director/
Conductor*

Billy Aronson
*Original Concept and
Additional Lyrics*

John Corker
General Manager

David Santana
*Wig, Hair and
Make-up Design*

Bernard Telsey,
Telsey + Company
Casting

Richard Kornberg &
Associates
*Press
Representative*

Brian Lynch,
Unitech Productions,
Inc.
*Technical
Supervision*

Jeffrey Seller
Producer

Kevin McCollum
Producer

Allan S. Gordon
Producer

James C. Nicola,
Artistic Director,
New York Theatre
Workshop
Producer

Mayumi Ando
*Alexi Darling,
Roger's mom,
and others*

Merle Dandrige
Joanne Jefferson

Tamyra Gray
Mimi Marquez

Caren Lyn Manuel
Mark's Mom

Andy Señor
Swing

Maia Nkenge Wilson
*Mrs. Jefferson,
woman with bags,
and others*

Rent

WIG AND MAKEUP
David Santana

BOX OFFICE
(L-R): Kelly Goode, Russ Hammel.

MANAGEMENT
(L-R): Justin Scribner, John Vivian,
Crystal Huntington.

ELECTRICS CREW
Jack Culver, Greg Freedman, Chaz Peek, Aaron
Straus, Susan Ash, Jason Penna.

FRONT OF HOUSE STAFF
Front Row (L-R): Casey (dog),
Michael McDonoughe, Joaquin Quintana,
Bernard "Sonny" Curry.

Second Row (L-R): Toni Ostoni,
Terrence Cummiskey, John Cuevas, Derek King,
Angel Serrano, Louise Angelino.

Third Row (L-R): Brandon Purves, Brian Baeza,
Kim Holmes, William Figueroa, Alverna Ivory,
Elena Mavoides.

Fourth Row (L-R): Whit Germano,
Renee Fleetwood, Junesse Cartagena, Trish Ryan.

Back Row (L-R): Ralph Hendrix, Edward Cuevas,
Kyle Luker.

PROPS
Front Row (L-R): Mike Yannotti, Billy Wright.

Back Row (L-R): Joe Ferreri, Sr. (carpenter), Jan
Marasek, Joe Ferreri, Jr. (carpenter).

Photos by Ben Strothmann

Rent

WARDROBE
(L-R): Jackie Freeman, Karen Lloyd, Kurt Alger.

DOORMAN
Sonny Curry

Photos by Ben Strothmann

STAFF FOR *RENT*

GENERAL MANAGER
JOHN CORKER

GENERAL PRESS REPRESENTATIVE
RICHARD KORNBERG & ASSOCIATES
Richard Kornberg   Don Summa
Alyssa Hart

CASTING
TELSEY + COMPANY
Bernie Telsey CSA, Will Cantler CSA, David Vaccari CSA,
Bethany Knox CSA, Craig Burns CSA,
Tiffany Little Canfield CSA, Rachel Hoffman CSA,
Carrie Rosson CSA, Justin Huff CSA,
Bess Fifer CSA, Patrick Goodwin

COMPANY MANAGER ....ANDREW JONES

PRODUCTION STAGE MANAGER ....JOHN VIVIAN
Stage Manager ....Crystal Huntington
Assistant Stage Manager ....Gay Merwin
Technical Supervision ....Unitech Productions, Inc.
Brian Lynch, Ken Keneally,
Manuel Becker & Jack Culver
Assistant Director ....Martha Banta
Resident Assistant Director ....Evan Ensign
Associate Conductor ....John Korba
Wig, Hair and Make-Up Designer ....David Santana
Assistant Costume Designer ....Lisa Zinni
Wardrobe Supervisors ......Karen Lloyd, Cleo Matheos
Hair and Make-up Supervisor ....David Santana
House Manager ....Louise Angelino
Treasurer ....Gary Kenny
House Electrician ....Richard J. Beck
Head Electrician ....Jack Culver
Follow Spot Operators ....Tom O'Neill, Charles Peek
Sound Board Operators ....Susan Ash, Greg Freedman
Deck Electrician ....Aaron Straus
House Carpenter ....Joe Ferreri
Assistant House Carpenter ....Joe Ferreri, Jr.
House Prop Master ....Billy Wright
Prop Master ....Jan Marasek
Assistant House Prop Master............William T. Wright
Dressers ....Jackie Freeman, Cleo Matheos,
Pamela Pierzina

Wardrobe Daywork ....Paula Inocent
Costume Construction ....Mary Beth Regan
Assistants to Messrs.
Seller & McCollum ....Ryan Hill, Caitlyn Thomson
Assistant to John Corker ....Kim Vasquez
Receptionist ....Nicholas Robideau
Office Intern ....Jennifer Collins
Dramaturg ....Lynn M. Thomson
Front of House/Lobby Creative Assistant ....Jamie Leo
Lobby Ceiling Murals ....Billy Miller
Music Preparation ....Eva Gianono
Marketing ....Allied Live/
Laura Matalon, Tanya Grubich,
Daya Wolterstorff, Allison Cabellon
Advertising ....Spotco
Peter Duffy, Peter Milano
Education Program ....Students Live!/
Amy Weinstein, President
Allyson Morgan
Merchandising ....Max Merchandising, LLC/
Toni Ostini, Manager
Title Treatment Design ....Spot Design
Poster Artwork ....Amy Guip
Legal Counsel ....Levine Plotkin & Menin, LLP/
Loren H. Plotkin
Accounting ....Lutz & Carr
Insurance ....DeWitt Stern Group
Banking ....JP Morgan
Payroll Service ....ADP
Production Photographers ....Joan Marcus/
Carol Rosegg
Theatre Displays ....King Display
Product Placement ....George Fenmore/
More Merchandising Internat'l

New York Theatre Workshop
Artistic Director   Managing Director
James C. Nicola   Lynn Moffat

The Producing Office
Kevin McCollum   Jeffrey Seller
John Corker   Debra Nir

Allan S. Gordon Productions
Allan S. Gordon
Elan Vital McAllister
Anne Caruso

Credits
Scenery by Hudson Scenic Inc. Lighting equipment by PRG
Lighting. Sound equipment by PRG Audio. Drums by Pearl
Drums. Bed linens by Martex. Additional musical instru-
ments courtesy of Sam Ash Music Stores. Motorcycle hel-
mets courtesy of Bell Helmets. 16 mm Projectors by Elmo
Mfg. Corp. Acrylic drinkware by US Acrylic, Inc. Candles
courtesy of Will & Baumer, Inc. Diamond Brand matches
used. Some skin care and hair products provided by Kiehl's.
Guitar strings supplied by D'Addario & Co. Some denim
wear by Lee Apparel and Rider. Make-up provided by
Francois Nars. Tattoos by Temptu Marketing. Throat
lozenges provided by Ricola, Inc. Plastic cups by Polar
Plastic, Inc. Emer'gen-C Super Energy Booster provided by
Alacer Corp.

Special Thanks to:
Allan and Nanette Larson; Julie Larson; Victoria Leacock.

"White Christmas" used by arrangement with the Irving
Berlin Music Company. "Do You Know the Way to San
Jose," written by Burt Bacharach and Hal David, used by
permission of Casa David and New Hidden Valley Music.
"The Christmas Song (Chestnuts Roasting on an Open
Fire)" by Mel Torme and Robert Wells, used by permission
of Edwin H. Morris & Company, a division of MPL
Communications, Inc. "Rudolph the Red-Nosed Reindeer"
written by Johnny Marks used by permission of St. Nicholas
Music, Inc.

⇒N⇐ NEDERLANDER

Chairman	**James M. Nederlander**
President	**James L. Nederlander**

Executive Vice President
Nick Scandalios

Vice President	Senior Vice President
Corporate Development	Labor Relations
Charlene S. Nederlander	**Herschel Waxman**

Vice President	Chief Financial Officer
Jim Boese	**Freida Sawyer Belviso**

Rent
SCRAPBOOK

Correspondent: Gwen Stewart (An original cast member who returned to the show for the final two months as "Mrs. Jefferson" and "Seasons of Love" soloist).

The Final Performance: I'd been connected to the show for almost thirteen years, so I know how much it meant to people. It's certainly the only show I've been connected with like this.

The final performance brought out so many emotions. It was exciting, nerve-wracking, sad and exhilarating. Everybody came in early to hand out closing night gifts of cards or little trinkets. So many people were backstage. And there were cameras everywhere you turned because they were filming the final performance. There was a guy at the theatre for almost two weeks just getting backstage footage and interviews to go into the special features section of the DVD. A lot of original cast members were there.

For me it was pretty nostalgic, because I started with the show 13 years ago. It was like the family you don't see for years, then you see them at a wedding and its like you were never apart. There were tons of *Rent* alumni in the audience, too, plus our families and a lot of *Rent* fans.

We got something like two and a half minutes of applause before the show even started. We had to yell out the first line to get things going. Before, during and after every number there was more applause. I'm sure we went over the usual time by half an hour.

Memories came flooding back of what it was like to work with Jonathan Larson, and then to lose him. I was just trying to do my show without bursting into tears. The theme of the show is "No Day But Today." My God, how could I sing those words without bawling? But everybody out there deserved a good performance, so I tried to give it to them.

After the final number we got the other original cast members on stage and we all took a bow. Jonathan's father Al came on stage and we all sang "Seasons of Love" together. The rest of the Larsons were standing in the aisle, and to see them was to see Jonathan. It was really intense. And the crowd was insane.

Afterward, I hugged a lot of the original cast members I hadn't seen in a long time. I live on the West Coast so it was good to see them and share a little time with them again. Then I cleared all my stuff from the dressing room and headed out to the party, which was phenomenal. A show is a show is show, but this show was special because when I lost Jonathan, I felt like I lost my brother. And that's something you carry with you all the time. Every time I would come back to New York I would always got back to the show to make sure the current cast was keeping up with the quality Jonathan wanted at the beginning.

My experience on this show is going to stay with me no matter what. It's in my mind and heart unlike anything else I've ever done. It's like my own baby, and that one little piece [the vocal solo] in "Seasons of Love"—that was me. I'm very sad that it's closed, but I'm really

happy that Sony shot the stage production, and people will get to see what everyone has been raving about.

It was a house full of love. Jonathan Larson was there in spirit, I have no doubt about that. I returned to the show in July for the last two

months of the run. On one of my first performances I was in the wings watching the show, and out of nowhere a little moth began flying around. I remember thinking, wow that's Jonathan! His spirit was always there with us.

Photos by Wilson Morales

1. Curtain call at the final performance.
2. Members of the final cast.
3. Director Michael Greif backstage with his childen.
4. (L-R): Al Larson, Daphne Rubin-Vega, Nan Larson and Julie Larson.
5. (L-R): Producer Kevin McCollum, director Michael Greif and producer Jeffrey Seller at the farewell performance.

Rock of Ages

First Preview: March 17, 2009. Opened: April 7, 2009.
Still running as of May 31, 2009.

CAST

(in order of appearance)

Lonny	MITCHELL JARVIS
Justice	MICHELE MAIS
Dennis	ADAM DANNHEISSER
Drew	CONSTANTINE MAROULIS
Sherrie	AMY SPANGER
Father	JAMES CARPINELLO
Mother	MICHELE MAIS
Regina	LAUREN MOLINA
Mayor	ANDRE WARD
Hertz	PAUL SCHOEFFLER
Franz	WESLEY TAYLOR
Stacee Jaxx	JAMES CARPINELLO
Waitress	SAVANNAH WISE
Reporter	KATHERINE TOKARZ
Ja'Keith Gill	ANDRE WARD
Record Company Men	ADAM DANNHEISSER/ MITCHELL JARVIS
Sleazy Producer	JEREMY WOODARD
Joey Primo	JEREMY WOODARD
Candi	LAUREN MOLINA
Young Groupie	ANGEL REED

THE ENSEMBLE

ANGEL REED, KATHERINE TOKARZ,
ANDRE WARD, SAVANNAH WISE,
JEREMY WOODARD

OFFSTAGE VOICES

ERICKA HUNTER, TAD WILSON

Continued on next page

⇒N⇐ BROOKS ATKINSON THEATRE
UNDER THE DIRECTION OF JAMES M. NEDERLANDER AND JAMES L. NEDERLANDER

MATTHEW WEAVER   CARL LEVIN   JEFF DAVIS   BARRY HABIB   SCOTT PRISAND   RELATIVITY MEDIA

in association with

CORNER STORE FUND   JANET BILLIG RICH   HILLARY WEAVER   RYAN KAVANAUGH   TONI HABIB
PAULA DAVIS   SIMON AND STEFANY BERGSON/JENNIFER MALONEY   CHARLES ROLECEK
SUSANNE BROOK   CRAIG COZZA   ISRAEL WOLFSON   SARA KATZ/JAYSON RAITT   MAX GOTTLIEB/JOHN BUTLER
DAVID KAUFMAN/JAY FRANKS   MIKE WITTLIN   PROSPECT PICTURES   LAURA SMITH/BILL BODNAR
HAPPY WALTERS and THE ARACA GROUP

present

ROCK OF AGES

book by
CHRIS D'ARIENZO

starring

CONSTANTINE MAROULIS   AMY SPANGER

ADAM DANNHEISSER   MITCHELL JARVIS   MICHELE MAIS   LAUREN MOLINA
PAUL SCHOEFFLER   WESLEY TAYLOR   *with* JAMES CARPINELLO

BAHIYAH SAYYED GAINES   ERICKA HUNTER   JEREMY JORDAN
MICHAEL MINARIK   ANGEL REED   KATHERINE TOKARZ   ANDRE WARD
TAD WILSON   SAVANNAH WISE   JEREMY WOODARD

set design BEOWULF BORITT	*costume design* GREGORY GALE	*lighting design* JASON LYONS	*sound design* PETER HYLENSKI	*projection design* ZAK BOROVAY
hair & wig design TOM WATSON	*make-up design* ANGELINA AVALLONE	*casting* TELSEY + COMPANY		*production stage manager* CLAUDIA LYNCH
production vocal coach LIZ CAPLAN VOCAL STUDIOS, LLC	*associate choreographer* ROBERT TATAD		*associate director* ADAM JOHN HUNTER	*associate producer* DAVID GIBBS
general management FRANKEL GREEN THEATRICAL MANAGEMENT LESLIE LEDBETTER		*press representative* BARLOW • HARTMAN		*technical supervisor* PETER FULBRIGHT
music director HENRY ARONSON		*music coordinator* JOHN MILLER		*original arrangements* DAVID GIBBS

music supervision, arrangements & orchestrations by
ETHAN POPP

choreographed by
KELLY DEVINE

directed by
KRISTIN HANGGI

NOW **THAT'S**
BROADWAY!

4/7/09

Constantine Maroulis (center)
and The Company

Photo by Joan Marcus

Rock of Ages

Cast Continued

UNDERSTUDIES

For Sherrie:
ERICKA HUNTER, SAVANNAH WISE
For Drew/Franz:
JEREMY JORDAN, JEREMY WOODARD
For Stacee Jaxx:
MICHAEL MINARIK, JEREMY JORDAN,
JEREMY WOODARD
For Lonny/Dennis/Hertz:
MICHAEL MINARIK, TAD WILSON
For Regina: KATHERINE TOKARZ
For Justice:
BAHIYAH SAYYED GAINES,
KATHERINE TOKARZ

SWINGS

JEREMY JORDAN, BAHIYAH SAYYED GAINES,
MICHAEL MINARIK

DANCE CAPTAIN

BAHIYAH SAYYED GAINES

BAND

Conductor/Keyboard:
HENRY ARONSON
Guitar 1:
JOEL HOEKSTRA
Guitar 2:
DAVID GIBBS
Drums:
JON WEBER
Bass:
WINSTON ROYE

Synthesizer Programming:
RANDY COHEN
Music Coordinator:
JOHN MILLER
Copyist:
FIREFLY MUSIC SERVICE/
BRIAN ALLEN HOBBS

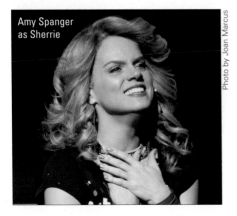

Amy Spanger
as Sherrie

Photo by Joan Marcus

Constantine Maroulis
Drew

Amy Spanger
Sherrie

James Carpinello
Stacee Jaxx/Father

Adam Dannheisser
Dennis

Mitchell Jarvis
Lonny

Michele Mais
Justice/Mother

Lauren Molina
Regina/Candi

Paul Schoeffler
Hertz

Wesley Taylor
Franz

Bahiyah Sayyed Gaines
Ensemble

Ericka Hunter
Ensemble

Jeremy Jordan
Ensemble

Michael Minarik
Swing

Angel Reed
Ensemble

Katherine Tokarz
Ensemble

Andre Ward
Ensemble

Tad Wilson
Ensemble

Savannah Wise
Ensemble

Jeremy Woodard
Ensemble

Henry Aronson
*Music Direction,
Keyboard*

Rock of Ages

Chris D'Arienzo
Book

Kristin Hanggi
Director

Kelly Devine
Choreographer

Beowulf Boritt
Set Designer

Gregory Gale
Costume Design

Jason Lyons
Lighting Design

Peter Hylenski
Sound Design

Tom Watson
Hair and Wig Design

Angelina Avallone
Make-up Design

John Miller
Music Coordinator

Bernard Telsey,
Telsey + Company
Casting

Robert Tatad
*Associate
Choreographer*

Barry Habib
Producer

Toni Habib
Producer

Stefany Bergson
Producer

Jennifer Maloney
Producer

Jayson Raitt
Producer

Bill Bodnar
Producer

2008-2009 AWARD

THEATRE WORLD AWARD
First Major New York Appearance
(Wesley Taylor)

BOX OFFICE
(L-R): Elaine Amplo, Peter Attanasio (Treasurer), Jillian Gloven

STAGE MANAGEMENT
(Clockwise from Top Left): Adam John Hunter, Claudia Lynch, Matt DiCarlo, Marisha Ploski

Photos by Brian Mapp

Rock of Ages

Photos by Brian Mapp

FRONT OF HOUSE STAFF

Front Row (L-R): Ilona Figueroa (Usher), Michelle Gonzalez (Usher), Marie Gonzalez (Usher), Jason Fonseca (Usher), Alisha Banyai (Usher), Carrie Spiller (Bartender)

Middle Row (L-R): Dewayne Queen (Merchandise), Kimberlee Imperato (Usher), Brenda Brauer (Head Usher), Sam Figert (Usher), Tara McCormack (Usher), Jimmy Holley (Ticket Taker), Kaitlin Dato (Usher), Marion Danton (Matron)

Back Row (L-R): Tom (Bartender), Louis Musano (Usher), Angel Diaz (Usher), Susan Martin (Manager), Austin Branda (Usher)

CREW

Front Row (L-R): Dawn Marcoccia, Michael Louis, Robert Guy, Joshua Schwartz, Marisa LeRette, Jake White, Jesse Stevens

Back Row (L-R): Danny Mura, Tommy Grasso, Steve Clem (Elec.), Tommy Lavaia (Head Carpenter), Craig VanTassel, Joe DePaulo (Head Prop Man), Manny Becker (Head Electrician)

Rock of Ages

Assistants to Mr. Weaver ....Tom Pelligrini,
Leigh Huser
Assistants to Mr. Levin ....B. Dannheisser, Anna Wood
Company Management Assistant ....Caitlin Fahey
Music Director/Conductor ....Henry Aronson
Music Coordinator ....John Miller
Assistant to John Miller ....Nichole Jennino
Synthesizer Programmer ....Randy Cohen
Music Copying/
   Music Preparation ....Firefly Music Service/
Brian Hobbs
Rehearsal Pianist ....Keith Cotton
Advertising ....Serino Coyne, Inc./
Scott Johnson, Sandy Block,
Ryan Cunningham, Andrea Prince,
Jill Falcone
Marketing & Promotions ....The Pekoe Group/
Amanda Pekoe, Alexa Shaughnessy
Marketing...............Leanne Schanzer Promotions, Inc./
Leanne Schanzer, Justin Schanzer,
Kara Laviola
Internet Marketing/
   Web Design ....Art Meets Commerce/
Jim Glaub, Mark Seeley
Press Associates ....Michelle Bergmann,
Melissa Bixler, Tom D'Ambrosio,
Juliana Hannett, Wayne Wolfe
Production Photography ....Joan Marcus
Insurance ....DeWitt Stern Group, Inc./
Peter Shoemaker, Mary E. De Spirt
Legal Counsel ....Sendroff and Baruch, LLP/
Jason Baruch
Banking ....Chase Manhattan Bank
Payroll Service ....Castellana Services, Inc.
Accounting ....Fried & Kowgios Partners, CPAs, LLP
Additional New York
   Rehearsals ....Ripley-Grier Studios
Group Sales ....Theatre Direct Group Sales
1.800.BROADWAY

FRANKEL GREEN THEATRICAL MANAGEMENT
Finance Director ....**Michael Naumann**
Assistant to Mr. Frankel ....Heidi Libby
Assistant to Ms. Green ....Joshua A Saletnik
Assistant Finance Director ....Sue Bartelt
Finance Associate ....Heather Allen
Information Technology
   Manager ....**Roddy Pimentel**
National Sales and
   Marketing Director ....**Ronni Mandell**
Director of Business Affairs ....**Michael Sinder**
Business Affairs Assistant ....Dario Dalla Lasta
Marketing Manager ....Nina Bergelson
Booking ....On the Road Booking, LLC/
Simma Levine, President
Office Manager ....**Lori Steiger-Perry**
Office Management Assistant ....Emily Wright
Receptionists ....Christina Cataldo, Allison Raines
Interns ....Carrie Brinker, Burke Campbell,
Caitlin Fahey, Stephanie Halbedel,
Rebekah Hughston, Collin Kim, Sue Lippa,
Katie Pope, Bailie Slevin

CREDITS AND ACKNOWLEDGEMENTS
Gibson, Ernie Ball, Baldwin Piano, Vic Firth, Vans, PRG
Audio, Showmotion and Spoon Group. Lighting equipment

from Hudson Sound and Light LLC, Mimi Bilinski. Costumes constructed by Jennifer Love Costumes and Jennifer Jacob. Custom leatherwear by www.rawhides.com. Shoes and boots constructed by T.O. Dey and Worldtone. Fabric painting and costume crafts by Jeffrey Fender. Hosiery and undergarments by Bra*Tenders. Keyboards by Yamaha.

Rehearsed at the New 42nd Street Studios

MUSIC CREDITS

"Anyway You Want It" written by Steve Perry and Neil Schon. © Published by Lacey Boulevard Music and Weed High Nightmare Music.

"Can't Fight This Feeling" written by Kevin Cronin. © Published by Fate Music (ASCAP).

"Cum on Feel the Noize" written by Neville Holder and James Lea. © Barn Publishing (Slade) Ltd.

"Don't Stop Believin'" written by Jonathan Cain, Stephen Ray Perry, Neal J. Schon © Published by Weed High Nightmare Music and Lacey Boulevard Music.

"Every Rose Has Its Thorn" written by Bobby Dall, Bruce Anthony Johannesson, Bret Michael, Rikki Rocket. © All rights owned or administered by Universal Music-Z Songs on behalf of Cyanide Publ./BMI. Used by permission.

"The Final Countdown" written by Joey Tempest. © Screen Gems-EMI Music Inc.

"Harden My Heart" written by Marvin Webster Ross. © 1980 WB Music Corp. (ASCAP), Narrow Dude Music (ASCAP) and Bonnie Bee Good Music. All rights administered by WB Music Corp. All rights reserved. Used by permission.

"Heat of the Moment" written by Geoffrey Downes and John K. Wetton. © 1982 WB Music Corp. (ASCAP), Almond Legg Music Corp (ASCAP) and Pallan Music. All rights on behalf of itself and Almond Legg Music Corp. administered by WB Music Corp. All rights reserved. Used by permission.

"Heaven" written by Jani Lane, Erik Turner, Jerry Dixon, Steven Sweet and Joey Allen ©.

"Here I Go Again" written by David Coverdale and Bernard Marsden. © 1982 C.C. Songs Ltd. (PRS) and Seabreeze Music Ltd. Administered by WB Music Corp. (ASCAP). All rights reserved. Used by permission.

"High Enough" written by Jack Blades, Ted Nugent and Tommy R. Shaw. © Published by Bicycle Music Company, Broadhead Publishing and Wixen Music.

"Hit Me With Your Best Shot" written by E. Schwartz. © Sony/ATV Tunes LLC/ASCAP.

"I Hate Myself for Loving You" written by Desmond Child and Joan Jett. © All rights owned or administered by Universal-PolyGram Int. Publ., Inc./ASCAP. Used by permission.

"I Wanna Rock" written by Daniel Dee Snider. © All rights owned or administered by Universal Music-Z Melodies on behalf of Snidest Music/SESAC. Used by permission.

"I Want to Know What Love Is" written by Michael Leslie Jones. © Published by Somerset Songs Publishing, Inc.

"Just Like Paradise" written by David Lee Roth and Brett Tuggle. © Diamond Dave Music c/o RS Plane Music.

"Keep on Lovin' You" written by Kevin Cronin. © Published by Fate Music (ASCAP).

"Kiss Me Deadly" written by Mick Smiley. © Published by The Twin Towers Co. and Mike Chapman Publishing Enterprises.

"More Than Words" written by Nuno Bettencourt and

Gary F. Cherone. © All rights owned or administered by Almo Music Corp. on behalf of Color Me Blind Music/ASCAP. Used by permission.

"Nothin' But a Good Time" written by Bobby Dall, Bruce Anthony Johannesson, Bret Michaels, Rikki Rocket. © All rights owned or administered by Universal Music-Z Songs on behalf of Cyanide Publ./BMI. Used by permission.

"Oh Sherrie" written by Steve Perry, Randy Goodrum, Bill Cuomo, Craig Krampf. © Published by Street Talk Tunes, April Music Inc & Random Notes, Pants Down Music and Phosphene Music.

"Renegade" written by Tommy Shaw. © All rights owned or administered by Almo Music Corp. on behalf of itself and Stygian Songs /ASCAP. Used by permission.

"The Search Is Over" written by Frank Sullivan and Jim Peterik. © Published by Ensign Music LLC (BMI). Used by permission. All rights reserved.

"Shadows of the Night" written by D.L. Byron. © Zen Archer/ASCAP.

"Sister Christian" written by Kelly Keagy. © Published by Bicycle Music Company.

"To Be With You" written by Eric Martin, David Grahame, William Sheehan, Pat Torpey and Paul Gilbert. © Dog Turner Music/EMI April Music/ASCAP.

"Too Much Time on My Hands" written by Tommy Shaw. © Stygian Songs/ASCAP.

"Waiting for a Girl Like You" written by Michael Leslie Jones and Louis Gramattico. © Published by Somerset Songs Publishing, Inc.

"Wanted Dead or Alive" written by Jon Bon Jovi and Richard S. Sambora. © All rights owned or administered by Universal-Polygram Int. Publ., Inc. on behalf of itself and Bon Jovi Publishing/ASCAP. Used by permission.

"We Built This City" written by Dennis Lambert, Martin George Page, Bernie Taupin and Peter Wolf. © All rights owned or administered by Universal-Polygram Int. Publ., Inc. on behalf of Little Mole Music Inc./ASCAP. Used by permission.

"We're Not Gonna Take It" written by Daniel Dee Snider. © All rights owned or administered by Universal Music-Z Melodies on behalf of Snidest Music/SESAC. Used by permission.

NEDERLANDER

Chairman ....**James M. Nederlander**
President ....**James L. Nederlander**

Executive Vice President
Nick Scandalios

Vice President
Corporate Development
Charlene S. Nederlander

Senior Vice President
Labor Relations
Herschel Waxman

Vice President
Jim Boese

Chief Financial Officer
Freida Sawyer Belviso

The Seagull

First Preview: September 16, 2008. Opened: October 2, 2008.
Closed December 21, 2008 after 18 Previews and 94 Perfomances.

PLAYBILL®

CAST

(in order of appearance)

Konstantin	MACKENZIE CROOK
Yakov	CHRISTOPHER PATRICK NOLAN
Masha	ZOE KAZAN
Medvedenko	PEARCE QUIGLEY
Sorin	PETER WIGHT
Nina	CAREY MULLIGAN
Polina	ANN DOWD
Dorn	ART MALIK
Shamrayev	JULIAN GAMBLE
Arkadina	KRISTIN SCOTT THOMAS
Trigorin	PETER SARSGAARD
A Housemaid	MARY ROSE
The Cook	MARK L. MONTGOMERY

The action takes place in the house and gardens
of Sorin's estate.

Two years pass between Acts Three and Four.

UNDERSTUDIES

For Masha, Polina:
MARY ROSE
For Trigorin:
MARK L. MONTGOMERY
For Sorin, Shamrayev, Dorn:
JARLATH CONROY
For Nina, Masha, A Housemaid:
JESSICA CUMMINGS
For Arkadina, Polina, The Cook:
LYNNDA FERGUSON
For Konstantin, Yakov, Medvedenko:
JONATHAN FIELDING

WALTER KERR THEATRE
A JUJAMCYN THEATRE
ROCCO LANDESMAN
President

PAUL LIBIN	JACK VIERTEL	JORDAN ROTH
Producing Director	Creative Director	Vice President

SONIA FRIEDMAN PRODUCTIONS   BOB BOYETT   ROBERT G. BARTNER   DEDE HARRIS
NORMAN & STEVEN TULCHIN   FOX THEATRICALS   DENA HAMMERSTEIN   SHARON KARMAZIN   OLYMPUS THEATRICALS   SPRING SIRKIN   TARA SMITH
MORTON SWINSKY   KARL SYDOW   THE WEINSTEIN COMPANY   FALKENSTEIN/DEROY   FLORIN/HIRSCHHORN   GUTTERMAN/McGINNIS

Present the ROYAL COURT THEATRE production of

KRISTIN SCOTT THOMAS   PETER SARSGAARD
MACKENZIE CROOK

in

the SEAGULL

By
ANTON CHEKHOV

In a new version by
CHRISTOPHER HAMPTON

with

ART MALIK   CAREY MULLIGAN   PEARCE QUIGLEY   PETER WIGHT   ZOE KAZAN
ANN DOWD   JULIAN GAMBLE   CHRISTOPHER PATRICK NOLAN   MARY ROSE   MARK L. MONTGOMERY

Scenic and Costume Design	Lighting Design	Sound Design	Composer
HILDEGARD BECHTLER	PETER MUMFORD	IAN DICKINSON	STEPHEN WARBECK

Production Stage Manager	U.K. Casting	U.S. Casting
ARTHUR GAFFIN	LISA MAKIN	JIM CARNAHAN, C.S.A.

Press Representative	Production Management	Associate Producer for RBT
BONEAU/BRYAN-BROWN	AURORA PRODUCTIONS	TIM LEVY

General Management	U.K. General Management
STUART THOMPSON PRODUCTIONS/DAVID TURNER	SONIA FRIEDMAN PRODUCTIONS

ROYAL COURT
IN NEW YORK

Directed by
IAN RICKSON

The Producers wish to express their appreciation to the Theatre Development Fund for its support of this production.

10/2/08

(L-R): Mackenzie Crook as Konstantin and Kristin Scott Thomas as Arkadina.

Photo by Joan Marcus

The Seagull

Kristin Scott Thomas
Arkadina

Peter Sarsgaard
Trigorin

Mackenzie Crook
Konstantin

Art Malik
Dorn

Carey Mulligan
Nina

Pearce Quigley
Medvedenko

Peter Wight
Sorin

Zoe Kazan
Masha

Ann Dowd
Polina

Julian Gamble
Shamrayev

Christopher Patrick Nolan
Yakov

Mary Rose
A Housemaid

Mark L. Montgomery
The Cook

Jarlath Conroy
u/s Sorin, Shamrayev, Dorn

Jessica Cummings
u/s Nina, Masha, A Housemaid

Lynnda Ferguson
u/s Arkadina, Polina, The Cook

Jonathan Fielding
u/s Konstantin, Medvedenko, Yakov

Anton Chekhov
Playwright

Christopher Hampton
New Version

Hildegard Bechtler
Scenic and Costume Design

Jim Carnahan
U.S. Casting

Stuart Thompson Productions
General Management

Sonia Friedman Productions
Producer

Bob Boyett
Producer

Dede Harris
Producer

Sharon Karmazin
Producer

Spring Sirkin
Producer

Tara Smith
Producer

Morton Swinsky
Producer

Bob Weinstein, The Weinstein Company
Producer

Harvey Weinstein, The Weinstein Company
Producer

Eric Falkenstein
Producer

Jamie deRoy
Producer

Larry Hirschhorn
Producer

Joe McGinnis
Producer

The Seagull

Jay & Cindy Gutterman
Producers

BOX OFFICE
(L-R): Harry Jaffie and Gail Yerkovich

Photos by Brian Mapp

FRONT OF HOUSE

STAFF FOR *THE SEAGULL*

GENERAL MANAGEMENT
STUART THOMPSON PRODUCTIONS

Stuart Thompson	David Turner
Caroline Prugh	James Triner

UK GENERAL MANAGEMENT
SONIA FRIEDMAN PRODUCTIONS

Diane Benjamin	Pam Skinner
Matthew Gordon	Sharon Duckworth

COMPANY MANAGER
Adam J. Miller

PRODUCTION MANAGEMENT
AURORA PRODUCTIONS INC.

Gene O'Donovan	W. Benjamin Heller II
Bethany Weinstein	Melissa Mazdra
Amy Merlino Coey	Laura Archer
	Dana Hesch

PRESS REPRESENTATIVE
BONEAU/BRYAN-BROWN
Adrian Bryan-Brown Jim Byk Matt Ross

Production Stage Manager ....Arthur Gaffin
Stage Manager ....Jamie Greathouse
U.K. Stage Manager ....Maddy Grant
U.K. Associate Scenic Designer ....Luke Smith
U.S. Associate Scenic Designer ....Charlie Smith
U.K. Associate Costume Designer ....Laura Hunt
U.S. Associate Costume Designer ....Katie Irish
U.K. Associate Lighting Designer ....Steve Andrews
U.S. Associate Lighting Designer ....Dale Knoth
U.S. Associate Sound Designer ....Joanna Lynne Staub
Production Carpenter ....George Fullum
Production Electrician ....Drayton Allison
Head Props ....Andy Meeker
Production Sound ....Bill Lewis
Wardrobe Supervisor ....Kelly A. Saxon
Dresser for Ms. Scott Thomas ....Amelia Haywood
Dressers ....Mickey Abbate, Ron Fleming
Hair Supervisor ....Valerie Gladstone
Production Assistant ....Adam Norrish
General Management
   Assistants ....Megan Curren, Geo Karapetyan,
      Aaron Thompson
General Management Intern ....Quinn Corbin
Banking ....City National Bank/
      Michele Gibbons
Payroll ....Castellana Services, Inc.
Accountant ....Fried & Kowgios CPA's LLP/
      Robert Fried, CPA
Controller ....Joseph Kubala
Insurance ....DeWitt Stern Group
Legal Counsel ....Lazarus & Harris LLP/
      Scott Lazarus, Esq.; Robert C. Harris, Esq.;
      Andrew Farber, Esq.
Advertising ....SPOTCO/
      Drew Hodges, Jim Edwards,
      Jim Aquino, Stacey Maya
Production Photographer ....Joan Marcus
Theatre Displays ....King Displays, Inc.
Opening Night ....Cristina Baldacci,
      Touch and reallyspectacular.com

SONIA FRIEDMAN PRODUCTIONS

Producer ....Sonia Friedman
Chief Executive Officer-NY ....David Lazar
General Manager ....Diane Benjamin
Creative Producer ....Lisa Makin
Head of Production ....Pam Skinner
Associate Producer......................Matthew Gordon
Associate Producer ....Sharon Duckworth
Literary Associate ....Jack Bradley
Production Assistant ....Lucie Lovatt
Production Assistant ....Martin Ball
Production Assistant ....Jamie Hendry
Executive Assistant-NY ....Dan Gallagher
Production Accountant ....Melissa Hay
SFP Board ....Helen Enright,
      Howard Panter, Rosemary Squire

FOR THE ROYAL COURT THEATRE

Artistic Director ....Dominic Cooke
Executive Director .... Kate Horton
Associate Producer .... Diane Borger
Production Manager ....Paul Handley
Head of Communications ....Kym Bartlett

CREDITS
Scenery by Souvenir Scenic Studios Ltd. Lighting equipment from PRG Lighting. Sound equipment from PRG Audio. Additional scenery work by Simon Kenny and crew, Hudson Scenic Studios. Hosiery and undergarments by Bra*Tenders.

Special thanks to Paul Handley.

🜋 JUJAMCYN THEATERS

ROCCO LANDESMAN
President

PAUL LIBIN	**JACK VIERTEL**	**JORDAN ROTH**
Producing Director	Creative Director	Vice President
DANIEL ADAMIAN		**JENNIFER HERSHEY**
General Manager		Director of Operations
MEREDITH VILLATORE		**JERRY ZAKS**
Chief Financial Officer		Resident Director

STAFF FOR THE WALTER KERR THEATRE
Manager ....Susan Elrod
Treasurer ....Harry Jaffie
Carpenter..................................George E. Fullum
Propertyman ....Timothy Bennet
Electrician ....Vincent Valvo, Jr.
Engineer ....Vladimir Belenky

Photo by Joan Marcus

(L-R): Peter Sarsgaard and Carey Mulligan

The Seagull
SCRAPBOOK

Photos by Aubrey Reuben

1. Leading Lady Kristin Scott Thomas at the opening night party at Sardi's.
2. Zoe Kazan and Paul Dano at the party.
3. Cast member Peter Wight and his daughter after the premiere.

Photos by Brian Mapp

CREW
(L-R): Peter J. "P.J." Iacoviello, George Fullum, Bill Lewis, David Holliman, Andy Meeker, Drayton Allison, Tim Bennet

STAGE MANAGERS AND COMPANY MANAGERS
Front Row: Jamie Greathouse

Back Row (L-R): Adam Miller, Arthur (Artie) Gaffin, Adam Norrish

WARDROBE AND HAIR
Front Row (L-R): Ron Fleming, Valerie Gladstone

Back Row (L-R): Mickey Abbate, Kelly Saxon, Amelia Haywood

Shrek The Musical

First Preview: November 8, 2008. Opened: December 14, 2008.
Still running as of May 31, 2009.

PLAYBILL

CAST

(in alphabetical order)

Ensemble	CAMERON ADAMS
Donkey	DANIEL BREAKER
Sugar Plum Fairy, Gingy	HAVEN BURTON
Shoemaker's Elf, Duloc Performer, Blind Mouse	JENNIFER CODY
Sticks, Bishop	BOBBY DAYE
Bricks	RYAN DUNCAN
Ugly Duckling, Blind Mouse	SARAH JANE EVERMAN
Princess Fiona	SUTTON FOSTER
Mama Bear	AYMEE GARCIA
Young Fiona (Wed., Fri., Sun.)	LEAH GREENHAUS
Baby Bear, Blind Mouse	LISA HO
King Harold, Big Bad Wolf, Captain of the Guard	CHRIS HOCH
Fairy Godmother, Magic Mirror Assistant, Bluebird	DANETTE HOLDEN
Shrek	BRIAN D'ARCY JAMES
Ensemble	MARTY LAWSON
Papa Ogre, Straw	JACOB MING-TRENT
Teen Fiona	MARISSA O'DONNELL
Peter Pan	DENNY PASCHALL
Young Fiona (Tue., Thu., Sat.)	RACHEL RESHEFF
Gnome, Pied Piper	GREG REUTER
Young Shrek, Dwarf	ADAM RIEGLER
White Rabbit	NOAH RIVERA
Lord Farquaad	CHRISTOPHER SIEBER

Continued on next page

⑤ BROADWAY THEATRE

1681 Broadway
A Shubert Organization Theatre

Gerald Schoenfeld, *Chairman*   **Philip J. Smith,** *President*

Robert E. Wankel, *Executive Vice President*

DREAMWORKS THEATRICALS

NEAL STREET PRODUCTIONS

present

SHREK THE MUSICAL

Based on the DreamWorks Animation Motion Picture and the Book by William Steig

Book and Lyrics by   Music by
DAVID LINDSAY-ABAIRE   **JEANINE TESORI**

Starring

BRIAN D'ARCY JAMES   SUTTON FOSTER   CHRISTOPHER SIEBER

JOHN TARTAGLIA and **DANIEL BREAKER**

CAMERON ADAMS   HAVEN BURTON   JENNIFER CODY   BOBBY DAYE   RYAN DUNCAN   SARAH JANE EVERMAN
AYMEE GARCIA   LEAH GREENHAUS   JUSTIN GREER   LISA HO   CHRIS HOCH   DANETTE HOLDEN   MARTY LAWSON
JACOB MING-TRENT   CAROLYN OCKERT-HAYTHE   MARISSA O'DONNELL   DENNY PASCHALL   GREG REUTER   RACHEL RESHEFF
ADAM RIEGLER   NOAH RIVERA   HEATHER JANE ROLFF   JENNIFER SIMARD   RACHEL STERN   DENNIS STOWE   DAVID F.M. VAUGHN

	Scenic & Costume Design **TIM HATLEY**	Lighting Design **HUGH VANSTONE**	
Sound Design **PETER HYLENSKI**	Hair/Wig Design **DAVID BRIAN-BROWN**	Make-up Design **NAOMI DONNE**	Puppet Design **TIM HATLEY**
Casting **TARA RUBIN CASTING, CSA**	Illusions Consultant **MARSHALL MAGOON**	Associate Director **PETER LAWRENCE**	Production Management **AURORA PRODUCTIONS**
Dance Arrangements **MATTHEW SKLAR**	Vocal Arrangements **JEANINE TESORI & TIM WEIL**	Associate Orchestrator **JOHN CLANCY**	Music Coordinator **MICHAEL KELLER**
Press Representative **BONEAU/BRYAN-BROWN**	Marketing Director **CLINT BOND JR.**	General Management **STUART THOMPSON PRODUCTIONS/ JAMES TRINER**	

Orchestrations
DANNY TROOB

Music Direction & Incidental Music Arrangements
TIM WEIL

Choreographed by
JOSH PRINCE

Directed by
JASON MOORE

The opening night performance of SHREK THE MUSICAL is dedicated to Gerald Schoenfeld.

12/14/08

Christopher Sieber (center) and company perform "What's Up, Duloc?"

Photo by Joan Marcus

Shrek The Musical

(L-R): Leah Greenhaus, Sutton Foster and Marissa O'Donnell perform "I Know It's Today."

MUSICAL NUMBERS

ACT I
"Big Bright Beautiful World"
"Story of My Life"
"The Goodbye Song"
"Don't Let Me Go"
"I Know It's Today"
"What's Up, Duloc?"
"Travel Song"
"Donkey Pot Pie"
"This Is How a Dream Comes True"
"Who I'd Be"

ACT II
"Morning Person"
"I Think I Got You Beat"
"The Ballad of Farquaad"
"Make a Move"
"When Words Fail"
"Morning Person" (Reprise)
"Build a Wall"
"Freak Flag"
"Big Bright Beautiful World" (Reprise)
"Finale"

Cast Continued

Queen Lillian, Wicked Witch,
   Magic Mirror Assistant .... JENNIFER SIMARD
Mama Ogre, Humpty Dumpty ...RACHEL STERN
Barker, Papa Bear, Thelonius .....DENNIS STOWE
Pinocchio, The Magic Mirror,
   Dragon Puppeteer ....JOHN TARTAGLIA

UNDERSTUDIES
Standby for Shrek:
BEN CRAWFORD
For Shrek:
JACOB MING-TRENT
For Princess Fiona:
HAVEN BURTON,
SARAH JANE EVERMAN
For Donkey:
BOBBY DAYE, RYAN DUNCAN
For Lord Farquaad:
CHRIS HOCH, GREG REUTER
For Pinocchio:
DENNY PASCHALL, NOAH RIVERA
For Teen Fiona:
HAVEN BURTON
For Young Shrek:
LEAH GREENHAUS, RACHEL RESHEFF

SWINGS
JUSTIN GREER,
CAROLYN OCKERT-HAYTHE,
HEATHER JANE ROLFF,
DAVID F.M. VAUGHN

DANCE CAPTAIN
JUSTIN GREER

(L-R): Brian d'Arcy James, Daniel Breaker and Sutton Foster

Photos by Joan Marcus

ORCHESTRA
Conductor:
TIM WEIL
Associate Conductor:
JASON DeBORD
Concertmaster:
ANTOINE SILVERMAN
Violins:
JONATHAN DINKLAGE, ENTCHO
TODOROV, SEAN CARNEY
Cellos:
JEANNE LEBLANC, ANJA WOOD
Acoustic Bass:
BILL ELLISON
Flutes:
ANDERS BOSTROM
Reeds:
CHARLES PILLOW, JACK BASHKOW,
RON JANNELLI
Trumpets:
ANTHONY KADLECK, BUD BURRIDGE
Trombones:
BRUCE EIDEM, MORRIS KAINUMA
French Horn:
ADAM KRAUTHAMER

Keyboards:
JOHN DELEY, JASON DeBORD
Guitars:
KEN BRESCIA, BOB BAXMEYER
Electric Bass:
LUCIO HOPPER
Drums:
WARREN ODZE
Percussion:
SHANE SHANAHAN

Electronic Music Design:
ANDREW BARRETT
FOR LIONELLA MUSIC LLC
Music Copying:
KAYE-HOUSTON MUSIC/
ANNE KAYE & DOUG HOUSTON

SPECIAL THANKS
The creative team would like to thank all the filmmakers and artists at DreamWorks and PDI/DreamWorks who opened and welcomed us into their SHREK world.

Shrek The Musical

Brian d'Arcy James
Shrek

Sutton Foster
Princess Fiona

Christopher Sieber
Lord Farquaad

Daniel Breaker
Donkey

John Tartaglia
*Pinocchio,
The Magic Mirror,
Dragon Puppeteer*

Cameron Adams
Ensemble

Haven Burton
*Sugar Plum Fairy,
Gingy*

Jennifer Cody
*Shoemaker's Elf,
Duloc Performer,
Blind Mouse*

Bobby Daye
Sticks, Bishop

Ryan Duncan
Bricks

Sarah Jane Everman
*Ugly Duckling,
Blind Mouse*

Aymee Garcia
Mama Bear

Leah Greenhaus
Young Fiona

Justin Greer
*Dance Captain/
Swing*

Lisa Ho
*Baby Bear,
Blind Mouse*

Chris Hoch
*King Harold,
Big Bad Wolf,
Captain of the Guard*

Danette Holden
*Fairy Godmother,
Magic Mirror
Assistant, Bluebird*

Marty Lawson
Ensemble

Jacob Ming-Trent
Papa Ogre, Straw

Carolyn Ockert-
Haythe
Swing

Marissa O'Donnell
Teen Fiona

Denny Paschall
Peter Pan

Rachel Resheff
Young Fiona

Greg Reuter
Gnome, Pied Piper

Adam Riegler
Young Shrek, Dwarf

Noah Rivera
White Rabbit

Heather Jane Rolff
Swing

Jennifer Simard
*Queen Lillian,
Wicked Witch,
Magic Mirror
Assistant*

Rachel Stern
*Mama Ogre,
Humpty Dumpty*

Dennis Stowe
*Barker, Papa Bear,
Thelonius*

David F.M. Vaughn
Swing

David Lindsay-Abaire
Book & Lyrics

Jeanine Tesori
Music

Jason Moore
Director

Tim Hatley
*Set, Costume &
Puppet Design*

Shrek The Musical

Hugh Vanstone
Lighting

Peter Hylenski
Sound Designer

Danny Troob
Orchestrator

David Brian Brown
Wig/Hair Design

Naomi Donne
Makeup Design

Tara Rubin Casting
Casting

Matthew Sklar
Dance Music Arranger

Michael Keller
Music Coordinator

Peter Lawrence
Associate Director

Andrew Barrett
Electronic Music Design

Stuart Thompson Productions
General Management

James Triner
General Manager

Sam Mendes,
Neal Street Productions
Producer

Ryan Worsing
Swing

2008-2009 AWARDS

TONY AWARD
Best Costume Design of a Musical
(Tim Hatley)

DRAMA DESK AWARDS
Outstanding Actor in a Musical
(Brian d'Arcy James)
Outstanding Set Design of a Musical
(Tim Hatley)
Outstanding Costume Design
(Tim Hatley)

OUTER CRITICS CIRCLE AWARDS
Outstanding Actress in a Musical
(Sutton Foster)
Outstanding Set Design
(Tim Hatley)
Outstanding Costume Design
(Tim Hatley)

CREW
Front Row (L-R): Roy Franks, James Cariot, Jason McKenna, Tommy Cole, Alan Grudzinski, Mike Martinez

Back Row (L-R): Bob Beimers, Bryan Davis, Charlie Grieco, Andy Miller, Peter Becker, Paul Davila, Mike Cornell, Declan McNeil, Drew Lanzarotta

Photo by Brian Mapp

Shrek The Musical

Photos by Brian Mapp

WARDROBE/HAIR/MAKE-UP
Front Row (L-R): Michael Sancineto, Julien Havard, Megan Bowers, Meghan Carsella, Angela Johnson, Christina Grant, David Presto, Jack Scott, Hiro Hosomizu

Back Row (L-R): Liz Mathews, Pam Hughes, James Roy, Joan Weiss, Dan Foss, Emily Ockenfels, Adam Bailey, Victoria Tjoelker, Cleo Matheos, Alessandro Ferdico, Pam Kurz, Richard Orton, Anthony Hoffman, Joel Hawkins, Julienne Schubert-Blechman

FRONT OF HOUSE STAFF
Back Row (L-R): Freddie Matos, Sean McMonoco, Karen Banyai, Mea Park, William Denson, Michael Harris, Lori Bokun, Ismeal Tirado, Robert Evans

Front Row (L-R): Lana Pinkhas, Ulises Santiago, Mattie Robinson, Andi Hopkins, John Hall, Nathan Wright, Jorge Colon

COMPANY MANAGEMENT
(L-R): Roeya Banuazizi, Scott Armstrong

DOORMAN
Fernando Sepulveda

STAGE MANAGEMENT
(L-R): Chad Lewis (holding picture of Peter Lawrence), Stacey Zaloga, Rachel A. Wolff, Beverly Jenkins

---

STAFF FOR *SHREK THE MUSICAL*

GENERAL MANAGEMENT
Stuart Thompson   James Triner
David Turner   Caroline Prugh

PRESS REPRESENTATIVE
BONEAU/BRYAN-BROWN
Adrian Bryan-Brown   Heath Schwartz
Matt Polk   Christine Olver

CASTING
TARA RUBIN CASTING
Tara Rubin, CSA   Eric Woodall, CSA
Laura Schutzel, CSA   Merri Sugarman, CSA
Rebecca Carfagna   Paige Blansfield   Dale Brown

PRODUCTION MANAGEMENT
AURORA PRODUCTIONS INC.
Gene O'Donovan   W. Benjamin Heller II
Bethany Weinstein   Melissa Mazdra
Amy Merlino Coey   Laura Archer   Dana Hesch

COMPANY MANAGER
Roeya Banuazizi

PRODUCTION
STAGE MANAGER ....PETER LAWRENCE
Stage Manager ....Rachel A. Wolff
Assistant Stage Manager .... Chad Lewis
Assistant Company Manager ....Scott Armstrong
Assistant Director ....Stephen Sposito
Associate Choreographer ....Sloan Just
Dance Captain ....Justin Greer
Puppet Captain ....John Tartaglia

Assistants to Stage Managers ....Stacey Zaloga,
Bryan Rountree
Associate Scenic Designer ....Paul Weimer
UK Scenic Associate ....Andrew Edwards
UK Scenic Assistant .... Tim Blazdell
UK Model Makers ....Ben Davies, Paul Tulley
Assistant Scenic Designers ....Derek Stenborg,
Zhanna Gervich
US Associate Costume
Designers ....Tracy Christensen, Brian J. Bustos
Associate Costume Designer ....Jack Galloway
Assistant Costume Designers ....Jessica Wegener,
Sarah Laux
Costume Department Assistants ....Leon Dobkowski,
Katie Irish, Roxana Ramseur
Associate Lighting Designer ....Philip Rosenberg
Assistant Lighting Designer ....Anthony Pearson
Moving Light Programmer ....Sharon Huizinga
Associate Sound Designer ....Keith Caggiano

Shrek The Musical

Associate Hair/Wig Designer ....Susan Corrado
Associate Makeup Designer ....Angela L. Johnson
Associate Prosthetics Designer ....Dave Presto
Assistant to the Makeup Designer ....Nicky Pattison
Media Associate and Programmer ....Laura Frank
Media Assistant.................................Joshua Fleitell
Production Carpenter ....Mike Martinez
Deck Carpenter ....Rick Styles
Fly Automation Carpenter ....Alan Grudzinski
Deck Automation Carpenter ....Bill Partello
Production Electricians ....James J. Fedigan,
Randall Zaibek
Head Electrician ....Mike Cornell
Deck Electrician ....Paul D.J. Davila
Follow Spot Operator ....Andrew Dean
Pyro/Special Effects Electrician ....Roy Franks
Production Sound ....Phil Lojo
Head Sound Engineer.....................David Dignazio
Assistant Sound Engineer....................Dan Hochstine
Production Props ....Jerry Marshall
Assistant Props ....Andrew Miller
Wardrobe Supervisor ....Michael Sancineto
Assistant Wardrobe Supervisor ....Meghan Carsella
Dressers ....Megan Bowers, Alessandro Ferdico,
Dan Foss, Sara Foster, Tony Hoffman,
Hiro Hosomizu, Pamela Hughes,
Kurt Kielmann, Pamela Kurz,
Emily Ockenfels, Julienne Schubert-Blechman,
Joan Weiss
Brian d'Arcy James' Dresser ....Jack Scott
Sutton Foster's Dresser ....Julien Havard
Production Hair Supervisor ....Carole Morales
Assistant Hair Supervisor ....Richard Orton
Hairdressers ....Joel Hawkins, Liz Mathews
Hair Day Worker ....Chelsea Roth
Production Makeup Supervisor ....Angela L. Johnson
Assistant Makeup Supervisor ....Christina Grant
Shrek Makeup Artist ....Dave Presto
Dialect Coach ....Stephen Gabis
Electronic Music Design Associate .... Jeff Marder
Rehearsal Pianists ....Jodie Moore, Matt Perri,
John Deley
Rehearsal Percussion ....Warren Odze
Production Assistant.......................Jacqueline Prats
Music Department Assistant ....Michael Gacetta
General Management Assistants .... Megan Curren,
Geo Karapetyan, Quinn Corbin
Management Intern ....Stevie Boothe
Child Wrangler ....Bridget Walders
Scenic Design Intern ....Melissa Shakun
Costume Interns ....Thomas Legalley, Robert Croghan
Banking ....JPMorgan/Chase
Payroll ....Castellana Services, Inc.
Production Accountant ....Erica Whelan
Insurance ....Marsh Risk and Insurance Services
Legal
Counsel .....Paul, Weiss, Rifkind, Wharton & Garrison
Merchandising ....Max Merchandising
Advertising...SPOTCO/
Drew Hodges, Jim Edwards,
Tom Greenwald, Tom McCann, Josh Fraenkel
Production Photographer ....Joan Marcus
NY Company Physical Therapists...............PhysioArts
NY Company Orthopaedist ....David S. Weiss, M.D.
Children's Tutoring ....On Location Education
Broadway Group Sales ....Shubert Group Sales

Prosthetic Makeup Design
Michael Marino
Prosthetic Renaissance
Hayes Vilandry   Roland Blancafor
Chris Kelly   Paul Komoda

CREDITS
Scenery fabrication by PRG-Scenic Technologies, a division of Production Resource Group, LLC, New Windsor, NY. Additional scenery and fly automation by Hudson Scenic Studios. Additional scenery by Scenic Art Studios, Inc., Souvenir Scenic Studios Ltd., Arquepoise Limited, Seattle Repertory Theatre. Deck effect show control and scenic motion control featuring Stage Command Systems® by PRG Scenic Technologies, a division of Production Resource Group, LLC, New Windsor, NY. Lighting equipment from PRG Lighting. Audio equipment from PRG Audio. Video projection system provided by Scharff Weisberg Inc. Pyrotechnical effects by Kelly Sticksel/Excitement Technologies Group. Props fabricated by Arnold S. Levine, Inc.; Zoe Morsette; Moonboots Productions, Inc.; Randy Carfagno Productions; Jerard Studio, Inc.; ICBA, Inc.; Paragon Innovation Group; Cigar Box Studios, Inc.; Peter Sarafin; Craig Grigg; Proof Productions; Seattle Repertory Theatre; Sean McArdle; Lewis Shaw; Spoon Group. Costumes executed by Tricorne, Inc.; Parsons-Meares, Ltd.; Eric Winterling, Inc.; Barbara Matera, Ltd.; Seams Unlimited; Crystal Thompson. Costume crafts by Marian Jean Hose, Leigh Cranston, Erik Andor. Costume mechanics by Jon Gellman Effects, Perfection Electricks, Michael Curry Design, Inc. Knitwear by Maria Ficalora Knitwear, Ltd. Custom fabric printing by Gene Mignola. Armor by Costume Armor. Custom millinery provided by Lynne Mackey Studio; Arnold S. Levine, Inc.; Rodney Gordon. Custom footwear by Capri Shoes by Oscar Navarro. Handmade shoes by Fred Longtin, LaDuca, Capezio, JC Theatrical. Custom and fabric painting by Jose Asiatico, Jeff Fender, Virginia Clow, Claudia Dzundza, Mary Macy, Parmelee Welles Tolkan, Margaret Peot. Costume flameproofing by Turning Star, Inc. Hosiery and undergarments by Bra*Tenders. Airbrushes supplied by Iwata. Mehron makeup. Wigs by Ray Marston Wig Studio, Victoria Wood Wigs, Bob Kelly Wigs. Drums from Yamaha Corporation of America. Performing Arts Short Term Housing. Road Rebel. Natural herb cough drops courtesy of Ricola USA, Inc.

Dragon and Travel Song puppets by Rick Lazzarini/ The Character Shop.

Rehearsed at the New 42nd Street Studios.

Makeup Provided by
MAKE UP FOR EVER

Magic Mirror Technology by
AUTODESK
Brett Ineson   Kamal Mistry
Kevin Smith   Jason Walter

CHASE is the official credit card of *Shrek the Musical*.

Sheraton Hotels & Resorts is the official hotel of
Shrek the Musical.

SPECIAL THANKS
Andrew Adamson, Guillaume Aretos, Denise Cascino, Ann Daly, Philippe Denis, Anne Globe, Vicky Jenson, Jim Mainard, Chris Miller, Terry Press, Chip Sullivan, Aron Warner, Sunny Ye.

A very special thanks to the amazing and talented artists at DreamWorks and PDI DreamWorks who contributed to the show: Sean Bishop, Doug Cooper, Martin Costello, David Doepp, John Dorst, Corban Gossett, Daniel Hashimoto, Anthony Hodgson, Pam Hu, Jucas Janin, Andrew Kim, Gina Lawes, Betsy Nofsinger, Alex Ongaro, Jason Reisig, Jason Schleifer, Scott Singer, Bill Stahl, Munira Tayabji, Mike Yamada

DREAMWORKS THEATRICALS
President ....Bill Damaschke
President's Office ....Carole Sue Lipman, Alex Loots
Marketing (NY) ....Clint Bond, Jr., David Carpenter,
Steven Rummer, Melissa Heller
Promotions ....Susan Spencer, Linda Kehn,
Chris Fahland
Consumer Products ....Kerry Phelan, Joel Ward
Operations/Finance .... Bruce Daitch
Business Affairs/Operations ....Jamie Kershaw
Finance ....Gary Raksis, Laura Fratianne,
Kathleen Frederickson
Insurance ....Ross Pebley
Administrative ....Cynthia Park, Belinda Arge,
Diane Stromer, Frank Hundley,
Alissa Wright, Andy Areffi

NEAL STREET PRODUCTIONS LTD.
Directors ....Sam Mendes, Caro Newling, Pippa Harris
Associate Producer Theatre ....Beth Byrne
Executive Coordinator ....Milly Leigh
General Assistant ....Caroline Reynolds

THE SHUBERT ORGANIZATION, INC.
Board of Directors

Gerald Schoenfeld	**Philip J. Smith**
Chairman	President
Wyche Fowler, Jr.	**John W. Kluge**
Lee J. Seidler	**Michael I. Sovern**

Stuart Subotnick

Elliot Greene	**David Andrews**
Chief Financial Officer	Senior Vice President Shubert Ticketing
Juan Calvo	**John Darby**
Vice President and Controller	Vice President Facilities
Peter Entin	**Charles Flateman**
Vice President Theatre Operations	Vice President Marketing
Anthony LaMattina	**Brian Mahoney**
Vice President Audit & Production Finance	Vice President Ticket Sales

D.S. Moynihan
Vice President – Creative Projects

Theatre Manager ....Michael S. R. Harris

Shrek The Musical
SCRAPBOOK

1. Leads and creators (L-R): Daniel Breaker, Brian d'Arcy James, Josh Prince, Sutton Foster, Jeanine Tesori, John Tartaglia, Jason Moore, David Lindsay-Abaire and Christopher Sieber.
2. Foster at the recording of the cast album.

Correspondent: Aymee Garcia, "Mama Bear," "Dragonette"

Memorable Opening Night Fax: Sam Mendes on opening night in Seattle. We copied down his fax number so we could stalk him.

Opening Night Gifts: Green iPods engraved with our logo and the opening night date from DreamWorks. Framed full-cast photos from DreamWorks. Engraved clocks that read "I'm a Morning Person Hooray!!" from Jason Moore. Personally illustrated storybooks with the tale of the creation of *Shrek The Musical* from Jeanine Tesori and David Lindsay-Abaire. A beautiful Shrek travel thermos from Josh Prince and Sloan Just … and much, much more!

Most Exciting Celebrity Visitors: Kevin Clash (Elmo). He left a voice message for Ellery Jo and Archer, Danette Holden's (Fairy Godmother) actual children in his Elmo voice. Cameron Diaz climbed up four flights of stairs just to say hello to EVERYONE. Steven Spielberg was amazing. Hugh Jackman was very sweet and, come on, it's Hugh Jackman!

Who Got the Gypsy Robe: Jen Cody. We made a panel with swatches from everyone's costume and bedazzled the crap out of it. Everyone signed the robe near their swatch of fabric.

"Easter Bonnet" Sketch: Jen Simard, Greg Reuter, David Vaughn, Ryan Duncan, and Rachel Stern wrote it. Bobby Daye helped with putting all the sound clips together. David Vaughn, Marty Lawson, Jen Cody, Cameron Adams, Heather Jane Rolff, Sarah Jane Everman, Noah Rivera, Haven Burton, Lisa Ho, Rachel Stern, Bridget Walders, Aymee Garcia, Ryan Duncan, Denny Paschall, Adam Riegler, Marissa O'Donnell, Leah Greenhaus, Rachel Resheff and Johnny Tartaglia performed it, with Chris Sieber doing voiceover.

Actor Who Performed the Most Roles: Denny Paschall: Festive Villager, Peter Pan, Guard, Duloc doll, skeleton, rat, monk, dragon puppeteer.

Most Shows in Career: Peter Lawrence (Production Stage Manager): 28 Broadway shows.

Special Rituals: Marty Lawson does a full dance and vocal warm-up before every show. He works it out. The women's ensemble also chooses a video to emulate during the finale on Saturday night.

Favorite Moment During Each Performance: The finale, when we're all spinning on the turntable.

Favorite In-Theatre Gathering Place: Women's ensemble dressing room or Sutton Foster's dressing room on SHOT NIGHT!!

Favorite Off-Site Hangouts: Swizz, Maison, Serafina, Lucky Burger, Ta Cocina, and Cosmic Diner.

Favorite Snack Food: Ketchup chips and Dill Pickle chips from Lisa Ho's homeland of Canada. Haven Burton's Puffins Cereal. Wine and cheese.

Mascots: Hi-ya, the fighting fish in the women's ensemble dressing room. Also the swimming penis toy that Bev sent us.

Favorite Therapies: Wine and cheese. Physical therapy twice a week.

Most Memorable Ad-Lib: Chris Sieber's "a Tony Award?" instead of "a pretty pony?" the night before the Tony Awards.

Memorable Publicity Events: The Food Network's 100th performance cake challenge and what really happened off camera. Judging the Macy's Pet-acular with dogs dressed up as Shrek.

Memorable Stage Door Fan Encounter: When our dresser/nurse Candace showed up at the stage door all the way from Seattle.

Fastest Costume Changes: Sutton Foster from Princess Fiona to Ogre Fiona. Full cast change into fairytale creatures.

Heaviest/Hottest Costume: Other than Shrek, the heaviest costume is the Humpty Dumpty Egg worn by Rachel Stern and Heather Jane Rolff. Tied for the hottest costumes are The Three Pigs, worn by Bobby Daye, Ryan Duncan, Jacob Ming-Trent, Justin Greer, David Vaughn, and the Three Bears worn by Lisa Ho, Aymee Garcia, Dennis Stowe, David Vaughn, Justin Greer, Heather Jane Rolff and Carolyn Ockert-Haythe.

Who Wore the Least: Haven Burton as the Sugar Plum Fairy.

Catchphrases Only the Company Would Recognize: "Your mama's a beaver." "Miss Thiiiiiiing." "Elfin Magic." "Thank-youuuuuu." "Ya ya ya ya yaaaaaaaaa YA!" "Crazy time…uh-oh… crazy time." "Rock bottom…."

Best In-House Parody Lyrics:
"Like donuts and Warren Beatty" instead "Like donuts and diabetes."
"Please accept this favor as a coconut of my gratitude" instead of "Please accept this favor as a token of my gratitude."
"Shrek and Donkey off on a whirlwind Big Titty adventure" instead of "Shrek and Donkey off on a whirlwind Big City adventure."
"I'll never act shoddy. If you kill a man hey laddy dahddy" instead of "I'll never act shoddy. If you kill a man I'll hide the body."
"With a sunset and a nice Jheri Curl" instead of "With a sunset and a beautiful girl."

Memorable Directorial Notes:
To Chris Sieber: "You get awkward plus one... no more"
To the rat tappers: "We can tell by your feet if you're smiling"

Company In-Jokes: Heckle and Jeckle. Don't talk sense. Ketchup and Mustard. Yippy Skippy.

Company Legends: Stephen Kramer Glickman, Dean Edwards, Chester Gregory, Kecia Lewis-Evans, Haneefah Wood, Leslie Kritzer, Ramona Keller.

Nicknames: We call the dragon fins "the Doritos." Duloc costumes are called "Tupperware."

Sweethearts Within the Company: Shrek and Fiona. Donkey and Dragon. Jack and Jill/Mary and Joseph. Mama Bear/Papa Bear.

Embarrassing Moments: Noses getting unglued or forgetting costume pieces. Fiona's transformation not working, which causes the actress playing Fiona to do an interpretive dance in place. Papa Bear's wig falling off in Seattle and someone posting it on YouTube.

Ghostly Encounters Backstage: There is a stinky sewage ghost at the top of Act II that haunts the women's ensemble dressing room.
There is also a ghost that stops the time on our battery-operated clocks and then knocks them over.

Coolest Things About Being in This Show: Hearing little kids laugh. Seeing a sea of green ogre ears out in the audience.

Slava's Snowshow

First Preview: December 2, 2008. Opened: December 7, 2008.
Closed January 4, 2009 after 7 Previews and 35 Performances.

PLAYBILL

Slava's
SNOWSHOW

7 Green Clowns

Photo by Veronique Vial

THE HELEN HAYES THEATRE

MARTIN MARKINSON   DONALD TICK

DAVID J. FOSTER, JARED GELLER, JOSEPH GORDON-LEVITT,
JUDITH MARINOFF COHN AND JOHN PINCKARD

PRESENT

Slava's
SNOWSHOW

CREATED AND STAGED BY SLAVA

BY ARRANGEMENT WITH SLAVA, GWENAEL ALLAN AND ROSS MOLLISON

THE ROLE OF YELLOW
WILL BE PLAYED BY ONE OF THE FOLLOWING:

SLAVA POLUNIN

ROBERT SARALP

DEREK SCOTT

PERFORMERS PLAYING GREEN CLOWNS:

SPENCER CHANDLER	**CHRISTOPHER LYNAM**
JOHNSON	**FYODOR MAKAROV**
TATIANA KARAMYSHEVA	**IVAN POLUNIN**
DMITRY KHAMZIN	**ELENA USHAKOVA**

SOUND DESIGN	LIGHTING DESIGN	ART DIRECTION
RASTYAM DUBINNIKOV	**ALEXANDER PECHERSKIY**	**GARY CHERNIAKHOVSKII**

RUSSIAN COMPANY	ASSOCIATE PRODUCERS	GENERAL MANAGER
ADMINISTRATOR	**JAY KUO &**	**FOSTER ENTERTAINMENT/**
NATASHA TABACHNIKOVA	**LORENZO THIONE**	**JENNIE CONNERY**

PRESS REPRESENTATIVES	ADVERTISING & MARKETING	PRODUCTION MANAGEMENT
BARLOW • HARTMAN	**ALLIED LIVE, LLC**	**JUNIPER STREET PRODUCTIONS**

12/7/08

Slava Polunin
Creator

Robert Saralp
Yellow

Derek Scott
Yellow

Spencer Chandler
Green Team

Slava's Snowshow

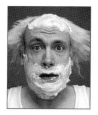
Johnson
Green Team

Tatiana Karamysheva
Green Team

Dmitry
Khamzin
Green Team

A moment of colorful audience participation.

Photo by Veronique Vial

Chris Lynam
Green Team

Fyodor Makarov
Green Team

Ivan Polunin
Green Team

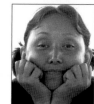
Elena Ushakova
Green Team

Guy Kwan, John Paull III, Hillary Blanken,
Kevin Broomell, Ana Rose Greene,
Juniper Street Productions
Production Manager

Joseph
Gordon-Levitt
Producer

STAFF FOR *SLAVA'S SNOWSHOW*

GENERAL MANAGER
FOSTER ENTERTAINMENT, INC.
Jennie Connery

GENERAL PRESS REPRESENTATIVES
BARLOW•HARTMAN
John Barlow   Michael Hartman
Tom D'Ambrosio   Michelle Bergmann

ADVERTISING & MARKETING SERVICES
ALLIED LIVE, LLC
Tanya Grubich   Laura Matalon
Victoria Cairl   Kara Eldridge

PRODUCTION MANAGEMENT
JUNIPER STREET PRODUCTIONS
Hillary Blanken   Ana-Rose Greene
Kevin Broomell   Guy Kwan

Assistant Company Manager	**Michael Altbaum**
Marketing Director	Natasha Montero
Group Sales Manager	Geoff Borman
Ensemble Members	Ivan Yaropolskiy, Vitaly Galich
Show Electrician	Alexander Percherskiy
Show Sound	Rastyam Dubinnikov
Technical Supervisor	Dmitry Ushakov
Production Carpenter	Doug Purcell
Production Electrician	Joe Beck
Production Props	Roger Keller
Production Sound	Robert Etter
Follow Spot Operators	Lorne MacDougall, Greg Fedigan

Assistant Props	Joe Moritz
Wardrobe Supervisor	Olga Devyatisilnaya
Slava's Manager	Gwenael Allan
Company Administrator, Europe	Anna Hannikainen
Company Administrator, Russia	Natasha Tabachnikova
Company Photographer	Veronique Vial
Production Assistant	Sean Richardson

Banking	Citibank/Kay Chow
Legal Counsel	David Friedlander, Esq.
Insurance	Wells Fargo/Barbara Buchwald
Immigration	Alexandre Tarelkine
Group Sales	Broadway Inbound, Inc.

CREDITS
Lighting equipment provided by PRG Lighting, North Bergen, NJ. Additional sound equipment provided by PRG Audio, Mount Vernon, NY. Additional soft goods provided by United Staging and Rigging, Bridgeport, CT. International freight and logistics services provided by Rock-It Cargo USA. Merchandise supplied by JSR Direct.

SPECIAL THANKS
Mollison Communications, The League of American Theatres and Producers, Theatre Development Fund, Jason Janicki and Sonia Kozlova.

STAFF FOR FOSTER ENTERTAINMENT

Producer	David J. Foster
Producer/Director of Development	Jared Geller
General Manager	Jennie Connery
Accounts	David Reynolds
Production Associates	Malinda Sorci, Hannah Mason

Interns	Lucy Foster, Edie Foster

22 W. 19th Street, Suite 5R, New York, NY 10011
Tel. (212) 245-1009

THE HELEN HAYES THEATRE
Owned and Operated by Little Theatre Group LLC
MARTIN MARKINSON and DONALD TICK

General Manager	SUSAN S. MYERBERG
House Manager	ALAN R. MARKINSON
Engineer	HECTOR ANGULO
Treasurer	DAVID HEVERAN
Assoc Gen Manager	SHARON FALLON
Assistant Treasurer	CHUCK STUIS
Head Usher	JOHN BIANCAMANO
Stage Door	ROBERT SEYMOUR, JONATHAN ANGULO, ROBERT SEYMOUR III
Accountant	CHEN-WIN HSU, CPA, PC

THEATRE RENOVATIONS

General Contractors	Susan Myerberg, Hector Angulo
Ceiling	Hector Angulo, Amelia Angulo, Jonathan Angulo
Walls and Mezzanine Façade	Hector Angulo, Raul C. Gomez, Juan C. Miranda
Seating	Irwin Seating Company/Paul Winter
Aisle Lighting	All Cinema Sales/Tom Kelly
Carpet	LJB Services Inc./Frank Bianchi
Seating	Roger E. Keller
Electrics	Joseph P. Beck
Stage House	Douglas G. Purcell

Soul of Shaolin

First Preview: January 13, 2009. Opened: January 15, 2009.
Closed January 31, 2009 after 3 Previews and 21 Performances.

CAST

Hui Guang (young man) ....YU FEI
Hui Guang (teenager) ....DONG YINGBO
Hui Guang (boy) ....WANG SEN
Na Luo (Master) ....ZHANG ZHIGANG
Abbot ....BAI GUOJUN
Hui Guang's Mother ....WANG YAZHI
Hui Guang's Mother (special appearance) .....LI LIN
Ensemble ....JIA HONGLEI, PAN FUYNAG,
     LI GUANGHUI, DONG XINGFENG,
     LU SHILEI, ZHANG XINBO, XIA HAOJIE,
     LI PANPAN, WANG YANSHUANG,
     SHI ZHENDONG, LIU WEIDONG,
     CAI KEHE, YANG WEI, YANG XIANYU,
     SUN SHENGLI, DONG JUNPENG,
     AN PUKANG, WANG XIAOGANG,
     HOU YANJIE, TIAN YINAN,
     WANG FEIHU, LIU WANCHENG,
     SHANG YAOFEI

The performers and stage managers in this show are represented by the American Guild of Variety Artists (AGVA), the AFL-CIO union of variety, comedy, circus and revue performers in the United States.

 **MARQUIS THEATRE**

UNDER THE DIRECTION OF JAMES M. NEDERLANDER AND JAMES L. NEDERLANDER

NEDERLANDER WORLDWIDE PRODUCTIONS, LLC
and
EASTERN SHANGHAI INTERNATIONAL CULTURE FILM & TELEVISION GROUP
present
A CHINA ON BROADWAY PRODUCTION

SOUL OF SHAOLIN

Featuring the
SHAOLIN TEMPLE WUSHU MARTIAL ARTISTS

Executive Producers
FANG JUN & ROBERT NEDERLANDER, JR.

Music Composed by
ZHOU CHENGLONG

Stage Design	Costume Design	Lighting Design
XIE TONGMIAO	HUANG GENGYING	SONG TIANJIAO

Sound Designers	Martial Arts Directors	Make Up Designer
WU FEIFEI	JIANG DONGXU	CHEN MEIPING
KEITH CAGGIANO	ZHU HUAYIN	

Shanghai Production Manager	Shanghai Marketing Director	General Management
FANG YONGNIAN	WANG ZAIPING	DON FRANTZ LAURIE BROWN

Press Representative	Marketing	Asian Marketing
BONEAU/BRYAN-BROWN	MARGERY SINGER COMPANY	WEI ZHOU

Shanghai General Manager	Executive Director	Director & Stage Supervisor
LI ZHIXIANG	XUE WEIJUN	WANG ZHENPENG

Shanghai Producer	Chief Martial Arts Director
WANG JINGBO	JIAO HONGBO

Directed & Choreographed by
LIU TONGBIAO

1/15/09

The cast

Photo by Joan Marcus

Soul of Shaolin

SYNOPSIS

Soul of Shaolin is set in ancient China during a time of war. After being separated from his mother when he was a baby, Hui Guang was rescued and raised by monks in the Shaolin Temple. Under the guidance of his mentor, Na Luo, Hui Guang is instructed in the unique ways and daily practices of Shaolin Kung Fu. The play *Soul of Shaolin* combines the action of Kung Fu and the inaction of Buddhist meditation with a heart-warming story to create an organic whole. By presenting the fist technique, the tempering of the body's internal organs and the wrestling skills and tricks of traditional Shaolin Kung Fu, the play brings out their underlying spiritual essence. As a brand-new form of artistic work, *Soul of Shaolin* showcases the beauty and skill of traditional Shaolin Kung Fu.

SHOW ORDER

Overture

SCENE I: Saving an Orphan

SCENE II: Learning Kung Fu Skills

SCENE III: Kung Fu Skills

SCENE IV: Encounter

SCENE V: Looking for Her Son

SCENE VI: Return Home

Photo by Joan Marcus

Li Zhixiang
Shanghai General Manager

Robert Nederlander, Jr.
Executive Producer

Margery Singer Company
Marketing Agency

Wei Zhou
Chinese Marketing Consultant

STAFF FOR *SOUL OF SHAOLIN*

CHINA BROADWAY PARTNERS, LLC
Robert Nederlander, Jr. .... President & CEO
Don Frantz .... Chief Operating Officer
David Groelinger .... Chief Financial Officer
Minhui Mark Ma .... VP China

EASTERN SHANGHAI INTERNATIONAL CULTURE FILM & TELEVISION GROUP
Fang Jun ....Chairman
Li Zhixiang ....General Manager
Fang Yongnian ....Vice General Manager

GENERAL MANAGEMENT
TOWN SQUARE PRODUCTIONS, INC.
Don Frantz   Laurie Brown

PRESS REPRESENTATIVES
Boneau/Bryan-Brown, Inc.
Chris Boneau   Aaron Meier
Christine Olver

Creative Consultant ....Charles (Chase) Senge

NEW YORK STAFF
Advertising ....Eliran Murphy Group/
Barbara Eliran, Jon Bierman,
Frank Verlizzo, Sasha DeFazio
Artwork ....Fraver
Directorial Consultant ....Charles Senge
Management Consultant ....Robert Nolan
General Management Associate ....Sue Abbott
Production Supervisor ....Mike Ward
Master Electrician ....Paul Ker
Associate Lighting Designer.....................Joyce Liao
Moving Light Programmer ....Paul Sonnleitner
Properties Supervisor ....John P. Lofgren
Wardrobe Supervisor ....I. Wang
Production Coordinator ....Danielle Ruddess
Educator ....Kelly Gilles
Banking ....Citibank Corp/
Linda Dunn

CHINA BROADWAY PARTNERS, LLC STAFF
VP of Finance & Marketing ....Katherine Potter
VP Production ....Toby Simkin
Production Coordinator ....Melissa Caolo
Director of Finance ....Shawn Coutu
Marketing ....Stanley Browne
Marketing Associate ....Yuanlei Leiley Zhang

Executive Assistant ....Diana Glazer
Interns ....Elizabeth Schwartz, Miranda Xu

SHANGHAI STAFF
Make-Up Design ....Chen Meiping
Sound Engineer ....Wu Feifei
Photographers ....Chen Lunxun, Zu Zhongren
Marketing Manager ....Ye Jianqui
Performance Managers ....Wang Zesheng,
Wu Lianna
Program Manager ....Liao Han
Public Relations Manager ....Zheng Luxiao
Administrative Director ....Yang Jie

ACKNOWLEDGEMENTS
The producers wish to thank the following partners for their generous support: Lee Sands, Denise Zhang, Fredrick Levin, Warren Loui, Herb Roimisher, Stanley Browne, Yinyin Zeng, Marvin Kaplan, Mike Bennett, Mary Lee, Susan Lee, and, of course, Chu-Chi Face Nederlander.

CREDITS
Scenery, props and costumes constructed by Eastern Shanghai. Lighting, sound and special effects equipment provided by PRG Lighting Services.

NEDERLANDER

Chairman ....**James M. Nederlander**
President ....**James L. Nederlander**

Executive Vice President
Nick Scandalios

Vice President
Corporate Development
Charlene S. Nederlander

Senior Vice President
Labor Relations
Herschel Waxman

Vice President
Jim Boese

Chief Financial Officer
Freida Sawyer Belviso

STAFF FOR THE MARQUIS THEATRE
Manager ....David Calhoun
Associate Manager ....Austin Nathaniel
Treasurer ....Rick Waxman
Assistant Treasurer ....John Rooney
Carpenter ....Joseph P. Valentino
Electrician ....James Mayo
Property Man ....Scott Mecionis

South Pacific

First Preview: March 1, 2008. Opened: April 3, 2008.
Still running as of May 31, 2009.

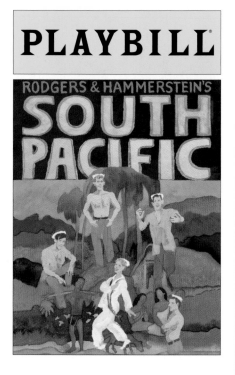

CAST OF CHARACTERS

Ensign Nellie Forbush	LAURA OSNES
Emile de Becque	DAVID PITTSINGER
Ngana, his daughter	LAURISSA ROMAIN
Jerome, his son	LUKA KAIN
Henry	HELMAR AUGUSTUS COOPER
Bloody Mary	LORETTA ABLES SAYRE
Liat, her daughter	LI JUN LI
Bloody Mary's Assistants	MARYANN HU, DEBORAH LEW, KIMBER MONROE
Luther Billis	DANNY BURSTEIN
Stewpot (Carpenter's Mate Second Class, George Watts)	ERIC ANDERSON
Professor	MATT CAPLAN
Lt. Joseph Cable, United States Marine Corps	ANDREW SAMONSKY
Capt. George Brackett, United States Navy	MURPHY GUYER
Cmdr. William Harbison, United States Navy	SEAN CULLEN
Lt. Buzz Adams	GEORGE MERRICK
Yeoman Herbert Quale, Sailor	CHRISTIAN DELCROIX
Radio Operator Bob McCaffrey, Sailor	PETER LOCKYER
Morton Wise, Seabee	GENSON BLIMLINE
Richard West, Seabee	NICK MAYO
Johnny Noonan, Seabee	MICHAEL ARNOLD
Billy Whitmore, Seabee	ROBERT LENZI
Tom O'Brien, Sailor	MIKE EVARISTE
James Hayes, Sailor	JEROLD E. SOLOMON
Kenneth Johnson, Sailor	CHRISTIAN CARTER

Continued on next page

Continued on next page

LINCOLN CENTER THEATER AT THE VIVIAN BEAUMONT

under the direction of
ANDRÉ BISHOP and BERNARD GERSTEN
in association with
BOB BOYETT
presents

RODGERS & HAMMERSTEIN'S SOUTH PACIFIC

Music
RICHARD RODGERS

Lyrics
OSCAR HAMMERSTEIN II

Book OSCAR HAMMERSTEIN II and JOSHUA LOGAN
Adapted from the Pulitzer Prize-winning novel *Tales of the South Pacific* by JAMES A. MICHENER
Original stage production directed by JOSHUA LOGAN

with
LAURA OSNES   DAVID PITTSINGER

DANNY BURSTEIN   LORETTA ABLES SAYRE   ANDREW SAMONSKY
ERIC ANDERSON   MATT CAPLAN   SEAN CULLEN   MURPHY GUYER
LUKA KAIN   LI JUN LI   LAURISSA ROMAIN

and
MICHAEL ARNOLD   BECCA AYERS   WENDI BERGAMINI   GENSON BLIMLINE
CHARLIE BRADY   CHRISTIAN CARTER   ERIC L. CHRISTIAN   HELMAR AUGUSTUS COOPER
MARGOT DE LA BARRE   CHRISTIAN DELCROIX   LAURA MARIE DUNCAN   MIKE EVARISTE
JULIE FOLDESI   ROB GALLAGHER   MARYANN HU   ZACHARY JAMES   ROBERT LENZI   DEBORAH LEW
PETER LOCKYER   GARRETT LONG   NICK MAYO   LIZ McCARTNEY   GEORGE MERRICK
WILLIAM MICHALS   KIMBER MONROE   GEORGE PSOMAS   GREG RODERICK   JEROLD E. SOLOMON

Sets	Costumes	Lighting	Sound
MICHAEL YEARGAN	CATHERINE ZUBER	DONALD HOLDER	SCOTT LEHRER

Orchestrations	Dance & Incidental Music Arrangements	Conductor
ROBERT RUSSELL BENNETT	TRUDE RITTMANN	FRED LASSEN

Casting	Production Stage Manager	General Press Agent	Musical Theater Associate Producer
TELSEY + COMPANY	MICHAEL BRUNNER	PHILIP RINALDI	IRA WEITZMAN

General Manager	Production Manager	Director of Development	Director of Marketing
ADAM SIEGEL	JEFF HAMLIN	HATTIE K. JUTAGIR	LINDA MASON ROSS

Music Direction
TED SPERLING

Musical Staging
CHRISTOPHER GATTELLI

Directed by
BARTLETT SHER

LINCOLN CENTER THEATER GRATEFULLY ACKNOWLEDGES THE CONTRIBUTORS WHOSE EXTRAORDINARY GENEROSITY HAS MADE SOUTH PACIFIC POSSIBLE:
Debra and Leon Black • The Susan and Elihu Rose Foundation • Catherine and Ephraim Gildor
The Joseph and Joan Cullman Arts Foundation • The Blanche and Irving Laurie Foundation • WolfBlock
Sir Thomas Moore/Laurence Levine Charitable Fund • Henry Nias Foundation courtesy of Dr. Stanley Edelman
The New York Community Trust - Mary P. Oenslager Foundation Fund • Leon Levy Foundation
Blanchette Hooker Rockefeller Fund • National Endowment for the Arts
American Airlines is the official airline of Lincoln Center Theater.

3/9/09

Photo by Joan Marcus

Laura Osnes
as Nellie Forbush

South Pacific

MUSICAL NUMBERS

The action of the play takes place on two islands in the South Pacific during World War II.
There is one week's lapse of time between the two acts.

ACT I

OVERTURE

Scene 1: The Terrace of Emile de Becque's Plantation Home
DITES-MOI ....Ngana and Jerome
A COCKEYED OPTIMIST ....Nellie
TWIN SOLILOQUIES ....Nellie and Emile
SOME ENCHANTED EVENING ....Emile
Reprise: DITES-MOI ....Ngana, Jerome and Emile

Scene 2: Another Part of the Island
BLOODY MARY ....Seabees
THERE IS NOTHIN' LIKE A DAME ....Billis and Seabees
BALI HA'I ....Bloody Mary

Scene 3: The Company Street
Scene 4: Inside the Island Commander's Office
Scene 5: The Company Street
MY GIRL BACK HOME ....Cable and Nellie

Scene 6: The Beach
I'M GONNA WASH THAT MAN RIGHT OUTA MY HAIR ....Nellie and Nurses
Reprise: SOME ENCHANTED EVENING ....Emile and Nellie
A WONDERFUL GUY ....Nellie and Nurses

Scene 7: Inside the Island Commander's Office
Scene 8: On Bali Ha'i
Reprise: BALI HA'I ....Island Women

Scene 9: Inside a Hut on Bali Ha'i
YOUNGER THAN SPRINGTIME ....Cable

Scene 10: Near the Beach on Bali Ha'i
Scene 11: Emile's Terrace
FINALE ACT I ....Nellie and Emile

ACT II

ENTR'ACTE

Scene 1: A Performance of "The Thanksgiving Follies" ....Nellie, Nurses and G.I.'s
Scene 2: Backstage at "The Thanksgiving Follies"
HAPPY TALK ....Bloody Mary and Liat

Scene 3: The Stage
HONEY BUN ....Nellie, Billis and Ensemble

Scene 4: Backstage
YOU'VE GOT TO BE CAREFULLY TAUGHT ....Cable
THIS NEARLY WAS MINE ....Emile

Scene 5: The Radio Shack
Scene 6: The Beach
Reprise: SOME ENCHANTED EVENING ....Nellie

Scene 7: The Company Street
Scene 8: Emile's Terrace
FINALE ULTIMO ....Emile, Nellie, Ngana and Jerome

Cast Continued

Petty Officer
    Hamilton Steeves ....CHARLIE BRADY
Marine Staff Sgt.
    Thomas Hassinger ....ZACHARY JAMES
Lt. Eustis Carmichael,
    Shore Patrolman ....ROB GALLAGHER
Lt. Genevieve Marshall,
    head nurse ....LIZ McCARTNEY
Ensign Dinah Murphy .LAURA MARIE DUNCAN
Ensign Janet MacGregor .....WENDI BERGAMINI
Ensign
    Connie Walewska .....MARGOT DE LA BARRE
Ensign Sue Yaeger ....GARRETT LONG
Ensign Cora MacRae ....BECCA AYERS
Islanders, Sailors, Seabees,
    Party Guests ....ERIC ANDERSON,
        MICHAEL ARNOLD, BECCA AYERS,
    WENDI BERGAMINI, GENSON BLIMLINE,
        CHARLIE BRADY, CHRISTIAN CARTER,
            HELMAR AUGUSTUS COOPER,
    MARGOT DE LA BARRE, MIKE EVARISTE,
        ROB GALLAGHER, MARYANN HU,
        ZACHARY JAMES, ROBERT LENZI,
    DEBORAH LEW, PETER LOCKYER,
        GARRETT LONG, NICK MAYO,
    LIZ McCARTNEY, GEORGE MERRICK,
    KIMBER MONROE, JEROLD E. SOLOMON

1st Assistant Stage Manager ......DANA WILLIAMS
2nd Assistant
    Stage Manager ....SAMANTHA GREENE

Dance Captain ....WENDI BERGAMINI
Asst. Dance Captain ....GEORGE PSOMAS
Swings ...JULIE FOLDESI, ERIC L. CHRISTIAN,
    GEORGE PSOMAS, GREG RODERICK

UNDERSTUDIES

For Nellie Forbush: WENDI BERGAMINI,
    LAURA MARIE DUNCAN,
    GARRETT LONG
For Emile de Becque: ROB GALLAGHER,
    WILLIAM MICHALS
For Ngana and Jerome: KIMBER MONROE
For Henry: CHRISTIAN CARTER,
    MIKE EVARISTE
For Bloody Mary: MARYANN HU,
    LIZ McCARTNEY
For Liat: WENDI BERGAMINI,
    DEBORAH LEW
For Luther Billis: NICK MAYO,
    GEORGE MERRICK
For Stewpot: MICHAEL ARNOLD,
    GENSON BLIMLINE

Continued on next page

South Pacific

Cast Continued

For Lt. Joseph Cable: CHARLIE BRADY,
 ROBERT LENZI, PETER LOCKYER
For Capt. George Brackett: ERIC ANDERSON,
 GENSON BLIMLINE
For Professor: CHRISTIAN DELCROIX,
 GEORGE MERRICK
For Cmdr. William Harbison:
 GENSON BLIMLINE, ROB GALLAGHER,
 GEORGE MERRICK
For Bob McCaffrey and Yeoman Herbert Quale:
 GEORGE PSOMAS, GREG RODERICK
For Ensign Dinah Murphy: WENDI BERGAMINI,
 JULIE FOLDESI, GARRETT LONG
For Lt. Eustis Carmichael and Lt. Buzz Adams:
 CHARLIE BRADY, NICK MAYO

ORCHESTRA

Conductor: FRED LASSEN
Associate Conductor: CHARLES DU CHATEAU
Violins: BELINDA WHITNEY (Concertmaster),
 KARL KAWAHARA,
 KATHERINE LIVOLSI-LANDAU,
 JAMES TSAO, LISA MATRICARDI,
 RENA ISBIN, MICHAEL NICHOLAS,
 LOUISE OWEN
Violas: DAVID BLINN, DAVID CRESWELL
Cellos: PETER SACHON, CARYL PAISNER,
 CHARLES DU CHATEAU
Bass: LISA STOKES-CHIN
Flute/Piccolo: LIZ MANN
Clarinet: TODD PALMER, SHARI HOFFMAN
Oboe/English Horn: KELLY PERAL
Bassoon: DAMIAN PRIMIS
French Horns: ROBERT CARLISLE,
 DANIEL GRABOIS, SHELAGH ABATE
Trumpets: DOMINIC DERASSE,
 GARETH FLOWERS, WAYNE DUMAINE
Trombones: MARK PATTERSON,
 NATE MAYLAND
Tuba: MARCUS ROJAS
Harp: GRACE PARADISE
Drums/Percussion: BILL LANHAM

Music Coordinator: DAVID LAI

Richard Rodgers' music is being presented in the 30-player orchestration created for the original production. The scores and orchestral parts were restored by The Rodgers & Hammerstein Organization using all existing material, including manuscripts (Rodgers, Trude Rittmann), the full orchestral scores (Robert Russell Bennett) and the individual instrumental parts played by the original orchestra.

Laura Osnes
Ensign Nellie Forbush

David Pittsinger
Emile de Becque

Danny Burstein
Luther Billis

Loretta Ables Sayre
Bloody Mary

Andrew Samonsky
Lt. Joseph Cable

Eric Anderson
Stewpot

Matt Caplan
Professor

Sean Cullen
Cmdr. William Harbison

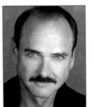

Murphy Guyer
Capt. George Brackett

Luka Kain
Jerome

Li Jun Li
Liat

Laurissa Romain
Ngana

Michael Arnold
Johnny Noonan

Becca Ayers
Ensign Cora MacRae

Wendi Bergamini
Ensign Janet MacGregor/ Dance Captain

Genson Blimline
Morton Wise

Charlie Brady
Petty Officer Hamilton Steeves

Christian Carter
Kenneth Johnson

Eric L. Christian
Swing

Helmar Augustus Cooper
Henry

South Pacific

Margot De La Barre
Ensign Connie Walewska

Christian Delcroix
Yeoman Herbert Quale

Laura Marie Duncan
Ensign Dinah Murphy

Mike Evariste
Tom O'Brien

Julie Foldesi
Swing

Rob Gallagher
Ensemble

MaryAnn Hu
Bloody Mary's Assistant

Zachary James
Thomas Hassinger

Robert Lenzi
Billy Whitmore

Deborah Lew
Bloody Mary's Assistant

Peter Lockyer
Ensemble

Garrett Long
Ensign Sue Yaeger

Nick Mayo
Richard West

Liz McCartney
Lt. Genevieve Marshall

George Merrick
Lt. Buzz Adams

William Michals
Understudy for Emile de Becque

Kimber Monroe
Bloody Mary's Assistant

George Psomas
Swing/ Asst. Dance Captain

Greg Roderick
Swing

Jerold E. Solomon
James Hayes

Joshua Logan
Co-Author (1908-1988)

Richard Rodgers
(1902-1979)
Music

Oscar Hammerstein II
(1895-1960)
Lyrics and Co-Author

James A. Michener
(1907-1997)
Author, Tales of the South Pacific

Bartlett Sher
Director

Christopher Gattelli
Musical Staging

Ted Sperling
Music Direction

Michael Yeargan
Sets

Catherine Zuber
Costumes

Donald Holder
Lighting

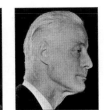
Scott Lehrer
Sound

Robert Russell Bennett
(1894-1981)
Orchestrations

Trude Rittmann
(1908-2005)
Dance and Incidental Music Arrangements

David Lai
Music Coordinator

Bernard Telsey,
Telsey + Company
Casting

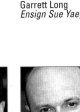

South Pacific

Bob Boyett

André Bishop and Bernard Gersten,
Lincoln Center Theater
Producer

Ana Maria Andricain
*Ensign Connie
Walewska, Ensemble*

Grady McLeod
Bowman
*Asst. Dance Captain,
Swing*

Jeremy Davis
*Johnny Noonan,
Ensemble, Swing*

Branch Fields
*Petty Officer
Hamilton Steeves,
Ensemble*

Laura Griffith
*Ensign Janet
MacGregor,
Ensemble*

Victor Hawks
*Stewpot (Carpenter's
Mate Second Class,
George Watts)*

Lisa Howard
*Lt. Genevieve
Marshall, Ensemble*

Emily Morales
*Bloody Mary's
Assistant, Ensemble*

Matthew Morrison
Lt. Joseph Cable

Darius Nichols
Swing

Kelli O'Hara
*Ensign Nellie
Forbush*

Lucia Spina
*Lt. Genevieve
Marshall, Ensemble*

Skipp Sudduth
*Capt. George
Brackett*

Paulo Szot
Emile de Becque

Noah Weisberg
Professor

Craig Bennett
*Marine Staff Sgt.
Thomas Hassinger,
Ensemble*

Marla Mindelle
*Ensign Cora
MacRae, Ensemble*

Paulo Szot
Emile de Becque

Photo by Ben Strothmann

WARDROBE
(L-R): Stacia Williams, Leo Namba, Linda McAllister, Lynn Bowling (Wardrobe Supervisor), Patti Luther,
Tammi Kopko, Mark Klein, Mark Caine

Not pictured: James Nadeaux

South Pacific

FRONT OF HOUSE
Front Row (L-R): Lydia Tchornobai, Jared Pachefsky, Bru Dye, Mim Pollock (Chief Usher), Margareta Shakeridge

Middle Row (L-R): Jeff Goldstein, Paula Gallo, Judith Fanelli, Barbara Hart, Margie Blair, Ann Danilovics, Jessica Clough, Beatrice Gilliard

Back Row (L-R): Nick Andors, Charles Blair, Roberto Debarros, Officer Douglas Charles, Farida Asencio

RUNNING CREW
Front Row (L-R): Fred Bredenbeck (Carpenter), Ray Skillin (Deck Carpenter), John Ross (Props), Pat Merryman (Production Electrician), Mark Dignam (Props), Karl Rausenberger (Production Propman), Bruce Rubin (Electrician/ Board Operator), Frank Linn (Electrician/ Automation Tech)

Middle Row (L-R): Gary Simon (Sound Deck), Marc Salzberg (Production Soundman), Matt Altman (Follow spot), Kristina Clark (Electrics), Jeff Ward (Follow Spot Operator), Juan Bustamante (Deck Automation), Bill Nagle (Production Carpenter), John Weingart (Production Flyman), Scott Jackson (Props), Julia Rubin (Sound Deck)

Back Row (L-R): Andrew Belits (Carpenter), Nick Irons (Follow spot), Joe Pizzuto (Follow Spot Operator), John Howie (Carpenter), Greg Cushna (Flyman), Kevin McNeil (Carpenter)

Not pictured: Bill Burke (Deck Electrician), Paul Gruen (Flyman), Takuda Moody (Sound Deck)

Photos by Brian Mapp

HAIR CREW
(L-R): Carrie Rohm (Hair Supervisor), John McNulty, Pat Marcus

STAGE MANAGEMENT
(L-R): Samantha Greene (2nd Assistant Stage Manager), Michael Brunner (Production Stage Manager), Dana Williams (1st Assistant Stage Manager)

South Pacific

LINCOLN CENTER THEATER

ANDRÉ BISHOP   BERNARD GERSTEN
ARTISTIC DIRECTOR   EXECUTIVE PRODUCER

ADMINISTRATIVE STAFF

GENERAL MANAGER ....ADAM SIEGEL
    Associate General Manager ....Jessica Niebanck
    General Management Assistant ....Meghan Lantzy
    Facilities Manager ....Alex Mustelier
    Associate Facilities Manager ....Michael Assalone
GENERAL PRESS AGENT ....PHILIP RINALDI
    Press Associate ....Barbara Carroll
PRODUCTION MANAGER ....JEFF HAMLIN
    Associate Production Manager ....Paul Smithyman
DIRECTOR OF
DEVELOPMENT ....HATTIE K. JUTAGIR
    Associate Director of Development ......Rachel Norton
    Manager of Special Events and
      Young Patron Program ....Karin Schall
    Grants Writer ....Neal Brilliant
    Manager, Patron Program ....Sheilaja Rao
    Assistant to the
      Director of Development ....Raelyn R. Lagerstrom
    Development Associate/
      Special Events ....Nicole Lindenbaum
    Development Assistant/Patron Program ..Terra Gillespie
DIRECTOR OF FINANCE ....DAVID S. BROWN
    Controller ....Susan Knox
    Systems Manager ....Stacy Valentine
    Finance Assistant ....Megan Wildebour
DIRECTOR OF MARKETING .LINDA MASON ROSS
    Marketing Associate ....Kristin Miller
    Marketing Assistant ....Ashley M. Dunn
DIRECTOR OF EDUCATION ....KATI KOERNER
    Associate Director of Education ....Alexandra Lopez
Assistant to the Executive Producer .....Barbara Hourigan
Office Manager ....Brian Hashimoto
Office Assistant ....Rhonda Lipscomb
Messenger ....Esau Burgess
Reception ....Brenden Rogers, Michelle Hamill

ARTISTIC STAFF

ASSOCIATE DIRECTORS ......GRACIELA DANIELE,
                             NICHOLAS HYTNER,
                             JACK O'BRIEN,
                            SUSAN STROMAN,
                            DANIEL SULLIVAN
RESIDENT DIRECTOR.............BARTLETT SHER
DRAMATURG and DIRECTOR,
    LCT DIRECTORS LAB ....ANNE CATTANEO
CASTING DIRECTOR ....DANIEL SWEE, CSA
MUSICAL THEATER
    ASSOCIATE PRODUCER ....IRA WEITZMAN
DIRECTOR OF LCT3 ....PAIGE EVANS
    Artistic Administrator ....Julia Judge
    Casting Associate ....Camille Hickman
    Lab Assistant ....Kate Marvin

HOUSE STAFF

HOUSE MANAGER ....RHEBA FLEGELMAN
Production Carpenter ....William Nagle
Production Electrician ....Patrick Merryman
Production Propertyman ....Karl Rausenberger
Production Flyman ....John Weingart
House Technician ....Linda Heard
Chief Usher .............................M.L. Pollock
Box Office Treasurer ....Fred Bonis

Assistant Treasurer ....Robert A. Belkin

SPECIAL SERVICES

Advertising ....Serino-Coyne/Jim Russek
           Roger Micone, Becca Goland-Van Ryn
Principal Poster Artist ....James McMullan
Poster Art for *Rodgers & Hammerstein's*
    South Pacific ....James McMullan
Counsel ....Peter L. Felcher, Esq.;
               Charles H. Googe, Esq.;
             and Carol Kaplan, Esq. of
       Paul, Weiss, Rifkind, Wharton & Garrison
Immigration Counsel ....Theodore Ruthizer, Esq.;
               Mark D. Koestler, Esq.
      of Kramer, Levin, Naftalis & Frankel LLP
Labor Counsel ....Michael F. McGahan, Esq.
           of Epstein, Becker & Green, P.C.
Auditor ....Douglas Burack, C.P.A.
               Lutz & Carr, L.L.P.
Insurance ....Jennifer Brown of DeWitt Stern Group
Photographer ....Joan Marcus
Video Services ....Fresh Produce Productions/
                        Frank Basile
Travel ....Tygon Tours
Consulting Architect ....Hugh Hardy,
       H3 Hardy Collaboration Architecture
Construction Manager ....Yorke Construction
Payroll Service ....Castellana Services, Inc.
Merchandising ....Marquee Merchandise, LLC/
                      Matt Murphy
Lobby Refreshments ....Sweet Concessions

STAFF FOR
RODGERS & HAMMERSTEIN'S SOUTH PACIFIC
COMPANY
    MANAGER ...JESSICA PERLMETER COCHRANE
Assistant Company Manager ....Daniel Hoyos
Assistant Director ....Sarna Lapine
Associate Choreographer ....Joe Langworth
Associate Set Designer ....Lawrence King
Assistant Set Designer ....Mikiko Suzuki
Assistant Costume Designers ....Holly Cain,
            David Newell, Court Watson
Associate Lighting Designer ....Karen Spahn
Assistant Lighting Designer ....Caroline Chao
Automated Light Programmer ....Victor Seastone
Associate Sound Designer ....Leon Rothenberg
Assistant Sound Designer ....Bridget O'Connor
Music Copyist ....Emily Grishman Music Preparation/
       Emily Grishman, Katharine Edmonds
Production Soundman ....Marc Salzberg
Wig and Hair Design ....Tom Watson
Make-up Designer ....Cookie Jordan
Properties Coordinator ....Kathy Fabian
Associate Props Coordinators ....Rose A.C. Howard,
       Carrie Mossman, and Propstar Associates
Prop Scenic Artist ....Curt Tomczyk
Wardrobe Supervisor ....Lynn Bowling
Dressers ....Mark Caine, Mark Klein,
       Tamara Kopko, Patti Luther,
       Linda McAllister, James Nadeaux,
       Leo Namba, Chuck ReCar, Stacia Williams
Hair Supervisor................................Carrie Rohm
Hair Assistants ....Pat Marcus, John McNulty
Production Assistant ....Brandon Kahn
Children's Guardian ....Vanessa Brown
Children's Tutoring ....On Location Education

Costume Shopper ....Nicole Moody
Electronic Percussion Programming ....Randy Cohen
Rehearsal Pianist ....Jonathan Rose

Vocal Coach ....Deborah Hecht

TELSEY + COMPANY
Bernie Telsey CSA, Will Cantler CSA, David Vaccari CSA,
Bethany Knox CSA, Craig Burns CSA,
Tiffany Little Canfield CSA, Rachel Hoffman CSA,
Carrie Rosson CSA, Justin Huff CSA, Bess Fifer CSA,
Patrick Goodwin, Abbie Brady-Dalton

FOR THE RODGERS & HAMMERSTEIN
ORGANIZATION
President & Executive Director .... Ted Chapin
Senior Vice President & General Manager ...... Bill Gaden
Senior Vice President &
    General Counsel ....Victoria G. Traube
Senior Vice President/Communications .... Bert Fink
Director of Music ....Bruce Pomahac

Performance rights to *South Pacific* are licensed by
R&H Theatricals: www.rnhtheatricals.com

For help with Michener matters, thanks to Selma Luttinger,
Shirley Soenksen at the University of Northern Colorado,
Alice Birney (Manuscript Division) and Mark Eden
Horowitz (Music Division) of the Library of Congress, and
the Vice President's Office at Swarthmore College.

The producers wish to thank the Naval Historical Center;
the Navy Medical Department; the CEC/Seabee Historical
Foundation; the Intrepid Sea, Air and Space Museum; the
New York City Marines; Major Seth Lapine, USMC; Dr.
Regina Anna Sekinger, Ph.D; and Katie McGerr for their
invaluable assistance with the military research for this
production.

CREDITS
Scenery construction by Hudson Scenic Studio, Inc. Show
control and scenic motion control featuring Stage
Command Systems® by PRG Scenic Technologies, a
division of Production Resource Group, LLC, New
Windsor, NY. Scenery fabrication by PRG Scenic
Technologies, a division of Production Resource Group,
LLC, New Windsor, NY. Costumes by Jennifer Love
Costumes; Angels the Costumiers; Parsons-Meares, Ltd.;
Euro Co. Costumes; and John Cowles. Men's tailoring by
Brian Hemesath and Edward Dawson. Millinery by Rodney
Gordon, Inc. and Arnold S. Levine, Inc. Fabric painting and
distressing by Jeffrey Fender. Fabric painting by Gene
Mignola, Inc. Undergarments and hosiery by Bra*Tenders.
Tattoos by Louie Zakarian. Sound equipment by Masque
Sound. Lighting equipment from PRG Lighting. Specialty
props construction by Costume Armour. Specific military
props and accessories provided by Jim Korn & Kaufman's
Army Navy. Special thanks to Frank Cwiklik at Metropolis
Collectibles, South Sea Rattan Collections and Carris Reels.
Cymbals provided courtesy of Paiste America Inc. Natural
herb cough drops courtesy of Ricola USA, Inc. Emergen-C
is the official health and energy drink of *South Pacific*.

For groups of 20 or more:
Caryl Goldsmith Group Sales, (212) 889-4300

Visit www.SouthPacificMusical.com

South Pacific
SCRAPBOOK

Correspondent: Greg Roderick, Swing

Most Exciting Celebrity Visitors: Hillary and Chelsea Clinton came to see us right after the Tony Awards. Afterward, the entire company lined up in the backstage hall, and they graciously met us all. Tom Cruise and Katie Holmes came—and sent us 200 cupcakes from Magnolia Bakery the next day. Sting and his wife sent us a case of wine, and we've had a lovely note from Tom Hanks and Rita Wilson. Other celebrities include: Mitzi Gaynor, Ted Danson, Mary Steenburgen, Danny DeVito, Rhea Perlman, George Wendt, Pierce Brosnan, Daniel Radcliffe, Martin Scorsese, Allison Janney and Captain "Sully" Sullenberger!

"Gypsy of the Year" Sketch: George Merrick wrote the sketch spoofing three actors who always seem to play the leading roles in every Sondheim musical: Raúl Esparza, Alex Gemignani and Michael Cerveris. George Merrick, Charlie Brady, Greg Roderick, Nick Mayo, George Psomas, Laurissa Romain, Luka Kain, Laurie Shephard, and stage crew member Kristina Melike-Clark performed in it. We didn't place in presentation, but *South Pacific* came in third for fundraising with more than $140,000!

Who Performs the Most Roles in the Show: The ensemble in this show mostly play the same characters throughout the entire show. But swings George Psomas, Greg Roderick, Eric Christian, and Julie Foldesi cover the entire ensemble of 13 seabees, six nurses, and two "island girls."

Special Backstage Rituals: Each night, as Emile DeBecque is singing "Some Enchanted Evening," the Seabees gather behind the sand dune to stretch and circle up like a sports huddle. All hands in, we chant "Seabees!" much like a sports team right before game play. The Asian girls do a similar routine they call "Wang Chung" before their entrance.

Favorite Moment Onstage: Personally, it's doing "Nothin' Like a Dame." The audience just loves it with all that testosterone filling the stage. But when I'm watching the show there are so many. One is towards the end of the show when the radio room is swept away, and Nellie stands alone on the huge stage with a shadow of the lone palm tree against the most incredible sky. It's an image you can never forget. And basically anything Danny Burstein does as Billis.

Favorite In-Theatre Gathering Place: One of the dressing rooms has been dubbed the HuLewLie Lounge, which stands for MaryAnn Hu, Deborah Lew and Julie Foldesi. It's a very social spot during the show, much more than the greenroom area, which only sees action before the show and during intermission when we have birthday cake.

Favorite Off-Site Hangout: The cast doesn't hang out together off-site as much as we did a year ago. But when we have a special gathering, we still enjoy O'Neals' across the street from Lincoln Center. Or occasionally Genson Blimline and former cast member Victor Hawks sponsor a Sunday night party at a bar/restaurant called Prohibition, on the Upper West Side. Also, the cast is pretty supportive at our softball

1. Male swings backstage (L-R): Greg Roderick, Eric L. Christian and George Psomas.
2. The nurses backstage. (Front Row L-R): Laura Osnes, Liz McCartney, Wendi Bergamini. (Back Row L-R): Marla Mindelle, Julie Foldesi, Margot de la Barre and Garrett Long.

games in the Broadway Show League and Garrett Long always brings after-game snacks like a softball mom.

Favorite Snack Food: Loretta Ables Sayre fixes a special treat on occasion called Hurricane Popcorn, which consists of popcorn, M&M's, dehydrated fruit, wasabi peas, and other things that only Loretta knows! It doesn't usually come out until the latter part of Act II, and it's usually gone in seconds!

Mascot: We don't really have a mascot at the show, but our bowling team for the Broadway Bowling League has a little bald karate guy that we rub for luck.

Favorite Therapy: Emergen-C!

Memorable Ad-Libs: Now that Skipp Sudduth has moved on, we don't get as many line-flub funnies. But Christian Delcroix amazingly comes up with a different ad-lib every night when his character Quale is introduced during the Follies. Most are hysterically funny, others, um…perplexing? But I'm fairly sure there has never been a repeat ad-lib in over a year. Very impressive.

Cell Phones, Texting or Tweeting Incidents: Surprisingly, we don't really get too many cell phone interruptions. But our house manager Rheba regales us with some audacious audience stories that have our jaws dropping!

Company Miscellaneous: The kids in our show produce a newspaper every few weeks called the "Island Times" which include news blurbs, short stories, cartoons, fashion advice and Dressing

Room of the Month.

With such a large company, we have birthday cakes almost every week, sometimes more than once in a week. By far the most common cake we have is carrot. Although we did have mac & cheese once instead. When we sing happy birthday to a company member, they are required to skip around the room before they can blow out their candles. NO ONE is exempt.

Memorable Fan Encounter: It is always great to be reminded of what a special experience our show is when we meet audience members at the stage door with tears still in their eyes. And seeing teenagers enamored with our show, which is so 'traditional,' is also very nice.

Heaviest/Hottest Costume: Catherine Zuber brilliantly designed the show with the tropics in mind, and most of the costumes are made of linen. So they are very cool and light. Probably the heaviest would be the deployment garb with backpacks and helmets.

Who Wears the Least: Nick Mayo and Bob Lenzi step out of the beach-showers in nothing but their birthday suits! Myself and George Psomas have to bare it all if we go on for either Nick or Bob.

Embarrassing Moments/Mishaps: There was some sort of noise-commotion in the audience just as two cast members were taking Bloody Mary's cart up over the dune. Because of the distraction, Rob Gallagher kept walking until he fell off the back of the dune. Luckily, it's only about a three-foot drop, and he didn't land on the footlights! From the front, it looked like Rob was suddenly chest-high in sand.

Another mishap was when the nurses first jog through the line of Seabees, and Liz McCartney fell flat on her face down centerstage right in front of the Seabees.

Then there was the night that a radio table partly rolled off the edge of the stage, through the orchestra netting and gave a heads-up to the percussion section.

Also, Nick Mayo gave a nice show to the audience one night when the stage was particularly slippery as he stepped out of the shower. The show was definitely PG-13 that night!

Other Special Moments: Performing "Dame" for the Macy's Thanksgiving Day Parade was an unforgettable and thrilling experience, even in 39 degrees.

On April 1, 2009, several members of the original 1949 Broadway and National Tour productions of *South Pacific* attended a Wednesday matinee to coincide with the 60th Anniversary of the show. It was a beautiful and emotional moment for both casts.

In late April, nine male cast members and our conductor Fred Lassen sang the National Anthem at the Mets vs Marlins game at Citifield. You can watch it on YouTube.

And certainly winning seven Tony Awards last June was a wee bit exciting. (I had joined the cast a week before. What a welcome!)

Coolest Thing About Being in this Show: In the world of commercial Broadway musicals, it still feels like we are doing a beautiful piece of art, which is what we as artists all dream about.

Speed-the-Plow

First Preview: October 3, 2008. Opened: October 23, 2008.
Closed February 22, 2009 after 24 Previews and 140 Performances.

PLAYBILL

CAST
(in order of appearance)

Bobby Gould .... JEREMY PIVEN
Charlie Fox .... RAÚL ESPARZA
Karen .... ELISABETH MOSS

TIME
1980s
PLACE
Hollywood

ACT I
Gould's office, morning
ACT II
His home, that evening.
ACT III
His office, the next morning

UNDERSTUDIES

For Gould and Fox:
JORDAN LAGE

For Karen:
ELOISE MUMFORD

---

⑤ ETHEL BARRYMORE THEATRE
243 West 47th Street
A Shubert Organization Theatre

Gerald Schoenfeld, *Chairman*   Philip J. Smith, *President*

Robert E. Wankel, *Executive Vice President*

JEFFREY RICHARDS   JERRY FRANKEL   JAM THEATRICALS
JK PRODUCTIONS   RONALD FRANKEL   OSTAR PRODUCTIONS   PEGGY HILL

BAT-BARRY PRODUCTIONS   KEN DAVENPORT   SCOTT DELMAN   ERGO ENTERTAINMENT   DEDE HARRIS
ALAN D. MARKS   PATTY ANN McKINNON   NICHOLAS QUINN ROSENKRANZ
ADAM SANSIVERI   JAMIE deROY/CARL MOELLENBERG

Present

JEREMY PIVEN   RAÚL ESPARZA
ELISABETH MOSS

In

SPEED-THE-PLOW

By

DAVID MAMET

Scenic Design   Costume Design   Lighting Design
SCOTT PASK   LAURA BAUER   BRIAN MacDEVITT

Casting   Production Stage Manager   Technical Supervision   Fight Director
TELSEY + COMPANY   MATTHEW SILVER   LARRY MORLEY   J. DAVID BRIMMER

Associate Producers   Press Representative   Company Manager   General Management
REBECCA GOLD/   JEFFREY RICHARDS ASSOCIATES   BRUCE KLINGER   RICHARDS/CLIMAN, INC.
DEBBIE BISNO   IRENE GANDY

Directed By
NEIL PEPE

SPEED-THE-PLOW is presented in association with The Atlantic Theater Company
Originally produced by Lincoln Center Theater, New York City
The Producers wish to express their appreciation to the Theatre Development Fund for its support of this production.

10/23/08

Photo by Brigitte Lacombe

(L-R): Raúl Esparza,
Jeremy Piven,
Elisabeth Moss

Speed-the-Plow

Jeremy Piven
Bobby Gould

Raúl Esparza
Charlie Fox

Elisabeth Moss
Karen

Jordan Lage
*u/s Bobby Gould,
Charlie Fox*

Eloise Mumford
u/s Karen

David Mamet
Playwright

Neil Pepe
*Director/
Artistic Director,
Atlantic Theater
Company*

Scott Pask
Scenic Design

Laura Bauer
Costume Design

Brian MacDevitt
Lighting Design

Bernard Telsey,
Telsey + Company
Casting

Matthew Silver
*Production Stage
Manager*

J. David Brimmer
Fight Director

David R. Richards
and Tamar Haimes,
Richards/Climan, Inc.
General Manager

Jeffrey Richards
Producer

Jerry Frankel
Producer

Arny Granat,
Jam Theatricals
Producer

Steve Traxler,
Jam Theatricals
Producer

Bill Haber,
Ostar Productions
Producer

Peggy Hill
Producer

Barry Weisbord,
Bat-Barry
Productions
Producer

Donny Epstein,
Ergo Entertainment
Producer

Yeeshai Gross,
Ergo Entertainment
Producer

Elie Landau,
Ergo Entertainment
Producer

Dede Harris
Producer

Jamie deRoy
Producer

Carl Moellenberg
Producer

Andrew D.
Hamingson
*Managing Director,
Atlantic Theater
Company*

Norbert Leo Butz
Bobby Gould

William H. Macy
Bobby Gould

Speed-the-Plow

Photos by Brian Mapp

MEMBERS OF CAST AND CREW
Back Row (L-R): Eileen Miller, Jordan Lage, Laura Beattie, Victor Verdejo, Irene Gandy, Kevin O'Brien, Eloise Mumford, Dan Landon, Jillian Oliver, Peter Condos, Bruce Klinger, Al Galvez

Front Row (L-R): Patrick Shea, David Lurie, Philip Feller, Matthew Silver, Raúl Esparza, Elisabeth Moss

FRONT OF HOUSE STAFF
Back Row (L-R): Kyle Lamont (Concessions), John Cashman, Conrad Wojciechowski

Middle Row (L-R): Victoria Heslin, Cookie Harlin, John Dancy, Sonia Moreno

Front Row (L-R): John Barbaretti, Rose Ann Cipriano, Aileen Kilburn, Jessica Cooke, Oksana Danrova, Dan Landon (Manager)

MANAGEMENT
(L-R): Bruce Klinger (Company Manager), David H. Lurie (Stage Manager), Matthew Silver (Production Stage Manager), Jillian Oliver (Production Assistant)

BOX OFFICE STAFF
(L-R): Joshua Skidmore, Diane Heatherington (Treasurer)

Not Pictured: Steven Deluca, Chuck Loesche

Speed-the-Plow
Scrapbook

Correspondent: Matthew Silver, Production Stage Manager

Opening Night Gifts: There were all kinds of wonderful things floating around, from cards with kind sentiments to really nice pens from the director and cool mugs from the playwright with the saying 'Industry produces wealth, God speed the plow' which is rumored to be where the title of the play came from. Also, an oldie but goodie in the form of Scotch, vodka and Champagne.

Special Backstage Rituals: Theatre being a truly politically incorrect sport our guys did not disappoint and found themselves pros at the game of Ass Tag. "You're it."

Favorite In-Theatre Gathering Place: "Club Alley."

Most Shows in Their Career: Prop Man Philip Feller.

Mascot: Prop Man Philip Feller.

Ghostly Encounters Backstage: Prop Man Philip Feller.

Favorite Snack Food: Wheat Thins.

Memorable Ad-lib: For those unaware, *Speed-the-Plow* takes place in the still-to-be-adorned office of a newly promoted studio exec. During one of the previews as Raúl was exiting the stage the doorknob to the office came off in his hand. As the audience showed that they understood the humor and possible humiliation of the situation without missing a beat Raúl showed that he was with them and said, "They don't make studios the way they used to," Then, later, as they discussed whether or not Jeremy's character would be able to date the temp, Raúl said, "Not if she can't get in here." Raúl, the pro that he is, turned lemons into lemonade.

Catchphrase Only the Company Would Recognize: "Enchanté."

Memorable Directorial Notes: When describing to the actors the moment immediately following a scene (a moment the audience doesn't see but you know happens) Neil used the phrase "Tasty Times" to describe what their characters were about to embark on. Neil also likes to remind folks not to "lose the forest for the trees."

Memorable Press Encounter: With Irene Gandy as our press rep how could they all not be memorable?

Memorable Stage Door Encounter: Jeremy was assaulted by an adoring fan with a pancake recipe. Actually she laid siege to the theatre and all members of the company and crew, eventually finding a weakness in our battlements.

Strange Audience Encounter: One night, when collecting money for Broadway Cares, Raúl got into a conversation with an audience member.

Photo courtesy Matthew Silver

Elisabeth, Jill, Raúl and Bruce revel in the large amount they raised for Broadway Cares/Equity Fights AIDS.

Audience Member: We gave money to Elisabeth because we know her.
Raúl: Oh, how do you know her?
Audience Member: We watch her every week on TV.

Cell Phone Rings: One night we had a phone ring and ring without anyone stopping it. It must have been 4 or 5 times. Then after a pause it beeped, telling us all that a message was left. I hate hang-ups.

Spring Awakening

First Preview: November 16, 2006. Opened: December 10, 2006.
Closed January 18, 2009 after 28 Previews and 859 Performances.

9 EUGENE O'NEILL THEATRE

A JUJAMCYN THEATRE

ROCCO LANDESMAN
President

PAUL LIBIN
Producing Director

JACK VIERTEL
Creative Director

JORDAN ROTH
Vice President

IRA PITTELMAN   TOM HULCE   JEFFREY RICHARDS   JERRY FRANKEL

ATLANTIC THEATER COMPANY
Jeffrey Sine   Freddy DeMann   Max Cooper

Mort Swinsky/Cindy and Jay Gutterman/Joe McGinnis/Judith Ann Abrams
ZenDog Productions/CarJac Productions
Aron Bergson Productions/Jennifer Manocherian/Ted Snowdon
Harold Thau/Terry Schnuck/Cold Spring Productions
Amanda Dubois/Elizabeth Eynon Wetherell
Jennifer Maloney/Tamara Tunie/Joe Cilibrasi/StyleFour Productions

present

SPRING AWAKENING
A NEW MUSICAL

Book & Lyrics by
Steven Sater

Music by
Duncan Sheik

Based on the play by
Frank Wedekind

with

Gerard Canonico   Tony Carlin   Amanda Castaños   Blake Daniel   Matt Doyle
Andrew Durand   Christine Estabrook   Glenn Fleshler   Emma Hunton   Morgan Karr   Emily Kinney
Caitlin Kinnunen   Alice Lee   Frances Mercanti-Anthony   Eryn Murman   Hunter Parrish
Zach Reiner-Harris   Alexandra Socha   Jesse Swenson   Jenna Ushkowitz   Gabriel Violett

Scenic Design	Costume Design	Lighting Design	Sound Design
Christine Jones	**Susan Hilferty**	**Kevin Adams**	**Brian Ronan**
Orchestrations	Vocal Arrangements	String Orchestrations	Music Coordinator
Duncan Sheik	**AnnMarie Milazzo**	**Simon Hale**	**Michael Keller**
Casting	Fight Direction	Production Stage Manager	Associate Producers
Jim Carnahan, C.S.A.	**J. David Brimmer**	**Heather Cousens**	**Joan Cullman Productions**
Carrie Gardner			**Patricia Flicker Addiss**

Technical Supervision	General Management	Press Representative
Neil A. Mazzella	**Abbie M. Strassler**	**Pete Sanders/Fifteen Minutes PR**

Music Director
Kimberly Grigsby

Choreography
Bill T. Jones

Directed by
Michael Mayer

Originally produced by the Atlantic Theater Company by special arrangement with Tom Hulce & Ira Pittelman.
The producers wish to express their appreciation to the Theatre Development Fund for its support of this production.

10/1/08

CAST
(in order of speaking)

Wendla	ALEXANDRA SOCHA
The Adult Women	CHRISTINE ESTABROOK
Martha	AMANDA CASTAÑOS
Ilse	EMMA HUNTON
Anna	EMILY KINNEY
Thea	CAITLIN KINNUNEN
The Adult Men	GLENN FLESHLER
Otto	GABRIEL VIOLETT
Hanschen	MATT DOYLE
Ernst	BLAKE DANIEL
Georg	ANDREW DURAND
Moritz	GERARD CANONICO
Melchior	HUNTER PARRISH
Ensemble	MORGAN KARR, ALICE LEE, ERYN MURMAN, ZACH REINER-HARRIS

TIME/PLACE

The play is set in a provincial German town
in the 1890s.

Continued on next page

(L-R): Caitlin Kinnunen, Emily Kinney, Alexandra Socha, Amanda Castaños and Emma Hunton

Photo by Joan Marcus

Spring Awakening

MUSICAL NUMBERS

ACT ONE

"Mama Who Bore Me" ....Wendla
"Mama Who Bore Me" (Reprise) ....Girls
"All That's Known" ....Melchior
"The Bitch of Living" ....Moritz with Boys
"My Junk" ....Girls and Boys
"Touch Me" ....Boys and Girls
"The Word of Your Body" ....Wendla, Melchior
"The Dark I Know Well" ....Martha, Ilse with Boys
"And Then There Were None" ....Moritz with Boys
"The Mirror-Blue Night" ....Melchior with Boys
"I Believe" ....Boys and Girls

ACT TWO

"The Guilty Ones" ....Wendla, Melchior with Boys and Girls
"Don't Do Sadness" ....Moritz
"Blue Wind" ....Ilse
"Left Behind" ....Melchior
"Totally Fucked" ....Melchior with Full Company
"The Word of Your Body" (Reprise) ....Hanschen, Ernst with Boys and Girls
"Whispering" ....Wendla
"Those You've Known" ....Moritz, Wendla, Melchior
"The Song of Purple Summer" ....Full Company

FRONT OF HOUSE STAFF

Photo by Brian Mapp

(L-R): Gerard Canonico as Moritz, Hunter Parrish as Melchior and Alexandra Socha as Wendla.

Photo by Joan Marcus

UNDERSTUDIES

For Melchior:
MATT DOYLE, JESSE SWENSON
For Moritz:
ANDREW DURAND, MORGAN KARR,
ZACH REINER-HARRIS
For Georg, Hanschen, Otto:
MORGAN KARR, ZACH REINER-HARRIS,
JESSE SWENSON
For Ernst:
MORGAN KARR, ZACH REINER-HARRIS
For Wendla:
EMILY KINNEY, ALICE LEE, ERYN MURMAN
For Ilse, Martha:
ERYN MURMAN, JENNA USHKOWITZ
For Anna, Thea:
ALICE LEE, ERYN MURMAN,
JENNA USHKOWITZ
For the Adult Men:
TONY CARLIN
For the Adult Women:
FRANCES MERCANTI-ANTHONY

Swings:
FRANCES MERCANTI-ANTHONY,
JENNA USHKOWITZ

Dance Captain:
JoANN M. HUNTER
Associate Dance Captain:
ERYN MURMAN

THE BAND

Conductor/Keyboards:
KIMBERLY GRIGSBY
Guitars:
THAD DEBROCK
Bass:
GEORGE FARMER
Associate Conductor/Drums:
TREY FILES
Cello:
BENJAMIN KALB
Violin/Guitar:
OLIVIER MANCHON
Viola:
HIROKO TAGUCHI

Spring Awakening

Gerard Canonico
Moritz

Tony Carlin
u/s Adult Men

Amanda Castaños
Martha

Blake Daniel
Ernst

Matt Doyle
Hanschen

Andrew Durand
Georg

Christine Estabrook
Adult Women

Glenn Fleshler
Adult Men

Emma Hunton
Ilse

Morgan Karr
Ensemble

Emily Kinney
Anna

Caitlin Kinnunen
Thea

Alice Lee
Ensemble

Frances Mercanti-Anthony
u/s Adult Women

Eryn Murman
Ensemble

Hunter Parrish
Melchior

Zach Reiner-Harris
Ensemble

Alexandra Socha
Wendla

Jesse Swenson
Swing

Jenna Ushkowitz
Swing

Gabriel Violett
Otto

Steven Sater
Book & Lyrics

Duncan Sheik
Music

Michael Mayer
Director

Bill T. Jones
Choreographer

Frank Wedekind
(1864-1918)
Author

Christine Jones
Set Designer

Susan Hilferty
Costume Designer

Kevin Adams
Lighting Designer

Brian Ronan
Sound Designer

Kimberly Grigsby
Music Director

AnnMarie Milazzo
Vocal Arrangements

Simon Hale
String Orchestrations

Michael Keller
Music Coordinator

J. David Brimmer
Fight Director, SAFD

Spring Awakening

Neil A. Mazzella
Technical Supervision

Jim Carnahan
Casting

Beatrice Terry
Associate Director

JoAnn M. Hunter
Dance Supervisor

Ira Pittelman
Producer

Tom Hulce
Producer

Jeffrey Richards
Producer

Jerry Frankel
Producer

Neil Pepe
Artistic Director, Atlantic Theater Company

Andrew D. Hamingson
Managing Director, Atlantic Theater Company

Freddy DeMann
Producer

Max Cooper
Producer

Morton Swinsky
Producer

Joe McGinnis
Producer

Jay and Cindy Gutterman
Producer

Judith Ann Abrams
Producer

Pun Bandhu,
ZenDog Productions
Producer

Marc Falato,
ZenDog Productions
Producer

Carl Moellenberg,
Carjac Productions
Producer

Jack M. Dagleish,
Carjac Productions
Producer

Tracy Aron
Producer

Stefany Bergson
Producer

Jennifer Manocherian
Producer

Ted Snowdon
Producer

Harold Thau
Producer

Terry E. Schnuck
Producer

Robert Bailenson
Producer

Amanda Dubois
Producer

Jennifer Maloney
Producer

Tamara Tunie
Producer

Joseph Cilibrasi
Producer

John Styles, Jr.,
StylesFour Productions
Producer

Pat Flicker Addiss
Associate Producer

Spring Awakening

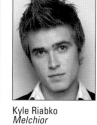

Skylar Astin
Georg

Blake Bashoff
Moritz

Lilli Cooper
Martha

Brian Charles Johnson
Otto

Kyle Riabko
Melchior

Matt Shingledecker
Ensemble

Phoebe Strole
Anna

Jesse Swenson
Melchior

Remy Zaken
Thea

Alice Lee
u/s Ilse

Jesse Swenson
Swing

CARPENTRY
(L-R): Guy Patria, Donald Robinson, Kevin Maher

STAGE MANAGEMENT
(L-R): Richard Rauscher, Heather Cousens, Bethany Russell

WARDROBE
(L-R): Susan Checklick, Danny Paul, Gayle Palmieri, Vanessa Valeriano

SOUND AND ELECTRICS
Front Row (L-R): Todd D'Aiuto, unknown, Francis Elers

Back Row (L-R): Rocco Williams, James Gardner, unknown

Spring Awakening

PRODUCTION PROPERTIES
Christopher Beck

BOX OFFICE
(L-R): Keith Stephenson, Stan Shaffer

Spring Awakening
SCRAPBOOK

Following the standing-room-only final perform-ance, the producing and creative team spoke about bringing the show to fruition. Excerpts from the speeches by lead producers Ira Pittelman and Tom Hulce and by co-creators Steven Sater (book and lyrics) and Duncan Sheik (music) follow:

Pittelman: "We've played almost 900 perform-ances; we've played more than two years on Broadway, and though this is the last night in New York, this is not the end of *Spring Awakening*. Over the next three years, our tour will play 45 cities in the U.S. and Canada. *Spring Awakening* will be produced in 18 coun-tries, in 14 different languages, so our beautiful, loving passionate transformative show will, in fact, run forever."

Hulce: "There are so many people we need to thank with this amazing, unprecedented adven-ture, first and foremost is the most amazing cast, our most incredible band members who have been with us from the beginning. . . . This is one of the most incredible rooms in New York to per-form in, and we are so grateful for the hospitali-ty and support of our friends at Jujamcyn. . . ."

Pittelman: "We also want to thank our produc-ing partners Jeffrey Richards and Jerry Frankel. . . . [and] all of our passionate, courageous and wonderful producing partners and investors—thank you so much. A very, very special thanks to our friend and mentor; he's been with us every step of the way—I don't think we could have done this without him—Manny Azenberg. . . . Can I just say, I'd like to thank Tom...."

Hulce: "I love you Ira. . . . Here we go. Ten years ago, Steven Sater had this genius, crazy idea, and he invited his friends Duncan Sheik and Michael Mayer to join him in making this seem-ingly impossible idea into something incredibly gorgeous. Along the way there have been many people who have given their support. We want to thank La Jolla Playhouse, we want to thank the Sundance Theatre Lab. We want to thank Todd Haimes and the Roundabout Theatre Company. A special thanks to Jon Nakagawa, who I think is here tonight, and the American Songbook Series of Lincoln Center. And now we come to the heart of this adventure: the Atlantic Theater Company. . . You gave us your guidance and your support and most of all and most crucially, you gave us your home: a spec-tacular and safe place where *Spring Awakening* could find itself and become itself and grow into the world. And for that we are forever, ever grateful. And, especially, you gave us a most remarkably, exceptionally talented cast of young people. Believe me, we are saving the best for last but before we do, the other thing the Atlantic helped us with was to assemble a bril-liant creative team, and with us here tonight is our extraordinary music director Kimberly Grigsby. Our resident director Bea Terry is here. But most noticeably absent tonight is our design team—our choreographer Bill T. Jones, his asso-ciate, and our director Michael Mayer. They are in London in final tech rehearsals for the launch of *Spring Awakening*, the British version, so they couldn't be with us, and we send them our boundless thanks for their inspired work. There's no greater honor or pleasure than for Ira

1. Cast members pose at an autograph session outside the O'Neill Theatre to benefit "Operation Backpack" July 9, 2008.
2. (L-R): Alexandra Socha and Gerard Canonico at "Broadway on Broadway 2008" in Times Square September 14, 2008.
3. The new cast, led by Hunter Parrish (center), takes bows at the August 11, 2008 performance.

and I and everyone gathered upon this stage than to give you Steven Sater and Duncan Sheik."

Sheik: "I'm not quite sure who organized the falling snow and the tolling bells as we entered the theatre, but it was a nice touch. As I sat in the audience tonight, I realized how much this is a show about partings, about saying goodbye and how beautiful and cathartic that can be, and I can't thank you all enough for sharing this moment—one of the best moments of my life."

Sater: "So I guess it really was ten years ago in February of '99 that I proposed to Duncan that we take this fearless children's tragedy written by Frank Wedekind and turn it into a piece of musical theatre. Shortly thereafter, Michael and Duncan and I really determined that we would touch the troubled heart of youth around the world and tonight at intermission this young man Tom came up to me and said, 'If you and Duncan hadn't decided to do this, I don't know what I would have done, I don't know what my life would have been,' and I just think we never could have dreamed—who can say what dreams are?—that we could touch this many hearts and have our own hearts touched in return. I was thinking much like Duncan; I was thinking this is a play filled with ghosts and learning to live with our ghosts, and it's only in the final scene, really, that we see that the ghosts in our minds and the ghosts in the moonlight can become a source of nurture and encouragement for the ghosts still left behind. Tonight, in some way, *Spring Awakening* on Broadway is becoming a ghost. It's a series of performances and actors and songs we've known, but I think for me—for many of us—those songs, those performances, those audiences will walk with our hearts and be a source of nurture through times of darkness and light and so in that sense the dream will never end. And for two and a half years, for all these incredible performances and for tonight most of all, I just want to thank you from the bottom of my heart."

The Story of My Life

First Preview: February 3, 2009. Opened: February 19, 2009.
Closed February 22, 2009 after 19 Previews and 5 Performances.

PLAYBILL

The Story of My Life

CAST

Thomas Weaver .... WILL CHASE
Alvin Kelby .... MALCOLM GETS

Voice of Young Thomas .... ALEX MAIZUS
Voice of Young Alvin .... AUSTIN McKINNIS

UNDERSTUDIES

For Thomas Weaver: BRADLEY DEAN
For Alvin Kelby: JIM STANEK

MUSICIANS

Conductor: DAVID HOLCENBERG
Associate Conductor: SUE ANSCHUTZ
Piano: DAVID HOLCENBERG
Drums/Percussion: BILL HAYES
Bass: MARC SCHMIED
Violin: ELIZABETH LIM-DUTTON
Viola: KEN BURWARD HOY
Cello: SARAH J. SEIVER
Clarinet: LES SCOTT
Bassoon: TOM SEFCOVIC
Trumpet: TIMOTHY L. SCHADT
Music Coordinator: JOHN MILLER

Music Copying:
EMILY GRISHMAN MUSIC PREPARATION
KATHARINE EDMONDS/EMILY GRISHMAN

BOOTH THEATRE
222 West 45th Street
A Shubert Organization Theatre
Philip J. Smith, *Chairman*   **Robert E. Wankel**, *President*

Chase Mishkin   Jack M. Dalgleish   Bud Martin   Carole L. Haber
in association with Chunsoo Shin
present

Will Chase   Malcolm Gets

The Story of My Life

A New Musical

Music and Lyrics	Book
Neil Bartram	**Brian Hill**

Set Design	Costume Design	Lighting Design
Robert Brill	Wade Laboissonniere	Ken Billington Paul Toben

Sound Design	Projection Design
Peter Fitzgerald Carl Casella	Dustin O'Neill

Orchestrations	Music Direction	Music Coordinator
Jonathan Tunick	David Holcenberg	John Miller

Casting	Production Stage Manager	Production Supervisor
Jay Binder/ Sara Schatz	Bess Marie Glorioso	Arthur Siccardi Patrick Sullivan

Associate Director	Press Representative	General Manager
Lisa Shriver	Keith Sherman Associates Glenna Freedman	Leonard Soloway

Directed by
Richard Maltby, Jr.

*The Story Of My Life received its world premiere at the Canadian Stage Company's Berkeley Street Theatre
in Toronto, Canada on November 2, 2006.
Subsequently produced by Goodspeed Musicals, Michael P. Price, Executive Producer.
The producers wish to thank Theatre Development Fund for its support of this production.*

NATIONAL ALLIANCE for MUSICAL THEATRE   THE STORY OF MY LIFE WAS PRESENTED AT NAMT'S FESTIVAL OF NEW MUSICALS IN 2007.

2/22/09

(L-R): Malcolm Gets and Will Chase

Photo by Aaron Epstein

The Story of My Life

MUSICAL NUMBERS

"Write What You Know"	Thomas
"Mrs. Remington"	Alvin
"The Greatest Gift"	Alvin & Thomas
"1876"	Thomas
"Normal"	Thomas
"People Carry On"	Alvin
"The Butterfly"	Thomas
"Saying Goodbye" (Part 1)	Thomas & Alvin
"Here's Where It Begins"	Thomas & Alvin
"Saying Goodbye" (Part 2)	Thomas & Alvin
"Independence Day"	Alvin
"Saying Goodbye" (Part 3)	Thomas & Alvin
"I Like It Here"	Thomas
"You're Amazing, Tom"	Alvin
"Nothing There/Saying Goodbye" (Part 4)	Thomas & Alvin
"I Didn't See Alvin"	Thomas
"This Is It"	Alvin & Thomas
"Angels in the Snow"	Alvin & Thomas

Photo by Aaron Epstein

(L-R): Malcolm Gets and Will Chase

Will Chase
(in 1st Grade)
Thomas Weaver

Malcolm Gets
(in 1st Grade)
Alvin Kelby

Bradley Dean
(in 1st Grade)
u/s Thomas Weaver

Jim Stanek
(in 1st Grade)
u/s Alvin Kelby

Neil Bartram
Music and Lyrics

Brian Hill
Book

Richard Maltby, Jr.
Director

Robert Brill
Set Design

Ken Billington
Lighting Design

Carl Casella
Sound Design

Jonathan Tunick
Orchestrations

David Holcenberg
Music Director

John Miller
Music Coordinator

Arthur Siccardi
Theatrical Services, Inc.
Production Supervisor

Lisa Shriver
Associate Director

Leonard Soloway
General Manager

Chase Mishkin
Producer

Jack M. Dalgleish
Producer

The Story of My Life
SCRAPBOOK

1. (L-R): Composer-lyricist Neil Bartram, librettist Brian Hill, co-stars Will Chase and Malcolm Gets, and director Richard Maltby. Jr. at Sardi's for the opening night party.
2. Orchestrator Jonathan Tunick arrives at the Booth Theatre for the premiere.

Photos by Aubrey Reuben

STAFF FOR *THE STORY OF MY LIFE*

GENERAL MANAGEMENT
Leonard Soloway

COMPANY MANAGER
Judith Drasner

GENERAL PRESS REPRESENTATIVE
Keith Sherman & Associates/Glenna Freedman
Scott Klein
Brett Oberman   Matt Ross

CASTING
JAY BINDER CASTING
Jay Binder CSA
Jack Bowdan CSA, Mark Brandon, Sara Schatz,
Nikole Vallins
Kate Sprance, Karen Young

PRODUCTION MANAGEMENT
Arthur Siccardi and Patrick Sullivan

Production Stage Manager ....Bess Marie Glorioso
Stage Manager ....Ana M. Garcia
Production Assistants ....Meg Friedman,
Melanie T. Morgan
Assistant to the Director ....Joshua Wellman
Assistant to the Costume Designer ....Mary Ann Smith
Assistant Scenic Designers ....Dustin O'Neill,
Angrette McCloskey,
Daniel Meeker
Associate Lighting Designer ....Cory Pattak
Assistant to the Lighting Designer ....Jim Milkey
Assistant to the Musical Contractor ....Nichole Jennino

Production Carpenter ....Kenneth McDonough
Production Properties ....Mike Pilipski
Production Electrician ....Susan Goulet

Production Sound ....Brad M. Gyorgak
Wardrobe Supervisor ....Jesse Galvan
Dresser.....................................Vangeli Kaseluris

Legal Counsel ....Fitelson, Lasky, Aslan,
Couture & Garmise, Attorneys at Law/
Richard Garmise
Legal Counsel to
JD Entertainment ....M. Graham Coleman, Esq./
Davis Wright Tremaine LLP
Accountants ....Rosenberg, Neuwirth & Kuchner/
Jana Jevnikar
Advertising...........................Eliran Murphy Group/
Barbara Eliran, Frank Verlizzo,
Elizabeth Findlay
Artwork ....Fraver
Cover Photography ....Jean-Marie Guyaux
Production Photographer ....Aaron Epstein
Marketing ....Type A Marketing/
Anne Rippey, Nick Pramik, Janette Roush
Website ....Bay Bridge Productions/
Laura Wagner, Jean Strong
Press Assistant ....Tamara Alfred
Press Interns.....................Taharah Nix, Lori Tiernan
General Management Intern ....Kristen Luciani
Banking ....JP Morgan Chase/Salvatore Romano
Insurance ....C&S International Insurance Brokers/
Debra Kozee
Street Team ....Big Frog Inc./
Paddy Haughey
Theatre Displays ....King Displays
Payroll ....CSI/Lance Castellana

CREDITS
Scenery by Hudson Scenic Studio, Inc. Lighting equipment from PRG Lighting. Sound equipment by Masque Sound. Costumes constructed by John David Ridge. Pianos courtesy of Baldwin Pianos. Men's costumes courtesy of Brooks Brothers. Makeup provided by M•A•C Cosmetics.

Special thanks to
Chris Choi, Bick Goss and Steven Rivellino.

To learn more about the production, please visit
www.TheStoryOfMyLife.com

THE SHUBERT ORGANIZATION, INC.
Board of Directors

House Manager ....Laurel Ann Wilson

Sunday in the Park with George

First Preview: January 25, 2008. Opened: February 21, 2008.
Closed June 29, 2008 after 32 Previews and 149 Performances.

PLAYBILL

SUNDAY IN THE PARK with George

CAST

(in order of appearance)

ACT I

George, an artist	DANIEL EVANS
Dot, his mistress	JENNA RUSSELL
An Old Lady	MARY BETH PEIL
Her Nurse	ANNE L. NATHAN
Franz, a servant	DAVID TURNER
The Bathers	SANTINO FONTANA, DREW McVETY, ALISON HOROWITZ
Jules, another artist	ANDREW VARELA
Yvonne, his wife	JESSICA MOLASKEY
A Boatman	ALEXANDER GEMIGNANI
Celeste #1	BRYNN O'MALLEY
Celeste #2	JESSICA GROVÉ
Louis, a baker	DREW McVETY
Louise, the daughter of Jules and Yvonne	ALISON HOROWITZ
Frieda, a cook	STACIE MORGAIN LEWIS
A Soldier	SANTINO FONTANA
Mr.	ED DIXON
Mrs.	ANNE L. NATHAN

ACT II

George, an artist	DANIEL EVANS
Marie, his grandmother	JENNA RUSSELL
Dennis, a technician	ALEXANDER GEMIGNANI
Bob Greenberg, the museum director	ANDREW VARELA
Naomi Eisen, a composer	JESSICA MOLASKEY
Harriet Pawling, a patron of the arts	ANNE L. NATHAN

Continued on next page

Continued on next page

STUDIO 54

ROUNDABOUTTHEATRECOMPANY

Todd Haimes, Artistic Director
Harold Wolpert, Managing Director
Julia C. Levy, Executive Director

in association with

Bob Boyett   Debra Black   Jam Theatricals   Stephanie P. McClelland
Stewart F. Lane/Bonnie Comley   Barbara Manocherian/Jennifer Manocherian   Ostar Productions

Presents

The Menier Chocolate Factory (David Babani, Artistic Director) production of

Daniel Evans   Jenna Russell
Alexander Gemignani   Jessica Molaskey

in

SUNDAY IN THE PARK with George

Music and Lyrics by Stephen Sondheim   Book by James Lapine

with

Mary Beth Peil

Ed Dixon Santino Fontana Jessica Grové Alison Horowitz Stacie Morgain Lewis
Drew McVety Anne L. Nathan Brynn O'Malley David Turner Andrew Varela
Colleen Fitzpatrick Kelsey Fowler Jeff Kready Hayley Podschun Steve Wilson

Set & Costume Design	Lighting Design	Sound Design	Projection Design
David Farley	Ken Billington	Sebastian Frost	Timothy Bird & The Knifedge Creative Network

Musical Supervisor	Orchestrations	Music Coordinator
Caroline Humphris	Jason Carr	John Miller

Production Stage Manager	Hair & Wig Design	Dialect Coach
Peter Hanson	Tom Watson	Kate Wilson

Casting	Technical Supervisor	Executive Producer	Press Representative
Jim Carnahan, C.S.A.	Steve Beers	Sydney Beers	Boneau/Bryan-Brown

Director of Marketing & Sales Promotion	Director of Development	Founding Director	Associate Artistic Director
David B. Steffen	Jeffory Lawson	Gene Feist	Scott Ellis

Musical Staging by Christopher Gattelli

Directed by Sam Buntrock

In association with Caro Newling for Neal Street Productions and Mark Rubinstein

Lead support provided by Roundabout's Musical Theatre Fund partners:
Perry and Marty Granoff, GVA Williams, The Kaplen Foundation,
John and Gilda McGarry, The Shen Family Foundation, Tom and Diane Tuft.

Playwrights Horizons produced the original production of *Sunday in the Park with George* in 1983
Originally directed on Broadway by James Lapine
Roundabout Theatre Company is a member of the League of Resident Theatres.
www.roundabouttheatre.org

6/29/08

(L-R): Alison Horowitz, Jessica Molaskey, Drew McVety, Brynn O'Malley, Jessica Grové, Daniel Evans, Michael Cumpsty, Jenna Russell.

Photo by Joan Marcus

Sunday in the Park with George

MUSICAL NUMBERS

ACT I

"Sunday in the Park With George"	Dot
"No Life"	Jules, Yvonne
"Color and Light"	Dot, George
"Gossip"	Celeste #1, Celeste #2, Boatman, Nurse, Old Lady, Jules, Yvonne
"The Day Off"	George, Nurse, Franz, Frieda, Boatman, Soldier, Celeste #1, Celeste #2, Yvonne, Louise, Jules, Louis
"Everybody Loves Louis"	Dot
"Finishing the Hat"	George
"We Do Not Belong Together"	Dot, George
"Beautiful"	Old Lady, George
"Sunday"	Company

ACT II

"It's Hot Up Here"	Company
"Chromolume #7"	Company
"Putting It Together"	George, Company
"Children and Art"	Marie
"Lesson #8"	George
"Move On"	George, Dot
"Sunday"	Company

Although suggested by the life of Georges Seurat and by his painting "A Sunday Afternoon on the Island of La Grande Jatte," all characters in *Sunday in the Park with George* are products of the author's imagination.

ORCHESTRA

Conductor:
THOMAS MURRAY
Associate Conductor:
SHAWN GOUGH
Music Coordinator:
JOHN MILLER
Music Director/Piano:
THOMAS MURRAY
Keyboard:
SHAWN GOUGH
Violin/House Contractor:
MATTHEW LEHMANN
Cello:
MAIRI DORMAN-PHANEUF
Woodwinds:
TODD GROVES
Music Copying:
EMILY GRISHMAN MUSIC PREPARATION—
KATHARINE EDMONDS/EMILY GRISHMAN

Original Broadway orchestrations by
MICHAEL STAROBIN

(L-R): Jenna Russell and Daniel Evans as Dot and George.

Photo by Joan Marcus

Cast Continued

Billy Webster, her friend	DREW McVETY
A Photographer	JESSICA GROVÉ
Charles Redmond, a visiting curator	ED DIXON
Alex, an artist	SANTINO FONTANA
Betty, an artist	STACIE MORGAIN LEWIS
Lee Randolph, the museum's publicist	DAVID TURNER
Blair Daniels, an art critic	MARY BETH PEIL
Elaine	BRYNN O'MALLEY

UNDERSTUDIES

For Yvonne/Naomi Eisen, Old Lady/Blair Daniels, Nurse/Mrs./Harriet Pawling:
COLLEEN FITZPATRICK
For George:
SANTINO FONTANA
For Louise:
KELSEY FOWLER
For Soldier/Alex, Louis/Billy Webster, Franz/Lee Randolph:
JEFF KREADY
For Dot/Marie:
BRYNN O'MALLEY
For Celeste #1/Elaine, Celeste #2/A Photographer, Frieda/Betty:
HAYLEY PODSCHUN
Standby for Mr./Charles Redmond, Boatman/ Dennis:
ANDREW VARELA
For Jules/Bob Greenberg:
STEVE WILSON

Dance Captain:
HAYLEY PODSCHUN

Production Stage Manager:
PETER HANSON
Stage Manager:
JON KRAUSE
Assistant Stage Manager:
RACHEL ZACK

Daniel Evans and Jenna Russell are appearing with the permission of Actors' Equity Association pursuant to an exchange program between American Equity and UK Equity.

TIME AND PLACE

ACT I takes place on a series of Sundays from 1884 to 1886 and alternates between a park on an island in the Seine just outside of Paris, and George's studio. **ACT II** takes place in 1984 at an American art museum and on the island.

Sunday in the Park with George

Daniel Evans
George

Jenna Russell
Dot/Marie

Alexander
Gemignani
Boatman/Dennis

Jessica Molaskey
Yvonne/Naomi Eisen

Mary Beth Peil
*Old Lady/
Blair Daniels*

Ed Dixon
*Mr./
Charles Redmond*

Santino Fontana
Bather/Soldier/Alex

Jessica Grové
*Celeste #2/
A Photographer*

Alison Horowitz
Louise

Stacie Morgain
Lewis
Frieda/Betty

Drew McVety
*Bather/Louis/
Billy Webster*

Anne L. Nathan
*Nurse/Mrs./
Harriet Pawling*

Brynn O'Malley
Celeste #1/Elaine

David Turner
Franz/Lee Randolph

Andrew Varela
*Jules/
Bob Greenberg*

Colleen Fitzpatrick
*u/s Yvonne/
Naomi Eisen,
Old Lady/
Blair Daniels, Nurse/
Mrs./Harriet Pawling*

Kelsey Fowler
u/s Louise

Jeff Kready
*u/s Soldier/Alex,
Louis/Billy Webster,
Franz/Lee Randolph*

Hayley Podschun
*u/s Celeste #1/Elaine,
Celeste #2/
A Photographer,
Frieda/Betty*

Steve Wilson
*u/s Jules/
Bob Greenberg*

Stephen Sondheim
Music & Lyrics

James Lapine
Book

Sam Buntrock
Director

Christopher Gattelli
Musical Staging

David Farley
*Set and Costume
Design*

Ken Billington
Lighting Design

Sebastian Frost
Sound Design

Timothy Bird
Projection Design

Jason Carr
Orchestrations

John Miller
Music Coordinator

Tom Watson
Hair and Wig Design

Dave Solomon
Assistant Director

Jim Carnahan
Casting

Bob Boyett
Producer

Debra Black
Producer

Sunday in the Park with George

Arny Granat,
Jam Theatricals
Producer

Steve Traxler,
Jam Theatricals
Producer

Stephanie P.
McClelland
Producer

Stewart F. Lane and Bonnie Comley
Producers

Barbara
Manocherian
Producer

Jennifer
Manocherian
Producer

Bill Haber,
Ostar Productions
Producer

Gene Feist
*Founding Director,
Roundabout Theatre
Company*

Todd Haimes
*Artistic Director,
Roundabout Theatre
Company*

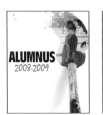

ALUMNUS
2008-2009

Michael Cumpsty
*Jules/
Bob Greenberg*

Photos by Ben Strothmann

CREW
Front Row (L-R): Dan Schultheis, Steve Jones, Dan Hoffman.

Middle Row (L-R): Erin Mary Delaney, Paul Ashton, Dorian Fuchs.

Back Row (L-R): Josh Weitzman, Lawrence Jennino and John Wooding.

HAIR AND WARDROBE
Front Row (L-R): Victoria Grecki, Mary Ann Oberpriller,
Nadine Hettel.

Back Row (L-R): Barry Ernst, Joe Godwin and Timothy Miller.

STAGE AND COMPANY MANAGEMENT
Front Row (L-R): Denise Cooper, Brent McCreary.

Back Row (L-R): Peter Hanson, Rachel Zack and Jonny Krause.

Sunday in the Park with George

Photos by Ben Strothmann

FRONT OF HOUSE STAFF
Front Row (L-R): Hajjah Karriem,
Jack Watanachaiyot, LaConya Robinson.

Middle Row (L-R): Nicole Ramirez,
Essence Mason, Delilah Rivera.

Back Row (L-R): José Cuello, Justin Brown,
Ana Bak-Kvapil and Nicholas Wheatley.

BOX OFFICE
(L-R): Pam Unger, Scott Falkowski
and Jaime Perlman.

ORCHESTRA
(L-R): Thomas Murray
and Mairi Dorman-Phaneuf.

ROUNDABOUT THEATRE COMPANY STAFF
ARTISTIC DIRECTOR ....TODD HAIMES
MANAGING DIRECTOR ....HAROLD WOLPERT
EXECUTIVE DIRECTOR ....JULIA C. LEVY
ASSOCIATE ARTISTIC DIRECTOR ...SCOTT ELLIS

ARTISTIC STAFF
DIRECTOR OF ARTISTIC DEVELOPMENT/
    DIRECTOR OF CASTING ....**Jim Carnahan**
Artistic Consultant ....Robyn Goodman
Resident Director ....Doug Hughes
Associate Artists ....Scott Elliott, Bill Irwin,
    Joe Mantello, Mark Brokaw, Kathleen Marshall
Artistic Associate ....Jill Rafson
Casting Director ....Carrie Gardner
Casting Associate ....Kate Schwabe
Casting Associate ....Stephen Kopel
Artistic Assistant ....Erica Rotstein
Literary Associate ....Josh Fiedler
Casting Assistant ....Jillian Cimini
Casting Interns ....Kyle Bosley, Erin Drake,
    Andrew Femenella, Quinn Meyers

EDUCATION STAFF
EDUCATION DIRECTOR ....**David A. Miller**
Director of Instruction and
    Curriculum Development ....Reneé Flemings
Education Program Manager ....Jennifer DiBella
Program Associate for
    School-Based Programs ....Amanda Hinkle
Education Associate for
    Theatre-Based Programs ....Jay Gerlach
Education Assistant ....Aliza Greenberg
Education Dramaturg ....Ted Sod
Teaching Artists ....Phil Alexander, Cynthia Babak,
    Victor Barbella, LaTonya Borsay,
    Rob Bronstein, Lori Brown-Niang,
    Miss Stella, Hamilton Clancy, Joe Doran,
    Katie Down, Amy Fortoul, Tony Freeman,
    Sheri Graubert, Matthew Gregory, Adam Gwon,
    Karla Hendrick, Jim Jack, Lisa Renee Jordan,
    Alvin Keith, Jonathan Lang, Rebecca Lord,

Tami Mansfield, Erin McCready, Jordana Oberman,
Evan O'Brient, Deirdre O'Connor, Andrew Ondrecjak,
    Laura Poe, Alexa Polmer-Spencer, Nicole Press,
    Jennifer Rathbone, Leah Reddy, Amanda Rehbein,
    Taylor Ruckel, Chris Rummel, Cassy Rush,
    Drew Sachs, Nick Simone, Derek Straat,
    Daniel Robert Sullivan, Vickie Tanner,
Olivia Tsang, Cristina Vaccaro, Jennifer Varbalow,
    Leese Walker, Eric Wallach, Gail Winar
Education Interns ....Sara Curtin, Steven Tarca

ADMINISTRATIVE STAFF
GENERAL MANAGER ....**Sydney Beers**
Associate Managing Director ....Greg Backstrom
General Manager, Steinberg Center ....Rebecca Habel
General Counsel ....Nancy Hirschmann
Human Resources Manager ....Stephen Deutsch
MIS Director ....Jeff Goodman
Assistant General Manager ....Maggie Cantrick
Operations Manager ....Valerie Simmons
Office Manager ....Scott Kelly
MIS Database Administrator ....Micah Kraybill
MIS Associate ....Dylan Norden
Assistant to the Managing Director ....Rebecca Skoff
Receptionists ....Dee Beider, Raquel Castillo,
    Elisa Papa, Allison Patrick, Monica Sidorchuk
Messenger ....Darnell Franklin
Management Interns ....Jason Butler, Jessica Segal

FINANCE STAFF
DIRECTOR OF FINANCE...............**Susan Neiman**
Assistant Controller.........................John LaBarbera
Accounts Payable Administrator ....Frank Surdi
Financial Associate ....Yonit Kafka
Business Office Assistant ....Joshua Cohen
Business Interns ....Aaron Esman, Jonathan Herger,
    Jaclyn Verbitski

DEVELOPMENT STAFF
DIRECTOR OF DEVELOPMENT .....**Jeffory Lawson**
Director, Institutional Giving ....Julie K. D'Andrea
Director, Special Events ....Steve Schaeffer

Director, Major Gifts ....Joy Pak
Director, Patron Programs ....Amber Jo Manuel
Manager, Donor Information Systems ....Lise Speidel
Manager, Patron Programs ....Kara Kandel
Telefundraising Manager ....Gavin Brown
Manager, Corporate Relations ....Corey Young
Patrons Services Assistant ....John Haynes
Development Assistants ....Joshua Poole, Daniel Curley
Special Events Assistant ....Ashley Firestone
Institutional Giving Assistant ....Nick Nolte
Assistant to the Executive Director ....Allyson Stewart
Development Interns ....Kaitlin Cherichello,
    Victoria Pardo-Posse

MARKETING STAFF
DIRECTOR OF MARKETING
    AND SALES PROMOTION ....**David B. Steffen**
Associate Director of Marketing ....Wendy Hutton
Marketing/Publications Manager .....Margaret Casagrande
Marketing Manager ....Stefanie Schussel
Marketing Assistant ....Shannon Marcotte
Website Consultant ....Keith Powell Beyland
DIRECTOR OF TELESALES
    SPECIAL PROMOTIONS ....**Daniel Weiss**
Telesales Manager ....Michael Pace
Telesales Office Coordinator ....Anthony Merced
Marketing Interns ....Ashleigh Awusie, Candace Simon

TICKET SERVICES STAFF
DIRECTOR OF
    SALES OPERATIONS ....**Charlie Garbowski, Jr.**
Ticket Services Manager ....Ellen Holt
Subscription Manager ....Ethan Ubell
Box Office Managers ....Edward P. Osborne,
    Andrew Clements, Jaime Perlman
Group Sales Manager ....Jeff Monteith
Assistant Box Office Managers ....Krystin MacRitchie,
    Robert Morgan, Nicole Nicholson
Customer Services Coordinator ....Thomas Walsh
Assistant Ticket Services Managers ....Robert Kane,
    Bill Klemm, Carlos Morris

The Playbill Broadway Yearbook 2008-2009

Sunday in the Park with George

Ticket Services ....Solangel Bido, Lauren Cartelli,
David Carson, Joseph Clark,
Barbara Dente, Nisha Dhruna, Adam Elsberry,
Lindsay Ericson, Scott Falkowski,
Catherine Fitzpatrick, James Graham, Tova Heller,
Nicki Ishmael, Kate Longosky, Elisa Mala,
Mead Margulies, Chuck Migliaccio,
Adam Owens, Kayrose Pagan, Ethan Paulini,
David Pittman, Thomas Protulipac,
Kaia Rafoss, DeeAnna Row, Benjamin Schneider,
Heather Siebert, Nalene Singh, Lillian Soto,
DJ Thacker, Pam Unger
Ticket Services Intern ....Andrea Finlayson

SERVICES

Counsel ....Paul, Weiss, Rifkind,
Wharton and Garrison LLP,
John Breglio, Deborah Hartnett
Counsel ....Rosenberg & Estis
Counsel ....Andrew Lance,
Gibson, Dunn, & Crutcher, LLP
Counsel ....Harry H. Weintraub,
Glick and Weintraub, P.C.
Immigration Counsel ....Mark D. Koestler and
Theodore Ruthizer, Esq.,
Matthew Dunn, Esq. of
Kramer Levin Naftalis & Frankel LLP
Government
Relations ....Law Offices of Claudia Wagner LLC
House Physicians ....Dr. Theodore Tyberg,
Dr. Lawrence Katz
House Dentist ....Neil Kanner, D.M.D.
Insurance ....DeWitt Stern Group, Inc.
Accountant ....Lutz & Carr CPAs, LLP
Advertising ....Spotco/
Drew Hodges, Jim Edwards,
Tom Greenwald, Y. Darius Suyama, Beth Watson
Sponsorship ....Allied Live/
Tanya Grubich, Laura Matalon,
Meghan Zaneski
Interactive Marketing ....Situation Marketing/
Damian Bazadona, John Lanasa,
Ryan Klink, Kristen Butler
Marketing ....Leanne Schanzer Promotions, Inc./
Leanne Schanzer, Justin Schanzer,
Kara Laviola
Events Photography ....Anita and Steve Shevett
Production Photographer ....Joan Marcus
Theatre Displays ....King Displays, Wayne Sapper
Lobby Refreshments ....Sweet Concessions
Merchandising ....Marquee Merchandise, LLC/
Matt Murphy

MANAGING DIRECTOR EMERITUS ....Ellen Richard

Roundabout Theatre Company
231 West 39th Street, New York, NY 10018
(212) 719-9393.

GENERAL PRESS REPRESENTATIVES
Adrian Bryan-Brown
Matt Polk   Jessica Johnson   Amy Kass

CREDITS FOR
SUNDAY IN THE PARK WITH GEORGE

Company Manager ....Denise Cooper

Company Manager Assistant ....Brent McCreary
Production Stage Manager ....Peter Hanson
Stage Manager ....Jon Krause
Assistant Stage Manager ....Rachel Zack
Assistant Director ....Dave Solomon
Associate Director/Choreographer, UK .....Tara Wilkinson
Assistant to the Choreographer ....Lou Castro
SSDC Observer ....Michael Schwartz
Dance Captain ....Hayley Podschun
Associate Costume Designer .... Matthew Pachtman
Costume Assistant ....Cathy Parrott
Assistants to the Scenic/
Costume Designer, UK ......Julie Bowles, Sarah Cant,
Machiko Hombu
Associate Lighting Designer ....Paul Toben
Associate Sound Designer ....Nick Borisjuk
Assistant to the Music Coordinator ....Charles Butler
Dialect Coach ....Kate Wilson
Production Carpenter ....Dan Hoffman
Production Electrician ....Josh Weitzman

Assistant Production Electrician ....John Wooding

Production Projection Engineer ....Sam Hopkins
Media Programmer ....Sam Hopkins
Synthesizer Programmer ....Bruce Samuels
Production Properties ....Kathy Fabian, Propstar Inc.
Assistant Production Properties ....Rose Howard
Wardrobe Supervisor ....Nadine Hettel
Dressers ....Joe Godwin, Victoria Grecki,
Mary Ann Oberpriller
Hair and Wig Supervisor ....Barry Ernst
Hair Assistant ....Timothy Miller
Make-up Designer ....Angelina Avallone
Production Sound Engineer ....Brad Gyorgak
House Properties ....Lawrence Jennino
Properties Running Crew ....Erin Mary Delaney
Automation Carpenter ....Paul Ashton
Flyman ....Steve Jones
Moving Light Programmer ....David Arch
Obsession Programmer ....Jessica Morton
Follow Spot Operator ....Dorian Fuchs
Deck Sound ....Larry White
Local One IATSE Apprentice .... Dan Schultheis
Production Assistant ....Rachel Bauder
Children's Tutoring Provided by ...On Location Education
Child Wrangler ....Lindsay Ericson
Dramatists Guild Intern.....................Andy Monroe
Scenery Constructed, Automated
and Painted by ....Hudson Scenic Studio, Inc.
Lighting Equipment
Provided by ....PRG, Production Resource Group
Sound Equipment
Provided by ....Masque Sound & Recording Corp.
Specialty Furniture Props ....Plumb Squares,
SPS Effects, Aardvark Interiors
Custom Parasols ..................D.P. Birch and Company
Flame Treatment ....Turning Star
Projected Visual and
Animation Content ....Knifedge Creative Network
Projection equipment provided by ....XL Video

Animation & Visual Effects
Production ....Knifedge The Creative Network
Creative Director ....Timothy Bird
Previsualization & Projection Strategy ....Sam Hopkins

& his Light Studio
Team Leader/AFX Animator ....Nina Wilson
Rigging ....Raf Anzovin for Anzovin Studio
Content Librarian ....Ciara Fanning
Character Animator ....Shaun Freeman
Animator & Technical Director ....John Keates
Matte Artist ....Alex Laurent
3D Animator ....Andy McNamara
Animator ....Stephen Millingen
AFX Animator ....Aaron Trinder
With Additional Animation by ....Sam Buntrock
"Putting It Together" Visual Effects
Producer ....Amy DiPrima
"Putting It Together" Visual Effects
Videographer ....John Chimples for ImageMaintenance

Credit: "Study for the Chahut," c. 1889 (panel) by Seurat, Georges Pierre (1859-91); © Samuel Courtauld Trust, Courtauld Institute of Art Gallery/The Bridgeman Art Library. Credit: "Young Woman Powdering Herself," 1889 (oil on canvas) by Seurat, Georges Pierre (1859-91); Museum of Fine Arts, Houston, Texas, USA/Gift of Audrey Jones Beck/The Bridgeman Art Library. Credit: "Un dimanche après-midi à l'Ile de la Grande Jatte," 1884-85 (oil on canvas) by Seurat, Georges Pierre (1859-91); Art Institute of Chicago, Chicago, Illinois, USA/PicturesNow. Credit: "Bathers at Asnieres," 1884 (oil on canvas) by Seurat, Georges Pierre (1859-91); National Gallery, London, UK/The Bridgeman Art Library.

Costumes by ....Euro Co. Costumes,
Giliberto Designs, Inc., Mardana,
Timberlake Studios, Inc., Tricorne, Inc.
Custom Fabric Painting and Dyeing ....Jeff Fender
Additional Fabric Dyeing ....Julianne Kroboth
Millinery by ....Leslie Norgate, Lynne Mackey, Inc.
Natural cough drops courtesy of ....Ricola USA Inc.
Original London lighting design by ....Natasha Chivers
and Mike Robertson
Special Thanks to ....101 Productions, Ltd.,
Wendy Orshan, Dave Auster
Special Events Wardrobe Styling
provided by ....Calvin Klein, Inc.
Associate Producer for
Robert Boyett Theatrical ....Tim Levy
Assistant to Mr. Boyett ....Diane Murphy
Lazarus and Harris ....Scott Lazarus, Esq.

Make-up provided by M•A•C

STUDIO 54 THEATRE STAFF
Theatre Manager ....Matthew Armstrong
Box Office Manager ....Jaime Perlman
House Manager ....LaConya Robinson
Associate House Manager ....Jack Watanachaiyot
House Staff................Elicia Edwards, Jason Fernandez,
Jen Kneeland, Kate Longosky,
Latiffa Marcus, Nicole Marino,
Jonathan Martinez, Dana McCaw,
Nicole Ramirez, Anthony Roman,
Nick Wheatley, Stella Varriale
House Carpenter ....Dan Hoffman
House Electrician ....Josh Weitzman
House Properties ....Lawrence Jennino
Security ....Gotham Security
Maintenance ....Ralph Mohan, Maman Garba

A Tale of Two Cities

First Preview: August 19, 2008. Opened: September 18, 2008.
Closed November 9, 2008 after 33 Previews and 60 Performances.

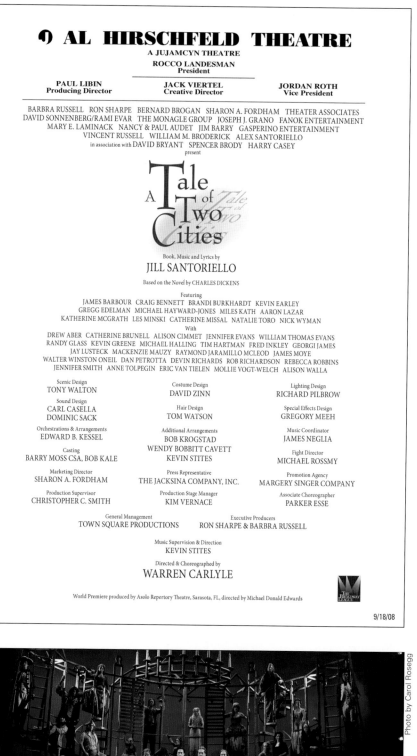

CAST

(in order of appearance)

Dr. Alexandre Manette	GREGG EDELMAN
Little Lucie	CATHERINE MISSAL
Marquis St. Evremonde	LES MINSKI
Mr. Jarvis Lorry	MICHAEL HAYWARD-JONES
Miss Pross	KATHERINE McGRATH
Lucie Manette	BRANDI BURKHARDT
Jerry Cruncher	CRAIG BENNETT
Madame Therese Defarge	NATALIE TORO
Ernest Defarge	KEVIN EARLEY
Gaspard	MICHAEL HALLING
Little Gaspard	MILES KATH
Seamstress	MACKENZIE MAUZY
Gabelle	KEVIN GREENE
Charles Darnay	AARON LAZAR
John Barsad	NICK WYMAN
Sydney Carton	JAMES BARBOUR
Stryver	FRED INKLEY
Attorney General	WILLIAM THOMAS EVANS
English Judge	JAMES MOYE
Cronies	TIM HARTMAN, WALTER WINSTON ONEIL
French President	RAYMOND JARAMILLO McLEOD
The Young Man	DREW ABER
Turnkey	JAY LUSTECK
Number Keeper	DEVIN RICHARDS

Continued on next page

9 AL HIRSCHFELD THEATRE

A JUJAMCYN THEATRE

ROCCO LANDESMAN
President

PAUL LIBIN
Producing Director

JACK VIERTEL
Creative Director

JORDAN ROTH
Vice President

BARBRA RUSSELL   RON SHARPE   BERNARD BROGAN   SHARON A. FORDHAM   THEATER ASSOCIATES
DAVID SONNENBERG/RAMI EVAR   THE MONAGLE GROUP   JOSEPH J. GRANO   FANOK ENTERTAINMENT
MARY E. LAMINACK   NANCY & PAUL AUDET   JIM BARRY   GASPERINO ENTERTAINMENT
VINCENT RUSSELL   WILLIAM M. BRODERICK   ALEX SANTORIELLO
in association with DAVID BRYANT   SPENCER BRODY   HARRY CASEY
present

A Tale of Two Cities

Book, Music and Lyrics by
JILL SANTORIELLO

Based on the Novel by CHARLES DICKENS

Featuring
JAMES BARBOUR   CRAIG BENNETT   BRANDI BURKHARDT   KEVIN EARLEY
GREGG EDELMAN   MICHAEL HAYWARD-JONES   MILES KATH   AARON LAZAR
KATHERINE MCGRATH   LES MINSKI   CATHERINE MISSAL   NATALIE TORO   NICK WYMAN

With
DREW ABER   CATHERINE BRUNELL   ALISON CIMMET   JENNIFER EVANS   WILLIAM THOMAS EVANS
RANDY GLASS   KEVIN GREENE   MICHAEL HALLING   TIM HARTMAN   FRED INKLEY   GEORGI JAMES
JAY LUSTECK   MACKENZIE MAUZY   RAYMOND JARAMILLO MCLEOD   JAMES MOYE
WALTER WINSTON ONEIL   DAN PETROTTA   DEVIN RICHARDS   ROB RICHARDSON   REBECCA ROBBINS
JENNIFER SMITH   ANNE TOLPEGIN   ERIC VAN TIELEN   MOLLIE VOGT-WELCH   ALISON WALLA

Scenic Design	Costume Design	Lighting Design
TONY WALTON	DAVID ZINN	RICHARD PILBROW
Sound Design	Hair Design	Special Effects Design
CARL CASELLA DOMINIC SACK	TOM WATSON	GREGORY MEEH
Orchestrations & Arrangements	Additional Arrangements	Music Coordinator
EDWARD B. KESSEL	BOB KROGSTAD	JAMES NEGLIA
Casting	WENDY BOBBITT CAVETT	Fight Director
BARRY MOSS CSA, BOB KALE	KEVIN STITES	MICHAEL ROSSMY
Marketing Director	Press Representative	Promotion Agency
SHARON A. FORDHAM	THE JACKSINA COMPANY, INC.	MARGERY SINGER COMPANY
Production Supervisor	Production Stage Manager	Associate Choreographer
CHRISTOPHER C. SMITH	KIM VERNACE	PARKER ESSE

General Management
TOWN SQUARE PRODUCTIONS

Executive Producers
RON SHARPE & BARBRA RUSSELL

Music Supervision & Direction
KEVIN STITES

Directed & Choreographed by
WARREN CARLYLE

World Premiere produced by Asolo Repertory Theatre, Sarasota, FL, directed by Michael Donald Edwards

9/18/08

The Cast

Photo by Carol Rosegg

A Tale of Two Cities

MUSICAL NUMBERS

ACT ONE

Prologue: "The Shadows of the Night" ....Dr. Manette, Lucie

Paris and Environs

"The Way It Ought to Be" ....Madame, Ernest, Men and Women of Paris
"You'll Never Be Alone" ....Dr. Manette, Lucie
"Argument" ....Marquis, Charles

London and Environs

"Dover" ....Sailors, Miss Pross, Cruncher
"The Way It Ought to Be" ....Sydney
"No Honest Way" ....Barsad, Cruncher, Sydney, Scoundrels
"The Trial" ....Attorney General, Stryver, Cruncher, Barsad, Sydney, Crowd
"Round and Round" ....Tavern Folk
"Reflection" ....Sydney

Six Months Later

"The Way It Ought to Be" (Reprise) ....Madame
"Letter From Uncle" ....Marquis

London

"The Promise" ....Dr. Manette, Charles
"I Can't Recall" ....Sydney
"Now at Last" ....Charles, Lucie
"If Dreams Came True" ....Charles, Sydney

Paris and London: Six Years Later

"Out of Sight, Out of Mind" ....Madame
"I Always Knew" ....Gabelle, Charles
"Little One" ....Gaspard, Little Lucie, Sydney, Ernest, Men
"Until Tomorrow" ....Ernest, Madame, Sydney, Men and Women of Paris

ACT TWO

Paris

"Everything Stays the Same" ....Madame, Ernest, Men and Women of Paris
"No Honest Way" (Reprise) ....Barsad
"The Tale" ....Madame, Dr. Manette, Young Man, Marquis, Crowd
"If Dreams Came True" (Reprise) ....Sydney
"Without a Word" ....Charles, Lucie
"The Bluff" ....Sydney, Barsad
"Let Her Be a Child" ....Sydney, Little Lucie, Charles
"The Letter" ....Sydney
"Lament" ....Ernest
"Finale: I Can't Recall" ....Seamstress, Sydney, Men and Women

ORCHESTRA

Conductor: KEVIN STITES
Associate Conductor: PAUL RAIMAN
Assistant Conductor: NICHOLAS ARCHER
Violins: MARTIN AGEE, CONRAD HARRIS
Viola: DEBRA SHUFELT-DINE
Cello: LAURA BONTRAGER
Bass: DAVID PHILLIPS
Flute/Piccolo: JUDITH MENDENHALL
Oboe/English Horn: MATTHEW DINE
B♭ Clarinet/Bass Clarinet/Bassoon:
    MARK THRASHER

Trumpet: TIMOTHY SCHADT, TERRY SZOR
French Horn:
    ANTHONY CECERE, WILLIAM DE VOS
Tenor Trombone/Bass Trombone/Tuba:
    CHRISTOPHER OLNESS
Drums/Percussion: JAMES MUSTO III
Timpani/Percussion: KORY GROSSMAN
Synthesizer: NICHOLAS ARCHER,
    PAUL RAIMAN
Music Coordinator: JAMES NEGLIA
Synthesizer Programming: DAVID ROSENTHAL

Cast Continued

ENSEMBLE

DREW ABER, CATHERINE BRUNELL,
ALISON CIMMET,
WILLIAM THOMAS EVANS, KEVIN GREENE,
MICHAEL HALLING, TIM HARTMAN,
FRED INKLEY, GEORGI JAMES,
JAY LUSTECK, MACKENZIE MAUZY,
RAYMOND JARAMILLO McLEOD,
JAMES MOYE, WALTER WINSTON ONEIL,
DAN PETROTTA, DEVIN RICHARDS,
ROB RICHARDSON, REBECCA ROBBINS,
JENNIFER SMITH, ANNE TOLPEGIN,
MOLLIE VOGT-WELCH, ALISON WALLA

SWINGS

JENNIFER EVANS, RANDY GLASS,
ERIC VAN TIELEN

Dance Captain ....RANDY GLASS
Fight Captain ....JAY LUSTECK

UNDERSTUDIES

Dr. Alexandre Manette:
RANDY GLASS, FRED INKLEY
Little Lucie:
GEORGI JAMES
Marquis St. Evremonde:
RANDY GLASS, JAMES MOYE
Mr. Jarvis Lorry:
WILLIAM THOMAS EVANS, TIM HARTMAN
Miss Pross:
JENNIFER SMITH, ANNE TOLPEGIN
Lucie Manette:
CATHERINE BRUNELL, REBECCA ROBBINS
Jerry Cruncher:
FRED INKLEY, JAY LUSTECK
Madame Therese Defarge:
REBECCA ROBBINS, ANNE TOLPEGIN
Ernest Defarge:
JAY LUSTECK, JAMES MOYE
Little Gaspard:
GEORGI JAMES
Charles Darnay:
MICHAEL HALLING, ERIC VAN TIELEN
John Barsad:
TIM HARTMAN, FRED INKLEY
Sydney Carton:
JAMES MOYE, ROB RICHARDSON

SETTING

Paris and London during the late eighteenth century

A Tale of Two Cities

James Barbour
Sydney Carton

Craig Bennett
Jerry Cruncher

Brandi Burkhardt
Lucie Manette

Kevin Earley
Ernest Defarge

Gregg Edelman
Dr. Alexandre Manette

Michael Hayward-Jones
Jarvis Lorry

Miles Kath
Little Gaspard

Aaron Lazar
Charles Darnay

Katherine McGrath
Miss Pross

Les Minski
Marquis St. Evremonde

Catherine Missal
Little Lucie

Natalie Toro
Madame Therese Defarge

Nick Wyman
Barsad

Drew Aber
Ensemble/ The Young Man

Catherine Brunell
Ensemble

Alison Cimmet
Ensemble

Jennifer Evans
Swing

William Thomas Evans
Ensemble/ Attorney General

Randy Glass
Ensemble/Swing/ Dance Captain

Kevin Greene
Ensemble/Gabelle

Michael Halling
Ensemble/Gaspard

Tim Hartman
Ensemble/Crony

Fred Inkley
Ensemble/Stryver

Georgi James
Ensemble

Jay Lusteck
Ensemble/Turnkey/ Fight Captain

Mackenzie Mauzy
Ensemble/ Seamstress

Raymond Jaramillo McLeod
Ensemble/ French President

James Moye
Ensemble/ English Judge

Walter Winston ONeil
Ensemble/Crony

Dan Petrotta
Ensemble

Devin Richards
Ensemble/Turnkey

Rob Richardson
Ensemble

Rebecca Robbins
Ensemble

Jennifer Smith
Ensemble

Eric Van Tielen
Swing

A Tale of Two Cities

Anne Tolpegin
Ensemble

Mollie Vogt-Welch
Ensemble

Alison Walla
Ensemble

Jill Santoriello and Warren Carlyle
*Book, Music and Lyrics;
Director/Choreographer*

Tony Walton
Scenic Designer

Carl Casella
Sound Designer

Tom Watson
Hair Design

Gregory Meeh
*Special Effects
Designer*

Margery Singer,
Margery Singer
Company
Promotion Agency

Michael Arden
Assistant Director

Christopher C. Smith/
Theatersmith Inc.
Technical Supervisor

Ron Sharpe
Producer

Barbra Russell
Producer

Greggory Brandt
Swing

ELECTRICS AND SOUND
Front Row (L-R): Sue Poulin, John Blixt, Michele Gutierrez

Back Row (L-R): Paul Ker, Mike Ward, Tom Burke, Greg Peeler,
Ty Lackey

PROPS
Front Row (seated): Dawn Makay

Second Row (L-R): Mike McCrindle, Jr.,
Laura Thomas-McGarty, Chris Makay

Third Row (seated): Sal Sclafani

HAIR DEPARTMENT
(L-R): Timothy Miller, Natasha Steinhagen, Katie Beatty,
Barry Ernst

CARPENTERS
(L-R): Tom Lowery, Russ Dobson, Michael Maher, Jr., Erik Hansen, Gabe Harris,
Morgan Shevett, Joe Maher, Jr., Dan Ansbro, James Sturek

Photos by Brian Mapp

A Tale of Two Cities

FRONT OF HOUSE STAFF
Front Row (L-R): Jose Nunez (Head Porter), Janice Rodriguez (Chief Usher), Albert Kim (Theatre Manager), William Meyers (Usher), Mary Marzan (Usher), Donald Royal (Usher)

Second Row (L-R): Jennifer DiDonato (Usher), Julie Burnham (Director), Kerri Gillen (Usher), Tristan Blacer (Ticket Taker), Hollis Miller (Usher), Terry Monahan (P&P Security)

Back Row (L-R): Frank Italiano (Engineer), Henry Menendez (Usher), Alex Gutierrez (Usher), Bart Ryan (Usher), Lorraine Feeks (Ticket Taker), Theresa Lopez (Usher)

Photos by Brian Mapp

MUSICIANS
Front Row: Christopher Olness

Middle Row (L-R): Mark Thrasher, Tony Cecere, Julie Ferrara, Martin Agee

Back Row (L-R): Emily Brausa, Timothy Schadt, Laura Covey, Kevin Stites (Music Director)

PRODUCTION CARPENTER
Erik Hansen

MANAGERS
(L-R): Jason A. Quinn (ASM), Kim Vernace (PSM), Paul J. Smith (SM), Megan Schneid (ASM), Austin Nathaniel (ACM), Robert Nolan (CM)

DRESSERS
(L-R): Dora Bonilla, Tara Delahunt, Kyle Wesson, Franc Weinperl, Dawn Divine, Robert Kwiatkowski, Maureen George, David Mitchell

---

GENERAL MANAGER
TOWN SQUARE PRODUCTIONS, INC.
Don Frantz & Laurie Brown
Scott Bartelson, Lauren Breuning, Hillary Reeves

PRESS REPRESENTATIVE
THE JACKSINA COMPANY, INC.
Judy Jacksina, Jamie Morris, Kaitlyn Marie Berg

COMPANY MANAGER
ROBERT NOLAN

MARKETING
FORDHAM ENTERTAINMENT MARKETING, LLC
Sharon A. Fordham

Production Stage Manager ....Kim Vernace
Stage Manager ....Paul J. Smith
Assistant Stage Managers ....Jason A. Quinn, Megan Schneid
Assistant Company Manager ....Austin Nathaniel

Dialect & Vocal Coach ....Deborah Hecht

Make-Up Designer ....Jon Carter

Stunt Coordinator ....GZ Entertainment/ Brian Schuley

Assistant Director ....Michael Arden
Associate Set Designer ....Heather Wolensky
Associate Costume Designer ....Jacob A. Climer
Associate Lighting Designer ....Michael Gottlieb
Lighting Programmer ....Robert Bell
Associate Sound Designer ....Wallace Flores

A Tale of Two Cities

Associate Production Supervision ....Donald J. Oberpriller
Associate Special Effects Design ....Jeremy Chernick
Assistant to the Producers ....Adele Magnolia
Assistant to the Author ....Molly Gachignard
Props Coordinator ....David Towlun
Set Model Builder ....Joanie Schlafer
Set Model Making Assistant ....Alexis Distler
Scenic Apprentices ....Justine Remy, Juliet Fox,
Georgia Warner
Dramaturg ....Tommy McArdle
Assistant Costume Designer ....Amelia Dombrowski
Assistant Lighting Designers ....Kathleen Dobbins,
Graham Kindred, Jay Scott
Assistant Hair Designer ....Ashley Ryan
General Assistant to the Set Designer ....Rebecca Lustig
Assistant to the Costume Designer ....Caitlin Hunt
Assistants to the Orchestrator ....Rosemary Barker,
Josh Green
Special Effects Design Assistant ....James Milkey
Child Wrangler ....Margaret Kath

Head Carpenter ....Erik Hansen
Assistant Carpenter, Deck Automation ....Russ Dobson
Fly Automation ....James W. Sturek
Production/Head Electrician ....Michael J. Ward
Production Spotlight ....Paul Ker
Spot Light Operators ....Tom Burke, Robert Miller,
John Blixt
Sound Operator ....Ty Lackey
Production/Head Properties ....Dawn Makay
Assistant Properties ....Chris Makay
Wardrobe Supervisor ....Debbie Cheretun
Assistant Wardrobe Supervisor ....Valerie Frith
Hair Supervisor ....Barry Ernst
Assistant Hair Supervisor ....Timothy Miller

Synth Programmer ....David Rosenthal/
Nocturnal Productions, Inc.
Assistant to the Synth Programmer ....Adam Schneider
Music Preparation ....Anixter Rice Music Service
Rehearsal Pianists ....Nicholas Archer,
AnnBritt DuChateau, Paul Raiman
Banking ....Commerce Bank, Barbara VonBorstel
Payroll ....Castellana Services, Inc./
Lance Castellana
Accountant ....Fried & Kowgios Partners CPA's LLC/
Robert Fried, CPA
Controller ....Galbraith & Company/
Sarah Galbraith
Insurance ....Dewitt Stern/
Pete Shoemaker, Susan Meegan
Legal Counsel ....Cowan, DeBaets,
Abrahams & Sheppard, LLP/
M. Kilburg Reedy, Fred Bimbler, Esq.
Tutoring ....On Location Education, Inc.
Advertising ....Serino Coyne, Inc.
Web Marketing & Design ....NetPlus Marketing, Inc.
Group Sales ....Group Sales Box Office
Corporate Marketing ....Plum Benefits, Inc.
Education Services provided by ....Camp Broadway
Education Distribution ....Roberta Nusim/
Young Minds Inspired
Logo Design ....Nicolas Creative, Inc.
Production Photographer ....Carol Rosegg
Physical Therapist ....PhysioArts
Massage Therapist ....Russ Beasley

Opening Night
Coordination ....The Lawrence Company Events/
Michael Lawrence
Production Assistants ....Christian Coulson,
Katherine Fanok, Danielle Federico
Music Interns ....Laura Fraenkel, Kevin David Thomas

ASOLO REPERTORY THEATRE COMPANY STAFF

Producing Artistic Director ....Michael Donald Edwards
Managing Director ....Linda M. DiGabriele
Associate Artistic Director ....Greg Leaming
Production Manager ....Victor Meyrich
Development Director ....Deborah Ann Trimble
Marketing Director ....Cheryl E. Ferreira
Finance/Human Resources Director ....Walker Croskey
Education Director ....Brian Hersh

CREDITS AND ACKNOWLEDGEMENTS

Additional scenic construction and automation by Showmotion, Inc., Rosebrand and I-Weiss. Horses constructed by Costume Armour, Inc. Translucent drops by Triumph Productions. Trees and horse silhouette by Michael Hagen, Inc. Original scenic construction by the Asolo Repertory Theatre: Victor Meyrich (Production Manager), David Ferguson (Technical Director), Bert Taylor (Metal Fabricator), JoAnn Waters-Atkins (Master Scenic Artist), Cathryn Dashiell and Jeffrey W. Dean (Property Masters) and Rick Alley (Prop Builder). Lighting equipment from PRG Lighting. VMS lighting software by Eric Cornwell West Side Systems. Sound equipment by Sound Associates, Inc. Synthesizer equipment by Nocturnal Productions, Inc. Special thanks to Kurzweil Music Systems. Costumes constructed by Donna Langman Costumes; John Kristiansen New York Inc.; Carelli Costumes Inc.; Tricorne, Inc.; Izquierdo Studio; Seams Unlimited; Timberlake Studios, Inc.; Marc Happel; Brian Hemesath. Custom knitting by Karen L. Eifert, Christine Szczepanski. Custom footwear by T.O. Dey, Capezio Professional Outfitters. Millinery and costume crafts by Rodney Gordon, Inc., Elizabeth Flauto. Fabric modification and distressing by Hochi Asiatico Studio. Wigs constructed by Tom Watson's Wig Studio. Makeup provided by M A C. Natural herb cough drops courtesy of Ricola USA, Inc. Rehearsed at New 42nd Street Studios. Tony Walton wishes to especially thank Kelly Hanson, Olga Rogova and Anais Godard.

THE PRODUCERS WOULD LIKE TO THANK...

Edward B. Kessel and Sound Imagination, LLC for production development and for support and belief from the beginning; Jeffrey Fanok from Team Fanok for warehouse and storage of show design materials; Spencer Brody from Globe Die Cutting for marketing and print materials; Roberta Nusim from Young Minds Inspired for creation of education materials for the schools; and to the creative team, co-producers, investors, actors, crew and musicians of *A Tale of Two Cities* who have given us this wonderful opportunity! Special thanks to Sharon A. Fordham, William M. and Susan Broderick, Ed and Peggy Monagle, Bernard and Maria Brogan, Mary E. Laminack, David and Shoshana Sonnenberg, Ron Sonnenberg, Rami and Lisa Evar, Nancy and Paul Audet, Tim O'Connor, YS Chi, Tim O'Connor, Regina and Richard Poworeznik, Charles and Helene Molineri, Gregg and Marie Gasperino, Alex Santoriello, Joseph J. Grano, David and Toinette Bryant, Jim and Sharon Barry, Harry Casey, Mary Hayes, Chris and Donna Karounos, Anthony and Lisa Coniglioni, Connie Kristan, Joseph DiMattina, Jim Orphanides, Joe and Chrissy Manello, Kevin and Jean Lynott, Richard Saxon, Wendy and Steve Start, Rosanne and Mike Juliano, Ilene and Steve Rosenthal, Rick Laminack, Joe Cositori, Phyllis and Dale Cunningham, Ken Beck, Jim Faulkner, Frank and Paula McSweeney, Dan Lacoff, Eve Jaffee, Alex and Susan Ford, Joanne Bonacci, Fern Lopez, Robert D'Anton, John Marciszewski, Dr. Don Carter, Joe Cheung, John Goodman, Robert Silver, Doug and Susan Whiteman, Xavier and Carol Gonzalez, Mary Insall, Leigh and Doug Conant, Vivien and Brent Legunn, Christopher Bouchur, Larry Weissfeld, Jane Shovel, Marge Falbo, Dr. Ira and Linda Abrahamson, Troy and Kim Skodmin, Adele and Frank Magnolia, Nasser Kazeminy, Laurie Brown, Robert Nolan, Don Frantz, Fred Bimbler, Robert Fried, Christopher Smith, Neil Berg, Rita Harvey, Linda Tilzner, Harvey Sabinson, The Asolo Repertory Theatre, Denise Zimmerman, Barbra Sellinger, R&D Circuits, Betty Ann Cluthe, Robert Manahan, Sharon Kessel, Tim Shew, Bob Duffy, Bob Nation, Dana Barbour, J. Mark McVey, Peter and Ann Nicolas, Tommy McArdle, Marjie and Steve Hanna, Jon Chironna, John Guy, the Howley Family, the Zorovich Family, the Fanok Family, the Mosello Family, the Byrnes Family, Marty Cooper, Bill Chi, Tom Fordham, Vince Russell, Debbie Mainger, Nancy Russell, Michele and Steve Corodemus, Kathy and Kim Redlich, Susan and Steve Sinofsky, Kathy and James Russell, Ellen Sides, Audrey and Ron Sharpe, Sr., Jordan Roth and to all of our voice students and their families who have been with us through this amazing adventure.

JUJAMCYN THEATERS

ROCCO LANDESMAN
President

PAUL LIBIN   **JACK VIERTEL**   **JORDAN ROTH**
Producing Director   Creative Director   Vice President

DANIEL ADAMIAN   **JENNIFER HERSHEY**
General Manager   Director of Operations

MEREDITH VILLATORE   **JERRY ZAKS**
Chief Financial Officer   Resident Director

Staff for the Al Hirschfeld Theatre

Manager ....Albert T. Kim
Treasurer ....Carmine La Mendola
Carpenter ....Joseph J. Maher, Jr.
Propertyman ....Sal Sclafani
Electrician ....Michele Gutierrez

Photo by Carol Rosegg

(L-R): Catherine Brunell and Kevin Greene

A Tale of Two Cities
SCRAPBOOK

Correspondent: Alison Cimmet, Ensemble
Favorite Opening Night Goodies: The night before opening, Fred Inkley (Stryver) got a huge Edible Arrangements bouquet for the company, and it was accompanied by a heartfelt poem. Warren Carlyle (director) wrote handwritten, personalized cards to every person in the cast. Kevin Earley (Defarge) transformed two-buck-chuck bottles into Defarge's Wine Shop wine, with intricately designed labels saying "Wine of the Revolution," and Natalie Toro (Mme. Defarge) gave everyone engraved corkscrews to go with the wine bottles. Ron and Barbra (producers) gave several gifts including a deck of cards each with a different *Tale* snapshot on it. Mollie Vogt-Welch (creator of "Christmas Balls of Joy"—see description of In-Jokes below) gave everyone a personalized Christmas ornament ball. The best was Drew Aber's: he (along with Gregg Edelman) made a techno-remix of his song "The Tale" and played it over the monitors for everyone to hear just after the half-hour call.
Most Exciting Celebrity Visitor: Julie Andrews, who later sent a personalized note to Tony Walton which he copied and hung on the callboard.
Who Got the Gypsy Robe (and What They Put on It): Devin Richards. The wardrobe department put a gorgeous *Tale* logo on it.
Actor Who Performed the Most Roles: Kevin Greene (Ensemble/Gabelle): 7 roles, 11 costume changes.
Most Seasoned Actor: Katherine McGrath
Backstage Rituals: I love how everyone mills around onstage just before the show begins, long after "places" has been called. Then, just before the show begins, everyone scampers off to the wings in the dark. Several cast members are involved in a prayer circle. Anne Tolpegin often stands at the scrim "listening" to the audience. My favorite is Alison Walla, stage left, enthusiastically chirping "This will be the best show EVER" every single night.
Highest Belted Note: Natalie Toro belted high E at least five times.
Favorite On-Stage Moment: Many people in the cast enjoy watching Michael Halling (Gaspard) killing Les Minski (Marquis)—he climbs the set like Spiderman then, with punctuating grunts, digs the knife into the Marquis.
Favorite Off-Stage Moments: Many company members enjoy watching sports on the TV in the men's quick-change room. Also, before the funeral scene there's often a vicious battle over candles. There are both long and short prop candles, but the long ones are so unwieldy nobody wants them. We have had an ongoing candle war, which involves hiding a short candle far in advance, and often finding someone else's hidden short candle and thwarting their plan. Animosity and hilarity ensue.

1. (L-R) Emma Walton, Steven Hamilton, Gen Walton, Daisy Pilbrow and set designer Tony Walton at the Al Hirschfeld Theatre on opening night.
2. Composer/author Jill Santoriello and director Warren Carlyle at a rehearsal at 42nd St. Studios.
3. James Barbour takes part in "Broadway on Broadway 2008."
4. Natalie Toro at the opening night party at Cipriani.
5. Producers Ron Sharpe and Barbra Russell at the premiere.

Favorite Off-site Hangout: Bill Evans loves encouraging everyone to go to Chelsea Grill, often.
Gathering Place: There's no greenroom in the Al Hirschfeld, nor any kind of proper gathering space. So we have the "green stairwell." The part of it just off left is a popular hang-out between scenes, much to the chagrin of dressers and actors who have to pass through. And the lower level of the stairwell is the hot spot for birthday cakes, and poster signing.
Snack Food: There's always candy around. There's a cake for everyone's birthday, and

A Tale of Two Cities
SCRAPBOOK

THE COMPANY

Front Row (L-R): Aaron Lazar, Rob Richardson, Randy Glass, Kathy McGrath, Catherine Missal, Nick Wyman, Gregg Edelman, Jennifer Evans, Kevin Earley, Walter Winston ONeil, Brandi Burkhardt

Second Row (L-R): Eric Van Tielen, Karen Missal, Kevin Greene, William Thomas Evans, Natalie Toro, Devin Richards, Michael Halling, Alison Cimmet, Craig Bennett, James Barbour, Rebecca Robbins, James Moye

Third Row (L-R): Georgi James, Jay Lusteck, Catherine Brunell, Jennifer Smith, Raymond Jaramillo McLeod, Fred Inkley, Drew Aber, Les Minski, Miles Kath, Tim Hartman, Anne Tolpegin, Mackenzie Mauzy, Mollie Vogt-Welch, Michael Hayward-Jones

with a big cast we usually have a cake at least once a week if not more! Also, before it was mysteriously shut down, our electrician, Michele hosted a marvelous wine and cheese party every Saturday night just before the end of the show.

Therapies: You would think having an endless supply of Ricola was in our contracts, the way we not only devour them and feel entitled to have them at our fingertips, but when the stash runs out, everyone is dismayed, and settles with reluctant despair for Halls. My favorite therapy is "Nick Wyman's Coffee Harem." He has a pot of fresh coffee going at all times in his dressing room, to seduce the young bleary-eyed hotties to come visit him and smother him with appreciation and gratitude.

Memorable Ad-lib: Everyone loved it when Ray McLeod called Aaron Lazar an AristocCAT instead of AristocRat. Also at the end of the show, the ad-libbing angry mob off right often picks a theme (such as pharmaceuticals, states of the U.S., kinds of liquor, bodies of water, etc.) and shouts appropriate words and phrases to go with the chosen theme.

Memorable Press Encounter: The time our *TOTC* commercial briefly cut into a live press conference that George Bush was holding!

Stage Door Fan Encounter: After the first preview a loving fan—wearing a handmade period corset—gave some of the principals and featured actors handmade dolls in costume. They were remarkable. And any coupled dolls (such as Charles & Lucie, Mr. & Mrs. Cruncher, etc.) had magnets behind their mouths and could "kiss"!!

Heaviest/Hottest Costume: Craig Bennett wore a costume that weighed more than 40 pounds.

Nicknames: Catherine Missal = Stealth
Miles Kath = James Bond
Kim Vernace = Lucky
Drew Aber = Sugar Hill
Kevin Earley = Ernie

Company Catchphrase: During rehearsals Warren Carlyle would often spontaneously choose an ensemble member to answer questions about their character's backstory, or to walk/perform their track alone while everyone watched. It was instructive,

horrifying, and often hilarious. The most memorable example was when he asked chorus-member Mollie Vogt-Welch to walk her track in the Christmas scene. Her character, she had decided, was a performer and she was wandering the streets of London inviting people to her show. Warren interjected a question putting her on the spot: "What is the show called?" Thinking quickly in the moment she responded (coining it just as she spoke it): "Christmas Balls of Joy!" It was truly hilarious, and everyone melted into fits of laughter. On opening night, many weeks later, Warren brought the cast together and said he had choreographed the first dance number of "Christmas Balls of Joy" and proceeded to perform it for the company. It involved himself, Parker Esse, and Mollie Vogt-Welch, complete with tap-dancing, a sexy Santa outfit, and lots of balloon-popping. Our opening night gift from Warren was a t-shirt that said "*A Tale of Two Cities*" on the back and "Christmas Balls of Joy" on the front.

Coolest Thing About Being in This Show: Dirt.

13

First Preview: September 16, 2008. Opened: October 5, 2008.
Closed January 4, 2009 after 22 Previews and 105 Performances.

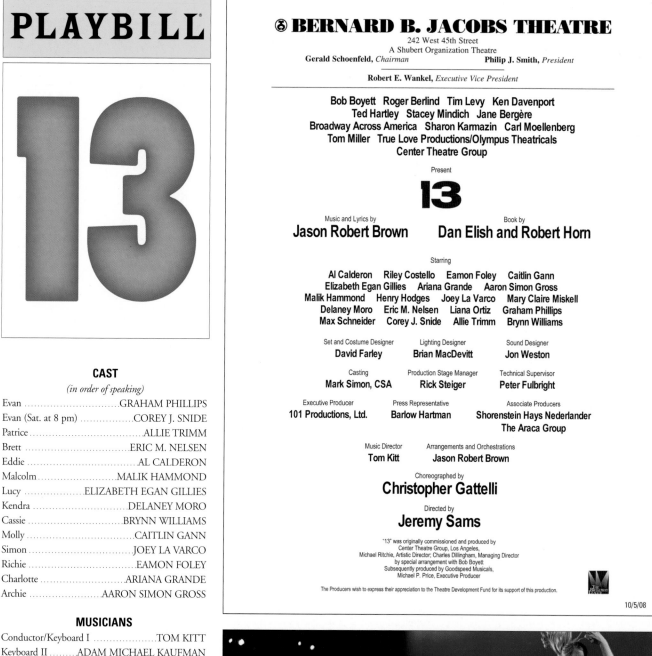

PLAYBILL

13

⊛ BERNARD B. JACOBS THEATRE

242 West 45th Street
A Shubert Organization Theatre
Gerald Schoenfeld, *Chairman*   Philip J. Smith, *President*

Robert E. Wankel, *Executive Vice President*

Bob Boyett   Roger Berlind   Tim Levy   Ken Davenport
Ted Hartley   Stacey Mindich   Jane Bergère
Broadway Across America   Sharon Karmazin   Carl Moellenberg
Tom Miller   True Love Productions/Olympus Theatricals
Center Theatre Group

Present

13

Music and Lyrics by   Book by
Jason Robert Brown   **Dan Elish and Robert Horn**

Starring

Al Calderon   Riley Costello   Eamon Foley   Caitlin Gann
Elizabeth Egan Gillies   Ariana Grande   Aaron Simon Gross
Malik Hammond   Henry Hodges   Joey La Varco   Mary Claire Miskell
Delaney Moro   Eric M. Nelsen   Liana Ortiz   Graham Phillips
Max Schneider   Corey J. Snide   Allie Trimm   Brynn Williams

Set and Costume Designer   Lighting Designer   Sound Designer
David Farley   **Brian MacDevitt**   **Jon Weston**

Casting   Production Stage Manager   Technical Supervisor
Mark Simon, CSA   **Rick Steiger**   **Peter Fulbright**

Executive Producer   Press Representative   Associate Producers
101 Productions, Ltd.   **Barlow Hartman**   **Shorenstein Hays Nederlander**
The Araca Group

Music Director   Arrangements and Orchestrations
Tom Kitt   **Jason Robert Brown**

Choreographed by
Christopher Gattelli

Directed by
Jeremy Sams

"13" was originally commissioned and produced by
Center Theatre Group, Los Angeles,
Michael Ritchie, Artistic Director; Charles Dillingham, Managing Director
by special arrangement with Bob Boyett
Subsequently produced by Goodspeed Musicals,
Michael P. Price, Executive Producer

The Producers wish to express their appreciation to the Theatre Development Fund for its support of this production.

10/5/08

CAST

(in order of speaking)

Evan	GRAHAM PHILLIPS
Evan (Sat. at 8 pm)	COREY J. SNIDE
Patrice	ALLIE TRIMM
Brett	ERIC M. NELSEN
Eddie	AL CALDERON
Malcolm	MALIK HAMMOND
Lucy	ELIZABETH EGAN GILLIES
Kendra	DELANEY MORO
Cassie	BRYNN WILLIAMS
Molly	CAITLIN GANN
Simon	JOEY LA VARCO
Richie	EAMON FOLEY
Charlotte	ARIANA GRANDE
Archie	AARON SIMON GROSS

MUSICIANS

Conductor/Keyboard I	TOM KITT
Keyboard II	ADAM MICHAEL KAUFMAN
Guitar	CHRIS RAYMOND
Guitar	ZACH PAGE
Percussion	ZAC COE
Bass	LEXI BODICK
Swing Keyboard	MAT EISENSTEIN
Swing Bass, Guitar, Percussion	CHARLIE ROSEN

The ensemble performs the title song.

Photo by Joan Marcus

Continued on next page

13

MUSICAL NUMBERS

ACT ONE

"13/Becoming a Man" .... Evan and Company
"The Lamest Place in the World" .... Patrice
"Hey Kendra" .... Brett, Malcolm, Eddie, Lucy and Kendra
"Get Me What I Need" .... Archie and Company
"What It Means to Be a Friend" .... Patrice
"All Hail the Brain" .... Evan
"Terminal Illness" .... Evan, Archie and Company
"Getting Ready" .... Company
"Any Minute" .... Brett, Kendra, Patrice and Archie
"Good Enough" .... Patrice
"Being a Geek" .... Evan and Company

ACT TWO

"Opportunity" .... Lucy and Girls
"Bad Bad News" .... Eddie, Malcolm, Simon and Richie
"Tell Her" .... Evan and Patrice
"It Can't Be True" .... Lucy, Molly, Cassie, Charlotte and Company
"If That's What It Is" .... Archie, Patrice and Evan
"A Little More Homework" .... Evan and Company
"Brand New You" .... Cassie, Charlotte, Molly and Company

Cast Continued

UNDERSTUDIES

Archie, Eddie, Simon, Richie:
RILEY COSTELLO
Kendra:
CAITLIN GANN
Patrice:
ARIANA GRANDE
Evan, Archie, Simon, Richie:
HENRY HODGES
Brett, Eddie:
JOEY LA VARCO
Patrice, Lucy, Molly, Cassie, Charlotte:
MARY CLAIRE MISKELL
Lucy, Kendra, Molly, Cassie, Charlotte:
LIANA ORTIZ
Brett, Malcolm, Simon, Richie:
MAX SCHNEIDER

Dance Captain: LOU CASTRO

Al Calderon
Eddie

Riley Costello
u/s Eddie, Archie, Richie, Simon

Eamon Foley
Richie

Caitlin Gann
Molly

Elizabeth Egan Gillies
Lucy

Ariana Grande
Charlotte

Aaron Simon Gross
Archie

Malik Hammond
Malcolm

Henry Hodges
u/s Archie, Evan, Richie, Simon

Joey La Varco
Simon

Mary Claire Miskell
u/s Lucy, Patrice, Molly, Charlotte, Cassie

Delaney Moro
Kendra

Eric M. Nelsen
Brett

Liana Ortiz
u/s Kendra, Lucy, Molly, Charlotte, Cassie

Graham Phillips
Evan

Max Schneider
u/s Brett, Malcolm, Richie, Simon

Corey J. Snide
Evan at Sat. eve. performances

Allie Trimm
Patrice

Brynn Williams
Cassie

Lexi Bodick
Bass

Zac Coe
Percussion

Adam Michael Kaufman
Keyboard

Zach Page
Guitar

Chris Raymond
Guitar

Charlie Rosen
Swing Musician

Jason Robert Brown
Music & Lyrics, Arrangements, Orchestrations

Dan Elish
Book

Robert Horn
Book

Jeremy Sams
Director

Christopher Gattelli
Choreographer

Brian MacDevitt
Lighting Designer

Tom Kitt
Music Director

Wendy Orshan,
101 Productions, Ltd.
General Management

Bob Boyett
Producer

Roger Berlind
Producer

Ken Davenport,
Producer

Ted Hartley
Producer

Jane Bergère
Producer

Sharon Karmazin
Producer

Carl Moellenberg
Producer

Graham Phillips (front) with members of the ensemble

Michael Ritchie
Artistic Director, Center Theatre Group of Los Angeles

Charles Dillingham
Managing Director, Center Theatre Group of Los Angeles

Gordon Davidson
Founding Artistic Director, Center Theatre Group of Los Angeles

Michael P. Price
Goodspeed Musicals

Carole Shorenstein Hays,
Shorenstein Hays Nederlander Associate Producer

STAFF FOR *13*

GENERAL MANAGEMENT
101 PRODUCTIONS, LTD.
Wendy Orshan   Jeffrey M. Wilson
David Auster

COMPANY MANAGER
Sean Free

GENERAL PRESS REPRESENTATIVE
BARLOW•HARTMAN
Michael Hartman   John Barlow
Leslie Baden   Matt Shea

CASTING
MARK SIMON CASTING
Mark Simon, CSA
Emma Freeman   Matthew Maisto

TECHNICAL SUPERVISOR
TECH PRODUCTION SERVICES, INC.
Peter Fulbright   Mary Duffe   Colleen Houlehen

VOCAL COACH
Liz Caplan

Production Stage Manager	Rick Steiger
Stage Manager	Karen S. Armstrong
Assistant Stage Managers	Alex Libby, Lou Castro
Assistant Company Manager	Chris D'Angelo
Associate Director	Mark Schneider
Associate Music Director	Mat Eisenstein
Assistant to Director	Anika Chapin
Associate Choreographer	Lou Castro
Assistant to Choreographer	Pamela Remler
Fight Director	Tom Schall
Associate Scenic Designer	Josh Zangen
Associate Costume Designers	Mary Ann D. Smith, Mary Fleming
Assistant to Costume Designer	Sydney Gallas
Stylist Consultant	Maya Evans Judd
Associate Lighting Designer	Jennifer Schriever
Assistant Lighting Designer	Peter Hoerburger
Assistant to Lighting Designer	Zach Blane
Moving Light Programmer	David Arch
Arcade Video Programming	Paul Vershbow
Associate Sound Designer	Jason Strangfeld
Assistant Sound Designer	Michael Eisenberg
Production Carpenter	Paul Wimmer
Assistant Carpenter/Automation	Scott "Gus" Poitras
Production Electrician	Michael Pitzer
Head Electrician	Jeremy Wahlers
Production Props Supervisor	Rob Presley
Assistant Props	Jacob White
Production Sound Supervisor	Jason McKenna
Assistant Sound	John T. Higgins
Wardrobe Supervisor	Linda Lee
Assistant Wardrobe Supervisor	Andrea Roberts
Dressers	Shana Albery, Andrea Gonzalez, John Webber
Hair Styled by	Jason Hayes
Music Preparation	John Blane
Music Assistants	Brian P. Kennedy, Thomas Murray
Keyboard Programmer	Randy Cohen
Children's Guardians	Ashley Gonzalez, Libby Stevens, Harry Turpin

Production Assistants	Zac Chandler, Deanna Weiner
Executive Assistant to Mr. Boyett	Diane Murphy
Assistant to Mr. Berlind	Jeffrey Hillock
Assistant to Mr. Levy	Evan Storey
Assistant to Ms. Bergere	Amanda Woods
Assistant to Mr. Hartley	Doris Schwartz
Assistant to Mr. Brown	Brooke Pierce
Legal Counsel	Lazarus & Harris LLP/ Scott Lazarus, Esq., Robert C. Harris, Esq.
Accountant	Rosenberg, Neuwirth, & Kuchner, CPAs/ Christopher Cacace
Comptroller	Kirill Baytalskiy
Advertising	Serino Coyne/ Greg Corradetti, Robert Jones, Joaquin Esteva
Marketing	HHC Marketing/ Hugh Hysell, Matt Sicoli, Nicole Pando
Promotions	The Nancy Richards Group
Educational Program	Camp Broadway
Promotional Partner	Verizon Wireless/ Rob Davis, Leo Arciniegas
Website Design	Mammoth Advertising/ Robert Neull, Kehvon Didehbani
Mobile Marketing	Vibes Media, Zach Davis
101 Productions	
Director of Finance & Marketing	Elie Landau
101 Productions, Ltd. Staff	Denys Baker, Mark Barna, Beth Blitzer, Danielle Fazio, Clinton Kennedy, Heidi Neven, Julie Anne Nolan, Mary Six Rupert, Samara Ungar, Hannah Wachtel
101 Productions, Ltd. Intern	Michael Rudd
Children's Tutoring	On Location Education/ Alan Simon, Jodi Green
Banking	City National Bank/Anne McSweeney
Insurance	DeWitt Stern, Inc./ Peter Shoemaker, Rebecca Alspector
Risk Managers	Stockbridge Risk Management/ Neil Goldstein
Immigration	Traffic Control Group, Inc./ David King
Theatre Displays	King Displays, Inc.
Merchandising	The Araca Group Ben Kaplan, Anne MacLean
Production Photographer	Joan Marcus
Payroll Services	Castellana Services, Inc.

www.13themusical.com

CREDITS

Scenery and automation by Showmotion Inc., Norwalk, CT. Lighting equipment from PRG Lighting. Sound equipment from PRG Audio. Costumes executed by Jennifer Love. Props by Cigar Box Studios. Natural herb cough drops courtesy of Ricola USA, Inc. Special thanks to Verizon for providing cell phones. Shoes provided by Famous Footwear. Cheerleading uniforms provided by OmniCheer. Jewelry provided by Claire's. Movie candy provided by Dylan's Candy. Dairy Queen props provided by Dairy Queen Corporation.

Piano by Steinway & Sons.

GROUP SALES
Theatre Direct, Inc.
(800) Broadway

13 rehearsed at Roundabout Rehearsal Studios

Original cast album available from
Ghostlight Records.

THE SHUBERT ORGANIZATION, INC.
Board of Directors

House Manager ....William Mitchell

(L-R): Delaney Moro and Elizabeth Egan Gillies

13

SCRAPBOOK

Correspondents: Al Calderon ("Eddie") and Malik Hammond ("Malcolm")

Opening Night Presents: Ariana Grande, who plays Charlotte, got us this awesome glass thing with a little hologram inside it. Delaney Moro, who plays Kendra, got us a photo album of *13* with our name etched on the cover in gold. All of our families were there, and everybody gave us good luck.

Opening Night Faxes: We got welcomes and good wishes from *In the Heights* (who said, "Welcome to the Hood"), *Avenue Q, Equus* and *Billy Elliot.*

Celebrity Visitors: Uma Thurman and Kirk Douglas talked to us and told us we did great. It was an honor. Bailey Hanks from *Legally Blonde* came up to us at "Broadway on Broadway," and said, "Omigod, your dance was so good!" It felt so good.

Who Got the Gypsy Robe: Eamon Foley, who has been in five Broadway shows. He's 15, a veteran!

Special Backstage Rituals: We have some cool rituals. On stage right Joey and I do a stupid thing each night: we pretend to have a random argument and then go, "Aw, I love you, man!" And hug twice. Joey and Ariana say "Break a leg" like 10 times really fast. To get our energy up Aaron and I go crazy dancing in our dressing room.

Favorite Moment During Each Performance: I look forward to doing "Brand New You"—not because it's the end of the show, but because it's such a fun number. We step like in "Stomp the Yard," and we have a blast onstage. It's like a party: it's loose. I love that.

In-Theatre Gathering Place: The basement of the theatre, that's our greenroom. We hang out there with the understudies, even during the show. It doesn't look too pleasant but it's pretty big and that's where we do our warm-ups.

Off-Site Hangouts: We used to go to the café next door to the place where we did rehearsals. But now, on matinee days, we go to dinner together or to each other's houses, sometimes for a sleepover.

Snack Food: Everybody's always eating Special K Bars...but we just like to eat.

Therapies: Pastilles for your voice. I use Emergen-C now and then if I'm feeling tired. Ariana and I also use Hall's cherry drops.

Mascot: During the tryout at Goodspeed we

1. The cast takes bows on opening night.
2. (L-R): Allie Trimm, Eric M. Nelsen and Brynn Williams at the opening night party at Opera.
3. *Yearbook* correspondent Malik Hammond at the cast party.
4. (L-R): Caitlin Gann and Delaney Moro at Opera.

had a scene where Patrice appeared in costume as the high school mascot, a quail. But the scene got cut and so did the costume.

Cell Phone Cameras: We see a lot of people with cameras. We were signing autographs one day and Eamon Foley asked a fan, "Were you the one videotaping?" The fan said, "Oh yeah I caught some realy cool pictures!" Eamon was, like, so serious and said, "Will you delete that right now, please?!" He was so serious, I was dying laughing! But she deleted it. I mean, you have to.

Web Buzz: Omigod, it's unbelievable. Two months ago on Facebook I had 126 friends; that was just the people I know. Two months later I have like 526, and I get like 50 friend requests a day. It's so great that people genuinely love the show, and that they're finding us and communicating with us. We also use 13Fans.com: it's like a *13* MySpace or Facebook. That's the fans' way of talking to us and putting up pictures and videos. People even start blogs about us: "Omigod, you talked to Al Calderon!" People know who we are now. It feels good.

Stage Door Fan Encounters: We're not allowed to sign people's arms anymore. One time this girl lost her Playbill, and asked if we could sign her hand. We signed it with a little heart, and suddenly EVERYBODY wanted a little heart on their hand. And now there's a new thing: "Can

I have a hug?"

Fastest Costume Change: Allie used to have maybe 45 seconds after the button on "13" to change out of her skater outfit in the New York scene and be ready for the Indiana scene.

Heaviest/Hottest Costume: We used to have a football number in which we wore full football gear. Malik and I had to do "Bad News" right after that, so we had to quickly change our clothes, then run around the stage to make our entrance. We barely used to make it.

Who Wears the Least: The cheerleading outfits for all the girls.

Catchphrase That Only the Company Would Recognize: "Babies."

Directorial Notes: Jeremy Sams, our director, is so British, it's amazing. We had a line where we used the insult, "Fagmo." When he cut it he said, "Your line 'Fagmo': We loved it. We lost it. It's gone. [Clap.]" Jeremy also keeps sending notes to Liz to articulate more. She now articulates so much that she winds up spitting everywhere.

Company Legends: In the movie scene we had fake buckets of popcorn, and when mine fell, I didn't want to pick it up and disrupt the scene. I just sat there hoping it would roll off. But it stayed on stage and when I tried to kick it off, it got caught under the lockers. In our Goodspeed tryout there was a really bad storm during "Get Me What I Need." Aaron was singing and the lights started going crazy like a disco box. Aaron just kept singing and I still think that was the most professional thing ever done.

Nicknames: We call Caitlin "Bubbles." Ariana Delaney sometimes calls me [Calderon] "Drain." I call her "D-Lane." Sometimes we call Malik "MAL-ik," instead of "Mah-LIQUE."

Coolest Thing About Being In This Show: We're all teenagers, both the cast and the band. There are no adults in this show.

Unforgettable: One thing we'll never forget is all of us being together and having a great time and being kids. We're all 13 to 17 years old, and we're already on Broadway, getting our foot in the door! I think that's amazing. I don't think there will ever be another Broadway show like this.

This Scrapbook originated as an interview broadcast on PlaybillRadio.com. This version was edited for print.

The 39 Steps

First Preview: January 4, 2008. Opened: January 15, 2008.
Still running as of May 31, 2009.

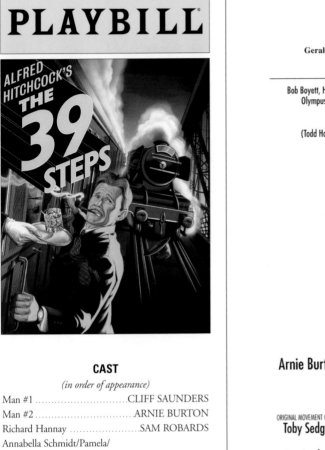

PLAYBILL

ALFRED HITCHCOCK'S THE 39 STEPS

CAST
(in order of appearance)

Man #1 ....CLIFF SAUNDERS
Man #2 ....ARNIE BURTON
Richard Hannay ....SAM ROBARDS
Annabella Schmidt/Pamela/
  Margaret ....JENNIFER FERRIN

UNDERSTUDIES

For Richard Hannay:
ROB BRECKENRIDGE
For Annabella Schmidt/Pamela/Margaret:
CLAIRE BROWNELL
For Man #1 & #2:
CAMERON FOLMAR

Production Stage Manager:
NEVIN HEDLEY
Stage Manager:
JANET TAKAMI

⑧ CORT THEATRE
138 West 48th Street
A Shubert Organization Theatre
Gerald Schoenfeld, *Chairman*   Philip J. Smith, *President*

Robert E. Wankel, *Executive Vice President*

Bob Boyett, Harriet Newman Leve/Ron Nicynski, Stewart F. Lane/Bonnie Comley, Manocherian Golden Prods.,
Olympus Theatricals/Douglas Denoff, Pam Laudenslager/Pat Addiss, Tim Levy/Remmel T. Dickinson
IN ASSOCIATION WITH
Roundabout Theatre Company
(Todd Haimes, Artistic Director; Harold Wolpert, Managing Director; Julia C. Levy, Executive Director)
Huntington Theatre Company
(Nicholas Martin, Artistic Director; Michael Maso, Managing Director)
Edward Snape for Fiery Angel Ltd.
PRESENT

ALFRED HITCHCOCK'S THE 39 STEPS

ADAPTED BY **Patrick Barlow**

BASED ON AN ORIGINAL CONCEPT BY **Simon Corble and Nobby Dimon**
BASED ON THE BOOK BY **John Buchan**
with

Arnie Burton   Jennifer Ferrin   Sam Robards   Cliff Saunders

LIGHTING DESIGN   SOUND DESIGN
Kevin Adams   **Mic Pool**

ORIGINAL MOVEMENT CREATED BY   ADDITIONAL MOVEMENT CREATED BY   PRODUCTION MANAGER   PRODUCTION STAGE MANAGER
Toby Sedgwick   **Christopher Bayes**   **Aurora Productions**   **Nevin Hedley**

CASTING   MARKETING   PRESS REPRESENTATIVE
Jay Binder/Jack Bowdan   **HHC Marketing**   **Boneau/Bryan-Brown**

DIALECT COACH   ASSOCIATE PRODUCER   EXECUTIVE PRODUCER   GENERAL MANAGER
Stephen Gabis   **Marek J. Cantor**   **101 Productions, Ltd.**   **Roy Gabay**

SET & COSTUME DESIGN
Peter McKintosh

DIRECTED BY
Maria Aitken

This production of *The 39 Steps* premiered at the Tricycle Theatre, London in August 2006.
We wish to express our appreciation to Theatre Development Fund for its support of this production.

10/1/08

(L-R): Sam Robards,
Arnie Burton, Cliff Saunders
and Jennifer Ferrin

Photo by Joan Marcus

The 39 Steps

Arnie Burton
Man #2

Jennifer Ferrin
*Annabella Schmidt/
Pamela/Margaret*

Sam Robards
Richard Hannay

Cliff Saunders
Man #1

Rob Breckenridge
u/s Richard Hannay

Claire Brownell
*u/s Annabella
Schmidt/Pamela/
Margaret*

Cameron Folmar
u/s Man #1 & 2

Maria Aitken
Director

Patrick Barlow
Adaptor

Peter McKintosh
*Set and Costume
Design*

Kevin Adams
Lighting Design

Mic Pool
Sound Design

Stephen Gabis
Dialect Coach

Jay Binder C.S.A.
Casting

Jack Bowdan C.S.A.
Casting

Bob Boyett
Producer

Harriet Newman
Leve
Producer

Ron Nicynski
Producer

Stewart F. Lane and Bonnie Comley
Producer

Jennifer
Manocherian
Producer

Barbara
Manocherian
Producer

Douglas Denoff
Producer

Pat Flicker Addiss
Producer

Michael Maso
*Managing Director,
Huntington Theatre
Company*

Todd Haimes
*Artistic Director,
Roundabout Theatre
Company*

Roy Gabay
General Manager

Wendy Orshan,
101 Productions
Producer

Charles Edwards
Richard Hannay

Mark Shanahan
u/s Richard Hannay

Francesca Faridany
*Annabella Schmidt/
Pamela/Margaret*

Jeffrey Kuhn
Man #1

Sean Mahon
Richard Hannay

The 39 Steps

(L-R): Jeffrey Kuhn, Francesca Faridany, Arnie Burton and Sean Mahon.

Photo by Joan Marcus

33 Variations
SCRAPBOOK

Correspondent: Don Amendolia, "Anton Diabelli"

Opening Night Gifts: I gave Beethoven action figures to the cast. To Jane I gave an 18th century cut-out black silhouette of Beethoven. I myself got an action figure, lots of flowers and chocolate. The theatre management gave us flowers when we first arrived.

Most Exciting Celebrity Visitors: My dressing room is on the same side of the stage as Jane's and, oh my God, the parade of people who come to see her every single night! James Earl Jones, Yoko Ono, Dolly Parton, Lily Tomlin—everyone on Broadway seems to have come. Colin's dad Tom has been back a couple of times and is always so pleasant. Liv Ullman was wonderful. Robert Redford was very nice, very complimentary.

Most Roles in This Show: Erik and I do all of the VOs, plus our onstage characters.

Who Has Done the Most Shows in Their Career: Maybe me. I've done dozens.

Special Backstage Ritual: There is a section of the show where we're all talking on top of one another, so every night at 15 minutes before "half-hour" we meet on stage and go over it once. But that's also become the time when people from dressing rooms on both sides of the theatre get a moment to yammer, talk and laugh, We fill each other in on the day's doings before we have to run and get our wigs on. That's always fun.

Favorite Moment: The Kyrie.

In-Theatre Gathering Place: The hallway underneath the stage, used for cross-unders. Jack Anderson, who runs the moving bookcases, operates from down there. He always has chocolate and pretzels and little snacks, and everybody stops and grabs something on their way past. It's right where the greenroom would be, and it's got a couple of old sofas. You bump into everyone from the show there at one point or another.

Favorite Snack Food: Whatever is there.

Off-Site Hangouts: Sometimes we just go around the corner to Thalia, but our favorite places are Orso and any of the Joe Allen restaurants. We also sometimes stop at Bar Centrale for a quick drink.

Mascot: Jane's dog Tulea. She is the sweetest little dog in the world. Twice during the show the dog-sitter brings her to me while I'm sitting downstairs on one of the sofas. Tulea got away from him only once, during previews, and ran out on stage. She heard applause, knew the show was over, and it was time to see Mom.

Favorite Therapies: There are Ricolas everywhere. Jane does Pilates. Michael does yoga. We all have Throat-Coat Tea. I make a special remedy of ginger-parsley tea when someone is ill and has to get well fast.

Memorable Ad-Libs: Jane once dropped something during the scene where she's packing to leave for Bonn. She ad-libbed, "See, I can get it! I can bend over. Watch!" The audience didn't know it was funny. During the La Jolla tryout, my tongue got completely tangled one night. I

1. Jane Fonda speaks to the press on opening night.
2. Opening night curtain call.
3. Cast members Don Amendolia and Susan Kellermann at the party.
4. Cast member Samantha Mathis at the party at Buddakan restaurant.
5. (L-R): Writer/director Moisés Kaufman with cast members Colin Hanks and Zach Grenier at Buddakan.

was supposed to say, "You don't understand what I mean by my waltz." And it came out, "You don't understand what I mean why buy balls. Bye-bye walls." I was lost. It simply wouldn't come out right—but I did it with full conviction!

Memorable Stage Door Fan Encounter: People don't usually know who I am because I wear a wig in the show, so I can usually slip. Every once in a while someone recognizes me and I stay for a while and chat with them. We have one fan who comes once a week with posters from the show and asks us to sign them, two at a time. I can't imagine what he does with them. Sometimes an older audience member will ask for an autograph and will tell me what a wonderful Beethoven I was!

Fastest Costume Change: Without a doubt, Colin. He has 19 costume changes.

Who Wore the Least: Samantha and Colin take their tops off.

Hottest Costume: Me. It's not the heaviest costume, but it has many layers. The period demands that kind of wardrobe.

Sweethearts Within the Company: We've had two engagements. The gal who played Clara in the first workshops, and who is understudy to Clara now, got engaged to the fellow who played Mike in La Jolla. The guy playing Schindler now is engaged to the gal who played Clara in La Jolla.

Catchphrases Only the Company Would Recognize: "Oh, Clara!"

Coolest Thing About Being in This Show: Playing Broadway is living the dream, and working with Jane is extraordinary. She's such a team player. It's a credit to Moisés that he seems to put really nice people together, so it's an absolute joy to go to work every night.

[title of show]

First Preview: July 5, 2008. Opened July 17, 2008.
Closed October 12, 2008 after 13 Previews and 102 Performances.

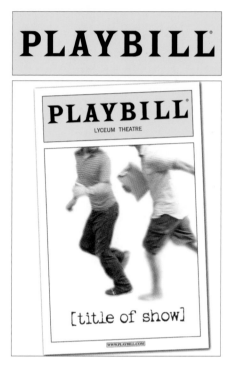

PLAYBILL

PLAYBILL
LYCEUM THEATRE

[title of show]

WWW.PLAYBILL.COM

CAST
(in order of appearance)
Jeff ....JEFF BOWEN
Hunter ....HUNTER BELL
Heidi ....HEIDI BLICKENSTAFF
Susan ....SUSAN BLACKWELL

PLACE:
[place]

TIME:
[time]

STANDBYS
Standby for Heidi and Susan:
COURTNEY BALAN

Standby for Jeff and Hunter:
BENJAMIN HOWES

Dance Captain:
BENJAMIN HOWES

Piano:
LARRY PRESSGROVE

◎LYCEUM THEATRE
149 West 45th Street
A Shubert Organization Theatre

Gerald Schoenfeld, *Chairman*   Philip J. Smith, *President*

Robert E. Wankel, *Executive Vice President*

KEVIN McCOLLUM JEFFREY SELLER ROY MILLER
LAURA CAMIEN KRIS STEWART VINEYARD THEATRE

present

[title of show]

Music and Lyrics by   Book by
JEFF BOWEN   **HUNTER BELL**

Starring

HUNTER BELL   SUSAN BLACKWELL   HEIDI BLICKENSTAFF   JEFF BOWEN

and

COURTNEY BALAN   BENJAMIN HOWES

Scenic Design	Costume Design	Lighting Design	Sound Design
NEIL PATEL	CHASE TYLER	KEN BILLINGTON JASON KANTROWITZ	ACME SOUND PARTNERS

Casting	Technical Supervisor	Vocal Arrangements	Production Stage Manager
TELSEY + COMPANY	BRIAN LYNCH	JEFF BOWEN LARRY PRESSGROVE	MARTHA DONALDSON

Associate Producers
RACHEL HELSON   SARA KATZ   LAMS ENTERTAINMENT   JAIMIE MAYER
HEATHER PROVOST   TOM SMEDES

Press Representative	Marketing	Promotions	General Management
SAM RUDY MEDIA RELATIONS	SCOTT A. MOORE	HHC MARKETING	THE CHARLOTTE WILCOX COMPANY

Music Direction and Arrangements by
LARRY PRESSGROVE

Directed and Choreographed by
MICHAEL BERRESSE

Originally presented at the 2004 New York Musical Theatre Festival
[title of show] was partially developed at The Eugene O'Neill Theater Center.
The producers wish to express their appreciation to Theatre Development Fund for its support of this production.

7/17/08

(Clockwise, from Top Left): Heidi Blickenstaff, Susan Blackwell, Hunter Bell and Jeff Bowen sing "Monkeys and Playbills."

Photo by Carol Rosegg

[title of show]

MUSICAL NUMBERS

"Untitled Opening Number"	Company
"Two Nobodies in New York"	Jeff and Hunter
"An Original Musical"	Hunter and Jeff
"Monkeys and Playbills"	Company
"Part of It All"	Hunter and Jeff
"I Am Playing Me"	Heidi
"What Kind of Girl Is She?"	Heidi and Susan
"Die Vampire, Die!"	Susan and Company
"Filling Out the Form"	Company
"Montage Part 1: September Song"	Company
"Montage Part 2: Secondary Characters"	Susan and Heidi
"Montage Part 3: Development Medley"	Company
"Change It, Don't Change It/Awkward Photo Shoot"	Company
"A Way Back to Then"	Heidi
"Nine People's Favorite Thing"	Company
"Finale"	Company

Jeff Bowen
*Music and Lyrics/
Jeff*

Hunter Bell
Book/Hunter

Susan Blackwell
Susan

Heidi Blickenstaff
Heidi

Courtney Balan
*Standby for Susan
and Heidi*

Benjamin Howes
*Standby for Hunter
and Jeff*

Michael Berresse
*Director/
Choreographer*

Neil Patel
Scenic Design

Ken Billington
Co-Lighting Design

Tom Clark, Mark Menard, and Nevin Steinberg,
Acme Sound Partners
Sound Design

Larry Pressgrove
*Musical Direction/
Arrangements*

Bernard Telsey,
Telsey + Company
Casting

Brian Lynch,
Theatretech, Inc.
*Production
Supervisor*

The Charlotte Wilcox
Company
General Manager

Kevin McCollum
Producer

Jeffrey Seller
Producer

Roy Miller
Producer

Rachel Helson
Associate Producer

Heidi Blickenstaff sings "I Am Playing Me," accompanied by
Larry Pressgrove.

Photo by Carol Rosegg

[title of show]

CREW
Front Row (L-R):
Alex Gushin Agosta (Company Manager)

Second Row (L-R):
Carlos Parra (Follow Spot), Martha Donaldson (PSM), Leah Nelson (Head Props), Kathleen Gallagher (Wardrobe Supervisor), Soomi Marano (Dresser)

Third Row (L-R):
Tom Reynolds (Stage Manager), Colin DeVerna (Follow Spot), Jonathan Cohen (Head Electrician), Adam Braunstein (Head Carpenter)

FRONT OF HOUSE STAFF
Front Row (L-R):
Carmen Sanchez (Asst. Porter), Rose Ann Cipriano (Ticket Taker), Merida Colon (Chief Usher), Roger Lakins (Usher)

Back Row (L-R):
Ethan Baker (Usher), Ramona Maben (Usher), Sonia Moreno (Usher), Robert Lugo (Usher), Elsie Grosvenor (Director), Gerry Belitsis (Usher), Kevin Pinzon (Usher), Victor Beaulieu (Sound Associates), Joann Swanson (Theatre Mgr.)

Photos by Brian Mapp

STAGE DOOR AND WARDROBE
John Donovan (Doorman) and Kathleen Gallagher (Wardrobe Supervisor)

TREASURERS
(L-R): Edvige Cadunz (Head Treasurer) and Jennifer Holze (Treasurer)

[title of show]

SCRAPBOOK

Correspondents: Susan Blackwell ("Susan"), Heidi Blickenstaff ("Heidi") and the Cast and Crew of *[title of show]*.

Memorable Opening Night Notes: In keeping with tradition, all the Broadway shows sent faxes welcoming us to Broadway. We even received a telegram, old-school style!!

Opening Night Gifts: *[title of show]* bags, *[title of show]* finger puppet theatres, *[title of show]* bathrobes, *[title of show]* tee-shirts, *[title of show]* clocks, *[title of show]* caricatures, *[title of show]* mugs, action figures based on each character, stationery, monkeys, Chicken-in-a-Biskit, Rice Krispies treats, lots of delicious food, and stakes and garlic to demolish our Vampires. Hunter and Jeff got original show jackets of *A Doll's Life* and *Grind* from Ken Billington. Susan got gold-

(L-R): Heidi Blickenstaff, Susan Blackwell, Hunter Bell, Michael Berresse, Jeff Bowen and Larry Pressgrove at Cafe De Ville for the opening night party (with snacks mentioned in the show).

STAFF FOR *[title of show]*

GENERAL MANAGEMENT
THE CHARLOTTE WILCOX COMPANY
Charlotte W. Wilcox
Seth Marquette
Matthew W. Krawiec, Dina Steinberg
David Roth, Steve Supeck, Margaret Wilcox

GENERAL PRESS REPRESENTATIVES
SAM RUDY MEDIA RELATIONS
Sam Rudy, Dale R. Heller,
Robert Lasko

COMPANY MANAGER
Alexandra Gushin Agosta

CASTING
TELSEY + COMPANY (CSA)
Bernie Telsey, Will Cantler, David Vaccari
Bethany Knox, Craig Burns
Tiffany Little Canfield, Rachel Hoffman
Carrie Rosson, Justin Huff, Bess Fifer
Patrick Goodwin

THE PRODUCING OFFICE
Kevin McCollum, Jeffrey Seller
John S. Corker, Debra Nir
Ryan Hill, Caitlyn Thomson
Director of Marketing: Scott A. Moore

THE VINEYARD THEATRE
Douglas Aibel .... Artistic Director
Jennifer Garvey-Blackwell .... Executive Director
Sarah Stern .... Associate Artistic Director
Reed Ridgley .... General Manager

PRODUCTION
STAGE MANAGER .... Martha Donaldson
Stage Manager .... Tom Reynolds
Assistant to Director .... Jennifer Ashley Tepper
Associate Scenic Designer .... David Barber
Assistant Lighting Designer .... Craig Stelzenmuller
Associate Sound Designer .... Nick Borisjuk

Advance Electrician .... Keith Buchanan
Head Electrician .... Jonathan Cohen
Head Spot Operator .... Colin DeVerna
Second Spot Operator .... Carlos Parra
Advance Carpenter .... McBrein Dunbar
Head Carpenter .... Adam Braunstein
Automation Flyman .... Paul Brydon
Head Properties .... Leah Nelson
Advance Sound .... Dan Robillard
Head Sound .... Brad Gyorgak
Wardrobe Supervisor .... Kathleen Gallagher
Dresser .... Soomi Marano
Production Assistant .... Zac Chandler
Management Intern .... Morrisa Gold
Intern .... Leah Harris
Legal Counsel .... Levine, Plotkin & Menin LLP/
Loren Plotkin, Susan Mindell
Accountants .... Fried & Kowgios Partners LLP
Comptroller .... Sarah Galbraith
Advertising/Website Design .... Spotco/
Drew Hodges, Jim Edwards,
Pete Milano, Pete Duffy
Promotions .... HHC Marketing/
Hugh Hysell, Michael Redman,
James Hewson, Todd Briscoe,
Matt Sicoli, Candice Beckmann,
Kayla Kuzbel, Nicole Pando,
Rachel Ellersieck, Sarah Moore
Production Photography .... Carol Rosegg
Theater Displays .... BAM
Banking .... City National Bank/Michelle Gibbons
Payroll Service .... Castellana Services, Inc.
Merchandise .... Marquee Merchandise
Insurance Consultant .... D.R. Reiff & Associates/
Dennis Reiff
Computer Consultant .... Marion Finkler Taylor

CREDITS
Scenery by Blackthorn Scenic Studios. Automation by Stage Machines, Inc. Lighting equipment supplied by PRG Lighting. Sound equipment by Sound Associates. Rehearsed at Ripley Grier Studios.

Performance rights to *[title of show]* are represented by

R&H Theatricals: www.rnhtheatricals.com

SPECIAL THANKS
Blue Man Group, Emilia Goldstein, Frank DenDanto III, James Compton, The York Theatre Company, Jonathan Dunkle, Josh Bradford, Kuuipo Curry, Lynda Barry, manhattan theatre source, Matt Vogel, Michael Bush, Rob Preuss, Sara Shives, Seth Rudetsky, Stacia Fernandez, The Weston Playhouse, Davis-Spylios, Harden-Curtis, Philip S. Birsh and Playbill, Inc.

Original cast recording available on
Ghostlight Records.

---

www.titleofshow.com

 **THE SHUBERT ORGANIZATION, INC.**
Board of Directors

| **Gerald Schoenfeld** | **Philip J. Smith** |
| Chairman | President |

| **Wyche Fowler, Jr.** | **John W. Kluge** |

| **Lee J. Seidler** | **Michael I. Sovern** |

Stuart Subotnick

Robert E. Wankel
Executive Vice President

Peter Entin	**Elliot Greene**
Vice President –	Vice President –
Theatre Operations	Finance

David Andrews	**John Darby**
Vice President –	Vice President –
Shubert Ticketing Services	Facilities

D.S. Moynihan
Vice President – Creative Projects

House Manager .... Joann Swanson

en ponies. Heidi got a dressing room full of flowers. Priceless.

Celebrity Visitors: Kitty Carlisle Hart to Susan: "How do you keep your feet so clean?"
Bernadette Peters to Hunter and Jeff: "When are we having lunch?"

Who Got the Gypsy Robe: Because we are all on principal contracts, no one was eligible for the Gypsy Robe ceremony. Sometimes we put on our bathrobes and run around the Lyceum stage while we play the OCR of *Gypsy* to assuage our grief.

Most Roles: Hunter and Jeff both play two characters. In addition to playing themselves, in the song, "An Original Musical" they are playing the characters of Blank Paper and Li'l Guy.

Most Shows in Their Career: We have all done lots of shows. From 1981's *A Puzzling Obsession* in the basement of Hunter Bell's aunt's house, to regional theatre, to national tours, to experimental downtown theatre, to Broadway.

Special Backstage Rituals: We circle up before every show. Each person shares an intention for the show (e.g.: 'Enjoyment,' 'Listening,' 'First Time,' 'Superfresh,' 'Focus,' 'Fun,' 'Off Road'…). Then we slowly inhale and exhale three times together. Then, like a sports team, we all put our hands in the middle of our circle and, as a group, we all shout out a word on the count of three: For instance, "One, Two, Three, Baby Goats!"

Favorite Moment During Each Performance: Standing on stage at the end of "Nine People's Favorite Thing" and realizing that we actually made it and we're doing *[title of show]* on a Broadway stage.

In-Theatre Gathering Place: Everyone gathers in the 'VIP Room,' which is actually an ensemble dressing room that we've seconded for group gatherings. This is where we stash gifts from friends and fans such as yummy treats, notes, cards and games. Also found in the VIP room are Jeff's charts from "The *[title of show]* Show."

Off-Site Hangout: Rosie O'Grady's on 46th Street. On a fancy night, Bar Centrale.

Favorite Snack Food: Haru Sushi. Cheddar bunnies and other treats fashioned by our exquisite ASM, Tom Reynolds.

Mascots: Heidi's doggie, Olive. Oliver the Comedy Chicken (currently on hiatus from the HBO special, "The Tiny Chickens Of Comedy"). Ice Bat. And Mindy, the drunken puppet, star of "The *[title of show]* Show."

Favorite Therapy: Ricola, yoga, pre-show vocal warm-ups led by Music Director Larry Pressgrove, Klonopin. And lots and lots of therapy.

What Did You Think of the Web Buzz on Your Show: Since we started all them web rumors about our show, we loved it.

Memorable Press Encounter: Meeting Roma Torre from NY1, a Golden Pony moment (see "Company Legends," below.)

Memorable Stage Door Fan Encounter: Hunter got serenaded by a cutie with a guitar.

Latest Audience Arrival: Benjamin was incredulous when an audience member came in 45 minutes late. He resisted walking up to her and saying, "You missed it."

1. The *[tos]* team on opening night, gathered around one of the hot dog carts mentioned in the show.
2. Bell and Bowen pretend to choke *Forbidden Broadway* cast members who are parodying them.
3. The original cast, overcome with emotion during curtain calls on the Broadway opening night.

Busiest Day at the Box Office: We had a "ticketganza" to celebrate the opening day at our box office. So many tossers, so many tickets.

Heaviest/Hottest Costume: Hunter's sandwich-board costume as the inspirational, foulmouthed "Blank Paper" weighs about 50 lbs.

Who Wore the Least: The trio of brave souls, Hunter, Heidi and Jeffy all are shirtless at some point in the play.

Catchphrases Only the Company Would Recognize: "Don't forget about the gingle gangle." "We'll never make nationals with Shannon on the end." "They're stale." "Many mumbling mice." "Pizzas." "That makes me hot."

Best In-House Parody Lyrics: We appreciate all the fun gifts from fans, and some of those gifts have misinformed lyrics that give us a giggle, like: "part of fancy captivate, preston navigate, part of a codal marmasette…." "I aimed for this guy" instead of "I aimed for the sky." You get the picture.

Memorable Directorial Note: "First time."

Company Legends: The *[title of show]* GOLDEN PONY: Mention your likes, desires or wishes in *[title of show]* and the *[title of show]* Golden Pony will poop it out for you.

Nicknames: Hunty, Jeppy, Jibs, Sibs, Hibs, Swasson, Benjermain, Heids, Lars, Tom-Tom, Court, Quartz, Tepps, Mee-yartha, Mikey.

Sweethearts Within the Company: Jeff Bowen and Michael Berresse have been a couple for seven years.

Embarrassing Moment: Jeff was making his one and only exit during the show and tripped over his own foot. He went down hard and fast. His upper body fell offstage, leaving his feet onstage, poking through the door like The Wicked Witch of the East. Hunter dragged him off by the ears and closed the door with the memorable ad-lib, "We'll be right back."

Understudy Anecdote: When Jeff had the incident, Benjamin was lying on the floor of his dressing room, barely awake from a quick catnap when he heard Martha, our stage manager frantically whispering his name over the monitor. By the time he realized that she was calling him down to the stage he was so frazzled he rushed down in full Jeff garb and only one shoe.

Coolest Thing About Being in This Show: Getting to perform a Broadway show that you love, with some of your closest friends.

Fan Club Info: titleofshow.com, supertossers.com

Also: Remember that time that *[title of show]* got to be in "The Playbill Broadway Yearbook"? That rocked!!!

To Be or Not To Be

First Preview: September 16, 2008. Opened: October 14, 2008.
Closed November 16, 2008 after 32 Previews and 40 Peformances.

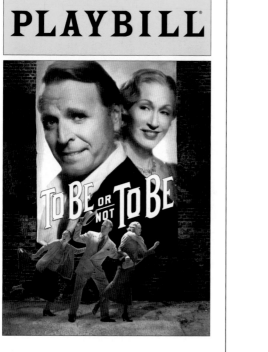

CAST
(in alphabetical order)

Rowicz ....PETER BENSON
Grunberg ....ROBERT DORFMAN
Sobinsky ....STEVE KAZEE
Dowasz ....PETER MALONEY
Maria ....JAN MAXWELL
Colonel Erhard ....MICHAEL McCARTY
Anna ....KRISTINE NIELSEN
Young Grunberg................BRANDON PERLER
Josef ....DAVID RASCHE
Silewski/Performer ....ROCCO SISTO
Walowski/Major Schweinlich ...JIMMY SMAGULA
Eva ....MARINA SQUERCIATI
Officer ....MARK J. SULLIVAN

TIME: 1939
PLACE: Warsaw, Poland

Stage Manager ....Elizabeth Moloney

UNDERSTUDIES

For Young Grunberg:
DANTE BALDASSIN
For Josef, Dowasz, Silewski/Performer, Officer:
RUFUS COLLINS
For Maria, Anna, Eva:
ANGELA PIERCE
For Colonel Erhard/Grunberg:
JIMMY SMAGULA
For Sobinsky, Rowicz, Walowski/Major Schweinlich:
MARK J. SULLIVAN

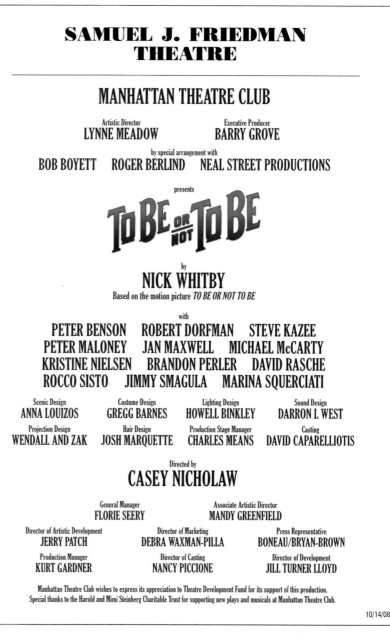

SAMUEL J. FRIEDMAN THEATRE

MANHATTAN THEATRE CLUB

Artistic Director
LYNNE MEADOW

Executive Producer
BARRY GROVE

by special arrangement with

BOB BOYETT   ROGER BERLIND   NEAL STREET PRODUCTIONS

presents

To Be or Not To Be

by
NICK WHITBY
Based on the motion picture *TO BE OR NOT TO BE*

with

PETER BENSON   ROBERT DORFMAN   STEVE KAZEE
PETER MALONEY   JAN MAXWELL   MICHAEL McCARTY
KRISTINE NIELSEN   BRANDON PERLER   DAVID RASCHE
ROCCO SISTO   JIMMY SMAGULA   MARINA SQUERCIATI

Scenic Design
ANNA LOUIZOS

Costume Design
GREGG BARNES

Lighting Design
HOWELL BINKLEY

Sound Design
DARRON L WEST

Projection Design
WENDALL AND ZAK

Hair Design
JOSH MARQUETTE

Production Stage Manager
CHARLES MEANS

Casting
DAVID CAPARELLIOTIS

Directed by
CASEY NICHOLAW

General Manager
FLORIE SEERY

Associate Artistic Director
MANDY GREENFIELD

Director of Artistic Development
JERRY PATCH

Director of Marketing
DEBRA WAXMAN-PILLA

Press Representative
BONEAU/BRYAN-BROWN

Production Manager
KURT GARDNER

Director of Casting
NANCY PICCIONE

Director of Development
JILL TURNER LLOYD

Manhattan Theatre Club wishes to express its appreciation to Theatre Development Fund for its support of this production.
Special thanks to the Harold and Mimi Steinberg Charitable Trust for supporting new plays and musicals at Manhattan Theatre Club.

10/14/08

(L-R): Michael McCarty and Jan Maxwell

Photo by Joan Marcus

To Be or Not To Be

Peter Benson
Rowicz

Robert Dorfman
Grunberg

Steve Kazee
Sobinsky

Peter Maloney
Dowasz

Jan Maxwell
Maria

Michael McCarty
Colonel Erhard

Kristine Nielsen
Anna

Brandon Perler
Young Grunberg

David Rasche
Josef

Rocco Sisto
Silewski/Performer

Jimmy Smagula
*Walowski/
Major Schweinlich*

Marina Squerciati
Eva

Dante Baldassin
*Understudy for
Young Grunberg*

Rufus Collins
*Understudy for
Josef, Dowasz,
Silewski/Performer,
Officer*

Angela Pierce
*Understudy for
Maria, Anna, Eva*

Mark J. Sullivan
Officer

Casey Nicholaw
Director

Anna Louizos
Scenic Design

Gregg Barnes
Costume Design

Howell Binkley
Lighting Design

Josh Marquette
Hair Design

Lynne Meadow
*Artistic Director,
Manhattan Theatre
Club, Inc.*

Barry Grove
*Executive Producer,
Manhattan Theatre
Club, Inc.*

Bob Boyett
Producer

Roger Berlind
Producer

Sam Mendes,
Neal Street
Productions
Producer

CHILD WRANGLER
(L-R): Dante Baldassin (Young Grunberg u/s), Cerissa Kimball (Child Wrangler),
Brandon Perler (Young Grunberg)

Photo submitted by Christine Olver

To Be or Not To Be

STAGE CREW
Front Row (L-R):
Jeff Dodson (Master Electrician), Angie Simpson (Wardrobe Supervisor), Lou Shapiro (Sound Supervisor), Paula Schaffer (Hair Supervisor), Michael DiMarco (Apprentice), Elizabeth Moloney (Stage Manager), Charles Means (Production Stage Manager)

Back Row (L-R):
Rebecca O'Neill (Flyman), Vaughn Preston (Automation), Marc Grimshaw (Props), Chris Walters (Props), Tim Walters (Props Head), Raynelle Wright (Sub ASM), Ian Harbor (Apprentice), John Fullum (Flyman), Adam Lang (Carpentry)

FRONT OF HOUSE STAFF
Front Row (L-R):
Tom Jarus (Usher), Nilsa Nairn (Usher), Ramon Pesante (Usher), Ed Brashear (Ticket Taker)

Back Row (L-R):
Cathy Burke (Usher), Jackson Ero (Usher), Dinah Glorioso (Usher), John Wyffels (Sweet Concessions Manager), Richard Ponce (Assistant House Manager), Russ Ramsey (Theatre Manager)

STAGE MANAGEMENT
(L-R:) Charles Means (Production Stage Manager), Elizabeth Moloney (Stage Manager), Raynelle Wright (Sub Assistant Stage Manager)

BOX OFFICE
(L-R): Dave Dillon (Box Office Treasurer) and Jeffrey Davis (Asst. Treasurer)

Photos by Brian Mapp

To Be or Not To Be

MANHATTAN THEATRE CLUB STAFF

Artistic Director ....Lynne Meadow
Executive Producer ....Barry Grove
General Manager ....Florie Seery
Associate Artistic Director ....Mandy Greenfield
Director of Artistic Development ....Jerry Patch
Artistic Consultant ....Daniel Sullivan
Director of Artistic Administration/
   Assistant to the Artistic Director .....Amy Gilkes Loe
Associate Director of
   Artistic Operations ....Lisa McNulty
Artistic Assistant ....Kevin Emrick
Administrative Assistant ....Rebecca Stang
Director of Casting ....Nancy Piccione
Casting Associate ....Kelly Gillespie
Casting Assistant ....Drew Ross
Literary Manager ....Raphael Martin
Play Development Associate/
   Sloan Project Manager ....Annie MacRae
Play Development Assistant ....Alex Barron
Director of Musical
   Development ....Clifford Lee Johnson III
Director of Development ....Jill Turner Lloyd
Director, Institutional Giving ....Roger Kingsepp
Director, Individual Giving ....Jon Haddorff
Director, Special Events ....Antonello Di Benedetto
Manager, Institutional Giving ....Andrea Gorzell
Manager,
   Institutional Giving ....Jessica Sadowski Comas
Manager, Individual Giving ....Emily Fleisher
Development Associate/
   Special Events ....Darra Messing
Development Associate/
   Institutional Giving ....Laurel Bear
Development Associate/
   Individual Giving ....Samantha Mascali
Development Associate/
   Database Coordinator ....Kelly Haydon
Patron Liaison ....Ryan Hudec
Director of Marketing ....Debra Waxman-Pilla
Marketing Manager ....Tom O'Connor
Marketing Associate ....Caitlin Baird
Director of Finance ....Jeffrey Bledsoe
Business Manager ....Holly Kinney
Human Resources Manager ....Darren Robertson
Business & HR Associate ....Adam Cook
Business Assistant ....Gillian Campbell
Receptionist/
   Studio Coordinator ....Christina Prints
IT Manager ....Mendy Sudranski
Systems Administrator ....Dilshan Keregala
Associate General Manager ....Lindsey Brooks Sag
Company Manager/
   NY City Center ....Erin Moeller
General Management Assistant ....Ann Mundorff
Assistant to the Executive Producer ......Emily Hammond
Director of Subscriber Services ....Robert Allenberg
Associate Subscriber Services Manager ......Andrew Taylor
Subscriber Services Representatives ....Mark Bowers,
   Rebekah Dewald, Eric Gerdts,
   Matthew Praet, Rosanna Consalva Sarto
Director of Telesales and Telefunding ....George Tetlow
Assistant Manager ....Terrence Burnett
Director of Education ....David Shookhoff

Asst. Director of Education/
   Coordinator, Paul A. Kaplan Theatre Management
   Program ....Amy Harris
Education Assistant,
   TheatreLink Coordinator ....Julia Davis
Education Assistant...........................Kelli Bragdon
MTC Teaching Artists ....David Auburn,
   Michael Bernard, Chris Ceraso,
   Charlotte Colavin, Dominic Colon,
   Allison Daugherty, Gilbert Girion,
   Andy Goldberg, Elise Hernandez,
   Jeffrey Joseph, Julie Leedes,
   Kate Long, Louis D. Moreno,
   Andres Munar, Melissa Murray,
   Angela Pietropinto, Alexa Polmer,
   Alfonso Ramirez, Carmen Rivera,
   Judy Tate, Candido Tirado, Joe White
Theatre Management Interns ....Ashley Dickerson,
   Taylor Gramps, E'bess Greer,
   Pamela Kierejczyk, Cerissa Kimball,
   Alan Lane, Nina Sacharow, Rebecca Schwartz,
   Manisha Snoyer, Thatcher Stevens,
   Sabrina Sydnor, Amber Wilkerson
Randy Carrig Casting Intern ....Caroline Pugliese

Production Manager ....Kurt Gardner
Associate Production Manager ....Philip Naudé
Assistant Production Manager ....Kelsey Martinez
Properties Supervisor ....Scott Laule
Assistant Properties Supervisor ....Julia Sandy
Props Carpenter ....Peter Grimes
Costume Supervisor ....Erin Hennessy Dean

GENERAL PRESS REPRESENTATION
BONEAU/BRYAN-BROWN

Chris Boneau   Aaron Meier
Christine Olver   Matt Ross

Script Readers ....Kyle Frisina,
   Branden Jacobs-Jenkins, Liz Jones,
   Portia Krieger, Aaron Leichter,
   Stephen Sanders, Kathryn Walat

SERVICES

Accountants ....ERE, LLP
Advertising ....SpotCo/Drew Hodges,
   Jim Edwards, Laura Price, Kristen Rathbun
Web Design ....Calico Systems
Legal Counsel ....John Breglio, Deborah Hartnett,
   Carol M. Kaplan/
   Paul, Weiss,
   Rifkind, Wharton and Garrison LLP
Real Estate Counsel ....Marcus Attorneys
Labor Counsel ....Harry H. Weintraub/
   Glick and Weintraub, P.C.
Immigration Counsel ....Theodore Ruthizer/
   Kramer, Levin, Naftalis & Frankel, LLP
Sponsorship
   Consultant ....Above the Title Entertainment/
   Jed Bernstein
Insurance ....Dewitt Stern Group, Inc./
   Anthony Pittari
Maintenance ....Reliable Cleaning
Production Photographer ....Joan Marcus
Event Photography ....Bruce Glikas
Cover Photo ....Henry Leutwyler

Cover Design ....SpotCo
Theatre Displays ....King Display

PRODUCTION STAFF FOR TO BE OR NOT TO BE

Company Manager ....Seth Shepsle
Production Stage Manager ....Charles Means
Stage Manager ....Elizabeth Moloney
Associate Director ....Casey Hushion
Make-Up Consultant ....La Sonya Gunter
Dialect Coach ....Charlotte Fleck
Fight Consultant ....Thomas Schall
Associate Scenic Designer ....Donyale Werle
Associate Costume Designer ....Matthew Pachtman
Associate Lighting Designer ....Ryan O'Gara
Associate Sound Designer ....Matthew Hubbs
Assistant to the Projection Designers ....Daniel Brodie
Hair Supervisor ....Paula Schaffer
Automation Operator ....Vaughn Preston
Flymen ....John Fullum, Patrick Murray
Assistant Propertyman ....Christopher Walters
Moving Light Programmer ....Marc Polimeni
Conventional Light Programmer ....Jane Masterson
Dressers ....Virginia Neinenger, Suzanne Sponsler
Production Assistant ....Paige Grant
Child Supervisor ....Cerissa Kimball

CREDITS

Presented by arrangement with Twentieth Century Fox and Thomas Sesler Verlag. Scenery by Global Scenic Services. Automation by Showmotion, Inc. Lighting equipment provided by PRG Lighting. Sound equipment provided by Masque Sound. Projection equipment provided by Scharff Weisberg, Inc. Costumes by Euro Co, Inc.; Giliberto Designs, Inc.; Mardana. Custom footwear by Capri Shoes. MTC wishes to thank the TDF Costume Collection for its assistance in this production. Natural herbal cough drops courtesy of Ricola USA. Make-up provided by M•A•C. Children's tutoring services provided by On Location Education.

SPECIAL THANKS

Christian Frederickson, Danusia Trevino, the Polish American Bookstore & Art Gallery

For more information visit
www.ManhattanTheatreClub.org

MANHATTAN THEATRE CLUB
SAMUEL J. FRIEDMAN THEATRE STAFF

Theatre Manager ....Russ Ramsey
Assistant House Manager ....Richard Ponce
Box Office Treasurer ....David Dillon
Assistant Box Office
   Treasurers ....Tevy Bradley, Jeffrey Davis
Head Carpenter ....Chris Wiggins
Head Propertyman ....Timothy Walters
Sound Engineer ....Louis Shapiro
Master Electrician ....Jeff Dodson
Wardrobe Supervisor ....Angela Simpson
Apprentices ....Michael DiMarco,
   Ian Harbor
Chief Engineer ....Deosarran
Maintenance Engineers ....Ricky Deosarran,
   Maximo Perez
Security ....Initial Security
Lobby Refreshments ....Sweet Concessions

To Be or Not To Be
SCRAPBOOK

Correspondent: Brandon Perler, "Young Grunberg"

Memorable Opening Night Note: David Rasche's note calling me a 'little imp' and that he really enjoyed working with me.

Opening Night Gifts: Huge candy bucket from my managers at J. Mitchell Mgmt., Frankenstein mug from David Rasche, Identity Crisis game from Marina Squerciati, chocolate from Kristine Nielsen, keychain from Rocco Sisto, framed *To Be or Not to Be* poster from Manhattan Theatre Club.

Most Exciting Celebrity Visitors and What They Did/Said: Jerry Stiller and Anne Meara who complimented me.

Which Actors Performed the Most Roles in This Show: Jimmy Smagula and Rocco Sisto play two roles each.

Special Backstage Rituals: I do a little jig before I go on. Peter Benson says the alphabet four times in a row really fast. Marina Squerciati does tongue twisters.

Favorite Moments During Each Performance: When I do my Shylock alone on stage at the end of the show. When we all sing the song at the end. When I grab the vodka bottle and try to open it.

Favorite In-Theatre Gathering Place: My dressing room because it's bright, festive and fun. We have lots of decorations, especially for Halloween. We play music and games. There is a lot of laughter with Dante Baldassin, my understudy, and Cerissa Kimball, our wrangler. The other actors love to come visit.

Favorite Off-Site Hangout: I spend most of my time in my dad's office at MTV which is only two blocks away. I eat in restaurants most days with my mom or dad, such as Cafe Pigalle, Bread Factory, Bella Vita Brick Oven, John's Pizzeria

Favorite Snack Food: Chocolate chip cookies.

Record Number of Cell Phone Rings, Cell Phone Photos or Texting Incidents During a Performance: So far, 12 cell phone rings. We like to keep count.

Memorable Press Encounter: Opening night red carpet at the theatre and at the party at Planet Hollywood. I didn't want it to end.

Memorable Stage Door Fan Encounter: When 60 of my friends came to see the show!

Fastest Costume Change: We all have really quick changes, but we did it! My quickest is a 30-second change from a Nazi youth uniform into a wool suit.

Who Wore the Heaviest/Hottest Costume: The capes that Robert Dorfman and Peter Benson wore in their *Hamlet* scene.

Memorable Directorial Note: When the director, Casey Nicholaw, told me I was doing great and I didn't need to change anything.

Coolest Thing About Being in This Show: I loved the creative process of rehearsals and tech week. I really enjoyed working with the other actors and getting to know the crew. It was also fun being a company deputy with Steve Kazee. It is so special to be a part of this show and part of Broadway history. I'll always appreciate this opportunity and hope to do more shows.

1. Curtain call on opening night.
2. Jan Maxwell arrives at Planet Hollywood for the cast party.
3. Director Casey Nicholaw at the premiere.
4. Kristine Nielsen at Planet Hollywood.
5. Michael McCarty at the cast party.
6. (L-R): Brandon Perler and Robert Dorfman on opening night.

Waiting for Godot

First Preview: April 3, 2009. Opened: April 30, 2009.
Still running as of May 31, 2009.

PLAYBILL

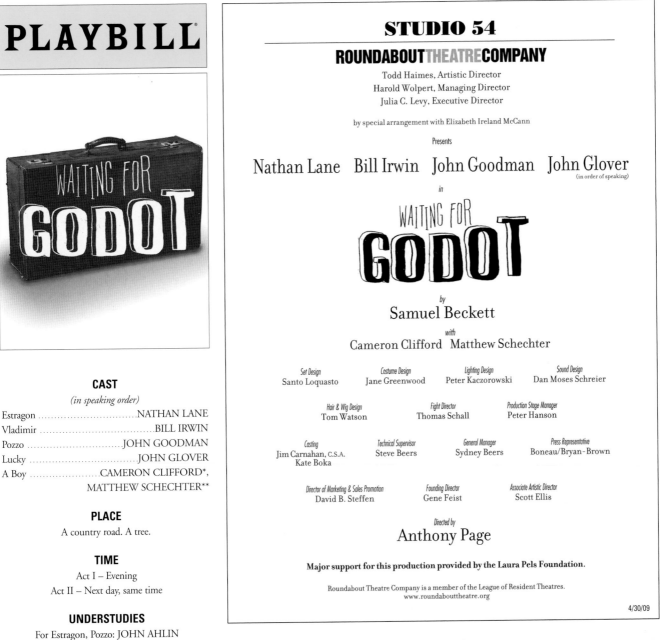

CAST
(in speaking order)

Estragon ....NATHAN LANE
Vladimir ....BILL IRWIN
Pozzo ....JOHN GOODMAN
Lucky ....JOHN GLOVER
A Boy ....CAMERON CLIFFORD*,
MATTHEW SCHECHTER**

PLACE
A country road. A tree.

TIME
Act I – Evening
Act II – Next day, same time

UNDERSTUDIES
For Estragon, Pozzo: JOHN AHLIN
For Vladimir, Lucky: ANTHONY NEWFIELD

*Mr. Clifford appears on Tuesday through
Saturday nights and Sunday matinees.
**Mr. Schechter appears on Wednesday matinees
and Saturday matinees.

Production Stage Manager: PETER HANSON
Stage Manager: JON KRAUSE

STUDIO 54

ROUNDABOUTTHEATRECOMPANY

Todd Haimes, Artistic Director
Harold Wolpert, Managing Director
Julia C. Levy, Executive Director

by special arrangement with Elizabeth Ireland McCann

Presents

Nathan Lane   Bill Irwin   John Goodman   John Glover
(in order of speaking)

in

WAITING FOR GODOT

by
Samuel Beckett

with
Cameron Clifford   Matthew Schechter

Set Design	*Costume Design*	*Lighting Design*	*Sound Design*
Santo Loquasto	Jane Greenwood	Peter Kaczorowski	Dan Moses Schreier

Hair & Wig Design	*Fight Director*	*Production Stage Manager*
Tom Watson	Thomas Schall	Peter Hanson

Casting	*Technical Supervisor*	*General Manager*	*Press Representative*
Jim Carnahan, C.S.A. Kate Boka	Steve Beers	Sydney Beers	Boneau/Bryan-Brown

Director of Marketing & Sales Promotion	*Founding Director*	*Associate Artistic Director*
David B. Steffen	Gene Feist	Scott Ellis

Directed by
Anthony Page

Major support for this production provided by the Laura Pels Foundation.

Roundabout Theatre Company is a member of the League of Resident Theatres.
www.roundabouttheatre.org

4/30/09

(L-R): John Glover, Bill Irwin, Nathan Lane and John Goodman

Photo by Joan Marcus

The Playbill Broadway Yearbook 2008-2009

Waiting for Godot

Nathan Lane
Estragon

Bill Irwin
Vladimir

John Goodman
Pozzo

John Glover
Lucky

Cameron Clifford
A Boy

Matthew Schechter
A Boy

John Ahlin
u/s Estragon, Pozzo

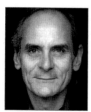
Anthony Newfield
u/s Vladimir, Lucky

Samuel Beckett
Playwright

Anthony Page
Director

Santo Loquasto
Set Design

Jane Greenwood
Costume Design

Peter Kaczorowski
Lighting Design

Dan Moses Schreier
Sound Design

Jim Carnahan
Casting

Gene Feist
*Founding Director,
Roundabout Theatre
Company*

Todd Haimes
*Artistic Director,
Roundabout Theatre
Company*

ROUNDABOUT THEATRE COMPANY STAFF
ARTISTIC DIRECTOR ....TODD HAIMES
MANAGING DIRECTOR ....HAROLD WOLPERT
EXECUTIVE DIRECTOR ....JULIA C. LEVY
ASSOCIATE ARTISTIC DIRECTOR ...SCOTT ELLIS

ARTISTIC STAFF
DIRECTOR OF ARTISTIC DEVELOPMENT/
DIRECTOR OF CASTING ....Jim Carnahan
Artistic Consultant ....Robyn Goodman
Resident Director ....Doug Hughes
Associate Artists ....Scott Elliott, Bill Irwin,
Joe Mantello, Mark Brokaw,
Kathleen Marshall
Literary Manager ....Jill Rafson
Casting Director ....Carrie Gardner
Casting Associate ....Kate Boka
Casting Associate ....Stephen Kopel
Artistic Associate ....Erica Rotstein
Literary Associate ....Josh Fiedler
The Blanche and Irving Laurie Foundation
Theatre Visions Fund Commissions ....Julia Cho,
Stephen Karam, Nathan Louis Jackson

Educational Foundation of
America Commissions ....Lydia Diamond,
Julie Marie Myatt
New York State Council
on the Arts Commission ....Nathan Louis Jackson
Roundabout Commissions ....Steven Levenson,
Robert Lopez & Kristen Anderson-Lopez,
Lynn Nottage
Artistic Intern ....Leslie Hart
Casting Interns ....Kyle Bosley, Jillian Cimini,
Erin Drake, Andrew Femenella,
Lauren Lewis, Quinn Meyers

EDUCATION STAFF
EDUCATION DIRECTOR ....**Greg McCaslin**
Director of Instruction and
Curriculum Development ....Renée Flemings
Education Program Manager ....Jennifer DiBella
Education Associate
for Theatre-Based Programs ....Jay Gerlach
Education Coordinator ....Aliza Greenberg
Education Dramaturg ....Ted Sod
Teaching Artists ....Cynthia Babak,

Victor Barbella, LaTonya Borsay,
Mark Bruckner, Joe Clancy, Vanessa Davis,
Joe Doran, Elizabeth Dunn-Ruiz,
Janet Edwards, Kevin Free, Tony Freeman,
Sheri Graubert, Matthew A.J. Gregory,
Melissa Gregus, Adam Gwon, Devin Haqq,
Carrie Heitman, Karla Hendrick, Jim Jack,
Jason Jacobs, Lisa Renee Jordan,
Jamie Kalama, Alvin Keith, Tami Mansfield,
Erin McCready, Deidre O'Connor,
Andrew Ondrejcak, Maya Parra, Laura Poe,
Jennifer Rathbone, Leah Reddy,
Amanda Rehbein, Bernita Robinson,
Christopher Rummel, Cassy Rush,
Nick Simone, Heidi Stallings, Daniel Sullivan,
Carl Tallent, Vickie Tanner, Jolie Tong,
Cristina Vaccaro, Jennifer Varbalow,
Leese Walker, Eric Wallach, Christina Watanabe,
Gail Winar, Conwell Worthington, III
Teaching Artist Apprentices ....Carrie Ellman-Larsen,
Deanna Frieman, Meghan O'Neill
Education Interns ....Sarah Best, Allison Bressi

Waiting for Godot

FRONT OF HOUSE STAFF
Front Row (L-R): Linda Gjonbalaj, Delila Rivera, Stella Varriale, Valerie Simmons, unknown.

Back Row (L-R): Nick Wheatley, Diana Trent, Nicole Ramirez, Elicia Edwards, Connie Robinson

CREW
Kneeling (L-R): Dan Schultheis, Dan Mendeloff

Standing (L-R): John Wooding, Steve Jones, Elisa Acevedo, Nadine Hettel, Joe Hickey

MANAGEMENT
(L-R): Peter Hanson, Denise Cooper, Jon Krause

BOX OFFICE
(L-R): Kayrose Pagan, Joe Clark, Krystin MacRitchie, Scott Falkowski

Waiting for Godot

ADMINISTRATIVE STAFF

GENERAL MANAGER ....**Sydney Beers**
Associate Managing Director ....Greg Backstrom
General Manager,
    American Airlines Theatre ....Rebecca Habel
General Manager, Steinberg Center ....Rachel Ayers
Human Resources Manager ....Stephen Deutsch
MIS Director ....Jeff Goodman
Operations Manager ....Valerie D. Simmons
Associate General Manager ....Maggie Cantrick
Office Manager ....Scott Kelly
MIS Database Administrator ....Micah Kraybill
MIS Associate ....Dylan Norden
Assistant to the Managing Director..........Rebecca Skoff
Archivist ....Tiffany Nixon
Receptionists ....Dee Beider, Raquel Castillo,
    Elisa Papa, Allison Patrick,
    Monica Sidorchuk
Messenger ....Darnell Franklin
Management Intern ....Jill Boyd

FINANCE STAFF

DIRECTOR OF FINANCE ....**Susan Neiman**
Assistant Controller.......................John LaBarbera
Accounts Payable Administrator ....Frank Surdi
Financial Associate ....Yonit Kafka
Business Office Assistant ....Joshua Cohen
Business Interns ....Laura Marshall, Richard Patterson,
    Jaclyn Verbitski

DEVELOPMENT STAFF

Director, Institutional Giving ....Julie K. D'Andrea
Director, Special Events ....Steve Schaeffer
Director, Major Gifts ....Joy Pak
Director, Patron Programs ....Amber Jo Manuel
Manager, Donor Information Systems ....Lise Speidel
Manager, Patron Programs ....Eric Scott
Manager, Telefundraising ....Gavin Brown
Manager, Corporate Relations ....Roxana Petzold
Patron Programs Associate ....Marisa Perry
Special Events Associate ....Ashley Firestone
Patron Services Associate ....David Pittman
Institutional Giving Associate ....Nick Nolte
Development Assistants........................Ryan Hallett,
    Nick Luckenbaugh
Assistant to the Executive Director ....David Jones, Jr.
Special Events Intern.....................Jennifer Whitton

MARKETING STAFF

DIRECTOR OF MARKETING
    AND SALES PROMOTION ....**David B. Steffen**
Associate Director of Marketing...........Wendy Hutton
Marketing/Publications Manager .....Margaret Casagrande
Marketing Manager ....Stefanie Schussel
Marketing Associate ....Shannon Marcotte
Website Consultant ....Keith Powell Beyland
DIRECTOR OF TELESALES
    SPECIAL PROMOTIONS ....**Marco Frezza**
Telesales Manager ....Anthony Merced
Telesales Office Coordinator ....Patrick Pastor
Marketing Interns ....Ashleigh Awusie, Candace Simon

TICKET SERVICES STAFF

DIRECTOR OF
    SALES OPERATIONS ....**Charlie Garbowski, Jr.**
Ticket Services Manager ....Ellen Holt

Subscription Manager ....Ethan Ubell
Box Office Managers ....Edward P. Osborne,
    Andrew Clements, Jaime Perlman
Group Sales Manager ....Jeff Monteith
Assistant Box Office Managers ....Krystin MacRitchie,
    Robert Morgan, Nicole Nicholson
Customer Services Coordinator ....Thomas Walsh
Assistant Ticket Services Managers ....Robert Kane,
    Bill Klemm, Carlos Morris
Ticket Services ....Solangel Bido, Lauren Cartelli,
    Joseph Clark, Barbara Dente, Nisha Dhruna,
    Adam Elsberry, Lindsay Ericson, Scott Falkowski,
    Catherine Fitzpatrick, James Graham,
    Kara Harrington, Tova Heller, Nicki Ishmael,
    Kate Longosky, Elisa Mala, Mead Margulies,
    Chuck Migliaccio, Kayrose Pagan,
    Thomas Protulipac, Jessica Pruett-Barnett,
    Kaia Rafoss, Josh Rozett, Ben Schneider,
    Kenneth Senn, Heather Siebert, Nalene Singh,
    Lillian Soto, Hannah Weitzman, Paul Winkler
Ticket Services Intern ....Reñe Bionat

SERVICES

Counsel ....Paul Weiss, Rifkind,
    Wharton and Garrison LLP,
    Charles H. Googe Jr., Carol M. Kaplan
Counsel ....Rosenberg & Estis
Counsel ....Andrew Lance,
    Gibson, Dunn, & Crutcher, LLP
Counsel ....Harry H. Weintraub,
    Glick and Weintraub, P.C.
Counsel ....Strook & Strook & Lavan LLP
Immigration Counsel ....Mark D. Koestler and
    Theodore Ruthizer
Government
    Relations ....Law Offices of Claudia Wagner LLC
House Physicians ....Dr. Theodore Tyberg,
    Dr. Lawrence Katz
House Dentist ....Neil Kanner, D.M.D.
Insurance ....DeWitt Stern Group, Inc.
Accountant ....Lutz & Carr CPAs, LLP
Advertising ....Spotco/
    Drew Hodges, Jim Edwards,
    Tom Greenwald, Kyle Hall,
    Beth Watson
Sponsorship ....Allied Live/
    Tanya Grubich, Laura Matalon,
    Meghan Zaneski
Interactive Marketing ....Situation Marketing/
    Damian Bazadona, John Lanasa,
    Ryan Klink, Kristen Butler
Events Photography ....Anita and Steve Shevett
Production Photographer ....Joan Marcus
Theatre Displays ....King Displays, Wayne Sapper
Lobby Refreshments ....Sweet Concessions
Merchandising ....Marquee Merchandise, LLC/
    Matt Murphy
Theatre and Lobby Rentals Available
    by calling ....Nancy Mulliner at Roundabout

MANAGING DIRECTOR
    EMERITUS ....Ellen Richard

Roundabout Theatre Company
231 West 39th Street, New York, NY 10018
(212) 719-9393.

GENERAL PRESS REPRESENTATIVES

BONEAU/BRYAN-BROWN
Adrian Bryan-Brown
Matt Polk   Jessica Johnson   Amy Kass

STAFF FOR *WAITING FOR GODOT*

Company Manager ....Denise Cooper
Production Stage Manager ....Peter Hanson
Stage Manager ....Jon Krause
Assistant Director ....Wes Grantom
Associate Set Designer ....Jenny Sawyers
Associate Costume Designer ....MaryAnn D. Smith
Assistant to the Costume Designer..........Anya Klepikov
Assistant Lighting Designer ....Keri Thibodeau
Associate Sound Designer ....David Bullard
Make-up Designer ....Angelina Avallone
Assistant Make-up Artist ....Benedetta Celada
Production Carpenter ....Dan Hoffman
Production Electrician ....Josh Weitzman
Assistant Production Electrician ....John Wooding
Production Properties ....Kathy Fabian, Propstar Inc.
Assistant Production Properties ....Carrie Mossman
House Properties ....Lawrence Jennino
Local One IATSE Apprentice ....Dan Schultheis
Production Sound Engineer ....David Gotwald
Wardrobe Supervisor ....Nadine Hettel
Dresser ....Joe Hickey
Hair & Wig Supervisor ....Elisa Acevedo
Production Assistant ....Rachel Bauder
Children's Tutoring
    provided by ....On Location Education
Child Wrangler ....Jill Valentine
Company Manager Intern ....Chris Minnick
Special Thanks ....Rachel Bress

CREDITS

Scenery fabrication by Showman Fabricators, Inc. and Global Scenic Services. Lighting equipment by PRG Lighting. Audio equipment by PRG Audio. Costumes by Eric Winterling, Inc. and John David Ridge, Inc. Custom boots by Montana Leatherworks, Ltd. Painting and dyeing by Izquierdo Studio. Soft goods by I. Weiss.

Make-up Provided by M•A•C

Waiting for Godot is presented through a special arrangement with Georges Borchardt, Inc., on behalf of the Estate of Samuel Beckett.

STUDIO 54 THEATRE STAFF

Box Office Manager ....Jaime Perlman
House Manager ....LaConya Robinson
Associate House Manager ....Jack Watanachaiyot
House Staff ....Justin Brown, Elicia Edwards,
    Linda Gjonbalaj, Hajjah Karriem,
    Jennifer Kneeland, Jonathan Martinez,
    Essence Mason, Nicole Ramirez,
    Delila Rivera, Diana Trent,
    Stella Varriale, Nick Wheatley
House Carpenter ....Dan Hoffman
House Electrician ....Josh Weitzman
House Properties ....Lawrence Jennino
Security ....Gotham Security
Maintenance ....Ralph Mohan, Maman Garba
Lobby Refreshments by ....Sweet Concessions

Waiting for Godot
SCRAPBOOK

Correspondent: John Ahlin, Understudy "Pozzo" and "Estragon"

On Performing the (Arguably) Greatest Play of the 20th Century: The four actors, inarguably great in their own rights, treated performing the play with a kind of reverence. The words are so deep, the characters so rich, the sadness so honest and the comedy so genuine that each show was an exhausting, exhilarating mountain to climb. There was no coasting.

The Preferred Pronunciation: A good deal of discussion was expended during rehearsal about the pronunciation of "Godot" and what American audiences would think. The director, Anthony Page, worked with Samuel Beckett in 1964 on the first English revival of *Waiting for Godot*. He told all that Beckett pronounced it "GOD-oh." And so it was.

Backstage Mood: With all the actors mostly onstage for the whole show and *Waiting for Godot* coming over the loudspeakers, the backstage mood was very low-key. Beckett's masterpiece of futility and hope had its way of seeping into the psyche. Crew members would catch themselves walking around pondering the meaning of life.

Celebrity Moment: One cast member met Jeremy Irons at an awards ceremony and Jeremy said "I'm coming Tuesday. Astound me." Well, karma reared its ironic head as this nameless actor began his long, famously dense speech as he usually does, by staring out into the yawning void of his character's memory. This particular Tuesday night he fixed his eyes on a point only to discover that the point was occupied by Jeremy Irons' eyes, staring back at him. The character's rambling incoherence was amplified by half a line of the actor's rambling incoherence. The actor recovered and did indeed "astound."

Favorite In-Theater Gathering Place: The wardrobe room. Actors would often gather before the play for gab and psychotherapy, calmly talking about life and show business and business in the show and analyzing the vast array of audience responses to the play.

Mascots: The show has three: Two 8-year-old boys with boundless energy, sharing the role of 'boy'; and one dog, Phoebe, a Morkie (half Maltese, half Yorkie) who was brought by the hairdresser on two-show days. You can tell the three mascots apart because the dog obeys commands.

Interesting Media Fact: Both Nathan Lane and John Goodman appeared on the David Letterman show. To do so they simply had to exit our stage door, turn left, walk exactly 39 steps and they were at Letterman's stage door.

An Audience Member to Remember: During a matinee early in the run, a patron jumped up screaming, "Let me outta here, let me outta here! I gotta get out of here!" He was ushered gently by the Studio 54 staff out to the street. It was a moment Beckett would have loved.

Favorite Moment During Each Performance: In a play of continually wonderful moments,

1. (L-R): Nathan Lane, director Anthony Page and Bill Irwin on stage before the opening night performance.
2. (L-R) Cast members Matthew Schechter and Cameron Clifford at the premiere.
3. (L-R): Cast members John Goodman and John Glover at the premiere.

both audience and cast enjoyed the moment when Gogo (Nathan Lane) and Didi (Bill Irwin) verbally abuse each other with escalating insults of the worst things to call someone. Lane's Gogo coup d'états by calling Didi a "Critic!" to a huge laugh. The laugh is then topped when Irwin's Didi collapses in humiliated defeat.

Most Memorable Ad-Lib: All the actors were careful to get every word correct, as the rhythm of Beckett is so beautiful in its precision. However, there was one moment when Gogo contemplates whipping Lucky in a fit of vengeance. Nathan Lane vividly demonstrated with both comic genius and a very loud whip just how he might do it. Often the whip would get tangled in the tree and Bill and Nathan's cleverness in getting it untangled was not to be missed. When that part of the play came up, all the backstage crew would rush to monitors to watch.

Busiest Day at the Box Office: The box office reported that on the day after opening, *Waiting for Godot* sold more tickets in one day than any previous show in Roundabout history, play or musical. It continued to "sell like a musical" all the way through its successful run.

Cell Phone Incident: Roundabout has a marvelous policy of including a school matinee in its runs, full of well-prepared and highly appreciative students. At this particular matinee a teacher's cell phone went off, and as ushers reported, every single student within a 30 seat radius turned and glared in unison. That teacher probably had a delightful bus ride home.

Fastest Costume Change: In a play with five actors and five costumes there are no costume changes. The previous show at 54, *Pal Joey*, had nearly 300 costumes, with 70 shirts needing ironing every night. The *Godot* costume crew got a lot of Sudoku in.

Heaviest Costume: John Glover as Lucky the lackey had heavy weights hidden in his costume to help him appeared beleaguered. His harrowing performance did indeed carry the weight of the world.

Nicknames: The two Johns, John Glover and John Goodman were known as J-Glo and Goodie to tell them apart. Bill and Nathan were called Bill and Nathan. Samuel Beckett's presence was felt throughout and he was referred to as Sam.

Favorite Catchphrase from the Show: "Nothing to be done." It accurately describes moments of a life in the theatre.

Ghostly Encounters Onstage: At a poignant moment in the show Gogo and Didi imagine they are hearing voices. It was marvelous to ponder that as the audience at Roundabout's Studio 54 filled the air with raucous laughs, they might be mingling with the still rolling remnants of long ago laughs generated by the likes of Johnny Carson and Jack Benny and the thousands of other actors and entertainers who have called the vast empty space home.

Coolest Thing About Being in this Show: The audience reactions. After the show, audience members were heard blocks away still discussing what it all means. Beckett's tragicomedy still resonates, and rarely fails to elicit a thoughtful laugh or emotional pang. As John Goodman's character, Pozzo, says: "The tears of the world are a constant quantity…The same is true of the laugh."

Photos by Aubrey Reuben

West Side Story

First Preview: February 23, 2009. Opened: March 19, 2009.
Still running as of May 31, 2009.

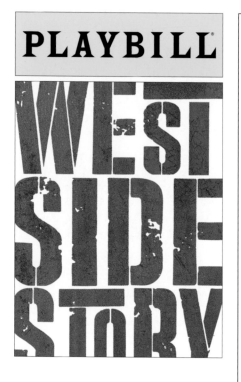

CAST

The Jets

Action	CURTIS HOLBROOK
Anybodys	TRO SHAW
A-rab	KYLE COFFMAN
Baby John	RYAN STEELE
Big Deal	ERIC HATCH
Diesel	JOSHUA BUSCHER
Graziella	PAMELA OTTERSON
Hotsie	MARINA LAZZARETTO
Kiddo	NICHOLAS BARASCH, KYLE BRENN (Wed. & Sat. mat.)
Mugsy	AMY RYERSON
Riff	CODY GREEN
Snowboy	MIKE CANNON
Tony	MATT CAVENAUGH
Velma	LINDSAY DUNN
Zaza	KAITLIN MESH
4H	SAM ROGERS

The Sharks

Alicia	YANIRA MARIN
Anita	KAREN OLIVO
Bebecita	MILEYKA MATEO
Bernardo	GEORGE AKRAM
Bolo	PETER CHURSIN
Chino	JOEY HARO
Consuela	DANIELLE POLANCO
Federico	MICHAEL ROSEN
Fernanda	KAT NEJAT
Inca	ISAAC CALPITO
Indio	MANUEL SANTOS

Continued on next page

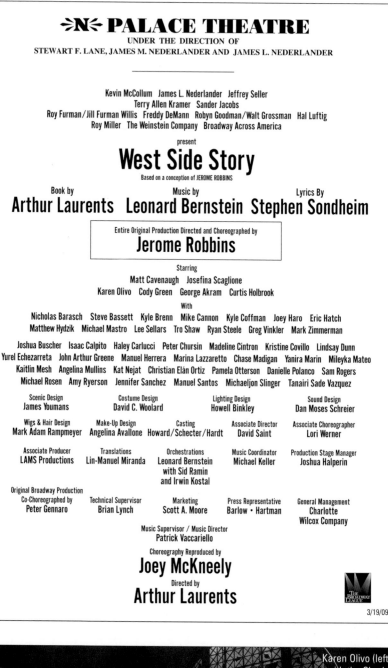

⊱N⊰ PALACE THEATRE
UNDER THE DIRECTION OF
STEWART F. LANE, JAMES M. NEDERLANDER AND JAMES L. NEDERLANDER

Kevin McCollum   James L. Nederlander   Jeffrey Seller
Terry Allen Kramer   Sander Jacobs
Roy Furman/Jill Furman Willis   Freddy DeMann   Robyn Goodman/Walt Grossman   Hal Luftig
Roy Miller   The Weinstein Company   Broadway Across America

present

West Side Story
Based on a conception of JEROME ROBBINS

Book by	Music by	Lyrics By
Arthur Laurents	**Leonard Bernstein**	**Stephen Sondheim**

Entire Original Production Directed and Choreographed by
Jerome Robbins

Starring

Matt Cavenaugh   Josefina Scaglione
Karen Olivo   Cody Green   George Akram   Curtis Holbrook

With

Nicholas Barasch   Steve Bassett   Kyle Brenn   Mike Cannon   Kyle Coffman   Joey Haro   Eric Hatch
Matthew Hydzik   Michael Mastro   Lee Sellars   Tro Shaw   Ryan Steele   Greg Vinkler   Mark Zimmerman

Joshua Buscher   Isaac Calpito   Haley Carlucci   Peter Chursin   Madeline Cintron   Kristine Covillo   Lindsay Dunn
Yurel Echezarreta   John Arthur Greene   Manuel Herrera   Marina Lazzaretto   Chase Madigan   Yanira Marin   Mileyka Mateo
Kaitlin Mesh   Angelina Mullins   Kat Nejat   Christian Elán Ortiz   Pamela Otterson   Danielle Polanco   Sam Rogers
Michael Rosen   Amy Ryerson   Jennifer Sanchez   Manuel Santos   Michaeljon Slinger   Tanairi Sade Vazquez

Scenic Design	Costume Design	Lighting Design	Sound Design
James Youmans	David C. Woolard	Howell Binkley	Dan Moses Schreier

Wigs & Hair Design	Make-Up Design	Casting	Associate Director	Associate Choreographer
Mark Adam Rampmeyer	Angelina Avallone	Howard/Schecter/Hardt	David Saint	Lori Werner

Associate Producer	Translations	Orchestrations	Music Coordinator	Production Stage Manager
LAMS Productions	Lin-Manuel Miranda	Leonard Bernstein with Sid Ramin and Irwin Kostal	Michael Keller	Joshua Halperin

Original Broadway Production Co-Choreographed by	Technical Supervisor	Marketing	Press Representative	General Management
Peter Gennaro	Brian Lynch	Scott A. Moore	Barlow • Hartman	Charlotte Wilcox Company

Music Supervisor / Music Director
Patrick Vaccariello

Choreography Reproduced by
Joey McKneely

Directed by
Arthur Laurents

3/19/09

Karen Olivo (left) with the Sharks

Photo by Joan Marcus

West Side Story

SCENES AND MUSICAL NUMBERS

ACT ONE

Scene 1: The Neighborhood
"Prologue" .... The Sharks and the Jets
"Jet Song" .... Riff and the Jets

Scene 2: Outside Doc's Drugstore
"Something's Coming" .... Tony

Scene 3: Bridal Shop

Scene 4: The Gym
"Dance at the Gym" .... Company
"Maria" .... Tony

Scene 5: Alleyways
"Tonight" .... Tony and Maria
"America" .... Anita, Rosalia and Shark Girls

Scene 6: The Drugstore
"Cool" .... Riff, Jet Boys and Jet Girls

Scene 7: Bridal Shop
"One Hand, One Heart" .... Tony and Maria

Scene 8: The Neighborhood
"Tonight" (Quintet) .... Company

Scene 9: Under the Highway
"The Rumble"

ACT TWO

Scene 1: Maria's Bedroom
"Siento Hermosa" ("I Feel Pretty") .... Maria, Rosalia, Consuela and Fernanda
"Somewhere" .... Kiddo, Tony, Maria and Company

Scene 2: The Neighborhood
"Gee, Officer Krupke" .... Action and the Jets

Scene 3: Maria's Bedroom
"Un Hombre Asi" ("A Boy Like That")/"I Have a Love" .... Anita and Maria

Scene 4: The Drugstore

Scene 5: The Cellar

Scene 6: The Neighborhood

Cast Continued

Lupe .... TANAIRI SADE VAZQUEZ
Maria .... JOSEFINA SCAGLIONE
Pepe .... MANUEL HERRERA
Rosalia .... JENNIFER SANCHEZ
Tio .... YUREL ECHEZARRETA

The Adults

Doc .... GREG VINKLER
Glad Hand .... MICHAEL MASTRO
Krupke .... LEE SELLARS
Lt. Schrank .... STEVE BASSETT

SWINGS

HALEY CARLUCCI, MADELINE CINTRON,
KRISTINE COVILLO,
JOHN ARTHUR GREENE, CHASE MADIGAN,
ANGELINA MULLINS,
CHRISTIAN ELÁN ORTIZ,
MICHAELJON SLINGER

UNDERSTUDIES

For Action: ERIC HATCH,
    JOHN ARTHUR GREENE
For Anita: YANIRA MARIN, KAT NEJAT
For Anybodys: PAMELA OTTERSON,
    KAITLIN MESH
For A-rab: SAM ROGERS, CHASE MADIGAN
For Baby John: CHASE MADIGAN,
    SAM ROGERS
For Bernardo: MANUEL HERRERA,
    MANUEL SANTOS
For Big Deal: JOSHUA BUSCHER,
    SAM ROGERS
For Chino: MANUEL SANTOS,
    MICHAEL ROSEN
For Consuela: YANIRA MARIN,
    TANAIRI SADE VAZQUEZ
For Diesel: MICHAELJON SLINGER,
    JOHN ARTHUR GREENE
For Fernanda: HALEY CARLUCCI,
    YANIRA MARIN

For Glad Hand: MICHAELJON SLINGER
For Graziella: AMY RYERSON, LINDSAY DUNN
For Maria: HALEY CARLUCCI, KAT NEJAT
For Riff: MIKE CANNON,
    JOHN ARTHUR GREENE
For Rosalia: HALEY CARLUCCI, KAT NEJAT
For Snowboy: MICHAELJON SLINGER,
    CHASE MADIGAN
For Tony: MIKE CANNON
Standby for Tony: MATTHEW HYDZIK
Standby for Doc, Glad Hand, Krupke, Lt. Schrank:
    MARK ZIMMERMAN

Dance Captain .... MARINA LAZZARETTO
Asst. Dance Captain ..... MICHAELJON SLINGER
Fight Captain .... JOSHUA BUSCHER

Josefina Scaglione appears with the permission of
Actors' Equity Association.

SETTING

Upper West Side of New York City

ORCHESTRA

Conductor: PATRICK VACCARIELLO
Associate Conductor: MAGGIE TORRE
Concertmaster: MARTIN AGEE
Violins: PAUL WOODIEL, ROB SHAW,
    VICTORIA PATERSON,
    FRITZ KRAKOWSKI, DANA IANCULOVICI,
    PHILIP PAYTON
Cellos: PETER PROSSER, VIVIAN ISRAEL,
    DIANE BARERE, JENNIFER LANG
Bass: BILL SLOAT
Reed 1: LAWRENCE FELDMAN
Reed 2: LINO GOMEZ
Reed 3: DAN WILLIS
Reed 4: ADAM KOLKER
Reed 5: GILBERT DeJEAN
Lead Trumpet: JOHN CHUDOBA
Trumpets: TREVOR NEUMANN,
    MATT PETERSON
Trombone: TIM ALBRIGHT
Bass Trombone: JEFF NELSON
French Horns: CHRIS KOMER,
    THERESA MacDONNELL
Piano: MAGGIE TORRE
Keyboard: JIM LAEV
Drums: ERIC POLAND
Percussion: DAN McMILLAN, PABLO RIEPPI
Music Coordinator: MICHAEL KELLER
Keyboard Programmer: RANDY COHEN

West Side Story

Matt Cavenaugh
Tony

Josefina Scaglione
Maria

Karen Olivo
Anita

Cody Green
Riff

George Akram
Bernardo

Curtis Holbrook
Action

Steve Bassett
Lt. Schrank

Mike Cannon
Snowboy

Kyle Coffman
A-rab

Joey Haro
Chino

Eric Hatch
Big Deal

Matthew Hydzik
Tony Standby

Michael Mastro
Glad Hand

Lee Sellars
Krupke

Tro Shaw
Anybodys

Ryan Steele
Baby John

Greg Vinkler
Doc

Mark Zimmerman
Adult Standby

Nicholas Barasch
Kiddo

Kyle Brenn
*Kiddo at Wed. & Sat.
mat. performances*

Joshua Buscher
Diesel

Isaac Calpito
Inca

Haley Carlucci
Maria Standby

Peter Chursin
Bolo

Madeline Cintron
Swing

Kristine Covillo
Swing

Lindsay Dunn
Velma

Yurel Echezarreta
Tio

John Arthur Greene
Swing

Manuel Herrera
Pepe

Marina Lazzaretto
*Hotsie;
Dance Captain*

Chase Madigan
Jet Swing

Yanira Marin
Alicia

Mileyka Mateo
Bebecita

Kaitlin Mesh
Zaza

West Side Story

Angelina Mullins
Swing

Kat Nejat
Fernanda

Christian Elán Ortiz
Shark Swing

Pamela Otterson
Graziella

Danielle Polanco
Consuela

Sam Rogers
4H

Michael Rosen
Federico

Amy Ryerson
Mugsy

Jennifer Sanchez
Rosalia

Manuel Santos
Indio

Michaeljon Slinger
Swing

Tanairi Sade Vazquez
Lupe

Arthur Laurents
Book, Director

Leonard Bernstein
Music

Stephen Sondheim
Lyrics

Jerome Robbins
Choreography

Joey McKneely and Lori Werner
*Reproduction Choreographer;
Associate Choreographer*

Patrick Vaccariello
Music Director

David C. Woolard
Costume Design

Howell Binkley
Lighting Design

Dan Moses Schreier
Sound Design

David Saint
Associate Director

Lin-Manuel Miranda
Translations

Charlotte Wilcox
The Charlotte Wilcox
Company
General Manager

Brian Lynch
Technical Supervisor

Kevin McCollum
Producer

James L.
Nederlander
Producer

Jeffrey Seller
Producer

Terry Allen Kramer
Producer

Freddy DeMann
Producer

Roy Furman
Producer

Jill Furman Willis
Producer

Robyn Goodman
Producer

Hal Luftig
Producer

West Side Story

Roy Miller
Producer

Bob Weinstein,
The Weinstein
Company
Producer

Harvey Weinstein,
The Weinstein
Company
Producer

Aléna Watters
Anita Standby

2008-2009 AWARDS

TONY AWARD
Best Featured Actress in a Musical
(Karen Olivo)

OUTER CRITICS CIRCLE AWARD
Outstanding Actress in a Musical
(Josefina Scaglione)

DRAMA LEAGUE AWARD
Julia Hansen Award
for Excellence in Directing
(Arthur Laurents)

THEATRE WORLD AWARD
First Major New York Appearance
(Josefina Scaglione)

STAFF FOR *WEST SIDE STORY*

GENERAL MANAGEMENT
THE CHARLOTTE WILCOX COMPANY
Charlotte W. Wilcox
Seth Marquette
Matthew W. Krawiec Dina S. Friedler Margaret Wilcox

GENERAL PRESS REPRESENTATIVE
BARLOW•HARTMAN
John Barlow   Michael Hartman
Wayne Wolfe   Matt Shea

COMPANY MANAGER
James Lawson

ASSISTANT COMPANY MANAGER
Erica Ezold

CASTING
STUART HOWARD ASSOCIATES, LTD.
Stuart Howard   Amy Schecter   Paul Hardt

Production Stage Manager ....Joshua Halperin
Stage Manager ....Lisa Dawn Cave
Assistant Stage Manager ....Jason Brouillard
Assistant to the Director ....Isaac Klein
Assistant to Mssrs. McCollum
& Seller ....Caitlyn Thomson
Assistant to Mr. Nederlander ....Ken Happel
Fight Director ....Ron Piretti
Associate Scenic Designer ....Jerome Martin
Assistant Costume Designers ....Robert Martin,
Daryl A. Stone, Maria Zamansky
Assistants to the Costume Designer ....Sara James,
Yuri Cataldo, Angela Harner
Associate Lighting Designer ....Ryan O'Gara
Assistant Lighting Designer ....Carrie Wood
Associate Sound Designer ....David Bullard
Moving Light Programmer ....David Arch
Head Carpenter/TheatreTech Associate ....Chris Kluth
Production Flyman ....Cory Schmidt
Automation Carpenter ....McBrien Dunbar
Advance Automation Carpenter ....Shaun Sites
Head Electrician ....Keith Buchanan
Moving Light Technician ....Chuck Fields
Spotlight Operator ....Patrick Harrington
Production Properties Supervisor ....George Wagner
Head Properties ....Chuck Dague
Sound Engineer ....Lucas Indelicato
Wardrobe Supervisor ....Scott Westervelt

Assistant Wardrobe Supervisor ....Jessica Dermody
Dressers ....Scotty Cain, Stephanie Fox,
Kasey Graham, David Grevengoed,
Sarah Hench, Hector Lugo,
Dorothy Manning, Herb Ouellette,
Roy Seiler, Keith Shaw, Hilda Suli-Garcia
Hair Supervisor ....Paula Schaffer
Assistant Hair Supervisors ....Jennifer Bullock,
Jeanette Harrington
Assistant to Makeup Designer ....Lazaro Arencibia
Assistant Keyboard Programmers ....Bryan Cook,
Jim Mironchik
Production Assistants ....Rachel E. Miller,
Zac Chandler
Language Consultant ....Desiree Rodriguez
Legal Counsel ....Levin, Plotkin & Menin/
Loren Plotkin
Accountants ....Fried & Kowgios LLP/
Robert Fried
Controller ....Galbraith & Co./
Sarah Galbraith
Advertising/Website Design ....SpotCo/
Drew Hodges, Jim Edwards,
Tom Greenwald, Y. Darius Suyama,
Pete Duffy
Children's Tutoring ....On Location Education
Children's Guardian ....Libby Stevens
Press Office Associates ....Leslie Baden,
Michelle Bergmann, Melissa Bixler,
Tom D'Ambrosio, Juliana Hannett
Production Photography......................Joan Marcus
Banking ....JP Morgan Chase/
Stephanie Daulton
Payroll Service ....Castellana Services, Inc.
Physical Therapy ....PhysioArts/
Jennifer Green
Massage Therapist ....Russell Beasley
Orthopedist ....Phillip Bauman, MD
Group Sales ....Nederlander Group Sales
Merchandise ....Creative Goods
Insurance Consultant ......Stockbridge Risk Management
Information Management
Services ....Marion Finkler Taylor
Travel Services ....Tzell Travel/
Andi Henig,
Road Rebel
Tour Booking Agency ....The Booking Group/
Meredith Blair

Rehearsed at New 42nd Street Studios

CREDITS
Scenery built by Hudson Scenic Studio, Inc.; Show Motion, Inc.; Blackthorn Scenic Studio, Inc.; Scenic Art Studios, Inc.; Blackwalnut; Center Line Studios, Inc. Costumes by Tricorne Inc., Barbara Matera Ltd., Eric Winterling Inc., Timberlake Studios Inc., Giliberto Designs Inc., Beckenstein Men's Fabrics Inc. Custom knitwear by Maria Ficalora Knitwear Ltd. Footwear by JC Theatrical & Custom Footwear Inc., Capezio. Millinery by Arnold S. Levine Inc. Undergarments by Bra*Tenders. Costume ageing and distressing by Hochi Asiatico Studio. Accessories by David Samuel Menkes Custom Leatherwear New York. Lighting equipment from PRG Lighting. Sound equipment from PRG Sound. Mannequins and sewing machine provided by Fox Sewing Machines, New York, NY. Cigarette lighters courtesy of Zippo Lighters. Certain props constructed by John Creech Design and Production, Brooklyn, NY. Doc's window and interior shelves set dressing provided by Ann Pinkus, Monmouth Antiques, Red Bank, NJ.

Makeup provided by M•A•C

SPECIAL THANKS
Tom Hatcher, Federico del Piño Gonzales,
Fernando Masorllones

NEDERLANDER

Chairman ....**James M. Nederlander**
President ....**James L. Nederlander**

Executive Vice President
Nick Scandalios

Vice President   Senior Vice President
Corporate Development   Labor Relations
Charlene S. Nederlander   **Herschel Waxman**

Vice President   Chief Financial Officer
Jim Boese   **Freida Sawyer Belviso**

STAFF FOR THE PALACE THEATRE
Theatre Manager ....Dixon Rosario
Treasurer ....Cissy Caspare
Assistant Treasurer ....Anne T. Wilson
Carpenter ....Thomas K. Phillips
Flyman ....Robert W. Kelly
Electrician ....Eddie Webber
Propertymaster ....Steve Camus
Engineer ....Rob O'Connor
Chief Usher ....Gloria Hill

Wicked

First Preview: October 8, 2003. Opened: October 30, 2003.
Still running as of May 31, 2009.

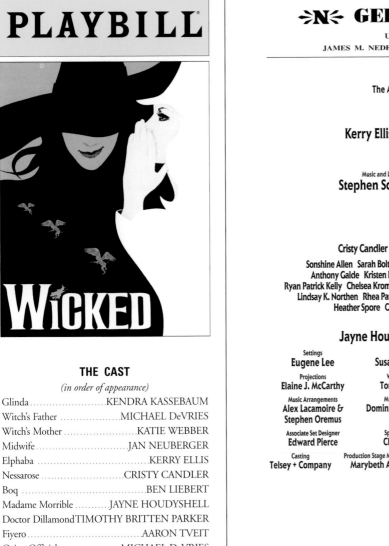

PLAYBILL

THE CAST

(in order of appearance)

Glinda	KENDRA KASSEBAUM
Witch's Father	MICHAEL DeVRIES
Witch's Mother	KATIE WEBBER
Midwife	JAN NEUBERGER
Elphaba	KERRY ELLIS
Nessarose	CRISTY CANDLER
Boq	BEN LIEBERT
Madame Morrible	JAYNE HOUDYSHELL
Doctor Dillamond	TIMOTHY BRITTEN PARKER
Fiyero	AARON TVEIT
Ozian Official	MICHAEL DeVRIES
The Wonderful Wizard of Oz	P.J. BENJAMIN
Chistery	SAM J. CAHN

Monkeys, Students, Denizens of the Emerald City,
Palace Guards and
Other Citizens of Oz .... SONSHINE ALLEN,
SARAH BOLT, JERAD BORTZ,
SAM J. CAHN, MICHAEL DeVRIES,
ADAM FLEMING, TODD HANEBRINK,
REED KELLY, CHELSEA KROMBACH,
KENWAY HON WAI K. KUA,
KYLE DEAN MASSEY, JAN NEUBERGER,
LINDSAY K. NORTHEN, RHEA PATTERSON,
EDDIE PENDERGRAFT,
ALEXANDER QUIROGA,
HEATHER SPORE, CJ TYSON,
BRIAN WANEE, KATIE WEBBER,
ROBIN WILNER

Continued on next page

⋙N⋙ GERSHWIN THEATRE

UNDER THE DIRECTION OF
JAMES M. NEDERLANDER AND JAMES L. NEDERLANDER

Marc Platt
Universal Pictures
The Araca Group and Jon B. Platt
David Stone

present

Kerry Ellis   **Kendra Kassebaum**

WICKED

Music and Lyrics   Book
Stephen Schwartz   **Winnie Holzman**

Based on the novel by Gregory Maguire

with

Aaron Tveit

Cristy Candler   Ben Liebert   Timothy Britten Parker

Sonshine Allen Sarah Bolt Jerad Bortz Sam J. Cahn Michael DeVries Adam Fleming
Anthony Galde Kristen Leigh Gorski Todd Hanebrink Lindsay Janisse Reed Kelly
Ryan Patrick Kelly Chelsea Krombach Kenway Hon Wai K. Kua Kyle Dean Massey Jan Neuberger
Lindsay K. Northen Rhea Patterson Eddie Pendergraft Alexander Quiroga Amanda Rose
Heather Spore CJ Tyson Brian Wanee Katie Webber Robin Wilner

and

Jayne Houdyshell   **P.J. Benjamin**

Settings	Costumes	Lighting	Sound
Eugene Lee	Susan Hilferty	Kenneth Posner	Tony Meola
Projections	Wigs & Hair	Production Supervisor	Technical Supervisor
Elaine J. McCarthy	Tom Watson	Thom Widmann	Jake Bell
Music Arrangements	Music Director	Dance Arrangements	Music Coordinator
Alex Lacamoire &	Dominick Amendum	James Lynn Abbott	Michael Keller
Stephen Oremus			
Associate Set Designer	Special Effects	Associate Choreographer	Associate Director
Edward Pierce	Chic Silber	Corinne McFadden Herrera	Lisa Leguillou
Casting	Production Stage Manager	General Management	Press	Executive Producers
Telsey + Company	Marybeth Abel	321 Theatrical Management	Barlow • Hartman	Marcia Goldberg & Nina Essman

Orchestrations
William David Brohn

Music Supervisor
Stephen Oremus

Musical Staging by
Wayne Cilento

Directed by
Joe Mantello

Grammy Award-winning Original Cast Recording on DECCA BROADWAY

10/1/08

(Center, L-R): Aaron Tveit, Kendra Kassebaum and Jayne Houdyshell with the Ensemble.

Photo by Joan Marcus

Wicked

MUSICAL NUMBERS

ACT I

"No One Mourns the Wicked" ....Glinda and Citizens of Oz
"Dear Old Shiz" ....Students
"The Wizard and I" ....Morrible, Elphaba
"What Is This Feeling?" ....Galinda, Elphaba and Students
"Something Bad" ....Dr. Dillamond and Elphaba
"Dancing Through Life"........................Fiyero, Galinda, Boq, Nessarose, Elphaba and Students
"Popular" ....Galinda
"I'm Not That Girl" ....Elphaba
"One Short Day" ....Elphaba, Glinda and Denizens of the Emerald City
"A Sentimental Man" ....The Wizard
"Defying Gravity" ....Elphaba, Glinda, Guards and Citizens of Oz

ACT II

"No One Mourns the Wicked" (reprise) ....Citizens of Oz
"Thank Goodness" ....Glinda, Morrible and Citizens of Oz
"The Wicked Witch of the East" ....Elphaba, Nessarose and Boq
"Wonderful" ....The Wizard and Elphaba
"I'm Not That Girl" (reprise) ....Glinda
"As Long As You're Mine" ....Elphaba and Fiyero
"No Good Deed" ....Elphaba
"March of the Witch Hunters" ....Boq and Citizens of Oz
"For Good" ....Glinda and Elphaba
"Finale" ....All

ORCHESTRA

Conductor: DOMINICK AMENDUM
Associate Conductor: David Evans
Assistant Conductor: Ben Cohn

Concertmaster: CHRISTIAN HEBEL
Violin: VICTOR SCHULTZ
Viola: KEVIN ROY
Cello: DANNY MILLER
Harp: LAURA SHERMAN
Lead Trumpet: JON OWENS
Trumpet: TOM HOYT
Trombones: DALE KIRKLAND,
    DOUGLAS PURVIANCE
Flute: HELEN CAMPO
Oboe: TUCK LEE
Clarinet/Soprano Sax: JOHN MOSES
Bassoon/Baritone Sax/Clarinets: JOHN CAMPO
French Horns: THEO PRIMIS,
    CHAD YARBROUGH
Drums: MATT VANDERENDE
Bass: KONRAD ADDERLEY
Piano/Synthesizer: BEN COHN
Keyboards: PAUL LOESEL, DAVID EVANS
Guitars: RIC MOLINA, GREG SKAFF
Percussion: ANDY JONES

Music Coordinator: MICHAEL KELLER

Aaron Tveit as Fiyero

Photo by Joan Marcus

UNDERSTUDIES and STANDBYS

Standby for Glinda:
KATIE ADAMS
Standby for Elphaba:
JULIE REIBER

Understudy for Elphaba:
CHELSEA KROMBACH
For Glinda:
LINDSAY K. NORTHEN, HEATHER SPORE
For Fiyero:
JERAD BORTZ, ANTHONY GALDE,
KYLE DEAN MASSEY
For the Wizard and Dr. Dillamond:
MICHAEL DeVRIES, ANTHONY GALDE
For Madame Morrible:
SARAH BOLT, JAN NEUBERGER
For Boq:
ADAM FLEMING, EDDIE PENDERGRAFT
For Nessarose and Midwife:
AMANDA ROSE
For Nessarose:
KATIE WEBBER
For Chistery: REED KELLY
RYAN PATRICK KELLY, CJ TYSON,
BRIAN WANEE
For Witch's Father and Ozian Official:
ANTHONY GALDE, ALEXANDER QUIROGA
For Witch's Mother:
KRISTEN LEIGH GORSKI, LINDSAY JANISSE,
ROBIN WILNER
For Midwife:
ROBIN WILNER

Swings:
ANTHONY GALDE,
KRISTEN LEIGH GORSKI,
RYAN PATRICK KELLY, AMANDA ROSE

Dance Captain/Swing:
LINDSAY JANISSE

Kerry Ellis is appearing with the permission of
Actors' Equity Association.

Wicked

Kerry Ellis
Elphaba

Kendra Kassebaum
Glinda

Jayne Houdyshell
Madame Morrible

P.J. Benjamin
The Wizard

Aaron Tveit
Fiyero

Cristy Candler
Nessarose

Ben Liebert
Boq

Timothy Britten Parker
Doctor Dillamond

Katie Adams
Standby for Glinda

Julie Reiber
Standby for Elphaba

Sonshine Allen
Ensemble

Sarah Bolt
Ensemble

Jerad Bortz
Ensemble

Sam J. Cahn
Chistery

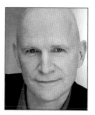
Michael DeVries
Witch's Father/Ozian Official

Adam Fleming
Ensemble

Anthony Galde
Swing

Kristen Leigh Gorski
Swing

Todd Hanebrink
Ensemble

Lindsay Janisse
Dance Captain; Swing

Reed Kelly
Ensemble

Ryan Patrick Kelly
Swing

Chelsea Krombach
Ensemble

Kenway Hon Wai K. Kua
Ensemble

Kyle Dean Massey
Ensemble

Jan Neuberger
Midwife

Lindsay K. Northen
Ensemble

Rhea Patterson
Ensemble

Eddie Pendergraft
Ensemble

Alexander Quiroga
Ensemble

Amanda Rose
Swing

Heather Spore
Ensemble

CJ Tyson
Ensemble

Brian Wanee
Ensemble

Katie Webber
Ensemble

Wicked

Robin Wilner
Ensemble

Stephen Schwartz
Music and Lyrics

Winnie Holzman
Book

Joe Mantello
Director

Wayne Cilento
Musical Staging

Eugene Lee
Scenic Designer

Susan Hilferty
Costume Designer

Kenneth Posner
Lighting Designer

Tony Meola
Sound Designer

Tom Watson
Wig and Hair Designer

Joe Dulude II
Makeup Designer

Thom Widmann
Production Supervisor

Stephen Oremus
Music Supervisor; Music Arrangements

William David Brohn
Orchestrations

Alex Lacamoire
Music Arrangements

James Lynn Abbott
Dance Arrangements

Michael Keller
Music Coordinator

Chic Silber
Special Effects

Corinne McFadden Herrera
Associate Choreographer

Bernard Telsey, Telsey + Company
Casting

Gregory Maguire
Author of Original Novel

Marcia Goldberg, Nancy Nagel Gibbs and Nina Essman,
321 Theatrical Management
General Management

Marc Platt
Producer

Jon B. Platt
Producer

David Stone
Producer

Ioana Alfonso
Ensemble

Brad Bass
Ensemble

Stephanie J. Block
Elphaba

David Burnham
Fiyero

Jason Davies
Swing

Kathy Deitch
Ensemble

Kristina Fernandez
Swing

Wicked

Lori Ann Ferreri
Ensemble, Swing

Lauren Gibbs
Ensemble

Lauren Haughton
Swing

Miriam Margolyes
Madame Morrible

Robert Pendilla
Swing

Adam Perry
Ensemble

Noah Rivera
Ensemble

Jonathan Richard Sandler
Chistery, Swing

Kathy Santen
Madame Morrible, Midwife, Ensemble

Steven Skybell
Doctor Dillamond

Barbara Tirrell
Ensemble, Midwife

Jonathan Warren
Dance Captain/ Swing

Lenny Wolpe
The Wonderful Wizard of Oz

TRANSFER STUDENTS 2008-2009

Todd Anderson
Swing

Kevin Aubin
Ensemble

Nova Bergeron
Ensemble

Alex Brightman
Boq

Jennifer DiNoia
Standby for Glinda

Marcie Dodd
Elphaba

Maia Evwaraye-Griffin
Ensemble

Kristina Fernandez
Ensemble, Swing

Brenda Hamilton
Swing

Lauren Haughton
Swing

Kevin Kern
Fiyero

Alli Mauzey
Glinda

Jonathan McGill
Ensemble

Mark Myars
Swing

Brynn O'Malley
Nessarose

Nicole Parker
Elphaba

Robert Pendilla
Swing

Adam Perry
Ensemble, Swing

Rondi Reed
Madame Morrible

Wicked

Kathy Santen
Midwife, Ensemble

Mark Shunkey
Chistery, Ensemble

Charlie Sutton
Ensemble, Swing

Jonathan Warren
*Dance Captain/
Swing*

Laura Woyasz
Standby

Briana Yacavone
Swing

Samantha Zack
Ensemble, Swing

CREW
First Row (L-R): Val Gilmore, Tim Shea, Mark Overton, John Curvan, Nick Garcia.

Second Row (L-R): Joe Schwarz, Jordan Pankin, Terry McGuarty, Danny Gadreau, Sean Kane.

Third Row (L-R): Ralph Perez, Wally Bullard, Brendan Quigley, Jeff Hahn and Jeff Schepis.

STAGE DOORMAN
Carlos Borja

HAIR AND MAKE-UP
Front Row (L-R): Chris Clark, Beverly Belletieri, Nora Martin.

Back Row (L-R): Jimmy Cortes, Ryan P. McWilliams.

WARDROBE
Seated (L-R): Bobbye Sue Albrecht, Kathe Mull, Alyce Gilbert.

Standing (L-R): Kevin Hucke, Randy Witherspoon, Barbara Rosenthal, James Byrne, Michael Michalski, Teri Pruitt, Jason Viarengo, Dianne Hylton, Laurel Parrish, Michelle Reisch, Robin Cook.

Not pictured: Trent Armstrong, Christina Cocchiara, Nancy Lawson.

Wicked

FRONT OF HOUSE STAFF
Front Row (L-R): Eileen Ruig, Peggy Boyles, Martha Boniface, Rick Kaye, James Gunn, Elizabeth Reed.

Second Row (L-R): Edda Sorrentino, Carmen Rodriguez, Philippa Koopman, Siobhan Dunne, Sharon Nelson, Penny Bonacci.

Back Row (L-R): Marianna Casanova, Jacob Korder, Albert Cruz, Lary Ann Williams, Gregory Woolard, Maria Szymanski, unknown, Brenda Denaris, Michele Belmond.

ORCHESTRA
Front Row (L-R): Victor Schultz, Danny Miller, Greg Skatt, Tuck Lee, Christian Hebel.

Second Row (L-R): Eric Weidman, Janet Axelrod, Theo Primis, David Evans, Jon Owens, Dale Kirkland.

Third Row (L-R): Ben Cohn, Andy Jones, Dominick Amendum (Conductor), Matt vanderEnde, Laura Sherman, Barry Nudelman, Kevin Roy, Ric Molina, Chad Yarbrough, Douglas Purviance, Tom Hoyt.

Back Row (L-R): unknown, Brian Hamm, Paul Loesel.

STAGE MANAGERS
(L-R): Chris Zaccardi, Christy Ney.

COMPANY AND STAGE MANAGERS
Front Row (L-R): Mark Gordon, Jason Daunter, Bob Brinkerhoff.

Back Row (L-R): Susan Sampliner, Marybeth Abel, Jennifer Marik.

Photos by Ben Strothmann

Wicked

STAFF FOR *WICKED*

GENERAL MANAGEMENT
321 THEATRICAL MANAGEMENT
Nina Essman   Nancy Nagel Gibbs
Marcia Goldberg

GENERAL PRESS REPRESENTATIVE
BARLOW•HARTMAN
Michael Hartman   John Barlow
Tom D'Ambrosio   Michelle Bergmann

CASTING
Telsey + Company, C.S.A.:
Bernie Telsey, Will Cantler, David Vaccari,
Bethany Knox, Craig Burns,
Tiffany Little Canfield, Rachel Hoffman,
Carrie Rosson, Justin Huff, Bess Fifer,
Patrick Goodwin

TECHNICAL SUPERVISION
JAKE BELL PRODUCTION SERVICES LTD.

COMPANY MANAGER .... SUSAN SAMPLINER

Stage Manager .... Bryan Landrine
Assistant Stage Managers .... J. Jason Daunter, Christy Ney
Associate Company Manager .... Eric Cornell
Assistant Director .... Paul Dobie
Dance Supervisor .... Patrick McCollum
Assistant to Mr. Schwartz .... Michael Cole
Assistant Scenic Designer .... Nick Francone
Dressing/Properties .... Kristie Thompson
Scenic Assistant .... Christopher Domanski
Oz Map Design .... Francis Keeping
Draftsman .... Ted LeFevre
Set Model Construction .... Miranda Hardy
Associate Costume Designers .... Michael Sharpe,
Ken Mooney
Assistant Costume Designers .... Maiko Matsushima,
Amy Clark
Costume Coordinator .... Amanda Whidden
Wig Coordinator .... J. Jared Janas
Associate Lighting Designer .... Karen Spahn
Associate Lighting Designer/
Automated Lights .... Warren Flynn
Assistant Lighting Designer .... Ben Stanton
Lighting Assistant .... Jonathan Spencer
Associate Sound Designer .... Kai Harada
Sound Assistant .... Shannon Slaton
Projection Programmer .... Mark Gilmore
Assistant Projection Designer .... Anne McMills
Projection Animators .... Gareth Smith, Ari Sachter Zeltzer
Special Effects Associate .... Aaron Waitz
Associate Hair Designer .... Charles LaPointe
Fight Director .... Tom Schall
Flying Effects .... ZFX Flying Illusions
Production Carpenter .... Rick Howard
Head Carpenter .... C. Mark Overton
Deck Automation Carpenter .... William Breidenbach
Production Electrician .... Robert Fehribach
Head Electrician .... Brendan Quigley
Deck Electrician/Moving Light Operator .... Craig Aves
Follow Spot Operator .... Valerie Gilmore
Production Properties .... George Wagner
Property Master .... Joe Schwarz
Assistant Property Master .... John Gentile

Production Sound Engineer .... Douglas Graves
Sound Engineer .... Jordan Pankin
Assistant Sound Engineer .... Jack Babin
Production Wardrobe Supervisor .... Alyce Gilbert
Assistant Wardrobe Supervisor .... Trent Armstrong
Dressers .... Bobbye Sue Albrecht, James Byrne,
Kevin Hucke, Dianne Hylton, Nancy Lawson,
Michael Michalski, Kathe Mull, Laurel Parrish,
Teresa Pruitt, Barbara Rosenthal,
Jason Viarengo, Randy Witherspoon
Hair Supervisor .... Chris Clark
Assistant Hair Supervisor .... Nora Martin
Hairdressers .... Beverly Belletieri, Ryan P. McWilliams
Makeup Design .... Joe Dulude II
Makeup Supervisor .... Jimmy Cortes
Music Preparation Supervisor .... Peter R. Miller,
Miller Music Service
Synthesizer Programming .... Andrew Barrett for
Lionella Productions, Ltd.
Rehearsal Pianists .... Matthew Doebler, Paul Masse
Rehearsal Drummer .... Gary Seligson
Music Intern .... Joshua Salzman
Production Assistants .... Timothy R. Semon,
David Zack
Advertising .... Serino Coyne/Greg Corradetti,
Natalie Serota, Leslie Barrett
Marketing .... Betsy Bernstein
Website .... Istros Media Corporation
Merchandise .... The Araca Group
Theatre Display .... King Displays
Group Sales .... Group Sales Box Office/
Stephanie Lee (800-223-7565)
Banking .... JP Morgan Chase Bank/
Margaret Wong
Payroll .... Castellana Services, Inc.
Director of Finance .... John DiMeglio
Production Administrator .... Robert Brinkerhoff
Accountant .... Robert Fried, C.P.A.
Insurance .... AON/Albert G. Ruben Insurance
Legal Counsel .... Loeb & Loeb/Seth Gelblum
Legal Counsel for Universal Pictures .... Keith Blau
Physical Therapy .... Encore Physical Therapy, P.C.
Orthopaedist .... David S. Weiss, MD
Onstage Merchandising .... George Fenmore, Inc.

Makeup provided by MAC Cosmetics

MARC PLATT PRODUCTIONS
Adam Siegel, Greg Lessans, Joey Levy,
Jared LeBoff, Nik Mavinkurve, Tia Maggini,
Dana Krupinski, Adam Wilkins, Conor Welch

STONE PRODUCTIONS
David Stone   Patrick Catullo   Aaron Glick

321 THEATRICAL MANAGEMENT
Eric Cornell, Tara Geesaman, Julie Griffith, Jeanette
Norton, Nicholas Porche, Greg Schaffert, Ken Silverman

UNIVERSAL PICTURES
President & COO, Universal Studios, Inc. ...... Ron Meyer
Chairman .... Marc Shmuger
Co-Chairman .... David Linde
President of Marketing & Distribution ..... Adam Fogelson
President of Marketing .... Eddie Egan
Co-President, Production
& EVP, Universal Pictures .... Jimmy Horowitz

The Time Hotel is the official hotel partner of *Wicked*.

For additional *WICKED* merchandise,
please visit www.wickedthemusical.com

CREDITS
Scenery built by F&D Scene Changes, Calgary, Canada. Show control and scenic motion control featuring Stage Command Systems© and scenery fabrication by Scenic Technologies, a division of Production Resource Group, New Windsor, NY. Lighting and certain special effects equipment from Fourth Phase and sound equipment from ProMix, both divisions of Production Resource Group LLC. Other special effects equipment by Sunshine Scenic Studios and Aztec Stage Lighting. Video projection system provided by Scharff Weisberg Inc. Projections by Vermilion Border Productions. Costumes by Barbara Matera Ltd., Parsons-Meares Ltd., Scafati, TRI-CORNE New York City and Eric Winterling. Millinery by Rodney Gordon and Lynne Mackey. Shoes by T.O. Dey, Frederick Longtin, Pluma, LaDuca Shoes NYC, and J.C. Theatrical. Flatheads and monkey wings built by Michael Curry Design Inc. Natural herb cough drops courtesy of Ricola USA, Inc. Masks and prosthetics by W.M. Creations, Inc., Matthew W. Mungle and Lloyd Matthews; lifecasts by Todd Kleitsch. Fur by Fur & Furgery. Undergarments and hosiery by Bra*Tenders, Inc. Antique jewelry by Ilene Chazanof. Specialty jewelry and tiaras by Larry Vrba. Custom Oz accessories by LouLou Button. Custom screening by Gene Mignola. Certain props by John Creech Designs and Den Design Studio. Essentials environmentally friendly detergent provided by Arm & Hammer. Additional hand props courtesy of George Fenmore. Confetti supplied by Artistry in Motion. Puppets by Bob Flanagan. Musical instruments from Manny's and Carroll Musical Instrument Rentals. Drums and other percussion equipment from Bosphorus, Black Swamp, PTECH, D'Amico and Vater. Emer'gen'C provided by Alacer Corp. Rehearsed at the Lawrence A. Wien Center, 890 Broadway, and the Ford Center for the Performing Arts.

NEDERLANDER

Chairman .... James M. Nederlander
President .... James L. Nederlander

Executive Vice President
Nick Scandalios

Vice President	Senior Vice President
Corporate Development	Labor Relations
Charlene S. Nederlander	**Herschel Waxman**

| Vice President | Chief Financial Officer |
| **Jim Boese** | **Freida Sawyer Belviso** |

STAFF FOR THE GERSHWIN THEATRE
Manager .... **Richard D. Kaye**
Assoc. Manager .... Dwayne Mann
Treasurer .... John Campise
Assistant Treasurer .... Anthony Rossano
Carpenter .... John Riggins
Electrician .... Henry L. Brisen
Property Master .... Mark Illo
Flyman .... Dennis Fox
Fly Automation Carpenter .... Michael J. Szymanski
Head Usher .... Martha McGuire Boniface

Wicked

SCRAPBOOK

Correspondent: Alex Brightman, "Boq"

Memorable Anniversary Celebration: I had such a blast at our star-studded concert of the very first draft of Act I. All of the cut songs and cut scenes were added back in and a whole slew of previous Elphabas and Glindas stopped by to perform. It was such a great celebration of the show.

Most Exciting Celebrity Visitor: My personal favorite was Will Forte from "Saturday Night Live." I had gotten tickets for him and his family and they had never seen the show before. After the curtain came down, I gave him a tour backstage. His whole family could not have been sweeter. And Will was blown away by the show. He loves to sing and he was already thinking about how he could incorporate some songs from the show into his life. It was great/hysterical/awesome!

"Easter Bonnet" Sketch: We did an "homage" to "Octomom." We used Stephen Sondheim's song "More" and changed the lyrics to make it apply to our sketch. Nicole Parker (our Elphaba) played the title role. There were sexy nurses, dancing babies, umbilical cord jump-roping, and eight births on stage. Our sketch was totally a group effort, starting with an enormous brainstorming session. Then Adam Fleming and "Cha Cha" Fernandez spearheaded the operation and held rehearsals and recording sessions. We just kept adding crazy stuff to the number and kept finding ways to make it work. It was a blast.

Actors Who Performed the Most Roles: Our swing performers do the most work. Some of them have to be ready to cover up to 12-15 tracks in the show. I tip my hat to anyone who can consistently swing in a show and not end up in a mental institution.

Favorite Snack Food: Adam Perry (one of our astounding dancers) makes cookies all the time and they are seriously addicting. Also...I have discovered a magical snack called Monkey Bread. I can't explain what it is because then I will be drooling on my computer. You'll just have to look it up. But I will tell you this...it fuels our cast. There is ALWAYS food backstage. Every time I walk down the principal hallway to the stage, there are cherries, entire pies, cakes, cookies, Swedish Fish, or pretzels just lying around. It's great.

Favorite Moment: I have a small moment with Alli Mauzey (our fabulous Glinda) right before "Dancing Through Life," that I love! We have a minute or two offstage before I chase her in and it's our first moment of the show to just sort of say hi and relax and make each other laugh. Often times we dance...she's better than I.

Favorite In-Theatre Gathering Place: Kevin Kern (our amazing Fiyero) always has people hanging out in his room before, during and after the show. He is just a great dude to talk to and he always has a good story to tell from past shows. Many times they are ridiculous backstage anecdotes that should probably NEVER be repeated. But they are always hilarious.

Favorite Off-Site Hangouts: The three places

Halloween came a few days early at the Empire State Building as the current Elphaba (Kerry Ellis) and *Wicked* composer Stephen Schwartz visited the building's observatory deck October 27, 2008 and relit the top of the building in green in honor of the show's fifth anniversary on Broadway.

I have found myself outside the theatre are Blockheads, Japas 55 and Sosa Borella. Blockheads is just a great place to hang outside and talk and they have great food and even greater margaritas. Japas 55 is a karaoke bar...need I say more? Sosa Borella is right around the corner from the theatre and it is open late for really good food and an amazing wine list.

Favorite Therapy: I love me a simple Halls Mentho-Lyptus Lozenge. I like to steam my voice when I'm feeling dry and worn out.

Memorable Ad-Lib: I don't want to be the one who calls out people flubbing lines, but I will say this. There was one incredible ad-lib during "Thank Goodness" where Rondi Reed (our Madame Morrible) completely made up a good four lines. Like...not even close. It was incredible and even more incredible that it all made sense. That's why she has the TONY!

Memorable Stage Door Fan Encounter: My favorite stage door encounter was when I was asked to sign a poster. Not a *Wicked* poster...but a *Glory Days* poster. It was surreal that people even owned them. It brought a tear to my eye.

Fastest Costume Change: When the witches leave the train station in "One Short Day," they have a twelve-second costume change to completely change outfits. It is insanity and a testament to our wonderful wardrobe crew!

Heaviest/Hottest Costume: Michael DeVries (our wonderful Witch's Father) wears a coat upwards of 50 pounds. I think that I wear the hottest costume in the opening of the show. I wear a mob coat that is made out of the same material as a comforter. It doesn't breathe and it's heavy and a sweatbox.

Catchphrase Only the Company Would Recognize: We have started to pronounce words differently. For example, instead of saying "pretzel," we would call it a "pretz-ZELL" with the emphasis on the second syllable. It started as a silly game and has now fully taken over at least the principal hallway.

Sweethearts Within the Company: I am not at liberty to say. But I do want to reveal my crush on Rondi Reed, although I think it may just be for her Tony Award.

Best In-House Parody Lyric: Changing "I'm not that girl" into "I'm not that squirrel."

Company In-Jokes: P.J. Benjamin (our Wonderful Wizard) will go around to the company and constantly ask them, "You're Equity, right?" or "Is the stage still raked?" Just some good old-fashioned humor.

Company Legends: Chelsea Krombach (one of our Elphie understudies) led the female ensemble to places playing her flute. She was the pied piper of the Gershwin for the night.

Nickname: Kevin Kern likes to call Alli Mauzey "Nugget." I don't know why. It's cute though.

Embarrassing Moment: For one glorious night, Kevin Kern (our Fiyero) referred to the lion cub as "The Lion King." It was awesomely embarrassing and a lovely shout out.

Ghostly Encounter Backstage: A couple of our dancers swore that they saw a ghost a couple weeks ago on the bridge.

Coolest Thing About Being in This Show: Probably...being in *Wicked*. It's the hottest ticket around. I wake up every single morning hoping that I haven't just been dreaming all this time. It's a literal dream come true.

Xanadu

First Preview: May 23, 2007. Opened: July 10, 2007.
Closed September 28, 2008 after 49 Previews and 512 Performances.

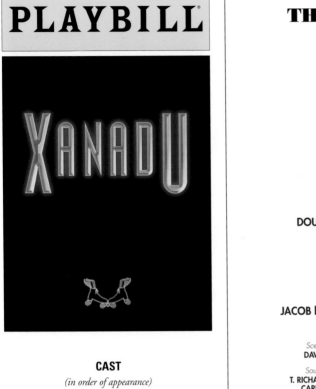

CAST

(in order of appearance)

Sonny ....CHEYENNE JACKSON
Euterpe, Siren, '40s Singer, Thetis ...PATTI MURIN
Erato, Siren, '40s Singer,
    Eros, Hera ....KENITA MILLER
Melpomene, Medusa ....MARY TESTA
Calliope, Aphrodite ....JACKIE HOFFMAN
Terpsicore, Siren, '80s Singer,
    Hermes, Centaur ....ANDRÉ WARD
Clio/Kira ....KERRY BUTLER
Danny Maguire, Zeus ....TONY ROBERTS
Featured Skater ....MARTY THOMAS

UNDERSTUDIES

For Clio/Kira:
KATE LOPREST, PATTI MURIN
For Sonny:
ANDRÉ WARD
For Danny Maguire:
PETER SAMUEL
For Melpomene:
ANNIE GOLDEN, ANDRÉ WARD
For Calliope:
ANNIE GOLDEN

SWINGS

JACOB ben WIDMAR, KATE LOPREST,
MARTY THOMAS

DANCE CAPTAIN

PATTI MURIN

THE HELEN HAYES THEATRE

MARTIN MARKINSON   DONALD TICK

ROBERT AHRENS   DAN VICKERY   TARA SMITH/B. SWIBEL
SARAH MURCHISON/DALE SMITH   CARI SMULYAN

present

KERRY BUTLER   CHEYENNE JACKSON

and

TONY ROBERTS

in

XANADU

Book by
DOUGLAS CARTER BEANE

Music & lyrics by
JEFF LYNNE & JOHN FARRAR

Based on the Universal Pictures Film Screenplay by
RICHARD DANUS & MARC RUBEL

Also Starring

JACKIE HOFFMAN   MARY TESTA

with

JACOB ben WIDMAR   KENITA MILLER   PATTI MURIN

MARTY THOMAS   ANDRÉ WARD

Scenic Design	*Lighting Design*	*Costume Design*
DAVID GALLO	HOWELL BINKLEY	DAVID ZINN

Sound Design	*Projection Design*	*Wig & Hair Design*
T. RICHARD FITZGERALD	ZACHARY BOROVAY	CHARLES G. LAPOINTE
CARL CASELLA		

Press Representative	*Marketing*	*Technical Supervision*
PETE SANDERS	HHC MARKETING	JUNIPER STREET PRODUCTIONS
FIFTEEN MINUTES PUBLIC RELATIONS		

Music Coordinator	*Casting*
JOHN MILLER	CINDY TOLAN

Associate Producers
MARC RUBEL   ALLISON BIBICOFF   CHRISTOPHER R. WEBSTER III/MAGGIE FINE   UDANAX LLC

Production Stage Manager	*General Manager*
ARTURO E. PORAZZI	LAURA HELLER

Music Direction and Arrangements by
ERIC STERN

Choreographed by
DAN KNECHTGES

Directed by
CHRISTOPHER ASHLEY

9/28/08

(L-R): Kerry Butler and Cheyenne Jackson

Photo by Paul Kolnik

Xanadu

MUSICAL NUMBERS

Time: 1980   Place: Los Angeles and Mount Olympus

Scene 1: Venice Beach
"I'm Alive" .... Muses and Clio/Kira
Scene 2: Santa Monica Pier
"Magic" .... Sonny, Kira and Muses
"Evil Woman" .... Melpomene, Calliope and Sirens
Scene 3: Outside the Auditorium
"Suddenly" .... Sonny and Kira
Scene 4: Danny Maguire's Office
"Whenever You're Away From Me" .... Danny Maguire, Kira and Young Danny
Scene 5: Inside Auditorium
"Dancin'" .... '40s and '80s Singers, Kira, Sonny and Danny
"Strange Magic" .... Sonny and Kira, Melpomene, Calliope and Eros
"All Over the World" .... Full Company
"Don't Walk Away" .... Sonny, Kira and Muses
Scene 6: Venice Beach
"Fool" .... Kira, Melpomene and Calliope
"The Fall" .... Sonny and Muses
"Suspended in Time" .... Kira and Sonny
Scene 7: Mount Olympus
"Have You Never Been Mellow?" .... Zeus, Hera, Aphrodite, Thetis, Cyclops,
Medusa, Centaur
Scene 8: Club Xanadu
"Xanadu" .... Full Company

BAND

Music Director:
ERIC STERN
Associate Music Director:
KARL MANSFIELD
Synths:
ERIC STERN, KARL MANSFIELD
Guitar:
CHRIS DELIS
Drums:
ERIC HALVORSON

Music Coordinator:
JOHN MILLER

Music Copying:
ANNE KAYE, DOUG HOUSTON
(KAYE-HOUSTON MUSIC)

SCRAPBOOK

Photos by Aubrey Reuben

1. (L-R): Cheyenne Jackson, Whoopi Goldberg and Kerry Butler with a glass of champagne on stage the night Goldberg joined the cast for a month's run in the roles of Calliope and Aphrodite in summer 2008.
2. (L-R): Jackson, Butler, Tony Roberts, Goldberg and Marty Thomas take curtain calls on Goldberg's first night at the Helen Hayes Theatre.

Xanadu

Kerry Butler
Clio/Kira

Cheyenne Jackson
Sonny

Tony Roberts
Danny, Zeus

Jackie Hoffman
Calliope, Aphrodite

Mary Testa
Melpomene, Medusa

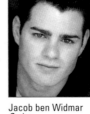
Jacob ben Widmar
Swing

Kenita R. Miller
Erato, '40s Singer, Eros, Hera

Patti Murin
Euterpe, '40s Singer, Thetis

André Ward
Terpiscore, '80s Singer, Hermes, Centaur

Kate Loprest
Female Swing

Annie Golden
Understudy for Melpomene and Calliope

Peter Samuel
Understudy for Danny Maguire

Marty Thomas
Featured Skater, Male Swing

Douglas Carter Beane
Bookwriter

Christopher Ashley
Director

Dan Knechtges
Choreographer

David Gallo
Scenic Design

Howell Binkley
Lighting Design

Carl Casella
Sound Design

John Miller
Music Coordinator

Tara Smith
Producer

Guy Kwan, John Paull III, Hillary Blanken, Kevin Broomell, Ana Rose Greene, Juniper Street Productions
Production Manager

Dana Iris Harrel
Associate Director

Whoopi Goldberg
Calliope, Aphrodite

Curtis Holbrook
Sonny; Thalia, Siren, Young Danny, '80s Singer, Cyclops

Kyle Dean Massey
Thalia, Siren, Young Danny, '80s Singer, Cyclops

Ryan Watkinson
Thalia, Siren, Young Danny, '80s Singer, Cyclops; Swing

Xanadu

FRONT OF HOUSE STAFF
Front Row (L-R):
Shykia Fields (Usher), Tyler Maley-Biancamano (Usher), Natasha Thomas (Usher), Berd Vaval (Ticket Taker), Chiyo Sakai (Usher)

Back Row (L-R):
Alan Markinson (House Manager), Ron Johnson (Usher), Bret Chisenhall (Merchandise), Caitlin Gold (Merchandise), Linda Maley (Ticket Taker), Ken Nero (Usher)

HAIR AND WARDROBE
Front Row (L-R):
Gina Leone (Hair Supervisor),
Cherie Cunningham (Assistant Wardrobe Supervisor)

Back Row (L-R):
Amy Kitzhaber (Dresser), Ryan Oslak (Wardrobe Supervisor)

Photos by Samantha Souza

STAGE CREW
Front Row (L-R):
Lorne MacDougall, Emile LaFargue, Joseph Redmond

Back Row (L-R):
Roger Keller, Ann Cavanaugh, Bob Etter, Doug Purcell

Young Frankenstein

MUSICAL NUMBERS

ACT ONE

Scene 1: A Village in Transylvania, 1934
"The Happiest Town" .... Villagers
Scene 2: Medical School, New York City
"The Brain" .... Frederick, Students
Scene 3: Hudson River, Pier 57
"Please Don't Touch Me" .... Elizabeth and Voyagers
Scene 4: A Railroad Station in Transylvania
"Together Again" .... Frederick, Igor
Scene 5: A Hay Wagon
"Roll in The Hay" .... Inga, Frederick, Igor
Scene 6: Castle Frankenstein
Scene 7: The Grand Hall of Castle Frankenstein
"Join the Family Business" .... Victor, Frederick, Ancestors
Scene 8: The Laboratory
"He Vas My Boyfriend" .... Frau Blucher
Scene 9: The Town Hall
"The Law" .... Kemp and Villagers
Scene 10: The Laboratory
"Life, Life" .... Frederick
Scene 11: The Courtyard of Castle Frankenstein
"Welcome to Transylvania" .... Transylvania Quartet
"Transylvania Mania" .... Igor, Frederick, Inga, Kemp and Villagers

ACT TWO

Scene 1: The Forest
"He's Loose" .... Kemp and Villagers
Scene 2: The Laboratory
"Listen to Your Heart" .... Inga
"Surprise" .... Elizabeth, Igor, Frau Blucher, Sasha, Masha, Basha, Tasha and Bob
Scene 3: A Remote Cottage in the Forest
"Please Send Me Someone" .... Hermit
Scene 4: The Dungeon of Castle Frankenstein
"Man About Town" .... Frederick
Scene 5: A Theatre in Transylvania
"Puttin' on the Ritz"
Music and Lyrics by Irving Berlin .... Frederick, The Monster, Inga, Igor, Frau Blucher, Ensemble
Scene 6: A Cave in the Forest
"Deep Love" .... Elizabeth
Scene 7: The Laboratory
Scene 8: The Village Square
Frederick's Soliloquy .... Frederick
"Deep Love" (Reprise) .... The Monster
Finale Ultimo .... The Company

ORCHESTRA

Conductor: PATRICK S. BRADY
Associate Conductor: GREGORY J. DLUGOS
Assistant Conductor: DAVID GURSKY

Woodwinds: VINCENT DELLA-ROCCA,
  STEVEN J. GREENFIELD,
  CHARLES PILLOW, FRANK SANTAGATA
Trumpets: DON DOWNS, GLENN DREWES,
  SCOTT HARRELL

Tenor Trombone: TIMOTHY SESSIONS
Bass Trombone: MIKE CHRISTIANSON
French Horns: PATRICK PRIDEMORE,
  JUDY YIN-CHI LEE
Concert Master: RICK DOLAN
Cello: CHUNGSUN KIM
String Bass: BOB RENINO
Drums: PERRY CAVARI

Percussion: CHARLIE DESCARFINO
Keyboard 1: GREGORY J. DLUGOS
Keyboard 2: DAVID GURSKY
Keyboard 3: PATRICK S. BRADY

Synthesizer Programming: RANDY COHEN

Music Coordinator: JOHN MILLER

Cast Continued

THE ENSEMBLE

JIM BORSTELMANN, JENNIFER LEE CROWL,
JACK DOYLE, LINDA GABLER,
AMY HEGGINS, ERIC JACKSON,
MATTHEW LABANCA, KEVIN LIGON,
BARRETT MARTIN, LINDA MUGLESTON,
CHRISTINA MARIE NORRUP,
JUSTIN PATTERSON, AARON RAMEY,
ANGIE SCHWORER, BRIAN SHEPARD,
SARRAH STRIMEL

UNDERSTUDIES

Inspector Kemp/Hermit:
JIM BORSTELMANN, KEVIN LIGON
Frederick Frankenstein:
MATTHEW LABANCA, AARON RAMEY
Elizabeth and Frau Blucher:
LINDA GABLER, LINDA MUGLESTON
Igor:
JAMES GRAY, BRIAN SHEPARD
Inga:
CHRISTINA MARIE NORRUP,
SARRAH STRIMEL
The Monster:
JIM BORSTELMANN, JUSTIN PATTERSON

SWINGS

JAMES GRAY, KRISTIN MARIE JOHNSON,
CRAIG WALETZKO, COURTNEY YOUNG

DANCE CAPTAINS

JAMES GRAY, COURTNEY YOUNG

Beth Leavel as
Frau Blucher

Photo by Paul Kolnik

Young Frankenstein

Roger Bart
Frederick
Frankenstein

Shuler Hensley
The Monster

Beth Leavel
Frau Blucher

Fred Applegate
Inspector Kemp/
Hermit

Christopher
Fitzgerald
Igor

Michele Ragusa
Elizabeth

Kelly Sullivan
Inga

Jim Borstelmann
Ensemble

Jack Doyle
Ensemble

Linda Gabler
Ensemble

Kevin Ligon
Ensemble

Linda Mugleston
Ensemble

Aaron Ramey
Ensemble

Jennifer Lee Crowl
Ensemble

James Gray
Swing/
Dance Captain

Amy Heggins
Ensemble

Eric Jackson
Ensemble

Kristin Marie
Johnson
Swing

Matthew LaBanca
Ensemble

Barrett Martin
Ensemble

Christina Marie
Norrup
Ensemble

Justin Patterson
Ensemble

Angie Schworer
Ensemble

Brian Shepard
Ensemble

Sarrah Strimel
Ensemble

Craig Waletzko
Swing

Courtney Young
Swing/
Dance Captain

Mel Brooks
Book, Composer &
Lyricist

Thomas Meehan
Book

Susan Stroman
Director/
Choreographer

Robin Wagner
Set Designer

William Ivey Long
Costume Designer

Peter Kaczorowski
Lighting Designer

Jonathan Deans
Sound Designer

Paul Huntley
Hair and Wig Design

Young Frankenstein

Angelina Avallone
Make-up Design

Tara Rubin Casting
Casting

Ira Mont
*Production
Stage Manager*

Julia P. Jones
*Assistant
Stage Manager*

Scott Bishop
Assistant Director

Jeff Whiting
*Assistant
Choreographer*

Doug Besterman
Orchestrations

John Miller
Music Coordinator

Laura Green,
Richard Frankel
Productions
*General
Management*

Neil A. Mazzella,
Hudson Theatrical
Associates
*Technical
Supervision*

Robert F.X. Sillerman
Producer

Marc Routh,
The R/F/B/V Group
Producer

Richard Frankel,
The R/F/B/V Group
Producer

Steven Baruch,
The R/F/B/V Group
Producer

Tom Viertel,
The R/F/B/V Group
Producer

Heather Ayers
Masha, Ensemble

Paul Castree
*Bob, Herald,
Transylvania Quartet,
Ensemble*

Renée Feder
Ensemble

Sutton Foster
Inga

Andrea Martin
Frau Blucher

Megan Mullally
Elizabeth

Jon Patrick Walker
*u/s Frederick
Frankenstein/Igor*

Cory English
Igor

DOORMAN
Bill Blackstock

Amanda Kloots-
Larsen
Ensemble

Beth Johnson Nicely
Swing

Lara Seibert
Ensemble

Photo by Ben Strothmann

Young Frankenstein

**STAGE MANAGEMENT, DANCE DEPARTMENT,
STAGEHANDS, WARDROBE, HAIR, MAKE-UP**
Front Row (L-R): Brian Dawson, Adam Girardet,
Charlene Belmond, Steve Kirkham,
Therese Ducey, Lair Paulsen, Jameson Eaton,
Ed Wilson, Tom Sherman, Julia P. Jones,
Juliet White, Mark Diaz, Ira Mont, Geoff Vaughn,
Thomas Ford, Douglas Petitjean,
Steven Zweigbaum, Mark Trezza

Middle Row (L-R): Scotty Cain, Dorothy DiComo,
Jessica Dermody, Steve Pulgliese,
John VanBuskirk, Norm Ballard

Back Row (L-R): Yanushka Kasabova,
Maura Clifford, Roy Seiler, John Rinaldi,
Barry Hoff, Deirdre LaBarre, Tom Galinski,
John Gibson, Tom McDonough, Eric Castaldo,
James Harris, John Warburton, Laura Beattie,
Sean Jones, John Sibley, Mark Davidson,
Chris Peterson, Simon Matthews

Photos by Ben Strothmann

FRONT OF HOUSE STAFF
Front Row (L-R): Juana Rivas, Delilah Lloyd,
Kirssy Toribio, Eddie Camacho, Adrian Zambrano,
Emily Fisher

Second Row (L-R): Katie Proctor,
Eroll Whittington, Denise Williams

Third Row (L-R): Howard Emanuel, Mike Chavez,
Kaitlin Becker, Edward Griggs, Bengey Asse,
Meghann Early, Danielle Doherty

Fourth Row (L-R): Peter Adamson,
Clinton Kennedy, Whitney Spears,
Jennifer Coolbaugh

Back Row (L-R): Adam Sarsfield,
Robert Parkinson, Karen Murray,
Sharon Hawkins, Stephanie Wilson

STAFF FOR *YOUNG FRANKENSTEIN*

GENERAL MANAGEMENT
RICHARD FRANKEL PRODUCTIONS
Richard Frankel   Marc Routh   Laura Green
Rod Kaats   Joe Watson

COMPANY MANAGER
Kathy Lowe
Associate Company Manager ....Bobby Driggers

GENERAL PRESS REPRESENTATIVE
BARLOW•HARTMAN
John Barlow   Michael Hartman
Leslie Baden   Michelle Bergmann

CASTING
TARA RUBIN CASTING
Tara Rubin, CSA, Eric Woodall, CSA
Laura Schutzel, CSA, Merri Sugarman, CSA
Rebecca Carfagna, Paige Blansfield, Dale Brown

Production Stage Manager ....**Ira Mont**

Stage Manager ....Ara Marx
Assistant Stage Manager ....Julia P. Jones
Associate Choreographer ....Chris Peterson
Assistant Director ....Scott Bishop
Assistant Choreographer ....Jeff Whiting
Dance Captains ....James Gray, Courtney Young
Dance Assistant ....Christina Marie Norrup
SSDC Observer ....Jennifer DiDonato
Technical Supervisor ....Neil Mazzella,
                                    Hudson Theatrical Associates
Associate Technical Supervisor ....Sam Ellis,
                                    Hudson Theatrical Associates

Young Frankenstein

Associate Set Designer ....David Peterson
Assistant Set Designers ....Atkin Pace,
       Thomas Peter Sarr, Robert F. Wolin
Associate Costume Designer ....Scott Traugott
Assistant to William Ivey Long ....Donald Sanders
Assistant Costume Designer ....Robert Martin
Assistants to the
    Costume Designer ....Brenda Abbandandolo,
       Cathy Parrott
Associate Lighting Designer ....John Viesta
Assistant Lighting Designers ....Joel E. Silver,
      Chris Reay, Keri Thibodeau
Assistant Sound Designer/Programmer ....Brian Hsieh
Assistant to the Wig Designer ....Giovanna Calabretta
Management Associate ....Ed Brooks
Management Assistant ....Randi Fields

Animations Designer ....Joshua Frankel

Frankenstein Puppet ....Michael Curry Design

Prosthetic Designer ....John Dods

Production Carpenter ....Todd Frank
Head Carpenter ....Geoffrey Vaughn
Automation Carpenters ....Mark Diaz, Angelo Grasso
Assistant Carpenter ....Bill Garvey
Production Electrician ....Richard Mortell
Head Electrician ....Brian Dawson
Assistant Electricians ....Thomas Ford, Tom Galinski
Moving Light Programmer ....Josh Weitzman
GrandMa/Hippotizer Programmer ....Thomas Hague
Production Sound Engineer ....Simon Matthews
Assistant Sound Engineer ....Carin Ford
Advance Sound Engineer ....David Dignazio
Production Properties Supervisor ....Laura Koch
Head Properties Supervisor ....Eric Castaldo
Props Production Assistants ....Dorothy DiComo,
      Eugene McGuinness
Wardrobe Supervisor ....Douglas Petitjean
Assistant Wardrobe Supervisor ....Deirdre LaBarre
Dressers ....Jessica Dermody, Mark Trezza
      Laura Beattie, Dennis Birchall,
      Tracey Boone, Scotty Cain, Maura Clifford,
      Dorothy DiComo, Adam Girardet,
      Kay Gowenlock, Tim Greer, Barry Hoff,
      Herb Ouellette, John Rinaldi, Roy Seiler
Hair/Wig Supervisor ....Edward J. Wilson
Hair Stylists ....Charlene Belmond, Therese Ducey,
      Jameson Eaton, Steven Kirkham,
      Carla Muniz
Makeup Artists ....Yanushka Kasabova,
      Juliet White
Dialect Coach ....Deborah Hecht
Production Assistants ....Emily Andres, Jarrod Carland,
      Annie L. Grappone, Emma Tammi
Physical Therapy Services ....PhysioArts

Additional Orchestrations ....Michael Starobin
Music Coordinator ....John Miller
Assistants to John Miller ....Kelly M. Rach, Joel Rieke
Associate Conductor ....Gregory J. Dlugos
Assistant Conductor ....David Gursky
Synthesizer Programming ....Randy Cohen
Rehearsal Drummer ....Perry Cavari
Music Preparation ....Anixter-Rice Services

Music Department Assistant ....Seth Sikes

Associate to Mr. Brooks ....Leah Zappy
Asst. to Mr. Brooks ....Shelby Van Vliet
Assts. to Mr. Sillerman ....Gini Smythe, Kyra Wiedenkeller
Asst. to Mr. Baruch ....Sonja Soper
Asst. to Mr. Viertel ....Tania Senewiratne
Advertising ....Spotco, Inc./
      Drew Hodges, Jim Edwards,
      Tom McCann, Tom Greenwald, Josh Fraenkel
Press Associates ....Melissa Bixler, Tom D'Ambrosio,
      Bethany Larsen, Ryan Ratelle,
      Matt Shea, Wayne Wolfe
Promotions/Marketing ....Broadway Print and Mail
Photographer ....Paul Kolnik
Insurance ....DeWitt Stern Group
Legal Counsel ....Elliot Brown, Dan Wasser/
      Franklin, Weinrib, Rudell & Vassallo, P.C.;
      Alan U. Schwartz; Greenberg Traurig, LLP
Banking ....Deutsche Bank
Payroll Service ....Castellana Service, Inc.
Accounting ....Fried and Kowgios Partners, LLP
Travel Agencies ....JMC Travel, Road Rebel,
      Road Concierge
Merchandising ....Dewynters
Rehearsals ....New 42nd Street Studios
Opening Night Party
    Coordination ....The Lawrence Company Events,
      Michael P. Lawrence

Group Sales ....Theater Direct International
      (800)-BROADWAY

RICHARD FRANKEL PRODUCTIONS STAFF

Finance Director ....**Michael Naumann**
Assistant to Mr. Frankel ....Heidi Libby
Assistant to Mr. Routh ....Katie Adams
Assistant to Ms. Green ....Joshua A. Saletnik
Assistant Finance Director ....Susan Bartelt
Information Technology Manager ....Roddy Pimentel
Finance Assistant ....Heather Allen
Finance Assistant ....Laura Burns
National Sales and Marketing Director ..**Ronni Mandell**
Marketing Manager ....Whitney Manalio
Marketing Coordinator ....Nina Bergelson
Marketing Associate ....Samantha Saltzman
Director of Business Affairs ....**Michael Sinder**
Office Manager ....**Lori Steiger-Perry**
Business Affairs Assistant ....Dario Dalla Lasta
Assistant Office Manager ....Shannon O'Neil
Receptionists ....Christina Cataldo, Chloe Hughes
Interns ....Beky Hughston, Leeann Kelley,
      Gloria Lai, Andrew Michaelson,
      Sarah Robinson, Sue Semaan,
      Nicole Sheetz, Owen Spruill,
      Amanda Tamny, Katharine Vandergriff

Makeup provided by M•A•C Cosmetics.

CREDITS AND ACKNOWLEDGEMENTS

Scenery, special effects and automation provided by Hudson Scenic Studio. Additional scenery and automation provided by Showmotion, Inc. Additional scenery provided by Showman Fabricators. Painted drops provided by Scenic Art Studios. Magic consultant: Charles Reynolds. Illusion builder: Bill Schmeelk. Lighting equipment provided by PRG Lighting. Sound equipment provided by PRG Audio. Stage properties provided by Cigar Box Studios, Rabbit's Choice and Costume Armour. Frankenstein puppet provided by Michael Curry Design. Hand props by Moon Boots - Jennie Marino. 3D visualization by Chris Nyfield/ Hindsight Studios. Costumes by Carelli Costumes, Inc.; David Quinn; EuroCo Costumes, Inc.; Jennifer Love Costumes, Inc.; John David Ridge, Inc.; Scafati Tailoring, Inc.; Tricorne, Inc. Shoes by T.O. Dey, J.C. Theatrical and LaDuca. Millinery by Carelli Costumes, Inc.; Rodney Gordon; Inc. Lozenges provided by Ricola, Inc. Umbrellas courtesy of TOTES.

World premiere at the Paramount Theatre,
Seattle, Washington, August 23, 2007.

HILTON THEATRE

General Manager ....Micah Hollingworth
Assistant General Manager ....Teresa Ryno
House Manager ....Emily Fisher
Facility Manager ....Jeff Nuzzo
Assistant Facility Manager ....Alex Becerra
Box Office Treasurer ....Spencer Taustine
Assistant Box Office Treasurer ....Kenny Klein
Head Carpenter ....James C. Harris
Head Electrician ....Art J. Friedlander
Head of Properties ....Joseph P. Harris Jr.
Head of Sound ....John R. Gibson
Staff Accountant ....Carmen Martinez
Payroll Administrator ....Tiyana Works
Shipping/Receiving ....Dinara Kratsch
Administrative Assistant ....Jenny Kirlin

LIVE NATION

President and
    Chief Executive Officer ....Michael Rapino
Chief Executive Officer,
    North America Music ....Jason Garner
Chairman, North East Region ....Jim Koplik
President, New York Music ....Kevin Morrow
Executive Assistant to
    Kevin Morrow and Jim Koplik ....Kodi Sparkman
Executive Vice President,
    Amphitheatre Operations ....Wilson Rogers
Senior Vice President, NY and CT ....John Huff
Vice President Ticketing Operations ......Wayne Goldberg
Vice President Marketing, New York ....Jim Steen
Head Booker, New York ....Phil Ernst
President, National Alliances ....Russell Wallach
Chief Financial Officer ....Kathy Willard
Chief Financial Officer, Venue Finance ....Ben Weeden
Senior Vice-President,
    North America Finance ....Kathy Porter
Vice President, Finance ....Dan Casale
Director of Accounting,
    New York & Connecticut Music ....Jennifer Douglas
Director of Accounting,
    New York & Connecticut Music ....Deborah Morrison

You're Welcome America. A Final Night With George W Bush

First Preview: January 20, 2009. Opened: February 5, 2009.
Closed March 15, 2009 after 18 Previews and 46 Performances.

PLAYBILL

★ You're Welcome America. ★
A Final Night with George W Bush

CAST

George W Bush .... WILL FERRELL
Secret Service Operative .... PATRICK FERRELL
Dr. Scott Blumeth .... MICHAEL DELANEY
Condoleezza Rice .... PIA GLENN
Pilot .... ADAM MUCCI

UNDERSTUDIES

For Condoleezza Rice/Pilot:
MINDY HAYWOOD
For Secret Service Operative/Dr. Scott Blumeth:
ADAM MUCCI

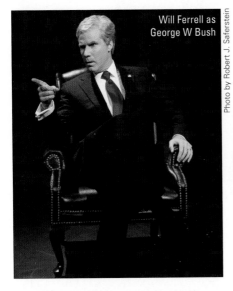

Will Ferrell as
George W Bush

Photo by Robert J. Saferstein

☎ CORT THEATRE
138 West 48th Street
A Shubert Organization Theatre

Philip J. Smith, *Chairman*   Robert E. Wankel, *President*

Jeffrey Richards   Jerry Frankel   Steve Traxler

Home Box Office, Inc.

in association with

Gary Sanchez Productions

&

Bat-Barry Productions   Ken Davenport   Ergo Entertainment

Ronald Frankel   Jon B. Platt   James D. Stern   The Weinstein Company

Tara Smith/b. Swibel   Dede Harris/Sharon Karmazin   Arny Granat

Present

★ You're Welcome America. ★
A Final Night with George W Bush

Written by and Starring

Will Ferrell

with

Michael Delaney   Patrick Ferrell   Pia Glenn   Adam Mucci

Scenic Design	Costume Design	Lighting Design	Sound Design
Eugene Lee	**Tom Broecker**	**Brian MacDevitt**	**Peter Fitzgerald**

Video Design	Choreography	Production Stage Manager
Lisa Cuscuna/Chris Cronin	**Matt Williams**	**Charles Means**

Flying Effects	Casting	Technical Supervision	General Press Representative
Flying by Foy	**Telsey + Company**	**Hudson Theatrical Associates**	**Jeffrey Richards Associates Irene Gandy/Alana Karpoff**

General Management	Executive Producer	Associate Producers
Stuart Thompson Productions/ David Turner	**Jessica Elbaum**	**Michael Filerman Seth Traxler**

Directed by

Adam McKay

NOW THAT'S BROADWAY!

2/5/09

Will Ferrell
*George W Bush/
Writer*

Michael Delaney
Dr. Scott Blumeth

Patrick Ferrell
*Secret Service
Operative*

Pia Glenn
Condoleezza Rice

You're Welcome America. A Final Night With George W Bush

Adam Mucci
Pilot

Mindy Haywood
u/s Condoleezza Rice/ Pilot

Adam McKay
Director

Eugene Lee
Set Design

Brian MacDevitt
Lighting Design

Chris Cronin
Video Design

Jeffrey Richards
Producer

Jerry Frankel
Producer

Steve Traxler
Producer

Barry Weisbord,
Bat-Barry
Productions
Producer

Ken Davenport
Producer

Donny Epstein,
Ergo Entertainment
Producer

Yeeshai Gross,
Ergo Entertainment
Producer

Elie Landau,
Ergo Entertainment
Producer

Jon B. Platt
Producer

Bob Weinstein,
The Weinstein
Company
Producer

Harvey Weinstein,
The Weinstein
Company
Producer

Tara Smith
Producer

Dede Harris
Producer

Sharon Karmazin
Producer

Arny Granat
Producer

Michael Filerman
Associate Producer

Bernard Telsey,
Telsey + Company
Casting

Neil A. Mazzella,
Hudson Theatrical
Associates
Technical Supervisor

Stuart Thompson
Productions
*General
Management*

STAGE MANAGEMENT
(L-R): Charles Means (Production Stage Manager), Jessica Elbaum (Executive Producer), Elizabeth Moloney (Stage Manager), Scott Cronick (Star Dresser) and Ed Galanek (Security).

You're Welcome America. A Final Night With George W Bush

SCRAPBOOK

Correspondents: Charles Means and Elizabeth Moloney, Stage Managers

Memorable Note, Fax or Fan Letter: Someone sent Will a newspaper clipping showing Will dressed as Bush with "You are an a**hole" written on it. Will posted it on his dressing room mirror along with his opening night cards.

Anniversary Parties and/or Gifts: Closing night sweatshirts with the Simianus logo on it from Adam and Will. Diego Luna mugs from Propstar.

Most Exciting Celebrity Visitors: Richard Holbrooke (Obama's Special Representative for Afghanistan and Pakistan), Jon Stewart, Chris Rock and Bob Costas.

Who Has Done the Most Shows: Smitty. He's seen it all....

Special Backstage Rituals: Pia and Will yelling "Thank you, Half Hour!" from their dressing rooms on the second floor. The company "bonesing it out" at places. Will, Adam, Beth and Scott singing "Slow Hand" as Will and Adam were getting into their harnesses for the top of the show.

Favorite Moments During Each Performance: The Nickname Section: Favorites include "Box of Wine," "Glug Glug," "Babaganoush" and "Flapjack." Pat's big dance. Pia's Condi dance.

Favorite In-Theatre Gathering Place: Will's first-floor dressing room with Jessica, Adam, Lauryn and Ed.

Favorite Off-Site Hangout: Vynl, Spotted Pig and Ruby Foo's.

Favorite Snack Foods: Dark chocolate M&M's. The Yellow Cake from the Gary Sanchez staff.

Mascot: Bigfoot.

Favorite Therapy: Ricola. Ricola. More Ricola.

Memorable Ad-Libs: "Amateur Historian Day." "That's My Stimulus Package." "The Tiger Woods Guy." Michael Delaney's "I want my 401-K back!" When Will left the stage during a performance, went out the side door into the alley and yelled up at some drunk audience members who got trapped on the fire escape while they were looking for the rest room.

Memorable Press Encounter: Will singing "Maria" from *West Side Story* on David Letterman.

Memorable Fan Encounter: The night three patrons sat in the front row dressed as characters that Will has played in movies, including Ron Burgundy and Elf.

Latest Audience Arrival: When patrons would go to the rest room during the show and then return during the Nicknames Section, Will would give them a hard time. Even better was when someone was walking down the aisle after late seating during the Prayer and Will would do a quick added prayer for them to be forgiven by the rest of the audience for being late.

Fastest Costume Change: Fifteen seconds.

Busiest Day at the Box Office: Most of the run—we were the highest grossing show at the Cort Theatre ever.

Who Wore the Heaviest/Hottest Costume: Will Ferrell in the Flight Suit. Pat Ferrell after his final dance.

Who Wore the Least: Pia Glenn as Condi.

Catchphrases Only the Company Would Recognize: "Spleef check." "Like it hurts!" "Was Val here tonight?"

Memorable Directorial Contribution: Adam McKay doing the pre-show announcement as Dick Cheney.

Sweethearts Within the Company: Scott Cronick and the Chipotle restaurant across the street.

Company In-Jokes: Rising Like A Spider. Checkmark!

Nicknames: Mr President, Queer Balls, and Hey 'Mo.

Embarrassing Moments: Most of these occurred in the house. There were several drunk patrons over the course of the run who either passed out or threw up in the balcony (much to the dismay of our follow-spot operator, Colin).

Superstitions That Turned Out *Not* To Be True: The Curse of the Cort.

Coolest Thing About Being in This Show: Having our first preview on the night of Obama's inauguration and working on Will Ferrell's Broadway debut!

Photo by Robert J. Saferstein

THE COMPANY
Front Row (L-R): Brian MacDevitt (Lighting Designer), Jen Schriever (Associate Lighting Designer), unknown, Colin DeVerna (Follow Spot), Lisa Cuscuna (Video Designer), Adam McKay (Director), Elizabeth Moloney (Stage Manager), Scott DeVerna (Master Electrician), Matt Williams (Choreographer), Megan Henninger (Assistant Sound Designer), Chris Cronin (Video Designer), Jens McVoy (Sound).
Back Row (L-R): Zach Blane (Assistant to the Lighting Designer), Marc Polimeni (Lighting Programmer), Keith DeVerna (Deck Sound), Peter Fitzgerald (Sound Designer), Jessica Elbaum (Executive Producer), Lauryn Kahn (Director's Assistant), Patrick Ferrell, Adam Mucci, Will Ferrell, Pia Glenn, Scott Cronick (Star Dresser), Yolanda Ramsay (Hair Supervisor), Lonnie Gaddy (Props), Smitty (Night Doorman), Lyle Jones (Wardrobe Supervisor), Michael Delaney, Raynelle Wright (Production Assistant), Charles Means (Production Stage Manager) and Cassidy Briggs (Company Manager).

You're Welcome America. A Final Night With George W Bush

Will Ferrell spoofs President Bush's premature declaration of victory in Iraq.

Photo by Robert J. Saferstein

STAFF FOR *YOU'RE WELCOME AMERICA. A FINAL NIGHT WITH GEORGE W BUSH*

GENERAL MANAGEMENT
STUART THOMPSON PRODUCTIONS
Stuart Thompson   David Turner
Caroline Prugh   James Triner

COMPANY MANAGER
Cassidy J. Briggs

PRODUCTION MANAGEMENT
HUDSON THEATRICAL ASSOCIATES
Neil Mazzella   Sam Ellis

GENERAL PRESS REPRESENTATIVE
JEFFREY RICHARDS ASSOCIATES
IRENE GANDY / ALANA KARPOFF
Elon Rutberg   Diana Rissetto   Shane Marshall Brown

CASTING
TELSEY + COMPANY
Bernie Telsey CSA, Will Cantler CSA, David Vaccari CSA,
Bethany Knox CSA, Craig Burns CSA,
Tiffany Little Canfield CSA, Rachel Hoffman CSA,
Carrie Rosson CSA, Justin Huff CSA, Bess Fifer CSA,
Patrick Goodwin, Abbie Brady-Dalton

FLYING EFFECTS
Flying by Foy

WIG DESIGNER
Bettie Rogers

Production Stage Manager ....Charles Means
Stage Manager ....Elizabeth Moloney
Scenic Design Associate ....Edward Pierce
Associate Scenic Designer ....Nick Francone
Assistant Scenic Designer ....Jen Price
Associate Costume Designer ....Eric Justian
Associate Lighting Designer ....Jennifer Schriever
Assistant Sound Designer ....Megan Henninger
Video Programmer ....Chris Herman
Sound Production Assistant ....Mallori Fitzgerald
Props ....Kathy Fabian/Propstar
Props Associates ....Carrie Mossman, Scott Keclik

Wardrobe Supervisor ....Lyle Jones
Star Dresser for Will Ferrell ....Scott Cronick
Hair Supervisor ....Yolanda Ramsay
Vocal Coach ....Louis Colaianni
Production Carpenter ....Edward Diaz
Production Electrician ....Scott DeVerna
Production Propertymaster ....Lonnie Gaddy
Production Sound ....Jens McVoy
Deck Carpenter ....Kevin Diaz
Followspot ....Colin DeVerna
Deck Sound ....Keith DeVerna
Assistant to Mr. Ferrell ....Betty Kay Overman
Assistant to Mr. McKay ....Lauryn Kahn
Associate to Jeffrey Richards ....Jeremy Scott Blaustein
Assistant to Jeffrey Richards ....Christopher Taggart
Assistant to Mr. Traxler ....Brandi Preston
Mr. Platt's Assistant ....Terrie Lootens
General Management Assistants ....Quinn M. Corbin,
                             Megan E. Curren, Geo Karapetyan
General Management Intern ....Brittany Levasseur
Production Assistant ....Raynelle Wright
Banking ....JPMorgan Chase/
                        Stefanie A. Boger, Salvatore A. Romano
Payroll ....Castellana Services, Inc.
Accountant ....Fried & Kowgios CPA's LLP/
                                            Robert Fried, CPA
Controller ...................................J.S. Kubala
Insurance ....DeWitt Stern Group
Legal Counsel ....Lazarus & Harris LLP/
                 Scott Lazarus, Esq.; Robert Harris, Esq.;
                                         Andrew Farber, Esq.
Advertising ....Serino Coyne/
                       Greg Corradetti, Tom Callahan,
                          Robert Jones, Vanessa Javier
Interactive Marketing ....Situation Marketing/
                        Damian Bazadona, John Lanasa,
                             Kristin Butler, Ryan Klink
Marketing Consultant ....Ken Davenport
Security ....Ed Galanek
Production Photographer ....Robert J. Saferstein
Theatre Displays ....King Display
Company Mascots ....Lottie, Skye, Gladys, Pips

CREDITS
Design services provided by Edward Pierce Studio. Scenery by Hudson Scenic. Lighting by Hudson Scenic and Production Resource Group. Sound and video by Sound Associates. Music licensing provided by Music Rightz. Specialty prop construction by Aardvark Interiors. Flameproofing by Turning Star.

Special Thanks: Jimmy Miller, Deborah Klein, Matt Lichtenberg, Jason Heyman, Jason Cooper, Martin Lesak, Matt Labov, Mark Flanagan, Joe Witt, Largo, Jerry Long and Joe Long, George W. Bush. This production rehearsed at the New 42nd Street Studios.

The following shows opened in 2007-2008 and closed shortly after the start of the 2008-2009 season with no changes to their casts or crews. For complete details and photographs from these shows, please consult the 2007-2008 Playbill Broadway Yearbook.

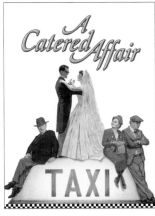

First Preview: March 25, 2008.
Opened: April 17, 2008.
Closed July 27, 2008 after
25 Previews and
116 Performances.

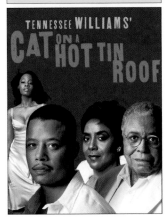

First Preview: February 12, 2008.
Opened: March 6, 2008.
Closed June 22, 2008 after
27 Previews and
125 Performances.

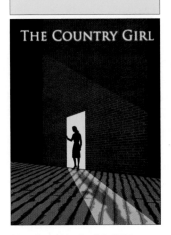

First Preview: April 3, 2008.
Opened: April 27, 2008.
Closed July 20, 2008 after
25 Previews and
97 Performances.

First Preview: April 11, 2008.
Opened: May 1, 2008.
Closed July 6, 2008 after
22 Previews and
77 Performances.

First Preview: December 20, 2007.
Opened: January 17, 2008.
Closed July 13, 2008 after
33 Previews and
205 Performances.

First Preview: February 8, 2008.
Opened: February 28, 2008.
Closed July 20, 2008 after
20 Previews and
165 Performances.

First Preview: April 12, 2008.
Opened: April 30, 2008.
Closed August 17, 2008 after
19 Previews and
126 Performances.

First Preview: April 15, 2008.
Opened: May 7, 2008.
Closed June 29, 2008 after
24 Previews and
63 Performances.

Events

Broadway Bares 18: Wonderland

June 22, 2008 at Roseland Ballroom

The 18th annual Broadway Bares, titled "Wonderland," raised $874,372 for Broadway Cares/Equity Fights AIDS, setting another record for the annual event.

The M•A•C AIDS Fund again sponsored the event that features scantily clad Broadway favorites performing sizzling numbers. The sponsor presented Broadway Bares with a check for $115,000 and added a surprise "challenge match" check of $50,000 for the event's closing "rotation" where performers dance for donations from audience members.

More than 200 Broadway gypsies and stars performed in the fundraiser, which featured the work of 14 choreographers. Denis Jones (*Legally Blonde, Dirty Rotten Scoundrels*) directed the "Alice in Wonderland"-inspired event that opened with a number penned by *[title of show]*'s Jeff Bowen and scenes by *[tos]*'s Hunter Bell.

Highlights of the event included Mary Birdsong (*Fame Becomes Me*) as Alice, and Tituss Burgess (*The Little Mermaid*) as the White Rabbit. The evening also boasted appearances by Matthew Morrison (*South Pacific*), Nathan Lane (*November*), Andrea Martin (*Young Frankenstein*), Tyler Maynard (*The Little Mermaid*), Jennifer Cody (*Shrek The Musical*), Julie White (*The Little Dog Laughed*) and Christopher Sieber (*Shrek The Musical*).

1. (L-R at front of passerelle): Susan Mosher, Mary Birdsong, Becky Gulsvig, Carla Hargrove, Tory Ross with the full company (a.k.a. "Friends of Alice") lead the audience in a medley of "Your Body Is a Wonderland" and "Boogie Wonderland."
2. Aerialist Armando Farfan of "The Living Art of Armando" as the Caterpillar turned Butterfly in "Smokin' Lotus."
3. A corps of Tweedledees and Tweedledums in "Dee, Dum and Then Some."

American Theatre Wing Spring Gala

May 19, 2008 at Cipriani Restaurant

The American Theatre Wing honored *Hello, Dolly!* and *Mame* composer Jerry Herman and corporate partner Visa at its Annual Spring Gala.

In a statement, Wing chairman Sondra Gilman said, "Jerry Herman has brought joy to theatregoers around the world with his inspired songs and shows. It is impossible to think of the American musical without thinking of Jerry Herman. He is deserving of every possible accolade, which is why we are so proud to be recognizing his lifetime of work as part of our work at the Wing."

(L-R): Doug Leeds of the American Theatre Wing, Jerry Herman and Howard Sherman of the Wing, at Cipriani.

Broadway Concierge

September 18, 2008 at the Times Square Information Center

The Broadway League, the national trade association for the Broadway industry, launched the Broadway Concierge & Ticket Center, located inside the Times Square Information Center at 1560 Broadway.

The new Ticket Center offers theatregoers customized free service for Broadway and Off-Broadway tickets. Actress Bebe Neuwirth was on hand to help roll out the Broadway Concierge service and to perform a song written for the occasion by Charles Strouse and Lee Adams (*Bye Bye Birdie*).

(L-R): Nina Lannan and Charlotte St. Martin of The Broadway League with Bebe Neuwirth and one of the concierges at the press conference for The Broadway Concierge & Ticket Center at the Times Square Information Center.

The Broadway Walk of Stars

September 15, 2008

The Broadway Walk of Stars Foundation held a reception at the home of producer Marty Richards September 15. Richards and MGM star Arlene Dahl, who have spearheaded the project, hosted the event, which featured a performance by current *South Pacific* star Kelli O'Hara.

The planned Broadway Walk of Stars will celebrate talent of the stage, screen, music and dance worlds as well as the cultural history of New York City.

(L-R): Marty Richards and Kelli O'Hara at a reception for the Broadway Walk of Stars at Richards' home in Manhattan.

Broadway Barks 10!

July 12, 2008 in Shubert Alley

Award-winning actresses, friends and animal activists Bernadette Peters and Mary Tyler Moore hosted the tenth annual "Broadway Barks" fundraiser and pet adopt-a-thon July 12, 2008 at the Broadhurst Theatre. The event benefits New York City animal shelters and adoption agencies. Produced by Broadway Cares/Equity Fights AIDS and sponsored by Pedigree and the ASPCA, the afternoon included celebrity presentations of pets from animal shelters throughout New York City.

Among celebrity presenters were Glenn Close, Nathan Lane, Christine Baranski, Harvey Fierstein, Laura Benanti, Bebe Neuwirth, Joel Grey, Victoria Clark, Orfeh, Peter Gallagher, Faith Prince, Cheyenne Jackson, Mario Lopez, Priscilla Lopez, Matthew Morrison, Kerry Butler, Boyd Gaines, Andrea Martin, Jackie Hoffman, Lacey Kohl, Sebastian Arcelus, Li Jun Li, Michael Longoria, Bill Berloni, Heather MacRae, Judy McLane, Michael Mulheren, Shuler Hensley, Sean Palmer, Loretta Ables Sayre and Andy Karl.

Photos by Aubrey Reuben

1. (L-R): Co-hosts Mary Tyler Moore and Bernadette Peters at the Broadhurst Theatre.
2. Lacey Kohl (of *Cry-Baby*) and friend at Broadway Barks 10!

Broadway Show League Softball Championship

September 6, 2008 at the Heckscher Ball Fields, Central Park

Broadway's top softball teams battled for the 2008 Broadway Show League softball championship, with top honors going to the team from The Actors Fund (right) which beat the combined *August: Osage County/ November* team 10-7.

The Broadway Show League consists of about three dozen teams from the casts and crews of various Broadway and Off-Broadway shows, as well as teams from theatre-related organizations. They play Thursday afternoon games throughout the summer on the Heckscher Fields in Central Park.

This year, awards were given in several categories:
Season Champions (11:30 AM Division vs 1:30 PM Division): The Actors Fund
Season Co-Champions (3:30 PM division): Jujamcyn and Nederlander
Regular Season Champions (11:30 AM Division): *Mary Poppins*
Regular Season Champions (1:30 PM Division): The Actors Fund
Regular Season Champions (3:30 PM Division): Nederlander
MVP (11:30 AM vs 1:30 PM): Jimmy Maresca, The Actors Fund
MVP (3:30 PM): Kenny McDonough, Jujamcyn
Women's MVP (11:30 AM vs 1:30 PM): Katy Lathan, *Young Frankenstein*

Photo by Bob Scofield

The Actors Fund Team - Season Champions
Front Row (L-R): Declan Henderson, Kevin Henderson, Tallula Henderson, Jo Tsai, Lexie Pregosin, Karyn Plonsky, Lauren Marcell, Patrick Edgar
2nd Row (L-R): Jason Rosenbaum, Juan Parra, Aaron Slavik, Fran Matola, Rich Cohen, Ted Smits, Adam Auslander, Jim Maresca, Andre Marcell
Back Row: John Quinn, Chris Lutkin, Tim Robbins, Michael McKeon, Mike Egan.

Women's MVP (3:30 PM): Cathy Tomlin, Equity
Manager of the Year (11:30 AM vs 1:30 PM): Paul Urcioli, Atlantic Theater Company
Manager of the Year (3:30 PM): Victor Hawks, *South Pacific*
Broadway Show League Spirit Award: Fran and Dick Connors
Broadway Show League Spirit Award: David Zuckerman, Photographer

Broadway on Broadway

September 14, 2008 in Times Square

A host of stage stars celebrated The Great White Way September 14 during the annual "Broadway on Broadway" concert in Times Square. Drew Lachey hosted the free outdoor event highlighting the new Broadway theatre season.

The 17th annual concert began at 11:30 AM with the casts of current and upcoming shows performing numbers backed by a 30-piece orchestra.

Among those in attendance were cast members of *Avenue Q, Billy Elliot, Chicago, Grease, Gypsy, Hairspray, In the Heights, Irving Berlin's White Christmas, Jersey Boys, Legally Blonde, The Lion King, The Little Mermaid, Mamma Mia!, Mary Poppins, Monty Python's Spamalot, The Phantom of the Opera, Pure Country, Spring Awakening, A Tale of Two Cities, 13, [title of show], Wicked, Xanadu* and *Young Frankenstein*.

An estimated 50,000 fans attended the concert which was presented by The Broadway League and the Times Square Alliance.

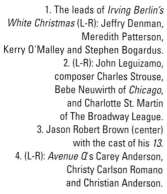

1. The leads of *Irving Berlin's White Christmas* (L-R): Jeffry Denman, Meredith Patterson, Kerry O'Malley and Stephen Bogardus.
2. (L-R): John Leguizamo, composer Charles Strouse, Bebe Neuwirth of *Chicago*, and Charlotte St. Martin of The Broadway League.
3. Jason Robert Brown (center) with the cast of his *13*.
4. (L-R): *Avenue Q's* Carey Anderson, Christy Carlson Romano and Christian Anderson.

Broadway Flea Market and Grand Auction

September 21, 2008 in Shubert Alley

The 22nd Annual Broadway Flea Market & Grand Auction, which was held in Shubert Alley September 21, raised a total of $496,380 for Broadway Cares/Equity Fights AIDS.

Seventy tables boasting a wide variety of theatre collectibles filled Shubert Alley this year and raised a total of $258,000. The booth that raised the most money was the "Broadway Beat" table, bringing in $17,133. The show table that raised the most for BC/EFA was the *Wicked* table, which took in $11,474.

The Autograph Table and the Celebrity Photo Booth, which allowed Broadway fans the chance to get up close and personal with dozens of Broadway favorites, raised $10,350.

The Silent Auction, which was hosted by Michael Goddard and Felicia Finley, raised $34,780. Among the high bids of the 80 items: a door panel from *Rent*, autographed by original cast member Jesse L. Martin went for $2,500.

The Grand Auction, featuring auctioneer Lorna Kelly and actor John Bolton, brought in $173,000. The top-selling item was a pair of house seats to *Spamalot* and a backstage tour hosted by "American Idol" finalist Clay Aiken, which fetched $10,000.

Among the celebs who took part in the event were Loretta Ables Sayre, James Barbour, Hunter Bell, Laura Benanti, Michael Berresse, Susan Blackwell, Heidi Blickenstaff, Jeff Bowen, Tituss Burgess, Danny Burstein, Kerry Butler, Mario Cantone, Kathleen Chalfant, Stephanie D'Abruzzo, Mandy Gonzalez, Bailey Hanks, Harriet Harris, Christian Hoff, Jayne Houdyshell, Beth Leavel, Norm Lewis, Priscilla Lopez, Rebecca Luker, Madeleine Martin, Julia Murney, Bebe Neuwirth, Karen Olivo, Lynn Redgrave, Tony Roberts, Marian Seldes, Robin Strasser, Caitlin Van Zandt and Patrick Wilson.

1. (L-R): Kevin Spirtas, Bebe Neuwirth (*Chicago*), Danny Burstein (*South Pacific*) and Rebecca Luker (*Mary Poppins*).
2. Autographed Broadway posters were hawked at one of the many tables.
3. (L-R): Malan Breton ("Project Runway"), Ilene Kristen ("One Life to Live") and Victorya Hong ("Project Runway") sign autographs.
4. Jayne Houdyshell (*Wicked*).
5. Autographed PLAYBILL posters were available for collectors.

Legends!

March 23, 2009 at Town Hall

James Kirkwood's *Legends!*, a comedy about showbiz divas, got a benefit reading featuring Charles Busch and Lypsinka.

Directed by Mark Waldrop, this was the first-ever New York City presentation of the bitchy comedy that originally starred Mary Martin and Carol Channing (in a 1986 tour that never made it to Broadway). John Epperson's (a.k.a. Lypsinka's) rewrite updated the story to 2009, beefed up the role of Aretha the maid for Goldberg, and included nips, tucks—and a new ending.

The event benefitted Friends in Deed-The Crisis Center for Life-Threatening Illness.

Curtain call for *Legends!*, including (2nd from L) Charles Busch, (3rd from L) Bryan Batt and (R) Lypsinka.

The 24 Hour Plays on Broadway

November 16-17, 2008 at the American Airlines Theatre

The eighth annual "The 24 Hour Plays on Broadway" featured Tony nominee Laura Bell Bundy and a collection of stars who wrote, rehearsed and performed an evening of six original plays within a single 24-hour period. Among the 2008 participants: Rachel Dratch, Pablo Schreiber, Anthony Mackie, Julianna Margulies, Cynthia Nixon, Sanaa Lathan, Justin Long, Annabella Sciorra, Rosie Perez and Terrence McNally. The event benefits Urban Arts Partnership, an organization that brings arts education into New York City classrooms.

1. Participants Alicia Witt and Josiah Early.
2. Participants Julia Stiles and Elijah Wood at the afterparty.

Leading Men IV

May 11, 2009 at Birdland

Actor John Tartaglia hosted the fourth annual "The Leading Men" benefit concert for Broadway Cares/Equity Fights AIDS. The evening of song, which raised $10,000, featured musical direction by Seth Rudetsky and direction by Alan Muraoka.

Men who took the stage included Paolo Montalban, Jonathan Groff, James Barbour, Norm Lewis, Tony Yazbeck, Cody Green, Nick Adams, Jim Caruso, Michael Kadin Craig, Kevin Earley, Graham Phillips, Nicholas Rodriguez, Tom Andersen and Jack Donahue.

The event was produced by Wayman Wong, who wrote the "Leading Men" column for Playbill.com 2003-2006.

(L-R): Tom Andersen, Jonathan Groff, Cody Green and John Tartaglia have a boys' night out at Birdland, singing for Broadway Cares.

Gypsy of the Year

December 8-9, 2008 at the New Amsterdam Theatre

The 20th annual Gypsy of the Year Competition, which celebrates the Broadway gypsy and was presented December 8 and 9 at the New Amsterdam Theatre, earned $3,061,148 for Broadway Cares/Equity Fights AIDS.

The Lion King won the Gypsy of the Year award for Best Stage Presentation, performing Ray Mercer's athletic "Guess Who's Coming To Dinner," a number in which dancers gamboled over, under and around a giant table, sometimes leaping off it into one another's arms.

The Chicago company of *Jersey Boys* was the biggest fundraiser, bringing in $220,000 for BC/EFA.

The cast of *Equus*—which stars Daniel Radcliffe and Richard Griffiths—was the top Broadway fundraiser, raising $203,747. (Radcliffe made headlines several times for auctioning the jeans he wears in the acclaimed production.) It was also the first time a non-musical raised the most cash since *The Dinner Party* in 2001.

Equus was also runner-up for the Best Stage Presentation, performing a homoeroticized parody musical version of their show, titled "The Love That Dare Not Speak Its Neigh," which included *Equus* and *Harry Potter* star Radcliffe performing a kick line with the show's horses.

Other top-raising Broadway productions included *Wicked* ($172,301), *South Pacific* ($140,552) and *Hairspray* ($125,291). The Chicago "Shiz Company" and Los Angeles productions of *Wicked* also brought in top dollars for BC/EFA, raising $178,500 and $161,868, respectively.

A special award was given for the top fundraising Off-Broadway company: *The Marvelous Wonderettes* raised $17,824.

Actor, musician and Playbill.com columnist Seth Rudetsky hosted the Competition, which also featured appearances by Tyne Daly and Jonathan Hadary, who hosted the first Gypsy of the Year Competition; Jen Cody and Don Richard, who reprised their comical turns as Little Sally and Officer Lockstock; and the cast of *[title of show]*—Hunter Bell, Jeff Bowen, Heidi Blickenstaff and Susan Blackwell—who made a special appearance.

1. In the opening number Tracee Beazer models one of the recent Gypsy Robes with items from *Pacific Overtures, La Cage aux Folles, Chitty Chitty Bang Bang* and other shows.
2. *Lion King* dancers Ray Mercer and Michelle Brugal celebrate winning Gypsy of the Year.
3. (L-R): Linda Balgord, costumed as VP candidate Sarah Palin, auditions for a job on Broadway.
4. The cast of *13* performs its skit.
5. Daniel Radcliffe reacts to word that *Equus* raised the most of any Broadway show.
6. (L-R): Tyne Daly shows off her *Equus* hoofs to host Seth Rudetsky and presenter Harvey Fierstein.
7. Gypsies from *Mamma Mia!* costumed as characters from other shows.

38th Annual Theater Hall of Fame Induction

January 26, 2009 at the Gershwin Theatre and the Friars Club

Photos by Aubrey Reuben

Five-time Tony nominee Dana Ivey hosted the 38th Annual Theater Hall of Fame ceremony in the Gershwin Theatre's North Rotunda.

Inductees included actors Nathan Lane and Richard Easton, playwright Alan Ayckbourn, producer Emanuel Azenberg, choreographer Patricia Birch, composer Marvin Hamlisch, orchestrator Jonathan Tunick and, posthumously, the late actor Roscoe Lee Browne.

Presenters for the starry evening included composer Stephen Sondheim, director Jack O'Brien, columnist Frank Rich, playwright Terrence McNally and actress Ann Reinking.

Eligible nominees for the Theater Hall of Fame must have had a minimum of five major credits and 25 years in the Broadway theatre. The inductees are elected by the American Theater Critics Association and the living members of the Theater Hall of Fame.

1. Orchestrator Jonathan Tunick with his Hall of Fame medallion at the Friars Club.
2. Inductee Pat Birch.
3. Emanuel Azenberg.
4. Anne Kaufman Schneider and presenter Jack O'Brien.
5. Host Dana Ivey.
6. Honoree Richard Easton.
7. (L-R): Honoree Nathan Lane with his *The Producers* director, Susan Stroman.
8. Inductee Marvin Hamlisch.

Broadway Bears XII

February 15, 2009 at B.B. King's Blues Club & Grill

①

For the second consecutive year, the *Spamalot* bear—signed by former "American Idol" finalist and *Spamalot* star Clay Aiken—raised the most money ($16,000) at the annual Broadway Bears fundraiser.

Hosted by Bryan Batt the event earned a total of $152,116 for Broadway Cares/Equity Fights AIDS. Other top money-makers were Alan Strang with Nugget from *Equus* ($10,000), Glinda from *Wicked* ($7,000) and Growltiger from *Cats* ($5,500). Lorna Kelly was the evening's auctioneer.

The yearly event features a host of teddy bears dressed as famous Broadway characters, many autographed by the original stars who wore the original (human-sized) outfits. Among the bears that were auctioned this year: Sir Thomas More from *A Man for All Seasons*, Be Our Guest Eggbeater from *Beauty and the Beast* and multiple Mama Roses in different costumes from *Gypsy*.

1. (L-R): Kiril Kulish, David Alvarez, Trent Kowalik with bears modeled on characters in their show *Billy Elliot*.
2. Michael Cerveris poses with *The Who's Tommy* bear.
3. Kerry O'Malley with the bear wearing her red dress costume from *Irving Berlin's White Christmas*.
4. Christopher Sieber with the Shrek bear from *Shrek The Musical*.

③

④

13th Annual Kids' Night on Broadway

February 3 and 4, 2009 at Madame Tussauds New York

Producer, actress, comic and former talk-show host Rosie O'Donnell helped kick off the Kids' Night on Broadway's Fan Festival with help from her youthful performance group Rosie's Kids.

Kids' Night on Broadway gives young people ages 6-18 a chance to attend a Broadway show for free when accompanied by a full-paying adult.

The event affords the young people the opportunity to experience the magic of live theatre and to participate in special activities hosted by the cast and crew of participating Broadway shows.

Among the shows participating in the 2009 Kids' Night on Broadway were *The 39 Steps, Altar Boyz, The American Plan, Avenue Q, Billy Elliot The Musical, Chicago, Disney's The Little Mermaid, In the Heights, The Lion King, Mamma Mia!, Mary Poppins, The Phantom of the Opera, Shrek The Musical, Stomp* and *Wicked.*

(L-R): Rosie O'Donnell and Charlotte St. Martin of The Broadway League roll out the 2009 event.

Third Annual Broadway Beauty Pageant

April 20, 2009 at Symphony Space

Anthony Hollock, a.k.a. "Mr. *Hair*," was crowned Mr. Broadway 2009 at the third annual Broadway Beauty Pageant held April 20, 2009 at Symphony Space in New York. The event raised $30,000 for New York's Ali Forney Center, which provides shelter for homeless LGBT youth, more than double the 2008 amount.

Formerly titled "Mr. Broadway," the event featured male cast members representing their respective Broadway shows. Other contestants included James Brown III ("Mr. *Little Mermaid*"), Adam Fleming (Mr. "*Wicked*"), Tony James (Mr. "*Lion King*") and David Larsen (Mr. "*Billy Elliot*"). Contestants competed for the title crown through talent, interview and swimsuit competitions.

The evening was hosted by *Irena's Vow* star Tovah Feldshuh. Though the audience votes on the winner, the event also features an honorary panel of celebrity judges: Ana Gasteyer (*Wicked*), Beth Leavel (*Young Frankenstein*), Charles Busch (*The Third Story*) and Seth Rudetsky (*The Ritz*).

Photo courtesy Wayman Wong

Anthony Hollock, "Mr. *Hair*," sports the tiara he earned for winning the "Mr Broadway" beauty pageant.

A Little Night Music Concert Performance

January 12, 2009 at Studio 54

Photo by Aubrey Reuben

Roundabout Theatre Company hosted a gala concert reading of Stephen Sondheim and Hugh Wheeler's musical *A Little Night Music*, starring Natasha Richardson (as Desirée Armfeldt), Vanessa Redgrave (Madame Armfeldt), Victor Garber (Frederick Egerman), Christine Baranski (Charlotte), Jill Paice (Anne Egerman), Marc Kudisch (Carl-Magnus), Steven Pasquale (Henrik Egerman) and Kendra Kassebaum (Petra).

Scott Ellis directed the fundraising production, which marked Richardson's final stage performance before her untimely death in a skiing accident a few weeks later.

(L-R): Natasha Richardson with her mother, Vanessa Redgrave at Studio 54.

Seventh Annual Red Ball

February 13, 2009 at the National Arts Club

Donald Smith was honored at the Seventh Annual Red Ball, the Valentine's Day-themed gala, which was hosted by the National Arts Club.

A variety of performers from the world of Broadway and cabaret spoke and performed. Smith is widely recognized for his leadership in the city's annual Cabaret Convention.

Donald Smith (center back row, holding box) surrounded by the various speakers and performers who honored him including (L) Karen Akers and Front Row (L-R): Lee Roy Reems, K.T. Sullivan and Marian Seldes.

Photo by Aubrey Reuben

Best Performance b
Musical
*David Alvarez, Ti
Kulish, *Billy Elliot,*
Gavin Creel, *Hair*
Brian d'Arcy James,
Constantine Maroul
J. Robert Spencer, *N*

Best Performance
Play
Hope Davis, *God o*
Jane Fonda, *33 Vari*
Marcia Gay Hard
Janet McTeer, *Mar*
Harriet Walter, *Ma*

Best Performance
Play
Jeff Daniels, *God o*
Raúl Esparza, *Spee*
James Gandolfini,
Geoffrey Rush, I
Thomas Sadoski, *i*

Best Performance
Musical
Jennifer Damiano
Haydn Gwynne, *I*
Karen Olivo, W
Martha Plimpton
Carole Shelley, *B*

Best Performanc
Musical
David Bologna, *I*
Gregory Jbara,
Marc Kudisch, *9*
Christopher Sieb
Will Swenson, *I*

Best Performan
in a Play
Hallie Foote, *Di*
Jessica Hynes, *T*
Marin Ireland, *i*
Angela Lansb
Amanda Root,

Best Performa
Play
John Glover, *W*
Zach Grenier, *J*
Stephen Manga
Paul Ritter, *Th*
Roger Robi
Gone

Best Origina
Written for th
Billy Elliot, Th
Music: Elton J
Lyrics: Lee Ha

Next to Nor
Music: Tom I
Lyrics: Brian

9 to 5: The M
Music and Ly

Shrek The Mu
Music: Jeanin
Lyrics: David

The 23rd Annual Easter Bonnet Competition

April 27-28, 2009 at the Minskoff Theatre

The 23rd annual Broadway Cares/ Equity Fights AIDS Easter Bonnet Competition thumbed its nose at the recession to raise $3,402,147 in six weeks of nightly curtain-call appeals by 58 participating Broadway, Off-Broadway and touring shows.

Susan Sarandon (*Exit the King*), Jeremy Irons (*Impressionism*) and Jane Fonda (*33 Variations*) presented the awards. *33 Variations* won both Best Bonnet and Best Presentation (pictured below) and collected $183,546, the most of any Broadway play or musical, and the all-time record for a non-musical.

However, the fundraising champ was the national touring company of *Rent*, which collected $352,000.

Runners-up for fundraising (all Broadway musicals): *Wicked* $176,714, *Billy Elliot* $155,103 and *Shrek* $139,304.

Runners-up for best bonnet and skit: *Billy Elliot* (a hat resembling a tutu) and *Naked Boys Singing* (a hat consisting of an outsize glittery ribbon spelling out the word "Live" in script).

1. The cast of *Wicked* pay their respects to fecund tabloid curiosity "Octomom."
2. Liza Minnelli (*Liza's at the Palace*) tops the opening number with a rendition of "New York, New York."
3. Perennial favorite, 105-year-old *Ziegfeld Follies* girl Doris Eaton Travis, teaches a dance to the girls' ballet corp of *Billy Elliot,* with a hand from Gregory Jbara.
4. Jane Fonda leads the cast of *33 Variations* in a "Voluntary Rehearsal" reminiscent of one of her 1980's "Jane Fonda's Workout" videos.
5. Don Richard and Jen Cody reprise their portrayals of *Urinetown*'s Officer Lockstock and Little Sally.

Photo by Tomas Vrzala

Photo by Carlos Gustavo Monroy

Photo by Aubrey Reuben

Photo by Tomas Vrzala

Photo by Carlos Gustavo Monroy

The A

June 7, 2009 at F

Billy Elliot,
Norman C
duction o
Awards.

The 63rd a
excellence in Bro
season, were pres
in a ceremony h
broadcast on CE
ients of the 6
"Tony" Awards
boldface, with

Best Musical
Billy Elliot, T
Next to Normal
Rock of Ages
Shrek The Musi

Best Play
Dividing the Es
God of Carna
reasons to be pr
33 Variations

Best Revival
Guys and Doll
Hair
Pal Joey
West Side Story

Best Revival
Joe Turner's C
Mary Stuart
The Norma
Waiting for G

Best Special
Liza's at Th
Slava's Snows
Soul of Shaol
You're Welcon
with Geor

Best Perfor
Musical
Stockard Ch
Sutton Fost
Allison Jann
Alice Ripl
Josefina Sca

1. Winner:
   Marc
   Kul
   Billy Ell
2. (L-F

3. Press a

4. The o
   prod

The Tony Awards

Best Scenic Design of a Play
Dale Ferguson, *Exit the King*
Rob Howell, *The Norman Conquests*
Derek McLane, 33 Variations
Michael Yeargan, *Joe Turner's Come and Gone*

Best Scenic Design of a Musical
Robert Brill, *Guys and Dolls*
Ian MacNeil, Billy Elliot, The Musical
Scott Pask, *Pal Joey*
Mark Wendland, *Next to Normal*

Best Costume Design of a Play
Dale Ferguson, *Exit the King*
Jane Greenwood, *Waiting for Godot*
Martin Pakledinaz, *Blithe Spirit*
Anthony Ward, Mary Stuart

Best Costume Design of a Musical
Gregory Gale, *Rock of Ages*
Nicky Gillibrand, *Billy Elliot, The Musical*
Tim Hatley, Shrek The Musical
Michael McDonald, *Hair*

Best Lighting Design of a Play
David Hersey, *Equus*
David Lander, *33 Variations*
Brian MacDevitt, Joe Turner's Come and Gone
Hugh Vanstone, *Mary Stuart*

Best Lighting Design of a Musical
Kevin Adams, *Hair*
Kevin Adams, *Next to Normal*
Howell Binkley, *West Side Story*
Rick Fisher, Billy Elliot, The Musical

Best Orchestrations
Larry Blank, *Irving Berlin's White Christmas*
TIE Martin Koch, Billy Elliot, The Musical
TIE Michael Starobin and Tom Kitt, Next to Normal
Danny Troob and John Clancy, *Shrek The Musical*

Best Sound Design of a Musical
Acme Sound Partners, *Hair*
Paul Arditti, Billy Elliot, The Musical
Peter Hylenski, *Rock of Ages*
Brian Ronan, *Next to Normal*

Best Sound Design of a Play
Paul Arditti, *Mary Stuart*
Gregory Clarke, Equus
Russell Goldsmith, *Exit the King*
Scott Lehrer and Leon Rothenberg, *Joe Turner's Come and Gone*

Special Tony Award for Lifetime Achievement in the Theatre
Jerry Herman

Regional Theatre Tony Award
Signature Theatre, Arlington, Virginia

Isabelle Stevenson Award
Phyllis Newman

Tony Honor for Excellence in the Theatre
Shirley Herz

Here's a tally of the 2009 Tony Award winners:

Billy Elliot, The Musical 10
God of Carnage 3
Next to Normal 3
Joe Turner's Come and Gone 2
Blithe Spirit 1
Equus 1
Exit the King 1
Hair 1
Liza's at The Palace... 1
Mary Stuart 1
The Norman Conquests 1
Shrek The Musical 1
33 Variations 1
West Side Story 1

1. At the Tony Brunch (L-R): Jeff Daniels, Hope Davis, Marcia Gay Harden and James Gandolfini of *God of Carnage*.
2. *33 Variations'* nominees (L-R): Zach Grenier, Jane Fonda and playwright Moisés Kaufman.
3. (L-R): Nominees Christopher Sieber (*Shrek*) and Marc Kudisch (*9 to 5*).

Photos by Aubrey Reuben

Other Theatre Awards

Covering the 2008-2009 Broadway Season

THE PULITZER PRIZE FOR DRAMA
Ruined by Lynn Nottage (Off-Broadway)

NY DRAMA CRITICS' CIRCLE AWARDS
Best Play: *Ruined* (OB)
Best Musical: *Billy Elliot, The Musical*
Best Foreign Play: *Black Watch* (OB)
Special Citation: Angela Lansbury
Special Citation: Gerard Alessandrini for *Forbidden Broadway* (OB)
Special Citation: Matthew Warchus and the cast of *The Norman Conquests*

DRAMA DESK AWARDS
Outstanding Play: *Ruined* by Lynn Nottage (OB)
Outstanding Musical: *Billy Elliot, The Musical* by Elton John and Lee Hall
Outstanding Revival of a Play: *The Norman Conquests* by Alan Ayckbourn
Outstanding Revival of a Musical: *Hair* by G. MacDermot, G. Ragni and J. Rado
Outstanding Actor in a Play: Geoffrey Rush, *Exit the King*
Outstanding Actress in a Play: Janet McTeer, *Mary Stuart*
Outstanding Actor in a Musical: Brian d'Arcy James, *Shrek the Musical*
Outstanding Actress in a Musical: Allison Janney, *9 to 5*
Outstanding Featured Actor in a Play: Pablo Schreiber, *reasons to be pretty* (OB)
Outstanding Featured Actress in a Play: Angela Lansbury, *Blithe Spirit*
Outstanding Featured Actor in a Musical: Gregory Jbara, *Billy Elliot, The Musical*
Outstanding Featured Actress in a Musical: Haydn Gwynne, *Billy Elliot, The Musical*
Outstanding Director of a Play: Matthew Warchus, *The Norman Conquests*
Outstanding Director of a Musical: Stephen Daldry, *Billy Elliot, The Musical*
Outstanding Choreography: Peter Darling, *Billy Elliot, The Musical*
Outstanding Music: Elton John, *Billy Elliot, The Musical*
Outstanding Lyrics: Stephen Sondheim, *Road Show* (OB)
Outstanding Book of a Musical: Lee Hall, *Billy Elliot, The Musical*
Outstanding Orchestrations: Martin Koch, *Billy Elliot, The Musical*
Outstanding Music in a Play: Dominic Kanza, *Ruined* (OB)
Outstanding Set Design of a Play: David Korins, *Why Torture Is Wrong and the People Who Love Them* (OB)

(L-R): Jerry Zaks and Stockard Channing help honor costume designer William Ivey Long as he picked up the TDF/Irene Sharaff Lifetime Achievement Award at the Hudson Theatre March 27, 2009.

Photos by Aubrey Reuben

Outstanding Set Design of a Musical: Tim Hatley, *Shrek the Musical*
Outstanding Costume Design: Tim Hatley, *Shrek the Musical*
Outstanding Lighting Design in a Play: David Hersey, *Equus*
Outstanding Lighting Design in a Musical: Rick Fisher, *Billy Elliot, The Musical*
Outstanding Sound Design: Paul Arditti, *Billy Elliot, The Musical*
Outstanding Solo Performance: Lorenzo Pisoni, *Humor Abuse* (OB)
Unique Theatrical Experience: *Celebrity Autobiography: In Their Own Words* (OB)
Outstanding Ensemble Performance: The cast of *The Norman Conquests*
Outstanding Ensemble Performance: The cast of *The Cripple of Inishmaan* (OB)
Special Award to Liza Minnelli
Special Award to *Forbidden Broadway*
Special Award to Atlantic Theater Company and artistic director Neil Pepe
Special Award to TADA! Youth Theater

OUTER CRITICS CIRCLE AWARDS
Outstanding New Broadway Play: *God of Carnage*
Outstanding New Broadway Musical: *Billy Elliot, The Musical*
Outstanding New Off-Broadway Play: *Ruined* (OB)
Outstanding New Off-Broadway Musical: *The Toxic Avenger* (OB)
Outstanding New Score (Bway or Off): *Billy Elliot, The Musical*
Outstanding Revival of a Play: *The Norman Conquests*
Outstanding Revival of a Musical: *Hair*
Outstanding Director of a Play (Lucille Lortel Award): Matthew Warchus, *The Norman Conquests*
Outstanding Director of a Musical: Stephen Daldry, *Billy Elliot, The Musical*

(L-R): Manhattan Theatre Club's Mandy Greenfield, Lynne Meadow, Lynn Nottage (author of *Ruined*) and Barry Grove at the New York Drama Critics' Circle Awards at the Algonquin Hotel May 11, 2009.

Other Theatre Awards

Covering the 2008-2009 Broadway Season

Outstanding Choreography: Peter Darling, *Billy Elliot, The Musical*

Outstanding Set Design: Tim Hatley, *Shrek the Musical*

Outstanding Costume Design: Tim Hatley, *Shrek the Musical*

Outstanding Lighting Design: Rick Fisher, *Billy Elliot, The Musical*

Outstanding Actor in a Play: Geoffrey Rush, *Exit the King*

Outstanding Actress in a Play: Marcia Gay Harden, *God of Carnage*

Outstanding Actor in a Musical: Brian d'Arcy James, *Shrek the Musical*

Outstanding Actress in a Musical: Josefina Scaglione, *West Side Story*

Outstanding Featured Actor in a Play: David Pearse, *The Cripple of Inishmaan* (OB)

Outstanding Featured Actress in a Play: Angela Lansbury, *Blithe Spirit*

Outstanding Featured Actor in a Musical: Gregory Jbara, *Billy Elliot, The Musical*

Outstanding Featured Actress in a Musical: Haydn Gwynne, *Billy Elliot, The Musical*

Outstanding Ensemble Performance: the cast of *The Norman Conquests*

Outstanding Solo Performance: Lorenzo Pisoni, *Humor Abuse* (OB)

John Gassner Award (New American Play): Gina Gionfriddo, *Becky Shaw* (OB)

Special Achievement Award: David Alvarez, Trent Kowalik, Kiril Kulish, *Billy Elliot, The Musical*

THE DRAMA LEAGUE AWARDS

Distinguished Production of a Play: *God of Carnage*

Distinguished Production of a Musical: *Billy Elliot, The Musical*

Distinguished Revival of a Play: *Blithe Spirit*

Distinguished Revival of a Musical: *Hair*

Distinguished Performance Award: Geoffrey Rush, *Exit the King*

Distinguished Achievement in Musical Theatre Award: Elton John

Julia Hansen Award for Excellence in Directing: Arthur Laurents

Unique Contribution to the Theatre: Angela Lansbury

THEATRE WORLD AWARDS

For outstanding Broadway or Off-Broadway debuts:

David Alvarez, Trent Kowalik, Kiril Kulish, *Billy Elliot, The Musical*
Chad L. Coleman, *Joe Turner's Come and Gone*
Jennifer Grace, *Our Town* (OB)
Josh Grisetti, *Enter Laughing, The Musical* (OB)
Haydn Gwynne, *Billy Elliot, The Musical*
Colin Hanks, *33 Variations*
Marin Ireland, *reasons to be pretty* (OB)
Susan Louise O'Connor, *Blithe Spirit*

(L-R): Cheyenne Jackson, Rosie Perez and Bobby Cannavale announced nominations for the Drama League Awards at Sardi's April 21, 2009.

Condola Rashad, *Ruined* (OB)
Geoffrey Rush, *Exit the King*
Josefina Scaglione, *West Side Story*
Wesley Taylor, *Rock of Ages*
Special Award to the cast of *The Norman Conquests*: Amelia Bullmore, Jessica Hynes, Stephen Mangan, Ben Miles, Paul Ritter, Amanda Root

THE CLARENCE DERWENT AWARDS

From Actors' Equity for "most promising female and male performers on the New York metropolitan scene."

Quincy Tyler Bernstine, *Ruined* (OB)
Aaron Tveit, *Next to Normal*

THE RICHARD SEFF AWARDS

From Actors' Equity, to "female and male character actors 50 years of age or older."

Lynn Cohen, *Chasing Manet* (OB)
Roger Robinson, *Joe Turner's Come and Gone*

OTHER ACTORS' EQUITY AWARDS

Joe A. Callaway Award for best performances in a classical play in the New York metropolitan area: Kathryn Meisle and Everett Quinton, both *Women Beware Women* (OB)

St. Clair Bayfield Award for the best supporting performance by an actor in a Shakespearean play in the New York metropolitan area: Stark Sands, *The Tempest* (OB)

ACCA Award for Outstanding Broadway Chorus: the opening night cast of *In the Heights*

THE IRENE SHARAFF AWARDS

From the Theatre Development Fund, for outstanding costume design

Robert L.B. Tobin Award for Lifetime Achievement: Bob Crowley

Memorial Tribute Award: Irene Sharaff

Artisan Award: Sally Ann Parsons

Lifetime Achievement Award: William Ivey Long

Young Master Award: Clint Ramos

FRED AND ADELE ASTAIRE AWARDS

Best Choreographer on Broadway: Peter Darling, *Billy Elliot, The Musical*

Best Female Dancer on Broadway: Pia Glenn, *You're Welcome America: A Final Night With George W Bush*

Best Male Dancer on Broadway: David Alvarez, Trent Kowalik and Kiril Kulish, *Billy Elliot, The Musical*

Douglas Watt Lifetime Achievement Award: Stanley Donen

HENRY HEWES DESIGN AWARDS

Given by the American Theatre Wing in December 2008 for work in the 2007-2008 Season

Scenic Design: Mark Wendland, *Next to Normal* (OB) and *Unconditional* (OB)

Costume Design: Katrina Lindsay, *Les Liaisons Dangereuses*

Lighting Design: Donald Holder, *Cyrano de Bergerac*, *Les Liaisons Dangereuses* and *South Pacific*

Notable Effects (Projection Design): Jim Findlay and Jeff Sugg, *The Slug Bearers of Kayrol Island* (OB)

GRAMMY AWARD

Best Musical Show Album: *In the Heights*

(L-R): Jim Dale and Faith Prince announced nominations for the Drama Desk Awards at the New York Friars Club April 27, 2009.

Faculty

The Shubert Organization

Philip J. Smith
Chairman

Robert E. Wankel
President

Jujamcyn Theatres

Rocco Landesman
President

Paul Libin
Producing Director

Jack Viertel
Creative Director

Jordan Roth
Vice President

Faculty

The Nederlander Organization

James M. Nederlander
Chairman

Freida Belviso
Chief Financial Officer

Jim Boese
Vice President

Susan Lee
Chief Marketing Officer

Jack Meyer
Vice President Programming

James L. Nederlander
President

Charlene S. Nederlander
Vice President Corporate Development

Kathleen Raitt
Vice President Corporate Relations

Nick Scandalios
Executive Vice President

Herschel Waxman
Senior Vice President Labor Relations

NEDERLANDER STAFF
Front Row (L-R): Rina Beacco, Alyce Cozzi, Phyllis Buono, Lisa Lent, Maleka Musliwala, Maria Manduca, Brian Harasek, Renee Pressley.
Second Row (L-R): Alice Gold, Blair Zwillman, Julia Barr, Carmen Santiago, Susan Knoll, Nancy Santiago, Josh Salez, Rachel Jukofsky, Rebecca Velazquez, Jennifer McKnight, David Perry, Nevolia Corbett-Williams, Marjorie Stewart.
Back Row (L-R): David Vaughn and Ken Happel.

Not pictured: Kim Angad-Jugmohan, Thuy Dang, Jey Moore and Erin Porvaznik.

Faculty

The Broadway League

Nina Lannan
Chair

Charlotte St. Martin
Executive Director

Back Row (L-R): Neal Freeman, Bob Davis, Chris Brockmeyer, Erin Rech, Colin Gibson, Mary McColl, Jon Levenson, Charlotte St. Martin, Jean Kroeper, Josh Cacchione
Middle Row (L-R): Erica Ryan, Ed Sandler, Thomas Ferrugia, Rachel Reiner, Britt Marden, Amy Steinhaus, Shoshana Parets, Jan Svendsen, Christina Boursiquot, Ben Pesner, Joy Axelrad
Front Row (L-R): Chelsi Conklin, Zenovia Varelis, Lindsay Florestal, Laura Fayans, Patty Casterlin, Jessica Storm, Elisa Shevitz

Not Pictured: Robin Fox, Karen Hauser, David Henry Hwang, Roxanne Rodriguez, Marva Smalls, Jennifier Stewart

Producers and Producing Companies

Roger Berlind

Bob Boyett

John Breglio,
Vienna Waits
Productions

Bill Haber/
Ostar Productions

Cameron Mackintosh

Arielle Tepper Madover

Barry and Fran
Weissler

Stewart F. Lane and
Bonnie Comley

Faculty

Manhattan Theatre Club

Front Row (L-R): Ann Mundorff, Philip Naudé, Nancy Piccione, Barry Grove, Lynne Meadow, Mandy Greenfield, Amy Loe.
Second Row (L-R): Thatcher Stevens, Kevin Emrick, Emily Hammond, Caitlin Baird, Julia Davis, Kristi Taylor, Lindsey Brooks Sag, Kelly Haydon, Darren Robertson, Gillian Campbell.
Third Row (L-R): Debra Waxman, Alex Barron, Andrea Gorzell, Lisa McNulty, Antonello Di Benedetto, Samantha Mascali, Annie MacRae, Jerry Patch, Kelsey Martinez.
Back Row (L-R): Carsten Losse, Laurel Bear, Adam Cook, Roger Kingsepp, Edward Allen, Drew Ross, Sunil Ayyagari, Mendy Sudranski, Kurt Gardner, unidentified.

Dodger Theatricals

Front Row (L-R): Lauren White, Pamela Lloyd

Second Row (L-R): Lauren Freed, Laurinda Wilson, Paula Maldonado, Reena Bahadur

Third Row (L-R): Michael David, Ashley Tracey, Annie Van Nostrand, Anne Ezell, Sally Campbell Morse, Julia McAnuff, Andrew Serna

Back Row (L-R): Lauren Mitchell, Jennifer Vaughan, John Haber, Jeff Parvin, Dean Carpenter, Tony Lance

Faculty

The Roundabout Theatre Company

Front Row (L-R): Harold Wolpert (Managing Director), Todd Haimes (Artistic Director), Julia Levy (Executive Director)
Second Row (L-R): Greg Backstrom, Greg McCaslin, Rachel Ayers, Shannon Marcotte, Ashley Firestone, Maggie Cantrick, Rebecca Habel, Susan Neiman, Valerie Simmons
Third Row (L-R): Steve Deutsch, Frank Surdi, Jill Rafson, Carly DiFulvio, Laura Marshall, Josh Cohen, Carolyn Levande, Margaret Casagrande, Kadeem Harris, Dee Beider
Fourth Row (L-R): Tova Heller, Lise Speidel, Stefanie Schussel, Wendy Hutton, Charlie Garbowski, Dylan Nordan, Joshua Allen, Scott Kelly, Kayla Carpenter, Jay Gerlach, Erica Rotstein, Yonit Kafka, Joy Pak, Nicholas Caccavo
Fifth Row (L-R): David Jones, Monica Sidorchuk, Ethan Ubell, Josh Rozett, Marisa Perry, Roxana Petzold, Gavin Brown, Amber Jo Manuel, Julie D'Andrea, Lauren Owens, John LaBarbera, Lindsay Ericson
Sixth Row (L-R): James Graham, Jeff Monteith, Nalene Singh, Robert Kane, Ted Sod, Nick Nolte, Crosby Clyse, Tiffany Nixon, Darnell Franklin, Elisa Papa, Aliza Greenberg, Ashanti McIntosh, Jennifer DiBella
Back Row (L-R): Ryan Hallett, Tyler Ennis, Nancy Mulliner, Ellen Holt, Jim Roma, Mead Margulies, Chris Rummel, Jill Boyd, Revanth Anne, Nick Luckenbaugh, Steve Ryan

Tony Award Productions

Alan Wasser

Allan Williams

TonyAwards.com

(L-R): Andrew C. McGibbon, Valerie Smaldone, Ben Pesner and Erin Rech

Not pictured: Laura Ellis

Faculty

IATSE Local One, Stagehands

Photos by Ben Strothmann

Replacement Room Chairperson Daniel Thorn, Administrative Secretary Edmond F. Supple, Sr. and Financial Secretary Anthony Manno.

Seated (L-R): Chairman, Board of Trustees John M. Diaz, Sr., Recording-Corresponding Secretary Robert C. Score, President James J. Claffey, Jr., Vice-President William J. Walters, Treasurer Robert McDonough.

Standing (L-R): Television Business Manager Robert C. Nimmo, Television Business Manager Edward J. McMahon, III, Theatre Business Manager Michael Wekselblatt, Theatre Business Manager Kevin McGarty, Trustee William Ngai and Trustee Daniel D. Dashman.

Coalition of Broadway Unions and Guilds

Photo by Robert Viagas

Seated (L-R): Deborah Alton (AGMA), Mim Pollock (Local 306 IATSE), Larry Lorczak (AEA), Kimberly Rimbold (AEA), Ira Mont (AEA), Mike McBride (USA 829 IATSE), Cecilia Friederichs (USA 829 IATSE), Laura Penn (SDC)

Standing (L-R): Valerie Gladstone (Local 798 IATSE), Eddie Wright (Local 32BJ SEIU), Jeff Abramson (Local 32BJ SEIU), David Faux (Dramatists Guild), Mary Landolfi (Local 802 AFM), Mauro Melleno (SDC), Gene McElwain (Local 751 IATSE), Tony DePaulo (IATSE International), Bill Dennison (Local 802 AFM) Pat Langevin (USA 829 IATSE), Michael Wekselblatt (Local One IATSE), Jeff LeFevre (Local 802 AFM), John Diaz (Local One IATSE), Frank Connolly (Local 817 IBT), Evan Shoemake (SDC)

Faculty

Actors' Equity Association

Mark Zimmerman
President

John Connolly
Executive Director

NATIONAL COUNCIL

(L-R):
Executive Director John Connolly,
Second Vice President
Rebecca Kim Jordan,
Eastern Regional Vice President
Kate Shindle,
First Vice-President Paige Price,
and President Mark Zimmerman

Photos by Brian Mapp

Front Row (L-R): David Lotz, Debbie Johnson, Barry Rosenberg, Walt Kiskaddon, Kenneth Naanep

Second Row (L-R): Adeola Adegbola, Kathy Mercado, Quin Chia, Michelle Lehrman, Mary-Kate Gilrein, Erica Palmisano, Ioanna Psaroudakis

Third Row (L-R): Diane Raimondi, Lincoln Hayes, Maria Cameron, Cathy Jayne, Louise Foisy, Erin Denton, Michelle Kelts, Tara Mora, Pearl Brady

Fourth Row (L-R): Ellen Carter, Tatiana Kouloumbis, Gary Dimon, Dwane Upp, David Westphal, Russell Lehrer, Rick Berg, Joe Erdey, Jessica Palermo

Back Row (L-R): Jeffrey Bateman, Zalina Hoosein, Valerie La Varco, Larry Lorczak, Tom Kaub, Melissa Colgan, Dragica Dabo

Front Row (L-R): Steve DiPaola, Carol Waaser, Marie Gottschall, Chris Williams

Second Row (L-R): Jenifer Hills, Joyce Vinzani, Stephanie Masucci, Tom Miller, Ann Fortuno

Back Row (L-R): Julie Coppola, Joe Chiplock, Karen Master, Robert Fowler, Joe De Michele

Front Row (L-R): Allison Plotkin, Kristine Arwe, Courtney Godan, Karlene Laemmie

Back Row (L-R): Jillian Williams, Calandra Hackney, David Thorn, Jonathan Black

Faculty

Association of Theatrical Press Agents and Managers

Front Row (L-R): Penny Daulton, Robert Nolan (President), Shirley Herz, Susan Elrod.
Back Row (L-R): Mark Schweppe, Nick Kaledin (Secretary-Treasurer), Alan Markinson, David Calhoun
(Vice President), David Gersten, Rina Saltzman and Jonathan Shulman.

Stage Directors and Choreographers Society

Seated (L-R): Larry Carpenter (Executive Vice President), Kathleen Marshall (Vice President), Karen Azenberg (President), Laura Penn (Executive Director),
Doug Hughes (Treasurer).
Second Row (L-R): Marcia Milgrom Dodge, Edie Cowan, Susan H. Schulman, Kim Rogers, Elizabeth Miller, Gerald Freedman, Lisa Peterson, Barbara Wolkoff,
Sue Lawless, Tom Moore, Lena Abrams, John Everson.
Back Row (L-R): Walter Bobbie, Sam Bellinger, Mauro Melleno, Daniel Sullivan, Rob Ashford, Randy Anderson, Richard Hamburger, Evan Shoemake,
Preston Copley.
Board members not present: Julie Arenal, Joe Calarco, Tisa Chang, Michael John Garcés, Wendy Goldberg, Paul Lazarus, Ethan McSweeny, Amy Morton,
Sharon Ott, Lonny Price, Mary B. Robinson, Oz Scott, Leigh Silverman, David Warren and Chay Yew.

Faculty

The Dramatists Guild

COUNCIL
Seated (L-R): Theresa Rebeck, John Weidman, Marsha Norman

Standing (L-R): Stephen Schwartz, David Ives, Jonathan Reynolds

STAFF
Seated (L-R): Abby Marcus, Gary Garrison, Ralph Sevush, David Faux

Standing (L-R): Robert Ross Parker, Roland Tec, Larry Pontius, John Minore, Tari Stratton and Patrick Shearer

Photos by Brian Mapp

American Federation of Musicians, Local 802

Mary Landolfi
President

Bill Dennison
Recording Vice President

(L-R): Bud Burridge, Maxine Roach, Jay Blumenthal, Andy Schwartz, Al Hunt, Ethan Fein, Mary Landolfi, Maura Giannini, Jay Schaffner, Ken Rizzo, Bill Dennison and Mark Johansen

Photos by Walter Karling

Faculty

United Scenic Artists, IATSE Local 829

Back Row (L-R): Jim Gilmartin, Cathy Santucci-Keator, Jeff Davis, Michael McBride
Front Row (L-R): Cecilia Friederichs, Beverly Miller and F. Mitchell Dana

IATSE Local 306 Motion Picture Projectionists, Video Technicians and Allied Crafts (Ushers)

Front Row (L-R): Raphel Cortez, LuLu Caso, Lorraine Lowery, Donna Vanderlinden, Mim Pollock, Rita Russell, Susan Lehman, Joe Coco, Barry Grafman
Second Row (L-R): Roseann Cipriano, Joe Rivierzo, Matt Loeb, Michael Goucher, Ken Costigan, Matt Barnaba
Back Row (L-R): Curtis Hucks, Margie Blair, Kevin Costigan, Marty Roller, Hugo Capra, Peter Riley

Faculty

Treasurers & Ticket Sellers Union, IATSE Local 751

OFFICE STAFF/BOSSES
(L-R): Patricia Garrison, Gene McElwain, Lawrence Paone and Kathy McBrearty.

THE EXECUTIVE COUNCIL
Standing (L-R): Mike McCarthy, Fred Bonis, Harry Jaffie, Stanley Shaffer, Peter Attanasio Jr., Robert Begin, Patricia DeMato and Michael Loiacono.
Sitting (L-R): John Nesbitt, Fred Santore Jr., Karen Winer, Lawrence Paone, Gene McElwain, Matthew Fearon and Noreen Morgan.

Theatrical Wardrobe Union, IATSE Local 764

Seated Front Row (L-R): Peggy Donovan, Erin Brooke Roth, Shannon Koger, Barbara Hladsky, Luana Michaels, unidentified, Cindy Chock, Marilyn Knotts, David Mitchell.
Second Row (L-R): Marcel Schmid, Danajean Cicerchi, Veneda Truesdale, Peggy Danz Kazdan, Bobby Condon, Kristin Gardner, Pat Sullivan, Vangeli Kaseluris, Charlie Catanese.
Standing (L-R): Kirsten Mogg, Joanna Viverto, Dennis Birchall, Pat White, Barbara Rosenthal, Rosemary Taylor, James Kabel, Anita Ali Davis, Michael Gemignani, Bart Daudelin, Joan Boyce, James W. Swift, Shelly Friedman, Frank Gallagher, Deborah Unger, Matthew Quinn, Martha Smith, Jenna Krempel, Warren Wernick, Terry LaVada.

Faculty

Theatrical Teamsters, Local 817

EXECUTIVE BOARD
Front Row (L-R): Francis J. Connolly, Jr. (Business Agent & Union Trustee), Jim Leavey (Recording Secretary), Ed Iacobelli (Vice President).
Back Row (L-R): Mike Hyde (Union Trustee), Thomas R. O'Donnell (President), Thomas J. O'Donnell (Secretary-Treasurer), Kevin Keefe (Union Trustee).

STAFF
Front Row (L-R): Christine Harkerss (Human Resources), Tina Gusmano (Union Secretary).
Back Row (L-R): Terry Casaletta (Casting Director Organizer), Marge Marklin (Fund Secretary).

Not Present: Kathy Kreinbihl (Fund Administrator), Margie Vaeth (Union Secretary).

Service Employees International Union Local 32BJ

EXECUTIVE OFFICERS
(L-R): Kevin Doyle (Executive Vice President), Héctor J. Figueroa (Secretary-Treasurer) and Michael P. Fishman (President).

International Union of Operating Engineers Local 30

BUSINESS MANAGER
John T. Ahern

Faculty

American Theatre Wing

Photo by Steve Shevett

BOARD OF DIRECTORS AND STAFF
Seated (L-R): Enid Nemy, Doug Leeds, Sondra Gilman, Dasha Epstein, Pia Lindström, Alan Siegel
Middle Row (L-R): Anita Jaffe, Jo Sullivan Loesser, Barbara Toy, Raisa Ushomirskiy, Randy Ellen Lutterman, Myra Wong, Gail Yancosek, Ted Chapin (Chairman)
Back Row (L-R): Howard Sherman (Executive Director), William Craver, Christopher Rovente, David Brown, Joanna Sheehan, Robb Perry, Lexie Pregosin
Not pictured: Lucie Arnaz, Kate Burton, Mallory Factor, James Higgins, Jeffrey Eric Jenkins, Ronald S. Konecky, Michael Price, Bruce Redditt, Jane Safer, Peter Schneider, Sally Susman and Sir Howard Stringer.

ATW Theatre Intern Group

Photo courtesy The American Theatre Wing

Kneeling (L-R): Louisa Balch, Eva Amesse, Andrea Barnett, Amy Lipson, Katie Chambers, Sarah Berk, Andrew Tejada, Samantha Schecter, Alex Parra, Andrea Zee
Seated (L-R): Rebecca Falcon, Tanis Parenteau, Bethany Pollock, Azure Osbourne-Lee, Aleeza Sklover, Tonianne Cincotta, Estafanía Fadul, Rachel Weiss, Jason Haft
Standing (L-R): Ruthie Fierberg, Alex Hadashi, Bradley Cherna, Jeffrey Simno, Liz Humphrey, Brian Carey, William Steinberger, Natalie Dominguez, Colin O'Rourke, David Bruin, Casey Keeler, Jordan Levine, Charity Schubert, Marie Huntley, Karl Hinze, Michael Piscadlo, Matt Gabbard, Sarah Packard, Stefanie Grassley, Zack Baer, unidentified, unidentified, Amy Claussen, Zarinah Washington

Faculty

Broadway Cares/Equity Fights AIDS

Front Row (L-R): Wendy Merritt Kaufman, Meagan Grund, Janie Smulyan, Scott Tucker, Ngoc Bui, K.T. Baumann, Jody O'Neil, Brian Schaaf.
Second Row (L-R): Director of Finance and Administration Larry Cook, Christopher F. Davis, Cat Domiano, Andy Halliday, Michelle Abesamis, Carol Ingram, Josh Blye, Denise Roberts Hurlin, Ed Garrison.
Third Row (L-R): Executive Director Tom Viola, Scott T. Stevens, Trisha Doss, Peter Borzotta, Frank Conway, Michael Simmons-DeFord, Michael T. Clarkston, Keith Bullock, Rose James, Madeline Reed.
Back Row (L-R): Nathan Hurlin, Skip Lawing, Chris Economakos, Michael Palm, Producing Director Michael Graziano.
Not Pictured: Chris Kenney, Yvonne Ghareeb, Charles Hamlen, Dennis Henriquez, Bobby McGuire, Joe Norton, Roy Palijaro, Andy Smith.

Hudson Scenic Studio

Faculty

Theatre Development Fund and TKTS

Photographed at the new TKTS Booth in Father Duffy Square.

Street Level (L-R): TDF Senior Staff: William Castellano, Doug Smith, Marianna Houston, Tymand Staggs, Veronica Claypool, Victoria Bailey, Joy Cooper, Eric Sobel, Lisa Carling, Julian Christenberry, Stephen Cabral

On Stairs (L-R): Cheryl Schoonmaker, Rob Kendt, Thomas Adkins, James Parks, Ginger Meagher, Patty Allen, Jonathan Calindas, Robert Gore, Jessica Kausen, Denyse Owens, James Crochet, Costas Michalopoulos, Catherine Lizima, Meagan Keener, Nicole Prosper-LaPene, Rob Neely, Eve Rodriguez, Thomas Westerman, Fran Plizzi, Michelle St. Hill, Richard Price, Ray Atherton, Howard Marren, Michael Yaccarino, Joseph Cali

Not Pictured: David LeShay

Photos by David LeShay

TKTS TREASURERS

Standing (L-R):
Rajesh Sharma,
Wesley Heron,
William Castellano,
William Roeder,
Brian Roeder,
Charles Stuis, Jr.

(Center): Joseph Monte

Faculty

The Actors Fund

TRUSTEES
Front Row (L-R): Lynn Redgrave, Jane Powell,
Kate Edelman Johnson, Anita Jaffe.
Standing (L-R): Dr. Marc Grodman, Charles Hollerith,
George Zuber, Charlotte St. Martin, Jeffrey Bolton,
Stewart Lane, Honey Waldman, Alan Levey, Dale Olson,
Paul Libin.
Partially Hidden (L-R): Merle Debuskey, Scott Weiner,
Kristen Madsen, Edward Turen, Brian Stokes Mitchell,
B.D. Wong, John Erman.
Back Row: Frank Horak.

NEW YORK STAFF
Front Row (L-R): Louie Anchondo, Ryan Dietz, Amy Picar,
Gail Perlman, Suzanne Tobak, Joy Pascua-Kim,
Connie Yoo, Li Yin Li.
Second Row (L-R): Tim Pinckney, Daniel Scholz,
Marieluisa Stern, Dalin Rivera, Stephanie Coleman,
Jay Haddad, Ina Sorens Clark, Victor Mendoza,
Erica Chung.
Third Row (L-R): Israel Duran, Zehava Krinsky,
Tony Lopez-Linus, Joe Benincasa (Executive Director),
Carol Wilson, Tamar Shapiro, Lucy Seligson,
Manira Hossain, Jose Delgado, Harry Ballard,
Barbara Davis.
Back Row (L-R): Sam Smith, DJ Brumfield, Charlene Nurse,
David Engelman, James Brown, Wally Munro, Gloria Jones,
Marjorie Roop, Renata Marinaro, Lynnell Herzer,
Ricardo Montero.

Photos by Brian Mapp

Photo courtesy The Actors Fund

**STAFF OF THE ACTORS FUND'S
LILLIAN BOOTH ACTORS' HOME (ENGLEWOOD, NJ)**
Nash Chien, Narine Gordon, Elaine Panton, Uraina Gray, Milagros Herbert,
Jennifer Hayden, Janet Hibbert, Gerry Gallyot, Adiela Sanchez, Charmaine
Mark, Frances McCain, Debra Dillard, Maritza Bonilla, Beverly Cushnie,
Jordan Strohl, Tolgonay Agamez, Lydia Hance, Emma Nichson, Maria Box,
Jeanette Rivera, Igor Denisenko, Taida Santana, Soo Donlin, Victor
Goldsmith, Grace Park, Luz Lopez, Susan Kang, Kim Eng, Hernando
Sepulveda, Stephanie Weeks, Rochelle Nuss, AnnMarie Defies, Wendy
Joseph, Florence Lynch, Cleveland Pickens, Lucy Palakudy.

Photo courtesy The Actors Fund

**STAFFS OF THE DOROTHY ROSS FRIEDMAN
RESIDENCES IN MANHATTAN, THE AL HIRSCHFELD
FREE HEALTH CLINIC IN MANHATTAN AND
SCHERMERHORN HOUSE IN BROOKLYN**
Front Row (L-R): Lorraine Chisholm, Ellen Celnik,
Linda Sax Craig, Jamie Trachtenberg, Hope Geteles,
Janet Pearl.
Back Row (L-R): Matthew Brookshire, Liz Lawlor,
Jonathan Margolies, John Barrow, Dr. James Spears.

LOS ANGELES STAFF
Front Row (L-R): Liz Morasso, Keith McNutt, Gabrielle
Forman, Gregory Polcyn, Tina Abas, Gregory King
Back Row (L-R): Dan Kitowski, Heather Vanian,
Michael Salerno, Lauren Trotter, Angelique Prahalis,
Roni Blau, Logan Speers, Linda Zimmerman,
Jan Kees Van Der Gaag.

Photo courtesy The Actors Fund

Faculty

Boneau/Bryan-Brown

Chris Boneau

Adrian Bryan-Brown

Photos by Joan Marcus

Jim Byk

Brandi Cornwell

Jackie Green

Kelly Guiod

Linnae Hodzic

Jessica Johnson

Kevin Jones

Amy Kass

Aaron Meier

Christine Olver

Joe Perrotta

Matt Polk

Rachel Stange

Heath Schwartz

Susanne Tighe

Faculty

The Hartman Group (formerly Barlow•Hartman Public Relations)

(L-R): Leslie Baden, Matt Ross, Holly Kinney, Wayne Wolfe, Michael Hartman, Juliana Hannett, Michelle Bergmann, Tom D'Ambrosio, Matt Shea and Frances Connelly

Photo courtesy The Hartman Group

Richard Kornberg & Associates

Richard Kornberg

Don Summa

Billy Zavelson

Alyssa Hart

Photos by Ben Strothmann

The Lawrence Company

(L-R): Nicole Harris, William Weaver, Suzanne Jakel, Michael P. Lawrence, Joanna B. Cepler, Richard Fromm, Emily Fisher

Photo courtesy The Lawrence Company

Faculty

Jeffrey Richards Associates

Standing (L-R):
Robert J. Saferstein,
Jeremy Scott Blaustein,
Jeffrey Richards, Elon Rutberg
Seated (L-R):
Kristin Piacentile, Irene Gandy,
Alana Karpoff, Diana Rissetto,
Charlie McAteer

Photo by Robert J. Saferstein

The Publicity Office

Standing (L-R):
Jeremy Shaffer
and Michael
Borowski.
Seated:
Marc Thibodeau
(with Berger).

Photo by Ben Strothmann

Cromarty & Co.

Peter Cromarty

Photo courtesy Cromarty & Co.

O&M Co.

Madeline
Miramontez
President

Maddie Barnett
Account Manager

Gizmo La Rosa
Carrubba
Account Manager

Charlie Dekker
Account Manager

Lysander Hillman
Account Manager

Photos courtesy O&M

Kame Kung
Office Manager

Roger Dimond
Snyder
Account Manager

Cleo Wagner
*Junior Account
Manager*

Interns

Faculty

G. ANDERSON
ART CLUB

B. AQUART
BASKETBALL

J. AQUINO
TRACK & FIELD

M. BARRY
BADMINTON

A. BIZJAK
JAZZ TEAM

G. COLEMAN
THEATRE TECHIE

J. COOPER
4-H

T. COPPOLA
CHORUS

D. COX
HISTORICAL SOCIETY

G. CRADDOCK
EAGLE SCOUTS

T. CREWS
TECHNOLOGY CLUB

A. CRUZ
GLEE CLUB

A. DAVIS
BLACK HISTORY CLUB

P. DUFFY
BALLET

T. FALOTICO
WATER POLO

C. FENTON
THATCHERITE

S. FITZPATRICK
CHEERLEADING

J. FRAENKEL
HILLEL

T. FRANCIS
STUDY CLUB

D. GANJOU
MODEL UN

R. GASKINS
DRILL TEAM

G. GREEN
PEP SQUAD

K. HALL
WEIGHTLIFTING

I. HILAIRE
SYNC. SWIMMING

L. HUNTER
ICE HOCKEY

L. JOHNSON
DANCE TEAM

L. KAISER
YEARBOOK

SpotCo Class of 2009

D. HODGES
PRINCIPAL

J. EDWARDS
VICE PRINCIPAL

B. BERK
DEAN OF STUDENTS

T. GREENWALD
AV SQUAD

K. LEVIN
HALL MONITOR

N. LINDEMAN
PING PONG

S. MAYA
FORENSICS

T. McCANN
EQUINE CLUB

M. McCRACKEN
DUNGEON MASTER

J. McNICHOLAS
BROADCAST CLUB

M. METTLER
CLOGGING

W. MITCHELL
DRAMA SOCIETY

D. PRESTON
MATHLETES

K. RATHBUN
QUIZ BOWL CAPTAIN

M. RHEAULT
WRESTLING

J. ROGERS
DRUMLINE

I. ROSEN
PROM COMMITTEE

A. ROTHENBERG
COLOR GUARD

V. SAINATO
DEBATE

S. SANTORE
CROSS COUNTRY

C. SEES
CLASS CLOWN

R. SIMNOWITZ
HOME ECONOMICS

C. SKENE
COMPUTER CLUB

J. SOCHACZEWSKI
EXCHANGE STUDENT

S. SOSNOWSKI
FENCING

A. SPIELMAN
NEWSPAPER

C. SPINNEY
BROWNIES

D. SUYAMA
SOCCER

L. TAYLOR
APIARIST CLUB

E. VICIOSO
BAND

B. WATSON
YOUNG DEMOCRATS

M. WILSTEIN
ASTRONOMY CLUB

Faculty

Andy Apostolides

David Barrineau

Sandy Block

Matt Britt

Denise Brown

Tom Callahan

Cara Christman

Greg Corradetti

Bruce Council

Nancy Coyne

Moira Deakin

Lauren D'Elia

Angelo Desimini

Joaquin Esteva

Joe Figliola

Peter Gunther

Lauren Houlberg

Noriko Ishikawa

Scott Johnson

Robert Jones

Marci Kaufman

Zack Kinney

Burt Kleeger

Jean Leonard

Kathryn Marotta

Chris Martin

Joette Martin

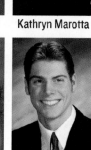
Roger Micone

Heather Millen

David Molina

Diane Niedzialek

Brad Pattinian

Andrea Prince

Catherine Reid

Jim Russek

Beth Schefflan

Aileen Siu

Caroline Thompson

Ginger Witt

Scott Yambor

Faculty

EMG
ELIRAN MURPHY GROUP
1040 Avenue of the Americas, Fifth Floor
New York, NY 10018
EMG-LTD.COM

a) Barbara Eliran b) Ann Murphy c) Richard Robertson d) Elizabeth Findlay
e) Janice Brunell (& chef) f) Jon Bierman g) DeWayne Snype h) Robert Marlin
i) Sasha DeFazio j) Randi Fields k) Adam Neumann l) Mary Costa m) Clint White
n) Suzanne Hereth o) Simona Tanasescu p) Frank "Fraver" Verlizzo q) Jeff Lilley
r) Pamela Bush s) Steve Knight & Terry Newberry t) Amy Lipson u) Patrick Flood
v) Shirley

Faculty

Faculty

Playbill

Philip S. Birsh
Publisher

Arthur T. Birsh
Chairman

Clifford S. Tinder
*Senior Vice President/
Publisher, Classic Arts
Division*

Joan Alleman
*Corporate Vice
President*

Photo by Brian Mapp

MANHATTAN OFFICE
Front Row Seated (L-R): Anderson Peguero and Robert Viagas
Second Row Seated (L-R): Rebeca Miller, Blake Ross, Clifford S. Tinder, Diana Leidel
Standing (L-R): David Gewirtzman, Jose Ortiz, Yajaira Marrero, Bruce Stapleton, Daniel Beaver-Seitz,
Jane Katz, Benjamin Finane, Irv Winick, Jolie Schaffzin, Glenn Shaevitz, Oldyna Dynowska, Maude Popkin,
Glenn Asciutto, Jill Napierala, Wanda Young, Theresa Holder, Jil Simon, Norman Miller, Silvija Ozols,
Samantha Souza and Ari Ackerman.

Not pictured: Clara Barragan-Tiburcio, Louis Botto, Esvard D'Haiti, Tiffany Feo, Arturo Gonzalez, Andrew Ku,
Alex Near, Kesler Thibert and Joel Wyman.

Photo by Brian Mapp

PLAYBILL.COM
(Seated L-R): David Gewirtzman,
Andrew Gans, Ernio Hernandez
(Standing L-R): Martha Graebner,
Matt Blank, Judy Samelson,
Kenneth Jones, Adam Hetrick
and Andrew Ku.

Michael Buckley
Columnist

Harry Haun
Columnist

Jennifer Lanter
Columnist

Mark Shenton
*London
Correspondent*

Robert Simonson
*Senior
Correspondent*

Steven Suskin
Columnist

Not pictured: Seth Rudetsky and Tom Nondorf.

Faculty

Playbill

CLASSIC ARTS DIVISION PROGRAM EDITORS
(L-R): Claire Mangan, Brian Libfeld, Rori Grable, Bill Reese and Kristy Bredin.
Not pictured: Silvia Cañadas, Maria Chinda and Andrew Rubin.

ACCOUNTING
(L-R): JoAnn D'Amato, John LoCascio, Beatriz Chitnis, Lewis Cole, Theresa Bernstein and James Eastman.

PROGRAM EDITORS
(L-R):
Scott Hale
(Off-Broadway)
and Pam Karr
(Broadway).

Carolina Diaz
Florida Production Manager

PLAYBILL RADIO
(L-R):
David Gewirtzman,
Robert Viagas
and Samantha
Souza

Ray Romano
Consulting Radio Producer

Regional Advertising Salespersons

Kenneth R. Back
Sales Manager Cincinnati

Elaine Bodker
Sales St. Louis

Dory Binyon
Sales Manager Chicago

Megan Boles
Sales Manager San Antonio

Carol Brumm
Sales St. Louis

Bob Caulfield
Sales San Francisco

Margo Cooper
Sales Manager St. Louis

Betsy Gugick
Sales Manager Dallas

Ron Friedman
Sales Manager Columbus

Tom Green
Sales Florida/Texas, etc.

Ed Gurien
Sales Florida/Dallas

Michel Manzo
Sales Manager Philadelphia

Marilyn A. Miller
Sales Manager Minneapolis

Judy Pletcher
Sales Manager Washington, DC

John Rosenow
Sales Manager Phoenix/Tucson

Kenneth Singer
Sales Manager Houston

Not Pictured: Jennifer Allington, Dick Coffee, Nancy Hardin, Karen Kanter, Jeff Ross, Sara Smith and Donald Roberts.

Faculty

Playbill / Woodside Office

PRODUCTION CHIEFS
(L-R): Louis Cusanelli, Robert Cusanelli and Patrick Cusanelli.

PRODUCTION
(L-R): Patrick Cusanelli, Benjamin Hyacinthe, David Porrello and Sean Kenny.

PRINTERS
Front Row (L-R): John Matthews, Domingo Pagan, Mary Roaid, David Rodriguez, Gilbert Gonzalez.

Second Row (L-R): Carlos Robinson, Manuel Guzman, Joseph Lucania, Ray Sierra, Nancy Galarraga, Arnold Jacklitsch, Scott Cipriano.

Back Row: Robert Cusanelli, Fabian Cordero, Louis Cusanelli, Fran Divirgilio, Ramdat Ramlall and Lennox Worrell.

PRINTERS
(L-R): Elias Garcia, Thomas McClenin, Sadu Greene, Frank Dunn, Kenneth Gomez, Maheshwari Moti, Thomas Pagliaro, Louis Cusanelli II and Carlos Moyano.

In Memoriam

May 2008 to May 2009

Doris Cole Abrahams
Edie Adams
Kenny Adams
Molly Adams
Bruce Adler
Jere Admire
Winifred Ainslee
John F. Altieri
Robert Anderson
Rose Arrick
Camila Ashland
Harrison Avery
Don Barnett
Joanne Belanger
Paul Benedict
Lynn Bernay
Shirl Bernheim
Marion Bertram
John E. Booth
Anne Brown
Buddy Bryan
Elaine Cancilla
Betty Carr
Carlene Carroll
Sydney Chaplin
Cyd Charisse
Keith Charles
Marilyn S. Cooper
Irene Dailey
Matthew Dalco
Linda Dangcil
Luther Davis
Nathan Davis
Bettina Dearborn
Sandra Deel
Dom DeLuise
Joseph Depauw
Hamp Dickens
James Dukas
Richard Durham
Richard Earle
George Eckert
Michael Ellis
Drummond Erskine
Walter Farrell
John Felton
Mel Ferrer
Bud Fleming
Gertrude Flynn
Nina Foch
William Francis
Abel Franco
David Fulford
George Furth

James Gallery
Gene Galusha
Estelle Getty
Cheryl Giannini
William Gibson
Steven Gilborn
Joey Ginza
Harry S. Gold
Dody Goodman
William Graham
Simon Gray
Louis Guss
A. Larry Haines
Lo Hardin
William Hardy
Naomi Hatfield
James Hawthorne
Jayne Heller
Eileen Herlie
Michael Higgins
Pat Hingle
Elijah Hodges
Louise Hoff
George Hoffman
Paul Huddleston
Ruth Jaffe
Ben Janney
Don Jay
Danny Joel
Van Johnson
Peter Kapetan
Peter Kass
Milton Katselas
Bob Kennedy
Neal Kenyon
John Michael King

Jay Kingwill
Eartha Kitt
Alvin Klein
Joan Kobin
Harvey Korman
Oni Faida Lampley
Edith Larkin
Ted Lawrie
Bill Lazarus
Hugh Leonard
K.C. Ligon
Stewart W. Little
Terrence J. Little
Nick Malekos
Anna Manahan
Howard Mann
Patricia Marand
Frank Marino
Kenneth Marsolais
John J. Martin
David Masters
Patrick McGoohan
Bob McClure
John McGlinn
Brooks McNamara
Harvey Medlinsky
Mario Melodia
John Messenger
Jerry Mickey
Lawrence Miller
Ralph Miller
Tom Miller
Philip Minor
Ricardo Montalban
Gavin H. Mooney
Jonathan Moore

Fred E. Morrow
Gladys Nederlander
Harriet Nichols
James Nichols
Rolla Nuckles
Marcia O'Brien
Jose Ocasio
Tom O'Horgan
Douglas Paasch
Moultrie Patten
Janet Pavek
Bruce Peyton
Arte Phillips
Howard Porter
Robert Prosky
Audree Rae
Alee Ralph
Mavis Ray
Terence Rigby
Tom Roland
Amelia Romano
Barbara Rubenstein
Dom Salinaro
Darrell Sandeen
Sarallen
Dorothy Sarnoff
Robert Shrewsbury
Lola Shumlin
Paul Sills
Lee Solters
Roy A. Somlyo
Robert St. Clair
Milan Stitt
Joyce Sullivan
Yma Sumac
Larry Swansen
A. Joseph Tandet
Eleanor Tauber
Barbara Ann Teer
Olice Thomas
Richard Thomsen
Matthew Tobin
Philip Truex
Richard Via
Daniel S. Walker
James M. Ward
Janet Ward
Jackie Warner
Dale Wasserman
Frank Wayne
James Whitmore
Donn Whyte
Clyde Williams
Van Williams

Index

Index

Index

Index

Index

Index

Index

Index

Index

Index

Index

Index

Index

Index

Maher, Joseph 70, 71, 96, 116, 117, 323, 325, 376
Maher, Kevin 70, 308, 309, 340
Maher, Michael Jr. 323
Mahon, John 32
Mahon, Melissa Rae iv, 41, 42, 43, 47
Mahon, Robert 227
Mahon, Sean 334, 335, 337
Mahoney, Brian 7, 10, 18, 32, 37, 53, 78, 82, 86, 90, 133, 197, 215, 223, 227, 253, 264, 286, 303, 313, 331, 336, 386
Mahoney, John 18
Mahshie, Jeff 224, 228
Maier, Charlotte 88, 89
Maier, Rachel 7
Mainard, Jim 286
Mainger, Debbie 325
Mais, Michele 272, 273
Maisto, Matthew 331
Maiuri, Brian 129, 202, 203, 258, 259
Maize, Jimmy 341
Maizus, Alex 311
Majidi, Shidan 211, 253
Major, Chris 190
Makarov, Fyodor 288, 289
Makay, Chris 323, 325
Makay, Dawn 323, 325
Makin, Lisa 40, 240, 277, 279
Makkoo, Susan 160
Mala, Elisa 129, 203, 245, 259, 319, 336, 356
Malabanan-McGrath, Alma 160
Malakoff, John 223
Malan, Jorie 95, 96
Malcolm, Graeme 80, 81
Maldonado, Katherine 239
Maldonado, Paula 160, 409
Malekos, Nick 432
Maley-Biancamano, Tyler 375
Maley, Linda 375
Malgiolio, Marco 77
Mali, Shanta 78
Malik, Art 277, 278
Malinowski, Tracey 185
Malkovich, John 18
Mallon, John 40
Malone, Steven 184
Maloney, James 178, 210
Maloney, Jennifer 169, 272, 274, 304, 307
Maloney, Jimmy Jr. 31, 303

Maloney, John 197
Maloney, Matthew 10, 163, 164
Maloney, Michael 196
Maloney, Peter 348, 349
Maltby, Richard Jr. viii, 311-313
Mamet, David iii, vii, ix, 9, 10, 300, 301
Manahan, Anna 432
Manahan, Robert 325
Manalansan, Mark 124, 125
Manalio, Whitney 125, 382
Manchon, Olivier 305
Mancina, Mark 173, 174, 177, 179
Mancuso, Catherine 18
Mancuso, Dave 218, 230
Mandell, Ronni 111, 125, 240, 276, 382
Manduca, Maria 407
Manello, Chrissy 325
Manet, Edouard 133
Manford, Gene 70
Mangan, Claire 430
Mangan, Stephen viii, 237-239, 401, 404
Manganaro, Al 210
Mangi, Nicole 105-107
Maniglia, Melissa 37, 221
Manilow, Barry 104
Manis, David 84, 85
Mann, David 120
Mann, Dwayne 370
Mann, Howard 432
Mann, Liz 294
Mann, Theodore 237, 240
Manners, Hilary 71, 335
Manning, Dorothy 362
Manning, Joanne 183
Manning, Robert 153
Manno, Anthony 411
Manocherian, Barbara 112, 115, 237, 239, 314, 317, 334
Manocherian, Jennifer 14, 16, 130, 132, 237, 239, 304, 307, 314, 317, 334
Manoff, Mark J. 336
Manolakos, Carrie 195
Manoy, Thomas 36
Mansbach, B. Thomas 227
Mansfield, Karl 373, 376
Mansfield, Tami 128, 202, 244, 258, 318, 336, 354
Mansker, Tony 205-208, 210

Mansur, Susan 146, 148, 152, 153
Mantello, Joe vii, 128, 202, 229, 231, 235, 241, 243, 244, 258, 318, 335, 354, 363, 366
Manuel, Amber Jo 129, 203, 244, 259, 318, 336, 356, 410
Manuel, Caren Lyn 268
Manye, Tshidi 173, 175
Manzo, Michel 430
Mapp, Brian i, iii, iv, 2, 7, 17, 23, 24, 30, 36, 37, 77, 89, 139, 143, 144, 149-151, 158, 159, 163, 193, 196, 202, 221, 239, 257, 258, 262, 263, 274, 275, 279, 280, 284, 285, 323, 324, 327, 340, 341, 345, 350, 409, 410, 412-416, 419, 421, 429, 430
Maraj, Anjie 179
Marambio, Freddy 3
Marand, Patricia 432
Marano, Melissa 111
Marano, Soomi 150, 153, 345, 346
Marasek, Jan 269, 270
Marcell, Andre 391
Marcell, Lauren 391
Marchica, Ray 193, 196
Marchione, Nicholas 181
Marchionni, Margie 252
Marcin, Brittany 65, 67
Marciszewski, John 325
Marcoccia, Dawn 275
Marconi, Daniel 209
Marcos, J. Elaine 48, 50
Marcotte, Shannon 129, 203, 244, 259, 318, 336, 356, 410
Marcum, Brian J. 217, 219
Marcus, Abby 414
Marcus, Daniel 241, 243
Marcus, Joan iv, 1, 3, 5, 7, 9, 14, 18, 38, 40, 58, 59, 64-66, 71, 75, 76, 78, 84, 86, 88-91, 96, 111-113, 129-131, 133, 135, 136, 140, 146, 149, 154, 160, 173, 179, 180, 181, 185, 192, 197, 200, 201, 203, 205, 211-213, 215, 217, 218, 223, 229, 230, 234, 241, 245, 247, 253, 256, 259, 270, 272,

273, 276, 277, 279, 281, 282, 286, 292, 298, 304, 305, 309, 314, 315, 319, 328, 330, 331, 333, 335, 338, 339, 341, 348, 351, 353, 356, 358, 362, 422
Marcus, Latiffa 319
Marcus, Pat 297, 298
Marden, Britt 408
Marder, Jeff 99, 102, 286
Mare, Kate 71
Maré, Quentin 256, 257
Maresca, Jim 391
Margolies, Jonathan 421
Margolyes, Miriam 367
Marguette, Dorothy 233
Margulies, Juliana 227
Margulies, Julianna 394
Margulies, Mead 129, 203, 245, 257, 259, 319, 336, 356
Marie, Cristina 239
Marik, Jennifer 369
Marin, Noah 37
Marin, Yanira 358- 60
Marinacci, Lori Eve 119-121
Marinaro, Renata 421
Maring, Christopher 309
Marino, Frank 432
Marino, Jennie 171
Marino, Kasey 119-121
Marino, Michael 286
Marino, Nicole 319
Marion, Dennis 196
Mariotti, Renee 335
Mark, Charmaine 421
Mark, Kimberly 62, 64, 132, 133
Markinson, Alan 375, 289, 376, 413
Markinson, Martin 288, 289, 372, 376
Markle, Lois 127, 128
Markley, Dan 146
Marklin, Marge 417
Markman, Neil 179, 185, 211
Markoff, Matthew 78
Markova, Alla 31
Markow, Rhonda M. 264
Marks, Alan D. 72, 300
Marks, Eddie 129
Marks, Johnny 270
Marks, Ken 119, 121
Marks, Lana 171
Marley, Susanne 14, 15
Marlin, Gary 158
Marlin, Robert 427
Marotta, Kathryn 426

Maroulis, Constantine viii, ix, 272, 273, 401
Marquette, Josh 197, 348, 349
Marquette, Seth 346, 362
Marquez, Amy 158
Marquez, David 18, 74
Marren, Howard 420
Marrero, Yajaira 429
Marroquin, Bianca 44
Marsden, Bernard 276
Marsh, Lane 57, 64
Marshak, Bob 253
Marshall, Herbert 4
Marshall, Jerry 286
Marshall, Karen 177
Marshall, Kathleen 38, 91, 93, 97, 128, 202, 244, 258, 318, 335, 354, 413
Marshall, Laura 259, 356, 410
Marsolais, Kenneth 171, 432
Marston, Ray 185
Martin, Andrea viii, 4, 84, 85, 87, 380, 389, 391
Martin, Barrett 101, 377-379
Martin, Brandon 335
Martin, Bud 229, 311
Martin, Elliot 9, 10
Martin, Eric 276
Martin, Gregory 197
Martin, Jerome 110, 362
Martin, Joette 426
Martin, John J. 432
Martin, Kat 129, 202, 203, 258, 259
Martin, Lucy 127, 128
Martin, Madeleine 14, 15
Martin, Marjorie 9
Martin, Mary 394
Martin, Michael X. 65-67, 229-231, 235, 236
Martin, Nicholas 333
Martin, Nora 368, 370
Martin, Raphael 351
Martin, Robert 223, 234, 362, 382
Martin, Ron 74, 109, 111
Martin, Susan 95, 96, 275
Martina, Tiger 187, 189-191
Martindale, Kelly 102-104
Martinez, Anthony 7, 52, 132
Martinez, Carlos 210
Martinez, Carmen 382
Martinez, Jonathan 245, 319, 356
Martinez, Kelsey 3, 13,

351, 409
Martinez, Maria 428
Martinez, Mike 284, 286
Marto, Ron 69
Martori, Gary 211
Marvel, Linda 338, 340, 341
Marvin, Kate 78, 298
Marx, Àra 37, 381
Marx, Jeff 20, 21
Marzan, Mary 69, 117, 324
Marzullo, Steve 193
Mascali, Samantha 3, 13, 351, 409
Masias, Felicia 23
Maskara, Meridith 151
Maso, Michael 333, 334
Mason, Essence 245, 318, 356
Mason, Hannah 289
Mason, Karen 119-121
Mason, Marsha viii, 130, 131, 134
Masse, Paul 151, 370
Massengill, David E. 336
Massey, Cara 166-168
Massey, Kyle Dean 363-365, 374
Massey, Rebecca 86
Mastascusa, Richie 146-148, 153, 246
Masten, Fritz 117
Master, Karen 412
Masters, David 432
Masterson, Jane 351
Mastro, Michael 358-360
Mastrone, Frank 247-249, 254
Masucci, Joe 125
Masucci, Stephanie 412
Matalon, Laura 31, 117, 129, 197, 203, 245, 259, 270, 289, 319, 356
Matarazzo, Gary 210
Mateo, Mileyka 358- 360
Matera, Barbara 78, 185, 370
Matheos, Cleo 270, 285
Mather, Ted 82, 90
Mathews, Liz 71, 285, 286
Mathis, Samantha 338, 339, 342
Matland, Michelle 129
Matola, Fran 391
Matos, Freddie 285
Matricardi, Lisa 294
Matsushima, Maiko 309, 370
Mattfeld, Quinn 241
Matthew, Ed 248, 252

Index

Index

Index

Index

Index

Index

Index

Index

Autographs

Autographs